D0049000

THE PELOPONNESIAN WAR

Also by Donald Kagan

The Heritage of World Civilizations
(with Albert M. Craig, William A. Graham, Steven Ozment
and Frank M. Turner)

The Western Heritage
(with Steven Ozment and Frank M. Turner)

While America Sleeps
(with Frederick W. Kagan)

On the Origins of War and the Preservation of Peace

Pericles of Athens and the Birth of Democracy

The Fall of the Athenian Empire

The Peace of Nicias and the Sicilian Expedition

The End of the Roman Empire: Decline or Transformation? (ed.)

The Archidamian War

The Outbreak of the Peloponnesian War

Great Issues in Western Civilization, vols. I and II
(ed. with L. P. Williams and Brian Tiernery)

Problems in Ancient History, vols. I and II (ed.)

Sources in Greek Political Thought (ed.)

*The Great Dialogue: A History of Greek Political Thought
from Homer to Polybius*

THE
PELOPONNESIAN
WAR *** *** ***

DONALD KAGAN

VIKING

VIKING
Published by the Penguin Group
Penguin Group (USA) Inc., 375 Hudson Street,
New York, New York 10014, U.S.A.
Penguin Books Ltd, 80 Strand, London WC2R 0RL, England
Penguin Books Australia Ltd, 250 Camberwell Road, Camberwell,
Victoria 3124, Australia
Penguin Books Canada Ltd, 10 Alcorn Avenue,
Toronto, Ontario, Canada M4V 3B2
Penguin Books India (P) Ltd, 11 Community Centre, Panchsheel Park,
New Delhi—110 017, India
Penguin Books (N.Z.) Ltd, Cnr Rosedale and Airborne Roads, Albany,
Auckland, New Zealand
Penguin Books (South Africa) (Pty) Ltd, 24 Sturdee Avenue,
Rosebank, Johannesburg 2196, South Africa

Penguin Books Ltd, Registered Offices: 80 Strand, London WC2R 0RL, England

First published in 2003 by Viking Penguin, a member of Penguin Group (USA) Inc.

1   3   5   7   9   10   8   6   4   2

Copyright © Donald Kagan, 2003
All rights reserved.

Maps by Jeffrey L. Ward

Title page art: Combat scene, red-figure krater (detail), 460–450 B.C.E., attributed to the Niobid Painter; Louvre, Paris, France. Copyright Réunion des Musées Nationaux/Art Resource, NY

LIBRARY OF CONGRESS CATALOGING-IN-PUBLICATION DATA

Kagan, Donald.
The Peloponnesian War / by Donald Kagan.
p. cm.
Includes bibliographical references and index.
ISBN 0–670–03211–5 (alk. paper)
1. Greece—History—Peloponnesian War, 431–404 B.C.   I. Title.

DF229 .K34 2003
938'.05—dc21   2002193377

This book is printed on acid-free paper. ∞

Printed in the United States of America
Set in Minion
Designed by Francesca Belanger

Without limiting the rights under copyright reserved above, no part of this publication may be reproduced, stored in or introduced into a retrieval system, or transmitted, in any form or by any means (electronic, mechanical, photocopying, recording or otherwise), without the prior written permission of both the copyright owner and the above publisher of this book.

The scanning, uploading, and distribution of this book via the Internet or via any other means without the permission of the publisher is illegal and punishable by law. Please purchase only authorized electronic editions and do not participate in or encourage electronic piracy of copyrighted materials. Your support of the author's rights is appreciated.

For David and Elena,
my grandchildren

ACKNOWLEDGMENTS

THE INSPIRATION FOR THIS BOOK came from John Roberts Hale of the University of Louisville, my old friend and former student. On a long airplane trip he convinced me that someone needed to write a history of the Peloponnesian War in one volume for the non-professional reader and that it might as well be me. I have enjoyed the writing of it, and I thank him for reading the manuscript and for his talent, enthusiasm and friendship. I am thankful, too, to my editor Rick Kot for his extraordinarily careful and helpful reading, which has much improved the book, and for his many kindnesses. I am grateful, as well, to my sons Fred and Bob, historians both, who have taught me so much in their written work and in countless wonderful conversations. Finally, I thank my wife, Myrna, for raising such boys and keeping their father up to the mark.

CONTENTS

Introduction   xxiii

Part One
THE ROAD TO WAR   1

CHAPTER ONE: The Great Rivalry (479–439*)   3

   SPARTA AND ITS ALLIANCE   3

   ATHENS AND ITS EMPIRE   7

   ATHENS AGAINST SPARTA   13

   THE THIRTY YEARS' PEACE   18

   THREATS TO PEACE: THURII   20

   THE SAMIAN REBELLION   22

CHAPTER TWO: "A Quarrel in a Far-away Country" (436–433)   25

   EPIDAMNUS   25

   CORINTH   28

CHAPTER THREE: Enter Athens (433–432)   30

   THE BATTLE OF SYBOTA   34

   POTIDAEA   36

   THE MEGARIAN DECREE   39

CHAPTER FOUR: The Decisions for War (432)   41

   SPARTA CHOOSES WAR   41

   THE ATHENIAN DECISION FOR WAR   47

*All dates are B.C.

Part Two
PERICLES' WAR   55

CHAPTER FIVE: War Aims and Resources (432–431)   57
    SPARTA   57
    ATHENS   60

CHAPTER SIX: The Theban Attack on Plataea (431)   64
    THE SPARTAN INVASION OF ATTICA   66
    ATTACKS ON PERICLES   68
    THE ATHENIAN RESPONSE   70
    PERICLES' FUNERAL ORATION   73
    THE WAR'S FIRST YEAR: AN ACCOUNTING   74

CHAPTER SEVEN: The Plague (430–429)   76
    EPIDAURUS   76
    THE PLAGUE IN ATHENS   78
    PERICLES UNDER FIRE   79
    PEACE NEGOTIATIONS   80
    PERICLES CONDEMNED   83
    THE SPARTANS GO TO SEA   84
    POTIDAEA RECAPTURED   85

CHAPTER EIGHT: Pericles' Last Days (429)   87
    SPARTA ATTACKS PLATAEA   87
    SPARTAN ACTION IN THE NORTHWEST   90
    ENTER PHORMIO   91
    THE SPARTANS ATTACK PIRAEUS   96
    THE DEATH OF PERICLES   97

CHAPTER NINE: Rebellion in the Empire (428–427)   99
    THE "NEW POLITICIANS" IN ATHENS   99
    CONSPIRACY ON LESBOS   100
    ATHENS REACTS   101

MYTILENE APPEALS TO THE PELOPONNESIANS   102

THE SIEGE OF MYTILENE   104

SPARTA ACTS ON LAND AND SEA   105

THE FATE OF MYTILENE   107

THE MYTILENE DEBATE: CLEON VERSUS DIODOTUS   109

CHAPTER TEN: Terror and Adventure (427)   113

THE FATE OF PLATAEA   113

CIVIL WAR AT CORCYRA   114

FIRST ATHENIAN EXPEDITION TO SICILY   118

Part Three

NEW STRATEGIES   123

CHAPTER ELEVEN: Demosthenes and the New Strategy (426) 125

THE SPARTANS IN CENTRAL GREECE   125

ATHENIAN INITIATIVES   128

DEMOSTHENES' AETOLIAN CAMPAIGN   129

THE SPARTANS ATTACK THE NORTHWEST   132

CHAPTER TWELVE: Pylos and Sphacteria (425)   137

ATHENS' WESTERN COMMITMENTS   137

DEMOSTHENES' PLAN: THE FORT AT PYLOS   138

THE SPARTANS ON SPHACTERIA   140

THE ATHENIAN NAVAL VICTORY   142

SPARTA'S PEACE OFFER   144

CLEON AGAINST NICIAS   147

THE SPARTAN SURRENDER ON SPHACTERIA   150

CHAPTER THIRTEEN: Athens on the Offensive:
Megara and Delium (424)   157

CYTHERA AND THYREA   157

DISAPPOINTMENT IN SICILY   159

THE ASSAULT ON MEGARA   162

ATHENS' BOEOTIAN INVASION   165

DELIUM   167

CHAPTER FOURTEEN: Brasidas' Thracian Campaign (424–423)   171

THE CAPTURE OF AMPHIPOLIS   173

THUCYDIDES AT AMPHIPOLIS   176

TRUCE   178

NICIAS' EXPEDITION TO THRACE   180

CHAPTER FIFTEEN: The Coming of Peace (422–421)   182

CLEON IN COMMAND   182

THE BATTLE OF AMPHIPOLIS   185

THE DEATH OF BRASIDAS AND CLEON   187

THE COMING OF PEACE   187

THE PEACE OF NICIAS   191

Part Four
THE FALSE PEACE   195

CHAPTER SIXTEEN: The Peace Unravels (421–420)   197

A TROUBLED PEACE   197

THE SPARTAN-ATHENIAN ALLIANCE   198

THE ARGIVE LEAGUE   200

SPARTA'S PROBLEMS   203

THE CORINTHIANS' MYSTERIOUS POLICY   206

THE BOEOTIANS   207

CHAPTER SEVENTEEN: The Alliance of Athens
         and Argos (420–418)   210

THE ATHENIAN BREACH WITH SPARTA   210

SPARTAN HUMILIATIONS   215

ALCIBIADES IN THE PELOPONNESUS   217

THE SPARTANS AGAINST ARGOS   218

CONFRONTATION IN THE ARGIVE PLAIN   221

CHAPTER EIGHTEEN: The Battle of Mantinea (418)   228

AGIS' MARCH TO TEGEA   228

TO FORCE A BATTLE   230

THE ALLIED ARMY MOVES   234

THE BATTLE   235

POLITICS INTERVENE   239

THE MEANING OF MANTINEA   241

CHAPTER NINETEEN: After Mantinea: Politics and Policy
   at Sparta and Athens (418–416)   244

DEMOCRACY RESTORED TO ARGOS   244

POLITICS AT ATHENS   245

OSTRACISM OF HYPERBOLUS   245

THE ATHENIAN CONQUEST OF MELOS   247

NICIAS AGAINST ALCIBIADES   249

Part Five

THE DISASTER IN SICILY   251

CHAPTER TWENTY: The Decision (416–415)   253

ATHENS' SICILIAN CONNECTIONS   253

THE DEBATE IN ATHENS   254

THE DEBATE TO RECONSIDER   256

CHAPTER TWENTY-ONE: The Home Front
   and the First Campaigns (415)   262

SACRILEGE   262

WITCH HUNT   264

ATHENIAN STRATEGY   267

THE SUMMER CAMPAIGN OF 415   270

THE FLIGHT OF ALCIBIADES   273

CHAPTER TWENTY-TWO: The First Attack on Syracuse (415)   275

THE ATHENIANS AT SYRACUSE   275

SYRACUSAN RESISTANCE   279

ALCIBIADES AT SPARTA   280

CHAPTER TWENTY-THREE: The Siege of Syracuse (414)   284

THE ILLNESS OF NICIAS AND THE DEATH
    OF LAMACHUS   286

ATHENS BREAKS THE TREATY   289

HELP ARRIVES AT SYRACUSE   289

NICIAS MOVES TO PLEMMYRIUM   291

NICIAS' LETTER TO ATHENS   293

THE ATHENIAN RESPONSE   295

CHAPTER TWENTY-FOUR: The Besiegers Besieged (414–413) 298

SPARTA TAKES THE OFFENSIVE   298

THE FORT AT DECELEA   299

REINFORCEMENTS FOR BOTH SIDES   300

THE CAPTURE OF PLEMMYRIUM   301

THE BATTLE IN THE GREAT HARBOR   303

THE SECOND ATHENIAN ARMADA:
    DEMOSTHENES' PLAN   306

THE NIGHT ATTACK ON EPIPOLAE   307

RETREAT OR REMAIN?   308

ECLIPSE   310

CHAPTER TWENTY-FIVE: Defeat and Destruction (413)   313

THE FINAL NAVAL BATTLE   313

THE FINAL RETREAT   316

THE FATE OF THE ATHENIANS   319

A JUDGMENT ON NICIAS   321

Part Six
REVOLUTIONS IN THE EMPIRE
    AND IN ATHENS   325

CHAPTER TWENTY-SIX: After the Disaster (413–412)   327

THE *PROBOULOI* 328

SPARTAN AMBITIONS 330

AGIS IN COMMAND 333

PERSIAN INITIATIVES 333

THE SPARTANS CHOOSE CHIOS 335

ALCIBIADES INTERVENES 337

TISSAPHERNES' DRAFT TREATY 339

CHAPTER TWENTY-SEVEN: War in the Aegean (412–411) 341

ATHENS FIGHTS BACK 341

DECISION AT MILETUS 344

ALCIBIADES JOINS THE PERSIANS 346

A NEW SPARTAN AGREEMENT WITH PERSIA 349

A NEW SPARTAN STRATEGY 351

REBELLION AT RHODES 354

THE IMPORTANCE OF EUBOEA 356

A NEW TREATY WITH PERSIA 357

THE SPARTANS IN THE HELLESPONT 358

CHAPTER TWENTY-EIGHT: The Revolutionary Movement (411) 361

THE ARISTOCRATIC TRADITION 362

DEMOCRACY AND THE WAR 364

THRASYBULUS AND THE MODERATES 365

THE REAL OLIGARCHS 367

PHRYNICHUS AGAINST ALCIBIADES 368

CHAPTER TWENTY-NINE: The Coup (411) 371

PEISANDER'S MISSION TO ATHENS 371

THE OLIGARCHS' BREACH WITH ALCIBIADES 373

DIVISIONS AMONG THE PLOTTERS 375

THE DEMOCRACY OVERTHROWN 376

THE OLIGARCHIC LEADERS 379

CHAPTER THIRTY: The Four Hundred in Power (411)   381

   THE DEMOCRACY AT SAMOS   384

   PHARNABAZUS AND THE HELLESPONT   387

   ALCIBIADES RECALLED   388

CHAPTER THIRTY-ONE: The Five Thousand (411)   392

   DISSENT WITHIN THE FOUR HUNDRED   392

   THE OLIGARCHIC PLOT TO BETRAY ATHENS   393

   THE THREAT TO EUBOEA   396

   THE FALL OF THE FOUR HUNDRED   398

   THE CONSTITUTION OF THE FIVE THOUSAND   398

   THE FIVE THOUSAND IN ACTION   400

CHAPTER THIRTY-TWO: War in the Hellespont (411–410)   402

   THE PHANTOM PHOENICIAN FLEET   402

   THE BATTLE OF CYNOSSEMA   403

   THE BATTLE OF ABYDOS   408

   THE BATTLE OF CYZICUS   410

Part Seven
THE FALL OF ATHENS   415

CHAPTER THIRTY-THREE: The Restoration (410–409)   417

   SPARTA'S PEACE OFFER   417

   DEMOCRACY RESTORED   420

   THE WAR RESUMED   424

CHAPTER THIRTY-FOUR: The Return of Alcibiades (409–408) 427

   ATHENS ATTEMPTS TO CLEAR THE STRAITS   427

   ATHENIAN NEGOTIATIONS WITH PERSIA   431

   ALCIBIADES RETURNS   432

CHAPTER THIRTY-FIVE: Cyrus, Lysander,
   and the Fall of Alcibiades (408–406)   437

PRINCE CYRUS REPLACES TISSAPHERNES   437

THE EMERGENCE OF LYSANDER   438

THE COLLABORATION OF CYRUS AND LYSANDER   441

THE BATTLE OF NOTIUM   442

THE FALL OF ALCIBIADES   446

CHAPTER THIRTY-SIX: Arginusae (406)   448

THE NEW NAVARCH   448

CONON TRAPPED AT MYTILENE   451

ATHENS REBUILDS A NAVY   452

THE BATTLE OF ARGINUSAE   454

RESCUE AND RECOVERY   459

THE TRIAL OF THE GENERALS   461

CHAPTER THIRTY-SEVEN: The Fall of Athens (405–404)   467

ANOTHER SPARTAN PEACE OFFER   467

THE RETURN OF LYSANDER   469

THE BATTLE OF AEGOSPOTAMI   471

THE RESULTS OF THE BATTLE   476

THE FATE OF ATHENS   478

THERAMENES NEGOTIATES A PEACE   480

Conclusion   485

Sources for the History of the Peloponnesian War   491

Index   495

LIST OF MAPS

Greece and Western Asia Minor   XXVIII–XXIX

1. Sparta and the Peloponnesus   6
2. The Athenian Empire ca. 450 B.C.   10–11
3. Aegean Sea   15
4. Attica, Megara, Boeotia   17
5. Southern Italy and Sicily   21
6. Samos and Miletus   23
7. Epidamnus and Corcyra   26
8. The Battle of Sybota   35
9. Chalcidice and Thrace   38
10. Peloponnesus, Pylos, Sphacteria, Cythera   58
11. Northwestern Greece   72
12. Corinthian Gulf   92
13. Sicily and Southern Italy   121
14. Central Greece   126
15. Pylos and Sphacteria   141
16. Amphipolis and Environs   174
17. Approaches to Argos 418   223
18. The Argive Plain in 418   225
19. The Battle of Mantinea   231

20. Sicily and Southern Italy   271

21. The Battle of the Anapus   276

22. The Siege of Syracuse   285

23. The Aegean and Asia Minor   343

24. The Straits   360

25. The Battle of Cyzicus   411

26. The Bosporus and Sea of Marmara   428

27. Arginusae   453

28. The Battle of Arginusae   455

29. The Battle of Aegospotami   472

INTRODUCTION

FOR ALMOST THREE decades at the end of the fifth century B.C. the Athenian Empire fought the Spartan Alliance in a terrible war that changed the Greek world and its civilization forever. Only a half-century before its outbreak the united Greeks, led by Sparta and Athens, had fought off an assault by the mighty Persian Empire, preserving their independence by driving Persia's armies and navies out of Europe and recovering the Greek cities on the coasts of Asia Minor from its grasp.

This astonishing victory opened a proud era of growth, prosperity, and confidence in Greece. The Athenians, especially, flourished, increasing in population and establishing an empire that brought them wealth and glory. Their young democracy came to maturity, bringing political participation, opportunity, and political power even to the lowest class of citizens, and their novel constitution went on to take root in other Greek cities. It was a time of extraordinary cultural achievement, as well, probably unmatched in originality and richness in all of human history. Dramatic poets like Aeschylus, Sophocles, Euripides, and Aristophanes raised tragedy and comedy to a level never surpassed. The architects and sculptors who created the Parthenon and other buildings on the Acropolis in Athens, at Olympia, and all over the Greek world powerfully influenced the course of Western art and still do so today. Natural philosophers like Anaxagoras and Democritus used unaided human reason to seek an understanding of the physical world, and such pioneers of moral and political philosophy as Protagoras and Socrates did the same in the realm of human affairs. Hippocrates and his school made great advances in medical science, and Herodotus invented historiography as we understand it today.

The Peloponnesian War not only brought this remarkable period to an end, but was recognized as a critical turning point even by those who fought it. The great historian Thucydides tells us that he undertook his history as the war began,

> in the belief that it would be great and noteworthy above all the wars that had gone before, inferring this from the fact that both powers were then at their best in preparedness for war in every way, and seeing the rest of the Hellenic people taking sides with one side or the other, some at once, others planning to do so. For this was the greatest upheaval that had ever shaken the Hellenes, extending also to some part of the barbarians, one might say even to a very large part of mankind. (1.1.2)[1]

From the perspective of the fifth-century Greeks the Peloponnesian War was legitimately perceived as a world war, causing enormous destruction of life and property, intensifying factional and class hostility, and dividing the Greek states internally and destabilizing their relationship to one another, which ultimately weakened their capacity to resist conquest from outside. It also reversed the tendency toward the growth of democracy. When Athens was powerful and successful, its democratic constitution had a magnetic effect on other states, but its defeat was decisive in the political development of Greece, sending it in the direction of oligarchy.

The Peloponnesian War was also a conflict of unprecedented brutality, violating even the harsh code that had previously governed Greek warfare and breaking through the thin line that separates civilization from savagery. Anger, frustration, and the desire for vengeance increased as the fighting dragged on, resulting in a progression of atrocities that included maiming and killing captured opponents; throwing them into pits to die of thirst, starvation, and exposure; and hurling them into the sea to drown. Bands of marauders murdered in-

---

[1] Adapted from the translation of Richard Crawley (Modern Library, New York, 1951). Throughout, references are to Thucydides' history of the Peloponnesian War unless otherwise indicated. The numbers refer to the traditional divisions by book, chapter, and section.

nocent children. Entire cities were destroyed, their men killed, their women and children sold as slaves. On the island of Corcyra, now called Corfu, the victorious faction in a civil war brought on by the larger struggle butchered their fellow citizens for a full week: "Sons were killed by their father, and suppliants dragged from the altar or slain upon it" (3.81.2–5).

As the violence spread it brought a collapse in the habits, institutions, beliefs, and restraints that are the foundations of civilized life. The meanings of words changed to suit the bellicosity: "Reckless audacity came to be considered the courage of a loyal ally; prudent hesitation, specious cowardice; moderation was held to be a cloak for unmanliness." Religion lost its restraining power, "but the use of fair phrases to arrive at guilty ends was in high reputation." Truth and honor disappeared, "and society became divided into camps in which no man trusted his fellow" (3.82.1, 8; 3.83.1). Such was the conflict that inspired Thucydides' mordant observations on the character of war as "a savage schoolmaster that brings the characters of most people down to the level of their current circumstances" (3.82.2).

Although the Peloponnesian War ended more than twenty-four hundred years ago it has continued to fascinate readers of every subsequent age. Writers have used it to illuminate the First World War, most frequently to help explain its causes, but its greatest influence as an analytical tool may have come during the Cold War, which dominated the second half of the twentieth century, and which likewise witnessed a world divided into two great power blocs, each under a powerful leader. Generals, diplomats, statesmen, and scholars alike have compared the conditions that led to the Greek war with the rivalry between NATO and the Warsaw Pact.

But the story of what actually took place two and a half millennia in the past, and its deeper meaning, are ultimately not easy to grasp. By far the most important source of our knowledge is the history written by the war's contemporary and participant Thucydides. His work is justly admired as a masterpiece of historical writing and hailed for its wisdom about the nature of war, international relations, and mass psychology. It has also come to be regarded as a foundation stone of historical method and political philosophy. It is not, however, completely satisfactory as a chronicle of the war and all that the war can teach us.

Its most obvious shortcoming is that it is incomplete, stopping in mid-sentence seven years before the war's end. For an account of the final part of the conflict we must rely on writers of much less talent and with little or no direct knowledge of events. At the very least, a modern treatment of accessible scope is needed to make sense of the conclusion of the war.

But even the period treated by Thucydides requires illumination if the modern reader is to have the fullest understanding of its military, political, and social complexities. The works of other ancient writers and contemporary inscriptions discovered and studied in the last two centuries have filled gaps and have sometimes raised questions about the story as Thucydides tells it. Finally, any satisfactory history of the war also demands a critical look at Thucydides himself. His was an extraordinary and original mind, and more than any other historian in antiquity he placed the highest value on accuracy and objectivity. We must not forget, however, that he was also a human being with human emotions and foibles. In the original Greek his style is often very compressed and difficult to understand, so that any translation is by necessity an interpretation. The very fact that he was a participant in the events, moreover, influenced his judgments in ways that must be prudently evaluated. Simply accepting his interpretations uncritically would be as limiting as accepting without question Winston Churchill's histories and his understanding of the two world wars in which he played so important a role.

In this book I attempt a new history of the Peloponnesian War designed to meet the needs of readers in the twenty-first century. It is based on the scholarship employed in my four volumes on the war aimed chiefly at a scholarly audience,[2] but my goal here is a readable narrative in a single volume to be read by the general reader for pleasure and to gain the wisdom that so many have sought in studying this war. I have avoided making comparisons between events in it and those in later history, although many leap to mind, in the hope that an

---

[2] These have been published by the Cornell University Press. Their titles are *The Outbreak of the Peloponnesian War* (1969), *The Archidamian War* (1974), *The Peace of Nicias and the Sicilian Expedition* (1981), and *The Fall of the Athenian Empire* (1987).

uninterrupted account will better allow readers to draw their own conclusions.

I undertake this project after so many years because I believe, more than ever, that the story of the Peloponnesian War is a powerful tale that may be read as an extraordinary human tragedy, recounting the rise and fall of a great empire, the clash between two very different societies and ways of life, the interplay of intelligence and chance in human affairs, and the role of brilliantly gifted individuals, as well as masses of people in determining the course of events while subject to the limitations imposed upon them by nature, by fortune, and by one another. I hope to demonstrate, also, that a study of the Peloponnesian War is a source of wisdom about the behavior of human beings under the enormous pressures imposed by war, plague, and civil strife, and about the potentialities of leadership and the limits within which it must inevitably operate.

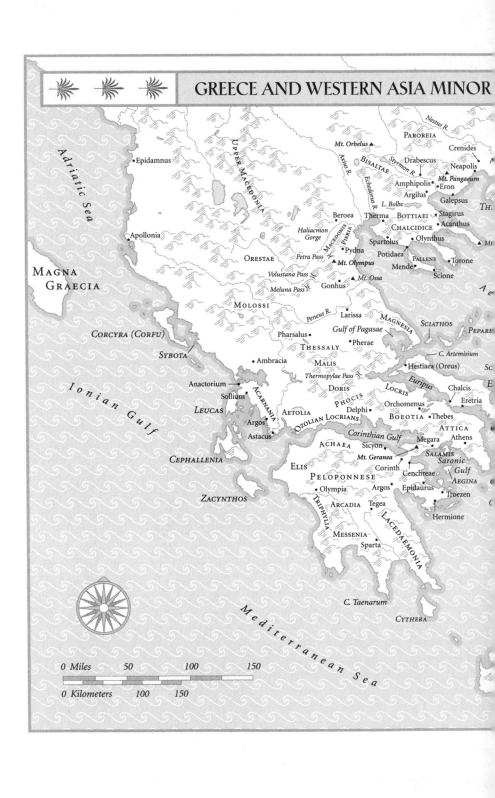

GREECE AND WESTERN ASIA MINOR

Nestus R.
PAROREIA
Mt. Orbelus ▲
Crenides
Drabescus
Styrmon R.
Neapolis
BISALTAE
Amphipolis
Mt. Pangaeum
Eron
Argilus
Echedorus R.
L. Bolbe
Galepsus
Beroea
Therma
BOTTIAEI
Stagirus
TH.
Haliacmon
CHALCIDICE
Acanthus
Gorge
MACEDONIS
Spartolus
Olynthus
Apollonia
ORESTAE
PIERIA
Pydna
Potidaea
PALLENE
Torone
Petra Pass
Mt. Olympus
Mende
Scione
Volustana Pass
▲ Mt. Ossa
Meluna Pass
Gonhus
Ae
MOLOSSI
Peneus R.
Larissa
MAGNESIA
SCIATHOS
PEPARE
CORCYRA (CORFU)
Pharsalus
Gulf of Pagasae
SYBOTA
THESSALY
Pherae
C. Artemisium
Ambracia
MALIS
Hestiaea (Oreus)
Sc
Anactorium
Thermopylae Pass
Euripus
Chalcis
E
Sollium
DORIS
LOCRIS
Eretria
LEUCAS
AETOLIA
PHOCIS
Orchomenus
Argos
Delphi
BOEOTIA
Thebes
Astacus
OZOLIAN LOCRIANS
ATTICA
Corinthian Gulf
Athens
ACHAEA
Sicyon
Megara
CEPHALLENIA
Mt. Geranea
SALAMIS
Saronic
ELIS
Corinth
Cenchreae
Gulf
PELOPONNESE
AEGINA
Olympia
Argos
Epidaurus
ZACYNTHOS
ARCADIA
Tegea
Troezen
TRIPHYLIA
Hermione
MESSENIA
LACEDAEMONIA
Sparta

Adriatic Sea

MAGNA GRAECIA

Ionian Gulf

Epidamnus

Mediterranean Sea

C. Taenarum
CYTHERA

0 Miles   50   100   150
0 Kilometers   100   150

Black Sea

Hebrus R.

T H R A C E

Rhodope

Propontis

Maronea
•Doriscus
Aenus•
Tyrodiza

rpedon
Melas Bay
•Cardia
•Cyzicus
CHERSONESE
•Lampascus
Sestus•
THRACE
•Abydus
ROS
Elaeus•
Sigeum•
•Troy
Scamander R.
EMNOS
•Colonae
•Antandrus
▲ **Mt. Ida**

•Adramyttium

Caicus R.
•Mytilene

LESBOS

Hermus R.
Phocaea•
•Sardis

Maeander R.
CHIOS
•Erythrae
Lebedus•
•Teos
Buthia•
•Ephesus

SAMOS
—Magnesia
•Priene
ROS
Miletus—
TENOS
•Teichiussa
MYCONOS
CARIA
DELOS
LEROS
ROS
NAXOS
•Pheselis
LYCIA
NOS
Cos
Chelidonian Is.

THERA

RHODES

CARPATHOS
Mediterranean Sea

CRETE

© 2003 Jeffrey L. Ward

Part One

THE ROAD TO WAR

THE GREAT PELOPONNESIAN WAR, undertaken, it was claimed, to bring freedom to the Greeks, began not with a formal declaration of war and a proud and open assault upon the homeland of imperial Athens, but with a stealthy and deceitful raid in peacetime by a powerful state against its much smaller neighbor. There was no brilliant parade led by the magnificent Spartan phalanx, their bright red cloaks gleaming in the Attic sunshine, at the head of the mighty Peloponnesian army, but a sneak attack by a few hundred Thebans, insinuated into the tiny city of Plataea in the dark of a cloudy night by traitors from within the city. Its onset indicated the kind of war it would be: a fundamental departure from the traditional character of the Greek way of warfare, based on the citizen-soldier fighting as a hoplite, a heavily armed infantryman in the serried block of soldiers, called a phalanx, according to fixed and well-understood rules that had governed Greek combat for more than two and one-half centuries. The only honorable way to fight, it had been believed, was in the open field in the daylight, phalanx against phalanx. The braver and stronger army would naturally prevail, place a trophy of victory on the ground it had won, take possession of the land in dispute, and march home, as would the defeated foe. The typical war, therefore, was decided in a single battle on a single day.

The events that led to the hostilities took place in remote regions,

far from the centers of Greek civilization, and represented as a Spartan
or Athenian might say, "a quarrel in a faraway country between people
of whom we know nothing."[1] Few of the Greeks who read Thucydides'
account even knew where the city where the trouble began was or who
lived there, and no one could have foreseen that an internal quarrel in
this remote region on the fringes of the Hellenic world would lead to
the terrible and devastating Peloponnesian War.[2]

---

[1] These were the words Neville Chamberlain used to describe the situation in
Czechoslovakia in 1938 that soon led to the Second World War: B.B.C. Archives;
record no. 1930. Cited by C. Thorne, in *The Approach of War 1938–39*, London, 1982,
p. 91.
[2] It is the "Peloponnesian War," of course, from the point of view of the Athenians; the Spartans, no doubt, thought about it as the "Athenian War."

CHAPTER ONE

The Great Rivalry (479–439)

THE WORLD OF THE GREEKS extended from scattered cities on the south coast of Spain at the far western end of the Mediterranean to the eastern shore of the Black Sea in the east. A concentration of Greek cities dominated the southern part of the Italian peninsula and most of the coastal area of Sicily, but the center of the Greek world was the Aegean Sea. Most of the Greek cities, including the most important ones, stood on the southern part of the Balkan peninsula that is modern Greece, on the eastern shore of the Aegean, in Anatolia (modern Turkey), on the islands of the Aegean, and on its northern shore.

At the outbreak of the war some of the cities in this region were neutral, but many, and the most important of them, had come under the hegemony of either Sparta or Athens, two states that were probably as different as any two in the Greek world and that looked upon each other with suspicion. Their rivalry shaped the Greek international system.

SPARTA AND ITS ALLIANCE

SPARTA LED the older organization, which was formed in the sixth century. In their own territory of Laconia the Spartans ruled over two kinds of subordinate peoples. The helots, who stood somewhere between serfdom and slavery, farmed the land and provided the Spartans with food, while the *perioikoi*, personally free but subject to Spartan control, manufactured and traded for what the Spartans needed. The Spartans alone had no need to earn a living and devoted themselves exclusively to military training. This enabled them to develop the best army in the Greek world, a group of citizen-soldiers with professional training and skill, unlike any other.

But the Spartan social structure was a potentially dangerous one. The helots outnumbered their Spartan masters by some seven to one and, as an Athenian who knew Sparta well put it, "They would gladly eat the Spartans raw" (Xenophon, *Hellenica* 3.3.6). To meet the challenge of their occasional rebellions the Spartans created a constitution and a way of life like no other, subordinating individual and family to the needs of the state. They allowed only physically perfect infants to live; boys were taken from their homes at age seven to be trained and toughened in military school until they were twenty. From twenty to thirty they lived in barracks, helping in turn to educate the new young recruits. They were allowed to marry but could visit their wives only by stealth. At thirty the Spartan male became a full citizen, an "equal" (*homoios*). He took his meals at a public mess with fourteen comrades, dining simply, often on a black soup that appalled the other Greeks. Military service was required until age sixty. The entire system aimed to produce soldiers whose physical powers, training, and discipline made them the best in the world.

In spite of their military superiority, the Spartans were usually reluctant to go to war, chiefly because of their fear that the helots would take advantage of any long absence of the army to rebel. Thucydides pointed out that "most institutions among the Spartans have always been established with regard to security against the helots" (4.80.3), and Aristotle said that the helots "are like someone sitting in wait for disasters to strike the Spartans" (*Politics* 1269a).

In the sixth century the Spartans developed a network of perpetual alliances to safeguard their peculiar community. Modern scholars usually call the Spartan Alliance the Peloponnesian League, but it was in fact a loose organization consisting of Sparta, on the one hand, and a group of allies connected to her by separate treaties on the other. When called upon, the allies served as soldiers under Spartan command. Each state swore to follow Sparta's lead in foreign policy in return for Spartan protection and recognition of its integrity and autonomy.

Pragmatism, not theory, provided the interpretive principle within the alliance. The Spartans helped their allies when it was to their ad-

vantage or unavoidable, compelling others to join in a conflict whenever it was necessary and possible. The entire alliance met only when
the Spartans chose, and we hear of few such gatherings. The rules that
chiefly counted were imposed by military, political, or geographical
circumstances, and they reveal three informal categories of allies. One
consisted of states that were small enough and close enough to Sparta
as to be easily controlled such as Phlius or Orneae. States in the second
category, including Megara, Elis, and Mantinea, were stronger, or
more remote, or both, but not so powerful and distant as to escape ultimate punishment if it was merited. Thebes and Corinth were the
only states in the third group, states so far removed and mighty in their
own right that their conduct of foreign policy was rarely subordinated
to Spartan interests. (See Map 1.)

Argos, a large state to the northeast of Sparta, was an old and traditional enemy, and not a member of the Spartan Alliance. The Spartans had always feared an Argive union with other enemies, and
especially its providing assistance to a helot rebellion. Anything that
threatened the integrity of the Peloponnesian League or the loyalty of
any of its members was considered a potentially deadly menace to the
Spartans.

Theorists regarded Sparta's political order as a "mixed constitution," containing monarchic, oligarchic, and democratic elements. The
monarchic constituent appeared in the form of two kings, each from a
different royal family. The *gerousia*, a council of twenty-eight men over
the age of sixty elected from a small number of privileged families,
represented the oligarchic principle. The assembly, consisting of all
Spartan men over thirty, was a democratic element, as were the five
ephors, magistrates elected annually by the citizens.

The two kings served for life, led Sparta's armies, performed important religious and judicial functions, and enjoyed great prestige
and influence. Since they often disagreed, factions formed around
them on different sides of an issue. The *gerousia* sat with the kings as
the highest court in the land, the one to which the kings themselves
were brought to trial. The prestige they held because of family connections, age, and experience in a society that venerated such things, and
the honor that accompanied their election, gave them great unofficial
influence.

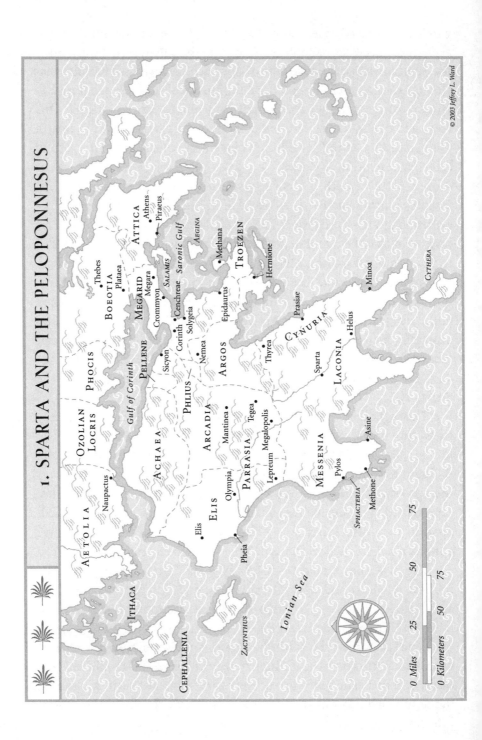

1. SPARTA AND THE PELOPONNESUS

ITHACA

CEPHALLENIA

ZACYNTHUS

Ionian Sea

AETOLIA

Naupactus

OZOLIAN LOCRIS

PHOCIS

Gulf of Corinth

ACHAEA

PELLENE

Thebes
BOEOTIA
Plataea

MEGARID
Megara
Crommyon

ATTICA
Athens
Piraeus

SALAMIS
Cenchreae *Saronic Gulf*
Corinth
Solygeia
Sicyon

AEGINA

Methana
TROEZEN
Hermione

PHLIUS
Nemea

ARGOS
Epidaurus

Thyrea

CYNURIA
Prasiae

Minoa

Helus

ELIS

Elis

Olympia

ARCADIA
Mantinea
Tegea
Megalopolis
PARRASIA
Lepreum

Sparta

LACONIA

CYTHERA

Pheia

MESSENIA
Pylos
SPHACTERIA
Methone
Asine

0 Miles   25   50   75
0 Kilometers   50   75

© 2003 Jeffrey L. Ward

The ephors, too, had important powers, especially in foreign affairs. They received foreign envoys, negotiated treaties, and ordered expeditions once war had been declared. They also summoned and presided over the assembly, sat with the *gerousia* and were its executive officers, and had the right to bring charges of treason against the kings.

Formal decisions on treaties, foreign relations, and war and peace belonged to the assembly, but its real powers were limited. Its meetings occurred only when called by officials. Little debate took place at them, and the speakers were usually the kings, members of the *gerousia*, or ephors. Voting was typically by acclamation, the equivalent of a voice vote; division and the counting of votes were rare.

For three centuries this constitution had been unchanged by law, coup d'état, or revolution. In spite of such constitutional stability, however, Sparta's foreign policy was often unsteady. Conflicts between the kings, between ephors and kings, and among the ephors themselves, and the inevitable disruption caused by the annual rotation of boards of ephors could weaken Sparta's control of its alliance. An ally could pursue its own interests and policy by exploiting Sparta's internal divisions. Sparta's mighty army and its command of the alliance gave the Spartans enormous power, but if they used it against a strong enemy outside the Peloponnesus, they ran the risk of a helot rebellion or an Argive attack. If they did not use it when called upon by their more important allies, they risked defections and the dissolution of the alliance on which their security rested. In the crisis leading to war both these factors would shape Spartan decisions.

ATHENS AND ITS EMPIRE

THE ATHENIAN EMPIRE emerged from a new alliance formed after the Greek victory in the Persian Wars. First its leader, then its master, Athens had a unique history that helped shape its character long before it became a democracy and rose to dominance. It was the chief town of the region known as Attica, a small triangular peninsula extending southeastward from central Greece. Because much of its area of about a thousand square miles is mountainous and rocky and unavailable for cultivation, early Attica was relatively poor, even by Greek standards. However, its geography proved a blessing when invaders from the north swept down and and occupied the more attractive lands of the Peloponnesus, regarding Attica as not worth the trouble of conquest. Unlike the Spartans, the Athenians claimed to have sprung from their own soil and to have lived in the same region since before the birth of the moon. As a result, they did not have to contend with the burden of an oppressed, alien, and discontented underclass.

Because Athens unified the entire region quite early in its history it was not troubled by quarrels and wars with other towns in Attica. Each of them became part of the Athenian city-state, and all their free, native-born inhabitants were Athenian citizens on an equal basis. The absence of intense pressures, internal and external, may help explain Athens' relatively untroubled nonviolent early history and its emergence in the fifth century as the first democracy in the history of the world.

The power and prosperity of the fifth-century Athenian democracy depended primarily on its command of its great maritime empire, centered on the Aegean Sea, the islands in it, and the cities along its coast. It began as an association of "the Athenians and their allies" called by modern scholars the Delian League, a voluntary alliance of Greek states that invited Athens to take the lead in continuing the war of liberation and vengeance against Persia. It gradually became an empire under Athenian command, functioning chiefly to the advantage of Athens (see Map 2). Over the years almost all its members gave up their own fleets and chose instead to make a money payment into the common treasury. The Athenians used these funds to increase the number of their own ships, and to pay the rowers to stay at their oars for eight months each year, so that eventually the Athenian navy had by far the biggest and best Greek fleet ever known. On the eve of the Peloponnesian War, of some 150 members of the league only two islands, Lesbos and Chios, had their own fleets and enjoyed relative autonomy. Even they, however, were unlikely to defy Athenian orders.

The Athenians made a large profit from their imperial holdings and used it for their own purposes, especially for the great building program that beautified and glorified their city and provided work for its people, and for the accumulation of a large reserve fund. The navy protected the ships of Athenian merchants in their prosperous trade throughout the Mediterranean and beyond. It also guaranteed the Athenians access to the wheat fields of Ukraine and the fish of the Black Sea, with which they could supplement their inadequate domestic food supply and, with the use of imperial money, even replace it totally if forced to abandon their own fields in the course of war. Once they completed the walls surrounding their city and connecting them by additional Long Walls to the fortified port at Piraeus, as they did in midcentury, the Athenians were virtually invulnerable.

In Athens the assembly made all decisions on policy, foreign and domestic, military and civil. The council of Five Hundred, chosen by lot from the Athenian citizens, prepared bills for the assembly's consideration but was totally subordinate to the larger body. The assembly met no fewer than forty times a year in the open air, on the Pnyx hill beside the Acropolis, overlooking the Agora, the marketplace and civic center. All male citizens were permitted to attend, vote, make proposals, and debate. At the start of the war about forty thousand Athenians were eligible, but attendance rarely exceeded six thousand. Strategic decisions were thus debated before thousands of people, a majority of whom had to approve the particular details of each action. The assembly voted on every expedition, the number and specific nature of ships and men, the funds to be spent, the commanders to lead the forces, and the precise instructions to be given those commanders.

The most important offices in the Athenian state, and among the few filled by election rather than by lottery, were those of the ten generals. Because they commanded divisions of the Athenian army and fleets of ships in battle, they had to be military men; because they were elected for only a one-year term, and could be reelected without limit, they also had to be politicians. These leaders could impose military discipline while on campaign, but not within the city. At least ten times a year they were required to face a formal presentation of any complaint against their behavior in office, and at the end of their term they had to make a full accounting of their conduct, military and financial. On each occasion they were subject to trial if accused and serious punishment if convicted.

The ten generals together did not constitute a cabinet or a

2. THE ATHENIAN EMPIRE ca. 450 B.C

Adriatic Sea

Epidamnus

THASOS

MACEDONIA

Apollonia

Potidaea

MAGNA
GRAECIA

Aeg

THESSALY

CORCYRA (CORFU)

Pagasae

SYBOTA

Ambracia

EUBOEA

Ionian Gulf

AETOLIA

LEUCAS

PHOCIS

Delphi

BOEOTIA

Eretria

Thebes

CEPHALLENIA

Sicyon

Megara

Athens

Elis

Corinth

ATTI

Olympia

Argos

Epidaurus

ARCADIA

LACONIA

Sparta

Mediterranean Sea

CYTHERA

0 Miles   50   100   150

0 Kilometers   100   150

© 2003 Jeffrey L. Ward

Black Sea

T H R A C E

Byzantium

Propontis

Sigeum

PHRYGIA

LEMNOS

Mytilene

LESBOS

LYDIA

Phocaea

CHIOS

Colophon

Ephesus

DROS

SAMOS

Magnesia

Priene

Miletus

DELOS

NAXOS

Ialysus

RHODES

CARPATHOS

CRETE

Autonomous Members

Subjects (formerly Dependent Members)

government; the assembly fulfilled the latter role. Sometimes, however, a remarkable general would gain so much political support and influence as to become the leader of the Athenians in fact, if not in law. Such was Cimon for the seventeen years between 479 and 462, when he appears to have been elected general annually, to have led every important expedition, and to have persuaded the Athenian assembly to support his policies at home and abroad. After the departure of Cimon, Pericles achieved similar success over an even longer period.

Thucydides introduces him into his history as "Pericles son of Xanthippus, the leading man in Athens at that time and the ablest in speech and in action" (1.139.4). Thucydides' readers knew far more than that about the most famous and brilliant individual ever to have led the Athenian democracy. He was an aristocrat of the bluest blood, son of a victorious general and hero of the Persian War. An ancestor on his mother's side was a niece of Cleisthenes, the founder of Athenian democracy. The family tradition was populist, however, and Pericles emerged as a notable figure on the democratic side early in his career. At about the age of thirty-five he became the leader of that political group, an informal but powerful position that he held for the rest of his life.

To that position he brought extraordinary powers of communication and thought. He was the foremost orator of his time, whose speeches persuaded majorities to support his policies and whose phrases rang in Athenian memories for decades, to be preserved for millennia afterward. Rarely has a political leader had the benefit of such serious intellectual training, associations, and tastes. From his youth Pericles identified with the enlightenment that was transforming Athens, earning him admiration from some and suspicion from many more.

His teacher, Anaxagoras, was said to have influenced Pericles' manner and style of speaking. Pericles' studies had given him:

> a lofty spirit and an elevated mode of speech, free from the vulgar and knavish tricks of mob-orators, but also a composed countenance that never gave way to laughter, a dignity of carriage and restraint in the arrangement of his clothing which no emotion was allowed to disturb while he was speaking, a voice

that was evenly controlled, and all the other characteristics of this sort which so impressed his hearers. (Plutarch, *Pericles* 5)

Such qualities made him appealing to the upper classes, while his democratic policies and other rhetorical skills won him the support of the masses. His extraordinary character helped him to win election after election over three decades and made him by far the most powerful political leader in Athens on the brink of the war.

During this period he seems to have been elected general each year. It is important to note, however, that he never had any greater formal powers than the other generals and never tried to alter the democratic constitution. He was still subject to the scrutiny provided in the constitution and required a vote in the open and uncontrolled assembly to take any action. Pericles was not always successful in obtaining support for his causes and, on some occasions, his enemies persuaded the assembly to act against his wishes. Nevertheless, it would be accurate to describe the Athenian government on the eve of the war as a democracy led by its first citizen. It would be wrong, however, to go as far as Thucydides in arguing that Athens in Pericles' time, though a democracy in name, was becoming the rule of the first citizen, for it always remained a thoroughgoing democracy in every respect. But in the crisis leading to war, in the formulation of a strategy to fight it, and into the second year of its conduct, the Athenians invariably followed the advice of their great leader.

ATHENS AGAINST SPARTA

IN THE EARLY YEARS of the Delian League the Athenians appeared to be continuing the good fight against the Persians for the liberty of all Greeks, while the Spartans were often embroiled in wars within the Peloponnesus. The rivalry between the two cities arose in the decades after the Persian War as the league grew in success, wealth, and power and gradually manifested its imperial ambitions. Immediately following the war a Spartan faction revealed its suspicion and resentment of the Athenians when it opposed the rebuilding of Athens' walls after the

Persians had fled. The Athenians boldly rejected their recommendation, and the Spartans made no formal complaint, "but they were secretly embittered" (1.92.1). In 475 a proposal to go to war to destroy the new Athenian alliance and gain control of the sea was rejected after heated debate, but an anti-Athenian faction in Sparta never disappeared and it rose to power when events favored its cause.

In 465 the Athenians besieged the island of Thasos in the northern Aegean (see Map 3) where they met fierce resistance. The Spartans had secretly made a promise to the Thasians to aid them by invading Attica and, Thucydides tells us, "they meant to keep it" (1.101.1–2). They were only prevented from doing so by a terrible earthquake in the Peloponnesus, which led to a major revolution of the helots. The Athenians, still formally tied to the Spartans by the Greek alliance against Persia sworn in 481, came to their assistance. Before they had a chance to accomplish anything, however, the Athenians were asked to leave, alone among Sparta's allies, on the specious grounds that they were no longer needed. Thucydides reports the true motive: "The Spartans were afraid of the boldness and the revolutionary spirit of the Athenians, thinking that . . . if they remained they [the Athenians] might be persuaded . . . to change sides. . . . It was because of this expedition that the Spartans and Athenians first came to an open quarrel" (1.102.1–3).

The incident, which offered clear evidence of the suspicion and hostility felt by many Spartans, caused a political revolution in Athens and ultimately a diplomatic revolution in Greece. The Spartans' insulting dismissal of the Athenian army brought down Cimon's pro-Spartan regime. The anti-Spartan group, which had opposed sending help to the Peloponnesus, now drove Cimon from Athens, withdrew from the old alliance with Sparta, and made a new alliance with Sparta's old and bitter enemy, Argos.

When the besieged helots could hold out no longer, the Spartans allowed them to leave the Peloponnesus under a truce, provided they never return. The Athenians settled them as a group at a strategic site on the north shore of the Corinthian Gulf, in the city of Naupactus, which Athens had recently acquired, "because of the hatred they already felt toward the Spartans" (1.103.3).

Next, two allies of Sparta, Corinth and Megara, went to war over

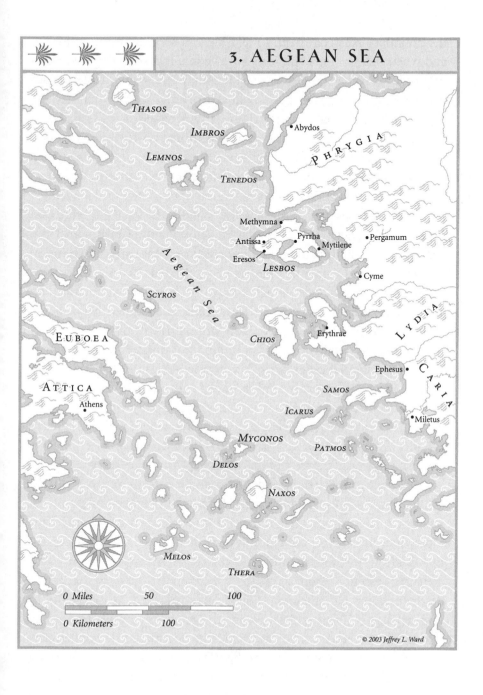

3. AEGEAN SEA

THASOS

IMBROS

Abydos

PHRYGIA

LEMNOS

TENEDOS

Methymna

Antissa   Pyrrha
Eresos   Mytilene   Pergamum

LESBOS

Cyme

Aegean Sea

SCYROS

LYDIA

EUBOEA

CHIOS   Erythrae

Ephesus   CARIA

ATTICA

Athens   SAMOS

ICARUS   Miletus

MYCONOS

PATMOS

DELOS

NAXOS

MELOS

THERA

0 Miles   50   100

0 Kilometers   100

© 2003 Jeffrey L. Ward

the boundary between them. In 459 Megara soon found itself losing, and when the Spartans chose to not become involved, the Megarians proposed to secede from the Spartan Alliance and join instead with Athens in exchange for help against Corinth. In this manner the breach between Athens and Sparta began to create a new instability in the Greek world. So long as the two hegemonal powers were on good terms, each was free to deal with its allies as it wished; dissatisfied members of each alliance had no recourse for their grievances. Now, however, dissident states could seek support from their leader's rival.

Megara, on Athens' western border, had great strategic value (see Map 4). Its western port, Pegae, gave access to the Corinthian Gulf, which the Athenians could otherwise reach only by a long and dangerous route around the entire Peloponnesus. Nisaea, its eastern port, lay on the Saronic Gulf, from which an enemy could launch an attack on the port of Athens. Even more important, Athenian control of the mountain passes of the Megarid, a situation possible only with the co-operation of a friendly Megara, would make it difficult if not impossible for a Peloponnesian army to invade Attica. An alliance with Megara would, therefore, promise Athens enormous advantages, but it would also bring war against Corinth and probably with Sparta and the entire Peloponnesian League as well. Nonetheless the Athenians accepted Megara, "and it was chiefly because of this action that Corinth's powerful hatred of the Athenians first arose" (1.103.4).

Although the Spartans did not become directly involved in the conflict for several years, this event represented the beginning of what modern historians call the "First Peloponnesian War." It lasted for more than fifteen years, including periods of truce and lapses of action, and, at one time or another, involved the Athenians in a military arena that extended from Egypt to Sicily. It ended when the Megarians defected from the Athenian alliance and returned to the Peloponnesian League, opening the way for the Spartan king Pleistoanax to lead a Peloponnesian army into Attica. A decisive battle seemed certain, but at the last moment the Spartans returned home without a fight. Ancient writers claim that Pericles had bribed the king and his advisor to abort the battle, and initially the Spartans were angry with the force's commanders, punishing both severely. A more likely explanation is that Pericles offered them acceptable peace terms, making

EUBOEA

LOCRIS (OPUNTIAN)

Atalante

PHOCIS

Orchomenus

Chaeronea

Lake
Copais

Coronea

BOEOTIA

Thespis

Thebes

Delium

Tanagra

Oropus

Oenophyta

Plataea

Dryoscephalae

Mt. Parnes

Mt. Cithaeron

Phyle

Decelea

Eleutherae

Oenos

Megalo Vuno

Corinthian Gulf

ATTICA

Acharnae

Pegae

Eleusis

Thria

MEGARID

Megara

AEGALIUS

Sicyon

Nisaea

Piraeus

Athens

Corinth

SALAMIS

Saronic Gulf

0 Miles   10   20

0 Kilometers   20

© 2003 Jeffrey L. Ward

hostilities unnecessary. In fact, a few months later the Spartans and Athenians did conclude a treaty.

THE THIRTY YEARS' PEACE

UNDER THE PROVISIONS of the Thirty Years' Peace, which took effect in the winter of 446/5, the Athenians agreed to give up the Peloponnesian lands they had acquired during the war, while the Spartans granted what amounted to official recognition of the Athenian Empire, for Sparta and Athens each swore the ratifying oaths on behalf of their allies. A key clause formally divided the Greek world in two by forbidding the members of either alliance to change sides, as Megara had done to initiate the recent war. Neutrals, however, could join either side—an apparently innocuous, and sensible condition that would nevertheless cause a surprising amount of trouble in years to come. Another provision required both sides to submit future grievances to binding arbitration. This seems to be the first attempt in history to maintain a lasting peace through such a device and suggests that both sides were seriously committed to avoiding armed conflict in the future.

Peace treaties are not all identical. Some end hostilities in which one side is destroyed or thoroughly defeated, such as the final war between Rome and Carthage (149–146 B.C.) Others inflict harsh terms on an enemy who has been defeated but not destroyed, such as the peace that Prussia imposed on France in 1871, or, as the common view has it, that the victors forced upon Germany at Versailles in 1919. This type of treaty often plants the seeds of a future war, because it humiliates and angers the loser without destroying its capacity for revenge. A third sort of treaty ends a conflict, usually a long one, in which each side has become aware of the costs and dangers of a protracted war and of the virtues of peace, whether or not an undisputed victor has emerged on the battlefield. The Peace of Westphalia in 1648, which ended the Thirty Years' War, and the settlement with which the Congress of Vienna concluded the Napoleonic Wars in 1815 are good examples. Such a treaty does not aim at destruction or punishment but seeks a guarantee of stability against the renewal of conflict. To succeed, such a peace must accurately reflect the true military and political situation and must rest on a sincere desire by both parties to make it work.

The Thirty Years' Peace of 446/5 falls into this last category. Over the course of a long war both sides had suffered serious losses, and neither could win a decisive victory; the sea power had been unable to sustain its triumphs on land, and the land power had been unable to prevail at sea. The peace was a compromise that contained the essential elements that should have guaranteed its success, for it accurately represented the balance of power between the two rivals and their alliances. By recognizing Sparta's hegemony on the mainland and Athens' in the Aegean it acknowledged and accepted the dualism into which the Greek world had been divided and so provided hope for a lasting peace.

Like any peace treaty, however, this one also contained elements of potential instability, and in each state minority factions were dissatisfied with it. Some Athenians favored expansion of the empire, and some Spartans resented sharing hegemony with Athens and were frustrated by the failure to achieve total victory. Others, including a number of Sparta's allies, feared Athenian territorial ambition. Athenians knew of these suspicions and in turn worried that the Spartans and their allies were only waiting for a favorable opportunity to renew the war. The Corinthians were still angry at Athens for its interference on behalf of the Megarians; Megara itself was now ruled by oligarchs who had massacred an Athenian garrison in gaining control of their city, and they had grown bitterly hostile toward Athens, as the Athenians were to them. Boeotia and especially its chief city, Thebes, were also under the control of oligarchs who resented the Athenians' emplacement of democratic regimes in their land during the recent war.

Any or all of these factors might one day threaten the peace, but the men who agreed to it, made weary and cautious by the war, intended to preserve it. To do so each side needed to allay suspicion and build confidence; to assure that the friends of peace were maintained in power rather than their warlike opponents, and to control any tendency its allies might have to create instability. When the peace was ratified there was reason to believe that all this was possible.

THREATS TO PEACE: THURII

AS ALWAYS, unforeseen events soon tested the treaty of 445 and its creators. In 444/3 both Sparta and Athens received a request from several former citizens of the recently reestablished colony of Sybaris in southern Italy. Decimated by quarrels and civil wars, the Sybarites sent to mainland Greece for assistance in founding a new colony nearby at a place called Thurii (see Map 5). Sparta was not interested, but the Athenians agreed to help in an unusual manner. They sent messengers throughout Greece to advertise for settlers for a new colony; it was not, however, to be an Athenian colony, but a Panhellenic one. This was a thoroughly novel idea, without precedent. Why did Pericles and the Athenians conceive it?

Some scholars believe that the Athenians were expansionists without limit and see the foundation of Thurii as merely part of an uninterrupted Athenian imperial growth, in the west as well as the east. But, apart from Thurii, the Athenians sought neither territory nor allies in the years between the Thirty Years' Peace and the crisis that brought on the Peloponnesian War, so the test of this theory must be Thurii itself. But Athenians were only one of the ten tribes that populated the city, and given that the largest single group was the Peloponnesians, Athens could not have hoped to gain power over it. Thurii's early history, moreover, demonstrates that Athens never intended to control it. No sooner was Thurii founded than it fought a war against one of Sparta's few colonies, Taras. Thurii lost, and the winners set up a trophy of victory and an inscription at Olympia for all the assembled Greeks to see: "The Tarantines offered a tenth of the spoils they took from the Thurians to Olympian Zeus." If the Athenians meant Thurii to be the center of an Athenian empire in the west they should have taken some action to protect it, but they did nothing, allowing the Spartan colony to flaunt its triumph in the most public gathering place in Greece.

A decade latter, in the midst of the crisis that led to war, a dispute arose in Thurii as to whose colony it actually was. The priests at Delphi settled the matter by declaring that Apollo was its founder, thereby reaffirming its the Panhellenic character. Although the connection with Athens was thus denied, again Athens did nothing, even though

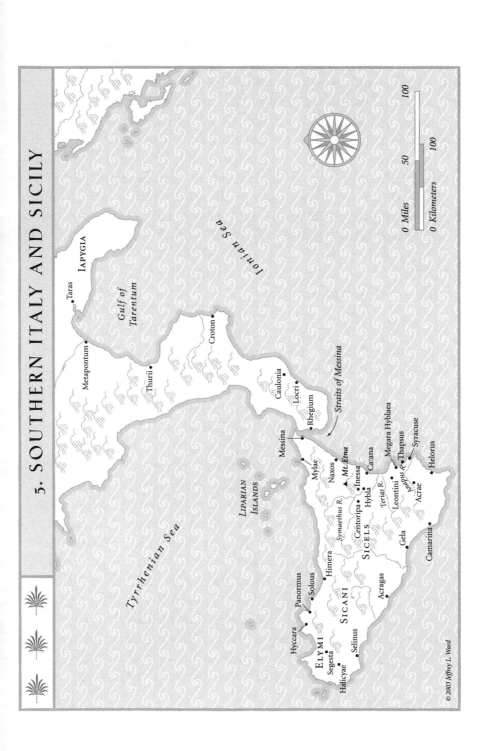

5. SOUTHERN ITALY AND SICILY

IAPYGIA

Taras

Gulf of
Tarentum

Metapontum

Thurii

Croton

Tyrrhenian Sea

Caulonia

Locri

Rhegium

Straits of Messina

LIPARIAN
ISLANDS

Messina

Ionian Sea

Mylae

Panormus

Solous

Himera

Naxos

Mt. Etna

Catana

Hyccara

ELYMI

SICANI

Inessa

Megara Hyblaea

Thapsus

Segesta

Centoripa

Hybla

Syracuse

Halicyae

Symaethus R.

Terias R.

Anapus R.

Acrae

Helorus

SICELS

Leontini

Selinus

Acragas

Gela

Camarina

© 2003 Jeffrey L. Ward

0 Miles   50   100

0 Kilometers   100

Delphic Apollo was friendly to Sparta, and the colony could be useful to the Spartans in case of war. The Athenians clearly did regard Thurii as a Panhellenic colony and consistently treated it as such.

The Athenians could simply have refused to take part in the establishment of Thurii. Such inaction would have attracted little notice, but by inventing the idea of a Panhellenic colony and situating it in an area outside Athens' sphere of influence, Pericles and the Athenians may have been sending a diplomatic signal. Thurii would stand as tangible evidence that Athens, rejecting the opportunity to found its own colony, had no imperial ambitions in the west and would pursue a policy of peaceful Panhellenism.

THE SAMIAN REBELLION

IN THE SUMMER OF 440 a war broke out between Samos and Miletus over control of Priene, a town lying between them (see Map 6). The island of Samos was autonomous, a charter member of the Delian League and the most powerful of the only three allies that paid no tribute and possessed their own navies. Miletus had also been one of the first members of the league, but it had twice revolted and been subjugated, deprived of its fleet, and forced to pay tribute and to accept a democratic constitution. When the Milesians asked for help the Athenians could not stand by and allow a powerful league member to impose its will on a helpless ally. The Samians, however, refused arbitration by the Athenians, who in turn could not ignore this defiance of their leadership and authority. Pericles himself led a fleet against Samos, replaced the ruling oligarchy with a democratic government, imposed a large indemnity, took hostages as a guarantee of good behavior, and left an Athenian garrison to guard the island.

The Samian leaders responded by turning from defiance to revolution, persuading Pissuthnes, the Persian satrap in Asia Minor, to aid them against Athens. He allowed them to hire a mercenary army in his territory and rescued the hostages from the island where the Athenians were holding them, thereby freeing the rebels to go forward. They defeated the democratic government and sent the captured garrison and other Athenian officials to the Persian satrap.

6. SAMOS AND MILETUS

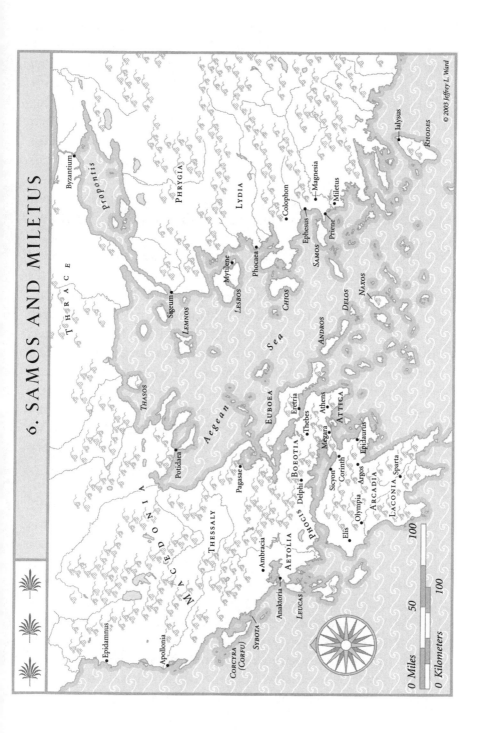

© 2003 Jeffrey L. Ward

News of the rebellion sparked an uprising at Byzantium, an important city located at a key point on the Athenian grain route to the Black Sea. Mytilene, the chief city of the island of Lesbos and another autonomous ally with a navy, awaited only Spartan support before joining the insurgents. Two of the elements that would later bring defeat to Athens in the great Peloponnesian War were now in place: revolt in the empire and support from Persia. Without Spartan participation, however, the rebellions would be crushed and the Persians would draw back. Sparta's decision about whether to become involved, in turn, was sure to be influenced by Corinth for, in the event of a war against Athens, the Corinthians would be the most important ally expected to produce a fleet.

How Sparta responded would be a test of both the peace and of Athenian policy since its conclusion. If that policy, especially in the west, seemed to Sparta and Corinth to be aggressive and ambitious, now was the time to attack Athens, while her sea power was engaged elsewhere. The Spartans called a meeting of the Peloponnesian League, proving, at least, that they took the matter seriously. The Corinthians later claimed to Athens that they intervened to decide the question, saying: "We did not vote against you when the other Peloponnesians were divided in their voting as to whether they should aid the Samians . . ." (1.40.5). The decision was made not to attack Athens, which was then free to crush the Samian rebellion and to prevent a general uprising aided by Persia, followed by a war that might have destroyed the Athenian Empire.

Why did the Corinthians, whose hatred of Athens dated back two decades and who would be the major agitator for war in the final crisis, intervene to preserve the peace in 440? The most plausible explanation is that they had understood the signal conveyed by the Athenian action at Thurii, and must have been sufficiently reassured by its establishment as a Panhellenic foundation and by Athens' subsequent restraint.

The outcome of the Samian crisis served to strengthen the prospects of peace. Since the agreement of 446/5 both sides had shown self-control and refused to seek advantages that might endanger the treaty. The outlook for the future was positive when a quarrel that arose in Epidamnus created new and unexpected problems.

CHAPTER TWO

"A Quarrel in a Far-away Country" (436–433)

EPIDAMNUS

"EPIDAMNUS IS A CITY on your right as a you sail into the Ionian Gulf. The Taulantians, a barbarian people of the Illyrian race live nearby" (1.24.1; see Map 7). Thucydides begins his narrative of the events that led to war with this explanation because few of his fellow Greeks would have known where Epidamnus was or anything else about it. In 436 civil war had driven the aristocratic party from Epidamnus, so they joined forces with the non-Greek Illyrians, who lived nearby, and attacked their native city. Under siege, the democrats within Epidamnus sent for help to Corcyra, the city's founder, which itself had originally been founded by Corinth. The Corcyraeans, who had done well by their policy of isolation from the brotherhood of Corinthian colonists as well as from other alliances, refused. The Epidamnian democrats then turned to Corinth, offering to become a Corinthian colony in return for assistance. As was the custom, Corinth had provided the founder for Epidamnus when it was established by its own daughter city, Corcyra. But relations between Corinth and Corcyra were uniquely bad. For centuries the two cities had quarreled and fought a series wars, often over control of some colony that both claimed as their own.

The Corinthians, nonetheless, enthusiastically accepted the invitation from Epidamnus, fully aware that their involvement would annoy the Corcyraeans, probably to the point of war. They dispatched a large garrison to reinforce the democrats in the city, accompanied by many permanent settlers for the reestablished colony, and the force traveled by the more difficult land route, "out of fear that the Corcyraeans might prevent them if they went by sea" (1.26.2). Scholars have failed to find a tangible, practical, material reason for Corinth's decision to

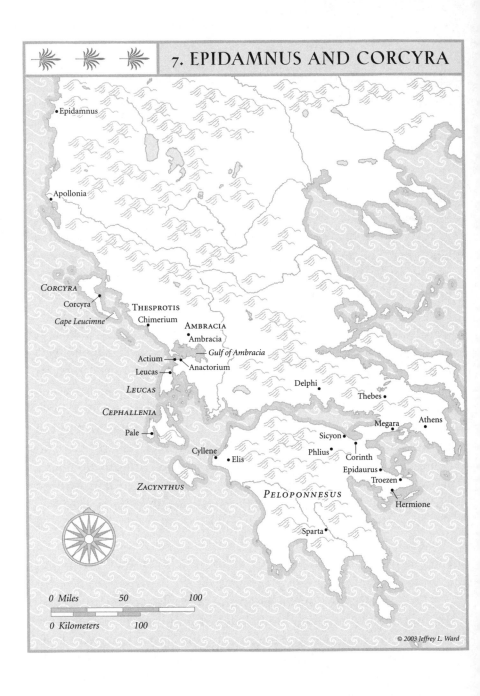

• Epidamnus

• Apollonia

CORCYRA
Corcyra •
Cape Leucimne

THESPROTIS
Chimerium •

AMBRACIA
• Ambracia
—— Gulf of Ambracia
Actium —•
Leucas —•
—Anactorium

LEUCAS

Delphi
•

Thebes
•

CEPHALLENIA

Pale —•

Megara
•

Athens
•

Cyllene
•

• Elis

Sicyon
•

Phlius
•

Corinth
•

Epidaurus •

Troezen
•

ZACYNTHUS

PELOPONNESUS

Hermione
•

Sparta •

0 Miles   50   100

0 Kilometers   100

© 2003 Jeffrey L. Ward

enter the fray, but Thucydides provides an explanation on other grounds: the Corinthians acted chiefly out of hatred for their disrespectful colony. "In the common festivals they did not give them the customary privileges, nor did they begin by having a Corinthian commence the initial sacrifices, as the other colonies did, but treated them contemptuously" (1.25.3–4).

The Corinthian decision was also, no doubt, part of the continuing contest over disputed colonies, a form of imperial competition familiar among European states late in the nineteenth century. It has long been clear that many of the European empires were unprofitable from a material point of view, and that the practical reasons given for acquiring them were excuses rather than plausible explanations. The real motives were often psychological and irrational rather than economic and practical; that is, they derived from questions of honor and prestige.

So it was with the Corinthians, who were determined to build a sphere of influence in the Greek northwest. This brought them into conflict with Corcyra, whose power had grown while Corinth's declined. The Corcyraeans had acquired a fleet of 120 warships, second in size only to that of Athens, and for years they had challenged Corinthian hegemony in the region. The public insults they suffered at festivals must have been the final provocation for the Corinthians, who seized the excuse offered them by the Epidamnian invitation.

Corinth's intervention ended the Corcyraeans' indifference to events in Epidamnus, and its fleet immediately and insolently delivered an ultimatum to the city: the democrats must dismiss the garrison and colonists sent by Corinth and take back the exiled aristocrats. Corinth could not accept such terms without disgrace, and the democrats in Epidamnus could not safely accept the loss of their reinforcements.

Corcyra's self-assured arrogance rested on its current naval power, while Corinth had no warships to speak of. The Corcyraeans sent forty ships to besiege Epidamnus, while the aristocratic exiles and their Illyrian allies enclosed it by land. But Corcyraean confidence was misplaced, for it ignored the fact that Corinth was rich, angry, allied to Sparta, and a member of the Peloponnesian League. In the past the Corinthians had been able to use those alliances to their own advantage, and they expected to do so again against Corcyra.

Corinth therefore announced the foundation of an entirely new colony at Epidamnus and invited settlers from all over Greece, who were sent to the area, accompanied by thirty Corinthian ships and three thousand soldiers. Additional ships and funds were provided by several other cities, including the major states of Megara and Thebes, members of the Spartan Alliance. While even a token force from the Spartans might have intimidated the Corcyraeans, the Spartans gave no assistance, perhaps already perceiving the danger inherent in the Corinthian expedition.

Shaken by these responses, the Corcyraeans sent negotiators to Corinth "with Spartan and Sicyonian ambassadors, whom they had invited along" (1.28.1). The Spartans' willingness to take part in the discussions clearly demonstrated their desire for a peaceful outcome. At the conference the Corcyraeans repeated their demands for a Corinthians withdrawal; failing that, Corcyra was willing to submit the dispute to arbitration by any mutually acceptable Peloponnesian state or, if the Corinthians preferred, to the oracle at Delphi. The Corcyraeans sincerely sought to reach a settlement, fully aware that they had underestimated Corinth's latent power. They also had little to fear from arbitration, for all the suggested parties in the judgment would be under the influence of Sparta and would, no doubt, require the Corinthians to remove themselves and the colonists, conditions that would satisfy the Corcyraeans. If the Corinthians refused and insisted on war, however, Corcyra would be forced to solicit aid elsewhere. The threat was unmistakable: if necessary, the Corcyraeans would seek an alliance with Athens.

CORINTH

A MINOR INCIDENT in a remote corner of the Greek world had produced a crisis that now began to threaten the stability of the Greek world as a whole. So long as the affair involved only Epidamnus and Corcyra the problem was purely local, for neither belonged to one of the two international alliances that dominated Greece. When Corinth became involved, however, and began to embroil members of the Spartan Alliance, prompting Corcyra to turn to Athens for help, a major war became conceivable. It was recognition of this very danger that had prompted the Spartans to agree to join the Corcyraean negotiators and lend support to a settlement of the quarrel.

The Corinthians, however, would not yield. While a flat refusal under the eyes of the Spartans would have been embarrassing, they made a counteroffer: if the Corcyraeans withdrew their ships from Epidamnus and the Illyrians departed, the Corinthians would consider Corcyra's proposal.

That proposal would have allowed the Corinthian forces to gain a strategic advantage in Epidamnus by strengthening their hold on the city, taking in supplies, and bolstering its defenses against a siege. The Corinthian suggestion was plainly not serious, but the Corcyraeans did not break off negotiations even then, and instead urged a mutual withdrawal of forces or a truce while the two sides negotiated in place. Again the Corinthians refused, this time declaring war in response and sending a fleet of seventy-five ships along with two thousand infantrymen to Epidamnus. They were intercepted en route by a Corcyraean force of eighty ships and were thoroughly defeated at the battle of Leucimne. On the same day Epidamnus surrendered to the Corcyraean besiegers. Corcyra now ruled the sea and the disputed city.

Burning with desire for revenge, the Corinthians spent the next two years building their largest fleet ever, and hired experienced rowers from throughout Greece, including cities in the Athenian Empire. The Athenians, still eager to stay out of the conflict, did not object, which may have strengthened the Corinthians' belief that Corcyraean claims of getting help from Athens were unfounded.

Their bluff called, the Corcyraeans finally did send an embassy to Athens to seek an alliance against Corinth. When the Corinthians learned of the mission they, too, dispatched ambassadors to Athens, "to prevent the addition of the Athenian fleet to the Corcyraeans' since that would impede their victory" (1.31). The original crisis, a small cloud in the blue sky, confined to the far northwest, just another in a long series of quarrels between Corcyraean colonists and their Corinthian metropolis, now threatened to reach a more dangerous level, involving at least one of the great powers of the Greek world.

CHAPTER THREE

Enter Athens (433–432)

IN SEPTEMBER 433 the Athenian assembly met on the Pnyx to hear the ambassadors from Corcyra and Corinth. Every argument was made, heard, and discussed before the full assembly. The same men who would be required to fight in any war that might result debated the issues and determined the course to take by their own votes.

The Corcyraeans faced a difficult task. No previous friendship existed between them and Athens, and material Athenian interests were involved in the quarrel. Why should the Athenians make an alliance that would entangle them in a war against Corinth, at the very least, and possibly against the entire Peloponnesian League? The Corcyraeans argued for the moral justness of their cause and for the legality of the alliance they proposed, since the Thirty Years' Peace expressly permitted affiliation with a neutral. Like most people, however, the Athenians were more concerned with questions of security and interest—issues on which the Corcyraeans were prepared to satisfy them: "We have a navy that is the greatest except for your own" (1.33.1–2), in other words, a force that could be added to consolidate Athenian power.

The Corcyraeans' most powerful appeal, however, was to fear. The Athenians needed the alliance, they argued, because a war between Athens and the Spartan Alliance by now seemed inevitable: "The Spartans are eager for war out of fear of you, and the Corinthians have great influence with them and are your enemies" (1.33.3). Athens should therefore accept the Corcyraean alliance for the most practical of reasons: "There are three fleets worthy of mention in Greece, yours, ours, and the Corinthians'; if the Corinthians get control of us first, you will see two of them become one, and you will have to fight against the Corcyraean and Peloponnesian fleets at once; if you accept us you will fight against them with our ships in addition to your own" (1.36.3).

The Corinthian spokesman had an even more difficult case to present. Corinth was, after all, the aggressor at Epidamnus and had rejected every offer for a peaceful solution, even against the advice of its allies. Their strongest case was to challenge the legality of an Athenian treaty with Corcyra. Technically, the Thirty Years' Peace did permit such an alliance, since Corcyra belonged to neither bloc, but the Corinthians argued that it violated the spirit of the treaty as well as common sense: "Although it says in the treaty that any of the unenrolled cities may join whichever side it likes, the clause is not meant for those who join one side with the intention of injuring the other" (1.40.2). No one who had negotiated or sworn to the original treaty could have imagined approving an alliance by one side with a neutral at war with the other. The Corinthians underscored this principle with a simple threat: "If you join with them, it will be necessary for us to include you in our revenge against them" (1.40.2–3).

The Corinthians went on to deny the Corcyrean claim that war was inevitable. They also reminded the Athenians of past favors, especially their service during the Samian uprising when they helped to dissuade Sparta and the Peloponnesian League from attacking Athens at a moment of great vulnerability. They believed they had confirmed on that occasion the key principle governing the relations between the two alliances, the one vital to the maintenance of peace: noninterference by each side in the other's sphere of influence. "Do not accept the Corcyraeans as allies against our wishes, nor help them to do wrong. In doing what we ask you will be behaving properly and serving your own interests in the best way" (1.43).

The Corinthian argument, however, was not entirely sound. Corcyra was not a Corinthian ally, as Samos had been allied to Athens, and even the broadest interpretation of the treaty did not prevent the Athenians from assisting a neutral attacked by Corinth. Athens would be on solid legal ground in accepting Corcyra's proposal. But the Corinthians were correct in a deeper sense: there could be no lasting peace if either side chose to help unaligned states at war with the other.

The behavior of the Athenians since 445 and throughout the period of the crisis makes it clear that they wanted to avoid war, but Corcyra presented a unique problem. Its defeat and the transfer of its navy would have created a Peloponnesian fleet strong enough to challenge Athenian naval supremacy, on which the power, prosperity, and indeed the very survival of Athens and its empire depended. Although the Athenians were thus threatened with a deadly change in the balance of power at one nearly immediate stroke, the Corinthians appear to have been confident that Athens would refuse a Corcyraean alliance, and would possibly even join the Corinthians against Corcyra, as they had the audacity to suggest. Why did they miscalculate so badly? For them, Corcyra was merely a local affair. In the pursuit of their narrow interests, intensified by a long-standing exasperation and anger at their humiliation by a lesser state, they underestimated the significance of their action to the balance of power in the international system. They made no effort to verify that the Athenians would stand aside while they made war on Corcyra. Instead, they ignored the danger and plunged ahead, hoping that all would proceed in their favor.

The Athenians seated on the hillside now faced the most difficult of choices. Almost all debates in the assembly ended within a single day, but the argument over the Corcyraean alliance lasted long enough to require a second meeting. On the first day opinion inclined toward rejection of the idea. We may assume feverish discussion overnight, and on the second day a new plan emerged. Instead of the full offensive and defensive commitment that was usual in a Greek alliance (*symmachia*) a proposal was made to enter into an alliance that was defensive only (*epimachia*), the first such relationship we hear of in Greek history. The chances are great that the innovative Pericles was its author. Throughout the crisis he had demonstrated his ability to shape Athenian policy, and Plutarch tells us that it was Pericles who "persuaded the people to send help to the Corcyraeans who were fighting the Corinthians and to attach themselves to a vigorous island with naval power" (*Pericles* 29.1).

Thucydides argues that the Athenians voted for the treaty because they believed that war with the Peloponnesians was inevitable, but the many who opposed it could not have agreed with that assessment. Why, they must have asked, should they risk war on behalf of Corcyra, when danger to Athens itself was still remote and problematical? The Athenians' action suggests, rather, the adoption of a policy aimed not at preparing for war but at deterring it: a middle way between the unpleasant choices of refusing the Corcyraeans, thereby risking the loss of their fleet to the Peloponnesians, and of accepting an offensive alliance likely to bring on an unwelcome conflict.

The defensive alliance was thus a precisely crafted diplomatic device meant to bring the Corinthians to their senses. To meet their new commitment the Athenians ordered a fleet of ten warships to Corcyra. If their intention had been to fight and defeat the Corinthians, they could easily have sent as many as two hundred from their sizable navy. Together with the ships of the Corcyraeans, a force of that size would either have forced the Corinthians to abandon their plans for war or guaranteed a smashing victory, the destruction of the enemy fleet, and the end of any threat from Corinth. The small number actually dispatched was therefore of more symbolic than military value, intended to show that Athens was serious in its pledge to deter the Corinthians. The choice of Lacedaemonius, the son of Cimon, as one of the fleet's commanders was also no coincidence, for it was clearly meant to disarm Spartan suspicion of his mission. He was a notable cavalryman, but we know nothing of any naval experience. His very name, which means "Spartan," is evidence of his father's close ties with the leaders of the Peloponnesian League.

Even more striking were the orders received by the Athenian commanders. They were not to fight unless the Corinthian fleet sailed against Corcyra itself, or one of its possessions, with the intention of making a landing. "These orders were given in order not to break the treaty" (1.45.3). Such commands are a nightmare for any naval officer, for in the melee of a naval battle, how can anyone be certain of the intentions of the enemy? Caution and patience might prevent a timely intervention; swift reaction to what might be a feint or a misunderstood maneuver could lead to an unnecessary engagement.

In modern language this was a policy of "minimal deterrence." The presence of an Athenian force demonstrated Athens' determination to prevent a shift in the balance of naval power; its small size showed that the Athenians did not intend to diminish or destroy Corinthian power. If the plan worked the Corinthians would merely sail home, and the crisis would pass. If the Corinthians did choose to fight, the Athenians might still hope to stay out of the battle. Perhaps the Corcyraeans might win without Athenian aid, as they did at Leucimne. Some Athenians also hoped "to wear the two sides out as much as possible against each other so that they might find Corinth and the other naval powers weaker in case it should be necessary to go to war with them" (1.44.2). Either way, the Athenians could avoid any engagement.

THE BATTLE OF SYBOTA

WHEN THE CORINTHIAN and Corcyraean fleets finally met at the battle of Sybota in September 433 the small Athenian squadron did not deter the Corinthians, as a larger contingent might have done. There is a considerable difference between the belief that one's actions may have unpleasant consequences at some time in the future and the fact of the presence of overwhelming forces that will bring immediate destruction. Eight allied cities had given help to Corinth in the previous battle at Leucimne; only two, Elis and Megara, joined it at Sybota. (See Map 8.) The others may have been deterred by Corinth's earlier defeat or by the new Corcyraean alliance with Athens. It is also possible that Sparta took steps to persuade its allies to stay out of the conflict. With 150 ships—90 of their own and 60 more provided by colonies and allies—the Corinthians attacked 110 Corcyraean vessels while the Athenians remained apart.

Soon, however, it became obvious that the Corcyraeans were being routed, and the Athenians could no longer stand aloof. "The situation had developed to the point where the Corinthians and Athenians necessarily had to fight one another" (1.49.7).

As the Corcyraean and Athenian forces prepared to defend Corcyra, the Corinthians, who had already launched their final attack, suddenly backed off. A second Athenian fleet had suddenly appeared on the horizon. In the heat of battle it was easy for the Corinthians to believe that its ships were part of a vast armada that would greatly outnumber and destroy them, and so they broke off the battle, and Corcyra was saved.

In fact, what they saw turned out to be a force of only twenty additional Athenian warships, sent out only days earlier to reinforce the

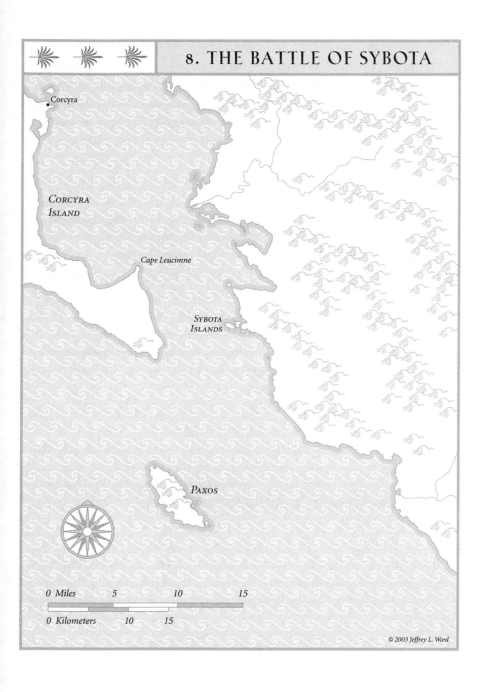

Corcyra

CORCYRA
ISLAND

Cape Leucimne

SYBOTA
ISLANDS

PAXOS

0 Miles   5   10   15

0 Kilometers   10   15

© 2003 Jeffrey L. Ward

original contingent. After the original ten had sailed, Plutarch tells us, Pericles' opponents criticized his plan: "He had provided little help for the Corcyraeans by sending ten ships, but a great pretext for complaint by their enemies" (*Pericles* 29.3). The best that could be achieved with this tactic was an unsatisfactory compromise. But the gods of war are capricious, and boldness often brings better results than reason would predict. Who could have imagined that the twenty ships of the reinforcement squadron, after days at sea and without any means of communicating with the forces off Corcyra, would arrive at exactly the moment that would enable them to save the island from conquest by Corinth?

The next day, bolstered by the presence of thirty undamaged Athenian ships, the Corcyraeans offered battle, but the Corinthians refused, fearful that the Athenians might regard the first day's skirmish as the beginning of a war against Corinth and seize the chance to destroy the Corinthian fleet. The Athenians, however, allowed them to sail away, and each side was scrupulous in disclaiming responsibility for a breach of the treaty. Corinth recognized that it could not win a war against Athens without enlisting the assistance of Sparta and its allies. But because the Spartans had already tried to restrain Corinth, the Corinthians could not expect to gain their support if they could be blamed for breaking the treaty. The Athenians, on the other hand, were careful not to give Sparta a reason to enter the quarrel.

Operationally, the Athenians' effort had succeeded: Corcyra and their fleet had been saved. But the policy of "minimal deterrence" was a strategic failure, for the Athenians' arrival had not deterred the Corinthians from fighting the battle nor had their intervention destroyed the Corinthians' capacity to fight. Frustrated and even angrier, they now were determined to bring the Spartans and their allies into the war to achieve their own goals and to gain vengeance against their enemies.

POTIDAEA

THE ATHENIANS NOW SAW that they must prepare for war, at least against Corinth, while they continued to try to avoid involving the

Peloponnesian League. Even before the battle of Sybota the Athenians had interrupted their grand building program to conserve their financial resources in case hostilities broke out. After Sybota they moved to shore up their positions in northwest Greece, Italy, and Sicily, and the following winter they sent an ultimatum to Potidaea, a city in the northern Aegean. (See Map 9). The Potidaeans were members of the Athenian alliance and at the same time colonists of Corinth, and unusually close to the mother city. Knowing that the Corinthians were planning revenge, the Athenians feared they might join with the hostile king of neighboring Macedon to spark a rebellion in Potidaea. From there it might spread to other states and cause serious problems in the empire.

Without any more specific provocation, the Athenians ordered the Potidaeans to pull down the walls that protected them on the seaward side, to send away the magistrates they annually received from Corinth, and to deliver to Athens a number of hostages. These steps were intended to remove the city from Corinthian influence and place it at the mercy of Athens. Once again, the Athenian strategy should be understood as a diplomatic response to a looming problem, a moderate choice between unwelcome extremes. Taking no action might invite rebellion while sending a military force to assert physical control over Potidaea would make the city safe for Athens, but it could be provocative. Issuing the ultimatum, however, delivered a powerful message to potential rebels at Potidaea, while remaining a matter of imperial regulation, clearly permitted by the Thirty Years' Peace.

Not surprisingly the Potidaeans objected to the demands, and discussions continued throughout the winter, until the Athenians finally ordered the commander of an expedition they had previously sent to Macedonia "to take hostages from the Potidaeans, pull down their walls, and keep watch on the cities near by so that they would not rebel" (1.57.6). Athenian suspicions proved to be justified; supported by the Corinthians the Potidaeans had already secretly petitioned Sparta for help in their uprising. In response the Spartan ephors had promised to invade Attica if the Potidaeans rebelled. What caused this reversal of policy at Sparta?

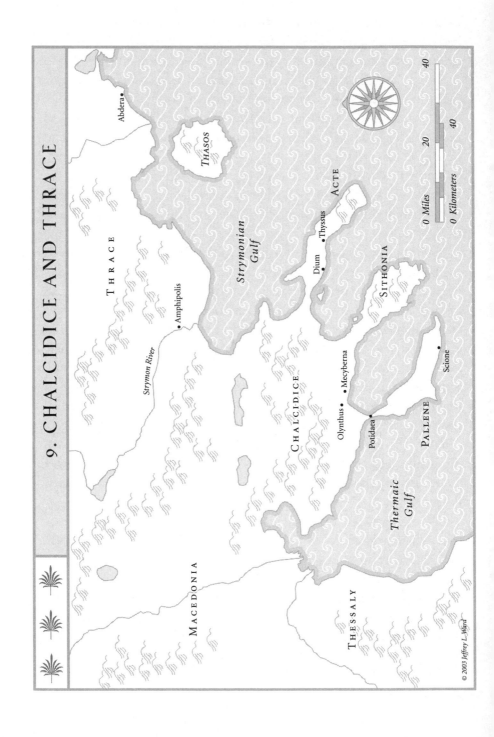

9. CHALCIDICE AND THRACE

MACEDONIA

THESSALY

THRACE

Strymon River

Amphipolis

Abdera

THASOS

Strymonian Gulf

ACTE

Thyssus

Dium

SITHONIA

CHALCIDICE

Mecyberna

Olynthus

Potidaea

PALLENE

Scione

Thermaic Gulf

0 Miles   20   40

0 Kilometers   40

© 2003 Jeffrey L. Ward

THE MEGARIAN DECREE

DURING THE SAME winter of 433–432 (in close proximity to the Potidaean ultimatum, but whether before or after is unclear) the Athenians had passed a decree barring the Megarians from the harbors of the Athenian Empire and from the Athenian agora. Economic embargoes are sometimes used in the modern world as diplomatic weapons, as a means of coercion short of war. In the ancient world, however, we know of no previous embargo employed in peacetime.

This was certainly another of Pericles' innovations, for contemporaries blamed the war on the decree and him for issuing it, though he defended it stubbornly to the end, even when it appeared to become the sole issue on which war or peace depended. Why did the Athenian leader introduce the embargo, and why did he and the majority of Athens' citizens approve and hold fast to it? Scholars have interpreted it variously as an act of economic imperialism, a device intended as a deliberate provocation to war, a statement of defiance to the Peloponnesian League, an attempt to enrage the Spartans into violating the treaty, and even the first act of war itself. The official explanation for the decree was that it was provoked by the Megarians' cultivation of sacred land claimed by the Athenians, their illegal encroachment upon borderlands, and their harboring of fugitive slaves.

Upon careful examination, however, the modern theories do not bear close scrutiny, and the ancient complaints can be dismissed as a mere pretext. The true purpose of the Megarian Decree was as a moderate intensification of diplomatic pressure to help prevent the spread of the war to Corinth's allies by ensuring that Megara was punished for its behavior at Leucimne and Sybota. The Corinthians could succeed only if the other Peloponnesians, especially Sparta, could be convinced to join the fight. Megara had both annoyed Athens and defied Spartan wishes by sending help to Corinth at Leucimne and Sybota, even when most of the Peloponnesian allies demurred. In time, these states might choose to join the Corinthians in another encounter with Athens; if enough of them took that step, the Spartans themselves could stay aloof only at the risk of their leadership of the alliance and their own security.

Once again, the Athenian action should be viewed as a middle path. To have done nothing might have encouraged Megara and other states to help Corinth. To attack the city by military force would have violated the treaty and brought Sparta into the war against Athens. The embargo, in contrast, would not bring Megara to its knees or inflict serious damage. It would cause discomfort to most Megarians and do significant harm to the men who prospered from trade with Athens and her empire—some of them, no doubt, members of the oligarchic council that governed the city. The punishment might also persuade Megara to stay out of future trouble and serve as a warning to other trading states that they were not immune from Athenian retaliation, even in a period of formal peace.

The Megarian Decree, however, was not without risks. The Megarians were certain to complain to the Spartans, who might feel compelled to come to their aid. But the Spartans might also easily refuse to do so, for the decree did not violate the treaty, which made no provisions for trade or economic relations. In addition, Pericles was a personal friend of Archidamus, by now the only king in Sparta (Pleistoanax had been sent into exile in 445). He knew that Archidamus favored peace and could expect that the Spartan leader would perceive his own peaceful intentions and the limited purposes of the decree, and would in turn help the other Spartans to understand them as well. While Pericles was correct in his assessment of Archidamus, he underestimated the passions aroused in some Spartans by the combination of events that had taken place since the alliance with Corcyra.

CHAPTER FOUR

The Decisions for War (432)

SPARTA CHOOSES WAR

THE SPARTAN EPHORS' pledge to the Potidaeans to invade Attica was a secret one, not endorsed by the Spartan assembly, and Sparta did not keep it when the Potidaeans launched their rebellion in the spring of 432. Neither their king nor a majority of their countrymen was yet prepared to go to war, but an influential faction was eager to change their minds.

The Athenian force dispatched to prevent an uprising in Potidaea was insufficient and arrived too late to be of much value. The Corinthians did not dare send an official expedition to help the rebels, which would have been a formal violation of the treaty. Instead, they organized a corps of "volunteers" commanded by a Corinthian general who led a force of Corinthians and Peloponnesian mercenaries. The Athenians, meanwhile, made peace with Macedon in order to free their forces fighting there for use against Potidaea and also committed additional reinforcements from Athens. By the summer of 432 a large force of men and ships surrounded the city, beginning a siege that would last more than two years and cost a vast sum of money.

With Potidaea under siege and the Megarians protesting bitterly about the Athenian embargo, the Corinthians were no longer the sole party with a case against Athens.[1] They therefore encouraged all the states that had any grievances to put pressure on the Spartans. Finally, in July 432, the ephors called a meeting of the Spartan assembly, inviting

---

[1] The island of Aegina, forced into the Athenian alliance during the First Peloponnesian War, secretly joined the Corinthians in complaining about mistreatment at the hands of Athens and stirring up the resentment of the other Peloponnesians (1.67.2), but the precise basis of their complaint is unclear.

any allied state with a complaint against Athens to come to Sparta and speak out. This was the only known occasion when allies were invited to address the Spartan assembly, rather than a meeting of the Spartan Alliance. Their resorting to this unusual procedure shows how reluctant the Spartans still were to fight in the summer of 432.

While the Megarians were the angriest participants, the Corinthians proved to be the most effective. They tried to persuade the Spartans that their traditional policy of prudence and reluctance to fight was disastrous in the face of the dynamic power of Athens, and underscored their argument by drawing a sharp distinction between the characters of the two peoples.

> They are revolutionary and quick to formulate plans and put them into action, while you preserve what you have, invent nothing new, and when you act do not even complete what is necessary. Again, they are daring beyond their power, run risks beyond wisdom, and are hopeful amidst dangers, while it is your way to do less than your power permits, to distrust your surest judgments, and to think you will be destroyed by any dangers. . . .
>
> With them alone it is the same thing to hope and to have, when once they have invented a scheme, because of the swiftness with which they carry out what they have planned. And in this way they wear out their entire lives with danger . . . because they consider tranquil peace a greater disaster than painful activity. . . . It is their nature neither to enjoy peace themselves nor to allow it to other men. (1.70)

However effective as polemic, both sides of the comparison were exaggerated. The Spartans could never have created their own great alliance and the one that led the Greeks to victory over the Persians had they been as sluggish as they were now being portrayed. Similarly, Athens had acted in full accord with the letter and spirit of the Thirty Years' Peace, as the Corinthians themselves implicitly acknowledged when they restrained their allies at the time of the Samian rebellion. Athens' troubling behavior over the previous year had plainly been a reaction to recent actions initiated by Corinth—actions about which the Corinthians said as little as possible.

The Corinthians concluded their address with a threat: the Spartans must come to the aid of Potidaea and their other allies and invade Attica, "lest you betray your friends and kinsmen to their worst enemies and turn the rest of us to some other alliance" (1.71.4). The threat was empty—there was no other alliance to which they could turn—but because Sparta's security and its way of life rested on the integrity of its alliance, even the suggestion of defections was alarming.

The next speaker was a member of an Athenian embassy who, Thucydides says, "happened to be present beforehand on other business" (1.72.1). We are not told what that "business" might be, and it seems clear that it was merely a pretext to allow the Athenians to present their views. Pericles and the Athenians did not want to send an official spokesman to a Spartan assembly to answer complaints, a gesture that would have conceded Sparta's right to judge Athenian behavior rather than obliging it to submit disagreements to arbitration, as the treaty required. They did, however, wish to prevent Sparta from yielding to the arguments of its allies, to argue that Athens had gained its power justly, and to demonstrate that that power was formidable. The ambassador ascribed the growth of the Athenian Empire to a series of necessities imposed by the demands of fear, honor, and a reasonable self-interest—matters that the Spartans should well understand. His tone was not conciliatory, but businesslike, and his conclusion insisted the parties adhere to the precise letter of the treaty: the submission of all disputes to arbitration. Should the Spartans refuse, however, "we shall try to take vengeance on those who have started the war when you have led the way" (1.78.5).

Was this speech deliberately provocative, intended to antagonize the Spartans into violating their oaths and starting the war? Such a view assumes that the only ways to seek peace are via attempts to appease anger, to explain differences charitably, and to make concessions. Sometimes, however, the best way to prevent war is through deterrence, by conveying a message of strength, confidence, and determination. This tactic can be especially effective when it leaves the other side an honorable way out, as the arbitration clause provided for the Spartans. The best contemporary witness, at any rate, tells us that war was still not the Athenians' goal: "They wanted to make clear the power of their city, to offer a reminder to the older men of what they already knew and to the younger men the things of which they were ignorant, thinking that because of their arguments the Spartans would incline to peace instead of war" (1.72.1).

The Athenians' strategy seemed especially reasonable given that Sparta's kings were traditionally influential in decisions of war and peace; in 432 the only active Spartan king was Archidamus, a personal friend of Pericles, "a man with a reputation for wisdom and prudence" (1.79.2), who would soon demonstrate his opposition to armed conflict.

After the foreigner had spoken the Spartans all withdrew. Although the assembly was hostile and confident that Athens could easily be beaten in a brief war, King Archidamus argued otherwise. Athens' power, he insisted, was greater than what Sparta had been accustomed to facing, and of a different kind. A walled city, with substantial financial resources, a naval empire, and command of the sea could wage a war such as the Spartans had never fought. Archidamus feared, he told them, "that we shall pass this war on to our children" (1.81.6).

The mood of the assembly was so contentious, however, that Archidamus could not simply recommend the Athenian offer, so he proposed a moderate alternative: the Spartans should limit themselves to registering an official complaint; at the same time, they should prepare for the kind of war they would really have to face if discussion failed, by seeking ships from the barbarians (primarily the Persians) and from the other Greeks. If the Athenians yielded, no action need be taken. If not, there would be plenty of time to fight when the Spartans were better prepared, in two or three years.

The king's plan was, not surprisingly, unwelcome to the Corinthians, the other complaining parties, and those in Sparta who were eager to take action. Any chance of saving Potidaea, they believed, required swift action. The Corinthians, in particular, did not want a settlement of grievances, but rather a free hand to crush Corcyra once and for all; they likewise wanted revenge against the Athenians, and indeed, the destruction of the Athenian Empire, a position with which the advocates of war in Sparta agreed. Taken together with a selective account of the history of the last fifty years, the affairs of Corcyra, Potidaea, and Megara seemed to confirm for most Spartans the Corinthian picture of the arrogance of the Athenians and the danger presented by their growing power.

The short and blunt response by the bellicose ephor Sthenelaidas, was typical:

> I don't understand the lengthy arguments of the Athenians. They praise themselves highly, but they don't deny that they are doing wrong to our allies and to the Peloponnesus. . . . Others may have much money, ships, and horses, but we have good allies whom we must not betray to the Athenians. Nor should we submit to judgments by courts or words, for we have not been injured by words. Instead, we must take swift vengeance with all our forces. And let no one tell us that we must take time to consider when we have been wronged; rather let those who contemplate doing a wrong reflect for a long time. So vote for war, Spartans, in a manner worthy of Sparta. Do not allow the Athenians to grow stronger and do not betray your allies, but let us, with the help of the gods, march out against those who are doing wrong. (1.86)

Claiming he could not tell which side of the debate was making the louder clamor, but "wanting to make them more eager for war by an open demonstration of their opinion," the ephor called for a division. When the count was taken, a large majority voted that the Athenians had broken the peace; it was in effect, a vote for war.

Why did the Spartans decide to undertake what might prove to be a long and difficult conflict against a uniquely powerful opponent, when they faced no immediate threat, stood to gain no tangible benefit, and were provoked by no direct harm to themselves? What had undermined the normally conservative Spartan majority favoring peace, led by the prudent and respected King Archidamus? Thucydides believed that the Spartans voted to fight, not because they were persuaded by the arguments of their allies, "but because they were afraid that the Athenians might become too powerful, seeing that the greater part of Greece was already in their hands" (1.88). His general explanation for the origin of the war was this: "I think that the truest cause, but the least spoken of, was the growth of Athenian power, which presented an object of fear to the Spartans and forced them to go to war" (1.23.6).

The fact remains, however, that the power of Athens had not grown during the dozen years between the peace and the battle of Sybota, nor had Athenian foreign policy been aggressive, as even the Corinthians had recognized as early as 440. The only increase in Athenian might had come as a result of its alliance with Corcyra in 433, made in response to a Corinthian initiative taken against Spartan advice, and the evidence was clear that in that case the Athenians had acted reluctantly and defensively, seeking only to prevent the Corinthians from causing a major shift in the balance of power.

But people in crisis are also moved by the fear of future threats. So it was with the Spartans, who grew alarmed when it seemed to them that "the power of the Athenians began to manifest itself and to lay hold on their allies. Then the situation became unendurable, and the Spartans decided they must try with all their resolution to destroy that power if they could and to launch this war" (1.118.2). All three versions of Thucydides' explanation justify his analysis of the fundamental motives that governed the relations between states: fear, honor, and interest. The deepest self-interest of the Spartans required them to maintain the integrity of the Peloponnesian League and their own leadership of it. Their concern was that the Athenians' growing strength and influence would enable them to continue to annoy Sparta's allies, to the point where those allies would abandon the Spartan Alliance to defend themselves, thereby dissolving the league and Sparta's hegemony. The Spartans' honor, their conception of themselves, depended not only on the recognition of that leadership but also on maintaining their peculiar polity, whose security, in turn, depended on the same factors. The Spartans were therefore willing to expose themselves to the great dangers of a war to preserve an alliance they had created precisely to save them from danger. To do so meant serving the interests of their allies, even if those interests threatened their own safety. It was not the last time in history that the leader of an alliance would find itself led by lesser allies to pursue policies it would not have chosen on its own.

Following the decision of the assembly the ephors called for a meeting of the Spartan Alliance to take a formal vote on the subject of war. The allies did not gather until August, and not all of them came to the meeting; presumably those who remained home disapproved of its purpose. Of those who attended, a majority (though not a large majority, such as Thucydides reports at the purely Spartan assembly) voted for war. Not all the allies, therefore, had concluded that the war was inevitable; not all of them believed it was just; not all of them judged the undertaking to be easy or of certain success; not all of them thought it was necessary.

The Spartans and their allies could have launched an invasion at once and redeemed their promise to the Potidaens only a few months late. Preparations for such an invasion were simple and would have required no more than a few weeks, and September and October would have provided favorable weather either for a battle or for the destruction of property if the Athenians should refuse to fight. Although the Athenian grain crop had long since been harvested, there was still time to inflict significant damage on grape vines and olive trees and to the farmhouses outside the city walls. If the Athenians were eager for an engagement, as the Spartans expected, a September invasion would give them plenty of incentive.

But the Spartans and their allies took no military action for almost a year. In the interim the Spartans sent three missions to Athens, of which at least one seems to have been a sincere effort to avoid war. The long delay before the onset of hostilities and the ongoing attempt at negotiation suggest that after the emotion of the debate had passed the cautious and sober arguments of Archidamus took effect and restored the mood in Sparta to its usual conservatism. Perhaps war might yet be averted.

THE ATHENIAN DECISION FOR WAR

THE FIRST SPARTAN mission to Athens, probably in late August, demanded that the Athenians "drive out the curse of the goddess," referring to an act of sacrilege committed two centuries earlier by a member of Pericles' mother's family with which Pericles was widely associated. The Spartans hoped that through this incident he would be blamed for Athens' troubles and discredited, because, "as the most powerful man of his time and the leader of his state, he opposed the Spartans in everything and did not allow the Athenians to yield but kept driving them toward war" (1.126.3). Pericles had indeed always opposed concessions without arbitration; once the Spartans and their allies voted for war, he rejected further negotiations as merely a tactical maneuver meant to undermine Athenian resolve.

Pericles crafted an Athenian response that demanded in turn that the Spartans expiate not one but two long-standing religious violations by expelling the responsible parties. The first sacrilege involved the killing of helots who had taken sanctuary in a temple, and called attention to the fact that the Spartans, who would wage the war under the slogan "freedom for the Greeks," ruled despotically over a vast number of Greeks in their own land. The second recalled the deeds of a Spartan king who had tyrannized his fellow Greeks before treasonously going over to the Persians.

The Spartans sent other envoys making various demands, but finally settled on one: "They proclaimed publicly and in the clearest language that there would be no war if the Athenians withdrew the Megarian Decree" (1.139.1). This retreat from their earlier position clearly indicates a change in Sparta's political climate since the vote for war. Plutarch says that Archidamus "tried to settle the complaints of the allies peacefully to soften their anger" (*Pericles* 29.5), but neither the king nor his opponents was firmly in command. Archidamus, apparently, was strong enough to force a continuation of negotiations, but his opponents could continue to demand concessions without arbitration. The compromise, therefore, still rejected arbitration but reduced the demands to one.

This concession amounted to a betrayal of Corinthian interests and, by supporting the Megarians without submitting to arbitration, the Spartans demonstrated their power and reliability as leaders of the alliance, thereby isolating Corinth. If the Corinthians threatened secession under those circumstances, Archidamus and the majority of Spartans were prepared to let them try. The Spartans had now made a serious effort, at some risk to themselves, to avoid war; the decision now lay with Athens.

The Spartans' offer persuaded many Athenians, who questioned the wisdom of the city's going to war simply over the Megarian Decree, which was, after all, originally a mere tactical maneuver and certainly not in itself worth fighting over. Pericles remained firm, however, insisting on the arbitration required by the treaty, but he could not ignore the pressure for a response. That came in the shape of a formal decree of official charges that had ostensibly provoked the embargo, which was sent to Megara and Sparta as a defense of the Athenian action. "This decree was proposed by Pericles and contained a reasonable and humane justification of this policy," says Plutarch (*Pericles* 30.3). Pericles explained his refusal to rescind the embargo by reference to an obscure Athenian law that forbade him from taking down the tablet on which the decree was inscribed. The Spartans countered: "Then don't take it down, turn the tablet around, for there is no law against that" (*Pericles* 30.1–3), but Pericles held fast and kept the majority with him.

At last the Spartans sent an ultimatum: "The Spartans want peace, and there will be peace if you give the Greeks their autonomy" (1.139.3). This amounted to a demand for the dissolution of the Athenian Empire, and Pericles would have preferred the argument in the Athenian assembly to focus on that obviously unacceptable requirement, but his opponents were able to set the terms of the debate. The Athenians "resolved to give an answer after having considered everything once and for all." Many spoke, some arguing that the war was necessary, others that "the decree should not be a hindrance to peace but should be withdrawn" (1.139.3).

Pericles' defense of his policy which rested publicly on what might seem a legal technicality, actually had a far more fundamental rationale. The Spartans consistently refused to submit to arbitration, as the treaty required, and instead sought to win their point by threats or force. "They want to resolve their complaints by war instead of discussion, and now they are here, no longer requesting but already demanding. . . . Only a flat and clear refusal of these demands will make it plain to them that they must treat you as equals" (1.140.2, 5). Pericles was prepared to yield on any specific point; had the Spartans submitted to arbitration, he would have been compelled to accept the decision. What he could not abide, however, was direct Spartan interference in the Athenian Empire at Potidaea and Aegina or with Athenian commercial and imperial policy as represented by the Megarian Decree. That concession would effectively grant that Athenian hegemony in the Aegean and control of her own empire required Spartan permission. If the Athenians gave way when threatened now, they would abandon their claim to equality and leave themselves subject to future blackmail. Pericles carefully articulated this danger in his speech to the assembly:

> Let none of you think that you are going to war over a trifle if we do not rescind the Megarian Decree, whose withdrawal they hold out especially as a way of avoiding war, and do not reproach yourselves with second thoughts that you have gone to war for a small thing. For this "trifle" contains the affirmation and the test of your resolution. If you yield to them you will immediately be required to make another concession which will be greater, since you will have made the first concession out of fear. (1.140.5)

For many Spartans, and for some Athenians as well, it must have been difficult to understand why this trifle of a decree merited a military engagement. Was Athens justified in its position? The grievances at hand were actually important only as they related to the quarrel between the two sides; Sparta's single nonnegotiable demand contained nothing of material or strategic significance. If the Athenians had withdrawn the Megarian Decree, the crisis would probably have been averted, and subsequently several circumstances might have encouraged a continuation of the peace. Sparta's betrayal of Corinth would surely have led to coolness between the two states, and possibly even a rift serious enough to have distracted the Spartans from the conflict with Athens. Other problems might also have arisen in the Peloponnesus, as they had in the past. The longer peace could be maintained, the greater was the chance that all would be reconciled to the status quo.

On the other hand one faction in Sparta, dating back at least half a century, remained jealous and suspicious of the Athenians and implacably hostile to their empire. An Athenian concession might have calmed the fears of a majority of the Spartans for a time, but the enemies of Athens would always be a disruptive force. Yielding in 431 might only have encouraged greater Spartan intransigence and have made war in the future all the more likely.

Such considerations were foremost in Pericles' mind, but his decision rested also on the strategy he had formulated for fighting the war. Strategy is not merely a matter of military plans, as tactics may be.

Peoples and leaders turn to war to achieve their goals when other means have failed, and they formulate a strategy that they believe will attain them through force of arms. Before the outbreak of war, however, different strategies can have different effects on the very decisions that bring on the war or avoid it. In the crisis of 432/1 both Sparta and Athens chose strategies that inadvertently helped foster the war.

The usual pattern of warfare between Greek states was for one phalanx to march into enemy territory, where it would be met by its foe's phalanx. The two armies would clash and, within the span of a single day, the issue that precipitated the conflict would be decided. Since Sparta's forces would greatly outnumber those of the Athenians the Spartans had every reason for confidence if the Athenians engaged them in the typical manner, and most Spartans had no doubt that they would. If they chose a different course of action, the Spartans were certain that a year, or two, or three, of ravaging Athenian territory would bring either the decisive battle they sought or an Athenian surrender. At the beginning of the war, the Spartans, as well as the rest of the Greeks, were convinced that this simple offensive strategy guaranteed swift and sure victory. Had they believed they would need to fight a long, difficult, costly war of uncertain outcome, as the Athenians and Archidamus tried to persuade them would be the case, they might have acted differently.

Pericles, however, devised a novel strategy made possible by the unique character and extent of Athens' power. Their navy enabled the Athenians to rule over an empire that provided them income with which they could both sustain their supremacy at sea and obtain whatever goods they needed by trade or purchase. Although Attica's lands and crops were vulnerable to attack, Pericles had all but turned Athens itself into an island by constructing the Long Walls that connected the city with its port and naval base at Piraeus. In the current state of Greek siege warfare these walls were invulnerable when defended, so that if the Athenians chose to withdraw within them they could remain there safely, and the Spartans could neither get at them nor defeat them.

Pericles' strategy, which Athens employed so long as he was alive, was fundamentally defensive, although it did contain some limited offensive elements. He believed that "if the Athenians would remain quiet, take care of their fleet, refrain from trying to extend their empire

in wartime and thus putting their city in danger, they would prevail"
(2.65.7). They were therefore to reject battle on land, abandon the
countryside, and retreat behind their walls, while the Spartans ravaged
their fields to no avail. Meanwhile the Athenian navy would launch a
series of raids on the coast of the Peloponnesus, not meant to do serious harm but merely to annoy and harass the enemy and to give it a
taste of how much damage the Athenians could do if they chose. The
intention was both to demonstrate to the Spartans and their allies that
they were powerless to defeat Athens, and to exhaust them psychologi-
cally, not physically or materially. The natural divisions within the
loose organization of the Spartans Alliance, such as the one between
the more vulnerable coastal states and the safer interior states, would
assert themselves in costly quarrels. It would soon become obvious
that the Peloponnesians could not win, and a peace would be negotiated. Thoroughly discredited, the Spartan war faction would lose
power to the reasonable parties who had kept the peace since 446/5.
Athens could then look forward to an era of peace more firmly
founded on the enemy's awareness of its inability to gain a victory.

This plan was much better suited to Athens than the traditional
one of confrontation between phalanxes of infantry, but it did contain
serious flaws, and reliance on it helped cause the failure of Pericles'
diplomatic strategy of deterrence. Its first weakness was its fundamental lack of credibility. Events would show that Pericles was indeed able
to persuade the Athenians to adopt his scheme and hold to it so long as
he was their leader, but few Spartans, and indeed few Greeks, would
believe it was feasible until they saw it put into practice. The Athenians
would, for example, have to tolerate the insults and accusations of
cowardice the enemy would hurl at them from beneath their walls.
That would represent a violation of the entire Greek cultural experience, the heroic tradition that placed bravery in warfare at the peak of
Greek virtues. Most of the Athenians, moreover, lived in the country,
and they would have to watch passively from the protection of the
city's walls while the enemy destroyed their crops, damaged their trees
and vines, and looted and burned their homes. No Greeks who had
ever had any chance of resisting had been willing to do that, and little
more than a decade earlier the Athenians had come out to fight rather
than allow such devastation.

A second weakness in the Periclean plan was that it would be hard to persuade the Athenians to go to war with such a strategy and harder still to keep them committed to it once the war began. When the Spartans invaded, the Athenians were "dejected and angered at having to abandon their homes and the temples that had always been theirs, ancestral relics of the ancient polity, at facing a change in their way of life, at nothing less than each man having to abandon his own polis" (2.16.2). When the invaders came closer to the city many Athenians, especially the younger men, insisted on going out to fight, and turned with fury against Pericles, "because he did not lead them out to battle, and they held him responsible for all their suffering" (2.21.3). Finally, Pericles was forced to use his extraordinary influence to prevent meetings of the assembly, "fearing that if the people came together they would make a mistake by acting out of anger instead of using their judgment" (2.22.1).

No one but Pericles could have persuaded the Athenians to adopt such a plan and hold to it. He was, however, in his mid-sixties, and if the crisis passed quickly but flared up again after his death, the strategy would no longer be possible, and the alternative was almost certain defeat. Such thoughts may have made Pericles' diplomacy more intransigent.

The Athenian scheme had still another flaw. At first glance its approach might seem to have been especially suitable: because Athens had defensive aims, it should also have adopted a defensive strategy. But since the most desirable goal was to avoid war by means of deterrence, a defensive plan was not appropriate. The objective of deterrence is to arouse such fear in the enemy as to make him to decide against fighting, but Pericles' strategy actually presented the Spartans with little to fear. If, for example, the Athenians refused to fight, the only cost to the Spartans would be the effort it took to march into Attica for a month or so and wreak what havoc they could. If the Athenians landed forces on the Peloponnesus, they could do little harm unless they built forts and remained for a considerable period. If they built forts away from the coast they could be surrounded, and starved out; if they built them on the coast, they could be cut off and prevented from doing any destruction. None of these efforts would be particularly painful or costly to the Spartans. More perceptive individuals might have seen that over time the Athenians would have been able to damage at least the coastal states by raids and by interfering with their trade, while Sparta's inability to protect them might have eroded its leadership of the alliance and encouraged dangerous defections. But few would have had the imagination to see that prospect in the dim future.

Had the Athenians been able to devise such a plan and to foresee such an outcome they might not have gone to war, but that option played no part in Pericles' plan. Without an obvious, credible, frightening offensive threat his diplomatic strategy of deterrence was crippled and doomed to failure.

Had he believed that he needed a more powerful offensive to deter war Pericles might not have imposed the Megarian Decree, or might have withdrawn it as the Spartans had asked, accepting the risks of future trouble. But Pericles was confident that his own defensive strategy would succeed, so he remained firm. He persuaded the Athenians to adopt his very language in their final answer to the Spartans: "They would do nothing under dictation, but they were prepared to resolve the complaints by arbitration according to the treaty on the basis of reciprocal equality" (1.145.1).

Part Two

PERICLES' WAR

IT IS CUSTOMARY to refer to the first ten years of the war as the "Archidamian War," by the name of the Spartan king who led the early invasions of Attica. But Archidamus was a player of the second rank in its origins and in the strategies that governed it. A more accurate title would be the "Ten Years War," but the first part of it would rightly be called "Pericles' War," for it was the Athenian leader who dominated its beginnings and its first direction. Although Pericles' diplomacy aimed at avoiding a war against Sparta and its alliance, the conflict that broke out in 431 deserves to bear his name. The failure of his plan of moderation and deterrence led to the war, and the strategy that he formulated and insisted upon shaped its course for its first years. It was not until several years after his death that the Athenians departed from his strategy and sought a new way to win. Even after his death his shadow influenced its course and the behavior of many of its chief figures.

CHAPTER FIVE

War Aims and Resources (432–431)

SPARTA

SPARTA'S SLOGAN in waging the war was "freedom for the Greeks" (2.8.4), which meant the destruction of the Athenian Empire and the liberation of the states it ruled. Penetrating the propaganda aimed at public opinion, Thucydides tells us that the Spartans' true motive was their fear of Athens' growing power, "and the Spartans decided they must try with all their might to destroy that power if they could and to launch this war" (1.118). Some Spartans also sought the restoration of their former position as the sole hegemonal state in the Greek world and the honor and glory that were attached to it.

Achieving any of these goals required the destruction of Athens' key resources: its walls, which made the city secure against the power of the Spartan army; its fleet, which gave it command of the seas; and its empire, which provided the money that supported its navy. A victory that left any of these intact was of limited value, so Sparta had to take the offensive.

The Spartan Alliance included most of the states in the Peloponnesus, the Megarians on its northeastern frontier, the Boeotians, northern Locrians, and Phocians in central Greece and, in the west, the Corinthian colonies of Ambracia, Leucas, and Anactorium. (See Maps 10 and 11.) In Sicily the Spartans were allied to Syracuse and all the Dorian cities except Camarina, and in Italy to Locri and their own colony Taras. The heart of the alliance, however, was its splendid, heavily armed infantry made up of Peloponnesians and Boeotians. This was two or three times the size of the Athenian hoplite phalanx and widely regarded as the best in the world. The Spartans' strategy rested on their confidence in the invincibility of this formidable force against any opponent.

At the beginning of the war Pericles admitted that in a single battle

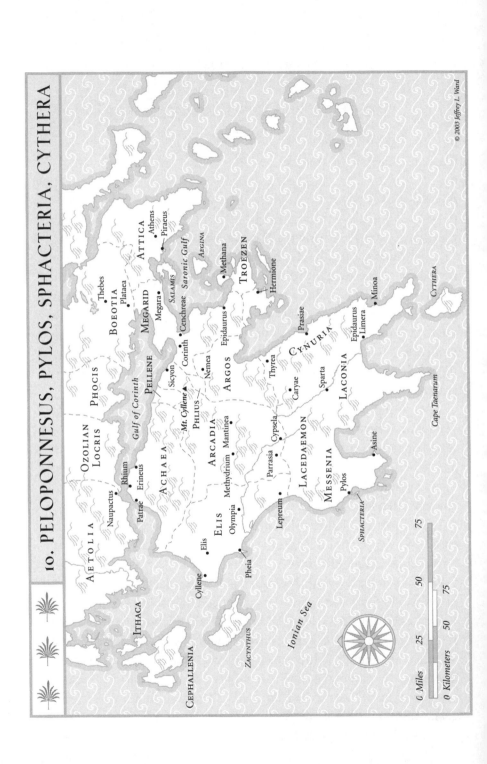

10. PELOPONNESUS, PYLOS, SPHACTERIA, CYTHERA

ITHACA

CEPHALLENIA

ZACYNTHUS

Ionian Sea

AETOLIA

Naupactus

Rhium
Erineus
Patrae

ACHAEA

Cyllene

Pheia

ELIS

Elis

Olympia

OZOLIAN
LOCRIS

PHOCIS

Gulf of Corinth

PELLENE

Mt. Cyllene ▲

PHLIUS

Sicyon

Corinth

Nemea

Methydrium Mantinea

ARCADIA

Parrasia

Lepreum

Cypsela

LACEDAEMON

MESSENIA

Pylos

SPHACTERIA

Asine

Thebes
Plataea

BOEOTIA

MEGARID

Megara

SALAMIS

Cenchreae

Saronic Gulf

ATTICA

Athens
Piraeus

AEGINA

Epidaurus

Methana

TROEZEN

Hermione

ARGOS

Thyrea

Caryae

Sparta

LACONIA

Prasiae

CYNURIA

Epidaurus
Limera

Minoa

Cape Taenarum

CYTHERA

© 2003 Jeffrey L. Ward

0 Miles   25   50   75

0 Kilometers   50   75

the Peloponnesian army was a match for all the rest of Greece. In 446, when a Spartan army had invaded Attica, the Athenians had chosen not to fight but to make peace, abandoning their land empire in central Greece and conceding Spartan dominance on the Greek mainland. That history helps explain why the Spartan war party was not persuaded by the arguments for caution made by King Archidamus. To them the traditional approach was bound to succeed: the Spartans needed merely to invade Attica during the growing season. Either the Athenians would yield as they had in 446, or, if their courage allowed, they would come out to fight and be defeated. In either case the war would be short and Spartan victory certain.

But Sparta's self-assurance rested on old thinking, and overlooked the fact that the creation of the Athenian Empire and its revenues, its vast and well-trained navy, and the erection of the city walls of Athens and of the Long Walls connecting it to the fortified port of Piraeus amounted to what we today would call a revolution in military affairs. They permitted a new style of warfare against which traditional methods would be ineffectual, but the Spartans could not or would not adjust to the new military realities.

Some Spartans believed that Athens, unlike any other Greek city, might choose neither to fight nor to surrender immediately, but most were confident that not even the Athenians could withstand siege conditions for long. When the war began the Spartans expected that "they would destroy the power of the Athenians in a few years if they wasted their land" (1.102.2). Most of the Greeks agreed: if the Peloponnesians invaded Attica, "some thought that Athens could hold out for a year, some for two, but no one for more than three years" (7.28.3).

King Archidamus, at least, knew that Athens could stand fast indefinitely without either giving battle or surrendering, so that superiority in hoplites would not guarantee victory. An alternate strategy of inciting rebellion in the empire, however, would require a navy able to defeat the Athenians at sea, and that called for sufficient funds. Archidamus pointed out, however, that the Peloponnesians had "neither money in the public treasury nor [could they] raise money from taxation" (1.80.4). When the war began the Peloponnesians had about a hundred triremes, but they lacked the rowers, steersmen, and captains skilled in the maneuvers of modern naval warfare perfected by the

Athenians. In any combat at sea the Peloponnesians would be inferior in ships, sailors, and tactics.

The Corinthians tried to argue against Archidamus' pessimistic but realistic assessment, but most of their proposals were impossible to carry out. They were reduced to wishful thinking, for in the end they relied on "all the other such devices as cannot now be foreseen" (1.122.1) and on the unpredictability of war, which "itself contrives its own devices to meet events" (1.121.1).

ATHENS

NO DEFENSIVE WAR plan like that proposed by Pericles had ever been attempted in Greek history, for no state before the coming of the Athenian imperial democracy ever had the means to attempt it. For all the difficulties it presented, however, it was better than the traditional method of warfare. Any thought of meeting the enemy in a land battle would have been foolish because of the great advantage in numbers held by the Peloponnesians. At the beginning of the war the Athenians had an army of thirteen thousand infantrymen of an age (twenty to forty-five) and condition to fight in battle, and another sixteen thousand above and below the age to serve in the phalanx, who were able to man the border forts and the walls surrounding Athens and Piraeus and those connecting them. Plutarch tells us that the Spartan army that invaded Attica in 431 numbered sixty thousand (*Pericles* 33.4). That number is too high, but the Spartan forces must have outnumbered Athens' fighting hoplites by a factor of between two and three to one.

The power and hopes of Athens rested on her magnificent navy. In her dockyards lay at least three hundred seaworthy warships, as well as others that could be repaired and used in case of need. Her free allies—Lesbos, Chios, and Corcyra—could also provide ships, perhaps over a hundred in all. Against this armada the Peloponnesians could provide only about a hundred ships, and the skill and experience of their crews were no match for those of the Athenians, as the first decade of the war would prove over and over again.

Pericles knew that the key to naval warfare was sufficient money to build and maintain the fleet and to pay its crews, and here, too, Athens had a vast advantage. In 431 the annual income of Athens was about 1,000 silver talents, of which 400 came from internal revenue and 600 from the tribute and other imperial sources.[1] Although about 600 talents were available for the cost of the war each year, that amount would not be sufficient to sustain the Periclean plan. Athens would also need to dip into her capital, and here, too, she was uniquely well provided. At the beginning of the war the Athenian treasury held 6,000 talents of coined silver, another 500 in uncoined gold and silver, and 40 talents worth of gold plating that covered the statue of Athena on the Acropolis and could be removed and melted down in an emergency. Against this extraordinary wealth the Peloponnesians were no match. Pericles was justified in telling the Athenians that "the Peloponnesians have no money, either public or private" (1.141.3). This was also true of most of their allies, and although the Corinthians were better off than the others, they had no reserve fund.

To evaluate the financial feasibility of Pericles' plan we need to know how long he expected the Spartans to hold out. Few scholars have investigated this question, assuming that a war of ten years was not outside his calculations. That idea rests, in part, on Pericles' speech to the Athenians on the eve of the war, in which he insisted that the Peloponnesians "have had no experience with wars overseas or extended in time; they only wage brief wars against each other because of their poverty" (1.142.3). He rightly argued that they lacked the resources to launch the kind of campaign that would have endangered the Athenian Empire, though nothing prevented them from launching a yearly invasion of Attica. These campaigns would last no longer than a month, and the only cost would be for the soldiers' food.

We can arrive at some estimate of the average annual cost of the Periclean strategy by examining the first year of the war, when Pericles was firmly in control and his plan applied to the letter. It was as inex-

---

[1] A talent represented a specified weight in silver. It is impossible to give a modern monetary equivalent, but it may be helpful to know that one talent was the cost of paying the crew of a warship for a month, that there were 6,000 drachmas in a talent, and that one drachma was a good day's pay for a skilled craftsman in Athens.

pensive a year as any could be while Athens was still in good fighting condition. When the Peloponnesians invaded Attica in 431 the Athenians sent 100 ships round the Peloponnesus. A squadron of 30 ships was dispatched to protect the crucial island of Euboea, and with another 70 already blockading Potidaea a total of 200 Athenian ships was in service for the year. It cost a talent to keep a ship at sea for a month, and eight months was the usual period they could be kept at sea. (The blockade, however, probably required the ships at Potidaea to stay the year round.) These estimates would result in an annual expenditure of 1,600 talents for naval forces. To this sum must be added the military cost, of which the greatest portion was spent at Potidaea. There were never fewer than 3,000 infantry posted in the siege there, and sometimes more; a conservative average is 3,500. The soldiers were paid a drachma a day and one for a retainer each day, so that the daily cost of the army was at least 7,000 drachmas, or one talent and one-sixth. If we multiply this by 360, a round number for a year, we arrive at 420 talents. There were certainly other military costs, as well, that need not be detailed here, but even if we include only the naval expenses and the cost of the troops at Potidaea, we arrive at an annual sum over 2,000 talents. (Two other calculations, based on different kinds of data, arrive at a similar figure.)

Pericles, then, must have expected to spend about 6,000 talents for a war of three years' duration.

In the second year the Athenians voted to set aside 1,000 talents from their reserves of 6,000 to be used only "if the enemy should make a naval attack against the city and they should have to defend it" (2.24.1), assigning the death penalty to anyone who might propose to apply it to any other purpose. This left a usable reserve fund of 5,000 talents in the treasury; if we include three years of additional imperial revenue for that period, a sum of 1,800 talents, we arrive at a total potential military budget of 6,800 talents. This would allow Pericles to maintain his strategy for three years, therefore, but not for a fourth.

Pericles was aware of these limitations, so he could not have anticipated a war of ten years, much less the twenty-seven it ultimately lasted. His ultimate goal was to bring about a change of opinion in Sparta, the true decision maker in the Peloponnesian League. To persuade the Spartans to consider peace required winning over only three of the five ephors. To get them and the Spartan assembly to accept peace the Athenians needed merely to help restore the natural majority that on balance kept Sparta conservatively and pacifically inside the Peloponnesus.

In this light, the plan of Pericles seemed to make excellent sense. The Spartan king, Archidamus, had already unsuccessfully warned his people that their expectations about the character of the coming war were mistaken: the Athenians would not fight a land battle and be defeated, and the Spartans had no other strategy available to meet that challenge. Pericles' tactic aimed to prove to the Spartans that their king had been right.

The main problem Pericles faced among his own people was to restrain them from offering battle in Attica, for any major offensive actions would conflict with his strategy. Not only would such aggression not bring victory but it might also provoke the enemy and prevent the reasonable policy of Archidamus from winning the upper hand. A policy of restraint at home and abroad, however, would likely bring the friends of peace to power in Sparta sooner or later.

Pericles might have expected such a change in Spartan opinion to come about relatively quickly, and surely in no more than three campaigning seasons, for it would be wildly unreasonable for Sparta to continue to beat its fists fruitlessly against the stone wall of the Athenian defensive strategy. But reason rarely predominates when states and their people have gone to war, and objective calculations of comparative resources are rarely enough to predict the course of an extended conflict.

CHAPTER SIX

The Theban Attack on Plataea (431)

AFTER THE FAILURE of the three Spartan missions the fighting finally began in March 431, in Boeotia, seven months after the declaration of war. It was launched not by Sparta, however, but by its powerful ally Thebes. For centuries the Thebans had quarreled and fought with their Athenian neighbors to the south. They had long sought to unify and dominate all of Boeotia but had been frustrated by resistance from some Boeotian states, occasionally assisted by Athens.

During the First Peloponnesian War the Athenians had defeated Thebes in battle, established democratic governments in most of the Boeotian towns, and dominated the Theban homeland for some years. The Thebans shared a long border with the Athenians, and in the event of war they wanted to possess Plataea, a small town with fewer than one thousand citizens, but one that presented both a danger and an opportunity. Its democratic government had always resisted membership in the Boeotian League, which was dominated by oligarchic Thebes, and since the sixth century the Plataeans had been a loyal ally to Athens. The town occupied a strategic position, less than eight miles from Thebes and immediately flanking the best roads from Thebes to Athens (see Map 5). In Athenian hands Plataea could serve as a base for attacks on Thebes and Boeotia and as a threat to any Theban army attempting to enter Attica. Even more important, perhaps, Plataea likewise flanked the only road connecting Thebes with Megara and the Peloponnesus that did not pass through Athenian territory. Were Plataea to come under Athenian control any collaboration between Athens' enemies in central Greece and in the Peloponnesus would be hindered. The onset of war also presented an ideal opportunity for Thebes to capture its old enemy while the Athenians were distracted by the Peloponnesians. For all these reasons the Thebans plotted to seize Plataea by surprise.

On a cloudy night early in March 431 over three hundred Thebans sneaked into Plataea guided by Nauclides, a leader of the Plataean oligarchic faction who, with his traitorous supporters, wanted to destroy the democrats who were in power and then turn the town over to Thebes. The Thebans expected the unprepared Plataeans to surrender peacefully and, threatening no reprisals, invited all the townspeople to join them. They preferred a Plataea under a friendly oligarchic government allied to Thebes rather than one decimated by executions and burdened with exiles waiting for revenge. The traitorous Plataeans, however, certain that their fellow citizens would fight back, wished to kill their democratic opponents immediately, but the Thebans ignored them. Indeed, as soon as the shock of the coup had worn off, the Plataeans began to mount a resistance, digging through the walls that separated their houses and gathering to plan their counterattack. Just before dawn they set upon the Thebans, who found themselves caught unexpectedly in the dark in an unfamiliar town.

A heavy rain had by now begun to fall, and the Plataean women and the town's slaves, screaming for blood, climbed to the rooftops and threw stones and tiles at the invaders. The disoriented Thebans fled for their lives, pursued by natives who knew Plataea's every feature. Many were caught and killed, and before long the survivors were forced to surrender.

The Theban army had intended to come and help the three hundred within Plataea in case they encountered trouble, but their plan went awry. The rain had swelled the Asopus River, which separated Theban from Plataean territory, and by the time the army arrived the invaders had been taken prisoner. Many of the Plataeans were not out of danger, however, for they were still at their farms in the countryside. The Thebans planned to seize them as hostages to exchange for the men in the city, but the Plataeans threatened to put their prisoners to death unless the army retreated from the country immediately. Although the forces withdrew, the Plataeans executed 180 of their captives regardless. By traditional standards of Greek warfare this was an atrocity, the first of many that only grew in horror as the years of war

went by. But a sneak attack at night in peacetime was also outside the
code of honor of the hoplite warrior and seemed therefore to merit no
protection for its perpetrators.

Meanwhile, learning of the attack and hostage taking from the
Plataeans, the Athenians had quickly recognized the value of the Theban prisoners. Greeks cities never took the loss of their citizens lightly,
and one of the captives, moreover, was Eurymachus, a leading politician influential with Thebes' ruling faction. As hostages, the prisoners
might have served as a disincentive to any Boeotian invasion of Attica,
as the capture of a similar number of Spartans in 425 would later discourage any further Spartan invasion of Attica. But an Athenian message to Plataea asking that the captives be spared had arrived too late;
passion had overcome calculation. The Thebans were now free to seek
vengeance, and the Athenians brought food and eighty Athenian hoplites to help garrison the city against the inevitable Theban attack. In
preparation they removed most of the women, the children, and all the
men but the hoplites, leaving a total garrison of 480 men, and 110
women to bake the bread.

THE SPARTAN INVASION OF ATTICA

As the attack on Plataea was a clear breach of the peace, the Spartans ordered their allies to send two-thirds of their fighting forces to
gather at the Isthmus of Corinth for the invasion of Attica. The remaining third was held at home where it could guard against Athenian
landings. The grand army was to be led by King Archidamus, who was
led by patriotism and honor to do his best.

Even on the march the king's actions suggest that he had not yet
abandoned hope of avoiding the conflict. He sent an ambassador to
inquire if the Athenians would yield now that they saw the great Peloponnesian army on the road to Attica. Pericles, however, had proposed
a decree forbidding the admission of any herald or embassy from the
Peloponnesians while their army was in the field, and the Athenians
turned away the Spartan envoy. As he crossed the frontier he said with
un-Spartan drama: "This day will be the beginning of great evils for
the Hellenes" (2.12.3).

Archidamus now had no choice but to proceed. The swiftest route from the isthmus was by way of the coastal road through the Megarid, to Eleusis, past Mount Aegalius, and into the fertile plain of Athens. Instead Archidamus delayed at the isthmus, marched in a leisurely fashion, and, when he passed through Megara, did not turn south toward Athens but marched north to besiege the town of Oenoe, an Athenian fortress near the Boeotian border. (See Map 4.) Oenoe was a powerful little post defended by stone walls armed with towers, but it presented no threat to so large an army and was unlikely to interfere with any immediate Peloponnesian plans. Taking it, moreover, was not easy and would have required an extended siege and the abandonment of the main purpose of the expedition, the ravaging of Attica.

The attack on Oenoe made no strategic sense; Archidamus' motives were political, for he still hoped to prevent a war. A year earlier he had argued that the Spartans should be very slow to ravage the land of Attica. "Do not think," he said, "of their land as anything but a hostage for us, and the better it is cultivated the better hostage it will be" (1.82.4). The Spartans, who were already blaming him for the delay that permitted the Athenians time to prepare for the invasion and to remove their cattle and property to safety, suspected his true intentions in the digression.

Eventually Archidamus was compelled to abandon the siege of Oenoe and to turn to the major purpose of the Peloponnesian invasion: the devastation of Attica. Eighty days after the Theban attack on Plataea, toward the end of May when the grain of Attica was ripe, the Peloponnesian army moved south and began to ravage Eleusis and the Thriasian plain, cutting down grain crops and damaging vines and olive trees.

Archidamus next moved east to Acharnae, instead of to the obvious target: the fertile plain of Athens, the lands of the city's nobility, where the greatest damage could be done. A march into those areas, which lay directly before the city, would have been the most provocative tactic and would have applied the greatest possible pressure on the Periclean policy of restraint. Archidamus continued to hope that the Athenians would see reason at the last moment; as long as possible he wanted "to hold as a hostage" the most prized fields of Attica by not cutting down their crops.

Meanwhile, the Athenians were following Pericles' plan and moving from their beloved countryside. Wives and children went to the city, sheep and oxen to the island of Euboea, just off the east coast of Attica. Because few Athenians were still alive who had seen the land devastated by the army of Xerxes in 480, many resented their displacement. "They were dejected and angered at having to abandon their homes and the temples which had always been theirs, ancestral relics of the ancient polity, at facing a change in their way of life, at nothing less than each man having to abandon his own polis" (2.16.2). At first they were all crowded within the city of Athens itself. Every vacant space was occupied; not even sanctuaries of the gods were exempt, including one called the Pelargikon, at the foot of the Acropolis, in spite of an oracular curse from the Pythian Apollo, an act that no doubt scandalized the pious. Later the displaced Athenians were dispersed to Piraeus and to the territory between the Long Walls, but for the time being the discomfort was extreme.

ATTACKS ON PERICLES

AT FIRST many Athenians hoped that the Peloponnesians would withdraw quickly and without a war, as they had done in 445, but when the enemy began to lay waste the land of Acharnae, less than seven miles from the Acropolis, the mood in Athens changed to fury, directed as much toward Pericles as toward the Spartans. He was accused of cowardice because he would not lead an army out against the enemy.

The most notable of his attackers was Cleon, who had opposed Pericles for several years. Cleon belonged to a new class of politicians in Athens: not aristocrats but rich men whose wealth came from trade and manufacturing, rather than from the traditional source, land. Such occupations were considered base and unworthy by the aristocratic code that had dominated the democratic but still deferential politics of Athens up to that time. Aristophanes mocked Cleon as a tanner and leather merchant, a thief and a brawler whose voice "roared like a torrent" and sounded like a scalded pig's. Cleon inevitably appears in his comedies in a state of anger, a lover of war who constantly stirs up hatred. Thucydides calls him "the most violent of the citizens" (3.36.6), and likewise describes his style of speech as harsh and bullying. Aristotle comments that Cleon "seems to have corrupted the people more than anyone by his attacks; he was the first to shout while speaking in the assembly, first to use abusive language there, first to hitch up his skirts [and move about] while addressing the people, although the other speakers behaved properly" (Aristotle, *Constitution of the Athenians* 28.3). In the comedy *Fates*, produced probably in the spring of 430, the poet Hermippus says to Pericles: "King of the Satyrs, why won't you ever lift a spear but instead use dreadful words to wage the war, assuming the character of the cowardly Teles? But if a little knife is sharpened on a whetstone you roar as though bitten by fierce Cleon" (Plutarch, *Pericles* 33–34). These mocking characterizations were all put forth by his enemies, but Cleon was actually a powerful figure in the assembly and would play an important role in the course of the war. He was only one of a number of enemies who attacked Pericles, and even some of the general's friends urged him to leave the city and fight.

By 431, however, Pericles' personal prestige had risen to the point where Thucydides could speak of him as "the foremost among the Athenians and the most powerful in speech and action" (1.139.4), and of Athens itself he could claim that it was "in name a democracy but really a government by the first citizen" (2.65.9). Pericles achieved such a position not only by virtue of his wisdom and rhetorical skill, or of his patriotism and incorruptibility. He was also a shrewd politician and had built up over the years a group of soldiers, administrators, and politicians who formed a group of colleagues that shared political opinions and served as generals along with him while accepting his informal leadership.

The support of such men made it possible for Pericles to withstand the storm of criticism he encountered and to restrain the many Athenians who urged him to attack the Peloponnesian army. Thucydides tells us that Pericles refused to call a meeting of the Athenian assembly or even any informal gathering, fearing that such groups might "make a mistake by obeying their anger instead of their judgment" (2.22.1). No one had the legal right to prevent a meeting of the assembly, so it must have been the respect in which Pericles was held, supported by his influence with the other generals, that dissuaded the prytanies (rotating presidents of the assembly) from calling one.

With no effective challenges to his strategy, Pericles was free to hold to it, responding to the Spartan devastations only by sending cavalry detachments to deter the Peloponnesians from approaching too close to the city. The invading army had been in Attica for a month, and its provisions were now exhausted. Archidamus, realizing that the Athenians would neither fight nor yield, abandoned his camp and moved eastward to ravage the area between Mounts Parnes and Pentelicus, and then returned home by way of Boeotia. He again avoided destroying the fertile Attic plain, persisting in his plan to hold it hostage as long as possible. The Spartans had little cause for satisfaction, for the strategy with which they had entered the war had thus far proven futile. The Athenians were essentially unharmed and were even now engaged in avenging what damage had been done.

THE ATHENIAN RESPONSE

WHILE THE PELOPONNESIANS were still in Attica the Athenians began to strengthen the defenses of their city, posting permanent guards to watch for sudden incursions by land or by sea. They also sent out a fleet of a hundred ships carrying a thousand hoplites and four hundred archers, supplemented by fifty ships from Corcyra and a number of the other western allies. This large force could easily defeat or drive from the seas any enemy fleet it might encounter, make landings, lay waste to enemy territory, and even capture and sack small cities. The expedition aimed to avenge the invasion of Attica and to impress upon the Peloponnesians the cost of such a war as they had chosen to fight.

The Athenians made landings on the Peloponnesian coast, probably in the region of Epidaurus and Hermione; then they landed at Methone in Laconia (see Map 1). They ravaged this latter territory, attacked the poorly defended walled town, and might have sacked it. Methone was saved only by the enterprise and bravery of Brasidas, a Spartan officer who took advantage of the scattered disposition of the Athenian forces to dash into the town and reinforce its garrison. The Spartans rewarded him with a vote of gratitude. The course of the war would show him to be the greatest of Spartan commanders, perhaps in all Spartan history—brave, daring, and brilliant as a soldier; clever, skillful, and persuasive as a speaker; and shrewd and respected as a diplomat.

After Methone the Athenians sailed to Pheia in Elis on the western coast of the Peloponnesus (see Map 1). One of their detachments captured the town of Pheia, but they abandoned it and sailed away, "for the entire Eleian army had come to the rescue" (2.25.5). The Athenian force was not of a size or of a mind to hold even a coastal city in the Peloponnesus against a full assault.

The armada then sailed northward to Acarnania (see Map 11). This was no longer Peloponnesian territory but within the Corinthian sphere of interest, and it was therefore treated differently. The Athenians took Sollium, a town belonging to Corinth, and held it throughout the rest of the war, entrusting it to some friendly Acarnanians to occupy. The town of Astacus they took by storm and incorporated into their alliance. Finally, they seized the island of Cephallenia, strategically located in regard to Acarnania, Corcyra, and the Corinthian island of Leucas, without a battle. Then the fleet sailed home, having carried out its limited and carefully controlled mission.

Meanwhile a smaller force of thirty ships sailed to Locris in central Greece as a safeguard for Euboea, an island vital to Athens. The Athenians ravaged some territory, defeated a force of Locrians in battle, and took the town of Thronium, well situated in regard to Euboea, which now served the Athenians as pasture and refuge.

To increase their security further, the Athenians sailed to Aegina, "the eyesore of the Piraeus," as Pericles called it (Aristotle, *Rhetoric* 1411a 15), and an old enemy. Aegina, an island in the Saronic Gulf, just off the coast of the Peloponnesus, stands in a position to dominate the approaches to Piraeus. Because a Peloponnesian navy contingent based on Aegina could disrupt Athenian trade, threaten Piraeus, and tie down a large Athenian defensive fleet, the Athenians expelled the entire Aeginetan population and resettled the island with colonists of their own. The Spartans in turn relocated the exiles in Thyrea, a borderland between Laconia and the Argolid, where they could be

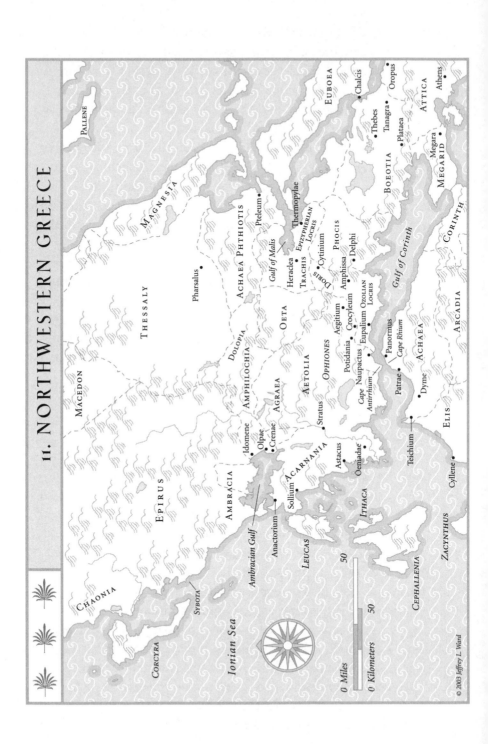

11. NORTHWESTERN GREECE

CHAONIA
CORCYRA
SYBOTA
Ionian Sea
EPIRUS
PALLENE
MACEDON
MAGNESIA
THESSALY
Pharsalus
ACHAEA PHTHIOTIS
Pteleum
Gulf of Malis
Thermopylae
Heraclea
TRACHIS
EPIZYPHERIAN LOCRIS
Cytinium
DORIS
PHOCIS
Delphi
Amphissa
OZOLIAN LOCRIS
EUBOEA
Chalcis
Oropus
Thebes
Tanagra
Plataea
BOEOTIA
ATTICA
Athens
Megara
MEGARID
Gulf of Corinth
CORINTH
AMBRACIA
Idomene
Olpae
Crenae
AMPHILOCHIA
DOLOPIA
AGRAEA
OETA
AETOLIA
OPHIONES
Aegitium
Crocyleum
Potidania
Stratus
Naupactus
Cape Eupalium
Antirrhium
Panormus
Cape Rhium
Patrae
ACHAEA
Dyme
ARCADIA
Ambracian Gulf
Anactorium
Sollium
ACARNANIA
Astacus
Oeniadae
ITHACA
LEUCAS
Teichium
ELIS
Cyllene
CEPHALLENIA
ZACYNTHUS

0 Miles   50
0 Kilometers   50

© 2003 Jeffrey L. Ward

counted on to keep a close watch on democratic Argos and to resist any Athenian landing in that region.

The Athenians also increased security in the important northeastern corner of their empire, winning over the formerly hostile prince Nymphodorus of Abdera, a city on the north shore of the Aegean Sea (see Map 9). They made him their diplomatic agent in the region, and he performed wonders. He brought Athens an alliance with his brother-in-law, the powerful Thracian king Sitalces. Athens' main problem in the region was the siege of Potidaea, which was draining the treasury. Nymphodorus promised to get Sitalces to lend the Athenians cavalry and light-armed infantry and bring the siege to an end. He also reconciled the Athenians with Perdiccas, king of Macedon, who immediately joined the Athenian army in attacking Potidaea's local allies.

As the autumn of 431 approached Pericles himself took ten thousand Athenian hoplites, three thousand metic (resident alien) hoplites, and a large number of light-armed troops—the largest Athenian army ever brought together—to ravage the Megarid. The Athenians planned to devastate Megara's fields and hoped that, with their embargo on its trade, the invasions would force the Megarians to succumb. A smaller army could have produced the same results, but well aware of the price the Athenians were paying in morale for his defensive strategy, Pericles launched the invasion on a grand scale both to relieve frustration and to demonstrate visibly the might of Athens.

PERICLES' FUNERAL ORATION

THIS CAMPAIGN of retribution reaffirmed Pericles' position among the Athenian people, and when they held funeral rites for those who had fallen in the first year of the war he "was chosen by the city as the wisest and most esteemed" to deliver their eulogy (2.34.6). The speech which has been preserved, demonstrates how Pericles' talents of persuasion were able to maintain the Athenians' support for his painful strategy.

Pericles' address is as unlike the standard Athenian funeral oration as Lincoln's Gettysburg Address was unlike the weary rhetoric spoken at length the same day by Edward Everett. Like Lincoln, Pericles' intention was to explain to the living in the midst of a difficult war why their sufferings were justified and why their continued dedication was necessary. In the process he painted the most glorious and attractive picture we have of the character of the Athenian democracy and its superiority to the Spartan way of life. He also called on the Athenians for the strongest commitment to their city:

> You must every day look upon the power of your city and become her lovers [*erastai*], and when you have understood her greatness consider that the men who achieved it were brave and honorable and knew what was necessary when the time came for action. If they ever failed in some attempt, they were determined that, at least, their city should not be deprived of their courage [*arete*] and gave her the most beautiful of all offerings. For they gave their lives for the common good. . . . (2.43.1–2)

In return he promised them a kind of immortality. The men who died fighting for Athens he explained:

> gave their lives for the common good and thereby won for themselves the praise that never grows old and the most distinguished of all graves, not those in which they lie, but where their glory remains in eternal memory, always there at the right time to inspire speech and action. For the whole world is the burial place for famous men; not only does the epitaph inscribed on monuments in their native country commemorate them, but in lands not their own the unwritten memory, more of their spirit even than of what they have done, lives on within each person. Now it is for you to emulate them; knowing that happiness requires freedom and freedom requires courage, do not shrink from the dangers of war. (2.43.2–4)

THE WAR'S FIRST YEAR: AN ACCOUNTING

THE FUNERAL ORATION brought the first year of the war to a close, and inspired by its power and brilliance, the Athenians stiffened their resolve to carry on. To many it must have seemed that the effort was going well, but the true picture was less bright.

In a war of attrition the side that does the most damage must ultimately win. The Athenian attacks on the Peloponnesians, apart from extra-Peloponnesian Megara, were relative pinpricks, irritating but not really harmful. Sparta itself was untouched; in all its territory of Laconia and Messenia only Methone had been briefly attacked. The Corinthians had lost a small town in Acarnania, and while they had been excluded from trade in the Aegean, their main commercial areas were in the undisturbed west. The Megarians continued to be barred from Aegean ports, and their land was seriously devastated, but they did not suffer badly enough to make them seek peace even after the first ten years of the war.

For Athens, on the other hand, the first year of the war was very costly. The Athenians had seen their crops destroyed, their vines and olive trees damaged, and their houses torn or burned down. The exports usually employed to maintain a balance of trade, olive oil and wine, had therefore been diminished, and as a result the importation of foodstuffs reduced both the resources of the Athenian commonwealth and the city's capacity to persist. The continuing siege of Potidaea had drained two thousand talents from the reserve fund, more than one-fourth of the disposable war chest.

Worst of all, the Peloponnesians showed no sign of discouragement, but would spiritedly return the following year to destroy the large portion of Attica they had left untouched. No evidence exists of any divisiveness within the Peloponnesian League and no growth in influence of the advocates of peace in Sparta. In Athens, however, tensions had already come to the surface. Cleon's complaints about the inefficacy of the Periclean strategy might still be a subject for comic poets, but they were indicative of the dissent that was bound to arise as the suffering continued. For the moment the occupation of Aegina, the attack on the Megarid, and the eloquence of Pericles might quiet the opposition, but it was certain to burst forth if the situation did not improve.

CHAPTER SEVEN

The Plague (430–429)

TOWARD THE BEGINNING of May 430 Archidamus again brought the invading Peloponnesian army into Attica to continue the destruction begun in the first year of the war. This time the Peloponnesians laid waste to the great plain before the city of Athens, then moved on to the coastal regions of Attica, both east and west. There was no longer any point in continuing the strategy of holding the land of Attica hostage, for the Athenians clearly would not yield or engage in battle. The invading army remained in Attica for forty days, the longest stay of the war, and left only when their provisions were exhausted.

EPIDAURUS

AT THE END of May Pericles himself led a fleet of a hundred Athenian triremes, aided by fifty from Chios and Lesbos. The expedition carried four thousand hoplites and three hundred cavalry, as numerous an infantry as later undertook the great Sicilian Campaign of 415, and one of the largest forces the Athenians ever assembled on ships. Some scholars think that the size of the army reveals a basic change from a defensive to an offensive strategy. Its goal, they believe, was to take the city of Epidaurus, place a garrison in it, and hold it. This would give Athens a stronghold in the Peloponnesus, well situated to harass and threaten Corinth and to encourage Argos to join the war against the Spartans.

While that effort would certainly have amounted to a sharp change in Pericles' strategy, there are powerful reasons for rejecting it as the purpose for the expedition. First, Thucydides mentions no shift in strategy but right up to the death of Pericles continues to describe it in the same terms: to "remain quiet, take care of their fleet, refrain from trying to extend their empire in wartime and thus putting their city in danger" (2.65.7). If the Athenians did mean to seize and retain Epidaurus, moreover, they went about it very badly, as their ravaging of the territory of the Epidaurians gave ample warning of their approach.

The expedition can best be understood as the foremost execution of the policy that lay behind all the Athenian seaborne raids during the first two years of the war, which included Methone, Pheia in Elis, Troezen, Hermione, Halieis, and Prasiae (see Map 1). Each time the Athenians began by destroying the nearby territory, and occasionally they attempted to sack the town if it was weakly defended. The attack on Epidaurus was merely an intensification of the same plan, motivated perhaps by domestic pressure to do the enemy more visible harm.

The sack of Epidaurus would have raised Athenian morale and helped Pericles with his continuing political battle. It might also have discouraged the neighboring Peloponnesian cities from sending their soldiers to join the Peloponnesian army invading Attica. It might also have led some Peloponnesian coastal cities to defect from the Spartan Alliance, although this did not happen.

The undertaking of the second Athenian naval expedition, then, suggests that Pericles himself began to recognize that his original strategy was not working. The Spartans continued to ravage Attica, and the Athenian treasury was being drained by the unexpected stubbornness of Potidaea. He realized that he must take more aggressive steps to persuade the enemy to make peace, even while he did not abandon the fundamental strategy of a defensive war.

In 430 the Athenians' force went no further than Prasiae on the eastern coast of the great peninsula and then turned back. No doubt, by then it had received news of the return from Attica of the Peloponnesian army, which would have forced the Athenians out of the Peloponnesus where their landings might now be met by overwhelming forces. Even so, they could have gone on to the northwest, as they had the previous year, where so powerful a force could have done great damage to Corinth and her colonies in the west. Why did the mighty armada return, having achieved so little?

THE PLAGUE IN ATHENS

PERICLES PROBABLY broke off his expedition because he received word of the effects of the plague that had broken out in Athens at the start of the campaigning season. It was said to have started in Ethiopia and moved on to Egypt, Libya, and through much of the Persian Empire before appearing in Athens. Thucydides, who was stricken with the plague himself, carefully described its symptoms, which have similarities to those of pneumonic plague, measles, typhoid, and many other diseases, but fit no known illness precisely. Before it had run its course in 427 it killed forty-four hundred hoplites, three hundred cavalrymen, and an untold number of the lower classes, wiping out perhaps one-third of the city's population.

The expedition returned sometime after the middle of June, when the plague had been established in Athens for well over a month. The Athenians, crowded into the city as a result of Pericles' policy, were particularly vulnerable to the contagion, which was deadly to some and demoralizing to all. The panic, fear, and collapse of the most sacred bonds of civilization were such that many neglected to give proper burial to the dead, the most solemn rite of the Greek religion. They had tolerated the first year's miseries with difficulty, but "after the second invasion of the Peloponnesians, the Athenians, since their land had been devastated a second time and the plague and the war together pressed hard on them, changed their minds and held Pericles responsible for persuading them to go to war and for the misfortunes that had befallen them" (2.59.1).

It was in this climate that the Athenians sent the force that had only recently returned from the Peloponnesus on a new expedition under Pericles' associates Hagnon and Cleopompus, with the charge of ending the resistance of Potidaea and of suppressing the Chalcidic rebellion in general. Potidaea still held out, and Hagnon's troops infected the original Athenian besieging army, which had been free of the plague. After forty days Hagnon took the remnant of his army back to Athens, having lost 1,050 of the original 4,000 men.

Pericles, attacked from two directions, had decided on this disastrous campaign chiefly because of the pressure of Athenian politics.

Any label used to describe political groups in the Greek cities is merely convenient shorthand and does not refer to anything resembling a modern political party. Athenian politics typically involved shifting groups that often came together around a man, sometimes around an issue, and occasionally with reference to both. There was little or no party discipline in the modern sense, and while the groups had only limited continuity, throughout the early years of the Ten Years War popular opinion seems to have fallen into three distinguishable categories: (1) those who desired immediate peace with Sparta; its advocates we call the peace party; (2) those who were determined to wage an aggressive war, to run risks in the attempt to defeat Sparta rather than to wear her out; this group we may call the aggressive war party; (3) those who were willing to support the policy of Pericles, avoiding risks, wearing down the Spartans, and working for a negotiated peace on the basis of the status quo ante bellum; these men we call the moderates. The peace forces, dormant since the first Spartan invasion, renewed their urging to make terms with the enemy. The advocates of more aggressive warfare could point to the great harm done to Attica and the meager results of the attack on the Peloponnesus. The war could not continue at the current rate of expenditure, with the siege of Potidaea continuing to represent a major item in the budget. Athens needed a significant victory to save money and to bolster Athenian morale. Instead it had suffered a painful failure.

PERICLES UNDER FIRE

LATE IN THE SUMMER of 430, with the plague raging, the Athenians turned against their leader. They had never experienced anything like this epidemic, and its crushing effect on the city had by now severely undermined Pericles' position, popular confidence in his strategy, and the continuation of a war that was blamed on his intransigence.

Traditional religion also played an important role in the change of opinion. The Greeks had always believed that plagues were divine punishments for human actions that angered the gods. The most familiar example is the one described at the beginning of Homer's *Iliad*, sent by Apollo to avenge Agamemnon's insult to his priest, but they were often connected with the failure to heed divine oracles and with acts of religious pollution. When the plague came to Athens the older men recalled an oracle from the past that had predicted: "A Dorian war will come and a plague with it." That implicitly cast blame on Pericles, the staunchest advocate of war against the Dorian Peloponnesians and a man likewise known for his rationalism and for associating with religious skeptics. The pious pointed out that the plague that ravaged Athens did not enter the Peloponnesus.

Others simply held Pericles responsible for causing the war and for imposing a strategy that made the effects of the plague far more terrible than if the Athenians had been scattered around Attica as they usually were. Plutarch explains how Pericles' enemies persuaded the people that the crowding of the city by the refugees from the countryside caused the plague: "They said that Pericles was to blame for this; because of the war he had poured the mob from the country within the walls and had given this mass of people no work to do" (*Pericles* 34.3–4). When the Spartans retired and the force Pericles led returned from the Peloponnesus he could no longer prevent a public debate, for an assembly had to be convened to vote the expenses and command for the expedition to Potidaea. The departure of that army and its generals weakened political support for Pericles, and it must have been in their absence that the attacks against him were finally successful.

PEACE NEGOTIATIONS

AGAINST PERICLES' WISHES and advice, the Athenian assembly voted to send ambassadors to Sparta to sue for peace, a decision that disproves more clearly than any incident of this period the claim of Thucydides that Athens at the time of Pericles was a democracy in name only, but in fact was or was becoming the rule of the first citizen. The nature of these negotiations is vital to understanding the further course of the war, but since the ancient writers are silent on the subject of what terms the Athenians proposed and how the Spartans answered, we must try to construct them as well as possible.

The Spartans probably asked of the Athenians what they had demanded in their penultimate proposal before the war: to withdraw from Potidaea, to restore autonomy to Aegina, and to rescind the Megarian Decree. In the favorable situation of 430, they probably added the condition of the last embassy: to restore autonomy to Greece, by which they meant the abandonment of the Athenian Empire.

Such unacceptable terms would have left Athens helpless before its enemies, and Sparta's insisting on them amounted to a rejection of the Athenian peace mission. The outcome only served to prove that Pericles was correct in arguing that the Athenians could achieve no satisfactory peace until they had convinced the Spartans that Athens would not yield and could not be defeated. But the peace party continued to regard him as the main obstacle to peace, and they were determined to remove him.

Sparta's rejection of the Athenian overtures also demonstrated that Archidamus and those of like mind had gained no ground among their compatriots. The Athenians' refusal to fight for their homes and crops served only to convince most Spartans that they were cowardly and would eventually yield if the pressure was maintained or increased. The attacks on the Peloponnesus had done no serious damage but caused considerable annoyance, inflaming the Peloponnesians even further. The plague in Athens provided additional incentive, for it weakened the enemy and promised early and easy victory.

But the aggressive faction in Sparta had misjudged badly, for while the plague did debilitate the Athenians, it did not destroy their ability to fight on. A more reasoned examination of developments to that point would have given the Spartans little justification for expecting victory in a long war. Once recovered from the plague, the Athenians would again be invulnerable behind their fleet and their walls, and the Spartans had still not formulated a plan that could overcome them. A more moderate approach might have consisted in persuading the Athenians to relieve Megara, to abandon Corcyra, and even to surrender Aegina and Potidaea. At the very least, that would have helped divide Athenian opinion, but because most Spartans believed that the enemy had no recourse, they set conditions that Athens could not accept even in its desperate condition.

In Athens, meanwhile, Pericles' enemies concentrated increased attacks on him, until he finally rose to defend himself and his policies.

He was that rare political leader in a democratic state who had told the people the truth, while pursuing disputed and even unpopular policies. Pericles' constant forthrightness left his angry listeners with no rejoinder, for they could not claim they had been uninformed or deceived. The responsibility, he made plain, was theirs as well as his. "If," he said to the Athenians, "you were persuaded by me to go to war because you thought I had the qualities necessary for leadership at least moderately more than other men, it is not right that I should now be blamed for doing wrong" (2.60.7).

On the occasion of this speech he also introduced a new argument for persisting. He extolled the greatness and power of the Athenian Empire, and the naval force upon which it rested, and which enabled it to master the entire realm of the sea. Compared to this, he argued the loss of land and houses was nothing, "a mere garden or other adornment to a great fortune. Such things can easily be regained if Athens retains her freedom, but should she lose her freedom all else will be lost as well" (2.62).

Although he had previously urged the Athenians not to extend their empire, in this oration he seems to encourage expansionist sentiment. We must recognize that here he speaks to address a new situation: while earlier attacks on him came from those, like Cleon, who wanted to fight more aggressively, the danger now came from those who did not want to fight at all, which called for a different emphasis. With the unique power they held, the Athenians need not fear losing the war but rather making a bad peace and withdrawing from empire. The Athenians had a tiger by the tail: "By now the empire you hold is a tyranny; it may now seem wrong to have taken it, but it is surely dangerous to let it go," for "you are hated by those you have ruled" (2.63.1–2).

Pericles' remarks indicate that the opposition had revived the moral argument against the empire and the war, but rather than rejecting their charge of the innate immorality of empire, he used it instead as a weapon to defend his policy. The time for morality was past; it was now a matter of survival. He called on the Athenians to look beyond their current sufferings, far into the future, for

the splendor of the present and the glory of the future remain in memory forever. And with the foreknowledge that you will have a noble future as well as a present free of shame, and that you will obtain both by your zeal at this time, do not send heralds to the Spartans and do not let them know that you are tormented by your present sufferings. (2.64.6)

PERICLES CONDEMNED

ALTHOUGH PERICLES WON the debate over policy, and the Athenians sent no further embassies to Sparta, his enemies did not withdraw. Unable to defeat him in the political arena, they turned now to the law courts. Athenian politicians frequently attacked a man and his policies by charging him with corruption; Pericles himself had begun his public career with such an accusation against Cimon. Probably in September 430, at the meeting when the usual vote confirming the magistrates in office was taken, Pericles was deposed and ordered to stand trial on a charge of embezzlement.

The peace faction was not strong enough to bring this about alone, but events played into their hands. After the failure of negotiations Hagnon and what was left of his decimated army returned from the unsuccessful attack on Potidaea. Their failure helped produce the widespread malaise reported by Thucydides: the Athenians "grieved over their private sufferings, the common people because, having started out with less, they were deprived even of that; the rich had lost their beautiful estates in the country, the houses as well as their expensive furnishings, but worst of all, they had war instead of peace" (2.65.2).

Pericles was eventually convicted and punished with a heavy fine. The jury was obviously not fully convinced of his guilt, or unwilling to take extreme action against a man who had been their leader for so many years, for the crime of peculation might have carried with it the death penalty. With the aid of his friends, he soon paid the fine, but he was probably out of office from about September 430 until the beginning of the next official year in midsummer 429.

THE SPARTANS GO TO SEA

THE SPARTANS, in the meantime, had grown increasingly frustrated by the stubbornness of the Athenians and the ineffectiveness of their own strategy. The attacks on the Peloponnesian coastal cities raised questions about their capacity to protect their allies against Athens' great naval power. Late in the summer of 430, therefore, they attacked Zacynthus, an island lying off the coast of Elis and an ally of Athens, with a hundred triremes and a thousand hoplites, commanded by the head of Spartan naval forces, the navarch Cnemus (see Map 11). Their purpose was to protect the western Peloponnesus and allies in the northwest by depriving Athens of the bases it needed in the region. The Spartans were unable to take the city, however, and could only ravage its territory before sailing home again.

It was becoming clear that the Spartans needed a new offensive strategy to win a decisive victory. For that they would need to take to the sea with a fleet greater than they had or could afford to build and man, so they sent an embassy to Artaxerxes I, the Great King of Persia, to seek an alliance. On the way the group stopped at the court of Sitalces in Thrace and asked him to abandon the Athenian alliance and join with the Peloponnesians, hoping he would send an army to help relieve the siege of Potidaea. Two Athenian ambassadors who were also present, however, persuaded Sadocus, the son of Sitalces, to arrest the Peloponnesians and convey them to Athens. When they arrived they were put to death immediately and without a trial, their bodies thrown into a pit and denied proper burial. This act of terror and reprisal took place when Pericles was out of power and was probably the work of the war party, which was in control in the autumn of 430, as the moderates were in disgrace and the peace party discredited. Thucydides believes that the Athenians committed this atrocity out of fear of one of the Peloponnesian ambassadors, Aristeus, the Corinthian most effective in the defense of Potidaea, lest that daring and brilliant man escape and do them further harm. The official explanation was that the summary execution was in retaliation for Spartan brutality. From the onset of the war the Spartans had made it a practice to kill all persons captured at sea, whether Athenians, Athenian allies, or neutrals. Such behavior by both sides was a harbinger of much worse crimes that would be committed in the years to come, illustrating Thucydides' observation that "war is a violent teacher" (3.82.2).

POTIDAEA RECAPTURED

THE WAR PARTY, probably led by Cleon, among others, reacted to Sparta's attack on Zacynthus, and to a further assault by the Ambracians on Argos in Amphilochia, by sending Phormio with twenty ships to Naupactus to safeguard the port from a sudden strike and to seal off the Gulf of Corinth. They also tried to increase revenue by tightening the collection of tribute in the empire, but their greatest achievement was the capture of Potidaea in the winter of 430/29. After a siege of two and one-half years the city's food supply was exhausted, and its people were reduced to cannibalism. The Athenian army posted there was exposed to the cold and suffering from disease, and some of the men may have been away from home since the force's arrival in the winter of 433/2. The Athenians had already spent over two thousand talents on the endeavor, and every day cost at least another talent from a depleted treasury. The Athenian generals—Xenophon, Hestiodorus, and Phanomachus—therefore offered the Potidaeans terms that were acceptable, if none too generous: "They were to depart with their children and wives and the mercenary soldiers, each with one garment, the women with two, with a stated sum of money for the journey" (2.70.3–4).

This was, under the circumstances, a reasonable settlement and one that was surely welcome to the Athenians, but the war party complained that the generals should have accepted nothing less than unconditional surrender and so brought them to trial. The complaint seems to have been that they overstepped their authority in making peace without consulting the Athenian council and assembly, but politics, no doubt, also played a part, for the generals had all been elected along with Pericles late in the previous winter, when he had great influence. The indictment of them was equally an indictment of Pericles and his moderate faction, but the attempt failed. The Athenians were relieved to have the long and costly siege ended and were not inclined to quibble over technicalities. Their acquittal of the generals may also suggest that the popular sentiment against Pericles was abating. Eventually a group of colonists was sent to hold the deserted city, which would henceforth be a key Athenian base in the Thraceward regions.

At the end of the second year of war the Athenians were far weaker than they had been twelve months earlier. They had shown restraint during two invasions, permitting their fields and houses to be destroyed without offering battle. However, with all of Attica devastated, there was little reason for the Spartans to believe that any future incursions would bring better results. The Athenian fleet, moreover, had proven that it could harass the coastal states of the Peloponnesus with relative impunity. Now was the time, according to the Periclean plan, for the discredited war party of Sparta to yield to Archidamus and his moderate colleagues and offer peace on reasonable terms.

Instead, the Spartans' determination was fiercer than ever. Deprived of a land battle, they had turned to a naval offensive, threatening Athenian control of the western seas and even the security of Naupactus. Their success challenged Pericles' confident prediction that the Peloponnesians would be "shut off from the sea." Although the Spartan embassy to Persia had been intercepted, there was no guarantee that future envoys would not get through, and the Great King might well be persuaded by them in the light of Athenian weakness. Should that happen, all calculations based on Athenian superiority in ships and money would be worthless. Encouraged by such prospects, the Spartans had made it clear that they were unwilling to make peace on any but their own terms.

In the meantime the plague was still devastating Athenian manpower and morale, and the city's financial condition was also a serious problem. Of the five thousand talents of expendable funds (excluding the emergency fund of one thousand talents) available at the beginning of the war, almost twenty-seven hundred—over half—had already been spent. While the expensive siege of Potidaea was over and its heavy drain on the treasury ended, Spartan activity on the sea meant that the Athenians might have to resume spending in order to man fleets and protect allies. At the rate of expenditure of the previous two years they could fight not more than two years more. Even the war party had to have realized that the city could not afford a major campaign in the coming year, yet a policy of inactivity was also dangerous. Though Spartan intransigence had restored the Athenians' will to fight, and though their walls, fleet, and empire were intact, the future of Athens seemed precarious.

CHAPTER EIGHT

Pericles' Last Days (429)

IN SPITE OF their suffering, their disappointments, and the apparent failure of his strategy, the Athenian people elected Pericles general once again in the spring of 429. His countrymen's respect for his demonstrated talent and their long-held confidence in him help explain this decision, but military and political realities supported their choice. When the Spartans refused a negotiated peace, they effectively nullified the appeal of the peace party for the next several years. Still, Athens could not take the offensive, as Cleon and others urged, with the plague still raging and the money in the treasury running out. The only alternative, it seemed, was a continuation of the original policy, which pointed to Pericles remaining as the Athenian leader.

The Pericles who returned to office in about July 429, however, had only a few months to live. Plutarch tells us that the disease that killed him did not attack him suddenly but lingered, "using up his body slowly and undermining the loftiness of his spirit" (*Pericles* 38.1). During the period neither he nor anyone else was able to keep a firm hand on Athenian policy, or to inspire and moderate the Athenian people. For the first time in many years the Athenians experienced the inconveniences inherent in the truly democratic management of a state in time of war.

SPARTA ATTACKS PLATAEA

HAVING ALREADY thoroughly laid waste to Attica, and fearing infection from the plague, the Spartans decided in May 429 to avoid the Athenian homeland and invade Plataea instead. The small Boeotian town actually had little strategic importance for Sparta and had done nothing to provoke it; the decision to attack had been initiated by the Thebans, who were eager to use the Peloponnesian army for their own purposes. Because the Thebans were both powerful and ambitious, as they would show increasingly during the war, their desires could not be entirely ignored, so its acquiescence was the price Sparta paid for continued Theban support. In the alliance politics that dominated the second half of the fifth century the old rules governing relations between states increasingly gave way to the exigencies of a new kind of war. Thucydides cuts through the hypocrisy to explain the true nature of Spartan motives: "The hostile attitude of the Spartans in the whole matter of Plataea was chiefly on account of the Thebans, for the Spartans thought that the Thebans would be useful to them in the war just then beginning" (3.68.4).

In 490 Plataea had been the only city to send an army to help the Athenians drive off the Persians at Marathon. After the battle of Plataea, which ended the Persian War in 479, the Spartans had administered an oath to all the Greeks who had taken part in it by which they restored to the Plataeans "their land and city, holding them in independence," and swore them to see to it "that no one should march against them unjustly or for their enslavement; if any one did the allies who were present should defend them with all their might" (2.71.2). The Spartan attack on Plataea, therefore, was not only an embarrassment but filled with a brutal irony.

Archidamus gave the Plataeans the option of exercising their freedom by joining in the fight against Athens, the enslaver of the Greeks or, at the very least, of remaining neutral. Neutrality was out of the question, however, for the Plataeans could not "receive both sides as friends" when the Thebans waited to pounce and Plataea's women and children were in Athens. Archidamus then invited the Plataeans to evacuate their city for the duration of the war; the Spartans would hold their land and property in trust, paying rent for its use, and restore it intact after the conflict ended. This offer, too, was a charade: once the city was in Peloponnesian hands the Thebans would never permit its restoration.

The Plataeans finally countered by requesting a truce to ask permission of the Athenians to surrender. Their plight illustrates the helplessness of small states caught between great powers. Independence, so highly cherished by the common man, was illusory in a world of such alliances, and a minor player could count at best on the protection and good will of one of the hegemonal states. The Plataeans hoped that the Athenians would allow some arrangement with the Spartans, since their city could not be rescued without a hoplite battle, which Athens could not win. But the Athenians, probably during a momentary ascendancy by the war party, urged the Plataeans to keep true to the alliance, promising that "they would not now stand aside and allow them to be wronged, but would aid them with all their power" (2.73.3).

The Plataeans now had no choice but to reject the Spartan proposal. Archidamus replied by insisting that the Spartans had broken no oaths; it was the Plataeans who were in the wrong by turning down all reasonable offers. The Spartans were, in fact, a religious people and fearful of the ill will of the gods; it was no less a god than Zeus himself who especially punished breakers of oaths. The king's specious argument, however, was also political propaganda, an attempt to justify a straightforward act of aggression and a violation of the principle of autonomy by the "champion of Greek freedom."

After a series of failed efforts to take Plataea without a long and expensive siege, in September the Spartans were compelled to build and guard a siege wall around the town. The defenders numbered only four hundred Plataeans and eighty Athenians, as well as women to cook, but Plataea had strong defensive walls and was so situated that a small force could defend it against assault by the entire Peloponnesian army.

While the Spartans were besieging Plataea, toward the end of May the Athenians took the offensive in the northeast. The rebellion in the Chalcidice had continued even after the fall of Potidaea, depriving Athens of imperial revenue and encouraging other local rebellions, so the Athenians sent Xenophon and two other generals with a force of two thousand hoplites and two hundred cavalry to crush the revolt. They attacked the town of Spartolus (see Map 16, page 174), counting on assistance from a treasonous democratic faction within the city. It was the beginning of a pattern that would be repeated throughout the war, as factional strife between oligarchs and democrats intensified. Patriotism would occasionally triumph over factional interest, but when love of party was greater than love of independence democrats would betray their cities to Athens, and oligarchs theirs to Sparta.

At Spartolus another pattern emerged as well, for as the democrats sought Athenian help for their faction their oligarchic opponents likewise sought outside assistance—in their case, from the neighboring city of Olynthus. The Olynthians provided a garrison, whose superiority in cavalry and light-armed troops led to the defeat of the Athenian hoplites. The Athenians lost all their generals, 430 men, and the initiative in the Chalcidice. This would not be the last time in the war that hoplite armies would be vanquished by forces other than hoplites.

SPARTAN ACTION IN THE NORTHWEST

AS THE ATHENIANS were failing to restore order to the northeast, the Peloponnesians undertook to protect themselves in the northwest. The campaign was instigated by allies in the region, the Chaonians and Ambraciots, who sought to keep Athens out of the region so that they could dominate it. They proposed, therefore, that the Spartans assemble a fleet of ships and one thousand hoplites from among members of the alliance and attack Acarnania. They presented this idea as but one step in a grand strategy to prevent the Athenians from attacking the Peloponnesus: Acarnania would fall easily, followed by Zacynthus and Cephallenia, and perhaps even Naupactus.

Here was another of many instances in which the Spartans were led into dangerous undertakings by the interests of their allies. On its surface, however, the plan seemed attractive: the Athenians had only twenty ships in western waters, at Naupactus, and the Ambraciots and Chaonians were enthusiastic allies who were familiar with the territory. The Corinthians also supported the suggestion of their Ambracian colonists, for Corinth was the city most threatened by Athenian presence in the west.

Once again Sparta placed the navarch Cnemus in charge of the Peloponnesian force. He slipped past Phormio's fleet at Naupactus and sailed to Leucas, where he joined with allies from Leucas, Ambracia, and Anactorium, and with barbarians from Epirus (see Map 11) who were friendly to Corinth. He then proceeded overland through Amphilochian Argos, sacking a village on the way, and without reinforcements, attacked Stratus, the largest city of Acarnania, which he believed was key to the campaign. The Acarnanians avoided a pitched battle, using their knowledge of the terrain and their skill with the sling, and the defeated Cnemus was forced to return to the Peloponnesus.

ENTER PHORMIO

THE ACARNANIANS HAD sent to Phormio for help as soon as Cnemus arrived at Stratus, but the Athenian general could not leave Naupactus unguarded while the Corinthian and Sicyonian fleets were still in the gulf. His task was to cut off the Peloponnesian reinforcements. Phormio was a distinguished and experienced general who had commanded ships alongside Pericles and Hagnon eleven years earlier at Samos; in 432 he had also led hoplites in a skillful campaign at the siege of Potidaea. His greatest talent, however, was as a naval commander, as he would soon demonstrate.

While Cnemus was marching against Stratus, his reinforcements had sailed into the Gulf of Corinth. Phormio had only twenty ships to the enemy's forty-seven, and the Peloponnesians believed that the Athenians would refuse to fight them against such odds. But the Peloponnesians were carrying many hoplites to Acarnania, so their vessels, which were inherently slower than the Athenians', were less fit for a modern sea battle. The greater maneuverability of their ships and the superior training of their crews and steersmen gave the Athenians an additional advantage to offset the enemy's superiority in numbers.

Phormio did not trouble the enemy ships as they sailed west along the Peloponnesian coast, biding his time until they cleared the narrow straits between Rhium and Cape Antirrhium and reached more open sea, where his tactics would be most effective (see Map 12). At last, when the Peloponnesians tried to sail across the open water from Patrae to the mainland, the Athenians attacked. The enemy tried to slip away under cover of the darkness, but Phormio caught them in mid-channel and forced them to battle.

Despite their great superiority in numbers the Peloponnesians adopted a defensive formation: a large circle with the fleet's prows facing outward, close enough together to prevent the Athenians from breaking through. At the center were five of the fastest vessels, prepared

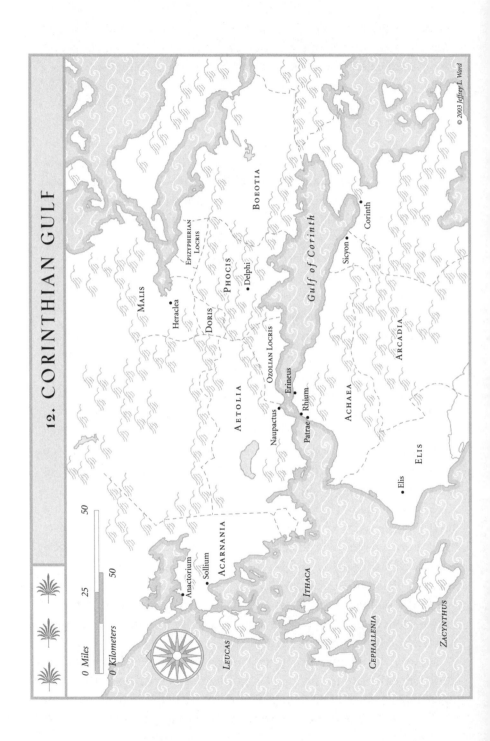

12. CORINTHIAN GULF

0 Miles   25   50

0 Kilometers   50

MALIS

Heraclea

DORIS

EPIZYPHERIAN LOCRIS

PHOCIS

Delphi

BOEOTIA

OZOLIAN LOCRIS

Erineus

AETOLIA

Naupactus

Rhium

Patrae

Gulf of Corinth

Sicyon

Corinth

ACHAEA

ARCADIA

ACARNANIA

Anactorium

Sollium

LEUCAS

ITHACA

ELIS

Elis

CEPHALLENIA

ZACYNTHUS

© 2003 Jeffrey L. Ward

to bring help to any breach in the defense. Phormio put his own ships in a line, sailing them around the circle formed by the enemy. This exposed the vulnerable sides of the Athenian ships, and a swift assault by the Peloponnesians might ram the Athenians and sink or disable them.

Phormio directed his ships around the enemy in an ever-tightening circle, forcing the Peloponnesians into a narrower and narrower space, "always just grazing by and giving the impression that they would charge at any moment" (2.84.1). He expected that in close quarters the Peloponnesians would not be able to maintain position and would foul one another's oars. He also knew that toward dawn a breeze usually blew in from the gulf and that in the choppy water it created the Peloponnesians would have difficulty managing their ships, burdened as they were with many troops on board. Thucydides gives a dramatic account of the ensuing battle:

> When the wind began to come up, the ships, which were already in close quarters, were thrown into disorder both by the wind and by the small boats [these were a number of light boats, not warships, placed in the center of the circle for safety]; one ship was colliding with another while the men tried to push them apart with poles, shouting at one another to watch out and cursing so that they could hear neither the words of their commanders nor the calls of the coxswains. At last, when the inexperienced rowers were unable to clear their oars in the high waves, just at that opportune moment Phormio gave the signal and the Athenians fell upon them. First they sank the ship of one of the generals and then they destroyed any one that they came upon, and they reduced the enemy to such a state that not one of the ships turned to defend itself, but all fled to Patrae and Dyme in Achaea. (2.84.3)

The Athenians captured twelve ships with most of their crews, set up a trophy of victory, and returned in triumph to Naupactus. At Cyllene the surviving Peloponnesian vessels met Cnemus limping home from his defeat at Stratus. The first major Peloponnesian effort at an amphibious offensive had ended in humiliating failure.

News of the routing of a larger Peloponnesian fleet shocked the Spartans, who blamed the commanders for the loss, and in particular

Cnemus, for as navarch he was responsible for the entire campaign. To address the problem they sent him three "advisers" (*xymbouloi*), among them the dashing Brasidas, with orders to fight a battle and "not to be driven from the sea by a few ships" (2.85.3).

Phormio, meanwhile, dispatched a messenger to Athens to announce his victory and to request reinforcements. The assembly's response, however, was strange: they granted a fleet of twenty ships, but ordered it to first to take the town of Cydonia in Crete, far to the south of the fastest route to Phormio. This seems an odd time to have pursued an offensive on another front, but the Athenians must have wanted to divert the Spartans from a concentration of their forces by causing trouble for their allies in Crete. Athens did not choose the moment arbitrarily, for the invitation from Crete came when it did and had to be immediately accepted or rejected. Although the effort in Crete failed and the mission may ultimately have been a mistake, it cannot be judged as absurd and did not prove costly. Even so, why did the Athenians send only twenty ships to Phormio, which continued to leave him badly outnumbered, when they had enough vessels to send a larger fleet to Naupactus and also a separate one to Crete? The most plausible answer is that they were restricted by shortages both of healthy men and of money.

At Naupactus, Phormio still had only twenty ships to face the Spartan force of seventy-seven. This time the Peloponnesians, free of heavy infantry, were eager to fight and commanded more vigorously, imaginatively, and skillfully than in the earlier battle. From Cyllene in Elis, they sailed eastward along the Peloponnesian shore until they met their infantry at Panormus, at the narrowest point in the Gulf of Corinth.

If Phormio refused to engage a force almost four times the size of his own the enemy would be free to sail west, break the Athenian blockade, and lock his fleet in Naupactus. The image of Athens as mistress of the seas would be destroyed, encouraging its restless subjects to revolt. Phormio was not, however, the man to let that happen, and he anchored just outside the narrows at Antirrhium, less than 'a mile across the gulf from Rhium in the Peloponnesus.

For a week the enemies glared at each other across the narrow water. The Athenians had no incentive to make the first move, for they were both outnumbered and compelled to protect Naupactus, their naval base on the gulf. The Spartans, therefore, took the initiative, sailing eastward along the Peloponnesian coast. On their right wing were their twenty best ships, heading toward Naupactus. Phormio had no choice but to keep pace with them as he sailed back into the narrower portion of the gulf. As he advanced, the Messenian hoplites, the Athenian allies who lived at Naupactus, followed along by land. Seeing the Athenian ships hurrying along the north shore in single file the Spartans wheeled about and cut off nine of them, driving them ashore. Eleven remained to face the twenty best Peloponnesian vessels. Even if the Athenians could defeat or elude them they would still have to deal with the remaining fifty-seven. Disaster seemed certain.

The Athenian eleven used their speed to get past the enemy. Ten reached Naupactus, waiting there with prows outward, ready to fight the overwhelming numbers that would soon arrive. The final Athenian ship was still making its way home, pursued by the Peloponnesians, who were already singing the chant of victory. A merchant vessel happened to be lying at anchor in the deep water off Naupactus; it became the device that produced a stunning reversal. The lone Athenian ship, instead of racing for the protection of Naupactus, whirled three-quarters of a circle, using the anchored merchantman to protect its exposed side as it turned, rammed the leading pursuer, and sank it. The Peloponnesians, believing the battle was already over, now fell into complete disorder. Some ran aground in ignorance of the waters. Others, stunned by the sight, put their oars into the water to stop their ships and wait for the rest of the fleet—a terrible mistake, for it left them motionless and helpless before a moving enemy.

The remaining Athenians, sparked by the amazing turn of events, now moved forward to attack the enemy who still outnumbered them two to one. By now, however, the Peloponnesians had lost all taste for battle and fled to Panormus, abandoning eight of the nine captured Athenian ships and losing six of their own. Each side set up a trophy as a mark of victory, but it was clear who had won. The Athenians retained their fleet, their base at Naupactus, and free movement on the sea. The Peloponnesians, fearing the arrival of Athenian reinforcements, sailed away in defeat. The reinforcements did soon arrive by way of Crete, too late for the battle but in time to discourage the enemy from attempting another offensive.

Had Phormio been defeated, the Athenians would have been

forced to surrender Naupactus and with it their ability to impede the commerce of Corinth and other Peloponnesian states trading with the west. A loss at sea would also have shaken Athenian confidence and encouraged the enemy to even more ambitious naval operations, which could spark rebellions in the empire, which, in turn, might gain support from the Great King of Persia. It is no wonder the Athenians remembered Phormio especially fondly, setting up a statue honoring him on the Acropolis and after his death burying him in the state cemetery on the road to the Academy near the grave of Pericles.

THE SPARTANS ATTACK PIRAEUS

CNEMUS AND BRASIDAS, reluctant to return home with news of their failure, were now driven to daring and agreed to the Megarians' proposal to attack Piraeus. The idea was incredibly bold, but the Megarians pointed out that the Athenian harbor was neither closed nor guarded. The Athenians were also overconfident and ill-prepared, for it was November, after the sailing season, and who would expect so audacious an attack from the defeated Peloponnesian navy, which had so recently abandoned the Gulf of Corinth in disgrace? The Peloponnesian plan, which depended on surprise, was to send the oarsmen from their fleet overland to the Megarian port of Nisaea on the Saronic Gulf. There they would find forty unmanned Megarian triremes, which they would sail immediately to the unsuspecting and unprotected Piraeus. The first step went as planned, but at Nisaea the Spartan commanders "were thoroughly frightened by the risk—and also there was some talk of a wind having prevented them" (2.93.4). Instead they attacked and ravaged Salamis, which gave the game away. Fire signals warned Athens, which was soon in panic, for the Athenians believed that the Spartans had already taken Salamis and were on their way into Piraeus. Thucydides believed they could have succeeded, but their timidity proved costly. At dawn the Athenians took courage, sending a force of infantry to guard the port and a fleet to Salamis. At the first sight of the Athenian ships the Peloponnesians fled. Athens was safe, and the Athenians took steps to guarantee that no such surprise attack in the future could succeed.

THE DEATH OF PERICLES

THE STRIKE ON Naupactus and Piraeus failed because the Peloponnesians lacked experience at sea, which led them to make costly errors and to be fearful in combat. Pericles had foreseen that behavior, but he did not live to enjoy the fulfillment of his predictions. In September 429, two years and six months after the outbreak of the war, he died. His last days were not happy. The "first citizen" of Athens had been removed from office, condemned, and punished. Many of his friends died in the plague, as well as his sister and his legitimate sons, Xanthippus and Paralus. Having lost his heirs, he now asked the Athenians for exemption from a law limiting citizenship to those with two Athenian parents—a law that he himself had introduced over two decades earlier. He requested citizenship for Pericles, his son by Aspasia, a Milesian woman who was his beloved mistress of long standing. The Athenians granted his wish.

Public problems also burdened Pericles in his final days. His policy of moderate deterrence exploded into war, and his conservative strategy seemed incapable of winning it. The plague had killed many more Athenians than would have been lost in any battle. His people blamed him for the war and the strategy that intensified the effects of the plague. Toward the very end of his life some friends who were attending Pericles, supposing him to be asleep, began to discuss his greatness, his power, and his achievements, especially the many victories he had won for Athens. Pericles, however, had heard their conversation and expressed his surprise at what accomplishments they chose to praise, for such things, he believed, were often due to chance and had been achieved by many. "But they had not spoken of the greatest and most beautiful thing. For no one of the Athenians now alive has put on mourning because of me" (Plutarch, *Pericles* 38.4). This was the response of a man with a burdened conscience to those who accused him of deliberately bringing on a war that he might have averted.

The death of Pericles deprived Athens of a leader with unique qualities. He was a military man and strategist of stature, but even more a brilliant politician of the rarest talents. He could decide on a policy and persuade the Athenians to adopt and remain committed to it, to restrain them from overly ambitious undertakings, and to encourage them when they lost confidence. The restored Pericles might have had sufficient power to hold the Athenians to a consistent policy, as no other Athenian could have. In his last recorded speech Pericles enumerated the characteristics necessary in a statesman: "To know what must be done and to be able to explain it; to love one's country and to be incorruptible" (2.60.5). No one had these traits in greater measure than Pericles himself, and if he made errors, he of all Athenians was most likely to put them right. His countrymen would miss him sorely.

In the same year Sitalces, king of the Thracians and ally of Athens, attacked the Macedonian kingdom of Perdiccas and the Chalcidic cities nearby. He managed to capture some fortresses, but ran into substantial resistance. Although he had a vast army of 150,000 men, a third of them cavalry, he delayed the attack on the Chalcidice, which depended on the collaboration of the Athenian fleet, but it never arrived. Perhaps the Athenians, once they saw its vast numbers in motion, feared that Sitalces' army might be tempted to move against their own empire in the region. Since the formation of the plan, moreover, the Spartans had attacked Naupactus and Piraeus by sea. Although these strikes failed, they may well have shaken the Athenians' confidence, leading them to decide that this was no time to undertake large expeditions far from home. Prudence and the shortage of manpower and money in the autumn and winter of 429/8 also probably account for the failure of Athens to send the promised navy to Sitalces.

The great size of the Thracian army frightened all the Greeks in the north, but it ran short of food and finally withdrew without having accomplished much. In the third year of the war Attica was free from invasion and had averted seaborne defeats, but the Athenian reserve fund continued to decline, leaving an estimated usable balance of 1,450 talents. There was now enough money to permit the war to continue at the level of the first two years for one additional year, or at half-speed for two. The original strategy for victory had failed, and the Athenians had as yet formulated no substitute. They could not continue as they had been without exhausting their financial resources, but they had no way to compel the enemy to make peace.

CHAPTER NINE

Rebellion in the Empire (428–427)

THE "NEW POLITICIANS" IN ATHENS

THE DEATH OF PERICLES brought a great change to Athenian political life. "Those who followed him," said Thucydides, "were more equal with one another" (2.65.10) and as a result were not able to provide the unified, consistent leadership necessary in a war. Formerly generals had almost always been aristocrats, but gradually a new set of politicians had arisen, individuals whose families had become rich through trade and industry. Such men were at least as wealthy as the landed aristocrats, and often as well educated, and they came to exercise political power no less ably than their predecessors.

The two competitors who now emerged as leaders of rival factions were Nicias son of Niceratus and Cleon son of Cleaenetus. Thucydides and most scholars since have judged the two men to have been cut from entirely different cloth: Nicias pious, upright, and reserved, a gentleman; Cleon, the longtime opponent of Pericles, an advocate of war, a demagogue, a vulgarian. Both, in fact, came from the same class of "new men" without noble lineage. Nicias had made his fortune by renting slaves to work in the silver mines of Attica; Cleon's father owned a successful tannery. In each case the father is the first member of the family known to us.

While few pairs of men could have been more unlike in personality, character, and style in their attitude toward the war they were not so different as they are usually portrayed. Neither favored the peace negotiations with Sparta, and both tried to find a way to win the war in the years following the death of Pericles. There is no record of any disagreement between the two until 425. In 428, their interests were virtually identical: the empire must be kept safe for Athens, the Athenians must be imbued with the spirit to carry on the war, resources must be husbanded and new ones found, and some strategy must be developed to resume offensive operations if the war was ever to be brought to a successful conclusion. The two men had a motive to cooperate, and there is no reason to believe that they did not do so.

CONSPIRACY ON LESBOS

IN 428 THE SPARTANS resumed their invasions of Attica near the middle of May and inflicted damage for about a month before withdrawing. The relief was brief, however, for a plot was already taking shape on the island of Lesbos that could threaten the empire and the survival of Athens itself. Along with Chios, Lesbos was one of only two important islands that retained its autonomy when the Delian League became the Athenian Empire. Mytilene, its chief city, was unusual among the allies of Athens in being governed by an oligarchy. The towns of Lesbos were also exceptional in that they still provided ships instead of tribute as their contribution to the league. In spite of this favored statue, however, Mytilene had considered withdrawing from the Athenian alliance even before the war, but had been deterred by the refusal of the Peloponnesians to accept the city into their own alliance. That rejection had taken place in peacetime, but during the war a rebellion on Lesbos would surely be welcomed by the enemies of Athens.

The plot was hatched at Mytilene, whose ambitions to dominate the island were at the root of the revolt. The time for an uprising could hardly have been better. Athens was widely known to be weak from the plague and short of men and money; an insurrection was likely to bring defections that would debilitate it even further. The success of the plot depended on help from Athens' enemies, which in 428 seemed certain, for the Boeotians as well as the Spartans were involved in the plans. The Mytileneans had appealed for assistance in a speech delivered at Olympia before the assembled Peloponnesians. The main motive for insurgency, they alleged, was their fear that at some time the Athenians would reduce them to subjection like all their other allies with the exception of Chios. Their true motive—the unification of all the cities of Lesbos under Mytilenean leadership—they concealed, for Athens would never have permitted it. The Athenians were in general opposed to the creation of larger units within their domain and in fact typically tried to break them up into smaller ones. The presence on the island of democratic Methymna, a city hostile to Mytilene, made it almost certain that the Athenians would intervene in the event of any revolt.

The Mytileneans nevertheless began to build defensive walls, block up their harbor, increase the size of their navy, and send to the Black Sea regions for grain supplies and mercenary bowmen. Before they completed these preparations, however, word of their intention got out as hostile neighbors hastened to warn Athens of the developments, in collaboration with Mytileneans who were *proxenoi*, representatives of the Athenians. They were probably democrats, hostile to the government, acting for their own political motives. The disclosure of their plans forced the rebels to move before they were ready.

ATHENS REACTS

In June the Athenians sent a fleet in the annual campaign around the Peloponnesus—economy kept it to forty ships instead of the hundred that had sailed in 431—but on verifying that the Mytileneans were unifying the island they made for Lesbos instead. They had hoped to surprise the rebels during a religious festival, but because secrecy was effectively impossible in the Athenian democracy, where every decision of policy had to be made in the full assembly on the Pnyx, a messenger had warned the Mytileneans in advance. When they refused the arriving fleet's order to surrender their ships and tear down their walls, the Athenians attacked.

Although the Mytileneans were caught before their supplies and archers had arrived, before their defenses were mounted, and their Peloponnesian and Boeotian alliances formally concluded, the Athenians recognized the relative weakness of their own force and reserves and feared "that they were not strong enough to fight all of Lesbos" (3.5.4). The Mytileneans "wanted, if they could, to get rid of the Athenian ships for the present" (3.4.2), while waiting for their allies, so they asked for an armistice. As part of their delaying tactics, they sent a mission to Athens promising to remain loyal to the alliance if the

Athenians withdrew their fleet. They said nothing about their forcible unification of the island, which was well on its way to completion. In effect, the Mytileneans were petitioning Athens to accept their domination of Lesbos in return for future loyalty. The Athenians, of course, could not abandon Methymna to Mytilene, and deny it the protection that guaranteed and justified their command of the empire. Knowing that the Athenians would refuse, the Mytileneans had also secretly ordered an embassy to the Spartans to request aid from their alliance.

MYTILENE APPEALS TO THE PELOPONNESIANS

TWO SETS OF Mytilenean envoys came to Sparta in July, a week apart, but neither was successful; the Spartans merely advised the Mytileneans to tell their story to the Peloponnesian alliance at a gathering at the Olympic festival. Sparta's declining any further involvement in the conflict was due in part to the fact that the idea for a rebellion at Mytilene had originally come from Boeotia, not from Sparta, and in part to its realization that to help Mytilene would have required a large and expensive fleet and fighting at sea. The memory of humiliating defeats by Phormio must have made the latter a particularly unappealing prospect.

In August the Peloponnesian alliance met in the sacred precinct of Zeus at Olympia after the conclusion of the games. The Mytilenean spokesman had to convince the allies that their intervention served the larger cause of Greek freedom and their own ends, not merely Mytilenean self-interest. He spoke of the encroachment of the Athenians on the autonomy of their allies, which would inevitably lead to the enslavement of Mytilene unless the rebellion succeeded. He argued that the timing of the insurrection was ideal: "There never has been such an opportunity before, for the Athenians have been ruined by the plague and the expenditure of money. Part of their fleet is sailing around your coast [Phormio's son Asopius set out on this expedition in July], and the rest is lined up against us. They are not likely to have any ships to spare if you make a second attack on them this summer both by land and sea. Either they will not resist you, or they will withdraw their fleet from both our territories" (3.13.3–4). The Mytileneans' final argument was that the war would be decided not in Attica but in the empire, whence came the money to fight it.

> If you come to our aid with vigor, you will enroll among your allies a state that has a great navy, which you need most of all, you will defeat the Athenians more easily by drawing their allies away from them (for every one will proceed more boldly after you have assisted us), and you will escape the charge which you now have of not helping those who rebel from Athens. If, however, you show yourselves openly to be liberators you will more surely have victory. (3.13.5–7)

The alliance accepted the Mytileneans immediately, and the Spartans ordered the allies to gather at the Isthmus of Corinth for the invasion of Attica. The Spartans themselves set to work preparing to haul their ships across the isthmus to the Saronic Gulf for a joint attack on Athens by land and sea. The allies, however, "collected slowly because they were in the midst of harvesting the grain and reluctant to serve" (3.15.2).

In this crisis the Athenians demonstrated that same determination and toughness of spirit that had saved their freedom and won them an empire. Although forty of their ships were still blockading Lesbos, they put to sea a fleet of a hundred triremes to raid the Peloponnesus, as they had in the first years of the war. This bold display of confidence and capability strained Athenian resources to the utmost. Besides the usual rowers from the lowest class, this time they drew upon men of the hoplite class, who normally fought as heavily armed infantrymen only; resident aliens were also pressed into service as rowers to meet the emergency. These crews were not as good as those commanded by Phormio, but the Spartans were still cowed by their defeats in 429.

The Athenians proceeded to land on the Peloponnesus wherever they liked, a demonstration of power that convinced the Spartans that the Mytileneans had misrepresented Athenian weakness, so they abandoned the attack and returned home. Once again the Mytileneans and their supporters on Lesbos were left to confront the Athenians alone.

Without allied help, they failed to take Methymna and had to be content with strengthening their hold on the subordinate cities of Antissa, Pyrrha, and Eresos, leaving the situation on Lesbos virtually unchanged. Sparta's apparent withdrawal, however, encouraged the Athenians to press harder, and they ordered a thousand hoplites to Lesbos under the general Paches, who built a wall around Mytilene, shutting it in by land and sea. The siege and blockade would not only protect Methymna but might also force Mytilene to surrender.

THE SIEGE OF MYTILENE

THE SIEGE OF MYTILENE, which became effective at the very onset of winter, strained Athenian financial resources beyond any prediction Pericles may have made at the beginning of the war. By the winter of 428/7 the available reserve had fallen to less than a thousand talents. The financial crisis was not a few years off; it was immediate.

The Athenians, therefore, undertook two extraordinary measures that had not been part of the publicly announced plan of Pericles. In the late summer of 428 they announced an increase in the tribute demanded from the allies. Months before the usual deadline for collection they dispatched twelve ships to gather the newly assessed taxes. We do not know how much they collected, but they did meet resistance in Caria, and the general Lysicles was killed in the effort to bring in new funds.

But even raising assessments and tightening collections, had they been successful, would not have been able to meet the financial needs of Athens, which had suddenly grown more intense with the siege of Mytilene. The Athenians, therefore, decided on a desperate solution: "Being in need of money for the siege, they themselves introduced for the first time a direct tax [*eisphora*] in the amount of two hundred talents" (3.19.1). Whether Thucydides means the first time ever or the first time in the course of this war, a direct tax had not been imposed in a very long time. Strange as it may seem to modern taxpayers—and to most people, in fact, since the birth of civilization—citizens of the Greek states hated the idea of direct taxation as a violation of their personal autonomy and an attack on the property on which their freedom rested. The new imposition was especially painful to the propertied classes, on whom the *eisphora* fell exclusively, a group that included the yeomen farmers who made up the hoplite army.

While raising financial demands on the allies was a dangerous tactic, it might produce rebellions that would undermine the source of Athenian power, the levying of a direct tax threatened to sap the very enthusiasm of the populace for the war. It is not surprising that Pericles never suggested these expedients in his public discussion of Athenian resources, but there is no reason to attribute their use in 428 only to Cleon and his faction. The men who rallied the Athenians to a major effort in the face of a possible attack on Athens by land and sea and the danger of rebellion in the empire must have been chiefly her generals: Nicias, and Paches, among others. They, no less than Cleon and his supporters, realized that the safety of Athens depended on putting down the rebellion of Mytilene before it spread throughout the empire and drained the treasury. They acted not out of partisan politics or class warfare but of prudent patriotism, responding to an emergency.

Throughout this period the Spartans had not been ignoring developments on Lesbos. Late in the winter they secretly sent a Spartan envoy, Salaethus, to Mytilene to inform the insurgents that the amphibious campaign originally planned for 428 would now take place in 427. They would invade Attica, and send forty ships to Mytilene under the Spartan commander Alcidas. This welcome news encouraged the rebels to hold out against Athens, and Salaethus himself stayed at Mytilene to coordinate actions on the island.

As the winter drew to a close the Athenians faced the greatest challenge they had yet confronted during this war. They had to put down a rebellion by a powerful member of their alliance while their own land was in danger of being invaded, and they must do so quickly, for a long siege like the one at Potidaea might finally exhaust their reserve and put an end to their defensive ability.

SPARTA ACTS ON LAND AND SEA

THE SPARTAN INVASION of Attica in 427 was meant to put pressure on the Athenians to prevent their sending a larger fleet to Mytilene.

The Peloponnesians were present in force but for the first time Archidamus, who must have been dying, did not lead the campaign. Because his son Agis may have been judged too inexperienced for the task, Cleomenes, brother of the exiled King Pleistoanax, took the command. At the same time, the Spartans sent the navarch Alcidas to Lesbos with a fleet of forty-two triremes, hoping the Athenians would be too preoccupied with the invasion of their own land to intercept them.

The aggressive faction of the Spartans had long believed that an invasion of Attica, combined with a naval attack in the Aegean, would lead to a general uprising among the allies that would destroy the Athenian empire, but the right opportunity had never presented itself. The rebellion of Samos in 440 might have been a good chance, but the Corinthians' refusal had spoiled it. Now, at last, the time had come.

In duration and amount of damage inflicted, the Attic land invasion was exceeded only by that of 430. Everything untouched by previous attacks and everything that had grown up since was cut down. At sea, because the Peloponnesian force could not hope to fight its way through the Athenian navy, its success depended on speed. Alcidas however, "wasted time in sailing around the Peloponnesus and proceeded in a leisurely manner on the rest of the voyage" (3.29.1). Still, he managed to avoid the Athenian fleet until Delos, but the delay was fatal, for at Icarus and Myconus he learned that Mytilene had already surrendered.

To formulate their next step the Peloponnesians held a council; even at this point boldness and enterprise might have accomplished much. The daring Elean commander Teutiaplus proposed an immediate attack on Mytilene, certain that the Peloponnesians could take the Athenians by surprise so soon after their victory there, but the cautious Alcidas rejected the idea. A better suggestion came from Ionian exiles, who urged the Spartans to use their fleet to support a rebellion of Ionian cities subject to Athens. Their plan was for Alcidas to seize one of the cities on the coast of Asia Minor and use it as a base for a general Ionian rebellion. Pissuthnes, the Persian satrap who had helped the Samian rebels in 440, might also again support the enemies of Athens. If the uprising succeeded, the Athenians would lose their income from the area at a time when they were especially vulnerable. Even a partial success would compel them to divide their forces in order to blockade the Ionian rebel cities. The most optimistic result would put in place the combination of the Spartan Alliance, rebellious Athenian subjects, and the Persian Empire—precisely the alignment that would one day defeat Athens.

The Ionians wanted to use the Spartan presence to support their rebellion, and their advice was excellent. Thucydides tells us that when the mainlanders saw the ships, "they did not run away but instead came closer to thinking that they were Athenian. For they did not have the slightest expectation that Peloponnesian ships would approach Ionia while Athens ruled the seas" (3.32.2). The support of such a fleet would surely have persuaded at least one city to rebel. Once that action dispelled the aura of Athenian naval invincibility, others would join, and the Persian satrap might take the opportunity to drive the Athenians from Asia.

But Alcidas would not hear of such an action. "After arriving too late to save Mytilene, the chief thing in his mind was to get back to the Peloponnesus as quickly as possible" (3.31.2). In a panic at the prospect of being caught by an Athenian fleet, he raced for home, and concerned that prisoners he had taken in Asia Minor might slow his escape, he put most of them to death. At Ephesus, friendly Samians warned him that such behavior was no way to free the Greeks but would alienate those Greeks who were already partial to Sparta. Alcidas yielded and freed the prisoners who were still alive, but Sparta's reputation was badly tarnished by the incident. When Paches learned of the Spartans' location he pursued their fleet as far as Patmos before giving up the chase, and Alcidas made it safely back to the Peloponnesus. The Spartans, as Thucydides said on a later occasion, were "the most convenient of all people for the Athenians to fight" (8.96.5).

THE FATE OF MYTILENE

THE FAILURE OF the Peloponnesian fleet to arrive in time doomed the rebels at Mytilene. As the blockade had been rapidly depleting the city's supply of food, Salaethus, the Spartan sent to bolster the morale of the rebels, had planned a desperate attack to break through the Athenians' besieging army. To have a chance he would need more hoplites than Mytilene could provide, so he took the extraordinary step of supplying the lower classes with hoplite equipment. Mytilene's oligarchic regime agreed to this plan, which reveals that they believed the common people to be reliable and trustworthy. Once the new recruits were armed, however, they demanded the distribution of the available food to all the town's citizens; unless the oligarchs agreed, they threatened to turn the city over to Athens and make a separate peace excluding the upper classes.

The evidence does not reveal whether the government could have met this demand or whether doing so would have guaranteed the loyalty of the people. Perhaps the stores of food were so low that a general distribution was impossible. In any case, the oligarchic government yielded to Paches on terms that amounted to unconditional surrender: the Athenians could "decide in whatever way they wanted about the Mytileneans" (3.28.3). Paches, however, promised not to imprison, enslave, or kill any Mytilenean until the return of an embassy he would allow to go from Mytilene to Athens to negotiate a permanent settlement.

The arrival of the Athenian army in the city had terrified the oligarchic Mytileneans who had been closest to the Spartans, and they had fled to the altars of the gods for sanctuary. Paches assured the suppliants that he would do them no harm and removed them to the nearby island of Tenedos for safekeeping. He proceeded to take control of the other Lesbian towns that had opposed Athens and after capturing Salaethus, who was hiding, also sent him to Athens along with the pro-Spartan Mytileneans on Tenedos and "any one else who seemed to him responsible for the rebellion" (3.35.1).

To understand the mood of the Athenians at the assembly that met to consider the fate of Mytilene in the summer of 427 we must recall the situation in which they found themselves. In the fourth year of the war they had suffered terribly from invasions and the plague, their original strategy had failed and no promising substitute was at hand. The rebellion at Mytilene and the penetration of the Spartan fleet to Ionia were terrifying harbingers of disasters that awaited. The men who sat on the Pnyx were dominated by fear for their survival and anger at those who had put it at risk.

They revealed the strength of these emotions by swiftly deciding to put Salaethus to death without a trial, even though he offered to persuade the Spartans to abandon the siege of Plataea in exchange for his life. The fate of Mytilene itself, however, was the subject of a contentious debate. Thucydides does not report the details of this meeting or any of the speeches made, but he tells us enough to reconstruct its course. The embassy from Mytilene, including both oligarchs and democrats, probably spoke first, and the two factions almost certainly split on the question of who was accountable for the rebellion. The oligarchs argued that all Mytileneans were to blame, trusting that the Athenians would not choose to destroy a whole people; the democrats claimed that the oligarchs alone were responsible and had forced the common people to join them.

Cleon's motion to kill all the adult males of Mytilene and sell its women and children as slaves became the focus of the debate. His chief opponent was Diodotus son of Eucrates, a man of whom we otherwise know nothing. While the assembly split into factions on the matter— the moderates represented by Diodotus, following the cautious policy of Pericles, and the more aggressive faction led by Cleon—all Athenians were angry: because the Mytileneans had rebelled in spite of their privileged status, because the rebellion had been long and carefully prepared and, most of all, because the revolt had brought a Peloponnesian fleet to the shores of Ionia. In the atmosphere, Cleon's proposal became law, and a trireme was dispatched to order Paches to carry out the sentence at once.

THE MYTILENE DEBATE: CLEON VERSUS DIODOTUS

IT WAS NOT LONG, however, before the Athenians began to reconsider their decision. Having expressed their anger, some of them recognized the frightfulness of their resolution. The ambassadors from Mytilene and their friends in Athens—including Diodotus, no doubt, and other moderates—took advantage of this shift in attitude and persuaded the generals, all of whom we know were moderates, to ask for a special meeting of the assembly to review the matter the following day.

In his account of that session Thucydides introduces Cleon into his history for the first time as "the most violent of the citizens and at that time by far the most influential with the people" (3.36.6). Cleon argued that the Mytileneans' rebellion was unjustified, the result of unforeseen good fortune that turned, as usual, into wanton violence (*hybris*); justice, therefore, required swift and severe punishment. No distinction, he insisted, should be made between common people and oligarchs, for both took part in the rebellion. Cleon, moreover, believed that leniency would only encourage further rebellion, while a uniformly harsh punishment would deter it: "We should never have treated the Mytileneans differently from the others and then they would not have reached this point of insolence. In general, it is the nature of man to despise flattery and admire firmness" (3.39.5). His implication was that the Athenians ought to have deprived Mytilene of its autonomy long since, and the failure to have done so was only one of many past errors. "Consider your allies: if you impose the same penalties upon those who rebel under constraint by the enemy and on those who rebel of their own free will, tell me who will not rebel on the smallest pretext when the reward for success is freedom and the price of failure is nothing irreparable?" (3.39.7).

If the Athenians continued their policy of softness, misplaced pity, and clemency, "we shall risk our lives and money against each rebellious state. If we succeed we will recover a state that has been destroyed, only then to be deprived for the future of its revenue, which is the source of our strength. If we fail we will add new enemies to those we have already, and the time we should devote to fighting our present enemies we will spend combating our own allies" (3.39.8). Cleon's address amounted to a full-scale attack on the imperial policy of Pericles and the moderates. He recommended instead a calculated policy of terror to deter rebellions, at least in wartime.

Cleon and Diodotus, who represented the extreme positions, were only two among several speakers. Others who "expressed various opinions" (3.36.6) surely spoke of justice and humanity, since Cleon's reported speech rebuts those considerations, and since the second assembly had been specifically convened to address the Athenians' feeling that the penalty chosen was "cruel and excessive" (3.36.4).

Because Cleon had implied that a rejection of his penalty in favor of a gentler one would be a sign of weakness at the very least, if not corruption and even treason, Diodotus shrewdly urged the Athenians to vote for his own proposal not out of clemency but from calculations of expediency. Diodotus genuinely desired a milder punishment for Mytilene, but his deeper purpose was to defend a continuation of a moderate imperial policy. He argued that because rebels always expect to succeed, no threat of punishment can prevent them. The current, more moderate policy, in contrast, encourages those who have rebelled "to reach an agreement while [they are] still able to pay the indemnity and the tribute in the future" (3.46.2). Taking Cleon's harsher line would only encourage rebels to "hold on to the very last when besieged," causing Athens "to spend money besieging an enemy who will not surrender and to be deprived of its revenue for the future, . . . the source of our strength against our enemies" (3.46.2–3).

Diodotus also claimed that "now the *demos* in all the cities is well disposed to you and either does not rebel along with the oligarchs or, if it is compelled, is immediately hostile to those who made the revolution, so that you go to war having the majority of the opposing city as an ally" (3.47.2). The evidence suggests he was wrong about the popularity of the empire, even with the lower classes, but he was less interested in establishing the facts than in prescribing a policy. The Athenians should blame as few men as possible among insurgents, he continued, for killing the commoners as well as the noble instigators of rebellion would only encourage the former to side against Athens in future uprisings. "Even if the *demos* were guilty you should pretend otherwise so that the only group that is still friendly to you should not become hostile" (3.47.4).

For Diodotus Mytilene was an isolated case, which made the policy of calculated terror proposed by Cleon not only offensive but ultimately self-defeating. His counterproposal was to condemn only those whom Paches had sent to Athens as the guilty parties. That suggestion was less humane than it might seem, for those arrested by Paches as "most guilty" numbered a little over a thousand, and constituted probably not less than one-tenth of the entire adult male population of the rebellious towns on Lesbos.

In the end the show of hands in the assembly was almost equal, but the proposal of Diodotus won. Cleon immediately proposed the death penalty for the "guilty" thousand, and his motion passed. The

Lesbians received no proper trial, either individually or en masse; the assembly simply assumed them guilty on the basis of Paches' opinion, and there is no evidence that the vote was close. This was the harshest action yet taken by the Athenians against rebellious subjects, yet however angry and callous their fear, frustration, and suffering had made them, they still shrank from the more brutal plan of Cleon.

The ship sent to Lesbos after the first assembly carrying the command to put all the men to death had a full day's head start, but a second trireme was sent off immediately to rescind the order. The Mytilenean envoys in Athens provided food and drink to the rowers and promised them a reward if they reached Lesbos first. Moved by the chance to accomplish a good deed and the hope of gain, the sailors set off at a great pace, refusing even to make the usual stops for eating and sleeping. The men on the first ship were in no hurry to accomplish their frightful task, but they arrived at Mytilene first. Thucydides tells the rest of the tale dramatically. "Paches had just read out the decree and was about to carry out its orders when the second ship put in and prevented the destruction. By so little did Mytilene escape its danger" (3.49.4).

CHAPTER TEN

Terror and Adventure (427)

THE ATHENIAN RESPONSE to the rebellion at Mytilene reflected a new, more aggressive spirit that began to challenge the old, moderate approach that was the legacy of Pericles. The elections of 427 brought to power two new generals, Eurymedon and Demosthenes, who soon would introduce bolder policies. Even the moderates felt the need to take the offensive, if cautiously. In the summer of 427 Nicias seized and fortified the little island of Minoa off the coast of Megara to tighten the blockade there.

THE FATE OF PLATAEA

ABOUT THE SAME TIME as the attack on Minoa, however, the defenders of Plataea surrendered. The Spartans could easily have stormed its walls, guarded by only a small number of starving men, but they gave orders not to take the city by force. Their rationale was that "if ever a peace were concluded with Athens, and if each side agreed to restore the places conquered in the war, Sparta could hold on to Plataea on the grounds that it had gone over of its own free will" (3.52.2).

This concern with sophistic legalism demonstrates that for the first time the Spartans were already considering a negotiated peace as a possibility in 427. Athens' toughness in surviving the plague and easy suppression of the rebellion in its empire as well as Sparta's own incompetence at sea, were sobering realities. Still, they were not yet ready to settle for anything but total victory.

To gain the Plataeans' surrender the Spartans promised the garrison a fair trial conducted by five judges from Sparta, but their treatment made a mockery of justice. No charges were brought against the Plataeans; each was merely asked if he had rendered any good service to the Spartans or their allies during the war. The Plataeans argued their case so convincingly and so embarrassed their interrogators that the Thebans, fearing that the Spartans might relent, found it necessary to answer with a long speech of their own. The Spartan judges then repeated the original question to the Plataeans, to which each one, of course, answered no. At least two hundred Plataeans and twenty-five Athenians were subsequently put to death, and the women who remained in the city were sold into slavery. The Spartans acted purely from political self-interest: "The behavior of the Spartans toward the Thebans was influenced almost entirely by concern for the Thebans, for they thought that they would be useful in the war that was just then beginning" (3.68.4). The Spartans were in effect preparing for a long war in which Boeotian power would be a more critical factor than a reputation for justice and decency.

Eventually, the Spartans turned Plataea over to the Thebans, who leveled the town entirely. They gave the city's land to deserving Thebans on ten-year leases, and by 421 the Thebans spoke of it as part of their own territory. Plataea had been obliterated, and the Athenians had not made any effort to intercede. Both developments were, in fact, inevitable. The city was strategically untenable, yet there was reason for the Athenians to feel embarrassment, even shame, at its fate. Plataea, a faithful ally, could have yielded on reasonable terms when attacked had not Athens held her to the alliance and promised help. The Athenians granted the surviving Plataeans the rare privilege of Athenian citizenship, but it was hardly adequate compensation for the loss of their homeland.

CIVIL WAR AT CORCYRA

A NEW DANGER soon threatened Corcyra, Athens' ally in the west, when fierce political strife threatened to bring Athens' enemies to power there and cause the loss of the island's great navy. The trouble began with the return to Corcyra of some 250 prisoners taken by the

Corinthians at the battle of Sybota in 433. The Corinthians had treated their captives well and won their loyalty. Early in 427 they sent them back home to subvert the policy and government of their native land at a time when hope was high among the Peloponnesians that a general rebellion of Athens' allies would soon take place.

No one on Corcyra was aware that these men had become agents of a foreign power against their own government; they explained their safe return by claiming that they had been ransomed for the incredibly high sum of eight hundred talents. Once returned at home they urged the end of the alliance with Athens and the resumption of traditional neutrality, concealing their intention to bring Corcyra into the Spartan Alliance. Despite their efforts the democratic Corcyraean assembly chose a middle path, reaffirming the defensive alliance, but voting also "to be friends with the Peloponnesians as they had in the past" (3.70.2).

The vote was nevertheless a victory for the oligarchic plotters, the first step in separating Corcyra from Athens. They next accused Peithias, a democratic leader closely attached to Athens, of trying to enslave Corcyra to the Athenians. The average Corcyraean, however, did not view an alliance with Athens as tantamount to treason and acquitted Peithias, who in turn successfully sued his five richest accusers on the charge of an alleged religious violation. Unable to pay an enormous fine, the defendants sought sanctuary in the temples.

The oligarchs, fearing that the victorious Peithias would use his victory to press for a full offensive and defensive alliance with Athens, turned to assassination and terror to prevent it. Armed with daggers they broke into a meeting of the council, killing Peithias and six others. A few democratic associates of Peithias escaped to the Athenian trireme that was still in the harbor. The ship immediately sailed off to Athens, where the refugees could tell their story and urge retaliation.

In this atmosphere of terror the assassins called a meeting of the assembly, but the Corcyraean people still refused to change alliances. The plotters in turn dared propose only neutrality, and even that measure passed only under compulsion. Fearing an Athenian attack, the oligarchs sent an embassy to Athens to plead that events at Corcyra were not aimed against Athenian interests. The Athenians, however, were unconvinced and arrested the ambassadors as revolutionaries. But the embassy to Athens was meant only to gain time while the oligarchs negotiated with Sparta, and encouraged by the hope of Spartan support, they defeated the common people in a pitched battle, although they were unable to destroy their democratic opponents. The democrats seized the acropolis and the other high places of the town, as well as the seaward harbor, while the oligarchs controlled the area around the marketplace and the harbor facing the mainland. The next day both sides sought support by offering freedom to the slaves; most of these joined the democrats, but the oligarchs hired eight hundred mercenaries from the mainland, and open civil war reigned on Corcyra.

Two days later the democrats turned the tables in a second battle, and the oligarchs saved themselves only by flight. The following day Nicostratus, commander of the Athenian forces at Naupactus, arrived with twelve ships and five hundred Messenian hoplites. He behaved with great moderation, taking no vengeance on the losing faction, but asked merely for a full offensive and defensive alliance to make the island safe for Athens. The only oligarchs brought to trial were the ten believed most responsible for inciting the revolution. The rest of the Corcyraeans were urged to make peace with one another.

But passions on Corcyra were now so inflamed that so gentle a solution proved impossible. The ten men selected for trial fled. The democratic leaders persuaded Nicostratus to leave them five Athenian ships in exchange for five of their own ships, manned by oligarchs of their choosing, their own personal enemies. The selected oligarchs, fearing they would be sent to Athens to meet some awful fate, likewise fled for sanctuary to the temples, and though Nicostratus tried to reassure them of their safety, they remained immovable. The democrats in turn prepared to kill all the oligarchs, but Nicostratus prevented so rash a response.

At this point the Peloponnesians took a hand. The forty ships under Alcidas straggling home from the Aegean picked up thirteen allied ships at Cyllene, and along with Brasidas in the role of *xymboulos* (adviser) hurried to Corcyra before a major Athenian fleet could arrive. Against the advice of the Athenians the Corcyraean democrats confronted this force with sixty ships, all in bad order, and with poor discipline. The Peloponnesians triumphed easily, but the twelve Athenian ships at Corcyra prevented them from exploiting the victory, and Peloponnesians sailed back to the mainland across from Corcyra with the ships they had captured. The next day Brasidas urged Alcidas to attack the city while the Corcyraeans were confused and frightened, but the timid navarch refused, and the delay was fatal: news that an Athenian fleet of sixty ships under Eurymedon son of Thucles was on its way from Leucas sent the Peloponnesians into flight.

Now, left to their own, the democrats unleashed the anger and hatred that are such powerful motivations in a civil war. Political execution degenerated into simple murder; men were killed for private revenge and for money; impiety and sacrilege were commonplace. "Father killed son, men were dragged from the temples and killed near them, some died when they were walled up in the temple of Dionysus" (3.81.5). These horrors gave Thucydides an opportunity to portray the evil consequences of civil strife during wartime, and few sections of his magnificent history are so full of dark and prophetic wisdom.

These atrocities, he tells us, were only the first among many that would result from the series of civil wars to which the great war gave rise. In each state democrats could call upon the Athenians for help against their enemies, while the oligarchs would ask the same of the Spartans. "In peacetime they would have had no pretext or desire to do so, but since the two opponents were at war, each faction in the different cities found it easy to call in one or the other as allies if it wanted to overthrow the local regime" (3.82.2). "Many and terrible things happened to the cities because of faction," says Thucydides, "such as happen and always will happen so long as the nature of human beings is the same" (3.82.2). In peaceful and prosperous times both people and nations behave reasonably because the tissue of material well-being and security that separates civilization from brutal savagery has not been torn away and people reduced to brutal necessity. "But war, which deprives people of the easy satisfaction of their daily needs, is a violent teacher that fits their dispositions to their circumstances" (3.82.2).

Party membership and loyalty came to be regarded as the highest virtues, overshadowing all others and justifying the abandonment of all the restraints of traditional morality. Fanaticism and the treacherous intention to plot the destruction of an enemy behind his back were regarded as equally admirable: to recoil from either of these was to disrupt the unity of the party out of fear of the enemy. Oaths lost their meaning and became tools of duplicity.

This state of terror arose as a result of the personal greed, ambition, and lust for power that typically emerge once factional war has broken out. While the leaders of each faction adapted a fine-sounding slogan—"political equality for the people" for one, and "the moderate rule of the best" for the other—they resorted to any evil trick available to them, and even murdered those who belonged to neither party "either because they would not join them in the fight or out of jealousy that they should survive" (3.82.8). This new species of evil-doing spread throughout the various states of the Greek world along with the revolutions. "In general, the men of lower intelligence won out. Afraid of their own shortcomings and of the intelligence of their opponents, so that they would not lose out in reasoned argument or be taken by surprise by their quick-witted opponents, they boldly moved into action. Their enemies, on the contrary, contemptuous and confident in their ability to anticipate, thought there was no need to take by action what they could win by their brains" (3.83.3–4).

In sharp contrast to the restraint practiced by Nicostratus, his predecessor in Corcyra, the Athenian general Eurymedon took no action for seven days, permitting the massacre to continue. Apparently he agreed with Cleon and deplored the moderation that seemed to be both ineffective in itself and to encourage revolution. His appearance as commander at Corcyra reveals that the recently elected board of generals had by now taken office, and his behavior there suggests that a new spirit was gaining ground in Athens.

THE FIRST ATHENIAN EXPEDITION TO SICILY

THAT SAME SPIRIT helped persuade the Athenians in September to send an expedition of twenty ships under Laches and Charoeades to Sicily, far from the previous theaters of war. The people of Leontini, a city on the eastern part of the island with whom Athens had an old alliance, complained that Syracuse, the major city in the region, had attacked them as part of a campaign to dominate all of Sicily. The war had quickly spread throughout the island and across the narrow strait to Italy. Opponents were divided, in part by ethnic divisions; the Dorians, as well as the Peloponnesians, were on the side of the Syracusans, while the Ionians and Athenians were against them. Impending defeat had led the Leontines to call on their Athenian allies for help.

Why would the Athenians, who were already engaged in a war of survival, send an expedition to a place so remote and apparently irrelevant to the major strategy of the war? Thucydides explains that their real goals were "to prevent the importation of grain from Sicily into the Peloponnesus and because they were making a preliminary test to see if they could bring the affairs of Sicily under their control" (3.86.4).

The instigation for the expedition is commonly attributed entirely to the group around Cleon, the "radicals" or "democrats" or the war party, but the evidence suggests otherwise. There is no reference to a divisive debate on the matter, such as the ones that decided the fate of Mytilene earlier in 427 or that led to the alliance with Corcyra in 433. The commanders were not "hawks" like Eurymedon or Demosthenes, but included men like Laches, an associate of Nicias. The expedition must have met little opposition.

We must also not overlook an obvious fact: the Athenians went to Sicily in 427 because they were asked and had been made aware of a potential danger that might become serious. At the beginning of the war the Peloponnesians had talked of obtaining a vast fleet from Sicily, which could pose a mighty threat to Athens if it ever materialized. Likewise if the Syracusans, colonists of Corinth, were allowed to conquer the other Greek cities in Sicily they might then be able to send critical assistance to their mother city and to the Peloponnesian cause in general. Every Athenian would have recognized the peril. The desire to prevent Sicilian grain from reaching the Peloponnesus was a new development reflecting changing conditions. To some extent, the length and severity of the Spartan devastations of Attica was dependent on the invaders' grain supply; the loss of harvests from Sicily might curtail future invasions. In that respect cutting off the grain traffic by sending limited military aid to Athens' western allies made sense.

But any attempt to subjugate Sicily would have been a clear violation of Pericles' advice not to expand the empire in wartime. To be sure, there were reckless expansionists among the Athenians, and some of them looked to the west as a likely area for conquest. There is no indication, however, that Cleon was among them or at any time sought expansion for its own sake. He, and men like Demosthenes and Eurymedon, wanted to gain control of Sicily to prevent the delivery of grain to the Peloponnesus and to prevent a Sicily dominated by Syracuse from providing aid to the enemy, but they may have sought more than simply a restoration of the earlier status quo. Athenian intervention followed by withdrawal would allow Syracuse to try to take over the island again, perhaps at a time when Athens could not afford to prevent it. Seeking to "bring the affairs of Sicily under their control" could mean only Athenian predominance, and perhaps the establishment of a garrison and naval base on Sicily to prevent future trouble.

The twenty ships sailed off just in time to avoid a second outbreak of the plague. Their mission initiated a new political reality in Athens. Events had moved the radicals into a position where they could now influence and even shape policy, and the moderates into one where they could not completely resist their opponents' agenda.

In Sicily the Athenians were remarkably successful in spite of the small size of their force. Leontini, an inland town, could provide no naval base, so Laches and Charoeades established one at the friendly Italian city of Rhegium, just across the strait from Messina (see Map 13). The Athenians intended to gain complete control of the Straits of Messina in order to hinder the transportation of grain from Sicily to the Peloponnesus by the normal route. The plan was to take Messina as a rallying point for Sicilian Greeks, especially Ionians, and for native Sicels hostile to Syracuse. With the support of local troops, the Athenians might also hope to defeat the Syracusans in battle, which could bring more support from the Syracusan side. A victory would at least prevent Syracusan domination of Sicily.

The first efforts accomplished little. Soon after their arrival at Rhegium the Athenians divided their forces into two squadrons to explore the coast of Sicily and assess the sentiment of the natives. Laches sailed along the southern coast off Camarina, while Charoeades headed for the eastern shore in Syracusan waters, where he was killed when he encountered a Syracusan fleet. The Athenian plan was predicated upon control of the sea, especially the waters near the Straits of Messina, so Laches attacked Syracuse's allies on the Liparian Islands, which lie at the western entrance to the straits, but the Liparians would not yield.

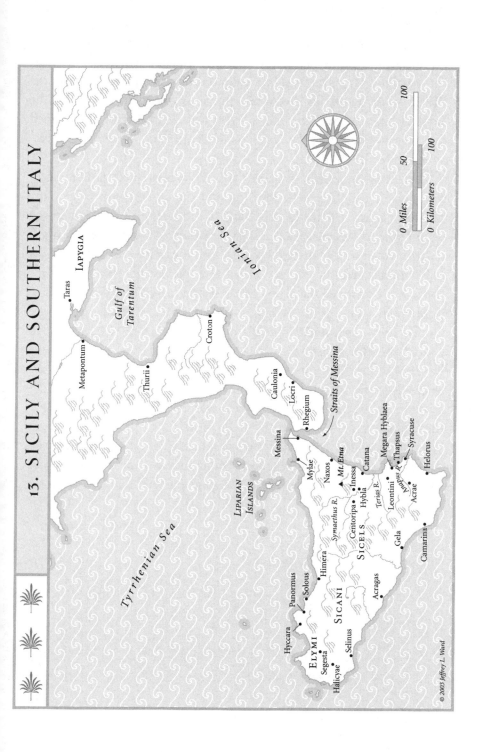

13. SICILY AND SOUTHERN ITALY

IAPYGIA

Taras

Gulf of
Tarentum

Metapontum

Thurii

Croton

Caulonia

Locri

Rhegium

Straits of Messina

Ionian Sea

Tyrrhenian Sea

Messina

LIPARIAN
ISLANDS

Mylae

Naxos

Mt. Etna

Inessa

Catana

Megara Hyblaea

Thapsus

Syracuse

Helorus

Acrae

Amenus R.

Leontini

Terias R.

Hybla

Gela

Camarina

SICELS

Centoripa

Syraethus R.

Himera

Panormus

Solous

Acragas

SICANI

Selinus

Hyccara

ELYMI

Segesta

Halicyae

0 Miles   50   100

0 Kilometers   100

© 2003 Jeffrey L. Ward

These and other failures were overshadowed when Laches captured Messina, which placed the straits under Athenian command, encouraged defections from Syracuse, and threatened its position on the
island. Many native Sicels who had previously been dominated by the
Syracusans came over to Athens. With their help, Laches maintained
the offensive, defeating the Locrians in a battle and attacking Himera,
although he could not capture it.

Laches' achievements were not trivial. He prevented the Syracusan
conquest of Leontini, took Messina and the straits, won over many
subjects of Syracuse to the Athenian side, and begun to threaten the
region around Syracuse itself. At sea the Athenians were unchallenged,
for the Syracusans were afraid to confront the small enemy fleet. They
fully appreciated the danger they were in, seeing "that the place
[Messina] controlled the access to Sicily and feared that the Athenians
would some time use it as a base for attacking with a larger force"
(4.1.2). They consequently began to increase the size of their fleet to
take on the Athenians.

In response the Athenian generals requested reinforcements; the
assembly sent forty more vessels under three commanders, "in part because they thought they could end the war there sooner, and partly because they wanted to give the fleet practice" (3.115.4). Pythodorus
sailed immediately with a few ships to take the command from Laches,
while Sophocles and Eurymedon would follow with the main force
later. The new fleet sailed away full of great expectations.

Part Three

NEW STRATEGIES

THE FIRST PART of the Ten Years War was shaped by the goals and strategy of Pericles, which guided Athenian policy even after his death. Whatever their merits, events had demonstrated their ultimate inadequacy, as expenditures depleted the treasury, rebellion broke out in the empire, and the Spartans showed no signs of seeking peace. Had he lived, Pericles himself would probably have adjusted to the new realities and changed his plan of war, but by 427 new generals and political leaders were emerging, some with ideas very different from those of the deceased leader. The next few years would see sharp departures from the original strategy, as the Athenians searched for some way to survive and win.

CHAPTER ELEVEN

Demosthenes and the New Strategy (426)

THE SPARTANS IN CENTRAL GREECE

IN 426 YOUNG AGIS came to the throne of Sparta at the death of his father, Archidamus, and Pleistoanax returned from exile, so the city once again had two kings. In one of his earliest official acts Agis led the army out of the Peloponnesus for the invasion of Attica, but a series of earthquakes compelled them to turn back when they reached the Isthmus of Corinth. So religious a people as the Spartans might have interpreted this as a divine sign that their insistence on continuing the war to complete victory was a mistake, but instead they reacted as men often do when their purposes have been thwarted: they merely intensified their determination to carry through their original plan by new means. Nevertheless some Spartans, like some Athenians, recognized that the original strategies had failed and that victory would require new ones.

In the summer of 426, therefore, Sparta undertook to open a new front in central Greece, where the Trachinians and the neighboring town of Doris—the traditional mother city of Sparta and the other Dorians—asked for help against the Oetaeans, who were at war with them (see Map 14). The Spartans thereupon established one of the few colonies in their history, at Heraclea in nearby Trachis, because: "The city also seemed to them to be well situated for the war against the Athenians, for a fleet could be equipped there against Euboea in such a way as to have only a short crossing, and the place would also be useful for a coastal expedition to Thrace. In short, they were eager to found the colony" (3.92.4).

It is tempting to conclude that Brasidas was the instigator of the Spartan decision, for it suits his temperament and imagination, and he would go on to exploit the new colony a few years later. Launching a

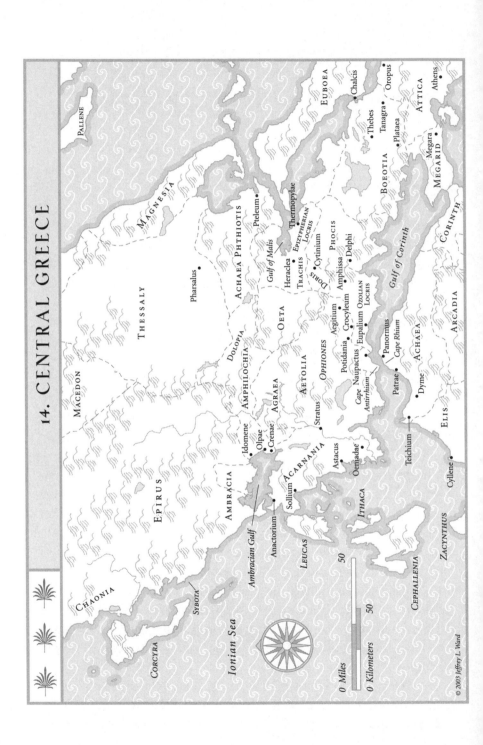

14. CENTRAL GREECE

CHAONIA

CORCYRA

SYBOTA

Ionian Sea

PALLENE

MACEDON

MAGNESIA

EPIRUS

THESSALY

Pharsalus •

DOLOPIA

AMPHILOCHIA

Idomene •
Olpae •
• Crenae
AMBRACIA

Ambracian Gulf

Anactorium •

LEUCAS

AGRAEA

Stratus •

ACARNANIA

Sollium •
Astacus •

Oeniadae •

ITHACA

CEPHALLENIA

ZACYNTHUS

AETOLIA

OETA

OPHIONES

Aegitium •
Crocyleum •
Potidania •
Cape Naupactus •
Antirrhium

Teichium •

Cyllene •

ELIS

ARCADIA

ACHAEA PHTHIOTIS

Peleum •

Thermopylae •
Heraclea • EPIZPHERIAN
• LOCRIS
Trachis • Cytinium
DORIS
Amphissa •
OZOLIAN
Eupalium LOCRIS
Panormus •
• Cape Rhium

Gulf of Malis

PHOCIS

Delphi •

Patrae •

Dyme •

ACHAEA

CORINTH

Gulf of Corinth

EUBOEA

Chalcis •

BOEOTIA

Thebes •
Plataea •

Tanagra •
Oropus •

MEGARID

Megara •

ATTICA

Athens •

0 Miles   50

0 Kilometers   50

© 2003 Jeffrey L. Ward

full-scale assault on Euboea by sea was a bolder scheme than most Spartans would have been willing to risk, in light of their recent encounters with the Athenian fleet, but the new colony could also be used as a base for piratical seizures of Athenian shipping and for commando raids on Euboea. A plan for an invasion of the northern areas of the Athenian Empire was even more promising. To win the war the Spartans would have to mount a full-scale attack on the empire, and without a bigger and better navy they could only harm the parts they could reach by land: Macedonia and Thrace, along the north shore of the Aegean. If they could march an army there they could encourage defections, reduce Athenian income, and incite rebellions elsewhere. Thrace, moreover, could serve as a base for the capture of Athenian-held cities on the Hellespont.

Turning the Athenian flank would not be an easy or entirely safe venture. The Spartans would first have to move their army through central Greece and hostile Thessaly to reach their goal. Once there they would have to build support while trying to persuade the local Athenian allies to rebel from the empire. At every step of the campaign precious troops might be lost. The Spartans would not take such a risk in 426, but the establishment of a colony at Heraclea was a necessary first step in any future effort.

Except as a base on the road to the north, though, Heraclea proved to be a disappointment. The Spartans built a walled town about five miles from Thermopylae and a wall to the sea across the pass that controlled the route from central Greece to Thessaly, and also began to construct dockyards for a naval base against Euboea. Having a Spartan colony on their borders, however, alienated the Thessalians, who attacked it repeatedly. The Spartan magistrates in the area only demonstrated the shortcomings of Sparta's dealings with other Greeks: "They themselves ruined the operation and reduced the city to a depopulated state. They frightened most away by their harsh and sometimes unwise orders so that their neighbors defeated them more easily" (3.93.3).

ATHENIAN INITIATIVES

THE ATHENIANS, meanwhile, continued their moderate effort to take the offensive, sending Nicias with sixty ships and two thousand hoplites against the island of Melos. Failing to take it, he landed in Boeotia and at Tanagra met up with the rest of the Athenian army, which had marched out from Athens under the command of Hipponicus and Eurymedon. After ravaging the country and defeating the Tanagrans and some Thebans in a pitched battle, Hipponicus and Eurymedon marched back to Athens, while Nicias' men returned to their ships, laid waste to some Locrian territory, and also returned home.

What was the point of these actions? Melos was the only Aegean island remaining outside the Athenian alliance, and although formally neutral in 426, it was a Spartan colony. Thucydides says the Athenians attacked because "the Melians, although they were islanders, did not want to be subjects nor even to join the alliance, and the Athenians wanted to bring them over" (3.91.2). It is not clear what led the Athenians to move so precipitously after having ignored Melos for more than fifty years. The continued pressing need for money may provide part of an answer, and an inscription of uncertain date may be evidence that the Melians gave financial support to the Spartan fleet in 427. If that is the case, the Athenian attack may have been intended as punishment for the Dorian "neutrals" who were helping the enemy.

The Athenians would have been glad to take Melos cheaply but they could not afford the cost of a siege. They had no intention of risking a land battle against the Theban hoplite army, with the associated danger that a Peloponnesian army might take them in the rear. The entire operation, including the raids on Locris, was conceived of as a unit, and no great risk or expense was involved. These were cautious, tentative steps toward a more aggressive strategy.

The Athenians also sent thirty ships around the Peloponnesus under the command of Demosthenes and Procles. The Athenian vessels carried only the usual contingent of ten marines each and no additional hoplites. Although they were assisted by some of their western allies they had no expectation of accomplishing anything decisive. In spite of the new, active spirit in Athens the shortage of men and money still limited the size and scope of campaigns.

This force ravaged the island of Leucas, a key stop on the route to Corcyra, Italy, and Sicily, and a loyal Corinthian colony that contributed ships to the Peloponnesian fleet. Its capture would have given the Athenians exclusive control of the Ionian Sea, and their Acarnanian allies argued for besieging the city and taking the island. Athens' Messenian allies from Naupactus, however, wanted Demosthenes to attack the Aetolians, who were now threatening their own city. They assured him that it would be easy to defeat the fierce but primitive Aetolian tribesmen, who lived in scattered, unfortified villages; they did not fight as hoplites did, but in light armor, and some of them were so barbaric as to eat their meat raw. These uncivilized people could easily be subdued one by one before they could unite.

DEMOSTHENES' AETOLIAN CAMPAIGN

DEMOSTHENES, who was in his first term as general, had probably been given vague orders, along the lines of, "aid Athens' allies in the west and do such harm to the enemy as you can." The safe and obvious course of action would have been to besiege Leucas and avoid angering the Acarnanians; his brief surely did not mention undertaking a campaign against barbarians who resided inland and well to the east of allied territory. While acceding to the Naupactians' request would be politically, as well as militarily, dangerous for the new commander, he did as they asked. In part, Thucydides tells us, Demosthenes wished to please the Messenians, who were even more critical allies to Athens than the Acarnanians, as they held a crucial position on the Corinthian Gulf whose loss would be a disaster. But his daring imagination saw greater possibilities in the enterprise than simply defending Naupactus, and in the bold style that would mark his entire career he conceived a grand plan. With the assistance of forces from Acarnania and Naupactus he would quickly conquer Aetolia and conscript the defeated Aetolians into his army. He would then pass through western Locris to Cytinium in Doris; from there he would enter Phocis, where the Phocians, who were old friends of Athens, would join him. With this large army, he could then attack Boeotia from the rear.

If he could reach Boeotia's western border at the same time as the joint armies of Nicias, Hipponicus, and Eurymedon marched in from the east, together they might win a great Athenian victory and drive Boeotia, Sparta's most powerful ally, out of the war. The democrats in Boeotia, who had cooperated with Athens before, could also be counted on for help. All this Demosthenes hoped to accomplish without the support of Athenian forces. His notion was to achieve great things at low risk to Athens, and he acted on his own authority, without the approval of the Athenian assembly, and without consultation.

Demosthenes ran into trouble almost immediately. The Acarnanians refused to accompany him to Aetolia, and the fifteen Corcyraean ships returned home, unwilling to fight outside their own waters and for causes not their own. It was probably in the following year that a character in a comedy by Hermippus remarked, "May Poseidon destroy the Corcyraeans on their hollow ships because of their duplicity,"[1] but the truth is that the decision to abandon Leucas to fight the Aetolians must have raised doubts among all the allies.

The loss of the greater part of his army and a third of his navy might have deterred a less confident general, but Demosthenes forged ahead. The Locrian allies of Athens were neighbors of the Aetolians, and used the same kind of armor and weapons, as well as knowing the enemy and the countryside. The plan was to have their entire army head inland and meet up with Demosthenes, who marched through the Aetolian lands, taking town after town. Then the scheme began to unravel. The Locrians were supposed to arrive with reinforcements, but they did not appear at all. This third defection troubled Demosthenes as the others had not: in the rough mountain country of Aetolia the very success of his campaign and the safety of his forces required the light-armed, javelin-throwing Locrians. Nevertheless, the Messenians assured him that victory would still be easy, if Demosthenes moved quickly enough before the scattered Aetolians could rally their forces.

In an age when military intelligence depended chiefly on word-of-mouth reports delivered directly by a messenger, Demosthenes' plan

---

[1] J. M. Edmonds, *The Fragments of Attic Comedy*, Leiden, 1957–1961, 304–306.

was even riskier than it might seem. The Messenian advice was already out of date, for the Aetolians had learned of the expedition and were even now preparing to resist it. Likewise Demosthenes was not aware that great numbers of their fellow tribesmen were on their way to help from all over Aetolia. The absence of his reinforcements argued for delay, but neither indecision nor caution was natural to Demosthenes, so he decided to advance against the Aetolians at once.

He easily took the town of Aegitium, but its swift capitulation was a trap: the inhabitants, with reinforcements, lay in ambush in the surrounding hills and attacked from all sides when the Athenians and their allies entered. The attackers were skilled javelin throwers in light armor who could inflict serious damage and retreat quickly before the heavily armed phalanx of the Athenians could do them harm. The Athenians now realized how badly they needed the javelin men whom their Locrian allies had promised. The efforts of the Athenian archers might have compensated, but when their captain was killed they scattered, leaving the hoplites undefended and worn down by the repeated sallies of the quicker light-armed Aetolians. When they finally turned to flee, one final misfortune turned the rout into a slaughter. The Messenian guide, Chromon, who might have led them to safety, was killed, and the Athenians and their allies were caught in rough, wooded, unfamiliar country. Many of them lost their way in the forests, so the Aetolians set fire to the woods. The casualties among Athens' allies were heavy, and the Athenians lost 120 of their 300 marines, as well as the general Procles. The defeated Athenians recovered their dead under a truce, retreated to Naupactus, and sailed off to Athens.

Demosthenes remained behind at Naupactus, "fearing the Athenians because of what had happened" (3.98.5), and with good reason. He had abandoned a successful and promising campaign for one not approved by those who had sent him on the mission. His plan may well have been far-sighted and brilliantly imaginative, but it was hastily conceived and poorly executed. Its success required speed, but that very speed prevented the careful preparation and coordination needed for so complex an operation. Demosthenes was also unfamiliar with the terrain and with the tactics of light-armed warfare. He may be held accountable for pushing ahead in the face of so many uncertainties, and even after things clearly began to go wrong. But extraordinary feats are not performed by cautious generals afraid to run risks, nor are great wars frequently won without bold leaders. Finally, we should not forget that Demosthenes was risking relatively very little, for Athens lost only 120 marines—a price, though regrettable, that was not excessive in light of the great rewards victory would have brought. Demosthenes, moreover, was that rare soldier who could profit from his mistakes, and he would use what he had learned from this experience to good advantage in the future.

THE SPARTANS ATTACK THE NORTHWEST

THE NEWS OF Demosthenes' defeat encouraged the Spartans to accept an invitation by the Aetolians to snatch Naupactus from Athenian control. They led a Peloponnesian army of three thousand into central Greece, forcing the Locrians to come over to their side. Near Naupactus they joined the Aetolians, and together they pillaged the countryside and occupied the suburbs. Learning of the Peloponnesian invasion, Demosthenes boldly went to the Acarnanians, whom he had deserted and angered, to ask their help. Remarkably, he persuaded them to send with him a thousand men on Acarnanian ships, and the fleet arrived in time to save Naupactus. The Spartans concluded that they could not storm the city, and withdrew into Aetolia.

The Spartan general Eurylochus, persuaded by the Ambracians, agreed to use the Peloponnesian army against their local enemy, Amphilochian Argos, and all of Amphilochia and Acarnania. "If they conquered these places," the Ambracians said, "they would bring the entire mainland into alliance with the Spartans" (3.102.6). Eurylochus accordingly dismissed the Aetolians and arranged to meet the Ambracians near Amphilochian Argos.

Three thousand Ambracian hoplites invaded Amphilochia in the autumn and took Olpae, a fortress near the sea less than five miles from Argos. To meet that threat the Acarnanians ordered troops to intercept the Spartan army of Eurylochus coming from the south before it could link up with the Ambracians traveling from the north. They also sent to Naupactus to ask Demosthenes to lead their armies. He was no longer a general and probably still in disfavor with the Athenians, since he had never returned to the city to render his accounts at the end of his term of office. Still, the Acarnanians' request was compelling evidence of the high regard in which he was held.

Eurylochus, meanwhile, slipped past the enemy troops and joined the Ambracians at Olpae. The united armies then moved northward and inland and camped at a place called Metropolis. Soon after, twenty Athenian ships arrived and blockaded the harbor of Olpae, and Demosthenes appeared, accompanied by two hundred of his faithful Messenians and sixty Athenians archers. The Acarnanians withdrew to Argos and placed their own generals under his command. He made camp between Argos and Olpae, protected by a dry riverbed separating him from the Spartans. There the two armies stood for five days.

Demosthenes' army was numerically inferior, but the plan he crafted to overcome this disadvantage reveals his native genius and how quickly he had benefited from his previous errors. On one side of the likely field of battle—a sunken road covered with bushes—he placed a force of four hundred hoplites and some light-armed troops. To counter a flanking movement against his phalanx, he ordered them to wait in ambush until the armies made contact and then to move against the enemy in the rear. This was an unexpected stratagem, far from the standard in hoplite battles, and it proved to be decisive.

The delay of five days before the commencement of the battle can be explained on the Athenian side by the desire to have the Spartans take the offensive and walk into Demosthenes' trap. For their part, the Spartans were waiting for the arrival of their Ambracian allies, but Eurylochus finally decided to attack. He has been judged harshly for this decision, but his task was to take Argos, and he could not wait indefinitely; expected reinforcements do not always appear, and even without them he still had numerical superiority. Nor can an army, particularly one made up of different peoples, be kept in check for long within sight of the enemy. In any case, additional troops would not have made a difference to the outcome—the battle was decided not by numbers but by superior tactics.

When the armies finally engaged, the Peloponnesian left wing, led by Eurylochus, outflanked the right wing held by Demosthenes and his Messenians. As they were on the point of encircling that end of the line and beginning to roll it up, the trap set by Demosthenes sprang shut. The Acarnanians leaped from their ambush at the rear of Eury-lochus and began to cut the back part of his army to pieces. Taken completely by surprise, they ran, and their panic was contagious. The Messenians under Demosthenes did the best fighting, and were soon chasing the greater part of the enemy army. At the other end of the battle line, however, the Ambraciots, whom Thucydides describes as the ablest warriors in that region, routed their opponents and pursued them to the city of Argos. As they turned back from its walls, however, they saw the main part of their army in flight and then came face to face with the victorious Acarnanians. They fought through to Olpae, suffering many losses. As night fell Demosthenes commanded the field, strewn with the bodies of the enemy, including two Spartan generals, Eurylochus and Macarius.

The next day Menedaius, the new Spartan commander, found himself besieged at Olpae by the enemy army by land and the Athenian fleet by sea. He had no idea when or if the second Ambracian army would appear, and there was no way to escape, so he asked for a truce to take up the dead and discuss the safe departure of his army. Demosthenes gathered his own dead and planted a trophy of victory on the battlefield, but then made another unorthodox maneuver: he did not, in the traditional way, agree to a general safe passage for the defeated enemy, but made a secret agreement to allow Menedaius, the contingent from Mantinea, the commanders of the other Peloponnesian troops, and "the most noteworthy" among the troops to depart if they did so quickly. Demosthenes permitted these soldiers to escape, says Thucydides, "to discredit the Spartans and the Peloponnesians with the Greeks of that region as betrayers and self-seekers" (3.109.2). This sort of political and psychological warfare was unknown in previous Greek conflicts.

The unsavory agreement was not easy to execute. Those in the besieged army at Olpae who learned of the deal pretended to gather firewood and started to slip away from camp. The chosen Peloponnesian notables did not keep the secret from their own men, most of whom seem to have joined in the escape. The others, who were not Peloponnesians, saw what was happening and ran to join the flight. When the Acarnanian army began to give chase their generals tried to stop them, trying to explain the terms of the tricky agreement in the chaos of events, an almost impossible task. In the end the Peloponnesians were allowed to escape, while the pursuing Acarnanians killed all the Ambraciots they could lay hands on.

Meanwhile the second army from Ambracia arrived at Idomene, a few miles north of Olpae, spending the night on the lower of two steep hills nearby. Warned of their approach, Demosthenes had sent out an advance guard to set ambushes and to seize strategic positions; these men had taken command of the higher hill without the knowledge of the Ambraciots below. Demosthenes was now ready to put into play all he had learned about mountain fighting and unconventional tactics.

Marching at night, he led one part of his army by the direct route and sent the rest through the mountains. He arrived before daybreak, while the Ambracians were asleep, making use of every natural advantage and inventing a few of his own. To add to the surprise Demosthenes placed the Messenians, who spoke a Dorian dialect similar to that of the Ambracians, at the front of the force so that they might get past the outposts without raising an alarm. The ruse was so successful that the awakened Ambracians initially believed the attackers were their own men. Most of them were killed immediately, and those who tried to escape through the mountains were caught by Demosthenes' reserves there. In disorder and in unfamiliar territory, the fact that they were light-armed troops facing hoplites worked against them. Some, in panic, ran to the sea and swam toward the Athenian ships, preferring to be killed by the Athenian sailors than to die at the hands of "the barbarian and hated Amphilochians." The Ambracian catastrophe was almost total. Thucydides refuses to report the number killed because, in relation to the size of the city, the figure was simply too great to believe; as he reports, "This was the greatest disaster to strike a single city in an equal number of days in this war" (3.113.6).

Demosthenes wanted to follow up the slaughter of the Ambraciots by seizing the city, but the Acarnanians and Amphilochians were not willing because "they now feared that the Athenians would be more difficult neighbors than the Ambraciots" (3.113.6). They gave the Athenians a third of the booty; the astonishing amount of three hundred suits of armor were set aside for Demosthenes. With these in hand and the glory they represented he was now willing to sail home; he was shrewd enough to dedicate his prizes to the gods and set them up in their temples, keeping none for himself—a suitably public demonstration of his piety, humility, and selflessness. The twenty Athenian ships returned to Naupactus, to the relief of their allies in the northwest. The Acarnanians and Amphilochians allowed the trapped Peloponnesians to return home safely as well as the surviving Ambracians, with whom they made a treaty for a hundred years in order to end old quarrels and keep the region free from further involvement in the great war. Corinth, the mother city of Ambracia, sent three hundred hoplites to provide a small garrison for its defense; the need for such a force shows how helpless the once powerful city had become.

Its arrival, however, also reveals that the Athenians had not achieved total control of the northwest. While the campaign managed to prevent the Peloponnesians from gaining control of the region, so that Athenian ships could still sail safely along the western coast of Greece and in the Ionian Sea, the limited Athenian commitment did not allow for greater achievements. Athens contributed no hoplites— only twenty ships, sixty archers, and a great general who was, however, a private citizen. The fighting in the northwest was characteristic of the Athenian efforts for the entire year, marked by a more daring and aggressive spirit but limited by caution and resources. Military expenses for the year 427/6 were trifling compared with what had been spent in the early period of the war. Only 261 talents came from the treasuries, one-fifth of the amounts borrowed in the first two years of fighting. Even with a new strategy, the Athenians could not win the war unless they could solve their financial problems, or meet with some unforeseen stroke of luck.

CHAPTER TWELVE

Pylos and Sphacteria (425)

ATHENS' WESTERN COMMITMENTS

IN THE SPRING of 425 the Athenians sent a fleet of forty ships around the Peloponnesus, commanded by Sophocles and Eurymedon, with orders to reinforce Pythodorus in Sicily. Before they arrived, however, troubles arose. The Syracusans and Locrians had recaptured Messina, and in Italy the Locrians had also attacked Rhegium, the Athenian base of operations and a major ally in that region. Each defeat damaged the Athenians' chances of winning other allies, a set of relationships that formed the core of their western strategy. The Athenian reinforcements would be able to restore the status quo, but the Sicilian news had not reached Athens before the fleet sailed, so it proceeded without haste.

There were difficulties at Corcyra, as well. When Eurymedon had sailed away from there after allowing the democrats to slaughter their opponents, five hundred potential victims had escaped to the mainland, where they occupied forts as a base for attacking the island. Their raids caused a famine in the city, and after they vainly sent to Corinth and Sparta for help, they finally hired mercenaries on their own. This combined force landed on Corcyra, burned their boats as evidence of their determination to stay until they were victorious, and fortified Mount Istome, from which they could dominate the countryside. Their success encouraged the Peloponnesians to send sixty ships to try to take the island. Though unaware of the Peloponnesian incursion, many Athenians still thought that saving Corcyra was a far more valuable use of the fleet than the campaign in Sicily.

Demosthenes had still a third proposal for deploying the west-bound Athenian squadron. His glorious campaign in Acarnania had banished the memory of the Aetolian disaster, and he had become a general-elect for the year that would begin in midsummer 425. Although he was now only a private citizen without a command, he had a scheme for landing on the coast of Messenia, from which he hoped to do the enemy serious harm; for this he, too, needed a fleet.

Each alternative had merit, and all three deserved to be pursued simultaneously by separate squadrons, but the Athenians had neither the money nor, perhaps, the men to undertake them all. In their new bolder mood, however, they sent their fleet off with orders that might otherwise seem strange. Sophocles and Eurymedon were commanded to sail to Sicily, "but also, as they were sailing past Corcyra, to look after the men in the city who were being attacked by the men on the mountain." They were also told to allow Demosthenes "to use these ships around the Peloponnesus if he wishes" (4.2).

DEMOSTHENES' PLAN: THE FORT AT PYLOS

IT WAS NOT UNTIL they reached the coast of Laconia that the Athenian generals learned that a Peloponnesian fleet was at Corcyra. Sophocles and Eurymedon were eager to hasten there, but Demosthenes had other ideas. Once at sea he was free to reveal to his colleagues the details of the plan he could not explain in the open Athenian assembly for fear it would reach the enemy. He meant to land at the place the Spartans called Coryphasium (the site of Homer's Pylos) and there build a permanent fort. Demosthenes must have taken note of the area on previous voyages and consulted with his Messenian friends about it. It had every natural benefit as a permanent base where the Messenian enemies of Sparta might be placed, both to ravage the land of Messenia and Laconia and to stir up a helot rebellion. It also had great utility for the war at sea, for it had the largest safe harbor (today called the Bay of Navarino) in that part of the world. Plenty of wood and stone were available to build fortifications; the surrounding territory was deserted, and it was about fifty miles from Sparta as the crow flies and perhaps half again as far by the route a Spartan army would most likely take, so that it could be made safe by its occupiers before they had to face a Spartan army. Demosthenes was right to believe that "this place was more advantageous than any other" (4.3.3).

Sophocles and Eurymedon, however, were worried about the safety of Corcyra and unconvinced by the imaginative daring of Demosthenes; they thought his scheme a reckless diversion and told him sarcastically that "there were many deserted promontories in the Peloponnese that they could occupy if they wanted to waste the state's money" (4.3.3). Demosthenes countered that he did not propose a lengthy campaign at Pylos but merely asked the fleet to put in long enough to build the fortifications, leave a small force to defend them, and then sail on to Corcyra. He was convinced that a successful landing on the Messenian coast would compel the withdrawal of the Peloponnesian fleet from Corcyra, thus achieving two purposes in the cheapest and easiest fashion.

At that point fortune took a hand: although Demosthenes failed to persuade the generals to land at Pylos, a storm carried the Athenian fleet there. As the generals waited for it to abate he went over the heads and against the will of his superiors and appealed directly to the soldiers but this effort, too, was unsuccessful. As the storm continued, however, the bored soldiers finally agreed to do what Demosthenes asked. The spirit of the venture took hold of them, and they hurried to fortify the most vulnerable places before the Spartans appeared, completing the defenses within six days. When the storm let up the generals left Demosthenes behind with a small force of men and five ships to defend the newly established fort and then sailed on to Corcyra.

At the time the Spartans were celebrating a festival, and their army was in Attica, so they took the matter lightly, for the Athenians had landed on the Peloponnesus before, and with much larger forces, but they had never stayed long enough to meet a large Spartan army. Even if the Athenians intended to make a permanent base at Pylos the Spartans had no doubt they could take it by force. Agis, who had marched his army into Attica as usual in the spring, was more alarmed. He was also short of food and troubled by unusually bad weather, and so returned home after only fifteen days, the shortest invasion by far.

The Spartans also reported the construction of the Athenian fort to the navarch Thrasymelidas at Corcyra, who perceived the danger as quickly as Agis had and headed for home immediately. He slipped past the Athenian fleet sailing north, and arrived safely at Pylos. Agis' army had in the meantime returned from Attica, and the Spartans also called on their Peloponnesian allies to send troops. An advance guard of those Spartans who had not gone to Attica and the *perioikoi* who lived closest to Pylos set forth at once to attack the Athenian stronghold.

THE SPARTANS ON SPHACTERIA

AS THE SPARTAN FORCES were gathering, Demosthenes sent two ships to intercept Sophocles and Eurymedon and tell them he was in danger. They found the Athenian fleet at Zacynthus whence it hurried to Pylos to help the contingent there. Although the Spartans had little doubt that they could take such a jerry-built structure guarded by only a few men, they knew that the Athenian fleet would soon arrive. They accordingly planned to launch an immediate attack on Pylos by land and sea and, if that should fail, to obstruct the entrances to the harbor to prevent the Athenian fleet from gaining access. They would also place troops on the island of Sphacteria as well as on the nearby mainland to prevent the Athenian fleet from coming ashore or establishing a base. The Spartans believed that "without risking a sea battle they could probably capture the place by siege because it had no grain, since it had been seized with little preparation" (4.8.8). In principle, the strategy made good sense, but in practice it could not be carried out, for the Spartans were unable to close off the channels.[1] (See Map 15.) Because the southern channel measures about fourteen hundred yards wide and about two hundred feet deep, not even the entire Peloponnesian

---

[1] There is considerable controversy over the geography of Pylos and Sphacteria. Some scholars have tried to explain the difficulties by suggesting that the bay discussed is not the whole Bay of Navarino but a smaller cove at the south end of Pylos or another nearby. As one of these scholars concedes, however, "while the Cove Harbor fits some parts of Thucydides' description of the site, and explains some parts of his story, it conflicts with others, and seems to be too small, in the opinion of many, for the action described to have taken place there." Robert B. Strassler, ed., *The Landmark Thucydides* (New York: Simon and Schuster, 1996), p. 228 note.

Hill of
Agio Nikolo

Bay of Voithio Kilia

Harbor
(now lagoon of Osmyn Aga)

Athenian Wall

Sandbar

PYLOS

Athenian Wall

Sikia Channel

Prehistoric Fort

Bay of
Navarino

Spartan camp

Well

SPHACTERIA

0 Miles   1

0 Kilometers   1

© 2003 Jeffrey L. Ward

fleet could have blocked it. The Spartans could therefore have protected the harbor only by engaging in a naval battle in the south channel with their sixty ships pitted against the Athenian forty—a contest that would have suited the Athenians perfectly, and one that there is no evidence the Spartans intended to undertake. Their plan to stop the Athenians remains a mystery to us, but it must have been either misconceived or badly executed. The Spartans placed 420 hoplites accompanied by their helot assistants on Sphacteria under the command of Epitadas. There they would become hostages to fortune and the enemy unless the Athenian fleet could be kept out of the Bay of Navarino, and we know that it could not.

Demosthenes, meanwhile, beached and fenced in his three triremes to protect them from the enemy fleet. Unable to procure conventional hoplite arms in hostile and deserted country, he equipped the crews of his ships, which numbered under six hundred men, with wicker shields. A Messenian privateer, however, arrived soon thereafter carrying weapons and forty hoplites, support that must have been arranged in advance by Demosthenes. He now probably had at least ninety hoplites, including ten from each of the five ships originally assigned to him, but the Athenian force defending the fort was still badly outnumbered and inferior in armament.

Demosthenes positioned most of his troops behind the fortifications facing inland. He himself, with sixty hoplites and a few archers, took on the more difficult job of defending the section of the coast that was most vulnerable to an enemy landing, the southwestern corner of the peninsula, where they situated themselves at the very edge of the sea.

THE ATHENIAN NAVAL VICTORY

IN HIS SPEECH before the battle Demosthenes shared with his troops a simple truth about ancient amphibious warfare: "It is impossible to force a landing from ships against an enemy on shore if he stands his ground and does not give way through fear" (4.10.5). The Spartans attacked precisely where Demosthenes expected, urged on by the conspicuous bravery of Brasidas, who was overcome by his wounds and lost his shield, but the Athenians stood firm, and the Spartans withdrew after two days of fighting. On the third day after the attack, Sophocles and Eurymedon arrived from Zacynthus with a fleet that had grown to fifty triremes by the addition of a number of Chian ships and several from Naupactus. The Spartans waited inside the harbor, preparing their ships for combat there. The battle that followed produced a great victory for the Athenian navy and a disaster for the Spartans, whose courage was spent mainly in wading into the surf after defeated and abandoned triremes and preventing the Athenians from towing them away. The Athenians set up a trophy of victory and sailed freely around the Spartan hoplites, who were cut off and imprisoned on the island of Sphacteria.

The stunning ramifications and importance of this naval triumph cannot be exaggerated. When the Spartans realized that their men could not be rescued they decided immediately to ask for a truce at Pylos, during which they would negotiate a general peace and recover the force on Sphacteria. We may marvel that so fierce a military state as Sparta should have been willing to seek peace merely to recover 420 prisoners. But this group represented fully one-tenth of the Spartan army, at least 180 of whom were Spartiates from the best families. In a state that practiced a strict code of eugenics, killing imperfect infants; whose separation of men from women during the most fertile years guaranteed effective birth control; whose code of honor demanded of its soldiers death rather than dishonor; and whose leading caste married only its own members, concern for the safety of even 180 Spartiates was not merely a sentimental gesture but an extremely practical necessity.

The truce allowed the Athenians to continue their blockade of Sphacteria but not to attack it, and they were to permit the delivery of food and drink to the men trapped there. In return the Spartans promised neither to attack the Athenian fort at Pylos nor to send any ships secretly to the island, and also agreed to turn over their sixty warships as hostage. An Athenian trireme carried Spartan envoys to Athens for peace talks; the truce would last until their return, when the Athenians were to restore the Spartan ships in the same condition they received them. Any violation of these terms would end the truce, which gave the Athenians a great opportunity: if the negotiations failed, they could easily claim some breach and keep the Spartan vessels. The Spartans, however, were in no position to refuse the conditions, even with such an unfavorable loophole.

SPARTA'S PEACE OFFER

SPARTA PRESENTED its terms of peace to the Athenian assembly, conceding that the Athenians had gained the upper hand but reminding them that their victory was not the result of a fundamental shift in the balance of power. They would be wise to make peace while the advantage was theirs. In exchange for the prisoners on Sphacteria the Spartans proposed an offensive and defensive alliance with Athens. As no mention was made of any territorial adjustment, the Athenians would have retained control of Aegina and Minoa, with a foothold in the northwest; in return they would abandon any claim to restore Plataea.

It might seem that the Athenians should have accepted the Spartan offer as representing the kind of peace Pericles had had in mind from the beginning of the war, but it is far from clear that such was the case. The aims of Pericles were largely psychological; he meant to convince the Spartans that they lacked the power to defeat Athens. Their speech to the assembly, however, reveals that they had not learned that lesson, but continued to believe that Athenian ascendancy was the result of circumstances that could be reversed at any time. "This misfortune we have suffered came not from our want of power or because, having grown great, we became arrogant. On the contrary, though our resources remained the same we miscalculated, to which error all men are equally liable" (4.18.2).

The Athenians must have understood that, after regaining its hostages, Sparta could resume the war any time it pleased, and in 425 they recognized that as long as the men on Sphacteria remained in their hands they had a virtual guarantee of peace. But, Thucydides says, "they grasped for more" (4.21.2), by which he means that greed, ambition, and the extension of empire were motivating the Athenians. This conclusion, however, is not inevitable, for the Athenians had good reason to want more than merely the promise of Spartan good will in the future and an alliance that depended on the continuation of that good will. Even if they were sincere in their offer, the Spartans who were now proposing peace and friendship might not continue in power. It was the volatility of Spartan internal politics that had helped bring on the conflict; similarly, the advocates of war had been strong enough to reject a peace offer from Athens in 430. Why should belligerence not take the upper hand again as soon as it was safe? Any reasonable Athenian might have wanted a firmer guarantee than what was being submitted.

Not surprisingly, the opposition to the Spartan offer was led by Cleon, who made a counterproposal that the Spartans being held on Sphacteria should surrender and be brought to Athens and held as hostages. The Spartans should also, he demanded, hand over Nisaea and Pegae, the ports of Megara, and Troezen and Achaea, since all these places had not been taken from Athens in the course of war but had been surrendered "by a previous agreement because of a misfortune, at a time when they were rather more eager for a treaty" (4.21.3). (He was referring to the year 445, when a superior Spartan army stood on the plain of Attica.) Only then would the Athenians return the prisoners and agree to a lasting peace.

Rather than reject these unwelcome conditions outright the Spartans requested the appointment of a commission with which they could negotiate further in private. Cleon responded by violently denouncing them for cloaking evil intentions with secrecy: if they had something honorable to say, let them present it before the open assembly. But because the Spartans could hardly discuss the possible betrayal of their allies in public, they gave up and went home.

It is tempting to blame Cleon for the breaking off of the negotiations, on the grounds that nothing would have been lost and much might have been gained by private discussions. But what, realistically, could have been achieved? Let us suppose that the Athenians had voted to negotiate by commission in secret. Given the political situation in Athens, Nicias and his supporters would have dominated the talks. Eager for peace, sincere in their desire for friendship with Sparta, and inclined to believe in its good faith, these men might have come to terms very attractive to the Athenians including, perhaps, an alliance, promises of eternal friendship, the restoration of Plataea, and even the abandonment of Megara. In return the Spartans might only have asked the release of the men on Sphacteria and the evacuation of Pylos, requests that would have been hard to reject.

The suggestion that the Spartans might have been willing to give up Megara, or at least its harbors, however, was unrealistic. Sparta could have abandoned the northwest and ignored Corinth's demands in regard to Corcyra and Potidaea, but to have surrendered Megara would have placed the power of Athens directly on the isthmus and cut Sparta off from Boeotia and central Greece. With that move its credibility as leader of its alliance and protector of its allies would have been effectively destroyed. Corinth, Thebes, and Megara would resist. To honor such a commitment Sparta would also have had to abandon its major allies, and even, under the terms of the proposed alliance with Athens, fight alongside the Athenians against them. Clearly, no such agreement was possible. The ensuing bitterness would soon lead to hostility and war, with the Spartan capacity to wage it undiminished. Cleon and the Athenians who supported him had ample reason to reject secret negotiations with Sparta.

If nothing stood to be gained by secret negotiation, however, the Athenians did have something to lose: delay might be useful to the Spartans in that the men on Sphacteria might find a way to escape. The Athenian blockade of the island could not be maintained in winter, and the trapped men could flee then if no peace had been made. Each day the truce permitted food to be brought to Sphacteria was another day the island could hold out, increasing the possibility that Athens might lose their trump card. Cleon saw that danger, and the majority supported him.

This debate marks a critical turning point in Athenian politics. In the period between the Spartan rejection of Athenian peace offers in 430 and the affair at Pylos in 425, there was a general consensus in Athens that the war should be waged as vigorously as possible to force the Spartans to seek peace. Disagreements as to the nature of that peace were superseded by dedication to the common effort. The victory at Pylos and the resulting Spartan peace mission, however, were transforming events. Up to then, to talk of reaching an agreement with Sparta was plainly treason; afterward it was a course patriotic men could advocate with a clear conscience. The Periclean war aims, the restoration of the prewar status quo, the preservation of the empire, and the end of the Spartan crusade against it, all now seemed to be within easy reach. Some Athenians might have argued that such a peace was insufficiently secure and that Pericles himself would have insisted on greater guarantees, but prudent men could respond that it was wise to trust Sparta and pave the way for a lasting accord. Nicias probably held such views in 425.

Cleon, however, had very different aims. He in effect demanded a return to the ideal state of affairs that existed before the Thirty Years' Peace of 445, when Athens controlled Megara, Boeotia, and other parts of central Greece, as well as a number of coastal cities of the Peloponnesus. The Athenians had been compelled to abandon these territories, he believed, as the result of a treaty they had signed under duress, because of certain "misfortunes." Because of the events at Pylos and Sphacteria, Cleon implied, the Athenians had to insist on a return to earlier conditions when peace did not depend on the vagaries of Sparta's politics or on the discretionary expression of its good will, but was guaranteed by Athens' possession of strategic defensive locations.

CLEON AGAINST NICIAS

THE SPARTAN AMBASSADORS' return to Pylos spelled an end to the truce, but the Athenians, alleging violations by Sparta, refused to return the ships they held in hostage. Henceforth the Spartans would have to fight on land alone, which may not have been too great a handicap in view of the ineffectiveness of their navy heretofore. The Athenians were now committed to capturing the men on Sphacteria, and they sent an additional twenty ships to enforce the blockade. They expected quick success, for Sphacteria was a desert island containing no food and only brackish water, and the Athenian fleet had complete control of all approaches to it. The Spartans, however, displayed surprising ingenuity in the face of this challenge, offering rewards to free men and freedom to any helots who would run the blockade with food and drink for the prisoners. Many risked the danger and took advantage of wind and darkness to reach the island. Some wrecked little boats on the harborless seaward shore and others crossed the channel underwater to keep the men on Sphacteria alive long after the time they were expected to surrender.

Eventually the Athenians themselves began to suffer from shortages of food and water. Over fourteen thousand men were dependent on a single small spring on the Pylian acropolis and what little potable water they could find on the beach. They were confined within a small space, and their morale had declined due to the unexpected length of the siege. They began to fear that the onset of winter would force them to lift the blockade by preventing the regular arrival of supply ships. As time passed and the Spartans sent no further embassies, the fear grew that they were confident of recovering their men, and that Athens might ultimately emerge from the impasse without either a great strategic advantage or a negotiated peace. Many in Athens began to feel that a mistake had been made and that Cleon, who had urged rejection of the peace offer, was to blame.

It was not until the Athenian assembly learned of the alarming state of affairs at Pylos that both Cleon and his policy finally came under open fire. The purpose of the meeting was probably to discuss a request by Demosthenes for reinforcements to attack Sphacteria. Cleon was certainly in close communication with Demosthenes and knew of his plan to assail the island; the kind of light-armed troops required for the campaign were already assembled at Athens when the debate took place, and Demosthenes had begun to make preparations for the assault, sending to the allies in the vicinity for additional troops. Demosthenes must also have asked for the specially trained troops he needed to capture the men on Sphacteria.

Cleon was the natural choice to serve as Demosthenes' advocate. He was the most outspoken proponent of rejecting the Spartan peace offer and would likely be held accountable if the men on Sphacteria were allowed to escape. He was also an effective politician and of a temperament to seize on the prospects for success in Demosthenes' bold plan. Nicias had by now come to favor a negotiated peace and feared that the capture of the Spartans would inflame the aggressive spirits in Athens and make such a peace impossible. He may therefore have been eager to delay an attack for as long as he could in the hope of reaching an agreement before it was too late. Since he had none of Demosthenes' experience in fighting on rugged terrain with light-armed troops and had no direct intelligence to judge the prospects of success, his native caution may also have led him to overestimate the dangers of attempting a forced landing on an island held by hoplites. In either case, he surely opposed the request for reinforcements to launch an assault on the island.

Because Cleon had accused the messengers who brought the bad news from Pylos of not telling the truth, they invited the Athenians to appoint a commission to verify the accuracy of their report. The Athenians complied and elected Cleon as one of its representatives, but he argued that the trip was a waste of time that might lose Athens a great opportunity. He urged instead that if the assembly believed the alarming reports they should immediately send an additional force to assault the island and capture the men, for "Cleon saw that the Athenians were now rather more eager to make an expedition" (4.27.4).

The assembly must have voted to dispatch such a force and appointed Nicias its commander, for Cleon's response was to point a finger at Nicias, insisting that it would be quite easy, if the generals were indeed valorous men, to take an adequate force to Pylos and capture the prisoners on the island. "He would do so himself, if he were in command" (4.27.5).

Now the Athenians, caught up in his game, asked Cleon why, if he believed the task was so easy, he didn't make the trip. Nicias, perceiving the mood of the crowd and "noticing Cleon's taunt," replied that the generals would gladly have him take any force he wished and attempt the task. At first Cleon was ready to accept the proposal, "thinking that the offer was only a ploy," but then he demurred, observing that it was Nicias and not he who was the general, "when he realized that the offer to relinquish the command was genuine." Nicias, detecting his opponent's embarrassment, repeated the offer in the hope of thoroughly discrediting Cleon, and the crowd soon joined in, some in earnest, others from hostility to Cleon, and still others for the sheer fun of it.

Nicias had no legal authority to make such an offer on his own behalf, much less on behalf of the other generals, but when the assembly took up his cry, it was clear that the Athenians would accept the suggestion. At last, Cleon, "not having any way to escape the consequences of his own proposal," agreed to lead reinforcements, taking

with him only a body of Lemnian and Imbrian troops who were present in Athens, some peltasts (light-armed troops) from Aenos, and
four hundred archers from elsewhere. With these men and those already at Pylos, he promised that within twenty days he would "either
bring back the Spartans alive or kill them on the spot!"

Cleon's pledge to succeed within twenty days and without the use
of any Athenian hoplites was neither bravado nor foolhardiness. Since
Demosthenes' plan was to attack at once, now that the necessary forces
of light-armed troops were at hand, a quick decision was inevitable:
Cleon knew he would succeed in twenty days or not at all. Still, the attitude Thucydides attributes to the *sophrones* (prudent men) seems
difficult to understand, let alone excuse. That patriotic Athenians
could have agreed to deliver the command of the Athenian expedition
and responsibility for the lives of allied soldiers and Athenian sailors
to a man they believed to be patently foolish, to say nothing of incompetent, strikingly reveals how potentially dangerous were the divisions
among Athenians that the events of 425 had produced.

THE SPARTAN SURRENDER ON SPHACTERIA

CLEON NAMED DEMOSTHENES as his fellow-commander and sent
word to him that help was on the way. At Pylos, Demosthenes nevertheless hesitated to attack the heavily wooded Sphacteria, on which an
unknown number of Spartan hoplites were concealed when, once
again, fortune seems to have favored the bold. A contingent of Athenian soldiers, prevented by the cramped conditions at Pylos from
preparing a hot meal there, made their way to the island, where one of
them accidentally started a forest fire. Before long most of the woods
had been burnt off, and Demosthenes could see that the Spartans were
more numerous than he had thought. He also noticed places at which
to make a safe landing that had been obscured before, and he realized
that one of the great tactical advantages of the enemy had been removed by the fire. When Cleon arrived with the fresh special troops,
Demosthenes was ready to put to use the valuable lessons he had
learned in Aetolia.

Just before dawn he landed with eight hundred hoplites on both the seaward side of the island and on the side facing inward toward the harbor. Demosthenes could now discern that most of the enemy troops were concentrated near the center of the island, guarding the water supply, while another force was near its northern tip, opposite Pylos, leaving only thirty hoplites to guard the point of landing at the southern end. After watching the Athenians sail by harmlessly for so many days, this small Spartan force was caught while still in bed and swiftly wiped out, as the Athenians had been at the battle of Idomene in the northwest the previous year. The Athenians landed the rest of their forces—hoplites, peltasts, archers, and even most of the barely armed rowers from the fleet—at dawn. Almost 8,000 rowers, 800 hoplites, the same number of archers, and over 2,000 light-armed troops faced the 420 Spartans.

Demosthenes divided his troops into companies of 200 who seized all the high places on the island, so that wherever the Spartans fought they would find an enemy in their rear or on their flanks. The key to the strategy was the use of light-armed troops, for they "were the most difficult to fight, since they fought at a distance with arrows, javelins, stones and slings. It was not possible to attack them, for even as they fled they held the advantage, and when their pursuers turned, they were on them again. Such was the plan with which Demosthenes first conceived the landing, and in practice that is how he arranged his forces" (4.32.4).

At first the Spartans lined up facing the Athenian hoplites, but the light-armed soldiers rained their weapons on them from the side and the rear, while the Athenian hoplites stood off and watched. The Spartans tried to charge their tormenters, who easily retreated to safety on high, rough ground that the hoplites could not reach. When the light-armed troops realized that the enemy was physically worn down by repeated vain pursuits and diminished by casualties they in turn charged at the Spartans, shouting and firing missiles as they came. The unexpected clamor disconcerted the Spartans and prevented them from hearing the orders of their officers. They fled to the northern end of the island where most of them hid behind the fortification to resist further attacks.

The Messenian general Comon came to Cleon and Demosthenes and asked for archers and light-armed troops to find a path around the precipitous shore of the island and take the enemy from the rear. The Spartans had not wanted to waste troops in guarding such an unlikely approach, so they were stunned by the appearance of Comon's men. They faced total destruction, for they were surrounded and outnumbered, weakened from exertion and hunger, and had no place to escape. As live prisoners were worth more than corpses, Cleon and Demosthenes offered them the opportunity of surrender. The Spartans accepted a truce to give themselves time to decide what to do. The island's commander refused to take the responsibility for capitulation, so he sent a herald to get orders from Sparta. There, the authorities likewise tried to avoid accountability, saying "The Spartans order you to decide your own fate yourselves, but to do nothing dishonorable" (4.38.3). The men on the island subsequently surrendered; of the 420 who came to Sphacteria, 128 were dead; the remaining 292, among them 120 Spartiates, were taken prisoner to Athens well within the period of twenty days that Cleon had promised. The Athenian casualties were few. "The promise of Cleon, mad as it was," Thucydides remarks, "was fulfilled" (4.39.3).

This outcome shocked the Greek world. "In the eyes of the Greeks it was the most unexpected event in the war" (4.40), for no one could believe that the Spartans could be brought to surrender. The Athenians garrisoned the fort at Pylos, the Naupactian Messenians sent a force to use it as a base for raids on Spartan lands, and the helots began to desert. The Athenians, moreover, threatened to kill their hostages if the Spartans again invaded Attica. The stunned Spartans sent repeated embassies to negotiate for the return of Pylos and the prisoners, to no avail.

The Athenians showered their gratitude on the hero of the hour, Cleon (Demosthenes seems to have stayed behind at Pylos to see to its security), with the assembly voting him the highest honors in the state, furnishing meals at the state's expense in the Prytaneum, as if he were an Olympic champion, and providing him with front seats at the theater. Some two months later the assembly ordered a new assessment, raising the tribute levied on the allies of Athens. Most scholars rightly see Cleon's hand in the matter, which reflects his harsh views toward the empire, as well as his domination of Athenian politics at that moment. From midsummer 425 at least until the spring of 424, when he was elected general, Cleon was supreme in Athens, and any bill he sponsored was likely to have passed through the assembly unchallenged.

The assessment was intended to raise more money to fight the war, and its total contribution seems to have been 1,460 talents, more than three times the earlier quotas. The new decree also provided for the tough and efficient collection of the revenue, including some regions that had not paid in some time and others, like the island of Melos, that had never contributed. These attempts to increase Athenian income, which would have been too dangerous to enact before the events at Pylos and Sphacteria made Athenian prestige soar while deflating Sparta's, reflect Cleon's determination to restore the empire to its full size, to govern it with a tight rein, and to draw from it the greatest revenue possible. The Athenians badly needed the money, and Cleon's great victory allowed them to demand it.

In the same summer Nicias, along with two unnamed generals, launched a campaign whose purpose the ancient writers do not explain, invading Corinthian territory with 80 ships, 2,000 Athenian hoplites, 200 cavalry, and a number of allied soldiers. The force landed near the village of Solygeia, six or seven miles from Corinth, but informers had warned the Corinthians of the invasion. Corinthian hoplites attacked the Athenians but were defeated in battle, losing 212 men to only 50 Athenians. The Athenians set up a trophy but could not exploit their victory, for when the older men of Corinth, who had remained in the city, came rushing up to help, Nicias thought they were Peloponnesian reinforcements and raced back to his ships.

The Athenians then sailed to the Corinthian town of Crommyon and ravaged its territory but made no attempt to take the town itself. The following day they stopped at Epidaurus before moving on to Methana, a peninsula between Epidaurus and Troezen. At Methana Nicias walled off the narrow neck of the peninsula and left a garrison that afterward raided the territory of Troezen, Halieis, and Epidaurus, all within easy reach. It seems likely that this venture was the expedition's chief purpose. Building a fort in the eastern Peloponnesus was probably influenced by the success at Pylos in the west; raids launched from Methana might force towns like Troezen and Halieis to come over to Athens; and the Athenians might even be able to intimidate or capture Epidaurus and then bring Argos into alliance. In the heady days after Pylos-Sphacteria everything seemed possible.

The Athenians also remained active in the west. Sophocles and Eurymedon took their fleet from Pylos to Corcyra, where the oligarchs on Mount Istome were still harrying the democratic friends of Athens in the city. The arrival of the fleet reversed the situation and, together with their allies, the Athenians captured the mountain fort and compelled the oligarchs to surrender, but only to the Athenians and on condition that they stand trial in Athens. The prisoners were placed on a nearby island for their protection, but the Corcyraean democrats wanted blood. They tricked the oligarchs into an attempt to escape, and the Athenians, declaring the truce broken, turned the prisoners over to their homicidal enemies. Those who were not killed with the greatest cruelty committed suicide; their women were sold into slavery. Sophocles and Eurymedon permitted these terrible atrocities. "In this way, the Corcyraeans from the mountain were destroyed by the demos, and the party strife which had lasted so long ended in such a manner, at least in so far as this war is concerned, for there were no longer any oligarchs left worth mentioning" (4.49.6).

As the fighting season drew to a close the Athenians' allies won another victory in the northwest. The garrison at Naupactus and the Acarnanians took Anactorium by treachery—so often the way with Greek sieges—after which the Acarnanians expelled the Corinthians and colonized the city. The Corinthians took the loss of Anactorium hard, for it damaged their waning prestige in an important region.

Throughout the war both sides had been attempting to get help from "barbarian" nations, the most important being Persia. Aristophanes' *Acharnians*, produced in 425, contains a hilarious scene in which an envoy from the Great King, "The King's Eye," appears on stage in Athens, which reveals that the Athenians had been in touch with Persia, perhaps as early as the beginning of the conflict. The Spartans, too, were wooing the Persians, and a Spartan embassy to the Persian court was intercepted by the Athenians in 430. In the winter of 425/4 the Athenians captured another envoy, this one carrying a message back to Sparta from the Persian monarch: "In regard to the Spartans the King did not know what they wanted. Though many envoys had come to him, they did not say the same things. If they wanted to say anything that was clear they should send men to him in the company of the Persian messenger" (4.50.2). The Spartans' opaqueness may have reflected their reluctance to abandon the Asiatic Greeks to Persia, surely a minimum demand for Persian cooperation, while they were claiming to fight for Greek freedom. The Athenians tried to take advantage of the situation by sending their own envoys back to the Great King with the intercepted messenger. When they reached Ephesus, however, they learned that King Artaxerxes had died, and they judged it a poor time to pursue negotiations. Neither side yet had reason to hope for Persian assistance.

The events of 425 had changed the course of the war entirely. The stalemate had been broken, and the Athenians held the advantage everywhere. Their financial problems were eased by the new imperial assessment. The capture of the enemy fleet ended the threat from the sea and any prospect of revolt in the maritime portions of the empire. The northwest was almost completely free of enemies. There was no immediate danger of a Persian intervention, and the Athenian campaign on Sicily guaranteed that the Greeks in the west would not help their Dorian cousins in the Peloponnesus. Finally, the prisoners taken at Sphacteria were being held safely in Athens, where their presence guaranteed that Attica would not be invaded. The Athenians had reasons to be pleased, and they were eager to press on to total victory. The question was how to proceed, and the answer depended on precisely what sort of victory they desired.

Those who would be satisfied with a negotiated peace in which Sparta would recognize the integrity of the Athenian Empire and make an alliance with Athens to prove it preferred a restrained strategy. They sought to avoid major land battles; to hold their fortified places in the Peloponnesus, even taking more of them when possible; and to use those fortifications to harass, discourage, and wear down the enemy—in other words, to continue or moderately extend the original policy of Pericles.

Cleon and men of like opinions could argue that such a peace would not be secure, since it rested ultimately on Spartan promises and good will, and insist that something tangible—a secure defense against renewal of the war—was needed. They set their sights on the control of Megara and the neutralization of Boeotia, concessions that the Spartans might even promise to Athens in negotiation, but which they could not deliver. To make peace when the enemy was weak and demoralized and when Athenian power was at its height would be a foolish plan; the correct strategy would be to move against Megara, Boeotia, and any other appropriate places. After they were subdued, the time might then be ripe to negotiate a peace that would be genuinely lasting. Such must have been the reasoning of Cleon and his friends, and it is not surprising that the Athenians chose to follow their advice.

CHAPTER THIRTEEN

Athens on the Offensive:
Megara and Delium (424)

CLEON'S GREAT SUCCESS at Sphacteria led to his election as general in the spring of 424, along with Demosthenes and Lamachus, two other aggressive men. Also elected were Nicias, Nicostratus, Autocles, and Thucydides son of Olorus, who would one day write the history of the war—all of whom were opposed to Cleon and his policies. While the Athenians were about to launch the most daring campaigns of the war, this did not so much reflect a change in the alignment of generals but rather the fact that, encouraged by their recent victories, the majority of Athenians were now ready to pursue a more militant strategy.

CYTHERA AND THYREA

EARLY IN MAY a trio of moderates—Nicias, Nicostratus, and Autocles—took sixty ships, two thousand hoplites, some cavalry, and a number of allies to capture the island of Cythera, just off the southeastern tip of Laconia (see Map 1). The invasion was part of a new strategy, modeled on the examples of Pylos and Methana, to place strongholds around the Peloponnesus from which the Athenians could damage, harass, discourage, and demoralize the enemy. Cythera was a Spartan base for trade with Egypt, which must have provided grain and other items, and for defending the Peloponnesian coast. Were the island to come under Athenian control, that trade could be cut off, and Cythera would serve not only as a springboard for raids on the Peloponnesus but as another convenient stopping place on the route to the west.

With ten ships and a small corps of hoplites Nicias swiftly seized the coastal city of Scandeia, while the main force marched straight to the town of Cythera in the interior and drove the enemy to its upper part. Nicias persuaded the Cytheraeans to surrender and offered generous terms, allowing the natives to remain on their island and keep their land at the cost of a tribute payment of four talents annually and the installation of an Athenian garrison.

The fall of Cythera struck the Spartans almost as hard as had the losses of Pylos and the men on Sphacteria, and they reacted by sending garrisons to guard various sites in the Peloponnesus and by organizing for the first time a corps of four hundred cavalry as well as a troop of archers. Thucydides vividly describes their state of mind:

> They were very much on guard for fear that there would be a revolution against the established order, for the disaster they had suffered on the island was great and unexpected, Pylos and Cythera were captured, and from every direction a war rose up around them which was swift and defied precaution. . . . In military affairs they now became more timid than ever before since they were involved in a naval contest, outside their normal conception of preparation for war, and in this unaccustomed area they fought against the Athenians, to whom the omission of an enterprise was always a loss in respect to what they had expected to achieve. At the same time, the misfortunes that had struck them in such numbers unexpectedly and in such a short time caused great terror, and they were afraid that another calamity might again strike them sometime like the one on the island. For this reason they were less daring in going into battle, and they thought that everything they undertook would turn out badly because they had no self-confidence as a result of having little previous experience with misfortune. (4.55)

The Athenians next attacked Thyrea in Cynuria, the border area that had long been a source of contention between Sparta and Argos (the Alsace-Lorraine of the Peloponnesus, as some historians have described it). The Spartans had given the town to the Aeginetans, whom the Athenians had expelled from their home island at the beginning of the war; together they were building a fort near the sea when the Athenians fleet appeared. A determined effort might have prevented their landing, but the Spartans' morale was not equal to the task. The unopposed Athenians marched straight to Thyrea, burning the city, taking booty, killing many Aeginetans, and seizing a large number of prisoners, refugees from Cythera among them. They scattered the Cytheraeans throughout the Aegean islands for safekeeping, but put all the Aeginetans to death "because they had always been enemies in the past" (4.57.5). Another atrocity was added to the growing list, as the war intensified old hatreds.

DISAPPOINTMENT IN SICILY

THE ATHENIANS WERE not enjoying the same degree of success in Sicily, where the loss of Messina and the siege of Rhegium left them without a base on either side of the narrows. (They eventually recovered Rhegium, but Messina remained in enemy hands.) They fought no more on the island in 425, but left the Sicilian Greeks to fight among themselves without interference. When Sophocles and Eurymedon arrived at Sicily they found their allies weary of the war and doubtful that the Athenians had the will and capacity to fight for their interests while engaged in their own battles on the Greek mainland. In 424 Gela, Syracuse's ally, and Camarina, an ally of Athens, made a separate peace. The two then invited the other Sicilian cities to a conference at Gela to seek a common accord, a diplomatic congress of a sort rare in Greek history. Addressing the gathering Hermocrates of Syracuse claimed to speak not in the interests of his own city but for all Sicily when he accused Athens, with its great power, of evil designs against it. The Greeks of Sicily should, he urged, abandon the conflict between Dorian and Ionian, which only made them easy prey for outsiders. Instead he presented the vision of a united nation of Greek Sicily, of a lasting peace including every one of the Greek cities on the island, of Sicily for the Sicilians.

> We are, generally speaking, neighbors, and together we inhabit a single land surrounded by the sea and are called by one name, Siceliots. We shall go to war, I imagine, when the situation arises, and we shall make peace again by employing common discussions

among ourselves. But if we are wise, when foreigners attack us we shall always act together to repel them, for if any of us is harmed individually we are all endangered. And we shall never again call in strangers as allies or mediators. If we do these things we shall not deprive Sicily, at the present time, of two advantages: to be rid of the Athenians and of our civil war. As for the future, we will live among ourselves in a free country and less exposed than now to dangers from outside. (2.64.3–5)

Hermocrates' speech has often been judged to be sincere and altruistic, a plea for the common good, but there is reason to question his motives. Syracuse, after all, stood to benefit if the weaker Greek cities of Sicily agreed not to call in the powerful states of the Greek mainland for aid. In 424, moreover, Syracuse, as the most powerful and aggressive state in Sicily, was most threatened by Athens. Hermocrates' later behavior also raises doubts about his sincerity. In 415 he urged the Syracusans to seek help against the Athenian invasion not only from the Greek cities of Corinth and Sparta but even from Carthage, and he also urged the Siceliots to join in the war the Peloponnesians were then waging against Athens even though the Athenians had already been driven from Sicily.

In 424, however, the battle-worn Siceliots at Gela were persuaded by the eloquence of Hermocrates, backed by the Syracusan evidence of good faith in ceding Morgantina to Camarina, and they agreed to a peace on the basis of the status quo. Their allies informed the Athenians and invited them to join the pact. Lacking a base in Sicily, with allies no longer willing to fight, and their own force inadequate to conquer the island, the Athenians accepted the peace and sailed for home.

Their generals may well have been satisfied with this outcome, for their mission had been to protect the allies of Athens, to prevent Syracuse from controlling all of Sicily, and, perhaps, to investigate the prospects for further gains. The Congress of Gela could be viewed as having accomplished all these purposes. On their return to Athens, however, they were soon charged with accepting bribes to withdraw when they could have subjugated Sicily. Such accusations were often leveled at unsuccessful commanders, or even those whose success had not been as complete as expected. The generals may indeed have taken some gifts from friends in Sicily, but there is no evidence of bribery. Nevertheless, they were all convicted; Sophocles and Pythodorus were exiled and Eurymedon was fined. Thucydides explains the condemnations as follows: "In this way, because of the good fortune they [the Athenians] enjoyed at this time, they expected that nothing would go against them but that they could achieve equally what was easy and more difficult whether their power was adequate or insufficient. The cause of this was their implausible success in most undertakings which gave them the strength of hope" (4.65.4).

By 424, after the victories at Pylos and Sphacteria, Methana and Cythera, the Athenians had greater expectations than before and may indeed have felt an unrealistic optimism, yet they did have some reason to be dissatisfied with the performance of the generals. After all, the first expedition of twenty ships to Sicily in 427 had prevented a Syracusan victory, taken Messina, gained support from Sicilian Greeks and native Sicels, and generated so much enthusiasm among the islanders that they sent a mission to Athens requesting additional assistance. It is not difficult to understand why in 424 the Athenians could so easily have believed that forty more ships might have brought the war on the island to a quick and gratifying end. We can well imagine their shock when the new generals announced that the conflict had been concluded on the basis of "Sicily for the Sicilians"—the slogan, after all, of a leading aristocratic politician from Syracuse—and that they had effectively been dismissed by their allies. The Athenians had justification in suspecting that Hermocrates' slogan might in fact be a cloak for "Sicily for the Syracusans," and in fearing a Sicily united under a Dorian state friendly to the enemy. They can also be excused for believing that a Sicily almost conquered by an expedition of twenty ships should not have been lost by one of sixty.

In fact, Sophocles, Eurymedon, and Pythodorus had shown minimal initiative and accomplished very little. Delayed at Pylos, they had allowed the Spartan fleet from Corcyra to slip by them, and arrived at Sicily too late to accomplish much because they had been forced into the long blockade that took up most of the summer. Had they been more vigilant, they could have landed in Sicily early enough to have made a great difference. In such circumstances any people might feel obliged to dismiss its officers. In this case, however, the Athenian response seems less unreasonable than excessive.

THE ASSAULT ON MEGARA

IN THE SUMMER of 424 Athens almost completely abandoned the strategy of Pericles, as it undertook aggressive operations against its neighbors with the intention of depriving the Spartans of crucial allies and providing Attica with full security against invasion. In July they tried to gain control of Megara and end the threat of attacks from the Peloponnesus. No people had suffered so much since the war began as the Megarians, for the Megarian Decree had destroyed their trade in the Aegean, and each year the Athenian army thoroughly ravaged their land. The Athenian capture of Minoa in 427, which made it impossible for a boat to slip out of the port of Nisaea into the Saronic Gulf, had pulled the noose still tighter. The resulting hardships had brought factional quarrels that led a democratic group to drive the extreme oligarchic regime into exile. Alarmed by this new leadership, Sparta and its mainly oligarchic allies had stationed a garrison of their own at Nisaea to watch the Megarians, while placing the Megarian exiles at the site of Plataea. A year later these oligarchs left Plataea and seized Pegae, the western port of Megara on the Gulf of Corinth, from where they closed Megara's last remaining access to the sea (see Map 4). By 424 the Megarians could obtain food and other supplies only overland from the Peloponnesus by way of Corinth, but because the allies disliked and suspected the Megarian democrats they were not cooperative.

Faced with so much pressure, the Megarian people recalled their exiles from Pegae, hoping to end their attacks and recover the use of their western port. The leaders of the democratic faction, meanwhile, fearing that their return would restore Megara to oligarchy and bring death or exile to themselves, conspired to hand their city over to Athens. Together with the Athenian generals Hippocrates and Demosthenes they planned to have the Athenians take the long walls connecting Megara to Nisaea, barring the Peloponnesian garrison from the city; the democrats would then betray Megara. If the plan succeeded

Megara would join the Athenian alliance, bringing an end to the annual invasions, commercial embargo, and blockade. With Athenian help the Megarians could also drive the exiles from Pegae, reclaim both their ports, and regain their old prosperity; they could man the forts on their southern frontier, and keep the Peloponnesians permanently out of the Megarid.

For the democratic leaders, who now found themselves in a perilous situation, the advantages of this scheme easily outweighed negative considerations, but most Megarians thought otherwise. The Megarians and Athenians had been enemies since at least the sixth century. The marriage of convenience between them in the First Peloponnesian War had ended with a Megarian slaughter of an Athenian garrison, and the years between the wars had been marked by boundary disputes, accusations of sacrilegious murder, and the imposition of the Megarian Decree. An alliance with a bitterly hated enemy, however expedient, was still too unpopular a concept for the people of Megara to accept. The democratic faction, therefore, could not propose a change of alliances publicly but could only conspire secretly with the Athenians.

The Athenian plan for seizing Nisaea was complicated and risky. Hippocrates sailed by night from Minoa with six hundred hoplites, and took cover in a trench near the walls. At the same time Demosthenes came overland by way of Eleusis with some light-armed Plataeans and a small number of Athenian hoplites and set up an ambush at Enyalius, a bit closer to Nisaea. Their success depended on surprise and secrecy; "throughout the night no one knew what was happening except the men whose business it was to know" (4.67.2).

At the same time the Megarian democrats were preparing for their role in the three-pronged attack on the walls. Each night the Peloponnesians let them open Nisaea's gates and wheel out a small boat on a cart, which was ostensibly used to attack Athenian shipping, and then bring it back into the city. On the night agreed they would allow the hidden Athenians to enter the walls through that same gate.

On the fixed night the Megarian traitors killed the guards, and Hippocrates took his men through the Nisaean gate. By daybreak the Athenians commanded the long walls, and at the prearranged time four thousand Athenian hoplites with six hundred cavalry arrived to make their position secure.

Even at this stage the Megarian democrats did not publicly suggest a change of alliances but instead had to play a terrible trick on their countrymen to gain their ends: they proposed to lead the Megarians out of their own gates and attack the waiting Athenian army, where the plotters would mark themselves so that the Athenians would spare them in battle; the others would be slaughtered unless they surrendered. The treachery was too much for one of the conspirators, however, who betrayed the plot to the oligarchs, who in turn convinced the rest of the Megarians to keep the gate shut. Had the democrats managed to open the gates the city would have fallen to the Athenians before the Spartans could send an army.

The Athenians might still have forced the surrender of Megara, but they were prevented from doing so by the unfortunate appearance of Brasidas, who happened to be near Corinth and Sicyon, gathering an army for a different purpose, when he heard of the events at Megara. He sent to Boeotia for reinforcements to meet his own force of thirty-eight hundred allies and a few hundred of his own troops, with which he hoped to save Nisaea. Too late for that, he led three hundred troops to try to rescue Megara.

The Megarians, however, were unwilling to admit him. The democrats knew the Spartans would destroy them and restore the oligarchic exiles, while the oligarchic friends of the exiles feared that the arrival of the Spartans would touch off a civil war, giving the Athenian army an opportunity to take the city. Both sides preferred to await the result of the battle they were certain would take place between the Athenian and Peloponnesian armies.

The Boeotians knew that Athenian control of the Megarid would cut them off from the Peloponnesus and leave them open to attack, and so had sent twenty-two hundred hoplites and six hundred cavalry to Brasidas. No more than five thousand Athenian hoplites would now be challenged by six thousand of the enemy. Rather than force a battle against the Megarians, the Athenians preferred to bide their time at Nisaea. Brasidas, too, chose to wait, for he believed his position would give him an advantage if the Athenians did attack, and that the very presence of his army might discourage them into retreat and save the city without a battle, and so it did. The Athenians withdrew behind the walls of Nisaea, while Brasidas returned to Megara, and this time he was admitted. The Athenians conceded failure by marching back to Attica, leaving a garrison at Nisaea. In Megara, the democrats, exposed as traitors, fled the city, and the oligarchic exiles returned to power intent on vengeance. They condemned as many of their enemies as were still in the city and established a very narrow regime, limiting political power to a small number. Henceforth Megara was a loyal ally of Sparta and an even more bitter enemy of Athens.

ATHENS' BOEOTIAN INVASION

ABOUT THE BEGINNING of August the Athenians undertook a bold and complicated action against Boeotia that had some of the earmarks of their earlier attack on Megara, suggesting that the two initiatives may in fact have been conceived at the same time as elements of a grand operation intended to change the course of the war. The failure at Megara, however, did not deter Demosthenes and Hippocrates from trying to carry out the second part of their plan.

In Boeotia democratic leaders in several towns had been plotting with the Athenians to bring their factions to power, and Demosthenes and Hippocrates gladly worked with them. In the west the democrats would betray Siphae, the port of Thespis, and Chaeronea to the Athenians. In the east, meanwhile, the Athenians would occupy the sanctuary of Apollo at Delium, just across the Athenian border (see Map 4). As at Megara, success required simultaneous attacks to prevent the Boeotians from massing their forces against the main Athenian army at Delium. Once again, secrecy was vital to enable treason to bring over Siphae and Chaeronea. It was hoped that the capture of three sites simultaneously might weaken Theban resolve and produce democratic, anti-Theban rebellions all over Boeotia. At the very least, Athens would have three fortresses on the borders of Boeotia for plundering expeditions and as refuges where exiles could escape. In this less optimistic form the plan would be part of the new strategy that placed permanent fortified bases in enemy territory, which was already working so well in Laconia. In time, the pressure from the three Athenian strongholds might make the Boeotians capitulate.

The Athenians would need a large army for the main blow against Delium and a smaller one for the landing at Siphae. Sending so massive a force would expose more soldiers to danger than the Athenians were willing to risk, but Demosthenes expected to recruit troops from the allies in the northwest. Gathering them, however, would take time, increasing the risk that the secret plan might get out, but the danger was unavoidable. Demosthenes took forty ships to the northwest, collected the men he needed, and waited for the date fixed for the attack on Siphae. Three months passed between his departure from Athens and his appearance at Siphae, probably because Boeotian democrats needed that long to prepare.

By the time Demosthenes' army finally sailed into the harbor at Siphae early in November everything had gone wrong. Traitors among the rebels had betrayed the plan to the Boeotians, who sent armies to occupy both Chaeronea and Siphae. If the timing of the double attack had been perfectly synchronized Boeotian troops might have been drawn off by Hippocrates' assault on Delium in the east, but this, too, misfired, for Demosthenes arrived at Siphae earlier, leaving the Boeotians free to concentrate on him. Demosthenes could not force his way onto the well-defended land, and the western part of the plan was a failure.

At Delium Hippocrates had some seven thousand hoplites and well over ten thousand metics (resident aliens) and foreign allies, as well as a large number of Athenians who had come to help build a fort. The army was present only to dissuade any challenging Boeotian force while the fort was being constructed; afterwards, a small garrison could hold it. Demosthenes and Hippocrates had never intended to risk a battle against an army of comparable size.

In seizing the area the Athenians had occupied the sacred ground of the sanctuary of the god Apollo, a serious violation of Greek taboos. This infraction represented yet another rejection of traditional practice that characterized this bloody and extended "modern" war.

DELIUM

HIPPOCRATES COMPLETED the fort in three days without any Boeotian interference and prepared to take his own army home, expecting
no trouble, for he had no idea of what had happened in the west. The
bulk of his army took the direct route south toward Athens, while the
hoplites stopped about a mile away from the city to wait for the general, who was completing his final arrangements at Delium. Meanwhile, the Boeotians had assembled at Tanagra, a few miles distant,
with seven thousand hoplites (the same number as the Athenians), ten
thousand light-armed troops, one thousand cavalry, and five hundred
peltasts. Although the Boeotian army was stronger, and the Athenians'
new fort sat on Boeotian soil, nine of the Boeotarchs, the magistrates
of the federal league of Boeotia, voted against combat; the only two
who sought battle were both Thebans.

However Pagondas son of Aeolidas, the commander of the army, a
distinguished aristocrat over sixty years old, perceived that the Athenians were vulnerable, and he persuaded the Boeotians to stand and
fight. In battles between Greek hoplites, the side defending its own soil
won almost three-quarters of the time, for the farmer-soldiers who
made up the phalanx fought more fiercely to protect their lands and
homes than on the offensive. Both generals took note of this tendency
in their prebattle speeches. Pagondas urged his men to do their utmost
even though the enemy troops were already withdrawing to their own
country. Normally, freedom meant safeguarding one's land, but when
fighting the Athenians, "who seek to enslave people near and far, how
can we do anything but fight to the bitter end?" (4.92.4). Hippocrates,
in turn, told his Athenians not to fear an engagement on foreign soil.
In reality, he explained, the battle was in defense of Athens, and he
spelled out the strategic goal of the campaign: "If we win, the Peloponnesians, without the Boeotian cavalry, will never invade Attica again,
and in one battle we will conquer their land and free our own"
(4.95.2).

Pagondas' words underscore the unique character of the battle of
Delium. It was not the usual quarrel over borderlands but a fight "to
the bitter end": namely, to destroy the Athenian army and stop the

greater war of which the battle at Delium was only a part. Marching to a position where a ridge separated the two armies, Pagondas arranged his forces with ingenuity and originality. On either flank he placed cavalry and light-armed troops to counteract any flanking movement. On the right of the hoplite phalanx he massed the Theban contingent to the extraordinary depth of twenty-five, compared to the usual eight, while the hoplites from the other cities lined up as they liked, probably in the standard fashion. This is the first recorded use of the very deep wing in a hoplite phalanx, a tactic that would be employed with devastating effect by Epaminondas of Thebes and Philip and Alexander of Macedon in the following century. While the Boeotian right wing would almost surely defeat the enemy's left, the enemy, arrayed at the typical depth of eight, would have a longer line, since the number of hoplites was equal, and could threaten a flank attack. Success for the Boeotians would therefore depend on a swift victory for the Thebans on the right, leading to a rout. At the same time the cavalry and light-armed men on the left flank would have to prevent the Athenians from turning that flank and starting a rout there. The Thebans also used three hundred elite hoplites, apparently specially trained and from the wealthiest class. This is the first recorded instance of separate training for what might be considered a professional corps, as opposed to the popular militia that constituted the normal phalanx. It is evidence of the growing complexity of Greek warfare, which accelerated during the Peloponnesian War, and would soon be emulated by other states.

When Pagondas began marching down from the top of the ridge Hippocrates had reached only the center of his line with his speech, which had to be repeated several times to reach all the troops. Standing with the right wing of his own army, Hippocrates quickly recognized that he could outflank the left wing of the enemy phalanx. He must have noticed, too, that the ravines on either side of the battlefield would hamper the activities of the cavalry and light-armed troops on the flanks, where he was inferior, so he ordered his men to charge up the hill on the run.

The Athenians on the right quickly routed the Boeotian left held by the men from Thespiae, Tanagra, and Orchomenus. At the opposite end of the field the Thebans were doing poorly, for the tough Athenians opposite them were giving ground slowly, step by step, and would not break and run. This was a moment of great peril for the Boeotians and hope for the Athenians, for if nothing intervened, the Athenian right would roll up the Boeotian line before the Theban right could do the same to the Athenians. The Thebans would consequently be caught in a pincers, with the Boeotian army routed and perhaps destroyed.

It was at this point that Pagondas displayed a touch of tactical genius that turned the tide of the battle. He sent two cavalry squadrons from the right wing around behind the hill, out of sight of the Athenians. They eventually reappeared behind the victorious Athenians and threw them into a panic, for they thought a completely new army had arrived to attack them from the rear. This broke the momentum of the Athenian charge and gave the Theban right time to break the Athenians opposite them and turn them to rout. The Athenian army was now a mob in flight, harried by the pursuit of the Boeotian and Locrian cavalry. Only the fall of night prevented an even greater slaughter. When the Athenians were finally permitted to take up their dead after long and complicated negotiations they discovered they had lost, in addition to many light-armed troops and noncombatants, almost a thousand hoplites, among them the general Hippocrates—the heaviest losses by far in the Ten Years' War. To remove the Athenian fortress at Delium the Boeotians constructed a kind of enormous flamethrower to set fire to the walls and drive the defenders off; the unprecedented war was encouraging the development of novel technology to meet military problems.

Few ancient battles were more famous in antiquity than Delium, chiefly because Socrates fought in it as a hoplite and Alcibiades with the cavalry. On the battlefield the brilliance of Pagondas was outstanding, and his strategic innovations were far in advance of their time. The contest also had significant military ramifications. The Athenians' failure to take Boeotia from the war encouraged the Spartan Alliance to hold out after victory had seemed impossible. In Athens the defeat and heavy casualties damaged the aggressive faction and helped those favoring a negotiated peace. Critics have condemned the Athenians for the strategy that led to the disaster at Delium, some for its un-Periclean aggressiveness, others because it rejected a direct assault for one of a complicated, circuitous character. By 424, however, the Periclean strategy had been demonstrated to be no longer feasible and a new one was unavoidable; nor would a strategy of forcing a set battle have been suited to an army inferior in numbers and morale to its enemy.

The Athenians were ultimately warranted in their decision to try to remove Boeotia as an enemy and, given their inferiority to the opposing coalition in hoplites, cavalry, and light-armed troops, they were correct in relying on surprise and the strategy of divide and conquer. The original plan, moreover, risked little. Demosthenes was not to have landed at Siphae unless the revolutions had made it safe to do so, and there was no intention to fight at Delium or anywhere else with a great army. If something had gone wrong in those areas, the road back home was still secure. Even with the failure of secrecy and confusion in timing, there would have been no disaster at Delium had Hippocrates retreated instead of standing to fight. With a bit of luck the campaign might have produced an important victory, but in 424, after a remarkable series of successes, luck was beginning to run against Athens.

CHAPTER FOURTEEN

Brasidas' Thracian Campaign (424–423)

IN MID-AUGUST 424, even before the disastrous Athenian invasion of Boeotia Brasidas had begun to turn the course of the war to Sparta's favor with a more daring exploit: taking an army northward toward Thrace to threaten the only accessible part of the Athenian Empire. (This was the same army—seven hundred helots armed as hoplites and a thousand mercenary hoplites from the Peloponnesus—that happened to be gathering near Corinth when the Athenians attacked Megara and enabled Brasidas to save that city.) By 424 the Athenian harassment of the Peloponnesus from Pylos and Cythera was becoming unbearable, and the Spartans were ready to try anything to relieve the situation. Brasidas' plan enabled them to be rid of seven hundred bold and able-bodied helots at a time when the Athenians and Messenians at Pylos were encouraging desertion, and the only Spartiate they risked in the effort was its commander. Their main goal was Amphipolis, a source of strategic materials and wealth in timber and gold and silver mines, and a key location from which to control both passage on the Strymon River and the road east to the Hellespont and the Bosporus, through which came the ships carrying Athens' vital grain supply. (See Map 16.)

The road to Amphipolis and to the other Athenian subjects in Macedonia and Thrace, however, was dangerous. Between them and Sparta's new colony at Heraclea lay Thessaly, formally allied to Athens, a broad, flat land difficult for a hoplite army to march through safely if challenged by the splendid Thessalian cavalry. The Spartans also lacked friends in northern Greece who could supply them with troops. Still, Brasidas was eager to attempt an assault, especially since events in 424 seemed to offer a favorable opportunity: the Bottiaeans and Chalcidians, who had been in revolt from Athens since 432, and Perdiccas, king of the Macedonians, who, though occasionally at peace or allied with Athens, were at heart always its enemy, invited the Spartans to send an army to Thrace. The rebels feared that the emboldened Athenians would soon send an army to crush them, while Perdiccas was involved in a private quarrel with Arrhabaeus, the king of the Lyncestians, and wanted to enlist the Peloponnesian army in his cause. Because Greek cities hostile to Athens might be trusted to support a Spartan campaign in the northeast, Brasidas was able to persuade his government to approve his plan.

His first challenge came in Thessaly, where the common people were friendly to Athens; furthermore, no Greeks wanted a foreign army to march through their territory. As Thucydides says, "If Thessaly had not been ruled by a narrow oligarchy, as is usual in that country, rather than a constitutional government Brasidas would never have gotten through" (4.78.3). Friends at Pharsalus sent guides to lead him through safely, and Brasidas' diplomacy and cleverness got them to Pharsalus. From there his Thessalian escort was able to take him the rest of the way to the territory of Perdiccas.

On learning that Brasidas had arrived in the north, the Athenians declared Perdiccas an enemy and began to keep closer watch on their suspected allies. To remain in Perdiccas' favor, Brasidas agreed to join in his attack against his neighbors, but disharmony soon broke out. Brasidas accepted the offer of Arrhabaeus to arbitrate the dispute and withdrew from the battle, deeply annoying the Macedonian king. Perdiccas responded by reducing his support from one-half to one-third of Brasidas' forces.

Brasidas had determined that Acanthus, on the Chalcidic peninsula, would be a good base for attacking Amphipolis and took his army there late in August (see Map 16). Although factional quarrels divided the town he did not try to take it by storm or treachery; instead he attempted to persuade its citizens to yield. Thucydides says of him, with either delicious irony or dismissive condescension, that "he was not an incompetent speaker, though a Spartan" (4.84.2). The Acanthians let him enter their city alone and unattended. Beginning with gentle words, he spoke of Sparta's role as liberator of the Greeks, promising to leave the city autonomous, to favor no faction, and to provide protection against Athenian retaliation; he concluded by threatening to destroy the Acanthians' crops, just ready for harvest, if they refused. The Acanthians voted to revolt from Athens and admit the Peloponnesians "because of the seductive words of Brasidas and fear for their crops" (4.88.1). Stagirus, a town nearby, joined the rebellion, a success that established momentum for the Spartan cause.

THE CAPTURE OF AMPHIPOLIS

EARLY IN DECEMBER Brasidas marched to Amphipolis, whose fall would surely lead to a general rebellion in the entire area and open the road to the Hellespont. Lying at a sharp bend in the Strymon River, Amphipolis was defended by water in three directions (see Map 16). A bridge across the river gave access to the city from the west, and an enemy crossing there would encounter a wall that surrounded the hill on which Amphipolis was built. An eastern wall effectively turned the city into an island. A small fleet could easily defend the city from any attack from the west.

Amphipolis contained only a few Athenians, its people consisting chiefly of what Thucydides calls "a mixed multitude," among them some settlers from nearby Argilus. Because the people of Argilus were secretly hostile to Athens, the Argilians within Amphipolis would not be trustworthy allies, so that in any attack or siege Amphipolis would be endangered from within as well as without.

Brasidas marched through a dark and snowy night to Argilus, which immediately declared its rebellion from the Athenian alliance. Before dawn, he reached the bridge over the Strymon, crucial for his plan. The snowstorm was still blowing, which helped him catch the guards by surprise, some of whom were traitors. The Peloponnesians easily seized the bridge and all the land outside the city walls, taking many prisoners from the shocked Amphipolitans caught there; inside, quarrels quickly broke out between settlers of different nationalities. Thucydides believes that if Brasidas had attacked Amphipolis immediately instead of pillaging the countryside he could have taken it easily. But storming a walled city with such a small army was sure to result in significant casualties and was likely to fail, so Brasidas counted on treachery. The Amphipolitans, however, soon recovered their courage and guarded their gates against treason.

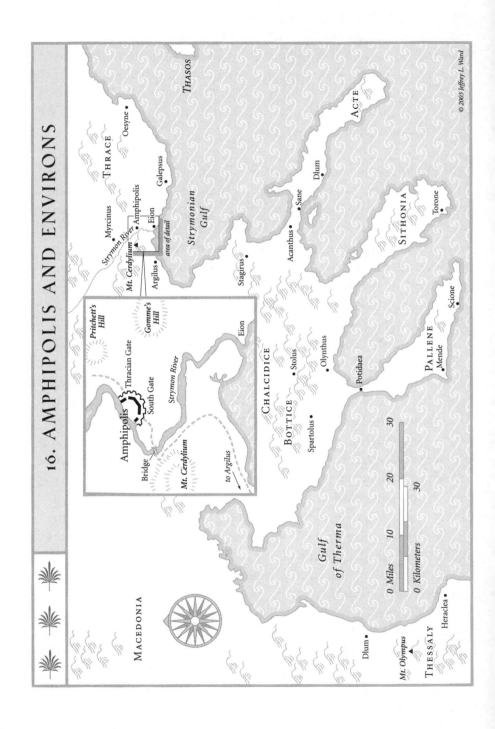

16. AMPHIPOLIS AND ENVIRONS

MACEDONIA

THRACE

Myrcinus

Oesyne

Amphipolis

Galepsus

Eion

Strymon River

Mt. Cerdylium

Argilus

area of detail

Strymonian Gulf

Thasos

ACTE

Dium

Sane

Acanthus

Stagirus

SITHONIA

Torone

CHALCIDICE

BOTTICE

Stolus

Olynthus

Potidaea

PALLENE

Mende

Scione

Spartolus

Pritchett's Hill

Thracian Gate

Gomme's Hill

South Gate

Amphipolis

Strymon River

Eion

Bridge

Mt. Cerdylium

to Argilus

Gulf of Therma

Dium

Mt. Olympus

THESSALY

Heraclea

0 Miles   10   20   30

0 Kilometers   30

© 2003 Jeffrey L. Ward

In Amphipolis, Eucles, the Athenian commander of the garrison, sent to Eion, asking Thucydides, the historian of the Peloponnesian War, who commanded the Athenian fleet in the Thraceward region, to come to the rescue. Thucydides, however, was not at Eion, less than three miles away near the mouth of the Strymon, but at Thasos, about a half-day's sail away. Thucydides' history offers no explanation for his absence; perhaps he was gathering troops to reinforce Amphipolis, though we have no evidence for such a purpose, or his trip may have had nothing to do with Amphipolis. Whatever the reason, his delay in arriving was a critical factor in the outcome.

Thucydides says that it was Brasidas' fear that Thucydides would soon arrive and stiffen resistance that caused him to offer easy terms of surrender to the Amphipolitans. Whatever the truth of that claim, the appearance of an Athenian fleet would have greatly undermined the chances of surrender, so Brasidas moved quickly and moderately. Eucles and the Amphipolitans, however, knew that Thucydides had only a few ships, which would be of little value once Brasidas had crossed the bridge. If the city was taken by force the results for the citizens would be grim—possibly exile, slavery, or even death. The Amphipolitans, therefore, accepted the conditions put forth by Brasidas: any resident of Amphipolis could either stay and keep his property with equal rights, or leave freely within five days, taking his property with him. The unstated condition was that Amphipolis must come over to the Spartan alliance and, "compared to what they had feared the proclamation seemed just" (4.106.1). At the news of Brasidas' offer resistance crumbled, and the city accepted the terms.

Not many hours after Brasidas entered Amphipolis Thucydides arrived at Eion with his seven ships. He had come quickly, traveling almost fifty miles in about twelve hours. The message had probably come to him by semaphore and said something like "bridge fallen, enemy here." Such news would explain the reaction of Thucydides as he himself reports it: "[Thucydides] wanted especially to arrive in time to save Amphipolis before it gave in, but if that was impossible to be early enough to save Eion" (4.104.5). He was in fact too late to save Amphipolis, but he did prevent the capture of Eion.

THUCYDIDES AT AMPHIPOLIS

THE LOSS OF Amphipolis frightened and angered the Athenians, who held Thucydides responsible. He was accordingly brought to trial and sent into an exile that lasted twenty years, until the end of the war. The ancient biographers of Thucydides report that Cleon was his accuser and that the charge was *prodosia* (treason), which, like peculation, was an accusation often leveled against unsuccessful generals. Cleon was still the leading politician in Athens and the likeliest candidate to introduce such a complaint. Historians have long argued over the justice of the court's decision, and the problem is compounded by the fact that the only useful account of the affair is by Thucydides, which itself is puzzling. Although Thucydides never directly discusses the sentence passed on him, and chooses instead an apparently objective description of the events, his bare narrative is a most effective defense. The proof of that assessment is that we can so easily convert his account into a direct answer to the charge that Thucydides was to blame for the fall of Amphipolis: "The emergency arose," he might say, "when Brasidas made a surprise attack on the bridge over the Strymon. The guard at the bridge was small, partly disloyal, and unprepared, so Brasidas took it easily. Responsibility for guarding the bridge belonged to Eucles, the commander of the city. The city was unprepared, but managed to rally in time to prevent immediate treason and send to me for help. I was at Thasos at the time, and set out immediately to relieve Amphipolis if I could, but to save Eion at least. I made amazingly good time because I knew the danger of treason would be great and that my arrival could turn the tide in our favor. If Eucles could have held on one more day we would have thwarted Brasidas, but he did not. My quickness and foresight saved Eion."

Thucydides' formal defense, whatever it was, did not convince an Athenian jury, although the implicit argument presented in his narrative has had much more success among modern historians. Still, if the statement he offered in court was essentially the same as the one presented in his history we can understand why it failed to exonerate him: it gives no answer to the key question—namely, why he was at Thasos rather than at Eion.

Thucydides had, no doubt, gone to Thasos on some legitimate mission, but that does not acquit him of the charge of failing to anticipate the arrival of the expedition of Brasidas and of being at the wrong place at the wrong time. The penalty, however, seems excessive, particularly when we consider Brasidas' daring and unusual tactics and the fact that Eucles, who allowed the bridge to be captured and the Amphipolitans to surrender, seems not to have been brought to trial or condemned. If the irrational *demos* was seeking scapegoats, why did it condemn only Thucydides? We know no reason why the Athenian jury would have made any distinctions between him and Eucles on political or other grounds. The Athenians did not automatically convict all accused generals or give those who were convicted the same penalty, but seem to have based their decisions on the precise details of the case, among other considerations.

Whoever was to blame, the fall of Amphipolis encouraged rebellions throughout the rest of the Thracian area, as factions in various regions sent secret messengers inviting Brasidas to bring their cities over to Sparta. Immediately after the capture of Amphipolis, Myrcinus, situated just up the Strymon, and then Galepsus and Oesyne on the Aegean coast defected, followed by most of the cities of the Acte peninsula.

The citizens of the Chalcidic towns counted on major Spartan assistance and underestimated Athenian strength, but they were wrong in both respects. The Athenians immediately sent garrisons to strengthen their hold on the Thracian district, and although Brasidas requested reinforcements while he began to build ships in the Strymon, the Spartan government at home refused, "because of jealousy toward him by the leading men and also because they preferred to recover the men from the island and put an end to the war" (4.108.7).

Jealousy, no doubt, played some part in the Spartan decision, but a real disagreement on policy was a more significant factor. Ever since the capture of the men on Sphacteria a faction favoring negotiated peace had dominated the state, persuading the Spartans to send mission after mission offering terms, only to be rejected by the Athenians. They now saw the victories of Brasidas as a powerful inducement for the peace they had vainly sought, for the capture of Amphipolis and other towns placed them in a powerful bargaining position from which to trade for the prisoners, Pylos, and Cythera.

One can easily sympathize with these conservatives. Perdiccas had shown himself to be unreliable. It would also be dangerous to move another army through Thessaly, and few Spartans wanted to send any forces away from home while the enemy was still at Pylos and Cythera and the helots were restless. At the same time the run of defeats at Megara, Boeotia, and Amphipolis had discredited the advocates of aggressive war in Athens, and the Athenians were ready to consider a negotiated peace. They had begun the year inflated by hopes of a complete triumph but ended it in a chastened mood, ready for compromise.

TRUCE

IN THE SPRING OF 423 the Athenians were at last prepared to discuss peace with the Spartans and agreed to a one-year truce for the purpose. Under its terms the Spartans promised the Athenians access to the sanctuary at Delphi and agreed not to put warships to sea, while the Athenians pledged not to receive helots escaping to Pylos. Athens was to keep Pylos and Cythera, but its garrisons were to remain confined within narrow limits at Pylos and to have no contact with the Peloponnesus from Cythera. The same provisions were made for the Athenian garrison at Nisaea and on the islands of Minoa and Atalante. Athenian presence at Troezen in the eastern Peloponnesus was permitted according to agreements previously made with the Troezenians.

To facilitate negotiations heralds and envoys from both sides were guaranteed safe conduct, and it was mutually agreed that any disputes would be settled by arbitration. The final clause reveals the genuineness of the Spartans' eagerness for peace: "These things seem to be good to the Spartans and their allies, but if anything seems fairer or more just to you than these proposals, come to Sparta and tell us. Neither the Spartans nor the allies will reject any just proposal you make. Only let those who come have full powers, just as you required of us. And the truce will last a year" (4.118.8–10).

The Athenian assembly accepted the truce late in March 423, but troubles soon arose. The Boeotians, elated by their victory at Delium, and the Phocians, nursing old grudges, rejected the pact, and as they controlled Athenian access to Delphi by land, implicitly threatened its first clause. The Corinthians and Megarians also objected to the terms that allowed the Athenians to keep the territory they had taken from them. By far the greatest barrier to peace, however, was the willful genius who commanded Sparta's armies in Thrace. As the truce was being concluded, the town of Scione in the Chalcidice revolted from Athens, and Brasidas at once crossed over by boat to exploit the new opportunity it presented. He won over even those who had not initially favored the rebellion, and a unified Scione made the unprecedented public gesture of granting Brasidas a golden crown as "liberator of Hellas." He soon stationed forces in the town, intending to use it as a base for attacks on Mende and Potidaea on the same peninsula.

Because of his ambitions, Brasidas must have taken news of the truce hard, especially when he learned that Scione was excluded from Spartan control, since it had revolted after the truce was signed. To protect Scione from Athenian vengeance, Brasidas falsely insisted that the rebellion had taken place before the truce. The Spartans believed him and claimed control of Scione, but he could only expect trouble when his deception was revealed.

The Athenians, however, already knew the truth about the chronology of the events in Scione and consequently refused to arbitrate its status. In their anger they agreed to Cleon's proposal to destroy the city and put the citizens to death; this time, there would be no second thoughts or reprieve. The dangerous defections of Amphipolis, Acanthus, Torone, and other towns in the northeast had further discredited Pericles' moderate imperial policy, and the Athenians were now willing to try Cleon's policy of deterrence through terror.

Brasidas, meanwhile, embarked on his own course, aimed at victory, not peace, contrary to the wishes of the Spartan regime. When the town of Mende revolted, unmistakably during the period of truce, he accepted the rebels. The angry Athenians at once prepared a force to move against both upstart cities, and Brasidas sent a garrison to defend them. Unfortunately, just when he needed the Spartan force for a quick action in the Chalcidice, Perdiccas demanded that it join his own in an attack on the Lyncestians; Brasidas, dependent on the Macedonian king for supplies, could not refuse.

The treachery of his Illyrian allies forced Perdiccas to retreat, but

his quarrel with Brasidas prevented cooperation against Athens between him and the Spartan general. The Macedonian ran off in the
middle of the night, leaving Brasidas' troops in a vulnerable position,
confronted by a large army of Lyncestians and the Illyrians who had
changed sides. With his usual brilliance, however, Brasidas brought his
army to safety. That episode ended the Spartan alliance with Perdiccas,
who, "Departing from his necessary interests sought how he could
most quickly make peace with the Athenians and get rid of Brasidas"
(4.128.5).

NICIAS' EXPEDITION TO THRACE

NICIAS AND NICERATUS assumed leadership of the Athenian expedition that set out for Pallene to put down the uprisings at Scione and
Mende, but not Torone, which had revolted earlier and under the terms
of the truce belonged to Sparta. They were determined not to violate
the pact, whatever Brasidas had done, for they truly sought peace. They
were, however, eager to recover Scione and Mende, for Brasidas' violations had angered the Athenians. If Nicias and his friends were not to
be completely discredited they would have to recover the rebellious
towns and restore the conditions in which the truce had been made.

The Athenians made their base at Potidaea before Brasidas returned from the campaign in the north. They found Mende defended
by the natives, three hundred men from Scione, and seven hundred
Peloponnesians under the Spartan general Polydamidas, Faithful to his
commander's orders he was no Brasidas but rather a typical specimen
of the Spartan abroad. He was preparing an attack on the Athenians
when some of the Mendaean democrats refused to fight. Polydamidas
berated and seized a democratic protester, which led his fellow Men-
daeans to attack the Peloponnesians and their own oligarchs, and then
to open the gates to the Athenians. Their forces burst into the city and
restored democracy to Mende and Mende to the Athenian alliance.

The escaping Peloponnesian troops fled to Scione, enabling its
people to hold out for the entire summer. Nicias and Niceratus built
an encircling wall around the city and then made an alliance with
Perdiccas—a valuable tactic, in that the Spartans were on the point of

sending a relief force to Brasidas in the hope of gaining the best bargaining position for peace negotiations. Like the peace party in Athens, their Spartan counterparts were in the awkward role of intensifying the war in order to make peace possible. Had an army reached Brasidas it might have destroyed all chance of a negotiated settlement, but the Macedonian king used his considerable influence in Thessaly and discouraged the Spartans from the attempt.

Although they barred the Spartan army, the Thessalians allowed its three generals to travel north. Their leader, Ischagoras, belonged to the peace faction and was no friend of Brasidas. He brought with him young and vigorous men to serve as governors—Clearidas for Amphipolis, and Cleonymus for Torone—who owed their posts and their allegiance entirely to the Spartan home government, and hence could be expected to follow orders. Their appointment also made a mockery of Brasidas' promise of freedom and autonomy to Amphipolis, Torone, Acanthus, and the other cities he had won, damaging his reputation and making any future defections from Athens unlikely.

As spring and the end of the truce approached, confusion reigned. Outside the Thracian region the armistice held, but Brasidas' violations bred suspicion and anger in Athens and prevented progress toward a stable peace.

CHAPTER FIFTEEN

The Coming of Peace (422–421)

FOR ALL THEIR outstanding grievances, neither Athens nor Sparta was willing to break the truce, which continued past its original expiration date in March well into the summer of 422. By August, however, the Athenians finally lost patience. The Spartans had refused to disown Brasidas and punish him but instead tried to reinforce his army and sent governors to rule the cities he had taken in violation of the truce. It was easy to conclude that they had entered into the armistice in bad faith simply to win time for Brasidas to gain even more successes and foment further rebellions, and thus to have the leverage to make greater demands in the bargaining for peace. The Athenians therefore sent thirty ships, twelve hundred hoplites, three hundred cavalry, and a larger force of excellent Lemnian and Imbrian light-armed specialists to recover Amphipolis and the other lost cities.

CLEON IN COMMAND

IN THIS CAMPAIGN CLEON, elected general for the year, gladly assumed leadership, but the force he and his anonymous associates assembled was not strong enough to guarantee success. In addition to the men doing garrison duty in Scione and Torone, Brasidas had about the same number of troops, as well as the great advantage of defending walled towns. Athens must have counted on help from Perdiccas and from some of its allies in Thrace, while Brasidas was effectively cut off and could expect no further assistance from Sparta. With reasonable luck Cleon might have won another important victory and restored the security of the Thracian district, giving Athens stronger bargaining power or, as Cleon hoped, encouraging the Athenians to resume the offensive in the Peloponnesus and central Greece on the way to victory.

Cleon initially did very well, making a feint at Scione, the obvious target, but attacking Torone instead, the chief Spartan base in the area. At the time Brasidas was away, and the forces left in the city were no match for the Athenians. Cleon arranged a rare joint attack from land and sea that drew the defending forces to his assault on the walls, while his ships assailed the unguarded shore. The Spartan commander Pasitelidas had stepped into a trap, and by the time he had disengaged from the front against Cleon and fled for Torone he found the Athenian fleet had taken the city, and he himself was captured. Cleon sent Torone's adult males to Athens as prisoners and sold the women and children as slaves. Brasidas' relief force was less than four miles from the city when it fell.

From Torone Cleon went to Eion to establish a base for the attack on Amphipolis. His assault on Stagirus in the Chalcidice failed, but he took Galepsus by storm. The imperial assessment list for 422/1 also shows the recovery of many other cities in the region, which must have been Cleon's work, as well. In the diplomatic realm he achieved alliances with Perdiccas and his Macedonians as well as the Thracian Polles, king of the Odomantians.

Cleon planned to wait at Eion until the arrival of these new allies would enable him to lock Brasidas up in Amphipolis and then to take it. Brasidas, however, anticipated the threat, and it was probably then that he moved his army to the hill called Cerdylium to the southwest of the city in the territory of the Argilians, leaving Clearidas in charge of Amphipolis itself (see Map 16). From Cerdylium he had a good view in all directions and could track Cleon's every move.

Thucydides says that Brasidas took up this position in the expectation that Cleon would attack with only his own army, as a sign of his contempt for the small number of men in the Spartan contingent. But Brasidas' forces were about equally matched with those of the enemy, as Cleon must surely have been aware, since he continued to wait for reinforcements. Cleon soon moved his army to a hill northeast of Amphipolis, a decision Thucydides dismisses as having had no military purpose but rather a response to the grumbling of the Athenian troops, whom he characterizes as annoyed by their inactivity and distrustful of the leadership of their general, contrasting his incompetence and cowardice with the experience and boldness of Brasidas. But even critics of Cleon would hardly have charged him with those particular shortcomings, and Thucydides himself portrays him as being too bold and optimistic. Brasidas, in fact, expected him to be rash enough to attack without waiting for his allies. Nor is the accusation of incompetence merited: Cleon had fulfilled his promise to take Sphacteria and had shown himself to be shrewd, skillful and successful at Torone. In fact, the men who are supposed to have doubted him at Amphipolis were the very ones who served under him when he stormed Galepsus and reclaimed the other towns in the region.

A better explanation for Cleon's move is that he meant to wait until the Thracians came, encircle the city, and then take it by storm. To accomplish that he needed to have an accurate assessment of its size, shape, the height and strength of its walls, the disposition of the forces and population within it, and the lay of the land outside it. That required a reconnaissance expedition of exactly the kind Thucydides describes Cleon as making: "He came and established his army on a strong hill in front of Amphipolis and himself examined the marshy portion of the Strymon and how the city was situated in respect to Thrace" (5.7.4). The soldiers may indeed have been restless, but the march was undoubtedly necessary, and it had to have been made in force in order to deter any attack from the city.

When Cleon reached the hill he saw no forces posted on the wall of Amphipolis and no troops rushing out of the gates to attack him. Thucydides says that Cleon believed he had made a mistake not to have brought siege equipment with him, for he realized he could have used it to take the city with the force he had at hand, but how he was able to know Cleon's intentions is unclear. Cleon died in the battle and therefore could not have been a direct source, and the Athenian soldiers who might have served as Thucydides' informants almost two decades later when he wrote his account were not likely to have been unbiased, even if they had been party to Cleon's private thoughts. We cannot determine with any certainty Cleon's reasoning, but there is no evidence that he underestimated the Peloponnesian force and foolishly endangered his army. In fact, when Brasidas saw Cleon marching north from Eion and joined up with Clearidas in the city he did not dare make an attack, judging his own force to be inferior in quality if not in actual numbers. Cleon had every reason to conclude that he could make his reconnaissance and return to Eion in safety.

THE BATTLE OF AMPHIPOLIS

BRASIDAS, HOWEVER, wanted to fight as soon as possible, for without financial and material support from Sparta or Perdiccas his position grew weaker each day, while Cleon would soon be greatly strengthened by Thracian and Macedonian troops. Leaving his army with Clearidas and choosing 150 men to accompany him, "He planned to make an immediate attack before the Athenians could get away, thinking that he would not again find them so isolated if their reinforcements should arrive" (5.8.4). As part of a scheme to deceive Cleon and lead him into a trap, he began with a great show of making the sacrifices that typically precede battle and sent the forces of Clearidas to the northernmost, or Thracian, gate of the city (see Map 16). By threatening to attack Cleon from that gate he would force him to move southward toward Eion, past the eastern wall of Amphipolis. Marching past the city the Athenian army would no longer be able to see movements behind its walls, and would believe they were now safe. Brasidas, however, planned to attack them with his select force of elite troops, which he had posted at the southern gate. The surprised Athenians, assuming that the entire army had followed them from the northern to the southern gates, would concentrate fully on defeating the men before them. Meanwhile, Clearidas could advance with the main force from the Thracian gate and take the Athenians in the flank.

Cleon seems to have taken a small force to scout the terrain north or northeast of Amphipolis. When he learned that the enemy army was massed at the Thracian gate, while most of the Athenians were south of that position, he judged it prudent and safe to order a withdrawal to Eion, for he had never planned to fight a pitched battle without reinforcements.

Thucydides reports that before any attack was made, Cleon, judging that there was sufficient time to get away, gave orders to retreat. A complicated maneuver by the left wing was needed to guarantee the safety of the retreating column, but this operation took some time to execute. Cleon posted himself at the most dangerous position on the right wing and wheeled it around to march left, leaving its unshielded right side highly vulnerable. This movement, or the failure to coordinate it with the movement of the left wing, caused confusion and a breach of order. Brasidas allowed the Athenian left wing to advance and took this tactical stumble as an opportunity to attack. He burst from the southern gates on the run and struck the Athenian center, which was taken wholly by surprise. The Athenians, "amazed by his daring and terrified by their own disorder, turned and ran" (5.10.6). At just the right moment Clearidas burst from the Thracian gate, catching the Athenians on the flank and throwing them into further disarray.

The men on the left wing hastened to Eion while those on the right, where Cleon was in command, stood their ground bravely. As for Cleon himself, who had never intended to stand and fight, Thucydides tells us that he "fled immediately," and was killed by the spear of a Myrcinian peltast. Although he has been accused of cowardice, the evidence does not support such an indictment. Cleon did not escape with the left wing; he stayed in the rear, the most dangerous place for an army in flight, for he was killed by a javelin thrown from a distance, and we have no evidence that he was struck in the back. As the Spartans had said in respect to their men at Sphacteria, "It would be quite a shaft that could distinguish the brave." His contemporaries among the Athenians, in any case, believed that Cleon served bravely at Amphipolis. He and those who fought with him were buried in the Cerameicus, where the state's honored war dead were entombed. We should not doubt his courage any more than his countrymen did.

In spite of his death his men stood their ground and struggled bravely; they were not routed until attacked by javelin throwers and cavalry. The Athenian cavalry seems to have been left behind at Eion, since no battle had been intended or expected. About six hundred Athenians were killed. While only seven Spartans fell, among whom was Brasidas, who was carried from the field still breathing, but he lived long enough to learn he had won his final battle.

THE DEATH OF BRASIDAS AND CLEON

THE BATTLE OF AMPHIPOLIS removed the two leaders whom Thucydides characterized as "the men on each side most opposed to peace" (5.16.1). The Amphipolitans buried Brasidas within the city in a spot facing the agora, built a monument to him, adopted him as founder of the city, and worshiped him as a hero whom they commemorated with annual athletic contests and sacrifices. He was deeply devoted to the destruction of the Athenian Empire and the restoration of the supremacy of Sparta in the Greek world. Had he lived, the war in the north would have continued, and his death was a serious setback for those who wanted to fight on to victory.

Like Brasidas, Cleon pursued an aggressive policy out of sincere conviction that it was the best course for his city. His public style, no doubt, lowered the tone of Athenian political life, and we need not approve of his harshness toward rebellious allies, but Cleon did represent a broad spectrum of opinion. He always carried his political positions forward energetically and bravely and presented them honestly and directly. No more than Pericles did he flatter the masses but addressed them in the same severe, challenging, realistic manner. He put his own life on the line, serving on the expeditions he recommended and dying on the last of them.

Whatever Thucydides' "sensible men" might think, Athens was not, in fact, better off after Cleon's death. His views endured through the efforts of other men, some of whom lacked his capacity, some his patriotism, others his honesty, and still others his courage. Thucydides is correct, however, in asserting that Cleon's death, like that of Brasidas, made peace a genuine possibility. No one now remaining in power in Athens had sufficient stature to oppose successfully the peace advocated by Nicias.

THE COMING OF PEACE

VICTORY AT AMPHIPOLIS had encouraged the Spartans to send reinforcements to Thrace, but when the news of Brasidas' death reached them they turned back, their chief commander, Ramphias being well aware of sentiment in Sparta: "They went back chiefly because they knew when they set out, that the Spartans were more inclined toward peace" (5.13.2). Recent events in the northeast had not substantially changed the realities of the war. Since the capture of their men at Sphacteria the Spartans had not ravaged Attica lest their men held prisoner in Athens be killed. The Peloponnesian navy no longer existed and had in any event failed to support rebellions by Athens' subjects. Brasidas' daring strategy needed a much greater commitment of men than Sparta could or would make, and reinforcements could not get through while Athens ruled the sea and Perdiccas and his Thessalian allies remained hostile on land.

Sparta also had much to fear from a continuation of the war. The Athenians could still launch assaults from Pylos and Cythera. The helots were deserting in increasing numbers, and the Spartans feared their inciting another great helot rebellion. A new threat loomed in the approaching expiration of Sparta's Thirty Years' Treaty with Argos. The Argives were insisting on the restoration of Cynuria, an unacceptable condition for renewing the agreement, but if the war continued the Spartans would risk the establishment of a deadly Argive-Athenian coalition, which might be further strengthened by the desertion of Spartan allies. Sparta had, for example, lately quarreled with Mantinea and Elis, both of which were democracies that feared Spartan retribution and would in all likelihood join with Argos.

Many leading Spartans, moreover, had private reasons for seeking peace. Members of Sparta's principal families were eager to bring home their relatives who were among the prisoners at Athens. Thucydides tells us that King Pleistoanax "was very eager for a treaty" (5.17.1), which would certainly ameliorate his difficult situation: his enemies, who had never forgiven him for failing to invade and destroy Attica in the First Peloponnesian War, had accused him of bribing the Delphic Oracle to bring about his restoration; considering the restoration illegal, they believed it was at the root of every defeat or misfortune the Spartans suffered. The conclusion of a treaty, Pleistoanax hoped, would reduce occasions for these personal attacks as well.

Objectively, the Athenians seem to have had less motivation for negotiating a peace. Their territory had not been ravaged for over three years, and they continued to hold the prisoners who guaranteed that immunity. Although the treasury reserve continued to shrink, the Athenians had enough resources to keep fighting in 421 and for at least three years longer, but most of them did not wish to. Their failures in Megara and Boeotia and the rebellions in Thrace were discouraging, and their losses at Delium were shocking. They were also afraid of more uprisings in the empire, though such concerns were more exaggerated than legitimate, for there was little danger of revolt in the Aegean or Asia Minor as long as Athens ruled the seas. Even the insurrections in the Chalcidice were no longer likely to spread. For the Athenians, however, such fears were a reality, and they helped move them toward peace.

In Athens the series of recent defeats and the loss of the main voices for war left Nicias and the peace party in a strong position. Thucydides, again, focuses on Nicias' private motives as a significant force, for as the most successful Athenian general of his time, he wanted "to hand down a name to posterity as a man who had never done harm to his city" (5.16.1). Nicias was also cautious by nature and subscribed to Pericles' policy of fighting with determination and restraint. After the victory at Pylos made a Periclean peace seem possible he consistently sought to convince the Athenians to adopt that plan because he sincerely believed it was was the best course for them.

Discouragement with the progress of the war, financial problems, and the removal of the leaders of the war party all help explain a movement toward peace, yet we still may wonder why the Athenians, after so many sacrifices, should have been willing to call a halt to the war at the very moment when their prospects were more favorable than at any time since Pylos. All they needed to do was wait for Argos to break off its treaty with Sparta and join with Athens in a renewed effort. A coalition of Argos, Mantinea, Elis, and perhaps others could be left to engage the Spartans in the Peloponnesus, while the Athenians could launch simultaneous attacks from Pylos and Cythera and try to stir up the helots. These incursions would completely occupy the Peloponnesians, leaving Athens free to invade Megara. There was a good chance that the Peloponnesian League might subsequently collapse, destroying Sparta's power and leaving Athens free to deal with an isolated Boeotia. At the very least, Sparta would be badly weakened and forced to make a peace more favorable to Athens.

But such rational calculations ignore the deep war-weariness also felt by the Athenians in 421. They had suffered heavy losses in battle and in the plague, they had wasted treasure long in the accumulation, and they had seen their homes in the country destroyed, their olive trees and grape vines cut down. The men of property and the farmers were the parties most receptive to peace, as Aristophanes makes humorously clear in his comedy *Acharnians*, produced early in 425. His hero Dicaeopolis represents the typical Attic farmer, crowded into Athens against his will, eager to return to his farm.

While peace talks were going on, men "longed for the old undefiled life without war," hearing with pleasure the line from a chorus in the *Erechtheus* of Euripides: "Let my spear he unused for the spider to cover with webs" (and gladly), recalling the saying that "in peace sleepers are awakened not by the trumpet but by the cock" (Plutarch, *Nicias* 9.5). Aristophanes' *Peace*, produced in the spring of 421, just before the peace was finally approved, is filled with the same longing, but expressed joyously at the prospect of an end to the war. The comedy's hero Trygaeus sings a paean to Peace:

> Think of all the thousand pleasures,
> Comrades, which to Peace we owe,
> All the life of ease and comfort
> Which she gave us long ago;
> Figs and olives, wine and myrtles,
> Luscious fruits preserved and dried,
> Banks of fragrant violets, blowing
>   hearts are yearning,
> Joys that we have missed so long,
> Comrades, here is Peace returning,
> Greet her back with dance and song!
>   (571–81)

Nicias was an excellent leader of the peace party, for his military success and public displays of piety made him popular in Athens. His well-known advocacy of peace and the special kindness he had shown to their prisoners had also won the confidence of the Spartans, which ought to have qualified him as the perfect negotiator. But the Athenians continued to resist a negotiated peace, probably because they were fully aware of the advantages that could soon come their way. The Spartans, therefore, risked a desperate gamble to force a peace. Toward the beginning of spring "there was a preliminary flourish of preparation on the part of the Spartans" as though for the building of a permanent fort in Attica, to make the Athenians "more inclined to listen" (5.17.2). Out of fear and anger the Athenians might well have responded by killing the prisoners at once and putting an end to the chance for peace, but the Spartan bluff worked. The Athenians finally agreed to make peace on the general principle of status quo ante bellum, with the necessary exceptions that Thebes was to keep Plataea and Athens would keep Nisaea and the former Corinthian territories of Sollium and Anactorium in the west.

THE PEACE OF NICIAS

THE PEACE, sworn for fifty years, allowed free access to common shrines, established the independence of the temple of Apollo at Delphi, and provided for the resolution of disputes by nonbelligerent means. Its territorial provisions restored the Athenian border fort of Panactum that had been betrayed to the Boeotians in 422. Sparta also promised to return Amphipolis to Athens, although its citizens and those of other cities were free to leave and take their property with them. The Spartans also abandoned Torone, Scione, and such other towns as the Athenians had recaptured or were still besieging. For the men of Scione this meant death, since the Athenian assembly had already decreed their fate. The other rebellious Thracian cities were divided into two categories. In the first were Amphipolis and the cities Athens had recovered, which were restored to Athenian control. Argilus, Stagirus, Acanthus, Stolus, Olynthus, and Spartolus, however, embarrassed the Spartans, who had encouraged their revolts in the name of Greek freedom. To save face for Sparta the Athenians allowed these cities to pay only the original tribute, and not the increased assessment of 425. They were to be neutrals, belonging to neither alliance, but the Athenians were permitted to use peaceful persuasion to try to win them back. For all its obfuscating legalisms, this amounted to the Spartans' betrayal of their northern allies.

The Athenians, too, made important concessions, giving an unusual degree of independence to the Chalcidians, and agreeing to restore their bases on the periphery of the Peloponnesus: Pylos, Cythera, and Methana. Athens also consented to give back the island of Atalante and Pteleum (perhaps a town on the coast of Achaea). The clause exchanging prisoners deprived the Athenians of their primary deterrent against Sparta, but it was an essential for peace. The final clause made clear that Athens and Sparta had also imposed the peace on their allies: "If either side forgets anything, about anything whatsoever, it shall be in accordance with the oath for both sides, employing just discussions, to make a change wherever it seems good to both sides, the Athenians and the Spartans" (5.18.11).

The Athenians ratified the treaty only a few days later than ten years after the first invasion of Attica, perhaps about March 12, 421. The peace brought great joy to the majority of Athenians and Spartans, and of the Greeks as a whole. In Athens, "it was the opinion of most men that it was manifestly a release from evils, and Nicias was in every mouth as a man dear to the gods, on whom, because of his piety, the divine forces had bestowed the honor of giving his name to the greatest and most beautiful of blessings" (Plutarch, *Nicias* 9.6).

The agreement has always been known as the Peace of Nicias, and he more than any other individual, was responsible for having brought it to fruition. It might appear that the Archidamian War had rewarded Athens with precisely the kind of victory Pericles had sought, but that was hardly the case. Pericles' goal had been to place the international order established in 445 on a secure footing by convincing the Spartans that they could not coerce Athens, that the Athenians were invulnerable, that the empire was a permanent reality, and that grievances had to be settled by discussion, negotiation, or arbitration and not by threats and force.

The peace did not bring that about, nor was it able to restore the territorial status quo. Amphipolis and Panactum, for example, were held by people hostile to Athens and not subservient to Sparta, so their return to Athens could not be assumed. Plataea, Athens' comrade in arms at Marathon and loyal ally ever since, was abandoned to Theban control. The loss of Amphipolis was compensated by the gain of Nisaea, but Pericles would surely have been appalled by the settlement made with the rebellious cities of Chalcidice. Their future status, even the amount of tribute they would pay, was fixed not by Athenians, but by a provision in a treaty between Athens and Sparta. This violated the principle for which Pericles had entered the war: the legitimacy, integrity, and independence of the Athenian Empire.

The manner by which peace had been achieved was even more unsatisfactory. There was no evidence that the Spartans had come to accept that Athens was invulnerable or that its empire was a permanent fact of life. The main forces compelling Sparta to peace were temporary difficulties: the desire to recover its prisoners, and the threat of an Argive alliance with Athens. The war faction was not destroyed or permanently discredited, and there was no assurance that, after restoring order in the Peloponnesus, the Spartans would not seek vengeance and supremacy. The peace gave them time to recover and left them capable of revenge, and did little to convince them of their inability to win the war. The Athenians, for their part, had been forced to make peace, by a military threat. In the end, the Ten Years' War brought no desired result to either side: it did not destroy the Athenian Empire, bring freedom to the Greeks, or put an end to Sparta's fear of Athenian power, nor did it guarantee Athens the security for which Pericles risked war. The expenditure of lives, suffering, and money was ultimately in vain.

The Peace of Nicias, like the Thirty Years' Peace that concluded the First Peloponnesian War, put a halt to a conflict that neither side had been able to win, but there the resemblance ends. The territorial provisions in 445 were realistic. The treaty of 421 was not, for it rested on implausible Spartan promises to restore Amphipolis and Panactum to Athens, and did not even mention Nisaea, Sollium, and Anactorium, which were certain to embitter Megara and Corinth and so threaten the peace. The earlier treaty was agreed to by an Athens firmly under the control of Pericles, a leader sincerely committed to observing both its letter and spirit, while the Spartans had reason to be satisfied with its terms.

The Athens of 421 lacked stable leadership; its policy had shifted many times in recent years, and the enemies of the peace were overcome primarily because of the temporary absence of influential voices among them. In Sparta many authoritative Spartans disapproved the peace. New ephors could bring opponents of the agreement to power, and even the ephors who had made it were less than zealous to carry out all its provisions. In 445 Sparta's allies accepted the peace without objection, but in 421 Boeotia, Corinth, Elis, Megara, and the Thracian allies refused to cooperate. In 445 the Argives were tied by treaty to Sparta; in 421 they belonged to neither alliance and were eager to regain their old hegemony in the Peloponnesus and to exploit the divisions in the Greek world in their own interest. All these obstacles made the prospects for peace dubious from the start.

Few war-weary Athenians considered such problems as they laughed at Aristophanes' *Peace* at the Great Dionysian festival in 421. Brasidas and Cleon, the mortar and pestle of war, as Aristophanes called them, were dead, and the god of war himself was forced to leave the stage. Trygaeus and the chorus of Athenian farmers were now free to draw the goddess of peace, Eirene, from the pit where she had been buried for ten years.

Part Four

THE FALSE PEACE

THE PEACE OF NICIAS lasted no more than eight years and was seriously damaged and broken in spirit at once and repeatedly before its formal demise in 414. The central figure in Athens throughout this period was Nicias, the most lastingly important Athenian political leader since the death of Pericles. His strengths and weaknesses would be crucial to the course of events. A critical force in shaping the treaty and bringing it into being, he also determined how it would be carried out.

CHAPTER SIXTEEN

The Peace Unravels (421–420)

A TROUBLED PEACE

NOT SURPRISINGLY, serious weaknesses in the peace emerged almost immediately. The Athenians had had good luck in drawing lots to determine who should take the initial step in carrying out the treaty, leaving the Spartans to be the first to return such Athenian prisoners as they held. They also ordered Clearidas to surrender Amphipolis and to force the other cities of the neighborhood to accept the pact. Sparta's allies in Thrace refused the demand, and Clearidas claimed to be unable to force their compliance, but, in fact, he was unwilling to do so. He hurried back to Sparta to defend himself and to see if the treaty could be changed, which the Spartans did by making a slight but significant modification: he was to "restore Amphipolis, if possible, but if not, to withdraw whatever Peloponnesians were in it" (5.21.3).

The Athenians' chief material aim in making peace had been to recover Amphipolis, and this amendment effectively denied them its possession, abandoning it instead to their enemies. In dealing with their first obligation the Spartans therefore broke the treaty in both letter and spirit.

Sparta's older and nearer allies also undermined the peace from its inception, for in spite of extended Spartan efforts at persuasion, they would not accept the agreement. Megara was outraged that Athens was to keep Nisaea, interfering with its trade to the east. Elis rejected the peace because of a private quarrel with Sparta. The Boeotians, led by the Thebans, refused to restore to the Athenians either the border fortress of Panactum, which they had seized in 422, or the Athenian prisoners taken during the war. The Thebans' power and prestige had grown greatly since 431 and, fearing that an Athens undistracted by a Peloponnesian war would undo their gains, they negotiated a series of ten-day truces with the Athenians to avoid fighting them alone. What they really wanted was to get the Spartans to renew the war and destroy Athenian power.

The Corinthians were even less pleased with the peace, for their colony at Potidaea was again firmly in Athenian hands, and its citizens driven from their homes and scattered. Athens had also taken the Corinthian colonies at Sollium and Anactorium in the northwest.

THE SPARTAN-ATHENIAN ALLIANCE

THESE MOUNTING OBSTACLES soon threatened to turn Athens against the accord, and it could well have responded by refusing to restore Pylos and Cythera or to return the prisoners taken at Sphacteria. Such repudiations of the peace terms would also have encouraged Argos and raised the threat of an Argive-Athenian alliance, probably joined by such disaffected states as Elis and Mantinea. This would have created a nightmare for the Spartans, who were now forced to seek some diplomatic way out of this dangerous situation. They eventually offered a fifty-year defensive alliance, the terms of which required each side to defend the other against attack and to regard the attackers as a common enemy, and committed the Athenians to give assistance to the Spartans in the event of a helot rebellion. A final clause permitted changes in the terms of the alliance by mutual consent. The Athenians agreed to the pact and at its approval, as a token of good faith in their new allies, they surrendered the Spartan prisoners, whom they had held since 425.

Why did the Athenians accept the alliance and hand over the prisoners, their security against a Spartan invasion, even though the Spartans had failed to carry out their agreements in the peace treaty? So long as they held the prisoners they were also safe from an attack by Sparta's allies, who would not dare attack Athens without Spartan support.

While Nicias and his Athenian supporters assented to the alliance as a means to shore up the faltering peace, they also welcomed it for itself. The prospect of a Spartan affiliation aroused visions of a return to the happy and glorious pro-Spartan policy of Cimon in the decades after the Persian War. This period had been a good one for Athens, preserving peace among the Greeks and allowing the Athenians to expand their Aegean empire and increase their prosperity, but by 421 the Cimonian approach was no longer feasible. Now the dominant memories in both parties' minds were of long and bitter civil wars rather than a united effort against a common enemy, which meant there was little good will on which to build an enduring peace. Under such circumstances trust could not be assumed but would have to be earned. From that perspective the alliance may even have undermined the chances for peace, for it allowed Sparta to continue to ignore its obligations under the peace treaty and thereby increased Athenian skepticism.

Nicias and his associates viewed the situation differently, however. To them, the failure of the Megarian and Boeotian campaigns and the defeats at Delium and Amphipolis only demonstrated the danger of continuing the conflict. The Athenians should act generously, and take the first step in creating a climate of mutual trust.

Had they rejected the alliance with Sparta, what alternative would the Athenians have had? In fact a rare opportunity seemed to present itself. The Athenians could encourage a new coalition led by Argos and joined by the other democratic states of the Peloponnesus, Elis and Mantinea. They could then join this new alliance themselves, send an army into the Peloponnesus, and force a battle with vastly improved chances for success. They could improve those chances by distracting the Spartans with helot raids launched from Pylos and raids on coastal towns from the sea. A victory in such a battle would probably have put an end to the Peloponnesian League and to Spartan power. But with war-weariness continuing to be the dominant sentiment, and Nicias still the dominant figure in Athenian politics, such a course was unlikely.

If an aggressive policy was impossible in 421, there remained one other choice: the Athenians could reject the alliance without breaking the Peace of Nicias and allow events to take their course. Without risking any lives or committing any other resources Athens could thereby keep the pressure on Sparta, while possession of the Spartan prisoners and the new Argive threat would guarantee Athens against attack. So long as Athens held aloof from Sparta, the Argives would be encouraged by the prospect of an alliance with Athens in the near future.

helots could escape to Pylos and, perhaps, foment a new rebellion in Messenia and Laconia. Athens could only have benefited from the turmoil in the Peloponnesian League caused by the allied defections, and an Athenian refusal to join with Sparta would have increased both that unrest and the danger to Sparta. So moderate, so safe, yet so promising a policy was available to the Athenians, but they chose instead to make the alliance.

THE ARGIVE LEAGUE

INEVITABLY THE NEW PACT between Athens and Sparta produced counteractions by the dissident states. The Corinthians met privately with Argive magistrates and warned them that the alliance was undoubtedly aimed at the "enslavement of the Peloponnesus," and urged the Argives to lead a new coalition to defend Peloponnesian freedom. This seemed to suggest the formation of a separate league that could stand apart from the two older power blocs and resist their combined force.

The success of Corinth's plan rested in large part on the quarrel between the various factions in Sparta. The men who accepted the peace and the subsequent Athenian alliance were motivated by concerns over Argos, and as long as that apprehension persisted Sparta would not be eager for war. Had the Corinthians not made their appeal, Argos would have been intimidated by the alliance into its customary inaction and thus eliminated the source of Spartan fear, even though experience had shown that such fear was an essential provocation to move Sparta to a major war. As they had exploited anxiety about the Athenians to drive the Spartans to war in 431, the Corinthians meant to employ similar concerns about Argos to do so again ten years later, though the task would now be more intricate and difficult. In the past Corinth had used the threat of secession and the prospect of an alliance with Argos as an effective weapon, but to succeed this time it would have to convince Sparta that the prospect of an Argive alliance was real.

The Argives accordingly appointed twelve men with full powers to make an alliance with any state with the exception of Athens and

Sparta, which could join only with the consent of the Argive assembly. Argos had good reasons, old and new, to make the attempt to form a new alliance system. Its hostility to Sparta dated back centuries, and it had never given up hope of winning back Cynuria. Because it would not extend its peace with Sparta without the region's return, war was, in any case, all but certain. To prepare for it, the Argives trained at public expense one thousand young men who were "strongest in body and in wealth" (Diodorus 12.75.7) as an elite corps capable of fighting the Spartan phalanx. With such means and the ambition of winning mastery of the Peloponnesus the Argives gladly took the road pointed out by the Corinthians.

The Mantineans were first to join with Argos, for they had good reason to fear an attack by Sparta: they had expanded their territory at the expense of their neighbors, fought the Tegeans, and built a fort on the Laconian border. Argos seemed a source of protection, so the Mantineans eagerly made the alliance, the more readily because Mantinea, like Argos, had a democratic constitution. The news of Mantinea's defection caused a great stir among Sparta's allies in the Peloponnesus, who concluded that the Mantineans "knew something more" (5.29.2) than they, and who were therefore eager to join the new Argive coalition themselves.

Learning of the alliance the Spartans accused the Corinthians of instigating the entire affair and reminded them that an affiliation with Argos would violate the oaths that bound Corinth to Sparta, as well as Corinth's agreement to accept the decision of the majority in the Peloponnesian League. The Corinthians, they pointed out, were already in violation of those pledges by having refused to accept the Peace of Nicias. The Corinthian activists responded to these charges at a meeting attended by the other dissident cities. Concealing their true motives—to regain Sollium and Anactorium—they instead "offered as a pretext their unwillingness to betray their allies in Thrace" (5.30.2). Their argument may be paraphrased as follows: "We have given our oaths to the Potidaeans and our other Chalcidian friends in the Thracian region. They are still in bondage to the Athenians, and if we agree to the Peace of Nicias, we will be in violation of our oaths to the gods and heroes. In addition, the oath we took to accept the majority decision includes the clause 'unless there be a hindrance on the part of gods and heroes.' To betray the Chalcidians would surely be such a hindrance. It is not we but you are breaking your oaths by abandoning your allies and collaborating with the enslavers of Greece."

This cunning and attractive refutation portrayed the new association as a continuation of the struggle against Athenian tyranny, a means of keeping faith with trusting allies betrayed by Spartan selfishness. The Spartans, of course, were not convinced.

Following the meeting the Argive ambassadors urged the Corinthians to join their alliance at once, but the Corinthians continued to procrastinate and asked the Argives to return for the next meeting of their assembly. The likeliest reason for the delay is that conservatives at Corinth still held back, waiting for more oligarchic states to join.

The next state to enter the coalition was Elis, whose formal constitution was democratic, but whose social system and customs were oligarchic. The Eleans made an alliance with the Corinthians before coming to Argos to conclude a pact there, "as they had been instructed" (5.31.1) by the Corinthians, and their adherence to the new league helped it get started. Only then did the Corinthians join the Argive alliance, bringing with them the loyal and fiercely anti-Athenian Chalcidians.

The Megarians and Boeotians, however, continued to reject Argive overtures, put off by the democratic constitution of Argos. Now the Corinthians turned to Tegea, a strategically located and solid oligarchy whose defection, they believed, would bring over the entire Peloponnesian League. The Tegeans, however, declined, striking a serious blow at the plan. "The Corinthians, who had worked eagerly up to then, slackened in their zeal and became afraid that no one else would join them" (5.32.4).

The Corinthian activists made one last effort to preserve their scheme, asking the Boeotians to join them in the Argive alliance and "to take other actions in common." They also requested that the Boeotians obtain for them the same ten days' truce that the Boeotians had with the Athenians, as well as assurances that if the Athenians declined this request, Boeotia would renounce its own armistice and make no further truce without the Corinthians.

The Corinthians' ploy was obvious, for the Athenians were sure to refuse, and the Boeotians would subsequently find themselves unprotected against Athens, tied to Corinth, and drawn into the Argive co-alition. The Boeotians' response was therefore friendly but cautious, and while they delayed a decision in regard to the Argive alliance, they did agree to go to Athens and ask for a truce for Corinth. The Athenians, of course, did not consent, answering that if they were indeed the allies of the Spartans, the Corinthians already had a truce. The Boeotians continued their own truce with Athens, angering the Corinthians, who claimed that the Boeotians had broken a promise, but to little effect.

While these complicated diplomatic negotiations went forward, the Athenians finally completed their siege of Scione, killing and enslaving its survivors in accordance with the decree proposed by Cleon in 423. Perhaps to remind themselves and others that the Spartans had been the first to take such measures, they settled the survivors of Plataea there. Even this act of terror, however, did not restore order in the Chalcidice and the Thracian district of the empire. Amphipolis remained in hostile hands and, later in the summer, the Dians captured the Chalcidic town of Thyssus on the promontory of Athos, though it was allied to Athens. Still, Athens took no action. The recovery of Amphipolis would have required a siege no less difficult than the one at Potidaea. No Athenian seems to have urged an attack on the rebellious colony, but there must have been great frustration and growing anger at the Spartans' failure to deliver Amphipolis.

SPARTA'S PROBLEMS

WHILE THE CORINTHIANS were working toward the creation of the Argive League, the Spartans proceeded to take the offensive against their enemies in the Peloponnesus. King Pleistoanax led the Spartan army into Parrasia, a district to the west of Mantinea, which the Mantineans had subjugated during the war (see Map 1). Their Argive allies sent a force to guard Mantinea itself, while its citizens tried in vain to protect the threatened territory. After restoring Parrasian independence and destroying the fort erected by the Mantineans, the Spartans withdrew. They next sent a garrison to dominate Lepreum, the region between Elis and Messenia and the source of their quarrel with the Eleans.

These actions established some degree of security on Sparta's frontiers and in the helot country, but the Spartans were facing internal problems as well. Clearidas had brought Brasidas' army back from Amphipolis, a force that included seven hundred helots whose service had won them their freedom and the right to live wherever they liked. Seven hundred helots moving freely about Laconia understandably unnerved the Spartans, as did the appearance of a new class of men, the *neodamodeis*. Men of this status, who are mentioned here for the first time in Spartan history, were liberated helots who seem to have lived freely; probably they, too, received their emancipation for military service well done. The Spartans also had to contend with the continuing shrinkage of the population from which they drew their army. For various reasons the number of "equals" who became Spartan hoplites decreased throughout the fifth and fourth centuries, from its level of five thousand at Plataea in 479. However, the need to place a garrison at Lepreum enabled the Spartans to address both matters simultaneously, as they sent both Brasidas' veterans and the *neodamodeis* to settle the land on the Elean frontier.

Another issue they faced was the return of the men who had surrendered at Sphacteria and spent years as prisoners in Athens. At first the former hostages simply resumed the often high and influential positions they had previously occupied in Spartan society; some of them even held public office. The Spartans, however, came to fear that the restored prisoners would cause trouble because of the dishonor that had incurred by their surrender, so they were disenfranchised, but this potentially dangerous group was allowed to remain in Sparta. The necessity of contending with such internal threats helps explain why most Spartans continued to support a cautious and peaceful foreign policy. The recently improved security on the Elean and Mantinean frontiers, the diminished challenge from the Argive coalition, and the pacific behavior of the Athenians all gave support to the cause of the peace faction.

The Athenians, however, continued to resent Sparta's failure to carry out its treaty obligations. Although the Spartans kept pledging to help Athens compel Corinth, Boeotia, and Megara to accept the peace, they failed to act each time the promise came due. Sparta's behavior at Amphipolis was even more vexing. By withdrawing their army instead of using it to force Amphipolis back into Athenian control the Spartans were in clear violation of the treaty terms, and the Athenians increasingly came to believe that the Spartans had deliberately deceived and cheated them. "Suspect[ing] the Spartans of evil intentions" the Athenians refused to restore Pylos, and "even regretted that they had restored the prisoners from the island and kept holding on to the other places, waiting until the Spartans should carry out their promises" (5.35.4).

In response the Spartans kept asking Athens to restore Pylos or at least to remove the Messenians and escaped helots currently living there. They claimed to have done all they could to return Amphipolis and assured the Athenians they would carry out their other commitments. In short, they offered nothing but new promises in place of the old, unfulfilled ones, but the peace forces at Athens were still strong enough to extract further concessions from their fellow citizens. The Athenians consequently withdrew the Messenians and helots from Pylos and settled them on the island of Cephallenia.

Even as the Athenians made this effort at appeasement, Sparta's commitment to the peace came further into question. At the beginning of autumn 421, new ephors took office, two of whom, Xenares and Cleobulus, "were most eager to break off the treaty" (5.36.1). They pursued a course intended to renew the war against Athens, and an opportunity to do so soon arose. The peace party, which was still dominant, had recently called a conference at Sparta, including the Athenians, the loyal allies, as well as the Boeotians and Corinthians, to try again to achieve a general acceptance of the treaty. Its complete failure probably encouraged Xenares and Cleobulus to attempt their complicated scheme.

While the Corinthians were trying to use an Argive alliance to frighten the Spartans into breaking the peace, the bellicose ephors took the opposite tack. The believed that the Spartans had made the peace and the Athenian alliance largely because of the threat from Argos and their desire to recover the Sphacterian prisoners and Pylos. Once these concerns were addressed, they reasoned, Sparta would be ready to resume the war. All that remained was to regain Pylos and put an end to the Argive League. Acting secretly, the two ephors proposed to the Corinthian and Boeotian ambassadors that their two states should cooperate, and that the Boeotians should make an alliance with Argos and then try to move the Argives into an alliance with Sparta. A pact with the Argives, they pointed out, would make it easier to fight a war outside the Peloponnesus. They also asked the Boeotians to give Panactum to the Spartans so that they could exchange it for Pylos, "and so more easily be in a position to go to war against Athens" (5.36.2).

THE CORINTHIANS' MYSTERIOUS POLICY

As the Corinthian and Boeotian ambassadors made their way home from Sparta they were stopped by two high Argive magistrates, who asked the Boeotians to join the Argive alliance. This time the Argives put the offer in deliberately ambiguous language: "Employing a common policy, they could make war against or a treaty with the Spartans or with any one else they might choose" (5.37.2). The Argives still aimed at Peloponnesian hegemony at the expense of Sparta, but their equivocal proposal allowed a different interpretation without committing Argos to anything. The Boeotians received the invitation with pleasure, "for by luck the Argives had asked them to do the same thing their Spartan friends had instructed them" (5.37.3). Back home, the Boeotarchs were equally gratified by the news. But the Spartans' and Argives' requests were identical only on the surface, for they aimed to achieve precisely the opposite results. Still, the Boeotarchs agreed to send ambassadors to Argos to conclude the alliance, pending approval by the Boeotian federal council.

The Corinthians must have been behind the next development: "The Boeotarchs, the Corinthians, Megarians, and the ambassadors from Thrace decided first to swear oaths to each other to assist any one of them who needed defense, should the occasion arise and to make neither war nor peace without a common agreement; and that only then should the Boeotians and Megarians (for they pursued the same policies) make a treaty with the Argives" (5.38.1). The Chalcidians in Thrace were satellites of Corinth, as were the Megarians of Boeotia.

The Boeotians themselves needed no such agreement, for they were ready to join with Argos and, since Corinth was already an Argive ally, the common agreement offered no benefit to Boeotia. Ultimately, this scheme for joint action was only an expanded version of the earlier one proposed by the Corinthians, without success.

The Corinthians knew that the Boeotians did not trust them, for they had rejected the earlier Corinthian proposal, regarded the Corinthians as rebels from the Spartan alliance, and feared that any agreement they entered into with Corinth would be certain to offend Sparta. The Boeotarchs presented to the Boeotian federal council, which was the sovereign power, resolutions for concluding the common agreement with Megara, Corinth, and the Chalcidians in Thrace. They concealed the secret plans behind the proposal, for Xenares and Cleobulus would have been in serious trouble if word of their private negotiations had reached Sparta. The Boeotarchs had been relying on their own authority to secure the passage of the proposal, but these were not normal times, and the council turned them down, "fearing that they might be acting against the Spartans by swearing oaths with rebels from their alliance" (5.38.3). Their rejection, unforeseen by the Boeotarchs but perhaps not by the Corinthians, put an end to the discussion. The Corinthians and the Chalcidians returned home, and the Boeotarchs did not dare bring up an Argive alliance. No envoys went to Argos to negotiate a treaty, "and there was neglect and a waste of time in the whole business" (5.38.4).

THE BOEOTIANS

MEANWHILE, the friends of peace in Sparta were also eager to recover Pylos and believed if they could convince the Boeotians to restore Panactum and the Athenian prisoners that they still held, the Athenians would return Pylos to Sparta. Since they continued to hold that view even after many talks with the Athenians, they must have been encouraged in it by the Athenian negotiators, presumably Nicias and his associates. With both factions in favor of the mission, the Spartans sent an official embassy to Boeotia to petition for the concessions to Athens. The Boeotians' response indicates that their war faction had by now developed a new plan: they said they would not return Panactum unless the Spartans made a separate treaty with them comparable to the one Sparta had negotiated with the Athenians. The Spartans knew that this would be a violation of their treaty with Athens, which implied that neither state could make peace or war without mutual consent. But a breach with Athens was precisely what the war faction wanted, so it supported the proposal for a Boeotian alliance. Without a majority, however the war faction needed additional support from the friends of peace. But much as all Spartans may have wanted to regain Pylos, why would any of them have believed that the Athenians would deliver it, especially when confronted with the treachery of a Spartan treaty with Boeotia? The only plausible explanation is that the Spartans put their faith in the apparently limitless forbearance of the peace faction at Athens and its ongoing control of Athenian policy. In early March 420 the Spartans accordingly made the treaty with Boeotia guaranteeing the Boeotians against an Athenian attack.

Even as the Boeotians welcomed the agreements as a blow against the Spartan-Athenian alliance, they were preparing to deceive their Spartan allies. They began at once to demolish the fort at Panactum, depriving Athens of an important border stronghold. Although the Spartans knew nothing of this plot the Corinthians were probably involved in it, for it accorded with their belief that conflict and fear, not comfort and security, would goad Sparta to fight.

Meanwhile, the Argives waited for Boeotian ambassadors to negotiate the promised alliance, but none was forthcoming. Instead they learned that Panactum was being demolished and that Sparta had made a treaty with Boeotia. They assumed that they had been betrayed, that Sparta was behind the whole affair, and that it had persuaded the Athenians to accept the destruction of Panactum by bringing Boeotia into their mutual alliance. The Argives were now in a panic; they could no longer make a treaty with either Boeotia or with Athens, and they feared that their own coalition would break up and its members go over to Sparta. Their greatest concern was that they would soon have to face a coalition of the Peloponnesians led by Sparta, the Boeotians, and the Athenians. The terrified Argives therefore sent envoys to Sparta "as quickly as possible" to try "to make a treaty however they could so that they might have peace" (5.40.3).

The Argive negotiations for an alliance with Sparta reflected eagerness on both sides. Argos wanted arbitration over Cynuria by a third party; the Spartans wanted a simple renewal of the old treaty, which left the disputed territory in their hands. The Argives offered to accept a fifty years' treaty for the present, provided that at any time in the future either side could request a battle of limited scope to decide control of Cynuria. The Spartans initially dismissed this proposal as absurd, but after considering it carefully, they agreed to the terms and signed the treaty, "for they were eager to have Argive friendship, regardless" (5.4.3). The Argive negotiators were to return to Sparta with official approval toward the end of June, but their delay in doing so allowed events to take a different course.

CHAPTER SEVENTEEN

The Alliance of Athens and Argos (420–418)

THE ATHENIAN BREACH WITH SPARTA

TO CARRY FORWARD their agreement with the Boeotians the Spartans went to take over Panactum and the Boeotians' Athenian prisoners so that they could restore both to the Athenians. They found the fort destroyed, but they received the prisoners and set forth for Athens to try to regain Pylos. They argued that Panactum, even though demolished, was properly reinstated for it could no longer harbor hostile forces. The Athenians, however, wanted their fort returned intact, and they were also furious at Sparta's pact with Boeotia, which not only violated the promise to make no new alliance without consultation but also exposed the deceit of Sparta's pledge to coerce its dissident allies. The Athenians accordingly "answered the envoys angrily and sent them away" (5.42.2).

Sparta's actions helped revive the Athenian war faction, dormant since the death of Cleon. Hyperbolus son of Antiphanes was a competitor for his position. Ancient writers call him "a leader of the masses," and in the *Peace*, performed in 421, Aristophanes speaks of him as the man who rules the assembly. He was a trierarch (a ship's captain and a man of means), an active member of the assembly who moved and amended decrees, and he may have been both a member of the council and a general. Some ancient writers treat him as a ridiculous and unworthy scoundrel, beneath even the other demagogues. Aristophanes may exaggerate in attributing to him imperial aims that reached as far as Carthage, but there is little doubt that he resisted the peace in 421 and the alliance with Sparta that followed it. He was a trained and skilled speaker, but he had neither the military reputation of Cleon nor the personal stature and influence of the rich and pious Nicias. Hyperbolus might well have emerged as leader of the war faction had he not been challenged by a potent and unexpected competitor.

Alcibiades son of Cleinias was between thirty and thirty-three years old when elected general in the spring of 420. (Thirty was the minimum age for the office.) He was wealthy enough to have entered chariots at the Olympic Games, so extraordinarily handsome that he was "hunted by many women of noble family" and "sought after by men as well" (Xenophon, *Memorabilia* 1.2.24), and was a talented speaker who had been trained by the best teachers of the day. His intellectual ability was widely admired, and his association with Socrates contributed significantly to that reputation, as well as having sharpened his skill in argumentation. Even his flaws seem to have helped him as much as they hurt. He had a speech defect, but people found it charming. He was willful, spoiled, unpredictable, and outrageous, but his antics won him at least as much admiration as envy and disapproval. This outsize character brought him attention and notoriety, which eased his early entry into public life.

It was Alcibiades' family that exerted the greatest influence on his political and military career, for the fame of his ancestors enabled him to reach a position of eminence in Athens unusually rapidly. The name "Alcibiades" is of Spartan origin and was acquired at least as far back as the sixth century as a result of the establishment of a relationship that made the family of Alcibiades Sparta's representatives (*proxenoi*) in Athens, although this role had lapsed by the time of the Peloponnesian War. Through his father he belonged to the noble clan of Salaminioi. His great-great-grandfather was an ally of Cleisthenes, the liberator of Athens and founder of the democracy. His great-grandfather fought as a trierarch in the Persian War on his own ship, manned at his own expense. His grandfather was an important enough political figure to be ostracized, and his father, an associate of Pericles, died fighting at the battle of Coronea in 447.

Alcibiades' mother was an Alcmaeonid, descendant of a most important family, which also included the mother of Pericles, so Pericles became the guardian of the boy Alcibiades and his brother Ariphron when their father died. From about the age of five Alcibiades and his wild and uncontrollable younger sibling were raised in the house of Athens' leading statesman. The childhood of Alcibiades coincided with the period when Pericles stood almost unchallenged as the most influential man in Athens. The talented boy, his ambition already whetted and his expectations elevated by the tradition of his father's house, conceived even greater ambitions by observing the power and glory of his guardian.

But great public success alone was not sufficient for the son of Cleinias and the ward of Pericles, and flatterers were not lacking to encourage his bold visions. As Plutarch put it: "It was . . . his love of distinction and love of fame to which his corrupters appealed, and thereby plunged him all too soon into ways of presumptuous scheming, persuading him that he had only to enter public life, and he would straightway cast into total eclipse the ordinary generals and public leaders, and not only that, he would even surpass Pericles in power and reputation among the Hellenes" (*Alcibiades* 7.3–4). Although in the still deferential democracy of the fifth century his noble family connections gave him a great advantage over his competitors, by 420 Alcibiades could also boast of a fine military record, having won a prize for valor from Phormio and fought with distinction at Potidaea and Delium as a cavalryman.

After the Spartan surrender at Sphacteria he tried to renew his family's old relationship with Sparta by looking after the Spartan prisoners. When the Ten Years' War ended, he hoped to negotiate with the Spartans and gain credit for the resulting peace, but the Spartans preferred to deal with the more experienced, reliable, and influential Nicias. Feeling slighted and insulted, Alcibiades reversed his position and attacked the Spartan alliance on the grounds that the Spartans were insincere. They had allied with Athens, he insisted, only to obtain a free hand against Argos; when Argos was dealt with, Sparta would again attack the isolated Athenians. Alcibiades sincerely preferred an alliance with Argos to one with Sparta; his assessment of Sparta's motives was certainly in line with those of Xenares, Cleobulus, and their faction.

When the demolition of Panactum and Sparta's alliance with Boeotia badly weakened Nicias' position, Alcibiades "raised a tumult in the assembly against Nicias, and slandered him with accusations all too plausible. Nicias himself . . . had refused to capture the enemy's men, who were cut off on the island of Sphacteria, and when others had captured them, he had released and given them back to the Lacedaemonians, whose favor he sought; and then he did not persuade those same Lacedaemonians, tried friend of theirs as he was, not to make a separate alliance with the Boeotians or even with the Corinthians, and yet when any Hellenes wished to be friends and allies of Athens, he tried to prevent it, unless it were the good pleasure of the Lacedaemonians" (Plutarch, *Alcibiades* 14.4–5). At the same time, Alcibiades privately urged the democratic leaders in Argos to come with Elean and Mantinean ambassadors and make an alliance with the Athenians: "The opportunity was ripe, and he himself would cooperate to the fullest" (5.43.3).

Alcibiades' invitation arrived in time to prevent the Argive alliance with Sparta, which they had sought only in the mistaken belief that Athens and Sparta were working together. Now that the truth was out, however, they abandoned all thought of the Spartan tie and rejoiced at the prospect of an alliance with Athens, "thinking that it was a city that had been friendly to them in the past, that it was a democracy like theirs, that it had a great power on the sea, and that it would fight on their side if war should break out" (5.44.1). After discovering the Argives' reversal, the Spartans tried to undo the damage by sending to Athens three men whom the Athenians regarded highly—Leon, Philocharidas, and Endius, the last from a family connected with that of Alcibiades—to prevent the Athenians from making an Argive alliance, to ask for the return of Pylos, and to assure the Athenians that Sparta's alliance with Boeotia in no way threatened them.

The Spartan envoys appeared before the Athenian council and announced that they had full powers to settle all differences. Alcibiades, fearing that if they made the same pronouncement to the assembly the Athenians would reject the Argive alliance, convinced them not to admit that they had come armed with such authority. In return he promised to use his influence to restore Pylos and settle all other differences. At the time of the actual assembly, however, when Alcibiades asked the envoys if they had full powers to make agreements and they said they did not, he stunned them by assailing their honesty. The assembly was soon ready to join with Argos, but an earthquake prevented conclusion of the alliance on the spot. The Spartan envoys had no opportunity to complain of Alcibiades' trick and must have left for

Sparta quickly, for we find no evidence that they attended the assembly the following day.

At that meeting Nicias sought a postponement of the vote. He insisted that a friendship with Sparta was more valuable than one with Argos and proposed an embassy to seek clarification of Sparta's intentions, since Alcibiades had prevented the Spartan ambassadors from saying what they had come to say. Nicias also argued that Athenian good fortune and security were at a high point and could only gain from peace; Sparta, on the other hand, threatened and insecure, stood to gain much from a quick battle that might reverse the situation. A contrary view might have focused on the perfidy and continuing hostility of Sparta and the danger it would present to Athenian safety after a period of recovery; according to this view, now, when Sparta was weakened and threatened by a powerful coalition, might be just the time to finish with it and eliminate the threat it had posed to Athens for so many years. But the Athenians were still so reluctant to resume the war that they postponed the Argive decision and instead sent Nicias as part of an embassy to Sparta. The ambassadors asked for the restoration of Panactum intact, the return of Amphipolis, and the relinquishment of the alliance with the Boeotians, unless they accepted the Peace of Nicias; they also announced that Athens would make an Argive alliance if Sparta did not abandon the Boeotians.

These demands destroyed any hope of conciliation, for the Spartans not surprisingly refused them. Nicias, nevertheless, asked Sparta to renew the oaths of the Peace of Nicias, "for he feared that if he came back with nothing accomplished he would be attacked, which, in fact, happened, since he was regarded as responsible for the peace with the Spartans" (5.47.4). Reluctant to recommence fighting, the Spartans agreed to that request, but they held to the Boeotian alliance. As Nicias had anticipated, the Athenian assembly flew into a rage when they learned the news, and they immediately made a treaty with Argos, Elis, and Mantinea. It was a mutual nonaggression pact and a defensive alliance on land and sea between the three Peloponnesian democracies and their dependencies on the one hand, and the Athenians and their subject states on the other, and was to last for one hundred years. The agreement was a triumph for Alcibiades and it set Athens on a new course inconsistent with the Peace of Nicias.

Still, for all their conflicts, both Athens and Sparta at least formally held to the treaties, because neither wished to assume the responsibility for breaking the peace. Meanwhile, the Corinthians, who were now free to make a more honest move, "pulled back from their allies and inclined once again to the Spartans" (5.48). Their tricky game had diminished the power of the Argive alliance, keeping it clear of oligarchic members and leaving it a coalition of democrats aligned with Athens, the kind of threat they hoped would move Sparta to renew the war. They also carefully preserved the defensive alliance they had made with Argos, Elis, and Mantinea, because the instability of Spartan politics might require them to make further strategic maneuvers and because their ambiguous position in respect to the Peloponnesian democracies might allow them to intervene at some crucial moment in the future.

SPARTAN HUMILIATIONS

THE ESTABLISHMENT of the Athenian alliance with the Peloponnesian democracies not only shifted the direction of politics in Athens but also encouraged Sparta's enemies to a new boldness. At the Olympic Games in the summer of 420 the Spartans suffered a great public insult when the Eleans leveled dubious charges against them for allegedly violating the sacred truce in which the festival took place and consequently barred them from the competition and from making the usual sacrifices. The Spartans appealed the decision, but the Olympic court, composed of Eleans, found against them and imposed a fine. The Eleans in turn offered to waive half the fine and pay the other half themselves if the Spartans would restore Lepreum to them. When the Spartans refused the Eleans made the humiliating demand that they swear an oath at the altar of Olympian Zeus, before all the assembled Greeks, to pay the fine later. The Spartans again refused, and were banned from temples, sacrifices, and competition in the games. Only their alliance with the other Peloponnesian democracies and Athens gave the Eleans the courage to undertake such provocative actions, and they defended the sanctuary against a possible Spartan attack with their own armed troops aided by a thousand men each from Argos and Mantinea and a troop of Athenian cavalry.

There was one Spartan, however, who refused to accept these insults tamely. Lichas son of Archesilaus stood out among his countrymen for the wealth and reputation of his family. His father had twice been an Olympic victor, and he himself had entered his chariot at the games as well as served as host for the foreigners who came to view the festival of the *Gymnopaediae* at Sparta. He was *proxenos* of the Argives and had close relations with the Boeotians. He may have been a supporter of the policy of Xenares and Cleobulus, and nobody was better suited to conduct the private negotiations that took place among Spartans, Argives, and Boeotians. His action at the Olympic Games of 420, at any rate, reveals a bold and defiant spirit.

Barred from taking part in the games as a Spartan, he formally gave his own chariot over to the Thebans and raced it in their name. When it came in first, Lichas strode onto the race course and placed a crown on the victorious charioteer, making it clear to all that the entry was his. The outraged Eleans sent the games' attendants to scourge him with whips and drive him out. In spite of fears that this might bring the Spartan army to the scene, the Spartans took no action, leaving the impression that they had been intimidated by Athens and its Peloponnesian allies. Just after the Olympic festival, perhaps encouraged by Sparta's disgrace, the Argives again invited the Corinthians to join in the new full alliance that included Athens. Spartan representatives came to Corinth, presumably to argue against the proposal, but an earthquake broke up the conference and prevented any action.

The general perception of their weakness soon caused the Spartans further embarrassment. In the winter of 420/19 neighboring peoples defeated their colonists at Heraclea in Trachis (see Map 14), killing the Spartan governor there. The Thebans sent a thousand hoplites, ostensibly to save the city, but in March they took control of it for themselves and dismissed the new Spartan governor. Thucydides says that they acted from fear that the Athenians would capture Heraclea, since the Spartans, distracted by their troubles in the Peloponnesus, could not defend it. We may guess that the Thebans, emboldened by Sparta's apparent impotence, seized the opportunity to reduce Spartan influence in central Greece and to increase their own. "The Spartans, nonetheless, were angry at them" (5.52.1), and these events further strained relations between Sparta and an important ally. Although Sparta had suffered little material harm as a result of it, the Athenian alliance with Argos, Elis, and Mantinea was achieving results even before Athens took any important action on its behalf.

ALCIBIADES IN THE PELOPONNESUS

EARLY IN THE SUMMER OF 419 the Athenians moved to strengthen the new league and to exploit Sparta's loss of prestige. Alcibiades, who had been reelected general, led a small force of Athenian hoplites and bowmen into the Peloponnesus, an expedition that had been planned in conjunction with the Argives and the other Peloponnesian allies. The ultimate target of Alcibiades' circuitous strategy was Corinth, whose defection would be a crippling blow to the Spartan alliance. The Athenians marched through the Peloponnesus from Argos to Mantinea and Elis, and from there to Patrae on the coast of Achaea, outside the Corinthian Gulf. He brought the city into an alliance with Athens and persuaded the people to build walls to the sea to keep communications open with Athens and provide resistance for any Spartan attack (see Map 1). The Corinthians, Sicyonians, and others in the neighborhood arrived in time to prevent the Athenians from constructing an Achaean fort at Rhium, opposite Naupactus at the narrowest point of the Gulf of Corinth.

All this was not a mere display of force but part of a plan to apply pressure to Corinth and other Spartan allies. The pact with Patrae and the fort at Rhium could effectively close off the mouth of the Corinthian Gulf to ships from Corinth, Sicyon, and Megara. Alcibiades brought only a small force of soldiers and no navy to Patrae, and its people could easily have withstood him had they desired. Their acceptance of the Athenian alliance shows how greatly the perception of Spartan decline, accentuated by Alcibiades' unchallenged march through the Peloponnesus, was hurting Sparta.

Alcibiades' second goal that summer was the capture of Epidaurus, which the Argives undertook. Thucydides reports that they made the usual complaint of a religious violation as the justification for their attack on the city, but their real purpose was to provide a shorter route by which the Athenians could come to their aid and, most important, "to keep Corinth quiet" (5.53.1).

The campaigns in Achaea and Epidaurus were both parts of a plan to threaten and isolate Corinth. The alliance with Patrae would help cut off the Corinthians' trade and communications with their western colonies, while the capture of Epidaurus would endanger them from two sides and demonstrate that Argos and Athens could defeat the Peloponnesian states allied to Sparta. With Epidaurus in hand, the Argives might march against Corinth from the south while the Athenians landed on the Corinthian coast, as Nicias had done in 425; such a threat might well force the Corinthians out of their Spartan alliance. Even their neutrality would prevent cooperation between the Boeotians and Spartans. In time Megara, and perhaps other Peloponnesian states, might also choose neutrality rather than to remain with a debilitated Sparta against the ever more powerful new league.

Here was a realistic strategy that offered the Athenians the promise of success without any great risk or investment. Alcibiades planned to use armed forces chiefly as a means of applying diplomatic pressure, aiming neither to bring the Peloponnesian enemy to battle, nor to exhaust its resources, but only to compel it to alter its course of action.

THE SPARTANS AGAINST ARGOS

THE ARGIVE INVASION of Epidaurian territory did indeed serve its intended purpose and convince the Spartans to act. Young King Agis marched the full Spartan army to Arcadia in a direction that would allow him to move toward Elis in the northwest, Mantinea to the north, or even northeast to Argos, if he chose. "No one knew where they were marching, not even the cities from which they were sent" (5.54.1).

The reason that Agis' real target was never revealed was that when he made the usual sacrifices at the border the omens proved unfavorable. The Spartans prepared to return home and sent word to their allies to plan to march again after the coming month, Carneius, which was a Dorian holy month. While the Spartans were sincerely religious, suspicion is aroused by the rare coincidence of two consecutive occasions in the summer of 419 on which omens were said to prevent the Spartan army under Agis from attacking the Argives or their allies. That suspicion is intensified by the knowledge that later in that same summer the Spartans, fearing that the Peloponnesian League might collapse, were not dissuaded from taking action by any unfavorable signs. The evidence strongly suggests that the unpropitious frontier sacrifices were merely a pretext.

Since he had been ordered out to fight, Agis could not merely withdraw, even in the face of adverse omens; the Epidaurians, their friends among the allies, and the many Spartans who did want to fight could not be restrained for any length of time. Agis, no doubt, gave the order to reassemble after the Carneian month to provide a pious justification for delay, while gaining time for the oligarchs to gain control of Argos. The anti-Spartan democrats who governed Argos resorted to religious chicanery of their own. They invaded Epidaurus on the twenty-seventh day of the month before Carneius and proceeded to call every day they remained in Epidaurian territory the twenty-seventh of that month, thus avoiding violation of the Carneian holiday. The Epidaurians asked their Peloponnesian allies for help, but some allies did not appear at all, pleading the holy month as an excuse, while others came no farther than the Epidaurian frontier.

Before the Argive League could take advantage of this opportunity to attack Epidaura the Athenians called a conference at Mantinea to discuss peace. Once again, Alcibiades chose military pressure and diplomacy rather than engaging in a hoplite battle, and planned to use Agis' hesitation as a means to persuade the Corinthians to abandon Sparta before they, too, were abandoned. At the conference, however, the equally cunning Corinthians accused the allies of hypocrisy, because while they spoke of peace, the Argives were in arms against the Epidaurians. They therefore demanded that both armies disband before the congress go forward. Perhaps they expected the Argives to refuse and thus provide an excuse for breaking up the gathering, but even after the Argives were persuaded to withdraw the meeting came to nothing. The Corinthians must have understood that their withdrawal from the Spartan alliance would probably have led to the triumph of Athens, so that when Alcibiades finally tried to force them to commit to the new league against Sparta, they rejected the peace terms, putting an end to the conference and to Alcibiades' hopes for a diplomatic victory.

The Argives quickly returned to ravaging Epidaurus, and once again the Spartans marched to their border in the direction of Argos, this time leaving no doubt where they were headed. The Athenians responded by sending a thousand hoplites to protect their Argive allies, while the Argives themselves withdrew to protect their own city. But once again, Agis' sacrifices produced unfavorable omens, and the army marched home. Even so, the mere threat of a Spartan attack had relieved the pressure on Epidaurus, which allowed Agis and his associates to avoid a direct confrontation with the Argives. Alcibiades took his own troops back to Athens, and the campaign of 419 came to an end with Corinth still allied to Sparta, making it clear that more than diplomacy would be needed to destroy the Peloponnesian League. This disappointing outcome not only created strains in the new alliance but revealed the tenuous balance of political power in Athens.

Over the following winter the Spartans sent three hundred men by sea to reinforce Epidaurus. Their route took them past Athenian bases at Aegina and Methana (see Map 1), which provoked complaints from Argos. Their treaty required the Athenians to prevent any enemy forces from crossing the territory of its allies, but the Athenians, despite controlling the sea, had permitted such a crossing. The Argives asked Athens to make amends by restoring the helots and Messenians from Naupactus to Pylos, from which they could harass the Spartans. This demand aimed to force the Athenians into a clearer commitment to fight Sparta.

In response Alcibiades persuaded the Athenians to inscribe on the stone bearing the Peace of Nicias the fact that the Spartans had broken their oaths, and to restore the helots to Pylos, from which they proceeded to ravage the countryside of Messenia. Still, the Athenians would not formally denounce the treaty, a further indication of the delicate political situation in Athens. While most Athenians supported the Argive alliance, no steady majority was in favor of renewing war against the Spartans. Alcibiades could persuade his countrymen to join an alliance where others would be responsible for most of the fighting, but not to take part in a war that would put many Athenian soldiers at risk. This division and ambiguity prevented the pursuit of any coherent, consistent policy.

The Spartans, too, were divided among, and perhaps within, themselves. Although none of the Athenian actions technically violated the treaties, each on its own terms was troubling, and Athenian assistance to the Argive attack on Epidaurus could simply not be ignored. Even so, the Spartans likewise did not declare the treaties ended and made no formal response to the Athenian declaration that Sparta had broken its oaths. Some Spartans were determined to maintain peace with Athens; others wished to resume the war but favored the adoption of different tactics. Some wanted a direct attack against Argos and its allies, including the Athenians; others hoped to detach Argos from the alliance by diplomacy and treason before resuming the war on Athens. In the end both Athens and Sparta stayed clear of any further involvement in the Epidaurian campaign, and the winter passed without incident.

The failure of Alcibiades' strategy to win immediate and decisive results and, perhaps, the fear of a renewed war against Sparta led to a fateful change in Athenian leadership. The Athenians elected Nicias and several of his friends as generals for 418, but rejected Alcibiades. The elections were in effect a vote for caution against adventure, and especially against the use of Athenian troops on Peloponnesian battle-fields, but because the Athenians did not abandon the Argive alliance they remained committed to helping their Peloponnesian allies. Perhaps they wanted their troops under more conservative leadership, not recognizing the contradiction of belonging to two alliances between hostile states.

CONFRONTATION IN THE ARGIVE PLAIN

IN MIDSUMMER 418 King Agis led 8,000 hoplites, including the full Spartan army, the Tegeans, and other Arcadians still loyal to Sparta, against Argos. Sparta's other allies, both inside and outside the Peloponnesus, were ordered to gather at Phlius; altogether these numbered about 12,000 hoplites, as well as 5,000 light-armed troops and 1,000 cavalry and mounted infantry from Boeotia. This extraordinarily large assembly was Sparta's answer to the menace posed by Alcibiades' policy. The Spartans launched the campaign "because their allies the Epidaurians were in distress, and of their other Peloponnesian allies, some were in rebellion and others ill-disposed. They thought that if they did not take action swiftly the trouble would go further" (5.57.2).

Against them the Argives mustered about 7,000 hoplites, the Eleans 3,000, and the Mantineans with their Arcadian allies about 2,000 more, for a total of about 12,000 troops; the Athenians agreed to send an additional 1,000 hoplites and 300 cavalry, but these had not yet arrived. If the Argives allowed the two enemy armies to join together they would be badly outnumbered: 20,000 hoplites from the Spartan alliance against 12,000 of their own, and 1,000 cavalry and 5,000 light-armed men from the Spartans against none of their own. They would, therefore, have to cut Agis off before his army could reach the northern army at Phlius, and so marched westward into Arcadia (see Map 17).

The direct route from Sparta to Phlius passed through Tegea and Mantinea, but Agis could not risk taking it, since he needed to avoid battle before meeting up with the northern army. Instead, he took a northwesterly route through Belmina, Methydrium, and Orchomenus. At Methydrium he encountered the Argives and their allies, who took up a position on a hill blocking the Spartans' path. They also obstructed the way to Argos and Mantinea, which meant that if Agis attempted to move eastward his army would be isolated in hostile territory and forced to battle alone against a numerically superior enemy. With the maneuver the Argives had achieved a great tactical success, and Agis could do nothing but occupy another hill facing the enemy. By nightfall Agis' situation seemed desperate: he would have to fight against bad odds or retreat and disgrace himself.

The arrival of dawn, however, revealed that the Spartan army had vanished: Agis had managed to elude the Argives by night and was well on his way to the rendezvous at Phlius, where he took command of "the finest Greek army assembled up to that time" (5.60.3). Some seventeen miles away lay Argos and its defending force, which had hurried home after the missed opportunity at Methydrium. Between the two armies

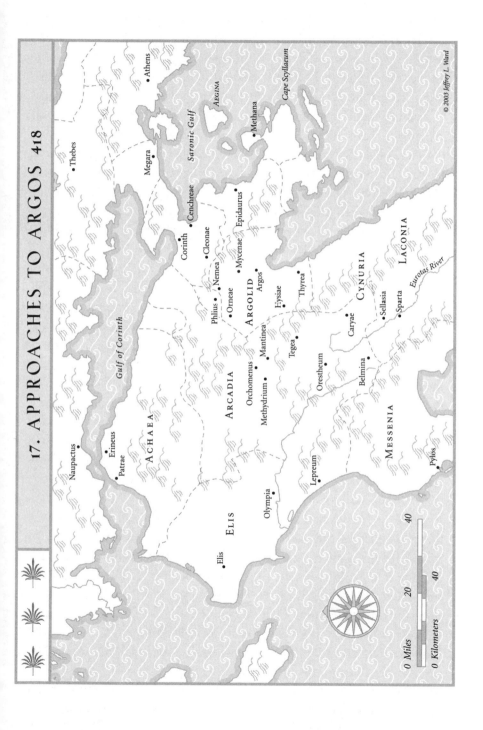

17. APPROACHES TO ARGOS 418

Thebes

Athens

Megara

Saronic Gulf

AEGINA

Cenchreae

Corinth

Cleonae

Methana

Epidaurus

Nemea

Mycenae

Phlius

Orneae

Argos

Cape Scyllaeum

ARGOLID

Hysiae

Thyrea

Orchomenus

Mantinea

CYNURIA

Caryae

LACONIA

ARCADIA

Tegea

Sellasia

Methydrium

Sparta

Eurotas River

Orestheum

Belmina

Naupactus

Erineus

Patrae

ACHAEA

Gulf of Corinth

Lepreum

MESSENIA

Elis

Olympia

ELIS

Pylos

© 2003 Jeffrey L. Ward

0 Miles   20   40

0 Kilometers   40

lay rough mountain country traversed by only one road suitable for cavalry, the Tretus Pass, which was entered south of Nemea and issued before Mycenae (see Map 18). A more direct path, however, led to the west of the Tretus, past Mount Kelussa and into the Argive plain. Although this route was not suitable for cavalry, foot soldiers could use it to reach Argos. The Argives must have known of its existence, yet their generals marched directly to Nemea to meet a frontal attack through the Tretus Pass, leaving themselves vulnerable to a flanking movement by way of Mount Kelussa. This was the Argives' second serious blunder of the same type within a few days—a blunder that avoided immediate battle and allowed the enemy to reach an operational target. Perhaps, once again, the Argive generals were playing for time in the hope that a reconciliation could still be effected.

Agis divided his forces into three columns. The Boeotians, Sicyonians, and Megarians and all the cavalry advanced through the Tretus Pass. The men from Corinth, Pellene, and Phlius proceeded by way of Mount Kelussa, probably reaching the plain near the modern village of Fikhtia. Agis himself led the Spartans, Arcadians, and Epidaurians by a third route, also steep and difficult, that may have taken him near the modern village of Malandreni; in any case, it led to a position still further to the rear of the Argive army. Agis had again made a successful march at night and by the next morning word reached the Argive army at Nemea that he was in their rear ravaging the town of Saminthus and its neighborhood, probably near the modern Koutsopodhi. Hurrying back to their city, the Argives were delayed by skirmishes with the Phliasians and Corinthians but broke through and found themselves between Agis and the allied armies. "The Argives were cut off in the middle: from the side of the plain the Spartans and those with them shut them off from the city; above them were the Corinthians, Phliasians, and Pellenians; on the side of Nemea were the Boeotians, Sicyonians, and Megarians. They had no cavalry, for the Athenians alone of their allies had not come" (5.59.3).

Facing the Spartans who stood between them and their city, the Argives prepared to fight. Just as the armies seemed about to engage, two Argives, Thrasyllus and Alciphron, stepped forward to speak to Agis. To the surprise of all they returned with a four months' truce, and no combat took place. Stranger still was the reaction of the two

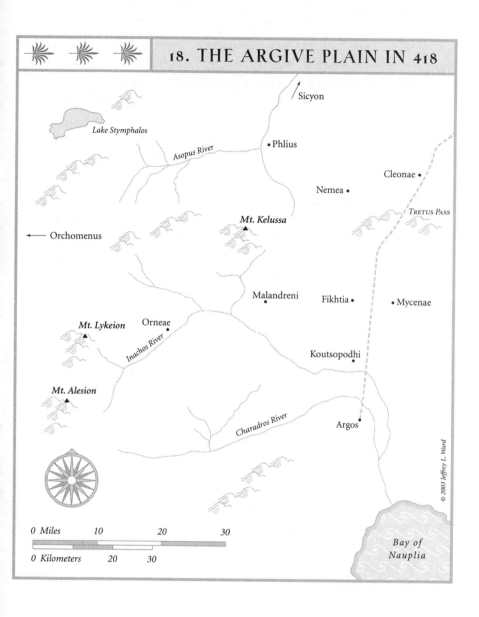

Sicyon

Lake Stymphalos

Asopus River

Phlius

Cleonae •

Nemea •

TRETUS PASS

← Orchomenus

Mt. Kelussa

Malandreni

Fikhtia •

• Mycenae

Mt. Lykeion   Orneae

Inachos River

Koutsopodhi

Mt. Alesion

Charadros River

Argos

© 2003 Jeffrey L. Ward

0 Miles   10   20   30

0 Kilometers   20   30

*Bay of
Nauplia*

armies: each was angered by the lost opportunity for warfare. The Argives believed from the beginning that "the battle was likely to be fought in favorable circumstances and that the Spartans had been cut off in their territory and close to the city of Argos" (5.59.4). When they returned to Argos they deprived Thrasyllus of his property and all but stoned him to death. The Spartans, on the other hand, "placed great blame on Agis because he had not conquered Argos when they thought the opportunity better than any they had before" (5.63.1).

When the Athenians finally arrived, too few and too late, the Argive magistrates (who must have been oligarchs) sent them away, refusing to let them appear before the assembly. With breathtaking boldness Alcibiades, who had accompanied the force in the role of ambassador, made no apology for the Athenians' tardy arrival but complained that the Argives had no right to make a truce without consulting the allies. Instead, he insisted, the allies should resume the war, since the Athenians were now there. Elis, Mantinea, and the other allies were easily persuaded, and the entire alliance decided to attack Orchomenus in Arcadia, a key position that could block an army coming from the Isthmus of Corinth and beyond from reaching the central and southern Peloponnesus. After some delay the Argives joined the siege of Orchomenus, which did not hold out for long and entered the new alliance. Even without a formal command Alcibiades had thwarted his Athenian rivals and given new life to the quadruple alliance.

The loss of Orchomenus outraged the Spartans and made them condemn the actions of Agis retrospectively. They resolved to destroy his house and to fine him ten thousand drachmas; only his promise to avenge the disgrace when he next took the field stopped them. Even so, the Spartans enacted an unprecedented law appointing ten *xymbouloi* to accompany Agis on his expeditions and "advise" him; without their consent he could not lead an army out of the city. What the Spartans found fault with was not his military performance, for if their intention was to blame him for the failure of his campaign or his nerve, they should have punished him immediately after his return to Sparta, and not some time later. They judged his error, rather, to be a political one, for Agis had meant to allow the Argive oligarchs to bring their city over to Sparta without having to resort to a fight. The capture of Orchomenus proved that his plan had failed and demonstrated the league's continuing vitality.

After the fall of Orchomenus Agis gave up hope of rapprochement with Argos and determined to retaliate for the apparent treachery of the Argives. Trouble at Tegea gave him the chance he needed. The successes of the new league and the hesitation of the Spartans had encouraged a faction that was eager to turn Tegea over to the Argives and their allies, and word came to the Spartans that unless they acted quickly the city would be lost. Hostile control of Tegea would effectively trap the Spartans in Laconia, end their authority over the Peloponnesian League, and interfere with their access to Messenia. Tegea's entry into an alliance in the sixth century had marked the beginning of the Peloponnesian League and of Sparta's rise to power; now, its defection would mean the end of both. Agis and the Spartans had no choice but to march north to save it.

CHAPTER EIGHTEEN

The Battle of Mantinea (418)

THE SPARTANS LEARNED of the threat to Tegea late in August 418 and at once called on their Arcadian allies to meet them there. They also asked their northern allies in Corinth, Boeotia, Phocis, and Locris to come to Mantinea as quickly as possible, but the ability of these troops to do so was uncertain, because the fall of Orchomenus put the most passable routes south in enemy hands. To get through safely the northern allies would first have to gather their forces, presumably at Corinth, and then overawe any opponents with their sheer numbers. Even with the best effort, however, the northern army could not reach Mantinea in less than twelve to fourteen days after the Spartans sent word to them. In addition, Thucydides' language hints that some of them found the summons inconvenient, and the Boeotians and Corinthians were probably still annoyed by the inconclusive outcome of their last march into the Peloponnesus. A combination of reluctance and resentment might further increase the delay in their arrival.

AGIS' MARCH TO TEGEA

AGIS COULD EXPECT to face at Mantinea an enemy army of about the same size as he had met earlier at Argos—about twelve thousand, men. His own army at Argos had numbered about eight thousand, and to that he now added some *neodamodeis*; with the Tegeans in full force at their own city, his total count would be as high as ten thousand hoplites. Even so, the enemy army would still be larger.

Agis also faced another problem in that the Spartans had come to lack confidence in his command. Twice he had led the army invading

Attica; the first time an earthquake had prevented the incursion, and the following year the grain of Attica had been too green to feed the soldiers, and violent storms added to the discomfort of his hungry men. After only fifteen days, the shortest invasion of the war, news of the Athenian fortification of Pylos forced Agis to lead his troops back to Sparta with nothing to show for their trouble. Neither campaign had given him any experience in battle, and both were attended by unusually bad luck. The expedition to Argos in 418 likewise had done nothing to increase the credibility of the young king. Twice he had turned back from the frontier, allegedly because of evil omens, and when he finally had the chance to fight an outnumbered and surrounded enemy, he had rejected it. Any sympathy he might have gained for his choice of diplomacy over war disappeared when the Argives and their allies later captured Orchomenus. The bad news from Tegea must have increased the Spartans' displeasure, and only the fact that their other king, Pleistoanax, was discredited can explain their willingness to allow Agis to lead the army once again, though they did take the cautionary step of keeping him subject to the guidance of ten advisers. Mantinea was his last opportunity to prove himself; success would bring redemption, and failure would mean disgrace.

In undertaking the campaign Agis faced a tricky strategic problem: he had to get to Tegea as soon as possible to prevent a coup, but after his arrival he would have to wait at least a week for the arrival of the northern contingent, while in the meantime being forced to confront a larger enemy army. A different Spartan leader could choose to stay within the walls of Tegea and refuse battle until his allies appeared, allowing the enemy to ravage the Tegean land, destroy farmhouses, approach the city, and hurl accusations of cowardice at the Spartans and their commander, but Agis could not afford to convey even the slightest hint that he was afraid to fight. Because he knew he would face superior numbers he also was forced to risk taking the entire Spartan army with him, leaving Sparta itself undefended at a time when the Messenians were perched at Pylos, threatening to launch a rebellion of the helots.

On his way to Tegea Agis received the welcome news that the Eleans had not joined their allies at Mantinea. The Mantineans wanted to attack Tegea, their neighbor and ancient enemy, while the Eleans preferred to move against Lepreum; the Athenians and Argives, meanwhile, recognized the strategic importance of Tegea, and both supported the Mantinean view. When the Eleans took offense and withdrew their commitment of 3,000 hoplites, Agis took advantage of this rift in the alliance to send back one-sixth of his army to guard Sparta. Even without these 500 to 700 men, however, he would still outnumber the enemy with over 9,000 Spartans and allies against about 8,000 for the Argive coalition.

TO FORCE A BATTLE

ALTHOUGH THE ELEANS' defection solved Agis' strategic conflict, they were certain before long to realize the foolishness of their withdrawal and return to swell the ranks of the Argive coalition's army, probably before Sparta's northern allies reached the area. Conditions now compelled Agis to force a pitched battle before the Eleans reappeared. Collecting his allies at Tegea, Agis marched to the sanctuary of Heracles (the Heracleum), more than a mile southeast of the city of Mantinea (see Map 19). The plain on which the ancient cities of Tegea and Mantinea were situated rises to a height of about twenty-two hundred feet and is surrounded by mountains. At its longest, north and south, it extends about eighteen miles, and at its widest, east to west, it is about eleven miles. The plain slopes down slightly from south to north, Mantinea being about one hundred feet lower in attitude than Tegea, ten miles away.

A little more than three miles south of Mantinea the plain narrows to a gap almost two miles wide between two ridges, Mytikas on the west and Kapnistra on the east. The border between the two states was probably at this gap or just to the south of it. Not far from Tegea the stream now called the Zanovistas rises and flows to the north into a sinkhole at the western edge of the Mantinean plain, north of Mytikas. Another stream, the Sarandapotamos, flows north past Tegea, makes a sharp turn to the east through a pass, and empties into three sinkholes near the modern town of Versova, still in Tegean territory. Two roads ran south from Mantinea, one of them leading southwest to Pallantion while the other, located near the eastern end of the gap, ran south to

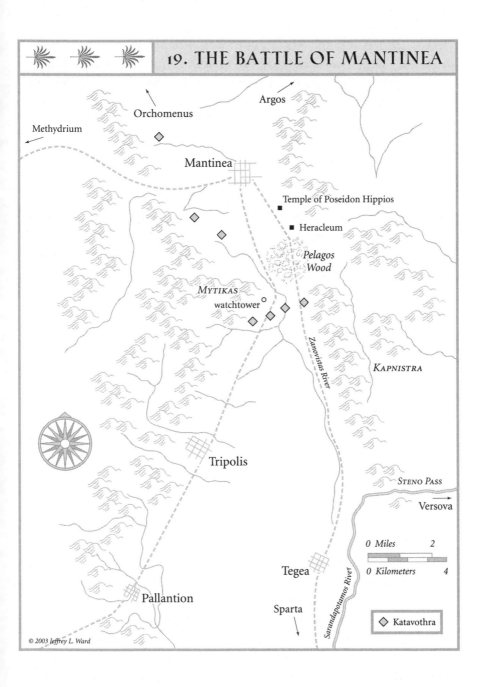

19. THE BATTLE OF MANTINEA

Methydrium

Orchomenus

Argos

Mantinea

Temple of Poseidon Hippios

Heracleum

Pelagos
Wood

MYTIKAS
watchtower

Zanovistas River

KAPNISTRA

Tripolis

STENO PASS

Versova

Tegea

Sparta

Sarandapotamos River

Pallantion

0 Miles 2

0 Kilometers 4

◇ Katavothra

© 2003 Jeffrey L. Ward

Tegea. To the east of Mantinea stood a mountain that the ancients called Alesion. The Tegea road ran past it, and, where the mountain shaded into plain, there stood a temple of Poseidon Hippios. South of Mount Alesion was an oak forest called Pelagos, which reached almost to Kapnistra and Mytikas. The Tegea road ran through this forest, and the Pallantion road skirted it on the west. The sanctuary of Heracles, at which the Spartans made camp, was located in the eastern part of the plain, south of Mount Alesion.

Agis began his offensive by ravaging the enemy's land to force him to defend it in a pitched battle, but the Spartans had arrived too late in the harvest season for the tactic to have exerted the usual pressure. Mantinea's grain had been gathered between the latter part of June and the end of July, so the crops, along with everything of value that could be moved, had already been safely stored, leaving the Spartans unable to do any unacceptable damage. The members of the Argive coalition, meanwhile, had taken up a strong defensive position on the lower slopes of Mount Alesion, a place "steep and hard to get at." By now the Eleans had been asked to rejoin their allies and were on their way, and reinforcements from Athens were also en route, a fact of which the generals of the confederacy were probably aware. When these reinforcements arrived the Argives would have a superiority in numbers and could choose the moment to fight, so long as the battle took place before Sparta's northern allies could appear. Until the reinforcements reached them, however, the Argive coalition had every reason to avoid battle, unless Agis was foolhardy enough to come to them.

That is exactly what Agis attempted to do, charging his men up the slopes of Alesion. It was the reckless act of a desperate man, for even with a small numerical advantage an uphill drive against a hoplite army in phalanx was doomed. The Spartans came "within a stone's throw or a javelin's cast" when the advance suddenly stopped. "One of the older men," gauging the impossibility of the situation, called out to Agis that what he had in mind was "to cure one evil with another" (5.65.2). The wise elder may have been one of the *xymbouloi*, who understood that with this impetuous action, the young king was trying to erase the memory of his behavior at Argos. Heeding the warning Agis led a rapid retreat without making contact with the enemy, and only the unwillingness of the allies to pursue him prevented a disaster.

By now Agis must have been more desperate than ever, for so far as he knew the enemy army would not come down from the heights until they were joined by their reinforcements. He therefore sent to Sparta asking that the men he had sent back earlier rejoin him at Tegea, for he now acknowledged that he would have to face a battle against odds at a time and place chosen by the enemy. To reduce those odds he would have to take the gamble of leaving Sparta unguarded for some days.

As King Pleistoanax led the requested troops toward Tegea, Agis conceived a plan to draw the enemy onto the plain and force a battle before its own reinforcements appeared. For years the Tegeans and Mantineans had fought over control of the waterways that ran through the plain. All the streams and mountain torrents in the region emptied into sinkholes in the limestone beneath the soil. When heavy rains choked the sinkholes Mantinea, because of the slope of the land, was in danger of being flooded. During the rainy season the Tegeans could stop up the sinkholes or divert the streams around them by digging simple ditches, which directed the overflow into Mantinean territory. Another device was to divert the more copious Sarandapotamos into the Zanovistas, flooding the Mantinean plain, damaging the crops and the city. This could be accomplished by digging a canal of about a mile and a half between the rivers at their closest point. At some time in the past they had probably done so and kept the trench they had created, merely building a barrier across it when they wanted to allow the Sarandapotamos to return to its normal channel. In their repeated conflicts with Mantinea, the Tegeans could then easily break down the barrier and resume inundating Mantinean land.

Agis marched back toward Tegea, probably to divert the Sarandapotamos into the Zanovistas; he may also have sent men to fill up sinkholes on the frontier or to dig ditches that would lead the water around them. Such efforts alone, however, would not have accomplished Agis' purpose, for "He wanted to make the men on the hill come down to help prevent the diversion of the water when they learned about it and so to make them fight a battle on the plain" (5.65.4). Because the sinkholes were some distance from Mount Alesion, where Agis had left the enemy army, and still farther from Mantinea, where it might be expected to withdraw once the Spartan forces had departed, and because the Pelagos Wood stood in between, the Argives probably would not have discovered the Spartan tactic immediately. Within a day, however, water would appear in the dry bed that wound its way well into Mantinean territory, and from bitter experience the Mantineans would realize what the Tegeans and their allies had done. Unless the Mantineans returned the Sarandapotamos to its own channel before the onset of the rainy season, which was due in a matter of weeks, their land would be flooded.

THE ALLIED ARMY MOVES

AGIS' PLAN—the best gamble available to a desperate man—assumed that anger and fear would immediately lead the enemy to seek a battle they would be wiser to delay. After a day near Tegea he marched again toward the Mantinean Heracleum, eager to put his army in battle order at the best place to fight and await the Argive advance. But Agis never reached the Heracleum, for the enemy did not behave as expected. Instead political suspicion and distrust within the army of the Argive coalition played directly into his hands.

After the Spartan withdrawal from Mount Alesion the allied troops began to complain of their Argive generals' inaction: "On the previous occasion the Spartans, though nicely trapped near Argos, had been allowed to get away, and now, when they were running away, no one pursued them; instead the Spartans were reaching safety without disturbance while we are being betrayed" (5.65.5). The last word here is revealing: the malcontent troops did not accuse their leaders of cowardice but rather of treason (*prodidontai*). The generals must have been from the aristocratic Argive Thousand, and as their earlier actions had already made them suspect among the democratic citizens of Argos, the intensification of such suspicious now compelled them to descend the hill and prepare for a battle.

Whatever Agis saw or did not see as he marched out of Tegea, he had to go north of the gap. If the enemy troops were in Mantinea, he would be forced to wait until the sight of water in the bed of the Zanovistas drew them out. If they were already on the plain, he could have his battle at once. As his army emerged in column from the forest, he was shocked to find the enemy army close by, well away from the hills, and in full battle order. The allies had camped in the plain overnight, and their lookouts on the heights must have informed the Argive generals of Agis' approach. As a result they were able to line up close to the place where the Spartans would emerge from the woods and wait in the battle formation of their own choosing. Agis had walked into a trap.

THE BATTLE

THE SPARTAN KING'S first task was to place his army, marching out of the forest in column, in line and in order of battle before the enemy could take advantage of its temporary disarray and attack. Here the unrivaled discipline and training of the Spartan army came into play, for Agis needed only to give his orders to the leaders of the six Spartan divisions, and the chain of command did the rest. Unlike other Greek armies, the Spartan army "was composed of officers commanding other officers, for the responsibility of carrying out orders is shared by many" (5.66.40). The Argive generals apparently chose not to strike the enemy as it emerged from the forest or to charge before the Spartans could form into line. Either tactic might have forced a Spartan retreat and led to another avoidance of battle, but, pressed by their soldiers' disgruntlement, the generals seem to have been determined to fight that day.

The allies placed their greatest strength—the Mantineans fighting for their homeland—on the right wing, while next to them were the other Arcadians with a similar motivation, and then the specially trained elite Argive Thousand. This right wing was meant to take the offensive and fight the decisive part of the battle. Next to them stood the ordinary Argive hoplites, and beside them the men of Orneae and Cleonae. On the left wing were a thousand Athenians supported by their own cavalry. The left wing was intended to stand on the defensive, to avoid encirclement, and to stave off a rout until the right wing could strike the decisive blow.

The Spartans' alignment indicates no particular plan of battle. The Sciritae, Arcadians who usually served as scouts or in connection with cavalry, held their traditional place on the left wing. Then came the troops who had fought with Brasidas in Thrace, along with a number of *neodamodeis*. The main Spartan army held the center, and next to them were their Arcadian allies from Heraea and Maenalia. The Tegeans took their place on the right, supported by a few Spartans who held the very end of the line. The cavalry was split, protecting both wings. The Spartan disposition was conventional and defensive, as we might expect from an army and a general taken by surprise. The initiative lay with the Argive generals.

The allied army of about eight thousand hoplites stretched across a front that extended about a kilometer, while the Peloponnesians, about nine thousand hoplites, formed a line about one hundred meters longer. The Tegeans and the small band of Spartans with them on the right wing extended beyond the Athenians on the allied left, but the slightly outnumbered allies did not try to compensate for that deficit by sending forces there. On the contrary, they extended their own right far beyond the Sciritae on the enemy left. The Spartans advanced at their usual slow pace, keeping time to the measured rhythm of the pipes they played to preserve the order of the phalanx, but the allied army "advanced eagerly and impulsively" (5.70). Plainly, the allied generals meant to have their best troops strike the decisive blow on the right and rout the enemy before their own left or center gave way.

On seeing his left wing in danger of encirclement, Agis signaled the Sciritae and the veterans of Brasidas' army on the left to break off contact with the rest of the army and to move further left to match the position of the Mantineans. Because this created a dangerous gap in the Peloponnesian line, he therefore ordered the officers Hipponoidas and Aristocles to take their companies—perhaps numbering a thousand Spartan troops altogether—from the right end of the main Spartan army to fill it.

There is no parallel to this maneuver in the history of Greek warfare. To change the line of battle while two armies were about to engage in battle, to open a gap in one's line deliberately, to open still another gap in order to fill the first—all of these tactics were unheard of. In fact, the shift to the right that alarmed Agis was typical of all armies, because of the natural tendency of hoplite phalanxes to move toward their unshielded side, and should have been anticipated by him, but once again he acted out of inexperience.

Agis' best plan would have been to hold formation, send his right wing to outflank and roll up the enemy left, throw his own powerful Spartan army against the unimpressive ordinary Argive contingent in the center, and hope that his left wing, bearing the brunt of the enemy onslaught, could hold out until he himself could bring relief. The risk in such a strategy was that the Peloponnesian left would be outflanked and rolled up too quickly. In the situation that surprise had forced on the Spartans, however, every alternative involved even greater risks. Under such circumstances Agis needed the judgment, confidence, and determination of an experienced commander, but, as his previous behavior shows, these were qualities he had yet to acquire. Instead he gave the unusual orders described above.

We can never know how Agis' maneuver might have worked had his orders been obeyed. The left wing moved out as ordered to prevent the flanking movement of the enemy, opening a gap between themselves and the Spartans in the center, but the soldiers from the right of that center did not proceed to fill that gap, for the captains of the two relevant companies, Aristocles and Hipponoidas, simply refused to carry out the command. Such insubordination was as unprecedented as Agis' order, and the two captains were later condemned and exiled for cowardice, so the Spartan court appears to have believed that Agis' strategy was feasible. But the truth of the matter is that while the two captains refused a direct order from their commander in the field, they kept their companies in their original positions in the phalanx, in the center, and they did not flee or seek sanctuary afterwards but returned to Sparta for trial. These are not the actions of cowards.

Still, disobedience by Spartan officers to a direct order in the field requires explanation, and the captains' refusal can be at least partially understood by the belief of these experienced soldiers that their army was led by an incompetent. Since first encountering the enemy, he had led his men in a reckless and abortive uphill charge, taken them back down after coming within a spear's throw of the enemy, and, finally, allowed the enemy to surprise him with a battle on a ground and in a formation of its choosing. A second reason for the captains' action may be that because Aristocles was the brother of Pleistoanax, Agis' royal colleague, he may have hoped for the effective protection of his brother and persuaded Hipponoidas of their security. But ultimately they must have reacted to an order that seemed sheer folly and attempted to prevent the terrible danger in which it would place the Spartan army.

In the end the Spartans won the battle even though the two captains had disobeyed Agis' orders—and perhaps even because of their refusal. Because they stood their ground there was no gap on the right side of the Spartan center. Instead, they were strengthening the Spartan center, where the victory was won. The Spartan victory also owed something to the enemy's mistakes. When Agis learned that he could not use troops from his right to close the gap he had created on the left, he reversed himself and ordered the left wing to close up the line again, but by then it was too late. The Mantineans routed the Spartan left wing and then, aided by the elite Argive corps, drove into the gap between the Spartan left and center.

For the Argives and their allies this was the decisive moment in the battle and the great chance for victory. If they had ignored the disorganized Sciritae, *neodamodeis*, and Brasidaeans on the left wing, or sent a small force to occupy them, and turned the main body left against the flank and rear of the Spartan center, they would almost surely have gained the victory, for the Spartan center was still fighting the enemy directly before it. Instead the allies turned to the right and destroyed the Spartan left wing, thus losing their great opportunity and with it the battle. The Mantineans and elite Argives charging through the opening in the Spartan ranks made the natural and easy decision: they turned to the right rather than to the left because at their right they faced the unshielded side of the enemy, a more tempting and safer target than the shielded Spartans to their left. Besides, the allies were probably surprised to see the gap open before them as they approached the enemy phalanx, for it had not been there when they started their advance. The allied generals must have ordered their right wing to concentrate all its force on the enemy left wing, to destroy it swiftly and totally, for only then could they hope to turn inward against the center. The sudden opening of the Spartan left center called for a change in strategy, but it was difficult if not impossible to revise a battle plan once a hoplite phalanx was under way, as Agis himself had discovered. Perhaps a great leader commanding a homogeneous, well-drilled, and familiar army could have succeeded in such a maneuver, but we do not know the identity of the allied general, and his army had been assembled from different states. The allied force did what it was most likely to do, and as a result the battle was lost.

While the allies needlessly pursued the Sciritae and the freed helots, Agis and the Spartan center repulsed the unimpressive forces in front of them: the "five companies" of older Argives and the hoplites from Cleonae and Orneae. In fact, "most did not even stand and fight but fled as the Spartans approached; some were even trampled in their hurry to get away before the enemy reached them" (5.72.4).

By this time the Spartan right wing was beginning to encircle the outflanked Athenians on the allies' left. The cavalry prevented a rout, but still disaster loomed, for the failure of the allies on the right to exploit their advantage had decided the issue.

Once the tide of battle had turned, Agis gave a number of orders that determined the character of the victory. Instead of allowing his right wing to finish off the Athenians who were retreating before it, he commanded his entire army to lend support to his defeated and hard put left wing, which allowed the Athenians and a part of the ordinary Argive army to escape. Agis' decision can be understood on purely military grounds, for the Spartan king surely wanted to protect his army from further losses and to destroy the flower of the enemy's forces—the Mantineans and the elite Argives—but it also had political value. Strange as it may seem, Athens and Sparta were still technically at peace. Destruction of the Athenian army at Mantinea would surely have strengthened the hand of Sparta's enemies at Athens, but Spartan restraint might persuade the Athenians to adopt a moderate policy and maintain the peace even while Sparta restored its power and prestige.

POLITICS INTERVENE

ON THE OTHER END of the field the Mantineans and elite Argives fled when they saw the collapse of their forces. The Mantinean casualties were heavy, but "most of the elite Argives were saved" (5.73.4). It is difficult to understand why of these two contingents fighting side by side one should have been almost annihilated while the other was almost unharmed. Thucydides reports that their flight was not pursued hotly or for any great distance, "for the Spartans fight their battles for a long time and stand their ground until the enemy is routed, but when he is, pursuit is brief and only for a short distance" (5.73.4). Still, that does not explain why the Mantineans were killed while the Argives escaped. For that we must turn to Diodorus, a much later historian, who gives a different interpretation:

> After the Spartans had routed the other parts of the army, killing many, they turned on the Thousand elite Argives. Encircling them with superior numbers, they hoped to destroy them entirely. The elite troops, though much inferior in number, were outstanding in courage. The king of the Spartans, fighting in the front ranks, persisted against the dangers, and he would have killed them all—for he was eager to carry out his promises to his fellow citizens to make amends for his previous disgrace by accomplishing great deeds—but he was not allowed to carry out his intention. For the Spartan Pharax, who was one of the advisers, and had a great reputation in Sparta, commanded him to give an escape route to the elite troops and not, by taking chances against men who had given up hope of living, to find out about the courage of men deserted by fortune. So the king was compelled by the orders he had recently received to allow their escape in accordance with the judgment of Pharax. (12.79.6–7)

The *xymboulos* Pharax was obviously thinking ahead to consider the political ramifications of the battle. To destroy the aristocratic elite of Argos when most of the ordinary, democratic Argives had escaped would guarantee the continued alliance of Argos with the other democracies, but if the Argive elite returned home after the great defeat of the anti-Spartan policy, they could gain control of the city and bring it into a Spartan alliance, striking a death blow to the enemy coalition. The vengeful, inexperienced Agis, determined to recover his honor, could not foresee this in the heat of battle, and the Spartans' decision to appoint advisers to him proved to be a well-considered idea.

THE MEANING OF MANTINEA

IF THE BATTLE of Mantinea did not succeed in destroying the defeated army, it nevertheless had tremendous importance. Its most significant result for the Spartans was the mere fact that they did not lose. Had the elite Argives exploited the gap in the Spartan line properly and defeated the Spartans and their allies, Spartan control of the Peloponnesus might have come to an end. The loss of Tegea, which would surely have followed an allied victory at Mantinea, would have destroyed Sparta's strategic position, cutting it off from all its allies and from Messenia. The blow to Spartan prestige, moreover, would have been fatal to its hegemony. An allied triumph at Mantinea would almost surely have brought victory in the greater war to Athens and its friends. Instead the Spartan victory restored Sparta's confidence and reputation: "The charges that the Greeks brought against them at that time, cowardice because of their disaster on the island Sphacteria, bad judgment and slowness on other occasions, were erased by this single action. Now it seemed they had suffered disgrace because of bad luck, but they were still the same in their resolve" (5.75.3).

The Spartan success was also a victory for oligarchy. An allied win at Mantinea would have fortified democratic rule at Argos, Elis, and Mantinea, lending it a prestige that would probably have encouraged other democracies in the Peloponnesus. Defeat, instead, weakened the hold of the Peloponnesian democrats on their own states and damaged democratic influence in general. The battle turned the tide away from democracy toward oligarchy throughout Greece.

The three thousand Elean and one thousand Athenian reinforcements finally arrived at Mantinea after the battle was concluded, but if they had arrived in time to strengthen the allied center, it would almost surely have ended differently. Now, all they could do was march against Epidaurus to relieve the attack on Argos their army had launched during the clash at Mantinea, and content themselves with building a wall around the city and leaving a garrison to hold it.

The democratic alliance survived, however tenuously, for morale was low. In November, after the allied forces had withdrawn, the Spartans moved their army to Tegea, but they intended to exploit their victory by diplomacy, not war. They sent Lichas, the Argives' *proxenos* at Sparta, to Argos with a peace offer. Even before this time there were Argives who were friends of Sparta, and "who wished to destroy the democracy," and the elite Thousand must have been among them. After their escape from Mantinea they were the only significant military force in Argos, and their bravery in the battle increased their prestige, at the same time that the half-hearted Athenian performance at Mantinea embarrassed and discouraged the Argive democrats. "After the battle the friends of the Spartans found it much easier to persuade the many to make an agreement with Sparta" (5.76.2).

When Lichas came to the Argive assembly to offer terms of peace he found there Alcibiades, still a private citizen, who himself had come to make the case for continuing the alliance with Athens. Even his skills, however, were no match for the new realities created by the outcome of Mantinea and the unopposed Spartan army at Tegea. The Argives accepted the Spartan treaty, which required them to restore all hostages, give up Orchomenus, evacuate Epidaurus, and join with the Spartans in forcing the Athenians to do the same. Beyond that, the confident oligarchs persuaded the Argives to renounce the alliances with Elis, Mantinea, and Athens and crowned their victory by concluding an alliance with Sparta.

The Argives' defection was a fatal blow to the democratic league, and when they demanded that the Athenians withdraw from Epidaurus the Athenians had to comply. Mantinea was so weakened that it, too, made a treaty with Sparta, relinquishing control of a number of Arcadian cities. The Argive Thousand joined an equal number of Spartans in an expedition to Sicyon, where they placed a trustworthy oligarchy. Finally, when the joint army returned, they put down the Argive democracy, and established an oligarchy there, as well.

By March of 417, then, the Spartans, by war and subversion, had shattered the democratic league. Yet while success at Mantinea averted disaster for Sparta, it did not guarantee its safety for the future. The

Athenians were still powerful, and Alcibiades continued to favor an active and aggressive policy. Athens continued to hold Pylos, which was a constant invitation to defection or rebellion by the helots. Elis, too, remained outside of Spartan control, and events would soon show that the rule of the Argive oligarchs was far from secure. Finally, differences of opinion on that policy to pursue continued to divide the Spartans themselves. The final significance of the battle of Mantinea was yet to be determined.

CHAPTER NINETEEN

After Mantinea: Politics and Policy at Sparta and Athens (418–416)

DEMOCRACY RESTORED TO ARGOS

AMONG THE GREEKS, wherever democracy had taken root, the people would not rest content with the imposition of oligarchy but sought a return to popular rule. In Argos, the newly installed oligarchs hastened this process by their oppressive behavior: "Taking hold of those accustomed to be popular leaders, [the oligarchs] put them to death; then, by terrorizing the other Argives, they destroyed the laws and began to take public affairs unto themselves" (Diodorus 12.80.3). In August 417 the democrats launched a rebellion during Sparta's celebration of the festival of the *Gymnopaediae*, killing or exiling many of the oligarchs, and reestablishing a popular government. The surviving oligarchs appealed frantically to Sparta for assistance, but the Spartans did not abandon their festivities. Eventually they did send an army to Argos, but it did nothing decisive while there.

Rejected by the Spartans, the democratic Argives took Alcibiades' advice, and with the help of the Eleans, built long walls connecting Argos with the sea. They also sought an alliance with Athens, to which the walls would keep open a sea route. The Argives finished the project by the end of summer, but alarmed by these actions, the Spartans sent an army under Agis against Argos, destroying what had been constructed. Agis also captured Hysiae, an Argive town, killing all the free men who had been captured before he broke off the campaign and returned home. Such atrocities were becoming more common, and Thucydides makes no comment about them.

Upon the Spartan departure the restored Argive democrats took steps against treason by attacking Phlius, where most of the oligarchic exiles had settled. In 416 Alcibiades, again an Athenian general, brought a fleet to Argos and removed three hundred suspected Spartan sympathizers, scattering them among the islands. Later the same year the Argives arrested more suspects, while others escaped into exile before they could be caught. Despite such measures, the Argives remained vulnerable to attack by the Spartans, and they urged the Athenians to be more active in defending them. For Athens, alliance with Argos now offered few opportunities and many dangers.

POLITICS AT ATHENS

IN THE SPRING of 417 the election of both Nicias and Alcibiades underscored the division and confusion that continued to govern Athenian politics. Alcibiades persevered in encouraging his friends at Argos, but without Elis and Mantinea there was no hope of resuming an active Peloponnesian campaign. Nicias' policy, meanwhile, was to turn away from the Peloponnesus and recover the Chalcidian and Macedonian territories. The region was crucial to Athens as a source of money and timber, and Athens also needed to recover lost territory, subjects, and prestige before the idea of rebellion spread any further. Since the peace in 421 there had been additional defections from Athens in the Chalcidice, and a new threat now arose from the king of Macedon.

In 418 the Spartans, accompanied by Argive oligarchs, had persuaded Perdiccas to swear an alliance with them, even though he was still too prudent to break completely with Athens. About May 417 the Athenians forced the king's hand by planning a campaign against the Chalcidians and Amphipolis under the command of Nicias. Perdiccas refused to do his part, compelling the Athenians to abandon the campaign, and they responded by imposing a blockade on the Macedonian coast, though to no good effect. The Athenians could not agree on any consistent policy, and the attempts of their two major leaders to pursue different policies simultaneously produced only failure and deadlock.

OSTRACISM OF HYPERBOLUS

HYPERBOLUS STEPPED IN to to break the impasse, using the old and neglected device of ostracism. Ostracism appeared perfectly suited to solve Athens' problems in 416, for it would give the Athenians a clear choice between the policies and leadership of Nicias and those of Alcibiades. No one had been ostracized for a quarter-century, however, for the cost of defeat—exile for ten years—was so high that only someone confident of a majority could favor so extreme a measure. Since Pericles, however, no Athenian could count on such confidence, and because in 416 Nicias and Alcibiades had about equal support, neither was willing to gamble on the tactic.

Hyperbolus, however, seemed to have had nothing to lose. Alcibiades' arrival as leader of the aggressive faction apparently placed Hyperbolus "out of the reach of ostracism," for in the past only major political figures—the leaders of factions—had been subjected to the procedure. Hyperbolus "hoped that when one of the other men was exiled he would become the rival of the one who remained" (Plutarch, *Nicias* 11.4). He is roundly condemned by the ancient writers, but he may in fact have sought more than just his own advantage, in the belief that the ostracism would bring Athens a steadier policy. Whatever his motives, Hyperbolus was the man most responsible for persuading the Athenians to hold an ostracism. Once the decision had been taken, Nicias and Alcibiades had no choice but to prepare for its dangers. In the end, Alcibiades suggested to Nicias that they collaborate to turn the decision against Hyperbolus, and their combined forces guaranteed their success; Hyperbolus himself was ostracized and died in exile.

The ostracism of March 416 revealed a fatal weakness in the institution: it could confirm a leader or a policy supported by a clear majority, but it was useless where such clarity was lacking. Perhaps the general realization of this flaw explains why ostracism was never again used at Athens. In retrospect, the city might have benefited greatly if the major rivals had run the risk of an honest competition between them; instead, the ostracism of Hyperbolus left it without a consistent policy or leadership. Not long afterwards, the Athenians again elected both Nicias and Alcibiades as generals, reflecting the continuing stalemate in their politics.

The behavior of the Athenians in these years reveals their great frustration. Sparta's unwillingness to carry out the terms of the peace dashed Nicias' hope for a sincere rapprochement between the two leading powers. Alcibiades' scheme of defeating Sparta through a great Peloponnesian alliance lay in shambles, while Nicias' more modest program of recovering Athenian losses in Thrace and the Chalcidice had never progressed beyond the planning stage. Peace, however, had allowed the Athenians to recover their financial strength; by 415 the reserve fund may have held as many as four thousand talents. Meanwhile a new generation of young men had come to maturity, without the bitter experience of war or sharp memories of the Spartan invasions. Although Athens had an unmatched naval power and a considerable army available, it seemed unable to use its strength and vitality either to enforce a true peace or to win the war. In the spring of 416 a campaign against Melos provided the Athenians with the outlet they needed for their energy and frustration.

THE ATHENIAN CONQUEST OF MELOS

THE MELIANS, alone of the Cycladic islanders, had refused to join the Delian League, which allowed them to enjoy the benefits of the Athenian Empire without bearing any of its burdens. They were Dorians and, during the Archidamian War, seem to have given aid to the Spartans, whose colonists they were. They fought off an Athenian attack in 426 and stubbornly maintained their independence, although the Athenians included them on their assessment lists beginning in 425. A further conflict was inevitable, for the Athenians could not long allow their will and authority to be flouted by a small Cycladic island. The Melians relied on their special relationship with Sparta for their security, a factor that, ironically, may help to explain the timing of the Athenian attack.

Frustrated by Spartan arms in the Peloponnesus and by Spartan diplomacy in the north, the Athenians may have been eager to demonstrate that, at least on the sea, the Spartans were powerless to do Athens harm. The Athenians sent 30 ships, 1,200 hoplites, 300 archers, and 20 mounted archers of their own to Melos; their allies, most of whom were probably islanders, sent 8 ships and 1,500 hoplites. The participation of such a high proportion of allies and islanders suggests that the attack was not perceived as especially unjustified, nor are we told of any dissension among the Athenians over the decision to undertake the invasion. The expedition did not seem important enough to invite the participation of either Nicias or Alcibiades, however, so Tisias and Cleomedes led the allied forces. Before laying waste the fields of Melos they sent ambassadors to the Melians to persuade them to submit.

The Melian magistrates refused to allow the ambassadors to address the people, presumably fearing that the masses would be willing to yield, and instead arranged for them to speak before the magistrates themselves and probably an oligarchic council. The purpose of the Athenians was to convince the Melians to surrender without fighting, a goal they may have hoped to achieve more readily by menace than by any other device. Such an approach, at any rate, was perfectly in keeping with their recent dealings with Scione, where the policy of mild treatment of fractious allies had been abandoned in favor of rule by terror. The blunt, hard language the Athenians used with Melos was not a unique occurrence in their political dialogue. In public speeches both Pericles and Cleon had been willing to term the Athenian Empire a tyranny, and the Athenian spokesman at Sparta in 432 used language not unlike that found in the Melian Dialogue: "We have done nothing amazing or contrary to human nature if we accepted an empire that was given to us and then refused to give it up, since we were conquered by the strongest motives—honor, fear and self-interest. And we are not the first to have acted this way, for it has always been ordained that the weaker are kept down by the stronger" (1.76.2).

The Melians, however, refused to yield, both because they believed that their cause was just, so the gods would not allow their defeat, and because they trusted the Spartans to come to their defense. The Athenians dismissed the threat of Spartan assistance as easily as they rejected divine intervention. The Spartans, they said, "most blatantly of all men we know, believe that what is agreeable is noble and what is expedient just," and that did not bode well for the Melians. The Spartans acted only when they had superior power and so, "it is not likely they will cross over to an island so long as we control the sea" (5.109).

The Athenians proceeded to besiege their city, until hunger, discouragement, and fear of treason finally compelled the Melians to surrender. The Athenians voted to kill all their men and to sell their women and children into slavery. Alcibiades is said to have proposed or supported the decree, but there is no evidence that Nicias or anyone else opposed it. By now the Athenians had thoroughly abandoned the moderate imperial policy of Pericles as a failure and chosen the harder one of Cleon in the hope of deterring future resistance and rebellion. Such would have been the reasoned explanation for their new course, but emotions must certainly have played at least as strong a part. Surely this was another of the events in Thucydides' mind when he spoke of war as a "violent teacher."

NICIAS AGAINST ALCIBIADES

WITHIN ATHENS Nicias and Alcibiades brought new sophistication and techniques to the practice of democratic politics, reminding a modern reader of political campaigns in our own time, when issues are subordinate to personalities and each politician tries to project a favorable "image" by means of some extraordinary display. Such novel methods, moreover, called for each competitor to possess and expend vast sums of money. In 417 Nicias, playing on his reputation for religious piety, gave a spectacular demonstration of his devotion to the gods, using the Athenians' dedication of a temple of Apollo at Delos to put on a great display, lending an unprecedented degree of opulence, precision, and drama to the choral procession. At sunrise he led the Athenian contingent from the nearby island of Rheneia over a bridge of boats he had built to span the exact distance between the two islands and decorated it with the richest tapestries in glorious colors. The beautifully costumed chorus, singing as it went, seemed to those on Delos as if it was walking on water into the rising sun. Then Nicias dedicated to Apollo a bronze palm three that soon became famous and gave the god a piece of land that cost no less than ten thousand drachmas, whose revenues were to endow sacrificial banquets where the gods were to be asked to bring blessings down upon the donor. Plutarch observes that "in all this there was much vulgar ostentation aimed at increasing his reputation and satisfying his ambition" (*Nicias* 3.4–4.1). Most Athenians, however, were deeply impressed by the spectacle and believed that the gods must favor so pious a man and smile on the city he led. In the following year Alcibiades matched this performance with one very different but no less grandiose. At the Olympic Games of 416 he entered seven teams in the chariot race, more than any private citizen had ever put forward, and three of them came in first, second, and fourth. Without embarrassment Alcibiades later explained the political motive behind this extravagant and expensive flamboyance at a religious festival: he wanted, he said, to demonstrate Athenian power. Because of this great show of wealth, "the Greeks believed our city to be more powerful than it was . . . though earlier they expected that we had been worn down by the war" (6.16.2). His more immediate target, however, was the Athenian voter. To the image of Nicias' mature piety he opposed one of the dash and boldness of a younger and more enterprising generation. These extravaganzas were part of a continuing campaign for political supremacy, but for the moment they afforded the competitors no clear advantage.

Neither Nicias nor Alcibiades was driven by greed for wealth, nor was either eager to turn policy decisions over to the masses. Both, however, had ambitions of being first in the Athenian state, while lacking the remarkable political gifts that occasionally appeared in a figure like Cimon or Pericles. The misfortune of Athens was that although the two men wanted to become the successor to the Olympian Pericles, the best each could do was to interfere with the plans of the other.

Part Five

THE DISASTER IN SICILY

THE ATHENIAN EXPEDITION to Sicily in 415 has been
compared with the British attempt to seize the Dardanelles
in 1915 or the American war in Vietnam in the 1960s and
1970s, undertakings whose purposes and feasibility remain
controversial, and which ended in defeat and different degrees of disaster. The Athenian venture produced the most terrible outcome, devastating losses in men and ships, rebellions in the empire and the entry
into the war against Athens of the mighty Persian Empire, all contributing to the general opinion that the Athenians were finished. So
great was the disaster that, even in retrospect, Thucydides marveled at
Athens' ability to hold out for almost a decade more. Such campaigns
always provoke heated debate as to why they were undertaken, why
they failed and who was to blame. The Athenian expedition to Sicily is
no exception.

CHAPTER TWENTY

The Decision (416–415)

ATHENS' SICILIAN CONNECTIONS

THE IMPETUS for a new Sicilian campaign in the winter of 416/5 came not from Athens but from Sicily, when two Greek cities on the island that had been allies for decades, Segesta and Leontini, sent to the Athenians for help against the neighboring city of Selinus and its protector, Syracuse. Athens had been particularly concerned about Sicily since the Congress of Gela in 424, when Hermocrates of Syracuse proposed a doctrine rejecting the interference of foreign states in Sicilian affairs. The advantages of such a policy for the Syracusans soon became apparent: with Athens out of the way, they intervened in a civil war in Leontini and launched a campaign to gain command of the city.

In 422, troubled by the growing power of Syracuse, the Athenians had sent Phaeax son of Erasistratus to assess the situation. His goal was to protect Leontini by urging Athens' allies and other Sicilian Greeks to unite against Syracuse. Although he gained support in southern Italy and in some Sicilian cities, a sharp rebuff at Gela put an end to his efforts. He had come with only two ships and abandoned his mission at the first negative response, but this evidence of continued Athenian interest in the island's affairs may have encouraged Syracuse's enemies to seek help from Athens in the future.

In 416/5 the Segestans, hard put in their war against Selinus, aided by Syracuse, turned to Athens for assistance. Their main argument was that "If the Syracusans, who had depopulated Leontini, were not punished and, after destroying their allies who were still left, took power over all of Sicily, there was the risk that at some time in the future, as Dorians to Dorians and as kinsmen and colonists of the Peloponnesians, they might send them help with a great force and help destroy the power of Athens" (6.6.2). They also offered to bear the costs of the

war and appealed to notions of traditional ties and obligations to allies, as well as stressing the importance of defense against future aggression. Thucydides, however, believed that the Athenians were not
especially interested in these issues, which only served them as a pretext: "The truest explanation" of the Athenians' favorable response, he
explained, was that "they longed for the rule of the whole island"
(6.6.1).

From his first mention of Sicily Thucydides insists that the Athenians had always intended to conquer and dominate it. He portrays
the Athenian masses as greedy, power-hungry, and ill-informed about
their enemy. "The many," he reports, "were ignorant of the magnitude
of the island and of the number of its inhabitants both Greek and barbarian and that they were taking on a war not much inferior to the one
against the Peloponnesians" (6.6.1).

Yet between 427 and 424 as many as twelve thousand Athenians in
the fleet had been to Sicily and traveled throughout it and its neighborhood. They could not have avoided learning a great deal about its
geography and population, and would surely have shared their knowledge with friends and relatives; in addition, most of them were still in
Athens in 415. The Athenians' consideration of Segesta's request, moreover, demonstrates little of what could be characterized as reckless ex-
uberance. They carefully sent ambassadors "to see if the money was
there, as the Segestans said, in the public treasury and the temples,
and, at the same time, to discover how the war against the Selinuntians
was going" (6.6.3). To be sure, the Segestans carried out elaborate deceptions to convince the Athenians of their great wealth, but the Athenians were more persuaded by the immediate presentation of sixty
talents in coined silver, a full month's pay for sixty warships. Only
when the ambassadors returned with the money did the assembly take
up the issue of intervention again in earnest.

THE DEBATE IN ATHENS

IN MARCH 415 the Athenian assembly discussed the merits of
Segesta's request once more and this time voted to send sixty ships to
Sicily under the command of Alcibiades, Nicias, and Lamachus. They

had full powers to help Segesta against Selinus; to restore Leontini, if they could; and "to settle affairs in Sicily in whatever way they judged best for Athens" (6.8.2). Nicias was chosen as general for the expedition "against his will, because he thought that the city had made a wrong decision" (6.8.4).

Even before this assembly had taken place Alcibiades, in contrast, had captured the imagination of the Athenian people, who "sat in groups drawing the map of Sicily and of the sea around it and the harbors of the island" (Plutarch, *Nicias* 12). While as the chief advocate of the expedition he would have been the natural choice for a single command, many in Athens suspected, envied, and disliked him. Although he could not be excluded, including Nicias would serve to balance Alcibiades' youthful, ambitious daring with the elder statesman's experience, caution, piety, and luck. Nicias must have made his reluctance to serve as general clear, but it would have been considered unpatriotic or cowardly of him to refuse the commission.

Assigning two generals who disagreed on all aspects of the projected campaign jointly to command it, however, was clearly an impossible situation, so the assembly also chose a third, Lamachus son of Xenophanes. Lamachus, an experienced soldier, was about fifty years old in 415; Aristophanes had presented him as something of a young *miles gloriosus* in the *Acharnians* and teased him about his poverty. He could be counted on to support the mission's purpose, while respecting the advice of Nicias.

To Thucydides' assertion that the stated purposes of the Sicilian expedition were only a pretext to disguise more ambitious goals, the size of the Athenian force provides an adequate response: the fleet was the identical size as the one that ventured to Sicily in 424. There had been no possibility of conquering Sicily with sixty ships in 424, and no plan for doing so. The decision to send the same number in March 415 indicates, once again, limited intentions.

The growth of Syracusan power since 424, however, may well have increased their scope of Athenian goals. Unchecked, Syracuse might gain control of much of Sicily and tip the balance in the Greek world in favor of the Peloponnesians. Many or most of the Athenians at the first assembly might have believed that settling affairs in the Athenian interest demanded the defeat or even the conquest of Syracuse. A surprise attack directly on the city from the sea might succeed with only sixty ships, as might an attempt to recruit Sicilian allies who could overawe or defeat the Syracusans. In either case, the risk to Athens would be low. A land attack on Syracuse would be carried out by Sicilian soldiers, for the Athenians were not sending an army. Even a naval attack need not present significant danger, for the fleet could draw back if it found the enemy ready and too strong. In the worst case, if the entire expedition was destroyed, it would have to be considered a great misfortune but not a strategic disaster. Many of the sailors would be allies, not Athenians, and the ships could be replaced. An expedition of the scope voted by the assembly, in any case, could not lead to the kind of catastrophe that might threaten Athenian survival, such as the eventual undertaking brought.

THE DEBATE TO RECONSIDER

ANOTHER ASSEMBLY MET a few days after the first to consider "how the fleet could be equipped most quickly and to vote anything else the generals might need for the expedition" (6.8.3). Nicias came to the session with the intention of turning the debate away from the subject of ways and means of conducting the campaign and instead to force a reconsideration of the entire project, so he must have spoken first. Proposing to repeal a decree just passed by the assembly, while apparently not strictly illegal, seems to have been unusual enough to have run the risk of introducing a number of different legal challenges both for Nicias and the president of the assembly, who granted his request. But Nicias believed that the importance of the subject was worth the gamble and urged the president "to become a physician to the state that has decided badly" (6.14).

Nicias offered a grim evaluation of Athens' current diplomatic and military situation, one that raises serious questions about the wisdom of his policy in making the peace that bears his name and the subsequent alliance with Sparta. The Athenians, he argued, could not afford to attack, for they already had powerful enemies at home. The peace treaty existed in name only; the Spartans had been forced into it and still disputed its terms, while some of their allies had simply rejected it.

A failed expedition to Sicily would not only weaken Athens but might also bring additional Sicilian forces over to the Spartan side. The Spartans were only waiting for the right moment to strike for victory, while the Athenians were still recovering from the war. "We must not," he said in an echo of Pericles' warning, "reach out for another empire until we have made the one we have secure" (6.10.5). He also reminded his listeners that the Carthaginians, though more powerful than Athens, had been unable to conquer Sicily.

The advocates of the expedition had evidently given serious credence to the appeals from the Sicilian allies, for Nicias took pains to disparage and discredit them as "a barbaric people" who involved the Athenians in trouble but offered no help in return. The threat posed by Syracuse, however, was obviously the main argument at the previous assembly, because Nicias devoted the majority of his effort to dismiss it at the next, but he could produce only vain and specious rebuttals, such as: "The Sicilians . . . would be even less dangerous than they are now if ruled by the Syracusans, for now they might attack us singly out of feeling for the Spartans, but if the Syracusans were in control it is not likely that an empire would attack another empire" (6.11.3). Another misguided assertion was that the Greeks in Sicily could best be deterred by the Athenians' not going there at all, for if the expedition was mounted and then failed, the Sicilians would readily join the Spartans in contempt of Athenian power. It would be best, he concluded, not to undertake the expedition at all, but if they must, the Athenians should make only a brief show of force and return home at once.

The most striking aspect of Nicias' speech is what it omitted, for it made no clear reference to any proposal to conquer and annex the island. Instead, he launched a personal attack on the main architect of the plan. Alcibiades, he said, was a member of a dangerously ambitious younger generation, and sought to endanger the state for his own glory and profit.

The target of this attack offered the chief response, and Thucydides takes this opportunity to characterize him vividly: "The most eager for the expedition was Alcibiades son of Cleinias. . . . He was eager to be designated general, hoping to capture both Sicily and Carthage and, if he succeeded, to increase his own private wealth and reputation" (6.15.2–3). Such desires ultimately had the most deadly consequences: "It was just this that later on did most to destroy the Athenian state. For the many were afraid of the extent of his lawless self-indulgence in his way of life and also of his purpose in each and every affair in which he became involved; they became hostile to him on the grounds that he was aiming at a tyranny. And so, although in public affairs he conducted his military functions in the best possible way, his activities in his private life offended everyone, so they turned the leadership of the state over to other men and before long brought the state to ruin" (6.15.3–4).

Alcibiades proudly defended his grand style of life and also the policy that led to the battle of Mantinea: "I brought together the greatest states of the Peloponnesus without great danger or expense to you and made them risk everything on a single day. As a result of that even today they do not conduct themselves with solid confidence" (6.16).

On the practical prospects for the expedition Alcibiades was no less biased than his opponent, but his arguments were better founded. He described Sicily's Greek cities as seriously unstable and lacking patriotic determination, and expressed the belief that Athenian diplomacy could win them over, as well as the barbarian Sicels, who hated Syracuse. Alcibiades' account of the situation in mainland Greece portrayed the Spartans as without hope or initiative. As they had no fleet to challenge the vast Athenian armada they could do no more decisive harm to Attica than their previous invasions had accomplished. Nothing short of an enormous disaster at sea could change the strategic balance to Athens' detriment, and at the moment they were planning to risk only sixty ships.

Alcibiades went on to emphasize the necessity of supporting their allies. "What plausible excuse could we give ourselves for shrinking back, or what defense could we offer to our allies in Sicily for not coming to their aid? We must assist them, for we have given our oath" (6.18.1). He then presented a novel analysis of the character of Athens and its empire. Just to maintain what they had achieved, he argued the Athenians must pursue an active policy on behalf of allies. "That is how we have acquired our empire and that is how others who have had empire acquired theirs—by always coming eagerly to the aid of those who called upon us, whether Greek or barbarian" (6.18.2). To

adopt a peaceful policy of limited ambition and to set arbitrary pa-
rameters for the boundaries of the empire would be disastrous.

Alcibiades then spoke of his larger goals for the Sicilian expedition: victory in Sicily, he insisted, would bring the Athenians control of
all Greece. In the second year of the war Pericles had expressed a similar sentiment, but he had done so to restore the confidence of the "un-
reasonably discouraged," Athenians to fight a war they could not
afford to lose, not to support an expedition for new conquests.

Alcibiades concluded with an argument that bears the stamp of
the Sophists, those teachers of rhetoric and other skills who trained the
wealthy young men of the day and who made much of the difference
between the natural world and the customs of human society. Athens,
he said, unlike some other states (Sparta being the obvious antithesis),
was active by its very nature and could therefore not afford to adopt a
passive policy. A long period of peace and inactivity would dull precisely the skills and character that had brought the city to greatness,
but even more serious were the consequences of going against its nature. "A city that is active would quickly be destroyed by a change to
passivity, and those people find the greatest safety who conduct their
affairs in the greatest harmony with their existing character and customs" (6.18.7). It was a remarkable rhetorical trick, lending a conservative coloration to what was in fact a daring departure.

When Nicias realized that the speech had increased the Athenians'
eagerness for the expedition, he turned from honest opposition to outright deception. He "knew that he could no longer turn them away
from the expedition with the same arguments, but thought he might
change their minds if he exaggerated the size of the force it required"
(6.19.2). This maneuver recalls the ruse he attempted in 425 concerning the Spartan men trapped at Sphacteria, when he attempted to defeat Cleon by offering him the generalship in the expectation that he
would refuse and be discredited. At the assembly of 415 his intention
was to sober the Athenians by making them appreciate the vastness of
the proposed undertaking and in so doing undermine Alcibiades. On
both occasions the trick failed and produced unintended results.

With biting sarcasm he rejected Alcibiades' image of a weak and
divided Sicily, depicting it instead as a powerful, wealthy, and militarily formidable opponent hostile to Athens and prepared to fight. The

enemy had a great numerical advantage, local grain to feed its armies, and plentiful horses to serve its cavalry; the latter two provisions were unavailable to the small force voted by the Athenians. The enemy cavalry, he pointed out, could easily pin the small Athenian force on the beach without adequate supplies. When winter came communication with Athens might take as long as four months. An Athenian triumph would require a vast armada of warships and supply vessels and a large army of many hoplites, as well as many light-armed troops to cope with the enemy cavalry. In addition, the expedition would require a great deal of money, for the Segestan promises of underwriting its costs, he insisted, could not be trusted.

Even if the Athenians did mount so large a force, Nicias continued, their victory would not be easy. Dispatching the expedition would be like sending off a colony to a far and hostile country. The venture would need careful planning, and good luck, but since luck was beyond human control, he would prudently depend on careful preparation. "I think that the preparation I have suggested provide the greatest security for the state and safety for those of us who go out on the expedition. But if anyone thinks otherwise, I offer to give up my command to him" (6.23).

With so pessimistic an analysis and such dire forebodings Nicias may have hoped to be contradicted and thereby to have an excuse to resign the command; perhaps he believed that such a gesture by the most experienced, pious, and fortunate member of the projected leadership team might temper the assembly. If so, he again miscalculated badly. Instead of being dissuaded by the prospect of assuming the burden of so large an expedition the assembly became more eager than ever, "and the outcome was exactly the opposite of what he expected" (6.24.2), for the people were convinced that he had given good advice.

A man called Demostratus, a nobleman but a leading radical politician in favor of the expedition and renewal of the war, now embarrassed Nicias with an unexpected challenge: precisely how large on increase in forces did he recommend? Forced to reply, Nicias proposed the figure of one hundred triremes, five thousand hoplites, and a proportional number of light-armed troops. In the heat of the debate, he neglected to ask for cavalry, in spite of the significant advantage he had predicted the enemy would gain from their own cavalry. The Athenians then voted to give the generals full powers to determine the size of the expedition and "to act in whatever way seemed best to them for Athens" (6.26.2).

Against his intentions, Nicias managed in the second assembly to convert an expedition of moderate size with limited goals and liability into a vast armada burdened with great ambitions and expectations, whose failure could bring disaster. No other Athenian politician could have dared to propose so large a force, and no other one did so in either of the assemblies. It was only after Nicias' speech in the second of them that the Athenians turned from a cautious and limited venture to a risky, ill-conceived and unplanned, unlimited commitment. Without his intervention they would undoubtedly have sailed against Sicily in 415, but there could have been no chance of their embarking on a major catastrophe.

CHAPTER TWENTY-ONE

The Home Front and the
First Campaigns (415)

SACRILEGE

THUCYDIDES DESCRIBES the mood in Athens in the spring of 415 as one of eagerness and enthusiasm for the Sicilian campaign: "A passion came upon all of them equally to sail off. The older men thought that either they would conquer or at least that such a great force could not come to harm. Those who were in their prime longed for distant sights and spectacles, being confident that they would be safe. The mass of the people and the soldiers hoped to get money at the moment and to make an addition to their empire from which they would have a never-ending source of income" (6.24.3).

Still, the expedition was not without controversy. Some priests warned against it, and others reported omens of disaster, but Alcibiades and proponents of the campaign produced counteromens and oracles. Even spectacular negative signs failed to halt the preparations, but soon before the scheduled departure more serious events became a cause for general alarm.

On the morning of June 7, 415, the Athenians awoke to find stone statues of Hermes throughout the city with their faces smashed and their distinctive phalluses hacked off. Apart from the outrage and fear generated by this terrible sacrilege, the details suggested that the religious violation had a political dimension, as well. The desecrators had carried out their attack over a wide area and in the course of a single night, proof that the perpetrators were not a few drunken revelers but a considerable group of men acting in concert. As Hermes was the god of travelers, the assault on his images was an obvious effort to prevent the planned expedition to Sicily. The Athenians "took the matter seriously, for it seemed to be an omen for the voyage and to have been done on behalf of a conspiracy to make a revolution and destroy the democracy" (6.27.3).

The assembly launched an investigation, offering rewards and immunity to witnesses who would offer evidence about this or any sacrilege. The council established a commission of inquiry including eminent democratic politicians. As the final plans for the expedition were under discussion a man called Pythonicus stunned the assembly with an accusation that Alcibiades and his friends had been discovered parodying the sacred mysteries of Eleusis. Under a grant of immunity a slave testified that he and others had seen the mysteries performed in the house of Pulytion, naming Alcibiades and nine others as the participants.

Although this event had no connection with the mutilation of the Hermae, the already charged atmosphere and the alleged involvement of Alcibiades made it the subject of great attention. Because few Athenians doubted that Alcibiades and his wild friends were capable of mocking a religious ritual, his enemies enthusiastically seized upon the charges, asserting that Alcibiades was involved in both the profanation of the mysteries and the vandalism of the statues, adding that he sought "the destruction of the democracy" (6.28.2).

Alcibiades denied all the charges and offered to stand trial immediately, wishing to avoid a hearing in absentia, when the soldiers and sailors who supported him would be away on the expedition and his enemies would be free to make their case against him with little opposition. Those enemies, in fact, wanted to delay the trial for the very same reason: "Let him sail off now with good luck," they said. "When the war is over let him come back here and defend himself. The laws will be the same then as now" (Plutarch, *Alcibiades* 19.4). The assembly agreed, and Alcibiades departed Athens with the charge hanging over his head.

The Athenian force finally left for Sicily in the second half of June, planning to stop first at Corcyra, where they would meet the allies. It was "the most expensive and glorious armament coming from a single city with a purely Greek force that put to sea up to that time" (6.31.1). The trierarchs had spent their own money in addition to state funds to make their vessels not only fast and strong but beautiful, as well, and even the hoplites competed in the splendor of their equipment. The entire city and the foreign allies who were present went down to the Piraeus to see the great spectacle. "It looked more like a display of power and wealth before the rest of the Greeks than an expedition against enemies" (6.31.1). A trumpet sounded, and the great throng offered the prayers customary on sending ships off to sea. "When they had sung the paean and finished the libations they set out, at first in column, then, as they sailed off, they raced each other as far as Aegina" (6.32.2). The great expedition, inflated to dangerous proportions by the failed stratagem of Nicias, rowed away as if taking part in a regatta rather than to a distant and dangerous adventure.

WITCH HUNT

WITH THE ARMADA safely at sea the investigating committee eagerly pursued its inquiries into the recent scandals. Teucrus, a resident alien who had fled to Megara, returned to Athens under a promise of immunity with sensational testimony: he claimed that he had participated in the parody of the mysteries and could identify the perpetrators of the mutilation of the Hermae, naming eleven other parodists and eighteen men he accused of attacking the statues. Alcibiades appeared on neither list. The committee arrested and executed one of these suspects, but all the others fled to safety.

Next a man called Diocleides testified about the Hermae affair, relating an account of a moonlight walk he had taken on the night of the crime during which he saw about three hundred conspirators gathered in the orchestra of the theater of Dionysus on the south slope of the Acropolis. Concluding the next morning that they must be the culprits, he went to some of those he could identify to attempt to extort money from them. Bribes were promised but not delivered, so Diocleides denounced forty-two of them, a group that included two members of the council and several rich aristocrats. These accusations fueled the fear of a general oligarchic plot against the Athenian democracy, and so great was the ensuing panic that the council suspended a law that forbade the torture of Athenian citizens to obtain their testimony. Peisander, who proposed the measure, planned to put the suspects on the rack in the hope of obtaining swift confessions. The two council members managed to avoid torture by promising to stand trial, but when they fled to Megara or Boeotia, and a Boeotian army subsequently appeared on the Athenian border, the city's alarm increased as fear of treason and invasion was added to fear of revolution, whether to oligarchy or tyranny.

That night the people of Athens put on their armor and did not sleep, and the council moved up to the Acropolis for safety. The grateful Athenians voted the informer Diocleides a hero's wreath and free meals at the Prytaneum—a treatment usually reserved for Olympic victors—but his glory was short-lived. Andocides, one of the accused prisoners and later a famous Athenian orator, also agreed to testify, and under a grant of immunity from the council revealed that his political dining club (*hetairia*) was responsible for the mutilation. He produced a list of the guilty, all of whom also appeared on the list of Teucrus; with the exception of four men who fled immediately, all were either already dead or in exile. The council then questioned Diocleides, who admitted his testimony had been false, claiming that he had acted on the instructions of Alcibiades' cousin, Alcibiades son of Phegus, and another man, who both took flight. Those implicated by his perjured testimony were cleared, and Diocleides was executed.

The Athenians were comforted, believing that the affair of the Hermae was now satisfactorily cleared up, and that they had escaped "many evils and dangers" (Andocides, *De Mysteriis* 66). The criminals had evidently been only a small number of men, members of a single *hetairia* with few important politicians, and not a major conspiracy. The matter of the profanation of the sacred mysteries, however, remained to be solved, so the inquisition was carried forward.

A new accusation came from the highest quarters of Athenian society in the person of Agariste, the wife of Alcmeonides; both names had a connection with one of Athens' greatest families, to which Cleisthenes, the founder of the Athenian democracy, and Pericles belonged. Agariste reported a profanation of the mysteries performed by Alcibiades, his uncle Axiochus, and his friend Adeimantus in the house of a nobleman. Once again Alcibiades' enemies used the testimony for their political ends, claiming that the mockery of sacred rites was part of "a conspiracy against the democracy" (6.61.1). The combination of enemy troop movements, the accusations against perhaps one hundred men of one or another sacrilege on the very eve of a great expedition to a distant land, and the alleged involvement of politicians, aristocrats, and especially Alcibiades himself only served to reignite anxieties about conspiracy, treason, and danger to the constitution. "Suspicion gathered about Alcibiades from all sides" (6.61.4). His formal accuser was Thessalus, son of the great Cimon, whose lineage and noble family lent weight to the charge, as did the detailed nature of its particulars. The matter was now serious enough that the council sent the state trireme *Salaminia* to retrieve Alcibiades and several other members of the expedition who had been accused to stand trial in Athens.

At this point it is worth considering the question of who committed the sacrileges, and why. The profanations of the mysteries were, no doubt, carried out by one of the dining and drinking clubs, *hetairiai*, which were then common among the young and wealthy aristocrats of Athens. The parodies of 415 did not have any political significance, however, for they were performed privately with no ability or intention to influence anyone outside the circle of revelers.

The assault on the Hermae was a more serious affair, and not merely a drunken joke. Organization, planning, and a much larger group of men were needed to undertake a plan as ambitious as the disfigurement of statues of the god all over Athens. Andocides, confirmed by other sources, gives the most plausible account when he tells us that his own *hetairia* was responsible, under the leadership of Euphilitus and Meletus. There is, however, no reason to believe the vandalism was an element in a plot to overthrow the constitution, whether for oligarchic or tyrannical ends. None of the informers, whether truthful or not, made such a claim, and no ancient evidence supports it.

It can be no coincidence, however, that the deed was executed just before the expedition to Sicily was set to depart, and there is no doubt that it was politically motivated. Some Athenians believed the Corinthians were responsible, intending to prevent the attack on Sicily. Whether or not any foreigners did take part in the sacrilege, it is completely plausible that the Athenians who plotted it had just such a purpose in mind. They knew that Nicias had already been appointed as one of the generals, and he was not only the most visibly pious man in Athens, much given to belief in omens and the patron of his own seer, but also famously cautious and opposed to the expedition. The Athenians, like most Greeks, were also superstitious, and on many occasions stopped public meetings because of natural events like thunderstorms and earthquakes. What could be a more likely result of the plotters' efforts than that Nicias would take alarm at so great a sacrilege against the god of travelers on the eve of this greatest of communal voyages?

The conspirators had no reason to anticipate the confusion the revelations about the mysteries would cause, but instead counted on generating a powerful fear and consternation that would lead to widespread questioning of the meaning of the attacks on the Hermae and their relevance for the expedition. One accidental consequence of the hysteria caused by the double sacrilege was a strong inhibiting effect on Nicias, who could no longer assume the role he might have been expected to play. Two of his brothers were among those named in the lists of the perpetrators, and one seems to have been guilty. As soon as their names were made public it was impossible for Nicias to use the mutilations as a reason for cancelling the expedition, for he would have immediately been suspected of being part of a conspiracy to achieve his failed policy by other means. The unexpected additional outrages destroyed whatever chances the bizarre plot may have had for success.

Also contrary to any expectations were the repercussions from Alcibiades' involvement in the affair of the mysteries. Although he played no part in the attacks on the Hermae, his political opponents took advantage of the widespread panic to discredit him just as he was ready to sail. His enemies on all sides later recalled him to a trial in Athens that would take place in the absence of his strongest supporters, at which he could not expect to prevail. In a way that no one could have foreseen the enemies of the Sicilian expedition took actions that, while they could could not prevent it, would ultimately contribute greatly to its disastrous failure.

ATHENIAN STRATEGY

THE ATHENIAN FORCE that left Piraeus contained 134 fighting triremes, 60 of them Athenian, and an unknown number of troop ships carrying 5,100 hoplites, 1,500 of them Athenians, the largest body of hoplites the Athenians had used to date during the war, except for those sent to ravage the land of Megara. Athens also supplied 700 thetes, who served as marines on the triremes, with most of the rest coming from the subject states of the empire and a few from free allies such as Argos and Mantinea. There were also about 1,300 light-armed troops of different kinds. One horse transport ship carried 30 men and their horses—the only cavalry on the expedition—and 30 cargo ships transported food, supplies, bakers, stonemasons, carpenters, and tools for building walls.

At Corcyra each general took command of one-third of the fleet, to enable individual actions and to ease the problem of supply. The entire fleet then crossed to the southern shore of Italy, where they met unanticipated resistance when the cities on which they had counted for supplies and bases shut them out. The key cities of Taras and Locris would not even permit them to anchor and obtain drinking water. The most important city of all was Rhegium, a strategic location from which to launch landings on the northern and eastern coasts of Sicily and to attack its major port of Messina across the strait. Although their Rhegian allies had cooperated fully with the Athenians in their previous venture on the island from 427 to 424, they now declared neutrality and barred entry to their city, allowing them only to beach their ships, make camp outside the walls, and buy supplies. What had changed the attitude of the Rhegians? The likeliest explanation is their perception of the vast size of this second expedition, which made it seem that the Athenians had come to conquer in the west as they had in the east, and not, as they claimed, to help their allies in local quarrels and to check the ambitions of Syracuse. The force of sixty ships that had originally been voted would probably not have made the same impression. The deflection of the great armada from its projected base was, in any case, a terrible blow to the expedition's prospects.

News from Segesta only added to the dismay of the Athenians. While Nicias was not surprised to learn that the Segestans had only thirty talents to offer to underwrite the campaign, his colleagues were appalled. All these developments compelled a reconsideration of aims and strategy, and Nicias therefore suggested a minimal approach: the Athenians should go to Selinus and demand pay for the entire force from the Segestans. If they agreed, which he knew was highly unlikely,

the Athenians "would consider the matter further" (6.47). If they refused, the Athenians should demand money to pay for the sixty ships
the Segestans had originally requested and then stay only until a peace
was arranged between Segesta and Selinus. After it was concluded,
they should sail along the Sicilian coast making a display of Athenian
power and sail home "unless they happened to find some quick and
unexpected way to help the Leontines or bring over any of the other
cities. But they should not endanger the state by spending its own resources" (6.47). These latter hypotheses were only fantasies, for Nicias'
true intention was to settle matters at Segesta in some way and then return immediately to Athens.

Such a plan would have been disastrous for Alcibiades, for to depart without having accomplished anything more would not only disgrace the chief proponent of the expedition but would also have a
negative impact on Athenian prestige, as it would leave Athens' Sicilian
allies at the mercy of their enemies and increase the chance of Syracusan domination of the island. Alcibiades proposed instead that the
Athenians try to gain the friendship of the Greek cities of Sicily and of
the native Sicels, who could provide food and troops. With such support they could attack Syracuse and Selinus, "unless Selinus came to
terms with Segesta and Syracuse permitted them to restore the Leontines to their homeland" (6.48).

Lamachus, in turn, wanted to sail directly to Syracuse and, "as soon
as possible fight a battle near the city while the city was unprepared and
most panic-stricken" (6.49.1). In the best case the Syracusans would surrender without a fight; failing that, the superior Athenians would prevail in a hoplite battle. In the worst case the Syracusans would refuse an
engagement and retreat behind their walls, but even in that case a swift
Athenian landing near the city would trap many Syracusans and their
goods outside the protection of the walls. The Athenians could then
seize their farms and use them for their own supply.

Lamachus' strategy could not have been the original one, for an attempt to attack Syracuse with only sixty triremes alone was inconceivable; he probably formulated it only when the refusal by Rhegium and
the revelation of Segestan deceit necessitated a new plan. Whatever its
origin, it had a number of shortcomings. Lamachus knew that a siege
of Syracuse would require a base nearby, so he recommended the

occupation of Megara Hyblaea, which had a good harbor in easy range (see Map 20). But the town had been deserted for decades and had neither farms nor markets, and could therefore not provide any supplies. The Athenians also lacked cavalry—a force with which the Syracusans were well supplied—which would be needed to guard the flanks of a hoplite phalanx or the builders of siege walls. If the assault did not achieve immediate success, these problems would loom large.

Even with these shortcomings, Demosthenes, an outstanding general, thought that Lamachus' advice was best. Thucydides' own judgment was that the Syracusans would have resisted an Athenian attack on their city and have subsequently lost in battle, in which case they could not have prevented the Athenians from cutting them off by land and sea and would have had to surrender. While no definitive assessment can be made in hindsight, it is entirely possible that Lamachus' strategy may have worked. His proposal, however, had no chance of adoption, for no plan could have been further from Nicias's wishes, and Alcibiades would hear of no plan other than his own. Lamachus, therefore, unwilling to accept Nicias' suggestion for inaction, lent his support to the scheme of Alcibiades, which became the Athenian strategy.

THE SUMMER CAMPAIGN OF 415

THE ATHENIAN FORCE now needed a large, secure, and convenient base from which to launch diplomatic missions and naval expeditions. With Rhegium unavailable, Messina was the most likely option, but the Messinians likewise prohibited Alcibiades from entering their town, offering only to provide a market. He was therefore compelled to take sixty ships from the armada—still camped uncomfortably outside Rhegium—and try his luck at Naxos, further along the coast. The Naxians were old enemies of Syracuse, so they received the Athenians into their city, but Catana, which lay to its south, was under the control of a pro-Syracusan faction and shut them out.

The Athenians established a camp near Leontini and from there ten ships eventually sailed into Syracuse harbor but found no fleet at anchor. The Athenians called out what amounted to an ultimatum but

20. SICILY AND SOUTHERN ITALY

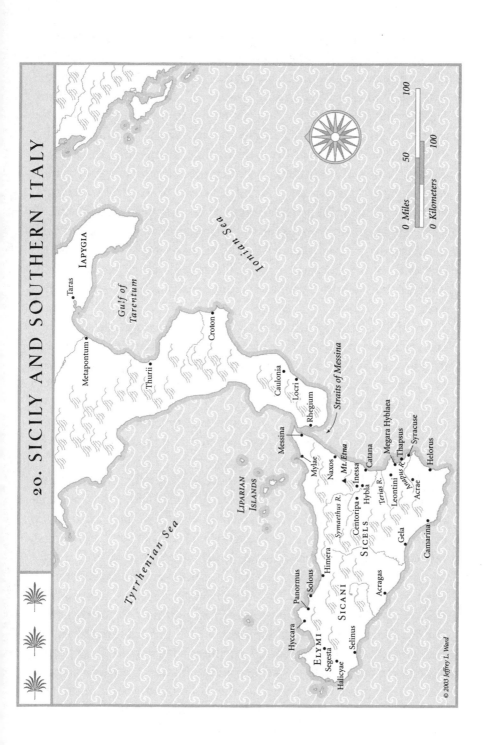

IAPYGIA

Taras

Gulf of
Tarentum

Metapontum

Thurii

Croton

Ionian Sea

Caulonia

Locri

Rhegium

Straits of Messina

Messina

Tyrrhenian Sea

Mylae

Naxos

Mt. Etna

LIPARIAN
ISLANDS

Inessa

Catana

Megara Hyblaea

Thapsus

Syracuse

Himera

Synaethus R.

Hybla

Amptus R.

Acrae

Helorus

Panormus

Solous

Centoripa

Terias R.

Leontini

SICELS

Hycara

ELYMI

Segesta

Acragas

Gela

Camarina

SICANI

Halicyae

Selinus

0 Miles   50   100

0 Kilometers   100

© 2003 Jeffrey L. Ward

received no answer, and after scouting the harbor and environs thoroughly they sailed out unharmed, but having effectively declared war. The enemy fleet was absent because the Syracusans had refused to believe the reports that the great armada was about to challenge them. The rich and powerful Syracusan state, a moderate democracy, took the warnings seriously enough to have a public discussion only when the Athenians were already at Corcyra. In the subsequent lengthy debate in the assembly Hermocrates son of Hermon, the dominant figure at the Congress of Gela in 424, which had driven Athens from the island, insisted that the great armada intended to conquer Syracuse and all Sicily. He urged the Syracusans to seek allies in Sicily, Italy, and even Carthage, the traditional enemy of the Sicilian Greeks, and to send for help to Corinth and Sparta. Meanwhile, they should dispatch a fleet to southern Italy where it could confront the armada before it reached Sicily.

Hermocrates' information was correct, but his strategic advice was open to question. Syracuse's navy was no match, either in numbers or in skill, for the Athenian fleet that was even now bearing down on Sicily. In any case, it would have been impossible for the Syracusans to build, man, and send a strong enough fleet to Italy in time to cut off the Athenians, as he must have known. Perhaps his advice was intended to overcome his countrymen's lethargy and reluctance with false hopes of a quick and easy success.

Some trick must have seemed necessary, for the Syracusans remained disinclined to take any action. A demagogue named Athenagoras insisted that the Athenians were not really coming, for it would be foolish of them to do so; those who believed they were, he claimed, intended to create conditions in which they could overthrow the democracy. In any case, the general consensus among the Syracusans was that they could easily defeat Athenian attackers. An unnamed Syracusan general of great common sense and personal authority pointed out that it could do no harm to prepare a defense in case the Athenians really did appear. The Syracusans should send envoys to the appropriate states to ask for help—a step, he admitted, the generals had already taken. He promised to report to the assembly anything more they might learn but passed over in silence the idea of sending an expedition to Italy, after which the assembly adjourned.

When they learned that the Athenians had landed at Rhegium, they finally began to take some measures for protection "on the assumption that war was coming swiftly, indeed was almost upon them" (6.45). These measures did not include the preparation of a fleet, as the Athenians learned when they sailed into an empty harbor.

From Syracuse the Athenians went back to Catana, which on a second attempt they were able to take by trickery and bring into their alliance. They now had a base from which they could either attack Syracuse or carry out the diplomatic warfare planned by Alcibiades. False reports that an opportunity existed to seize Camarina and that the Syracusans had built a fleet caused them to take their force to both cities to no purpose, but so as not to waste the effort they raided Syracusan territory. As they withdrew, a few straggling light-armed troops were killed by Syracusan cavalry, an omen for the future.

THE FLIGHT OF ALCIBIADES

AT CATANA the Athenians had found the state trireme *Salaminia* waiting to bring Alcibiades and the others indicted for mutilating the Hermae or profaning the mysteries back to Athens to stand trial. Plutarch believes that Alcibiades could have started a mutiny if he had wished, but the disappointing results of the expedition to date may have undermined his popularity, and he submitted quietly. He promised to follow the *Salaminia* on his own trireme, but he must have learned from the crew the nature of the situation in Athens and decided to escape. At Thurii in Italy he fled inland and made for the Peloponnesus.

In Athens he was convicted in absentia; with the others accused he was condemned to death, his property was confiscated, his name was inscribed on a stele of disgrace erected on the Acropolis, and a reward of a talent was promised to whoever succeeded in killing any who had fled. Another decree ordered that Alcibiades' name, and presumably the names of the rest of the guilty, be cursed by the Eleusinian priests. In response the fugitive Alcibiades is supposed to have said: "I will show them I am alive" (Plutarch, *Alcibiades* 22.2).

The departure of Alcibiades left Nicias as the de facto leader of the expedition. While he would have liked to pursue the passive strategy he had proposed and return home as soon as possible, the passage of time and the expenditure of much money and several lives to no purpose made that option impossible. Neither his troops nor the Athenians would have been satisfied with such a result, so Nicias moved the entire armada toward Segesta and Selinus to see what could be done about the situation that had originally brought the Athenians to Sicily.

He sailed through the Straits of Messina toward northwestern Sicily, "as far as possible from the Syracusan enemy" (Plutarch, *Nicias* 15.3). Although the armada was not permitted to land at Himera, the only Greek city in chiefly Carthaginian territory, the Athenians attacked Hyccara, a town of native Sicans hostile to Segesta, turned it over to the Segestans and enslaved the "barbarian" inhabitants. Nicias himself went to Segesta to collect the money that had been pledged and to try to settle its quarrel with Selinus. The results must have been completely discouraging, for he collected only thirty talents from Segesta, presumably all the money he could find, and rejoined his army at Catana. By now the Athenians had approached almost every Greek city in Sicily. (So far as we know they did not appeal to Gela or Acragas, probably because they knew their overtures would be futile.) The strategy of Alcibiades had also failed, and emblematic of the entire campaign was a subsequent unsuccessful assault on a small town near Catana.

The first campaigning season was a great disappointment; the departure of Alcibiades left the venture in the hands of a leader who did not believe in its goals and who had no strategy of his own to achieve them. Plutarch described the situation as follows: "Nicias, though theoretically one of two colleagues, held sole power. He did not stop sitting about, sailing around, and thinking things over until the vigorous hope of his men had grown feeble and the astonishment and fear that the first sight of his forces had imposed on the enemy had faded away" (*Nicias* 14.4). Since he still dared not leave Sicily, Nicias and his men would now be compelled to face the main enemy at Syracuse without a clear plan of action.

CHAPTER TWENTY-TWO

The First Attack on Syracuse (415)

NICIAS' DELAYS and evasions in confronting their city restored confidence to the Syracusans, who insisted that their generals lead them against the Athenians at Catana. Syracusan cavalrymen rode up to the Athenians and insulted them by asking, "Have you come to settle here with us on someone else's land instead of resettling the Leontines on their own?" (6.63). Nicias could hesitate no longer, but faced the problem of how to get his forces into position to attack Syracuse. The fleet could not land against an armed opponent who was now ready to face it, and while the hoplite army could march to Syracuse safely, the Athenians also had many light-armed soldiers and a vast mob of bakers, masons, carpenters, and camp followers with no cavalry to protect them against the substantial force of Syracusan horsemen.

THE ATHENIANS AT SYRACUSE

THE ATHENIANS, therefore, resorted to trickery, using a double agent to deceive the Syracusan generals and lure the entire enemy army to Catana. While the Syracusans were marching the forty miles there, the Athenians landed their ships and men unopposed in Syracuse harbor on a beach south of the Anapus River, opposite the great temple of Olympian Zeus (see Map 21). They took up a position protected by houses and natural barriers from flank attacks by the Syracusan cavalry and built further fortifications to defend themselves from a frontal assault or an attack from the sea.

When the Syracusans, duped and angry, returned to find the Athenians firmly encamped before their city, they challenged them to fight,

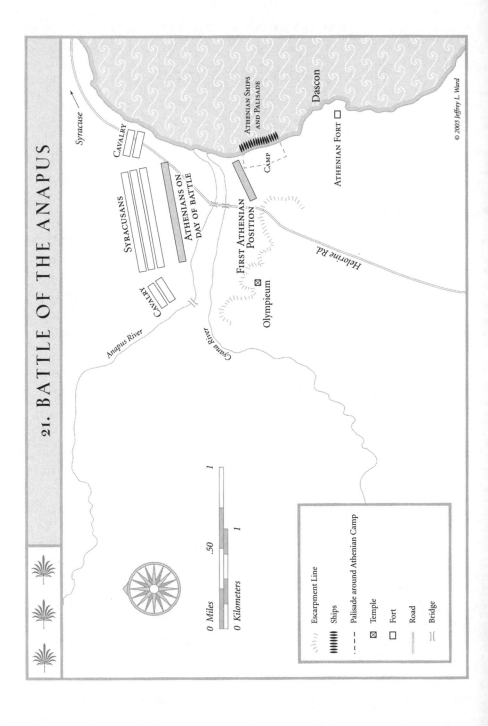

21. BATTLE OF THE ANAPUS

Syracuse

Cavalry

Syracusans

Athenians on
day of battle

Cavalry

Anapus River

Cyana River

First Athenian
Position

Olympieum

Helorine Rd.

Athenian Ships
and Palisade

Camp

Dascon

Athenian Fort

© 2003 Jeffrey L. Ward

0 Miles   .50   1

0 Kilometers   1

- ⦚⦚⦚ Escarpment Line
- ▨ Ships
- --- Palisade around Athenian Camp
- ⊠ Temple
- ☐ Fort
- — Road
-)(Bridge

but the Athenians did not rise to the bait, and the Syracusans could do nothing but make camp for the night. The Athenians attacked the next morning. Half the army stood eight deep, with the Argives and Mantineans on the right, the Athenians in the center, and the other allies on the left, where the danger from the cavalry was greatest. Behind them, well to the rear, another group of Athenians formed a hollow square surrounding the supply-carrying civilians; they remained near the Athenian camp as a reserve force. The Athenian advance across the river took the enemy by surprise. Some soldiers had gone home to Syracuse for the night and had to hurry back and find a place in the ranks wherever they could. The Syracusans and their allies matched the length of the Athenian line but had twice its depth, as well as fifteen hundred unopposed cavalry. To counter that disadvantage the Athenians must have placed themselves at an angle to the river, using it to guard the left end of their line and some marshes to protect their right, which effectively prevented the enemy cavalry from flanking their phalanx. The Athenians also positioned their slingers, archers, and stone-throwers on the wings, where they helped fight off the enemy cavalry. In spite of the depth of the Syracusan phalanx and the individual bravery of its soldiers, the superior discipline and experience of the Athenians and their allies carried the day.

As they fought, rain, thunder, and lightning terrified the Syracusans, probably helping to break their spirit, but the practiced Athenians took it in stride. Soon the Argives drove the enemy left wing back, the Athenians pushed back the center, the enemy line broke, and the Syracusans and their allies fled. Here was the Athenians' great opportunity to score a decisive victory, for if they undertook an aggressive pursuit and inflicted many casualties they might break Syracusan resistance or, at least, hamper the enemy's prospects of withstanding a siege. To achieve that, however, cavalry, which could pursue faster and farther than hoplites, was essential, but the Athenians had none. The unopposed Syracusan cavalry was able to check the pursuit, enabling their army to regroup and send a garrison to the temple of Zeus to protect its treasures before reaching safety behind the city walls. For the Athenians it was a tactical victory without strategic result: Syracuse stood fast, ready and able to continue the fight, and some way had to be found to make it yield. Instead of launching a siege at once, however, the Athenians set up a trophy of victory on the battlefield, returned the enemy dead under truce and buried their own—50 to the enemy's 260—and sailed back to Catana.

Thucydides explains Nicias' withdrawal on the lateness of the season, and the need to store up grain, to get more money from Athens and elsewhere, and especially to "send to Athens for cavalry and recruit some from their allies in Sicily so that they would not be completely dominated by the enemy cavalry" (6.71.2). Nicias' contemporaries blamed him for not acting more resolutely. In his *Birds*, performed soon after the battle, Aristophanes makes a joke about "Nicias-delays," and Plutarch reports the common opinion in Athens that, "by calculating too carefully and delaying and being overly cautious he destroyed the opportunity for action" (*Nicias* 16.8).

Nicias' caution in response to the lack of cavalry was not unreasonable, for Athenian detachments sent to dig trenches or build encircling walls could not fight off attacks by Syracusan cavalry unless defended by horsemen of their own. But wars are often decided by issues other than material considerations. Demosthenes, a far more brilliant general, thought that had Nicias been bolder in the winter of 415, the Syracusans would have offered battle, suffered defeat, and found their city shut in by a wall before they could send for help, and consequently been forced to surrender. Still, it is most unlikely that the Athenians could have built a wall enclosing the city without the protection of cavalry, and so long as such a wall was not in place the Syracusans remained free to send for assistance and make good use of it. On balance, Nicias chose the correct plan and executed it with great skill, for which he deserves no blame as a tactician.

As a strategist, however, Nicias did make an error that was the chief cause of the expedition's failure. Cavalry was essential to the capture of Syracuse. Had it been available from the first, the Syracusans would have been forced to surrender; no outside help could have saved them. The lack of provisions for cavalry is particularly astonishing in that Nicias himself had emphasized its importance before the expedition's departure, telling the Athenian assembly: "The thing in which the Syracusans most surpass us is in their possession of many horses and their use of grain that is home-grown and not imported" (6.20.4).

But in his list of forces the Athenians should vote for the expedition he omitted any mention of horsemen, and although he had plenty of time before they sailed to remedy the problem at a subsequent assembly, he never did so. Even after the council at Rhegium, when it was obvious that a siege of Syracuse would be likely, there was still time to send home for horsemen.

Perhaps the oversight was more a failure of purpose than of judgment. Nicias, as we have seen, never wanted to attack Sicily, and forced to take part in the campaign, intended to pursue a minimal course that would avoid any serious engagement. He had probably refused to consider any step as serious as an attack on Syracuse until circumstances made it unavoidable and then found himself without the forces to carry it out.

Although the siege of Syracuse would therefore have to be delayed a number of months until the arrival of money and cavalry from Athens, there was no reason to waste the winter of 415/4. The Athenians accordingly sailed to Messina, hoping to gain control of the faction-ridden town by treason, but Alcibiades had revealed their plot on his way to the Peloponnesus, the first of many of his actions that would prove that he was still alive. When the fleet arrived, the hostile faction barred the Athenians from the city, and they withdrew to build a new base at Naxos.

SYRACUSAN RESISTANCE

AT SYRACUSE, MEANWHILE, Hermocrates encouraged the people to undertake a series of major military reforms. To increase the size of the army they gave arms to poorer men to enable them to fight as hoplites and introduced compulsory training, an unusual measure among the amateur citizen-armies of the Greeks. The number of generals was reduced from fifteen to three, one of whom was Hermocrates, and they were granted full powers to make decisions without consulting the assembly, which allowed for more effective leadership and better secrecy of plans. The Syracusans willingly curtailed their democracy in the extreme emergency of the moment.

On the diplomatic front they not only sent to Corinth and Sparta for help in defending their city but also asked the Spartans "to make war against the Athenians openly and more persistently so that the Athenians might have to withdraw from Sicily or be less able to send reinforcements there" (6.73). At the same time they extended the city walls to include more territory, which would force the Athenians to build an even larger siege wall to enclose Syracuse. They also placed garrisons at Megara Hyblaea and the Temple of Zeus and built palisades at likely landing places along the coast.

On hearing that the Athenians were trying to win over Camarina Hermocrates went there and argued that they had come not to assist their allies but rather to conquer Sicily. The Athenian spokesman Euphemus argued in turn that Syracuse was the true threat to the freedom of the Greek cities in Sicily. For their part the Camarinans felt kindly toward the Athenians, "except insofar as they thought they would enslave Sicily," and their formal response was that "since they were allied to both sides that were at war, it would be most consistent with their oaths to aid neither" (6.88.1). This apparent neutrality was helpful to Syracuse but not to the Athenians, who needed to gain allies in Sicily quickly or not at all. The great size of the Athenian armada probably influenced the Camarinan decision, again working against the original strategy.

The Athenians did better with the non-Greek Sicels, some of whom came over to Athens freely, bringing food and money, while others required compulsion. Moving their base to Catana for better contact with the Sicels, the Athenians also sought help as far away as Etruria in Italy and Carthage in Africa, both former enemies of Syracuse. While a few Etruscan cities sent a number of ships to Sicily in 413, the appeal to Carthage failed entirely, though the request itself undermines claims made by Alcibiades, Hermocrates, and Thucydides that the aims of the expedition included the conquest of Carthage.

ALCIBIADES AT SPARTA

THE SYRACUSANS had better luck in their search and Corinth, their city's founder, gladly agreed to support their colonists and sent their own envoys along to help persuade the Spartans to do the same. The leading Spartans, however, were not eager for a major commitment to Sicily and decided to send no tangible assistance, only an embassy to urge Syracuse to hold out against the Athenians. At Sparta, however, the Syracusans and Corinthians did find a valuable ally in the person of Alcibiades. The Athenian reprobate had made a remarkable adjustment to Spartan ways—he took vigorous bodily exercise and cold baths, let his hair grow long in the Spartan manner, and ate the coarse bread and the black porridge of the Spartan mess—but it is unlikely that he meant to spend the rest of his life in Sparta. He was determined to return to Athens either as a leader and returning hero or as an avenger.

Because he was still a fugitive and an outlaw with a price on his head wherever the Athenian writ was in force, Alcibiades' first goal was to make a name for himself among the Spartans and win influence and power by persuading them to defeat the Athenians in Sicily and then to resume the war in Greece. A major goal of the introductory speech he delivered in the Spartan assembly was to allay the distrust and antipathy the Spartans felt toward him. As a demagogue supported by the Athenian mob; as the chief opponent of Sparta's friend Nicias; as the author of the deadly policy that brought Athens into alliance with Argos, Mantinea, and Elis, and, indirectly, of the battle of Mantinea and of the Sicilian expedition itself; and as a traitor to his own city, he was not the obvious man to give trustworthy advice to the Spartans.

He argued his case by lightly explaining away or rejecting his past and presenting his flight from Athens as a liberation from democracy, which he described as "recognized foolishness" (6.89). He claimed to reveal the true motives of the Athenian expedition to the west: far from being limited to an assault on Syracuse on behalf of allies, it was meant to take the entire island and more. Beyond Sicily, the Athenians sought to subdue southern Italy, Carthage and its empire, and even far-off Iberia. When all this had been accomplished the Athenians would use the vast resources of these conquests to attack the Peloponnesus itself, and "after that they would rule over the entire Hellenic people" (6.90). The Athenian generals, he insisted, would carry out this program even in his absence.

But the Spartans had to act quickly, he argued, before the Syracusans surrendered. "Let no one," he said, "believe you are deliberating only about Sicily, for the fate of the Peloponnesus is also at stake" (6.91). The Spartans should send an army to Sicily at once under a Spartiate commander but also resume the war on the mainland to encourage the Syracusans and to distract the Athenians. To that end they must undertake the one move the Athenians feared most and build a permanent fort at Decelea in Attica. From there the Spartans could cut them off entirely from their homes and crops and the silver mines of Sunium and further reduce revenues by encouraging resistance and rebellion in the empire.

The traitor Alcibiades recognized the need to defend his own credibility. "The true patriot is not the man who, having lost his own homeland, does not attack it, but the one who tries in every way to recover it because of his passion for it" (6.92.4). We have no indication of whether this sophistry impressed the Spartans, but Alcibiades concluded his speech by urging them to turn away from the past and appreciate the future benefits he could bring them: "If I did you great harm as an enemy I could also do you considerable good as a friend, since I know the plans of the Athenians while I only guessed at yours" (6.92.5).

The Spartans had sufficient reason to suspect this exiled traitor with a price on his head and a reputation for clever deceptions, but one of his claims ought to have cast doubt on everything else he said, for it was so patently false: "The generals who are left will carry out the same plans, if they can, without any change" (6.91.1). It should have been inconceivable to the Spartans, who knew and respected him, that Nicias would pursue the grand design of conquest Alcibiades had described. On that point Alcibiades simply lied, and there is good reason to suspect that he also invented the grandiose Athenian goals he claimed to reveal to the Spartans for his own purposes: to frighten Sparta into resuming the war against Athens.

To understand Alcibiades' performance in Sparta we need to examine his career and achievements as they appeared in 415/4, before he attained the status of a legend. He had not yet commanded an Athenian victory on land or sea, and all his plans had produced strategic failures. His campaigns carried a distinctive stamp, usually relying on the persuasiveness of his personal diplomacy and the use of allied forces to do the brunt of the fighting, with a consequent low risk to

Athens. Such an approach might seem clever and safe, but it brought no decisive result. The culmination of his Peloponnesian strategy was the battle of Mantinea in 418, but victory there required a larger Athenian hoplite force than appeared, and his consistent reluctance to risk large numbers of Athenians in battle makes it questionable whether he would have sent a larger force, even had he been general in that year.

His absence at Mantinea underscores another of his shortcomings as an Athenian leader: he could not win the consistent political support year after year that a general needed to carry out a coherent policy. His strategy for Sicily in 415 was unoriginal, largely a repetition of the plan pursued unsuccessfully in the years 427–424. No doubt he thought his personal leadership and persuasiveness would succeed where Sophocles and Eurymedon had failed, but he was unable to prevent Nicias from expanding the expedition into an elephantine force that would frighten the Greek cities of the west into neutrality or opposition. When the price of that expansion became clear at Rhegium he did not change his plan to meet the new realities. Finally, the distrust his fellow citizens felt toward him allowed his political opponents to drive him into exile. That was the Alcibiades the Spartans saw before them, a defeated and hunted man who badly needed to convince them of the magnitude of the danger that threatened and of the benefit they stood to gain from his advice and help. We must marvel at his boldness and imagination and at the enormity of his bluff.

While the Spartans did send a general to Sicily, the force he commanded contained only two Corinthian and two Laconian ships. No Spartiate soldiers went to Sicily, nor was the general, Gylippus, a true Spartiate. As the son of Cleandridas, an exile condemned to death for accepting bribes, and, it was said, of a helot mother, he was a *mothax*, a man of inferior status. Every element of the Spartan mission to Sicily was therefore expendable. Reasonable Athenian precautions could have prevented even this pitiful force from reaching Sicily.

CHAPTER TWENTY-THREE

The Siege of Syracuse (414)

IN THE FIFTH century, to capture a strongly walled and defended city required a careful and well-conducted siege to cut it off from supplies and reduce it by starvation, or to take it by treason. In the spring of 414 the Athenians commanded the sea and had sufficient troops to enclose the city thoroughly by land, and as soon as money and cavalry arrived from Athens they would be ready to begin their assault. Once they completed a siege wall about Syracuse a watchful Athenian fleet could intercept any help from the Peloponnesians.

News of the cavalry's appearance stirred the Syracusans to place guards at the approaches to Epipolae, the plateau overlooking their city (see Map 22), "for they thought that if the Athenians could not control Epipolae the Syracusans could not easily be walled in, even if they were defeated in battle" (6.96.1), but they were too late. Before the Syracusan garrison could reach there Nicias sailed the Athenian army to Leon, not far from Epipolae's northern cliffs. Before the Syracusans could prevent it the Athenian army ascended to the plateau, from where they could easily repel the Syracusan attempt to dislodge them. The Athenians then built a fort at Labdalum on the northern cliffs of Epipolae where they stored their supplies, equipment, and funds.

Soon the horses arrived, along with additional cavalrymen from their Sicilian allies. With their hoplites and a total of 650 cavalrymen they could now protect the men who would construct the siege walls. At a place called Syce, northwest of the city and not far from the edge of the plateau, they built a fort that Thucydides calls "The Circle." This was to be the center of their operations while they conducted the siege.

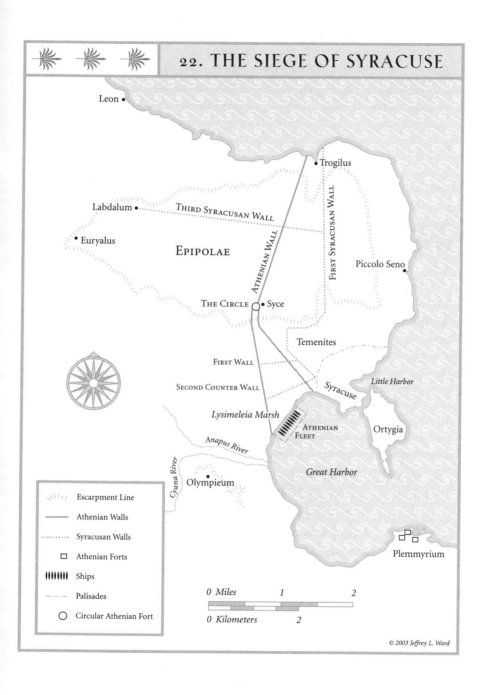

22. THE SIEGE OF SYRACUSE

Leon •

Trogilus

Labdalum •   THIRD SYRACUSAN WALL

• Euryalus

EPIPOLAE

FIRST SYRACUSAN WALL

Piccolo Seno •

THE CIRCLE ○ • Syce

Temenites

FIRST WALL

SECOND COUNTER WALL

Syracuse

Little Harbor

Lysimeleia Marsh

ATHENIAN FLEET

Ortygia

Anapus River

Great Harbor

Cyana River

Olympieum •

Plemmyrium

Escarpment Line

Athenian Walls

Syracusan Walls

□ Athenian Forts

||||||| Ships

Palisades

○ Circular Athenian Fort

0 Miles   1   2

0 Kilometers   2

© 2003 Jeffrey L. Ward

The Syracusans went out to challenge the enemy, but when their generals saw the disorder of their badly disciplined troops they soon retreated behind the city's walls, leaving part of their cavalry behind to prevent the Athenians from continuing to raise their wall. With their own cavalry and one contingent of hoplites the Athenians were able to rout the Syracusans and protect the construction, and the following day they began to extend their wall northward from "The Circle" toward Trogilus. Unless the Syracusans acted quickly, they would soon be shut in by land, but their generals were still fearful of sending their army against the Athenians. Instead they decided to construct a counterwall that would cut across the line of the projected siege works, constructing it of stone and timber and placing towers along its length. The Athenians continued raising their own wall on the plateau, and instead of attacking the counterwall turned their attention to the water supply of the besieged city, destroying the pipes that ran underground into Syracuse.

Soon Syracusan carelessness gave the Athenians an opportunity to show their daring. Lolling in the midday heat, they left the walls lightly and carelessly defended, and three hundred Athenian hoplites, supported by a corps of light-armed soldiers supplied with heavy armor for the occasion, assaulted them on the run. Nicias and Lamachus followed directly behind with the rest of the army, each leading a wing. The shock troops drove the guards from the counterwall to the wall around the suburb called Temenites. The pursuing forces managed to get in through the gate, but there were too few of them to hold their position. While the Athenians failed to take Temenites, they destroyed the counterwall and set up another trophy of victory.

THE ILLNESS OF NICIAS AND THE DEATH
OF LAMACHUS

IT WAS AROUND this time that Nicias became ill with the kidney ailment that would trouble him until his death. Perhaps he was already unwell when the surprise raid was planned, for its audacity and dash suggest the touch of Lamachus. The following day the Athenians began to build the southern portion of their siege wall, from "The Circle" on Epipolae to the Great Harbor south of the city. When it was completed a key part of Syracuse would be surrounded, and the Athenians could move their fleet from Thapsus, whence they had to haul supplies overland to Epipolae, to a safe anchorage in the Great Harbor, for without the wall, protection of the Athenian fleet on the beach of the Great Harbor would require a dangerous division of Athenian land forces.

The new construction alarmed the Syracusans, who immediately proceeded to raise another counterwall across the Lysimeleia marsh. The Athenians, meanwhile, had extended their own wall to the edge of the cliff and were already preparing a new attack, this time both from land and sea. They moved their fleet into the Great Harbor, and came down from Epipolae. Placing planks and doors on the firmest parts of the marsh, they again caught the Syracusans by surprise, the assault splitting their army in two, with the right wing fleeing to the city, and the left heading to the Anapus. The latter group ran for the bridge, and three hundred Athenian shock troops hurried to cut them off, but the Syracusan cavalry was waiting at the river and, with the hoplites, routed the three hundred and turned against the right wing of the main Athenian army. The right wing of a phalanx is its most vulnerable part, especially when threatened by a combined attack from infantry and cavalry, and the first regiment on the Athenian right was thrown into panic. The brave and bold Lamachus, though he was on the left wing, hurried to help. He steadied the line but, finding himself isolated across a ditch with only a few of his soldiers beside him, he died fighting. The Syracusans took his body with them as they retreated across the river toward their fortress at the Olympieum. The Athenian victory came at a high price, for it left the ailing Nicias alone in command, and the skill and daring of Lamachus would be sorely missed.

The Syracusans, seeing the Athenian army in the plain before the city, sent one force to occupy its attention while another attacked "The Circle" up on the heights. They captured and demolished the incomplete and undefended wall running south from the fort, within which Nicias lay. In spite of his illness he was alert enough to order the building of a fire, which drove the enemy back at the same time that it warned the army down in the plain that the fort was in danger. The timing was fortunate, for the Athenians near Syracuse had already driven the enemy off, just as the Athenian fleet sailed into the harbor. It was now safe to race up to Epipolae in time to protect the fort and their only remaining general, as the Syracusans fled back to their city.

Nothing now prevented the Athenians from continuing their southern wall to the sea. If they carried a northern wall across the plateau of Epipolae, their fleet's control of the sea would complete the enclosure of Syracuse and, by maintaining a properly careful watch, they could force the enemy either to surrender or starve. News of the desperate situation of the Syracusans spread quickly and brought alliances with those Sicels who had previously remained uncommitted, as well as supplies from Italy and three ships from as far off as Etruria.

The Syracusans "no longer thought they could win the war, for no help had come to them from the Peloponnesus" (6.103.3). Intimations of surrender were rife, as the Syracusans replaced their generals with three new ones. They discussed peace terms among themselves and even with Nicias, and there were rumors of a treasonous plot to surrender the city. As always, Nicias had excellent intelligence, and the Athenians had every reason to believe that the city might soon give up without a fight.

At this point, however, Nicias became careless and overconfident, ignoring the one distant cloud in the otherwise bright Athenian sky: the four ships coming from the Peloponnesus, one of them carrying the Spartan Gylippus. Although news had reached Nicias of the Spartans' arrival in Italy some time before, he had taken no action against such a contemptible force. The correct course would have been to hurry to complete the enclosure of Syracuse, send a squadron of ships to the straits or to Italy to prevent the passage of the Peloponnesians, blockade both Syracusan harbors to prevent access if even a single ship got past the forward interceptors, and guard the approaches to Epipolae, especially Euryalus, in case any of the Peloponnesians managed to reach Sicily and came to Syracuse by land. Nicias did none of these things, with disastrous results.

ATHENS BREAKS THE TREATY

DURING THIS ENTIRE PERIOD the Peace of Nicias was still formally in effect, but low-level hostilities continued. Sparta and Argos continued to raid and invade each other's territory. Athens made frequent raids of its own into Messenia from Pylos and elsewhere in the Peloponnesus, but refused the Argives' requests to attack Laconia. By the odd interpretation tacitly adopted by both sides these actions were not judged as constituting violations of the Peace, but a direct Athenian assault on Laconia would have to be. By 414, however, the Athenians could no longer deny their ally's pleas for more vigorous assistance, for Argive soldiers were serving the Athenian cause in Sicily, so the Athenians sent thirty ships to make seaborne raids against several places on the Laconian shore. In this way the Sicilian expedition had significant ramifications for the war as a whole, for the Athenians' actions "violated the treaty with the Spartans in the most flagrant way" (6.105.1).

Meanwhile, Gylippus and the Corinthian admiral Pythen, each in command of two Peloponnesian ships, were making their way toward Sicily under the impression that the Athenians had already completed their circumvallation of Syracuse, but at Locri in southern Italy they learned the truth and set out to save the city, sailing to Himera to avoid the Athenian fleet. When Nicias learned of their arrival at Locri he decided to send four ships to intercept them, but the response came too late. The men of Himera joined the Peloponnesian expedition and provided arms for its crews. More help came from Selinus and Gela and from the Sicels, who changed sides because of the death of their pro-Athenian king and the persuasive zeal of Gylippus. By the time he set out for Syracuse he commanded a force of about three thousand infantry and two hundred cavalry.

HELP ARRIVES AT SYRACUSE

ADDITIONAL SUPPORT was already on the way to the Syracusans in the shape of eleven triremes manned by the Corinthians and their allies. One of them, under the Corinthian general Gongylus, slipped through the blockade and arrived at the city even before Gylippus could reach it overland. Gongylus appeared in the nick of time, for the Syracusans were about to surrender. He persuaded them not to hold the decisive assembly, reporting that more ships were on the way and that the Spartan Gylippus had come to take command. Not surprisingly this news convinced the Syracusans to change their plans, and they sent their entire army out to greet the Spartan general.

Gylippus came onto Epipolae from the west, through the Euryalus pass, the same route the Athenians had taken, so it is hard to understand why they left it unguarded. He arrived at a critical moment, for the Athenians were about to complete their double wall down to the Great Harbor, needing only to finish a short section near the sea. "The wall toward Trogilus and the other sea stones had already been laid out for the greater part of the distance, and some parts were left half-finished while others had been completed. That is how close Syracuse had come to danger" (7.2.4–5).

At their siege wall Gylippus insolently offered the Athenians a truce if they would leave Sicily within five days. Although the Athenians did not bother to respond, the Syracusans must have been impressed by his boldness. For all his bravado, however, his forces lacked discipline and training. As the two armies arrayed for battle Gylippus saw that his men were confused and not in proper order, vulnerable to a sudden Athenian attack. A defeat at this point could both discredit the new Spartan general and discourage further resistance, but Nicias was not the man to exploit the opportunity. When Gylippus withdrew toward open country, Nicias let the chance to pursue him pass, and remained where he was.

The following day Gylippus took the offensive, feinting an attack on the Athenians' wall, while he sent another force to Epipolae, where the Athenians had not yet completed the wall, and against their fort at Labdalum. He seized the fort and all its contents, killing the Athenians who were manning it. Nicias' carelessness in failing to safeguard the fort, supply depot, and treasury was another terrible oversight, but Gylippus proceeded to exploit yet another error. Nicias should have completed the walls enclosing Syracuse as quickly as possible, for a purely naval blockade would not be sufficient to isolate the city, yet he had chosen instead to build a double wall to the sea in the south before completing the single northern section on Epipolae from the round fort to Trogilus. The time and manpower used on the second southern wall, however much security it may have provided, were resources the Athenians could not afford to divert so long as the northern sector was incomplete. Gylippus responded by beginning to erect a counterwall that would cut across the path of the Athenian wall as it moved north toward Trogilus.

NICIAS MOVES TO PLEMMYRIUM

BY NOW, however, Nicias had abandoned any plans of conquering Syracuse. Sick and in pain, confronted for the first time by daring and aggressive enemies, he worried chiefly about the safety of his forces and their escape from Sicily. Instead of hastening to prevent the construction of Gylippus' counterwall and to complete the Athenian wall to Trogilus, Nicias decided to build three forts at Plemmyrium on the south of the entrance to the Great Harbor to make it his new naval base and the storehouse to replace Labdalum. But the site had disadvantages: what little water and firewood were available were not close to the forts, so the Athenian patrols that went to collect these essentials were easy prey for the Syracusan cavalry, who set up a base near the Olympieum from which they could attack them. "For these reasons, especially, the crews began to deteriorate at that time" (7.4.6).

The relocation to Plemmyrium also dangerously divided Nicias' forces. The main army on the heights of Epipolae was far from its supplies, and the enemy could force it to come down to defend the forts whenever they chose to attack them. Nicias offered no persuasive defense of his new tactics, which reflected a fundamental change in goals and strategy. Because the loss of Labdalum had cut off an escape route overland to the north, he had moved his army to Plemmyrium as the safest base from which to escape by sea. Only after the Athenian forces were established there did he send twenty ships to intercept the Corinthian fleet that was approaching Sicily from Italy.

At the same time, Gylippus continued with the erection of his counterwall, using the same stones the Athenians had laid out for their own wall. He regularly challenged them to fight, well aware that the decision would rest on a battle, not on a wall-building contest, and he rightly perceived that Nicias did not wish to engage in any hostilities. Their general's timidity undermined the morale of the Athenian soldiers as it boosted the confidence of the enemy. Gylippus, however, chose a site for the first battle that kept his superior cavalry out of play, so he was defeated, producing a dangerous situation. He took the blame for defeat entirely on himself, winning the Syracusans' respect and fealty by assuring them that they were in no way inferior to the enemy, as he would soon prove by leading them into battle again.

A new opportunity arose when Gylippus' counterwall finally met the line of the Athenian wall to Trogilus, forcing Nicias to fight or forfeit all hope of enclosing the city. The battle took place in the open, where the enemy cavalry and javelin throwers gave them the advantage over the Athenian hoplites. The cavalry proved to be decisive, driving the exposed Athenian left flank before it, which caused a general rout, and the Athenians avoided destruction only by running to the safety of the round fort. The battle brought Gylippus a great strategic victory: the Syracusans built their counterwall across the line of the Athenian siege wall.

With all their attention focused on the heights of Epipolae, the Athenians were unable to prevent the Corinthian fleet, commanded by Erasinides, from sailing into Syracuse harbor unharmed. The crews of these ships supplied Gylippus with well over two thousand men to help complete the counterwall and probably to extend it the entire length of Epipolae, cutting the Athenians off from the plain and the sea to their north. All hope of enclosing Syracuse and starving it into surrender with their present forces was now gone.

The talented and zealous Gylippus built a fort at the Euryalus pass and placed six hundred Syracusans there to guard the entrance to the Epipolae, installing the Syracusans and their allies in three camps on the plateau. Backed by the news of his successes he embarked on a tour to recruit neutrals and gain help from allies who had held back from involvement while the Athenians seemed sure to win. He also sent to Sparta and Corinth to ask for reinforcements in ships and men. Even at sea, where the Athenians still had control, Gylippus' victories gave the Syracusans the will and courage to train their crews in preparation for a battle against the great Athenian fleet.

NICIAS' LETTER TO ATHENS

BY THE END of the summer Nicias believed that the Athenian expedition was in such danger that it must either withdraw or be supported with major reinforcements. He surely preferred withdrawal, for he had never favored the campaign or had any faith in its prospects, and recent events were deeply discouraging. As the only remaining general he retained the authority that the Athenian assembly had given all three, so he had the power to order a retreat, and would have had the guarantee of safe passage through the dominance of the Athenian navy.

Still, he did not give up the command, for to have done so would have brought dishonor and, perhaps, even more unwelcome consequences. Until the time of the Sicilian expedition Nicias' record contained many victories and no defeats, but a retreat from Sicily with no significant goals achieved was bound to be regarded as a failure, and possibly worse. Throughout the the course of the war the Athenians had shown themselves unforgiving toward generals who disappointed their expectations, humiliating and punishing even the great Pericles himself when the results of his policy and strategy displeased them. In the same year they brought to trial two generals who had taken Potidaea after a long and costly siege because they made a peace the assembly considered unfavorable. Sophocles, Pythodorus, and Eurymedon, the generals who concluded the peace of Gela in 424, by which the Athenians abandoned their first expedition to Sicily, were nominally convicted for taking bribes, but Thucydides tells us that they were actually punished for their unsatisfactory performance. Eurymedon's punishment was only a fine, but the others were sent into exile. In the same year Thucydides was exiled for his part in the loss of Amphipolis.

Nicias was certain to face severe criticism on his return to Athens, for news that Spartan and Corinthian forces were now playing an important part in Sicily would have been shocking, and the Athenians were not likely to believe that Nicias had come home because their mighty expedition was in grave danger. Many disgruntled veterans of the campaign would undoubtedly complain that he had ordered the retreat with the fleet unbeaten and in command of the sea, and the army intact. Nicias' errors, delays, and omissions would be made known and would become the main topic of discussion. By ordering a withdrawal without prior permission from the Athenian assembly Nicias would have risked the reputation he had spent his life building and guarding, not to speak of his property and, perhaps, his life.

He proceeded, therefore, with still another attempt at clever duplicity. With his official report that reached Athens in the fall of 414 he sent a letter to the assembly. It told of the Athenian reverses without discussing their causes and set forth the current state of affairs: the Athenians had ceased besieging Syracuse and were now on the defensive; Gylippus was recruiting reinforcements and planning an attack on the Athenians by land and sea; the Athenian situation was beyond repair. He cast no blame on his own leadership, explaining that the ships and their crews had suffered in quality because of the length of the campaign and requirements of the blockade, which kept them always at sea. The enemy, free from the need to maintain a blockade, could easily dry its ships and give its crews practice, but if the Athenians relaxed their guard at all their supplies could be cut off, since everything had to be brought by sea from Italy and past Syracuse. The reversal of Athenian fortunes in Sicily brought other troubles, as well. Sailors leaving camp to collect water, wood, and forage for the horses were attacked and killed by the enemy cavalry. Slaves, mercenaries, and volunteers deserted, and the resulting shortage of experienced rowers deprived the Athenian fleet of its usual tactical advantage. Soon, Nicias warned, their Italian suppliers, perceiving that the Syracusans were likely to win, would stop sending food, which would put an end to the Athenian expedition. For none of these problems, he stressed, were the generals or the army responsible. The Athenians "must either recall the force that is here or reinforce it with another just as large, infantry and a fleet and a great deal of money" (7.15). He also requested to be relieved of his command because of his illness, but whatever it was to decide, the assembly had to do so quickly, he insisted, before the enemy forces in Sicily grew too powerful.

Nicias' message painted a darker picture than reality justified. The Athenians were still superior at sea, and there was no good evidence that they would soon be short of supplies. His attempt to explain the reversal of Athenian fortunes was still less accurate. The lion's share of the responsibility for the situation rested with Nicias' lethargic, over-confident, and careless leadership. He had allowed Syracuse to move swiftly from imminent surrender to a recovery of morale, seizure of the initiative, and the real prospect of victory. He failed to intercept Gylippus' pitifully small squadron, and allowed Gongylus' fleet to slip through his blockade. He neglected to protect the approaches to Epipolae, and wasted time building a double wall to the sea south of the heights and three forts at Plemmyrium while his northern wall was incomplete. He allowed his storehouse and treasury at Labdalum to be captured, permitted the Corinthian squadron to get to Syracuse, and moved his navy to its untenable position at Plemmyrium. The deterioration of the navy was not inevitable but a product of Nicias' negligence: he could have dried and repaired his ships in rotation in the months before the arrival of Gylippus, and if Athenian sailors died and deserted it was because their ships had been placed in a bad location at Plemmyrium.

The true purpose of Nicias' inadequate, self-serving, and less than honest account was to convince the assembly to order the expedition home; failing that, he wished to be relieved of his command with honor and replaced. If he had simply stated that, in his judgment there was now little prospect of victory, the Athenians might have agreed to withdraw. If he had only explained he was too ill to do the job, they might have recalled him and sent a healthy general in his place. Instead, he offered them a choice. Concerned for his reputation and himself, he asked the Athenians either to do as he proposed or to send a second expedition as large as the first. This seems to have been yet another version of the ploy that had not been successful in deterring the Athenians from making the voyage in the first place, but Nicias had evidently learned nothing from that experience.

THE ATHENIAN RESPONSE

ONCE AGAIN, the Athenians confounded Nicias' expectations and voted to send another fleet and army, while refusing to relieve him. Instead they named Menander and Euthydemus, two men who were already at Syracuse, as his temporary fellow-generals. As regular generals to head the reinforcements and join with Nicias in the command they chose Demosthenes, the hero of Sphacteria, and Eurymedon, who had led the Athenian forces in Sicily from 427 to 424. Eurymedon was to depart for Sicily at once with ten ships, 120 silver talents, and the encouraging news that Demosthenes would follow later with much greater forces.

Both elements of the Athenian decision can only evoke surprise. The majority of the promises and expectations of the proponents of the initial expedition had proven to be unfounded, while most of the fears of the opponents had been justified. The Italians and Sicilians had not joined the Athenians with enthusiasm and in great numbers, the Peloponnesians were now engaged, and the Syracusans were resisting with renewed morale. We might expect the Athenian people to have felt deceived by the optimists, and to have conceded the wisdom of the doubters and recalled the expedition and its pessimistic and unwell commander.

Most historians agree with Thucydides in blaming the continuation of the Sicilian campaign on the greed, ignorance, and foolishness of the direct Athenian democracy. But the behavior of the Athenians on this occasion is the opposite of the flighty indecision that is usually imputed to their democracy. They showed constancy and determination to carry through what they had begun, in spite of setbacks and disappointments. Their error, in fact, is one common to powerful states, regardless of their constitutions, when they are unexpectedly thwarted by an opponent they anticipated would be weak and easily defeated. Such states are likely to view retreat as a blow to their prestige, and while unwelcome in itself, it is also an option that puts into question their strength and determination and with it their security. Support for ventures such as the Sicilian campaign generally remains strong until the prospect of victory disappears.

But why did the Athenians insist on keeping in place the ailing and discouraged Nicias? An answer may be found in the unique regard in which the Athenians held their general. It was not the awe they felt for the brilliant imagination and rhetorical genius of Pericles, whose intellect always seemed able to devise a plan or invent a device to meet every challenge and then to explain it convincingly to the people. In the case of Nicias, rather, it was their view of his character, his way of life, and the success and good fortune that had always accompanied him. He had typically tried to behave in the same dignified manner as traditional aristocratic politicians, but without their objectionable haughtiness. "His dignity was not the austere, offensive kind but was mixed with a degree of prudence; he won over the masses because he seemed to fear them." His inadequacies as a debater, oddly, won him sympathy: "In political life his timidity ... even made him seem a popular, democratic figure" (Plutarch, *Nicias* 2.3–4).

After one battle he had won near Corinth he discovered that he had failed to notice and bury two Athenian soldiers. Asking the enemy for permission to bury one's dead was regarded as a symbol of defeat, but Nicias returned and made the request, rather than commit the impiety of leaving the corpses unattended. As Plutarch says, "He preferred to give up the honor and glory of the victory than to leave two citizens unburied" (*Nicias* 6.4). Plutarch may have been correct in criticizing him for having carefully chosen his commands with an eye toward those that were likely to be quick, easy, successful, and safe, but the Athenians knew only that he never lost, any more than his choruses lost in the dramatic competitions of Dionysus. Even his name was connected to *nike*, the word meaning victory.

It is not surprising, therefore, that, less than two years after the gods had been insulted by the desecration of the mysteries and the mutilation of the Hermae, the Athenians refused to excuse from service the one man most beloved of the gods, the man who was their talisman of victory. If he was ill, he would recover; meanwhile, healthy and vigorous colleagues would assist him. With the original force alone he had very nearly succeeded in taking Syracuse; surely, with reinforcement and able colleagues, his skill and good fortune would soon achieve victory.

CHAPTER TWENTY-FOUR

The Besiegers Besieged (414–413)

SPARTA TAKES THE OFFENSIVE

WHILE THE ATHENIANS WERE occupied with matters in Sicily the Spartans were preparing to put an end to the uneasy and artificial peace. Two important practical changes in the status quo convinced them to resume the war by invading Attica and building a permanent fort in the Athenian homeland. The first was the reversal of the strategic balance in Sicily, where the Athenians now seemed poised to lose to the Syracusans. Instead of freeing the great armada for duty at home, the Sicilian campaign would now drain Athens' strength even further. The second critical event was the Athenian decision to conduct retaliatory raids into Spartan territory. For some time the Athenians had been making raids around the Peloponnesus, but they had always avoided an attack on Laconia itself. The Spartans chose not to regard these annoyances as breaches of the peace, but in the summer of 414 the Athenians assaulted the coast of Laconia, changing the situation critically. Their actions "violated the treaty with the Spartans in the most flagrant way" (6.105.1) and liberated them from the sense of guilt that had haunted them since the onset of the war. The Spartans were well aware that the fighting had begun when their Theban allies had violated a truce with their attack on Plataea, that they were in the wrong when they refused to submit to arbitration in 432–431, and that they had broken their sworn oaths and violated the Thirty Years' Peace. "For this reason they believed that they deserved their misfortunes, meaning their disaster at Pylos and the other things that had befallen them" (7.18.2)

Now, however, it was the Athenians who had broken the treaty and dishonored their oaths. During previous years, when the Athenians were fighting in the Peloponnesus alongside their allies, it was the

Spartans who had asked for the arbitration of grievances and the Athenians who had refused. "At this time, therefore, the Spartans thought that the violations, of which they had been guilty previously, had turned around and now were committed by the Athenians, and they were eager to go to war" (7.18.3).

THE FORT AT DECELEA

KING AGIS RESUMED ravaging Attica early in March 413, at which time he also began to fortify and garrison the hill that dominated the plain at the town of Decelea, some fourteen miles to the north-northeast of Athens and about the same distance from Boeotia. This exerted unprecedented pressure on the Athenians, for while previous incursions had lasted no more than forty and as few as fifteen days a year, henceforth they were barred from their homes and fields entirely. "Instead of a city Athens became a garrisoned fortress" (7.28.1). Day and night soldiers of all ages took turns, standing watch against a Spartan attack, a state of affairs that went on winter and summer for the duration of the war. Each day the cavalry went out to skirmish to keep the Spartans at bay, tiring the men and laming the horses. Needed to defend their city, they were not available for the effort in Sicily, where they were sorely missed.

In several notable ways the occupation of Decelea was comparable to the Athenian occupation of Pylos. In the first year, for example, some twenty thousand slaves deserted, many of them fleeing from the silver mines at Laurium whose revenues would now be lost to the Athenians. Cattle and pack animals were also part of the Peloponnesian booty. The Thebans, who joined the Spartans in raiding Attica, were the most opportunistic and assiduous of the allies in their appropriation of Athenian property. A fourth-century historian tells us that they "took over the prisoners and all the other spoils of the war at a small price, and, as they inhabited the neighboring country, carried off to their homes all the furnishing material in Attica, beginning with the wood and tiles of the house." (*Hellenica Oxyrhynchia* 12.3).

The Spartans at Decelea also blocked the overland route to Euboea by way of Oropus. Since the beginning of the war most of the Athenian livestock had been pastured on Euboea, from which they received essential supplies and which was an important point of departure for some of their exports. The Decelean occupation forced them to receive and send everything by the long sea voyage around Cape Sunium, a much more costly alternative. All this put great pressure on Athens.

It was the shortage of money that underlay what turned out to be the most horrible atrocity of the war. As they gathered reinforcements for Sicily the Athenians hired a corps of light-armed specialists from Thrace, but thirteen hundred of these knife-carrying barbarians arrived in Athens too late to take part in the campaign. To save money they were sent home under the guidance of Dieitrephes, an Athenian commander who was given orders to use them to do what harm they could on their way. One morning at daybreak they attacked the little town of Mycalessus in Boeotia, whose inhabitants were defenseless. "The Thracians burst into Mycalessus, sacked the houses and the temples, and butchered the people, sparing neither old nor young, but killing every one they met in whatever order they came upon them, even children and women, and pack animals, too, and anything they saw that was alive" (7.29.4). They also assaulted a boys' school: "The children had just come in, and they cut down every one of them" (7.29.5).

REINFORCEMENTS FOR BOTH SIDES

As THE ATHENIANS prepared to strengthen their position in Sicily, Gylippus' success also convinced the Peloponnesians to send additional forces to the island. They planned to dispatch three contingents: one, made up of six hundred helots and *neodamodeis* commanded by a Spartan general, Eccritus, and a second, consisting of three hundred Boeotians under their own generals, would leave from Cape Taenarum in the south and sail together across the open sea. A third force of seven hundred hoplites made up of Corinthians, Sicyonians, and Arcadian mercenaries would sail west through the Gulf of Corinth past the Athenian base at Naupactus, protected by a convoy of twenty-five Corinthian triremes.

In Athens, meanwhile, Eurymedon went ahead with money and a

small force while Demosthenes readied the main relief armada. Early in the spring of 413 two fleets set out from Piraeus under Charicles and Demosthenes; they did not sail directly to Sicily but attacked Laconia, aided by the Argives. Their main goal was a cape across from the island of Cythera where they landed and fortified its isthmus. It was intended to be what Pylos was in the west—a place to which helots could escape and from which they could raid Laconia—but the new base proved to be too far from Messenia to attract desertions, and as the Athenians never launched any attacks from it, they abandoned it the following year.

Charicles returned to Athens, but Demosthenes sailed along the coast on the route to Sicily, causing trouble for the Corinthians and recruiting allies along the way. At Acarnania he met Eurymedon, who had come back to notify him of Athenian reverses and the need to hurry with the reinforcements. But before they could set off, Conon, the Athenian admiral at Naupactus, arrived with the complaint that he had only eighteen triremes there and so could not take on the Corinthian convoy of twenty-five. Conon would later prove himself to be one of the greatest of all Greek admirals, so his hesitancy suggests that the ships at Naupactus were manned by inferior crews and steersmen, the best having been drained off by the force already in Sicily and by the one heading there. To assist him, Demosthenes and Eurymedon sent him the best ships they had before hurrying off to Sicily.

THE CAPTURE OF PLEMMYRIUM

ALTHOUGH GYLIPPUS HAD WON a series of important victories, the prospect of a new Athenian armament's landing in Sicily threatened all he had accomplished. The Syracusans, who were paying for the services of as many as seven thousand foreign soldiers, were short of money, and the Athenian blockade, however imperfect, had succeeded in cutting off income for private citizens and stopping the trade that produced import duties for the public treasury. In addition the cost of building, fitting out, and manning warships came as an enormous burden to the Syracusans, for they had no empire to provide the funds to pay for the fleet, and their allies offered no money. The arrival of fresh reinforcements from Athens, therefore, might well lead the Syracusans once again to consider surrender.

Gylippus consequently moved swiftly against the Athenians where they were vulnerable, at Plemmyrium, planning a diversionary naval attack to disguise an assault on the enemy base by land. To persuade the Syracusans to undertake a naval battle even as a distraction to the fearsome Athenians he relied on Hermocrates, who was no longer in office but still a powerful figure. Hermocrates' eloquence convinced the Syracusans, who took to their ships with enthusiasm. Under cover of darkness Gylippus led his army toward Plemmyrium at the same time that eighty Syracusan triremes approached it from the sea at different points.

The Athenian fleet reacted swiftly, putting sixty triremes into the water, and though outnumbered fought the enemy to a standstill. The situation on land, however, was different, for the Athenian army, unaware of the enemy advance, watched the sea battle from the shore. At daybreak Gylippus attacked the ill-defended forts and captured all three, although many Athenian soldiers escaped. Meanwhile, Athenian naval superiority asserted itself, as the Syracusan vessels ships fell foul of one another and "bestowed the victory upon the Athenians" (7.23.3). The Athenians sank eleven ships, while losing only three of their own, and regained domination of the sea. But they suffered many casualties, and their food and naval supplies in the forts (the sails and tackle of forty triremes, as well as three entire triremes caught on shore) were seized. The strategic cost of the capture of Plemmyrium was even greater. The Athenians could no longer bring in supplies, and "the loss of Plemmyrium brought bewilderment and discouragement to the army" (7.24.3).

The Syracusans sent word of their victory to their Peloponnesian friends, asking them to press the war against Athens even more vigorously, and dispatched a fleet to Italy to cut off supplies coming from Athens. They also reported the fall of Plemmyrium throughout Sicily, using ambassadors from Corinth, Sparta, and Ambracia to lend credibility to the claims. The effort was crowned with great success, for "almost all of Sicily . . . , the others who previously stood by and watched, now joined with and came to the aid of the Syracusans against the Athenians" (7.33.1–2).

THE BATTLE IN THE GREAT HARBOR

THE SYRACUSANS RECRUITED a corps of Sicilian Greeks to march against the Athenians at Syracuse. Nicias, however, arranged to have them ambushed before they got far, thwarting the Syracusan hopes of attacking the Athenians by land before their reinforcements could arrive. The Syracusans, therefore, needed a victory at sea, and fresh news from the Corinthian Gulf increased their hopes for success. Diphilus, now the Athenian commander at Naupactus, had thirty-three ships to the thirty under the Corinthian commander Polyanthes. To overcome the usual Athenian advantage of greater experience and training Polyanthes made a small but important alteration in the design of his triremes to permit a new tactic. At the bow of each trireme was an *epotis*, a plank projecting from each side like a cathead on a modern sailing vessel from which an anchor can be slung. On the trireme the *epotis* was the terminal of the outrigger, which was attached to the gunwale on each side of the ship and on which were fixed the oar pins of the top-level rowers.

In the normal course of battle triremes avoided ramming each other head on, for that would damage both ships in a way that would not necessarily bring the advantage to either. Polyanthes, however, had powerfully reinforced his *epoteis*, so that when the Athenians came forward his strengthened catheads were able to smash the more fragile Athenian ones, taking the attached outriggers with them and crippling the Athenian ships. Three Corinthian vessels were sunk in the battle, and seven Athenian ships totally disabled by Polyanthes' maneuver. The results were indecisive, for both sides set up victory trophies, but the strategic victory went to the Peloponnesians. The Athenians had failed to destroy the enemy forces and put an end to their ability to protect merchant ships and troop carriers traveling west. For the first time a Peloponnesian fleet had fought a numerically superior Athenian fleet to a standstill. In the open sea, against an enemy who was prepared for them, the new tactics could be overcome, but in restricted waters, against an unprepared enemy, they could continue to be successful.

The triumph in the Corinthian Gulf encouraged the Syracusans to challenge the Athenian fleet once again as part of a complicated plan of attack on land and sea. The Syracusan vessels now used thickened catheads, buttressed by fixed stay-beams, both inside and outside the ship. In the narrow space of Syracuse harbor the Athenians would not easily be able to break through the Sicilian line (*diekplous*) or to circle around it (*periplous*), so the tactic of crashing the heavy crossbeams against the lighter Athenian beams promised to bring success. Because the Syracusans controlled the land surrounding the Great Harbor (with the exception of the small stretch of coastline between the Athenians' walls and both Ortygia and Plemmyrium) they dominated access to it (see Map 22); as a result an Athenian defeat there could turn into a disaster, for fleeing ships would be unable either to land or to escape by water. Although the Athenians had by now learned of the efficacy of the head-on attacks made by the Peloponnesians in the Corinthian Gulf, such was their confidence in their own superiority and their disdain for the enemy's incompetence that they judged them to be not carefully planned tactics but rather inadvertent moves, the result of inferior Peloponnesian helmsmen.

In the land part of the plan Gylippus marched an army to the Athenian wall facing the city, while Syracusan forces from the garrison at the Olympieum, hoplites, cavalry, and light-armed soldiers approached it on the opposite side. This drew the Athenians' full attention to defending the walls and thus left them unprepared to face the Syracusan fleet when it came sailing down on them. Some Athenians ran to one wall, some to the other, and some hastened to man the fleet. Still, they managed to put seventy-five ships to sea against the eighty enemy vessels challenging them, and the first day's combat brought no result. The following day there was no fighting, so Nicias used the lull to prepare for another attack. The Athenians had built a palisade sunk into the sand beneath the water some distance offshore to protect their ships when drawn onto the beach. To make it easier to defend vessels pulling out of battle Nicias placed a merchant ship in front of every entrance of the palisade, two hundred feet apart. Each ship carried a crane armed with heavy metal weights in the shape of a dolphin. The crane could drop the "dolphin" onto a pursuing enemy vessel and sink or disable it.

On the third day the Syracusans attacked, and again the battle became a long skirmish, which lasted until the Syracusans withdrew for rest and dinner on the beach, where merchants were setting up a food market for the hungry men. The Athenians likewise headed for shore, believing that fighting was done for the day. As the men were eating, however, the Syracusans suddenly launched another assault, and the tired, hungry, and stunned Athenians barely succeeded in putting their ships to sea. The Athenian commanders saw that the strain of having to continue to move about the sea would soon wear down their men, leaving them no match for the rested Syracusans. But retreat before an enemy facing one in line in restricted waters is neither easy nor safe, and in any case, the notion of Athenian admirals choosing to refuse battle to an enemy of almost equal numbers was unheard of, so they ordered an immediate attack.

The Syracusans met the Athenians with the head-on charge as well as a few new tricks. They loaded their decks with javelin throwers whose missiles disabled many Athenian rowers. Small boats carrying additional javelin throwers rowed in under the oar banks of the Athenian triremes, allowing them to kill even more rowers. Their unorthodox tactics, and the disparity in the physical condition of the sailors in the two fleets, brought victory to the Syracusans; the Athenians were able to escape disaster only by fleeing to safety behind the merchantmen and the palisade. Two reckless Syracusan ships that pursued too aggressively were destroyed by "dolphins." Seven Athenian ships were sunk and a large number were damaged; many Athenian sailors were killed and many taken prisoner. The Syracusans dominated the Great Harbor and set up a trophy of victory. They now believed they were superior to the Athenians at sea and would soon defeat them on land, and they made preparations to attack again on both fronts.

THE SECOND ATHENIAN ARMADA: DEMOSTHENES' PLAN

THE SYRACUSANS' EXULTATION WAS short-lived, for soon after the battle in the harbor the Athenian reinforcements under Demosthenes and Eurymedon arrived in a splendor that had both a psychological and military purpose. The armada "was decked out theatrically so that the decorations of the weapons and the ensigns of the triremes ... might terrify the enemy" (Plutarch, *Nicias* 21.1). The force, almost the same size as the original expedition, consisted of seventy-three ships, carrying almost five thousand hoplites, many javelin throwers, slingers, and bowmen, as well as supplies for all. This vast reinforcement, sent even as the Spartans dominated Attica from their fort at Decelea, amazed and intimidated the Syracusans, who wondered if there would ever be an end to their city's peril.

Demosthenes had studied the Athenian campaign as it had been conducted up to that point and concluded that a quick assault and siege would have caused the Syracusans to surrender before they could have sent for help to the Peloponnesus. With characteristic clarity and boldness he planned to remedy that mistake at once. "Knowing that at that moment he was most frightening to the enemy, he wanted as swiftly as possible to take advantage of their present panic" and attack immediately (7.42.3).

He was confident that his fleet could blockade the city by sea; the crucial assignment was to take the Syracusan counterwall on Epipolae that prevented the enclosure of the city by land. Despite the fact that access to the heights of Epipolae was guarded by the formidable Spartan commander Gylippus, Demosthenes was prepared to take the gamble, for even defeat was preferable to wasting Athenian resources and risking the safety of its men. If he could seize Epipolae he could defeat Syracuse and have a reasonable expectation of gaining control of Sicily; if he failed he would take the expedition home to fight again another day. In either case the war in Sicily would come to an end with the expedition essentially intact.

THE NIGHT ATTACK ON EPIPOLAE

DEMOSTHENES' FIRST DIRECT ATTACK on the Syracusan counter-wall on Epipolae failed, demonstrating that any assault by daylight was bound to fail. Undaunted and ever ingenious, he planned a daring attack by night. Early in August he led about ten thousand hoplites and the same number of light-armed troops through the darkness before the rising of the moon to the pass at Euryalus, at the western end of the plateau, where they surprised the Syracusan garrison and took their fort. Escapees spread the word that the Athenians were on the plateau in force, but the elite Syracusan guard that first came to the rescue was quickly routed. The Athenians now raced ahead to exploit their success, an initial corps clearing the way while a second force headed swiftly for the counterwall. The Syracusans guarding it fled, allowing the Athenians to capture and tear down parts of it.

Gylippus and his troops, dazed by this daring and unexpected tactic, tried to stop the rampaging Athenians, who forced them back and continued to race ahead eastward on Epipolae. Eager to exploit the enemy's surprise, the Athenians themselves fell into disorder, and were routed by a regiment of Boeotian hoplites. This proved to be the turning point of the battle, for as soon as a single Athenian force was turned back toward the west, confusion set in. In the dim light of the moon the advancing Athenians could not tell whether the men running toward them were friends or foes, a problem that was compounded by the fact that the generals appear not to have placed anyone at the pass to direct traffic. As the different companies came onto the plateau they found some Athenian forces advancing eastward unchecked, others running back toward Euryalus in retreat, and still others who had just come up through the pass and were not yet in motion. No one instructed the men newly arrived on the plateau which group they should join.

The Syracusans added to the chaos by shouting and cheering, and as they began to sense their victory they and their allies, also Dorians, reverted to the Dorian custom of singing a paean. Their war cry blasting out of the darkness terrified the Athenians. Although their own force was mainly Ionian, it included such important Dorian contingents as the Argives and Corcyraeans, who now began to sing out their own paeans, which were indistinguishable from the enemy's, adding to the Athenians' terror and making it still harder to distinguish enemy from ally. "Finally, when they had once been thrown into confusion, they attacked one another in many different parts of the battlefield, friends against friends and citizens against fellow citizens; not only did they fall into a panic but they even came to blows and were separated only with difficulty" (7.44.8).

No one on the Athenian side was as familiar with the plateau as the Syracusans, and those who had just arrived with Demosthenes and Eurymedon had no knowledge of it at all. In the darkness, as victory turned to defeat, advance to retreat, and retreat to rout, this ignorance was disastrous. Trying to escape, many Athenian soldiers jumped off the cliffs to their deaths, and many must have met the same fate by accident. The experienced men from Nicias' army ultimately found their way back to camp and safety, but the new men from the reinforcing expedition wandered about until daybreak, when the Syracusan cavalry hunted them down and killed them. The result was the greatest disaster yet suffered by the Athenians: between two thousand and twenty-five hundred men were killed, and all hope of a quick victory at Syracuse abandoned.

RETREAT OR REMAIN?

AS THE TRIUMPHANT SYRACUSANS set out to recruit additional Sicilian allies for the assault on the Athenians' walls that would bring final victory, Athenian morale sunk ever lower. Apart from the defeat in battle, their spirits suffered from the malaria and dysentery that came with being encamped on marshy ground in a late Sicilian summer. "The situation appeared to them to be as hopeless as it could be" (7.47.2). Demosthenes argued for sailing home while Athens still had naval superiority. "He said it would be of more use to Athens to fight the war against an enemy who was building a fort against it in its own country than against Syracuse, which it was no longer easy to subdue, nor was it right, besides, to expend a great deal of money to no purpose by continuing the siege" (7.47.4). This was wise counsel, for it had become clear that there was no way to take the Syracusan counterwall on Epipolae and no chance of a successful siege, and no reinforcements were forthcoming. It was time to cut losses before a disappointing failure became a disaster.

Demosthenes must have been surprised, therefore, when Nicias did not agree. Nicias knew that the Athenians were in danger but, privately undecided, did not want to make a firm decision to retreat, for fear that the enemy might learn of it and cut off escape. He had also learned from his private sources that the enemy might be suffering more greatly than his own forces, since the superior Athenian fleet could still prevent supplies from reaching Syracuse by sea. His greatest hope came from a report that there was a group in Syracuse that continued to press for surrender to Athens. Nicias was in touch with them, and they continued to urge him to hold his ground.

Neither reason, however, was compelling. Even if the sea lanes were cut off Syracuse could still get supplies overland, and hopes of treason from within the city were chimerical. Those wanting surrender lacked adequate support, and they were not likely to gain more after Syracuse's recent victories. The arrival of Gongylus and Gylippus had ended their only real chance for capitulation.

In the debate among the Athenian generals Nicias suppressed his own uncertainty and insisted on staying in Sicily. His main argument aimed to counter the powerful financial considerations raised by Demosthenes. The Syracusans, he claimed, were in even worse straits; the cost of a navy and the many mercenary soldiers they employed had already claimed two thousand talents of their own money and forced them to borrow still more. They would soon run out of funds to pay their mercenary force.

The Syracusans were undeniably short of money, but their victories would have improved their credit and encouraged their allies and others to lend them what they needed to achieve complete success. Besides, they still had native wealth of their own that could be tapped by taxation in the current emergency. Unless Syracuse could be cut off by land and sea it could hold out indefinitely, but there was no longer hope of shutting the city in.

Nicias revealed his true motives in the remainder of his speech: he feared that once back in Athens his soldiers would turn against him and convince the assembly that it was he who was to blame for the failure. They would complain "that their generals had been bribed to betray them and withdraw. He himself, at any rate, knowing the character of the Athenians, did not wish to be put to death unjustly on a disgraceful charge by the Athenians but preferred, if he must, to take his chances and meet his own death himself at the hands of the enemy" (7.48.4).

Although Demosthenes and Eurymedon opposed Nicias' decision to stay, they were outvoted when Menander and Euthydemus, the two men elected to assist the ailing Nicias, supported their prestigious senior commander. With their backing he also rejected the compromise proposal made by Demosthenes and Eurymedon, urging the Athenians at least to withdraw from the swamps outside Syracuse to healthier and safer positions at Thapsus or Catana, from which they could raid the Sicilian countryside and live off the land. Once away from Syracuse harbor, they could also fight in the open sea, where the new Syracusan tactics would be ineffective and where their own greater skill and experience would give them the advantage. Nicias' dismissal of this plan may have been motivated by his fear that once the army boarded the ships and sailed out of Syracuse harbor, it would be impossible to keep the Athenians in Sicily much longer.

Meanwhile, Gylippus had recruited a large army of Sicilians and added to his forces six hundred Peloponnesian hoplites, helots, and *neodamodeis* who had been delayed by storms but arrived in Sicily in time to take part in another assault on the Athenians. As disease caused by the malarial swamps continued to diminish the Athenian forces in numbers and morale, even Nicias softened his opposition to withdrawal. He asked only that there be no open vote to retreat that might forewarn the enemy. The road to safety was thus still open when fate, the gods, or chance intervened.

ECLIPSE

ON THE NIGHT OF August 27, 413, between 9:41 and 10:30 P.M., the moon was totally eclipsed. Fear overcame the superstitious Athenian army, and the men read the event as a divine warning against sailing immediately. Nicias consulted a soothsayer who recommended that the Athenians wait "thrice nine days" before departing. Even for credulous men, however, this interpretation of the eclipse was not the only one possible. Philochorus, a historian who lived in the third century B.C., himself a seer, gave a different reading: "The sign was not unfavorable to men who were fleeing but, on the contrary, very favorable; for deeds of fear require concealment, while light is an enemy to them" (Plutarch, *Nicias* 23.5). A commander who wished to escape could easily have conceived and used such an interpretation to good effect, but Nicias unquestioningly accepted the omen as unfavorable, confident that the gods had intervened to confirm his own judgment. He "refused to discuss further the question of their departure until they waited thrice nine days as the soothsayers recommended" (7.50.4).

Word of the debate and decision to remain leaked when deserters informed the Syracusans that the Athenians were planning to sail home but were delayed by the lunar eclipse. To prevent their escape the Syracusans decided to force another sea battle at once in Syracuse harbor. While the Athenians patiently obeyed their soothsayer the Syracusans practiced their crews in naval tactics, even though their first attack was by land, when a sortie lured a company of Athenian hoplites and cavalry out through a gate and crushed them, forcing a retreat. The main assault came the following day. As the army attacked the Athenian walls, the Syracusan navy sent seventy-six triremes against the Athenian base, and the Athenians met them with eighty-six ships.

The Athenian numerical superiority enabled Eurymedon's ships on the right wing to extend beyond the Syracusan left, so he ordered the circling maneuver, the *periplous*. He started southward, toward the part of the bay off Dascon, but seems to have been too close to the shore to attain full speed. Before he could make his way around the end of the enemy line the Syracusans broke through Menander's ships in the Athenian center. At that point the Corinthian admiral Pythen decided not to pursue the fleeing Athenians before him but to turn south and join the attack against Eurymedon. The Syracusans forced the Athenian right wing back toward shore, destroying seven ships and killing Eurymedon. That was the turning point in the battle, as the entire Athenian fleet was routed and driven toward the shore, many of the men disembarking to find themselves outside the stockade and away from the area protected by their own walls. Gylippus killed fleeing

Athenians as they beached their ships or swam ashore, and the Syracusans at sea hauled away the abandoned triremes. As Gylippus' troops attempted to overrun the Athenian camp they were surprised by a band of the Athenians' Etruscan allies, who, aided by the Athenians themselves, were able to save most of the ships. Even so, eighteen triremes were lost, with every member of their crews.

The Syracusans set up trophies to mark their victories on land and sea, as did the Athenians, who were entitled to do so to mark their repelling of Gylippus at the seawall, but it was a pathetic gesture. The Athenian forces, even with augmentation by powerful reinforcements, had suffered major defeats on land and sea. Thucydides believes that the Athenians miscalculated in two major respects: they underestimated the strength of Syracuse in both ships and cavalry, and they ignored the fact that Syracuse was a democracy, whose unity it would be much harder to undermine. It seems less than fair to blame the Athenians' plight on the assembly that voted the vast forces for the expedition and for its reinforcement, for in both instances they followed the advice of Nicias. It is equally wrong to hold them responsible for the second error, for there is no evidence that they had ever counted on internal revolution or treason to deliver Syracuse into their hands. That was the notion of Nicias alone and, by delaying the enclosure of the city and pursuing the hope of victory through treason long after there was any chance of it, he doomed the Athenians, and they finally understood that victory was impossible. "Even before this they did not know what to do, and when they were defeated even with their fleet, something that they did not think possible, they were much more at a loss than ever" (7.55.2). All they could hope for now was escape.

CHAPTER TWENTY-FIVE

Defeat and Destruction (413)

THE AMAZING NAVAL VICTORY in the harbor reinvigorated the Syracusans, who were now determined to secure not merely the salvation of their city but the complete destruction of the Athenian expedition and freedom for all the Greeks they ruled. These great achievements, they believed, would bring their city honor and fame; "they would be regarded with wonder by the rest of the world and even by those who came after them" (7.56.2). They accordingly set out to shut the Athenian fleet in the Great Harbor by anchoring triremes and other boats across its entrance, bridging them over with boards, and connecting them with iron chains. Since the Athenians needed their ships to get back to Athens and their only feasible escape route was by sea, they decided to try to break out of the harbor, however daunting that attempt might be.

THE FINAL NAVAL BATTLE

THE FORCE THAT now prepared to fight for its very existence was not the proud, smart fleet that had rowed out of Piraeus as if in a regatta but a ragtag assembly that had a very old-fashioned look, carrying many hoplites, javelin throwers, and bowmen, and ready for the antiquated fighting style that was based on missiles, grappling, and hand-to-hand fighting, rather than the sleek ramming tactics that had made Athens queen of the seas. To meet the enemy's offense of ramming head-on with thickened catheads they invented "iron hands," or grappling hooks that would seize an attacking ship and prevent it from backing away after driving into the prow of an Athenian ship. With the enemy so held, the Athenians' many foot soldiers would give them superiority in the closed waters of the harbor, where finer tactics would be impossible. Deserters, however, again warned the enemy of the Athenian measures, so the Syracusans stretched hides across the prows and upper portions of their ships to make grappling them impossible.

Nicias had command of the troops on land, but after he spoke to the entire assembled force on the beach he took a boat through the Athenian fleet, stopping at each trireme, addressing the captain by his name, his father's name, and his tribe, and appealing to old ancestral and family feelings. As Pericles had done, he reminded them of the liberty their homeland provided its citizens, but, in his own way, he also spoke on a less exalted level, saying, "the kind of thing that men call out in much the same language on every occasion, about wives and children and ancestral gods, but which, in the fear of the moment, they think will be useful" (7.69.1–3). While Nicias lacked the aristocratic birth, intellectual power, and political skill of a Pericles, his simple, old-fashioned manner and common touch had a powerful appeal of its own in the Athenian democracy.

The other Athenian generals now took the fleet out into the harbor, aiming at its mouth, through which they hoped to force an escape. The Syracusans guarded the exit with one detachment of their ships and spread the others all around it, in position to attack the Athenian fleet from all directions simultaneously when the time was ripe. Sicanus and Agatharcus commanded the wings and Pythen the center. Syracusans foot soldiers lined the shore around most of the harbor, while the Athenian troops occupied the small part they controlled. The battle was fought before what amounted to a gallery of spectators at an athletic contest, for the families of the Syracusan warriors had occupied every high place from which the fighting might be visible.

The Athenian fleet made its way for the small opening the Syracusans had left in the barrier to allow their own ships to pass, and its advantage in numbers enabled it to break through. As they began to cut the chains holding the line of vessels together, the remaining Syracusan squadrons attacked from all sides, pressing the Athenians on the flanks and in the rear. In the confined waters of the harbor almost two hundred ships fought at close quarters, for ramming was impossible. Everything worked to strip from the Athenians the advantages of experience and skill they had earned from long years of practice and naval warfare. Their men shot arrows and hurled javelins at the enemy, but they had done their previous fighting on solid ground, not bobbing about the waves on swiftly moving ships, so they had no accuracy. The Syracusans, on the other hand, were ordered by the wily Corinthian commander Ariston, who died in the battle, to throw stones at the enemy, which were easier to control and more effective in the conditions of this battle. Much of the combat involved boarding and hand-to-hand engagement between marines on both sides. In the constricted space, ships were struck or boarded from one side even as they were in the process of attacking on the other. The shouting of the men was so loud that the rowers could not hear the commands or easily keep the beat of their stroke, another negation of an important Athenian advantage. After a while the coxswains themselves grew so excited that they shouted encouragement to their men, which interfered with their calling out of the stroke.

The drama of this battle at sea was witnessed by a vast audience of soldiers on both sides watching from different vantage points on the shore as well as by the Syracusan civilians, all of whom exulted or suffered, in turn, as the battle seemed to go well or badly. It was a thrilling and fearful spectacle whose outcome was vital to the spectators. In the end the Syracusans routed the Athenians, who fled to shore in panic, leaving their ships behind and running to seek safety at their camp. Their order and spirit broken, most thought only of saving themselves. They did not even ask for a truce to permit the burial of their dead, an astonishing omission. Nothing could be allowed to delay their flight, for they believed that only a miracle could save them.

One Athenian managed to keep his wits and composure at this terrible moment. Demosthenes saw that the Athenians still had sixty viable ships to fewer than fifty for the enemy, and proposed that they collect their forces and try another breakout from the harbor at daybreak. The plan might have worked, for the Syracusans would not have expected another such attempt, the reduced number of combatants would have left the Athenians room to use their tactical superiority, and Nicias was persuaded to make the effort. It was too late, however, for the morale of the men had collapsed entirely. They refused the generals' orders to board the ships again and insisted on endeavoring to escape by land.

THE FINAL RETREAT

THE SYRACUSANS' DISCIPLINE had likewise collapsed, but for the opposite reasons: they had taken to rejoicing in their victory and salvation, drinking and reveling without a thought of the defeated enemy. One Syracusan, however, was thinking strategically. Hermocrates knew that the Athenians were still dangerous, and recognized that were they to succeed in escaping to another part of Sicily, they could rally, recover their spirit and discipline, and return to threaten the city again. He meant to destroy the Athenian force there and then, while he had the opportunity, and proposed to block the roads and passes leading from Syracuse. Gylippus agreed, but he and the other generals thought that in their current condition their men would be unlikely to obey any commands, so Hermocrates resorted to trickery. He sent horsemen to the Athenian camp at twilight. Pretending to be the Syracusans who had hoped to betray the city to Nicias, they stood at a distance, called out the names of selected Athenians, and urged them to tell Nicias that it would not be safe to move the army that night, for the Syracusans were guarding the roads. The Athenians' own fear of traveling through enemy territory in the darkness would probably have led to the same outcome, and they delayed their march. Then they lingered another day while the men packed supplies and equipment before getting under way, by which time the enemy had had sufficient time to block the escape routes.

About forty thousand men set off on the march, of whom about half were soldiers and the rest noncombatants. "They looked like nothing more than a city, and one of considerable size, sneaking away in flight after being reduced by a siege" (7.75.5). The men were riddled with shame for their sacrilege in failing to bury their dead and for abandoning their sick and wounded, who piteously cried out to friends and relatives, clinging to them as they marched away. "As a result the army was plunged so completely into tears and disarray that it could not easily depart, even from a hostile country and although they had already endured suffering beyond tears and feared unknown sufferings in the future" (7.75).

Tired, ill, and in great pain, Nicias spoke to the men to raise their spirits and calm their anxieties. He urged them not to blame them-

selves for their defeat and misery and held out the hope that their fortunes might soon be reversed. They were still, he reminded them, a
mighty army: "You should realize that wherever you settle down you
are immediately a city and that there is no other city in Sicily that
could easily sustain an attack from you or drive you out once you have
established yourselves anywhere" (7.77.4). There was, therefore, the
possibility of salvation if they would keep their morale and discipline
and move swiftly in good order. "Know the whole truth, soldiers,"
Nicias said. "You must be brave men, for there is no place nearby to
which you can safely escape if you are cowards. And if you get away
from your enemy now you will all some time see again what you most
desire, while those of you who are Athenians will raise up again the
great power of your city, however fallen it may be. For it is men that
make up the city and not walls or ships empty of men" (7.77.7).

The first destination was Catana, a city loyal to Athens that could
furnish a friendly welcome and supplies, and then serve as a base for
further operations. The usual route, around Epipolae, would expose the
retreating army to attack from the Syracusan cavalry, so the plan was to
march westward along the course of the Anapus, meet friendly Sicels
somewhere in the highlands, and turn northward toward Catana at
some appropriate place, well to the west of Epipolae and away from the
Syracusan forces. Nicias and Demosthenes each commanded a hollow
rectangle of troops surrounding the civilians. Almost four miles from
Syracuse, at a point along the Anapus, they fought through a force of
Syracusans and their allies, but the Syracusan cavalry and light-armed
troops stayed with them, harrying them with constant attacks and a
rain of missiles. The next morning they marched about two miles to the
northwest, seeking food and water, and spent the entire day at the task.

Barring further progress was what is now called Monte Climiti, a
large plateau that ends in a high cliff-face eight miles northwest of Syracuse. The Athenians hoped to make their way over it through the large
ravine now called the Cava Castelluccio on their way to safety at Catana.
Here, again, however, their delays undid them, for the Syracusans had
sufficient time to build a wall across the ravine to the east of what was
then called the Acraean Bald Rock. When the Athenians started out the
next morning the Syracusans and their allies attacked with cavalry and
javelin throwers, forcing them back to camp. The next day they tried to

force their way up Monte Climiti against a fortified position and an entrenched enemy, and got as far as the Syracusans' wall. There spears and arrows rained on them from higher up on the sides of the ravine, and they were again pushed back. A sudden torrential rainstorm broke upon them in the mountain pass, a dangerous and terrifying event, and many Athenians took it as a sign of divine disfavor. Harassed by enemy missiles, fearful, soaking wet, and exhausted, they could not rest, for Gylippus was already building a wall behind them. Because that barrier could cut them off and allow them to be destroyed on the spot, they quickly sent a force to prevent its completion and moved the entire army back to camp on level country, away from the Syracusan force.

Their new plan was to march northwest along the Anapus with Monte Climiti on their right and then head for Catana. On the fifth day they reached the flat land today called Contrada Puliga, where the Syracusans' cavalry and javelin throwers again rode and ran in front of the Athenian army, alongside it, and behind it, avoiding close contact with the hoplites and raining missiles on them from a distance. The cavalry cut off stragglers and rode them down. If the Athenians attacked, the Syracusans retreated; when the Athenians withdrew, the Syracusans charged. They concentrated their assault on the rear, hoping to cause a panic in the rest of the army. The Athenians fought bravely and with discipline, marching more than half a mile before being forced to make camp and rest.

Nicias and Demosthenes now decided to turn southeast toward the sea, follow one of the rivers that flowed into it to its upland source, and there either to join the Sicels or turn toward Catana by a more roundabout route. To steal past the Syracusans they lit as many campfires as they could, as a decoy, and marched back toward the coast under cover of darkness toward the little town of Cassibile. Nicias led the first division through the frightening alien darkness, and Demosthenes followed with the rest of the army. By dawn they met near the shore and headed for the Cacyparis River (today, the Cassibile), planning to move inland along its banks to meet their Sicel friends. Once again the Syracusans intercepted them, but the Athenians fought their way across the river and marched southward toward the next stream in their path, the Erineus.

THE FATE OF THE ATHENIANS

NICIAS MADE CAMP just beyond the river, about six miles ahead of Demosthenes. The Syracusans continued to harass Demosthenes' men, slowing his retreat, and then the main Syracusan force from the camp at Monte Climiti, including cavalry and light-armed troops, arrived in force about noon on the sixth day of the Athenian retreat. They cut the Athenians off not quite a mile south of the Cacyparis, trapping them in an olive grove surrounded by a wall with a road on either side, where the Syracusans could throw and shoot missiles at them from every direction. The Athenians suffered great losses throughout the afternoon until Gylippus and the Syracusans tried to divide them by offering freedom to Athenian allies who would desert. Only a few allied contingents surrendered, but when the situation became hopeless Demosthenes, at last, surrendered on these terms: if the Athenians gave up their weapons "none of them would be killed, either by violence, or by imprisonment, or by being deprived of the necessities of life" (7.82.2). The Syracusans captured the six thousand men who were left from the twenty thousand soldiers who began the retreat less than a week before and filled four shields with the booty taken from them. Demosthenes tried to kill himself with his own sword, but his captors prevented him from taking his life.

The next day the Syracusans overtook Nicias, reported the capture of Demosthenes, and ordered him to surrender, as well. Instead, he sent them an offer to have Athens pay the full cost of the war in exchange for letting his army go free, leaving as hostages one soldier for each talent. The Syracusans refused, for they saw the chance to wipe out their hated enemy in a total victory and would not trade it for any amount of money. They surrounded Nicias' men and devastated them with missiles, as they had the trapped army of Demosthenes. The Athenians again tried to escape in the dark, but this time the Syracusans were ready. Three hundred men, nonetheless, dared to make the effort and broke through the Syracusan guard, but the rest gave up the attempt.

On the eighth day Nicias tried to force his way through the surrounding enemy to the next river, the Assinarus, some three miles south. The Athenians no longer had a plan, only a blind wish to escape and a parching thirst. Through the onslaught of missiles, cavalry attacks, and hoplite assaults, they reached the Assinarus, where all discipline collapsed as each man rushed to get across the river first. The army became a mob that clogged the passage and made it easier for the enemy to prevent the crossing. "Since they were forced to go forward in a close mass they fell on top of and trampled one another; some were killed immediately, impaled on their own spears, while others got tangled in their equipment and with each other and were carried away by the stream. The Syracusans stood along the opposite bank of the river, which was steep, and threw missiles down on the Athenians below, most of them drinking greedily and heaped together in disorder in the hollow bed of the river. The Peloponnesians also came down and butchered them, especially those in the river. And the water immediately became spoiled, but it was drunk, nonetheless, though it was muddy and full of blood, and most of them even fought over it" (7.84).

All that remained of the great Athenian army was destroyed at the Assinarus. The Syracusan cavalry, which had caused the Athenians so much trouble through the campaign, killed the few men who did make their way across the river. Nicias gave himself up, but to Gylippus, "trusting him rather than the Syracusans" (7.85.1); only then did the Spartan commander order an end to the killing. Of Nicias' troops only about one thousand were still alive. Some escaped from the Assinarus, and others later escaped after being captured, all fleeing to Catana.

The triumphant Syracusans took their prisoners and booty and stripped the armor from the dead enemy, hanging it from the finest and tallest trees along the river. They crowned themselves with wreaths of victory and decorated their horses. On returning to Syracuse they held an assembly at which they voted to enslave the servants of the Athenians and their imperial allies and to place Athenians citizens and their Sicilian Greek allies into the city's stone quarries for safekeeping. A proposal to put Nicias and Demosthenes to death provoked more debate. Hermocrates objected, on lofty grounds of generosity, but the assembly shouted him down. Gylippus had a more practical argument: he wanted the glory of bringing the Athenian generals home to Sparta. Demosthenes was its bitterest enemy because of his victories at Pylos and Sphacteria, and Nicias, a friend who had once argued for releasing the prisoners and made first a peace and then an alliance with the Spartans. But the Syracusans rejected the request, as did the Corinthians, so the assembly voted to put both Athenian generals to death.

A JUDGMENT ON NICIAS

THUCYDIDES WRITES an extraordinary eulogy of Nicias: "For this reason, or for one very much like it, he was killed; of all the Greeks, in my time, at any rate, he least deserved to meet with such extreme misfortune because he had led his entire life in accordance with virtue" (7.86.5). The citizens of Athens held a different opinion. The antiquarian Pausanias once saw a stele in the public cemetery of Athens on which were engraved the names of the generals who died fighting in Sicily, all except that of Nicias. He learned the reason for the omission from the Sicilian historian Philistus: "Demosthenes made a truce for the rest of his men, excluding himself and was captured while trying to commit suicide, but Nicias surrendered himself voluntarily. For this reason Nicias' name was not written on the stele: he was condemned as a voluntary prisoner and as an unworthy soldier" (1.29.11–12).

The Syracusans were now holding over seven thousand prisoners in their stone quarries, crowded together in inhuman conditions, burned by the sun during the day and chilled by the autumn cold at night. They were given about a half-pint of water and a pint of food each day, much less than what the Spartans had been permitted to send to the slaves on Sphacteria, and they suffered terribly from hunger and thirst. Men died from their wounds, from illness and exposure, and the dead bodies were thrown in piles on top of one another, creating an unbearable stench. After seventy days all the survivors, except the Athenians and the Sicilian and Italian Greeks, were sold into slavery. Plutarch tells the tale of slaves freed for their ability to recite the verses of Euripides, for the Sicilians were mad for his poetry. Neither poetry nor anything else could help the remainder of the men left in the quarries, who were kept there for eight months; presumably no one survived any longer.

Thucydides calls the Sicilian expedition "the greatest action of all those that took place during the war and, so it seems to me, at least, the greatest of any which we know to have happened to any of the Greeks;

it was the most glorious for those who won and the most disastrous for those who were defeated. For the losers were beaten in every way and completely; what they suffered was great in every respect, for they met with total destruction, as the saying goes—their army, their ships, and everything were destroyed—and only a few of many came back home" (7.87.5–6). To most Greeks it seemed the war was all but over.

Who should ultimately bear responsibility for this terrible disaster? Alcibiades was the author of the Sicilian expedition, but Nicias played a more central role. Thucydides regarded the expedition as a mistake by the unguided and misguided democracy. He does not blame Nicias but praises him in the highest terms, even though his narrative account offers a very different impression from his own interpretation of the events. In the end, it was only Nicias' failed rhetorical trick that turned a modest undertaking, taking few risks, into a massive campaign that made the conquest of Sicily seem possible and safe. He also made a critical technical error in omitting cavalry from his list of requirements for the campaign.

Once in command in Sicily, he embarked upon a series of errors of commission and omission that brought destruction to the expedition. He failed to complete the siege of Syracuse by delaying the construction of a single circuit of walls before undertaking any other projects. He wasted more time in discussions with dissidents in Syracuse; he did not send a squadron to intercept Gylippus' arrival in Sicily; he did not mount a competent blockade to prevent Gongylus and the Corinthian ships from reaching Syracuse by sea; he did not fortify and guard Epipolae to prevent a surprise attack. He thereby allowed the revival of the enemy, who responded by driving the Athenians from their dominance. He then moved the Athenian navy, the supply depot, and the treasury to an untenable position at Plemmyrium, where the morale and quality of the fleet deteriorated and from which Gylippus was able to expel them, capturing the money and supplies.

Instead of abandoning the doomed campaign after the summer of 414, Nicias refused to withdraw out of fear for his reputation and safety. Instead he asked the Athenians to choose between a retreat and sending huge reinforcements and to relieve him of the command. A straightforward and honest assessment of the dangerous situation and his own incapacity might well have led to a withdrawal and thus avoided the great disaster. Even after the terrible defeat on Epipolae, Nicias refused to take his expedition home. To save his reputation and avoid punishment he seized on the lunar eclipse as a last chance to avoid the inevitable and let slip away the Athenians' final opportunity to escape.

Part Six

REVOLUTIONS IN THE EMPIRE AND IN ATHENS

Predictions that Athens would collapse right after the Sicilian campaign were widespread among the Greeks in 413, but they turned out to be premature. Still, such expectations were not unreasonable, for in the next few years the Athenians confronted uprisings in their empire and upheavals at home that could easily have brought them down. Only remarkable determination and effort allowed Athens to keep fighting.

The rest of the war was powerfully shaped by the Persian Empire. When the Athenians' empire and war effort failed to collapse as expected it became evident that the Spartans and their allies could not win without building a fleet and defeating Athens at sea. This could be done only by gaining support of the Persians who, alone, could supply the needed financial and military assistance. Although Spartans and Persians shared a desire to destroy Athenian power, Persian aims conflicted with Spartan goals and ambitions. The Athenians, too, needed money to rebuild their shattered fleet and, most of all needed to prevent the Persians from aiding the enemy. After the war in Sicily, therefore, attention shifted eastward, to the Great King of Persia and the satraps of his western provinces.

CHAPTER TWENTY-SIX

After the Disaster (413–412)

THE NEWS OF the disaster in Sicily probably reached Athens toward the end of September 413, when, it is said, a foreigner told the story to his barber in Piraeus, who carried it to Athens, where no one believed him. For some time people doubted even the accounts of those soldiers who escaped from Sicily about the scope of the calamity. When they finally accepted the truth the angered and frightened Athenians vented their fury on the politicians they held responsible for the Sicilian expedition, "as if they had not voted for it themselves" (8.1.1), and on the seers who had predicted success.

They mourned their lost countrymen and desperately feared for their own safety when they calculated their losses and the enemy's gains. They expected massive rebellions in their empire, accompanied by an attack on Athens by the Peloponnesians, and they knew how poorly equipped the city was to face such dangers. They were, for one thing, desperately short of fighting men. Not only had the plague killed about a third of the population and disabled still others, but the Sicilian campaign had probably claimed at least 3,000 hoplites and 9,000 thetes as well as thousands of metics. By 413 the Athenians probably had only 9,000 hoplites of all ages, perhaps 11,000 thetes, and 3,000 metics, fewer than half of the number available when the war started. They had also lost 216 triremes, of which 160 were Athenian; only about 100, not all of which were seaworthy, remained.

Money for repairs and new construction was also in short supply. Of the nearly five thousand expendable talents available in 431 fewer than five hundred now remained in the treasury. The forces at the Spartan fort at Decelea had helped more than twenty thousand slaves escape, the permanent Spartan danger kept the Athenians from working their farms, and Boeotian raiders stripped their houses and took their farm animals. Many had to move from the countryside to the city, where demand for all goods drove up prices. More imports were needed and had to be carried greater distances at increased costs. Charitable concerns further strained the public treasury, for the state had to support the needy widows and orphans created by the war.

The losses suffered by individual Athenians reduced their ability to provide ships for the state. In the past, rich men had been able to fit out a warship independently when their turn came to perform that public service but they now had to introduce the syntrierarchy, which allowed two men to share the expense. Wealthy Athenians were also unable to pay much direct tax, even in this emergency.

THE *PROBOULOI*

THE SICILIAN EXPEDITION had also deprived the Athenians of their best and most experienced generals: Demosthenes, Lamachus, Nicias, and Eurymedon were dead, Alcibiades was in exile, and the other four known generals in 413/2 had held no previous command. Among political leaders, not only were Nicias and Alcibiades lost to them, Hyperbolus was also in exile. To fill this vacuum the Athenians decided "to elect a board of older men to serve as *probouloi*, offering advice and proposing legislation, concerning current problems as the situation may require" (8.1.3). They chose ten *probouloi*, one man over the age of forty from each tribe, who were probably granted the right to present bills to the assembly, thereby replacing the council in this primary function. Whatever their formal powers, their seniority, their election for an unlimited term, and the vagueness and generality of their commission gave them unprecedented influence and authority.

The names of only two *probouloi* are known: Hagnon and Sophocles, the great tragic poet. Hagnon was a general alongside Pericles during the Samian campaign of 440, so probably more than sixty years old in 413. He was a defender of Pericles, and a public figure of great repute. Sophocles, who was probably well into his eighties when elected *proboulos*, had also been a general, elected to the high position of treasurer of the Athenian alliance, but was most celebrated for having won prizes for tragedy for more than half a century, making him one of the most famous and admired men in Greece. Like Hagnon, he had been associated and worked with Pericles. Both were wealthy, experienced, respected, and, in the context of 413, conservative, though their association with Pericles guaranteed that they were neither oligarchs nor enemies of the democracy.

Thucydides could not resist a jibe at the post-Periclean democracy: "In the terror of the moment, as is the way of the demos, they were ready to do everything with discipline" (8.1.4). The Athenian assembly did indeed act with Periclean restraint and prudence, placing a limit on itself by bestowing extraordinary powers on a board of respected and trusted moderates in his tradition. As one of their first acts "They decided, so far as the situation permitted, not to give in but instead to prepare a fleet, obtaining timber and money wherever they could, to see to the security of their alliance, especially Euboea, and to reduce public expenditures" (8.1.3).

As well as new ships the Athenians built a fort at Sunium at the southern tip of Attica to protect the grain-carrying vessels that sailed by. They abandoned the fort in Laconia, which had proved to be both costly and ineffective: "If they judged any expenditure useless they curtailed it in the interests of economy" (8.4). They kept a close watch on their allies "so that they might not revolt from them" (8.4), and also replaced the collection of tribute on the basis of assessments imposed on each allied city with a uniform five-percent duty on all goods imported or exported by sea. This measure was undertaken to increase revenue over what could reasonably be obtained from an empire that was on the point of rebellion. The new tax would also shift the burden from landowners to merchants, who benefited from the empire and might be more willing to pay taxes and better disposed to Athens. Nevertheless, "the subjects of the Athenians were ready to rebel against them even beyond their power" (8.2.2), and within a year major regions, such as Euboea, Chios, Lesbos, Rhodes, Miletus, and Ephesus had revolted, even though they could not win their freedom without the help of Sparta and its allies.

SPARTAN AMBITIONS

THE ATHENIAN DEFEAT IN Sicily gave the Spartans new confidence, and a set of more ambitious war aims. While they had initially entered the war, they claimed, "to free the Greeks," they now believed that after triumphing over Athens, "they themselves would safely hold the hegemony of all Greece" (8.2.4). More Spartans had come to hope that "they would enjoy great wealth, Sparta would become greater and more powerful, and the houses of the private citizens would receive a great increase in their prosperity" (Diodorus 11.50).

Not only military success but also changes in Spartan society contributed to the enlargement of this particular faction. The number of full Spartan citizens was in decline: about five thousand hoplites had fought at Plataea in 479, but only about one thousand would be at Leuctra in 371; no more than thirty-five hundred were present at Mantinea in 418. Spartan practices such as enforcing separation of spouses in their most fertile years and pederasty continued to limit the number of offspring, and Spartiates also deliberately chose to have few children to maximize their inheritances. They also tried to acquire as much private land as possible and other wealth when it was available to supplement the public grant.

As the number of Spartiates decreased, moreover, the proportion of free men in Laconia who were not Spartiates increased. In 421 there were a thousand *neodamodeis* in the region, helots who had fought in the Spartan army and were given their freedom and a piece of land as a reward; by 396 there were at least two thousand. Most likely they and their offspring could hope to achieve Spartiate status, for the title implies some degree of citizenship. Another such group consisted of *hypomeiones*, or "inferiors," who seem chiefly to have been men born to the Spartiate class, and were hence eligible for Spartan citizenship, but whom poverty prevented from contributing to the common meals; they were consequently excluded from citizenship, respect, and honor.

Still other free men outside the body of Spartiates were called *mothakes*. Some of them seem to have been the illegitimate sons of Spartiate men and helot women, but it is likely that others were Spartan-born on both sides but too poor to contribute to the common meals. They would, however, have gone through Spartan training and would have been elected to a common mess, their portion contributed by a wealthier Spartan patron. Three men of this class—Gylippus, Callicratidas, and Lysander—rose to high military commands during the war. That these individuals of inferior origins could attain positions of such honor and eminence meant that others could aspire to do the same, if only they could acquire enough wealth to gain admission to a mess and to full citizenship. Those who lacked the means for citizenship could hope to gain it through the spoils of warfare, conquest, and Spartan hegemony. Such men would naturally provide powerful pressure for a more aggressive policy than was normal for Sparta.

In 413 there was less resistance to the ambitious Spartan faction than at any previous time in the war. Agis, esteemed for the glory he had earned at Mantinea, stood at Decelea with powers greater than were usual for Spartan kings, and was eager to increase Sparta's and his own reputation and strength. The traditionalists who opposed adventures outside the Peloponnesus had no equally formidable figure on their side. The discredited King Pleistoanax could do no more than remain outside the fray and pray silently for peace.

Still, the task of ending the war with a quick victory was more difficult for the Spartans than it might seem. As had always been the case, the Athenians could not be beaten unless defeated at sea, but the Spartans still lacked ships, capable crews, and the money to build the former and pay the latter. They had depended heavily on their allies to supply these needs, and even though the war had badly damaged the allies' economies, in 413 the Spartans set a quota of ships to be built by each of them: twenty-five for themselves and the same number for the Boeotians; fifteen for the Corinthians and fifteen for the Locrians and Phocians together; ten for the consortium of Arcadia, Pellene, and Sicyon; and another ten for the group of Megara, Troezen, Epidaurus, and Hermione. These are very low figures compared with what was possible before the war, and the total of a hundred triremes was far from sufficient to defeat the Athenians. It appears that not even that quota was filled, however, and by the spring of 412 only thirty-nine ships were ready for battle. For the rest of the war at sea very few ships were constructed for the Spartans by their mainland allies, and though they hoped for great things from their allies in Sicily, by 412 only twenty-two ships came from Syracuse and Selinus, and an additional five from Syracuse in 409.

Given the economic realities of the alliance the only prospect for providing adequate help was Persia, but obtaining it would be no easy task. Because the Spartans had fought the war under the slogan of "Freedom for the Greeks," they were committed to the destruction of the Athenian Empire and the restoration of autonomy for its subjects, many of whom had also been under Persian control at one time or another.

The Persians wanted to restore their rule over the majority if not all of them, so a clash of goals was inevitable—a situation complicated by the fact that a number of influential Spartans were already planning on keeping the "liberated" cities for their own exploitation.

Although the Persians and Spartans had remained in regular communication during the first ten years of the war, their relationship had never been, given their conflicting aims, a productive one. In 425 the Athenians had intercepted a Persian envoy carrying a letter from the Great King who expressed confusion at the variety of the messages from Sparta.

The Athenians had tried to open negotiations with the Persians at the same time, but King Artaxerxes died before anything could be accomplished. His death unleashed a struggle for the succession, and the winner took the name Darius II. He was one of seventeen bastard sons of the late king, and because the other sixteen remained, his throne was insecure. In 424/3 the Athenians and Persians made the treaty of Epilycus "establishing friendship forever" between them (Andocides, *On the Peace* 29.) Threatened by Brasidas' campaign around Amphipolis, Athens was eager to prevent Persian aid to Sparta however it could. When uprisings challenged the new king over the next few years he had reason to be glad of this agreement.

The Peace of Nicias had offered no temptation for Darius to change his policy, for with the Athenian navy in control of the sea and Athens' treasury that paid for the ships being filled by increased tribute payments without the drainage of military expenditures, there was no reason to tamper with the status quo. The disaster in Sicily upset that balance, but even when the time seemed ripe for the Persians to recover their lost Greek possessions it would not be easy for them to come to terms with the Spartans to achieve their ends.

AGIS IN COMMAND

AFTER THE SICILIAN campaign "both sides made preparations as though the war was just beginning" (8.5.1). The Spartans again took the offensive, but this time the Athenians could only prepare a defense. Before the war Archidamus had warned that the Spartans would pass the conflict on to their sons, and indeed in 413 his son Agis commanded the Spartan forces at Decelea, where he had full authority "to send the army wherever he liked, to gather troops and collect money. And during this period the allies obeyed him more than those in the city of Sparta, one might say, for having an army under his own control, he could swiftly appear anywhere and inspire fear" (8.5.3).

Fighting now to extend Spartan power and his own glory, Agis took an army into Central Greece on a campaign that reveals his and Sparta's new, more aggressive program. Late in autumn he marched to the region of Oeta near to the Gulf of Malis (see Map 14), in an effort to recover the colony of Heraclea in nearby Trachis. The Spartans had founded Heraclea in 426, but in 420/19 the Boeotians had taken control of it on the pretext of preventing its fall to the Athenians. In 413 it would be useful to the Spartans as a base from which to stir up rebellion in the Aegean, and by 409 it would be back under Spartan control. But Agis, who had more ambitious plans, began to extort money from a number of the local peoples and to take hostages in an attempt to force them into the Spartan alliance. These actions represent an expansion of Spartan power into Central Greece, a policy they would continue after the war in establishing what modern scholars call "The Spartan Hegemony."

PERSIAN INITIATIVES

UPON HIS RETURN to Decelea Agis agreed to help the Euboeans' rebellion against Athens, but before he could act an embassy arrived from Lesbos to ask for aid with their own revolt. He decided in favor of supporting Lesbos, sending ten ships and three hundred *neodamodeis* there, while the Boeotians provided ten additional triremes. Now two other delegations, each with Persian support, came directly to Sparta itself to petition for assistance with their uprisings. One came from Chios and Erythrae, accompanied by an envoy from Tissaphernes, the Persian satrap of Sardis; the other appeared on behalf of Pharnabazus, satrap of the Hellespontine province of the Persian Empire. The Greek envoys who spoke for the Persians urged the Spartans to support the rebellions of Greek cities in the Hellespontine region. The satraps had the authorization of the Great King; Persia was ready to join in the war against Athens.

Darius had been pressing his satraps to collect tribute and arrears from the Greek cities that Persia had lost in 479, a step that would not only break his treaty with Athens, which was less than a dozen years old, but also subvert the Persian policy of maintaining peace with Athens, which dated from midcentury. Why was the Great King willing to fight Athens again? Some scholars have pointed to his displeasure at an Athenian alliance of uncertain date with Amorges, bastard son of the satrap Pissuthnes, who was in rebellion against the Great King in Caria, but the likeliest explanation of the Persian reversal is the most obvious: the disaster in Sicily, which portended Athens' doom. Now was an opportune time for the Great King to join in the war against a desperately weakened opponent and recover his lost lands, revenues, and honor.

The satraps' envoys at Sparta were actually rivals, each trying to win Spartan support for a rebellion against Athens in his own province as well as credit for bringing the Spartans into alliance with the Great King. The Spartans were even more divided among themselves on the issue of involvement in foreign affairs. First, there was a divergence of opinion between Sparta and Agis at Decelea. Although the king had decided to assist the Lesbians, in Sparta "there was great conflict, so that some tried to persuade the assembly to send an army and navy to Ionia and Chios first, while others argued for the Hellespont" (8.6.2). In fact, good arguments could be made in support of any of the four proposals. The Athenians kept their flocks and herds on Euboea, and they counted on it for provisions. When it revolted in

411 they were even more frightened than after the Sicilian disaster, for "they got more benefit from it than from Attica" (8.96.2). Lesbos was a large, rich, and populous island, strategically located as a base for a campaign to cut off Athens' lifeline to the Black Sea. Pharnabazus' offer likewise had great appeal, offering access to the Hellespont itself, with the additional attraction of Persian financial support.

THE SPARTANS CHOOSE CHIOS

IN THE END, however, Spartans favored the request from the Chians and Tissaphernes, for those from Euboea and Lesbos included neither a Greek fleet nor the promise of Persian support. On its surface, the proposal of Pharnabazus might have seemed the most attractive, for success in the Hellespont promised the quickest victory over Athens, and his envoys brought with them twenty-five talents in cash. But Tissaphernes seems to have held a superior command in the west for the war against Athens, and the Chians brought a significant fleet of their own with them. The Spartan decision was also favored by Alcibiades, who needed to prove his value to his justly suspicious hosts, and the campaign in Ionia begun by a Chian revolt offered him a unique opportunity to do so. He had a number of well-placed friends in the Ionian region, where he might hope to present himself to the Spartans as an indispensable figure.

The Spartans carefully checked to verify that the Chian navy was as large and the city's power as great as the Chians claimed, and then voted to bring them and the Erythraeans, who lived across the bay, into their alliance. They decided to send forty triremes—of which ten should sail immediately under their admiral Melanchridas—to join the Chian fleet of sixty ships. Before they could leave, however, an earthquake frightened them into reducing the first mission to five ships commanded by Chalcideus. Even then they proceeded slowly, so by well into the spring of 412 they still had not launched a fleet.

While the Spartans did take earthquakes and omens seriously, strategic and political factors must also have played a considerable part in the delay. Agis could not have been pleased to see his own plan rejected for another. The Peloponnesian League had to be consulted before undertaking any naval expedition, for most of the ships belonged to the allies and were anchored in the Corinthian Gulf for safety. When the congress finally met at Corinth it decided to send Chalcideus to Chios but also to dispatch a fleet to Lesbos, as Agis had desired, under Alcamenes, "the same man whom Agis had in mind" (8.8.2). In a third mission, to commence after the Lesbian campaign, Clearchus was to take a force into the Hellespont. This overly intricate tripartite strategy most likely reflected a similar complication in the political situation in Sparta.

The League congress voted that the various forces set off at once without concealing their movements, "for they were contemptuous of the impotency of the Athenians, since no large Athenians fleet was yet in evidence" (8.8.3–4). But they moved with great caution, for the memory of their humiliations by the Athenian navy was still strong, and then the Corinthians refused to depart until the Isthmian Games were completed. Although Agis offered to take command of the expedition to Chios and allow the Corinthians to remain at home for the duration of the festival, they turned down the proposal and gained enough allied support to have their way.

Not surprisingly, the resulting delay gave the Athenians time to discover the plot. They accused the Chians, the last of their allies with a fleet of their own, of planning rebellion and demanded that they turn a number of their ships over to the imperial fleet as a token of good faith. Because the oligarchs feared that their plot would be opposed by the common people of Chios and by pro-Athenian oligarchs, and because the Peloponnesian hesitation made them begin to doubt that the promised aid would be forthcoming, they delivered seven ships to the Athenians, as ordered.

The delay also allowed the Athenians to attend the Isthmian Games, where they learned more about the Chian plot and the details of the Peloponnesian plans. When Alcamenes finally took the first twenty-one Peloponnesian ships out to sea in July 412, an Athenian fleet of the same size was waiting for them, so Alcamenes turned back to harbor at once. The Athenians, meanwhile, withdrew to Piraeus for reinforcements, bringing the number of their vessels up to thirty-seven. Alcamenes tried to sneak away to the south along the Peloponnesian shore, but the Athenians chased him down. At the sight of them he fled for safety to the deserted port of Spiraeum, just north of the Epidaurian border, and lost only one straggler. The others reached the harbor but not safety, for the Athenians attacked by land and sea, destroying most of the enemy ships on the beach and killing Alcamenes. The Athenians set up a camp nearby and reinforced the fleet to keep watch on the enemy, determined to let no Peloponnesian vessel sail into the Aegean.

In Sparta the ephors waited for news, having ordered Alcamenes to send word as soon as his ships set sail so that they could dispatch the five ships under Chalcideus to join him. Spirits were high, and the men were eager to embark. Then came word of the defeat, the death of Alcamenes, and the blockade at Spiraeum, and the mood changed at once. "Having failed in their first undertaking in the Ionian war they no longer thought of sending out their ships but even wanted to recall those that had already put out to sea" (8.11.3).

ALCIBIADES INTERVENES

NEWS OF THE Peloponnesian losses might have prevented the rebellion of Chios entirely, but at this point Alcibiades appears to have played a key role in moving Sparta back to action. He persuaded the ephors to send the five ships under Chalcideus directly to Ionia, with himself on board, before the news of the defeat could arrive there. Alcibiades would tell the Ionians of Athens' weaknesses and assure them of Spartan eagerness, and he would be believed because of his intimate knowledge of both Athens and Sparta and because of his influence with leading Ionians. His private message to the ephor Endius reveals that contests for personal honor and factional considerations still played an important part in Spartan policy. "It would be good, through the agency of Alcibiades, for him to cause Ionia to revolt and to make the King an ally of the Spartans and not to allow this to become an exploit of Agis." Alcibiades had reasons of his own to assume this role, "for he happened himself to be at odds with Agis" (8.12.2). That remark evokes a famous scandal at Sparta, when an earthquake, it was said, drove Alcibiades from the chamber of Agis' wife into public view, probably in late February of 412. By July, Agis would have learned of the incident and would soon seek revenge. Alcibiades' best hope was to achieve a success so great as to make him invulnerable even to Agis; if not, he would have to escape to the last possible refuge available to him, the Persian Empire. The expedition to Ionia presented both possibilities.

To maintain secrecy, the little fleet under Chalcideus seized everyone they encountered on the crossing to Chios. Their oligarchic allies had planned the Spartans' arrival to coincide with an assembly of the council. That body appears to have been a blend of the few and the many, and "the many were in a state of amazement and panic" at the appearance of the fleet (8.14.2). Alcibiades, fortified by the Spartan ships and soldiers, told them that a large additional force was on its way. This encouraged the Chians to launch the rebellion, bringing Erythrae with them. Alcibiades' characteristic ploy was a great success: with only a tiny fleet and brilliant chicanery he succeeded in gaining sixty warships, a safe base of operations, and the first crucial defections from the Athenian Empire. He appears to have done Athens more harm in this particular affair than ever before, and once again he had dramatically given notice to the Athenians that he was still alive.

Alcibiades and Chalcideus swiftly raised rebellions in a few nearby cities, and before long, the powerful example of Chios inspired revolts on the mainland in Erythrae, Clazomenae, Haerae, and Lebedus, and Teos was an open city. Farther to the south, the great city of Ephesus joined the uprisings, as did Anaea, a small city strategically located opposite Samos and close to Miletus. Now Alcibiades was ready to bring over Miletus, the jewel of Ionia. He replaced Peloponnesian crews with Chians because he "wanted to win the Milesians over before the arrival of the Peloponnesian ships and, upon the Chians and himself and . . . as he had promised, upon Endius who had sent them out, to confer the prize for having . . . caused the rebellion of the greatest number of cities possible" (8.17.2). Alcibiades and Chalcideus arrived just in time to bring Miletus into the general rebellion before the Athenians could prevent it. Its defection served as a base for the spread of revolts into southern Ionia and Caria and the islands offshore.

TISSAPHERNES' DRAFT TREATY

THE CAPTURE OF MILETUS prompted Tissaphernes to go there to negotiate an alliance between the Spartans and the Great King. This one-sided document restored to Darius whatever territory and cities he or his ancestors had held, while the Persians and Spartans agreed to work together to halt payments to Athens from those regions. The Spartans committed to help the Great King against any rebellious subjects, and the king to aid them if any ally rose up against them. The two would also fight together against Athens and make no separate peace. As it happened, the Spartans then faced no prospective trouble from their allies, whereas the Persians were at war with Amorges and might well consider that all the Greek cities they had lost since 480 were still in a state of rebellion. The agreement, taken literally, would return to the Persians whatever Greek territory they had held before Salamis. In contrast, nothing was stipulated about what support, financial or otherwise, the Persians would provide to Sparta. Later, a distinguished Spartan would proclaim his outrage at the alliance's full implications: "It was dreadful," he said, "that the King should even now claim to rule the lands that he and his ancestors had previously held, for that involved the enslavement again of all the islands and Thessaly and Locris and everything as far as Boeotia, instead of freedom the Spartans would be imposing Persian domination upon the Greeks" (8.43.3). Not surprisingly, the Spartans chose to keep this agreement secret from their allies.

Alcibiades, no doubt, was instrumental in the Spartans' willingness to accept so unbalanced an accord. A veteran of many negotiations, he was the senior partner in the discussions, and Chalcideus followed his advice. He must have argued that a quick agreement would give Chalcideus credit for achieving an alliance with Persia; details were unimportant and could be changed later. The main goal was to obtain a commitment from the Persians before some other Spartan—perhaps a member of Agis' faction—arrived to claim the prize. These arguments surely suited Alcibiades' own desires, for he needed great achievements immediately.

Whatever its ultimate fate, the treaty of Chalcideus was deemed a great success in 412, even though the Athenian exile who engineered it was suspected of having cuckolded a Spartan king and was living from moment to moment as a result. Still, the rebellions in Ionia and the treaty with the Great King fulfilled Alcibiades' promises to Endius, the ephors, and Sparta, and though time would reveal the treaty's flaws, Alcibiades had shaken Sparta from its timidity and lethargy and opened the door to victory.

CHAPTER TWENTY-SEVEN

War in the Aegean (412–411)

ATHENS FIGHTS BACK

FOR THE ATHENIANS the revolt at Chios was a terribly dangerous development, as they knew that "the remaining allies would not want to remain quiet when the greatest state was in rebellion" (8.15.1). In the summer of 412, therefore, they voted to use the reserve fund of a thousand talents they had set aside early in the war for extreme emergencies. They recalled the ships blockading the enemy on the Peloponnesian shore and dispatched them to Chios, and planned to send thirty more. Each day the uprising continued was a drain on the Athenian treasury, another day for the Persians to intervene, and another day of practice for the enemy fleet to improve its skills.

Nineteen Athenian ships sailed from Samos to stop the rebellion at Miletus, but they arrived too late. Although outnumbered by an enemy force of twenty-five, however, they were able to set up a blockade of the city. While Athenian reinforcements might appear at any time and seize the advantage, Chalcideus, who was in command of the Peloponnesian fleet, did not attack, and even turned down the Chians when they offered their services. Like most Spartan commanders, he was reluctant to risk a fight at sea, even against a smaller Athenian fleet. If he had added the Chians to his forces, bringing the number of vessels of thirty-five to nineteen in his favor, he could not have refused an engagement. Events would show that he should not be judged foolish or cowardly; the battles at Cynossema and Cyzicus that took place in subsequent years would demonstrate quite convincingly that the Athenians retained their superiority at sea.

Chalcideus' unwillingness to fight did, however, permit the Athenians to send reinforcements into the Aegean and to develop Samos as their main naval base in the Aegean. As they did so, a civil war broke out on that island, marked by bitter class hatred. Aided by Athenian sailors, the common people rose up against the aristocrats of the governing oligarchy, killing two hundred Samian noblemen, exiling forty more, distributing their lands and houses among themselves, and stripping the aristocrats of their civic rights, including the right of intermarriage with the lower class.

Meanwhile, the Chians sailed to Lesbos and incited rebellions at Methymna and Mytilene (see Map 23). At the same time, a Peloponnesian army marched northward along the mainland coast, passing through Clazomenae, Phocaea, and Cyme, and bringing these important cities over to their side. On the Peloponnesian shore, the Spartan fleet at Spiraeum finally broke through the blockade and sailed to Chios under Astyochus, the new navarch sent to take command of the entire Peloponnesian fleet. He joined the main Chian force at Lesbos and landed at Pyrrha, moving on to Eresus the following day. Twenty-five Athenian ships under the generals Leon and Diomedon had put into Lesbos only hours earlier, and they defeated the Chian ships in the harbor, won a battle on land, and took the main city of Lesbos at the first assault. Astyochus brought Eresus into the rebellion and set out along the northern coast of the island to try to save the revolt at Methymna and to encourage one at Antissa, but "everything on Lesbos was going against him" (8.23.5), so he sailed back to Miletus. Without the support of a fleet, the land army had to turn back from the road to the Hellespont, sending each allied contingent back home. So ended the Peloponnesians' first effort to end the war swiftly.

With Lesbos secure, the Athenians set out for Chios, recapturing Clazomenae before they left. Under Leon and Diomedon they occupied a group of islands off the northeast point of Chios, and two fortified towns on the mainland just opposite Chios, as bases for conducting a blockade and assaults from the sea. The Athenians now controlled the sea locally and could land where they liked. They also used hoplites to serve as marines in place of the usual thetes, so were stronger in any land battles. After their ships defeated the enemy consistently, the Chians refused any further battle at sea, so the Athenians came ashore to ravage the rich, well-cultivated, and well-stocked Chian lands. By now some Chians were seeking to end these attacks by overthrowing the government and restoring the alliance with Athens, but the ruling

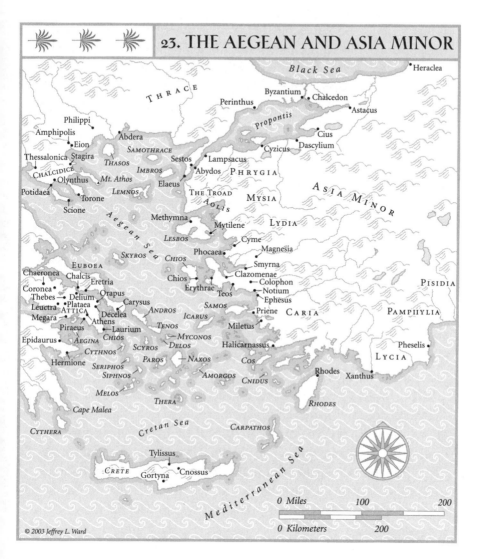

23. THE AEGEAN AND ASIA MINOR

Black Sea

Heraclea

THRACE

Perinthus
Byzantium • Chalcedon

Propontis
Astacus

Philippi
Cius

Amphipolis
Abdera
Cyzicus • Dascylium

Eion
SAMOTHRACE

Thessalonica Stagira
THASOS
Sestos • Lampsacus

CHALCIDICE
IMBROS
Abydos • PHRYGIA

Olynthus
Mt. Athos
Elaeus

Potidaea
LEMNOS
THE TROAD
MYSIA

Torone
AOLIS

Scione
Aegean Sea
Methymna

Mytilene
LYDIA

LESBOS
Cyme

SKYROS
Phocaea
Magnesia

CHIOS
Smyrna

Chaeronea
EUBOEA

Coronea
Chalcis
Eretria
Chios
Clazomenae
Colophon
PISIDIA

Thebes
Delium
Orapus
Erythrae
Teos
Notium

Leuctra
Plataea
Carysus
Ephesus

Megara
ATTICA
Decelea
ANDROS
SAMOS
Priene
CARIA
PAMPHYLIA

Piraeus
Athens
ICARUS

Laurium
TENOS
Miletus

Epidaurus
AEGINA
CHIOS
MYCONOS

Hermione
CYTHNOS
SCYROS
DELOS
Halicarnassus
LYCIA

SERIPHOS
PAROS
NAXOS
Cos
Pheselis

SIPHNOS
AMORGOS
Rhodes
Xanthus

MELOS
CNIDUS

THERA
RHODES

Cape Malea

Cretan Sea
CARPATHOS

CYTHERA

Mediterranean Sea

Tylissus

CRETE
Gortyna
Cnossus

ASIA MINOR

0 Miles 100 200

0 Kilometers 200

© 2003 Jeffrey L. Ward

oligarchs called on Astyochus for help, as they wondered "how they might put an end to the plot most moderately" (8.24.6). Astyochus took hostages, which kept the situation quiet for a time. Still, Chios remained under siege and exposed to constant attack, and was no longer the focus of rebellion in Ionia but instead in imminent danger of defeat.

DECISION AT MILETUS

THE ATHENIANS' NEXT TARGET was Miletus, the only other major Ionian city still in revolt. In October the generals Phrynichus, Onomacles, and Scironides sailed from Samos with forty-eight vessels, some of them troop ships, carrying 3,500 hoplites—1,000 from Athens, 1,000 from their Aegean allies, and 1,500 from Argos—which represented a remarkably large force so soon after the Sicilian disaster. They faced an army that included 800 hoplites from Miletus, an unknown number of Peloponnesians, mercenaries in the service of the satrap Tissaphernes, and Tissaphernes himself with his cavalry.

The Argives charged impetuously, breaking the order on the Athenian side, and paid for their rashness with defeat and the loss of three hundred men. The Athenians and their Ionian allies did better, routing the Peloponnesians and driving off the Persians and their mercenaries, after which the Milesians prudently fled within their city walls. A great victory was celebrated, for the Athenians now dominated on both land and sea. All that remained was to wall off the city and wait for it to surrender, as they were certain that the fall of Miletus would put an end to the rebellions.

On the day of their triumph, however, news came that fifty-five ships commanded by the Spartan Therimenes were on their way to Miletus, among them twenty-two from Sicily led by Hermocrates, their Syracusan nemesis. After the fleet had sailed into the Gulf of Iasus and camped at Teichiussa, it was Alcibiades himself who rode up and told them of the Athenian victory at Miletus, saying, "If they did not wish to destroy their position in Ionia and their cause in general, they should go to the aid of Miletus as fast as possible and not stand by while it was walled off" (8.26.3).

Although the other Athenian generals wanted to stay and fight, Phrynichus opposed them, arguing: "After the disasters they had undergone it was hardly justified voluntarily to undertake any offensive action whatever, unless it was absolutely necessary; it was even less justified, without being compelled, to rush into dangers of their own choosing" (8.27.3). Phrynichus prevailed, and the Athenians sailed to Samos, "their victory incomplete" (8.27.60), leaving Miletus free from both siege and blockade. In response, the Argives angrily went home and played no further part in the war.

The retreat had another costly result when Tissaphernes came to Miletus and persuaded the Peloponnesians to attack Amorges at Iasus. Unaware of the Athenian withdrawal, Iasus' people assumed that the approaching fleet was Athenian and did not mount a defense. The Peloponnesians captured Amorges alive and delivered him to Tissaphernes, took Amorges' Peloponnesian mercenaries into their own army, and sacked Iasus, selling its people to Tissaphernes and turning the remains of the town over to him. The result was that the Athenians had lost another ally, the Persians were rid of an annoying distraction, and the Spartans and Persians had cooperated to achieve their first victory together.

While some praised Phrynichus and his strategy—"Later on no less than on the present occasion, in this matter but also in all the others in which he took part, he appears not to have been lacking in intelligence" (8.27.5)—most of his fellow Athenians took a contrary view, and the following year formally charged him with the loss of Iasus and Amorges. There is good reason to agree with their verdict. Modern scholars defend Phrynichus' decision on the grounds that after Sicily the Athenian navy was no longer what it had once been and, having lost its tactical superiority, could not risk a naval battle against odds too dangerous. These judgments, however, do not fit the facts. Even though the glory days of Phormio had passed, the Sicilian disaster had not put an end to the Athenian navy's tactical dominance. Earlier in 412 the Athenians had successfully forced the Peloponnesian fleet to land at a deserted and inconvenient base; at Chios and Lesbos they had swept the enemy ships from the sea. In the spring of 411, even though the entire Ionian coast was no longer in Athens' hands, the Spartans remained so fearful of the Athenian fleet that they sent an army to the

Hellespont by land. In the same year the Athenians, outnumbered seventy-six to eighty-six, routed the Peloponnesians at Cynossema in the Hellespont.

The flaw in Phrynichus' argument is that by following his advice the Athenians could never be certain of their ability to force a battle. The Spartans could simply refuse naval conflict and instead send armies by land; even if they chose to travel by water they could elude the Athenian navy and cause further rebellions. The Athenians' best hope of getting the enemy to fight at sea, in fact, lay in luring it out against an apparently inferior fleet. The opportunity Phrynichus refused might have compelled Therimenes to do battle to save Miletus. Had the Athenians stayed to fight, the entire war might have taken a different course. Not only did their departure give the rebels breathing space and new hope, but on the domestic front it deprived the moderate democracy of the *probouloi* of a victory that would have given it the prestige and credibility that would have enabled it to resist the oligarchic plots that were even now forming in Athens.

For the moment the Spartans had an advantage in numbers at sea, with which they could raise the blockade of Chios, the key to rebellion in Ionia on the road to the Hellespont, but they were slow to act. They still feared confronting the Athenian navy in the open sea and lacked experienced and able leaders. Their obligation to collaborate with the Persians was also problematic, for their separate agendas inevitably led to delay and inactivity.

ALCIBIADES JOINS THE PERSIANS

AFTER ATTACKING AMORGES at Iasus, Therimenes returned to Miletus; the Spartan navarch Astyochus was still at Chios, separated from his navy by the Athenian fleet at Samos. Probably early in November 412 Tissaphernes came to Miletus to deliver the pay he had promised: each sailor received a month's wages at an Attic drachma per day. He announced that in the future, however, he would pay only half that amount, but Hermocrates, the fiery Syracusan commander, compelled a compromise that produced a small rise in that figure.

Although Alcibiades took no part in these discussions, since the battle of Miletus he had changed sides again, leaving the Spartans to join Tissaphernes. Public suspicion of him had arisen among the Peloponnesians "after the death of Chalcideus and the battle of Miletus" (8.45.1). The Athenian renegade had worked closely with Chalcideus, but when the Spartan commander was killed in a raid Alcibiades lost important support. At about the same time Endius' term as ephor came to an end, removing still another friend from a position of influence just when he needed it, for by now "he was a personal enemy of Agis and for other reasons did not inspire confidence" (8.45.1). His origins, his personality, and his record had always made him suspect, but no ancient writer explains why the Peloponnesians then in Ionia should suddenly have believed him involved in treason and pressed for a letter to be sent to Astyochus ordering the navarch to kill Alcibiades.

Perhaps the reason was the failure of the plan he had recommended at Sparta. The Athenians seemed to have quickly put down the rebellion in the empire; Chios was not the center and instigator of a general uprising but was besieged and draining Peloponnesian resources. Alcibiades also seemed to have persuaded the Spartans to play Persia's game. The Persians had been slow to pay the promised wages to Spartan forces and now planned to cut the rate. Advised by Alcibiades, Chalcideus had made a treaty with the Persians that was unfavorable to Sparta and seemed to concede the enslavement of Greeks to Darius. At Miletus the Athenians defeated the Peloponnesians in a land battle in which Tissaphernes' mercenaries had brought them little benefit. The Peloponnesian army under Therimenes was used not to defeat the Athenians but to oblige Tissaphernes by giving him Amorges and Iasus.

Alcibiades probably changed sides when he learned of the letter ordering his death, so that when Tissaphernes came to Miletus early in November, Alcibiades would already have been with him for several weeks. Thucydides says that Alcibiades became the satrap's "adviser in everything" and that Tissaphernes "gave his confidence" to him" (8.45.2; 46.5). The Persian, however, was a clever and sophisticated man himself and had good reasons for lending his patronage to the double fugitive.

For Tissaphernes as for the Spartans, the situation had not worked out as expected. Because the rebellion had not spread rapidly through the empire and brought a swift victory, the war would go on, require large forces, and cost a great deal of money, at least some of it from his own funds. Alcibiades had valuable contacts in both camps and could be helpful in dealing with them by serving as Tissaphernes' spokesman. Alcibiades, for his part, needed the Persian satrap for protection but also for the status of the relationship: his service as the trusted, intimate, and necessary adviser to the man who might decide the outcome of the war might make it possible for him to return to Athens one day. Meanwhile, it suited him to be a constant presense at the side of Tissaphernes and to seem to have his ear, just as it suited Tissaphernes to allow him to do so.

Alcibiades also offered strategic advice, proposing that Tissaphernes "not be in too great a hurry to end the war and not to wish to give command of the land and sea to the same power, either by bringing on the Phoenician ships he was preparing or by increasing the number of Greeks to whom he provided pay." The best course would be "to wear the Greeks out, one against the other" (8.46.1–2). Here again he was perhaps belaboring the obvious, for the Persians had no navy in the Aegean with which to win the war. As for the Phoenician fleet, this is the first we hear of any plan to use it. Whether Tissaphernes ever intended to do so is not clear, but in the early winter of 412 /1 no such fleet was ready for use.

Alcibiades also suggested that Tissaphernes break with Sparta and draw closer to Athens, arguing that the Athenians, as cynical imperialists, would readily abandon the Greeks in Asia Minor to the Persians and be "more suitable partners in empire," while the Spartans, as liberators of the Greeks, would continue to support them. Tissaphernes, therefore, should "first, wear out both sides, then reduce Athenian power as much as possible, then finally, drive the Peloponnesians from his land" (8.46.3–4). Such counsel was fundamentally absurd, grossly misrepresenting the character of both sides, but it did suit Alcibiades' needs. For the moment his greater danger came from the Spartans. If he could win the Persians away from Sparta, moreover, he could claim the gratitude of the Athenians and, perhaps, return in honor and glory. Tissaphernes was not deceived by such advice but pursued the policies that suited him. He paid the Peloponnesians their reduced salaries irregularly, keeping them bound to him by continuing to promise that the Phoenician fleet would soon arrive, which helped keep them inactive.

A NEW SPARTAN AGREEMENT WITH PERSIA

DURING THE LAST three months of 412 the Peloponnesian fleet stayed at Miletus while the Athenians gathered 104 ships at Samos and continued to dominate the sea. They sent fleets on various missions, but the Spartans continued to refuse battle, even when they had the greater numbers. Only Astyochus at Chios was more enterprising. He seized hostages, as we have seen, to prevent a revolution on the island and took the offensive in that area, but his assaults on Athens' mainland strongholds failed, and bad weather put an end to the campaign. When envoys from Lesbos asked for his help in their rebellion, he was ready to join them, but the allies, led by the Corinthians, rejected the idea because of the earlier failure there. The Lesbians repeated their request a little later, and this time Astyochus urged Pedaritus, the Spartan governor of Chios, to join him in the expedition, in which "either they would gain more allies or, if they failed, do harm to the Athenians" (8.32.3). But Pedaritus, backed by the Chians, refused. Astyochus bitterly abandoned his plan, swearing as he left Chios not to come to the aid of its people if they should ever need him.

Astyochus next set off to Miletus to take command of the main Spartan fleet, but before he arrived the Spartans and Persians had begun to revise their first draft treaty. Renegotiation of the unbalanced agreement was a Spartan initiative carried out by Therimenes, and the resulting accord bears his name. In some respects he achieved improvements in the terms. A new clause spoke in the familiar language of mutual nonaggression instead of the former provision stating that the Greek cities of Asia "belonged" to the Great King. The requirement that each side help the other put down rebellions, which favored Persia exclusively, was dropped. The new version specified the Great King's obligation to pay the Greek forces he called upon, and went beyond that to stipulate the alliance as "a treaty and friendship" (8.37). But these changes amounted only to verbal niceties, for Persia had already achieved its goal by using Peloponnesian forces to capture Amorges and Iasus and had no imminent need of any further assistance.

Sparta, on the other hand, had once again made significant concessions. The agreement negotiated by Chalcideus had bound both sides to stop the Athenians from collecting tribute, while the new one forbade the Spartans from collecting any by themselves—a measure that effectively prevented the establishment of a Spartan empire to replace the Athenian one. The Persian promise to pay Greek forces was limited to the number the Great King summoned, and yet the others must be fed. The agreement said nothing about the specific amount to be remunerated. The main change in the new agreement appears in its first clause: "Whatever territory and cities belong to King Darius or belonged to his father or their ancestors, against these neither the Spartans nor their allies shall go either for war or to do any harm" (8.37.2). What Tissaphernes had to fear in the near future was Spartan attacks on his own territory and their attempts to raise money from the cities the Persians regarded as their own. The treaty negotiated with Therimenes bound the Spartans not to take those actions.

Why did the Spartan leaders make another unfavorable agreement? While Therimenes was neither an outstanding individual nor an experienced negotiator, even a brilliant and veteran diplomat would have had a hard time doing much better in the circumstances, for the Spartans' bargaining position was abysmal. Tissaphernes had already achieved what he wanted, and if the Spartans were irked with him, so be it, for it was they who needed Persian money and support more than ever against the revived Athenians. After completing the agreement with the Persians, Therimenes formally handed his fleet over to the navarch Astyochus and sailed off in a small boat, never to be seen again, his fate unknown.

Although at Miletus Astyochus had a numerical advantage of about ninety triremes against the Athenians' seventy-four moored nearby at Samos, he refused to fight, even when the Athenian fleet made sorties against him. His crews began to complain that his policy of disengagement would undermine the Peloponnesian cause, that he had been bribed, that "he attached himself to Tissaphernes . . . for his own gain" (8.50.3). But Astyochus' inactivity can readily be explained without resorting to charges of corruption and treason. Like most Spartan commanders at sea, he was naturally cautious and reluctant to take on the Athenians, and in any case, he probably believed Tissaphernes' promise to bring on the Phoenician fleet to overwhelm the enemy, and so patiently awaited its arrival.

Turning to Chios, the Athenians landed on the east coast of the island and began to fortify Delphinium, a strong point with good harbors north of the capital city. Pedaritus, meanwhile, executed those accused of Athenian sympathies and replaced the moderate regime with a narrow oligarchy, and his harsh measures seem to have crushed pro-Athenian activity. Chios was filled with frightened people suspicious of one another and afraid of the Athenians. In these straits they sent for help to Astyochus, but he continued to refuse to aid them. Pedaritus wrote home to Sparta to complain, accusing the navarch of wrongdoing, but his efforts accomplished nothing for the moment. The Athenian fort at Delphinium proceeded to cause the same kind of harm to the Chians as the Spartan fort at Decelea had to the Athenians, and in some ways more. The Chians owned an unusually large number of slaves and treated them with particular harshness. Many of them fled to the safety of Delphinium, ready to help the Athenians in any way they could. Because the Athenians also continued to control the sea, the Chians could not import any necessities. In desperation, they once again appealed to Astyochus, begging him "not to look on while the greatest of the allied cities in Ionia was shut off from the sea and devastated by raids on land" (8.40).

But Astyochus still held back, and for good reason: between him and the Chians stood 101 Athenian warships, 74 at Samos and 27 at Chios. The allies were so moved by the Chian appeals, however, that they pressed Astyochus to go to their aid. Faced with the combination of that pressure and, perhaps, the fear of criticism or worse from back in Sparta he finally capitulated and agreed to sail.

A NEW SPARTAN STRATEGY

BEFORE ASTYOCHUS could set out, however, news came that Antisthenes was on the way with a fleet carrying eleven "advisers" (*xymbouloi*) with orders "to share in the conduct of affairs in whatever way should be best" (8.39.2; 41.1). The leader of the group was the rich, famous, and influential Lichas, an Olympic victor in the chariot race and a man of significant diplomatic experience who, alone, could overshadow the navarch. Lichas and the other *xymbouloi* had the unprecedented power to depose Astyochus, if they saw fit, and replace him with Antisthenes. Pedaritus' letter of complaint had, no doubt, given rise to their mission, but it was also prompted by dissatisfaction in Sparta with Astyochus' performance. The *xymbouloi* also had instructions to take as many ships as they chose, put them under the command of Clearchus son of Ramphias, and send that fleet to Pharnabazus in the Hellespont in an effort to close the straits to Athens.

This was a basic shift in strategy, surely influenced by the failure of the first plan, but also reflecting a political shift. It was Endius and Alcibiades who initially supported the decision to go to Chios, but now the ephor was out of office, and the Athenian renegade was in the service of Tissaphernes. With Chios under siege, the Athenians resurgent, the Peloponnesian forces inept or inert, and negotiations with Persia having produced only unsatisfactory agreements and unreliable support, most Spartans now believed it was time for a change. The letter from Pedaritus was in a large part a catalyst for a rethinking of policy that was already under way.

Antisthenes' ships took a roundabout route to avoid the Athenian fleet, landing at Caunus on the southern coast of Asia Minor. From there they requested a convoy to take them to Miletus, now the main Peloponnesian base in Ionia, for they expected an Athenian challenge. Astyochus at once set aside any idea of sailing to Chios, "thinking that nothing should come before convoying so great a fleet, so that together they might dominate the sea, and bringing across in safety the Spartans who had come to investigate him" (8.41.1). That meant the abandonment of Chios and the Spartan forces on it, but the summons from Caunus gave him so valid an excuse to avoid the expedition that even the desperate allies would have to accept it.

When the Athenians learned of Antisthenes' arrival at Caunus they sent twenty ships south to intercept him, against the sixty-four that Astyochus brought with him. The Athenians did not hesitate to send so small a fleet against a much larger force, and left only fifty-four ships at Samos to face ninety of the enemy at Miletus. The twenty Athenian triremes heading south would have to sail past Miletus, but their commander, Charminus, seemed unconcerned by the threat of a Spartan attack.

As Astyochus sailed south to bring his convoy to Antisthenes as quickly as possible, rain and fog scattered his fleet, and in the confusion he stumbled upon the Athenian force. Although Charminus was also taken by surprise—he knew nothing of Astyochus' plans and was expecting to encounter only the twenty-seven ships of Antisthenes, not the sixty-four of the navarch—he decided to attack. Under cover of fog the Athenians were mauling Astyochus' left until, to their astonishment, the entire Spartan fleet surrounded them. They managed to break out, nevertheless, losing only six ships. Astyochus did not pursue them but went to Cnidus, where he joined the force from Caunus. Only then did the combined grand fleet sail to Syme to set up a trophy of victory over the twenty ships of Charminus.

The Athenians, however, did not let them enjoy their triumph for long. Although their Samian fleet, together with the ships of Charminus, now contained fewer than seventy triremes to face the ninety or so under Astyochus, they sought him out to avenge their "defeat," but to no avail. Even with such an advantage, Astyochus refused to fight. With the Peloponnesian fleet united, the *xymbouloi* conducted their investigation of the charges against Astyochus, ultimately acquitting him and confirming him in office.

The stage was now set for the Spartans to present their grievances to Tissaphernes, with the prestigious Lichas as their spokesman. Although Sparta's commanders had been behaving as though the two treaties with Persia were binding, they had never been formally ratified at Sparta, and Lichas now treated them with contempt. "It was scandalous," he said, "that the King still claimed to rule all the territory that he and his ancestors ruled in the past, for that would mean that all the islands would again be enslaved by him, as well as Thessaly, Locris, and everything as far as Boeotia; instead of freedom the Spartans would bring the Greeks subjugation to the Persian Empire." Unless the agreements were improved, he warned, "the Spartans would not abide by these, nor did he ask for support on such terms" (8.43.3-4).

It is hard to attribute Lichas' aggrieved tone solely to an outraged love of Greek liberty, because he would soon take part in negotiating a third treaty that conceded the Greek cities of Asia to Persia and then announced to the unhappy Milesians that they "and all the other cities in the King's land should be slaves to him, in a moderate way" (8.84.5). Perhaps he believed that the earlier negotiators had been intimidated and too pliable, and that a tougher approach would bring better results, including language about the status of the Greek cities that was less embarrassing to the "liberators of Greece" and clearer and better terms for financial support. If so, he was disappointed, for Tissaphernes simply walked out of the meeting in a rage. He recognized quite clearly that the Spartans needed him more than he needed them, and he could afford to wait until they understood that.

Another explanation for the behavior of Lichas may be found in the orders he carried from Sparta, which instructed the commanders to move the war from Ionia to the Hellespont, away from the satrapy of Tissaphernes to that of Pharnabazus, who might be a more comfortable partner. Perhaps Lichas wanted Pharnabazus to hear of the tenor of his discussions with Tissaphernes, which might serve as a useful warning to the satrap as the Spartans entered a new theater of operations.

REBELLION AT RHODES

AN UNEXPECTED OPPORTUNITY, however, delayed the move to the north. A group of oligarchs from Rhodes came to Cnidus to persuade the Spartan leaders to support a rebellion of the democratic cities from Athens, install oligarchies, and bring the rich resources and abundant manpower of the island over to the Peloponnesian side.

The Spartans were quick to agree, hoping this potential influx of wealth and men would enable them to support their fleet without having to turn to Tissaphernes for money. With ninety-four ships they sailed to Camirus on the western shore of the island, catching the city by surprise. Together with Lindus and Ialysus, Rhodes went over to the Peloponnesians in January 411.

It was now that the failure of Athens to capture Miletus took its toll, for by the time the Athenians reached Rhodes from Samos, they were too late to prevent the rebellion. Phrynichus had claimed that the Athenians would be able "to fight at a later time . . . having prepared adequately and at leisure," but events at Rhodes demonstrated how wrong that judgment was. The seventy-five Athenian triremes stood off the island's coast, challenging the ninety-four Spartan vessels to come out to sea and fight, but the Spartans refused, pulling their ships onto the Rhodian shore in mid-January and not putting them into the water again until well into the following spring.

Finally struck, no doubt, by the high cost of the decision not to fight the Peloponnesian fleet at Miletus the previous year, the Athenians deposed Phrynichus and Scironides, replacing them with Leon and Diomedon. The new generals immediately attacked Rhodes while the Peloponnesian ships remained beached on the island, defeated a Rhodian army, and then moved to Chalce, an island close by, from which they continued to launch raids and keep watch on the Peloponnesians.

To the paralyzed Spartans at Rhodes Pedaritus now sent an appeal for help at Chios. The Athenian fortification was complete, he explained, and unless the entire Peloponnesian fleet came quickly, the island would be lost. While waiting for their arrival Pedaritus himself attacked the Athenian stronghold with his mercenaries and the Chians, and captured a few beached ships, but the Athenians launched a successful counterattack, killing him in the process. The Chians "were blockaded still more than before by land and sea and there was great famine there" (8.56.1).

The Spartan commanders at Rhodes could not ignore the appeal from Chios and were ready to sail to its rescue, in spite of a competing appeal of great urgency. A rebellion had broken out on Euboea, encouraged by the Boeotian capture of Oropus, just across a narrow strait, and the rebels had asked for help from the Peloponnesian fleet. No revolt could be more threatening to the Athenians, but the Peloponnesian armada at Rhodes ignored the Euboeans' request and set out for Chios in March. On the way they caught sight of the Athenian fleet from Chalce sailing north, but the Athenians did not seek a fight, continuing on to Samos. Even this glimpse of the Athenians, however, was sufficient to send the Spartans back to Miletus, "seeing that it was

no longer possible for them to bring help to Chios without a naval battle" (8.60.3).

THE IMPORTANCE OF EUBOEA

THE ACTIONS of both sides in this matter require explanation. The
Spartans, after having beached their ships at Rhodes all winter in fear
of the Athenian fleet, now sailed north toward that fleet, from which
they must expect attack. At the first sight of the enemy, however, the
Spartans fled to port. The Athenians, on the other hand, had come to
Chalce specifically to catch the Spartans at sea and force a battle. Yet
when the opportunity finally presented itself, they let it pass.

The key to this behavior is the importance of Euboea to each of
the combatants. Euboea was vital to Athens; when the entire island revolted later in the year "there was greater panic than ever before. For
neither the disaster in Sicily, though it seemed great at the time, nor
any other event had ever before frightened them so" (8.96.1). Because
Euboea "was of more value to them than Attica" (8.96.2), the primary
impulse of the Athenian commanders in the Aegean must have been to
sail at once to defend it, even though that would free the great Spartan
fleet at Rhodes to raise new rebellions, to rescue Chios, to threaten
Samos and Lesbos, and to make its way to the Hellespont and the
Athenian lifeline. Instead, they went to Samos, from which they would
be able to move swiftly either to Euboea or to cut off the Spartan fleet.
The reason they did not seek a fight with the Spartans on their way
north was because of their desire to reach Samos as quickly as possible, in case they were summoned on to Euboea immediately.

The Spartans, on the other hand, having been informed about
Oropus and the rebellion on Euboea, expected the Athenians would
sail there without delay, leaving the route to the north free, and
thereby allowing the relief of Chios. But when they saw the Athenian
fleet directly in their path, they abandoned Chios and chose to return
safely at last to their main base at Miletus, since that way had been left
open.

Events unfolding in the Aegean, meanwhile, had changed Tissaphernes' assessment of the situation. He had turned away from Sparta

because it appeared to be the stronger of the two powers, and his strategy had been to wear out both sides. Lichas' harsh language may also have made the Athenians seem an attractive alternative, but the events of the winter had proved his calculations wrong: the Athenians, though fewer in number, again ruled the sea, and the Spartan fleet was clearly afraid to fight. Tissaphernes was no longer concerned about a Spartan victory so much as what their desperation might lead them to do. The money the Spartans collected from Rhodes would be insufficient to maintain the crews of the Peloponnesian ships for a month, much less the eighty days that they stayed there. As their funds ran out, Tissaphernes worried that the Spartans "would be compelled to fight a naval battle and lose, or that their ships would be emptied by desertions and the Athenians would attain their ends without his aid; but beyond that, what he feared most was that they would ravage the mainland in search of subsistence" (8.57.1). He wanted the Spartan fleet under his control at Miletus, where it could defend that strategically important port from Athenian attack and where he could monitor its activities.

A NEW TREATY WITH PERSIA

THE SPARTANS were at least as eager for a reconciliation. Persian talks with the Athenians had grown increasingly alarming, money was short, and the events of the winter had shown that any chance they had of beating Athens at sea depended on major assistance from the Persians. The Spartan leaders, therefore, negotiated a new treaty with Tissaphernes at Caunus in February. Like the earlier agreements it contained a nonaggression clause, reference to Persian financial support, and a commitment to wage war and make peace in common, but the differences in this most recent version were crucial. It was to be a formal treaty requiring ratification by both home governments. King Darius himself must have approved the first clause that reads: "All the territory of the King that is in Asia shall belong to the King; and about his own territory the King may decide whatever he wishes" (8.58.2). For all the grandiosity of the claim, it abandons all reference to the European lands included in the earlier agreements, a concession to the complaints made by Lichas. There can be no mistake, however, about Darius's claim to sole domination of Asia.

One of the most important elements that distinguishes this agreement from the earlier ones is its reference to the proposed use of "the King's ships." The assumption in the previous versions was that the Spartans and their allies would do the fighting while the Great King would have only financial obligations. In the new agreement, however, it is Darius's navy that bears the burden of expectations for military success. His representatives now agree to maintain the Peloponnesian forces only until the Great King's ships arrive; after that those forces may stay on at their own expense or receive money from Tissaphernes, not as a grant but as a loan to be repaid at the end of the war, and that war is to be waged by both sides in common.

In the actual combat the record of Persian warships against Greeks was dismal, and, in the event, the Persians never did bring a fleet of their own into play. Whatever their abilities, however, the firm promise of such a reinforcement was the major factor in persuading Lichas, as well as the other Spartan leaders, to approve an agreement that was not substantially better than the one he had so vehemently denounced.

Even the Persians' renunciation of extra-Asiatic claims was of little practical importance, because it was never intended seriously. The Spartans, however, formally abandoned the Greeks of Asia and their own role as liberators, a deeply embarrassing concession in the new treaty. They would not have agreed to such a provision unless the failure of the campaigns since the Sicilian disaster had convinced them that they could hope to win the war in no other way.

THE SPARTANS IN THE HELLESPONT

ALTHOUGH NO PERSIAN FLEET ever materialized, Persian money did help restore the Spartans' initiative, and news of the reconciliation seems to have gained support even from some Greeks in Asia Minor. Because the Spartans could not challenge Athens at sea, they now took the only course available: sending an army under the general Dercylidas overland toward the Hellespont. Their first target was the Milesian colony of Abydos on the Asian side, but once they reached the Straits they hoped to raise rebellions in the entire region and threaten to cut off the Athenians' trade and food supply. At the very least, the presence of a Peloponnesian army on the Hellespont would force the Athenians to bring their fleet north from the Aegean, leaving the empire open to revolt.

Dercylidas reached the Hellespont in May 411, and quickly incited uprisings in Abydos and nearby Lampsacus (see Map 24). The Athenian general Strombichides took twenty-four ships, some of them transports carrying hoplites, and recovered Lampsacus but was unable to reclaim Abydos. At Sestos on the European side he established "a fortress and a lookout post for the whole Hellespont" (8.62.3), but he could not dislodge the Spartans from their foothold on that vital waterway.

The new Spartan strategy soon had an effect on the Aegean theater of the war. Some time earlier the Spartans had sent Leon, an officer, to replace Pedaritus as governor of Chios. With twelve ships from Miletus he had joined twenty-four Chian triremes, to form a fleet of thirty-six. Against it the Athenians had sent thirty-two ships, but some of them were troops transports, not useful in a sea battle. Although the Peloponnesian forces gained the upper hand they were unable to win a decisive victory before darkness came. The blockade continued, but the Peloponnesians and their allies had demonstrated that they could more than hold their own in a naval battle.

Strombichides was then forced to take the better part of the Athenian fleet to the Hellespont, leaving behind only eight ships to guard the sea around Chios. This gave Astyochus the courage to slip past Samos to Chios from where, with more than a hundred warships gathered from Chios and Miletus, he went to Samos, challenging the Athenians to fight for command of the sea. His newly found courage was met with apparent timidity, for the Athenians refused to be engaged. Thucydides explains that they did not come out against Astyochus because "they were suspicious of one another," referring to an internal conflict that had recently broken out at Athens, dividing its citizens into hostile factions and posing a serious threat to the city's survival. Suddenly the situation had completely reversed: Athens had lost control of the sea and the initiative in the war, and was torn by civil strife.

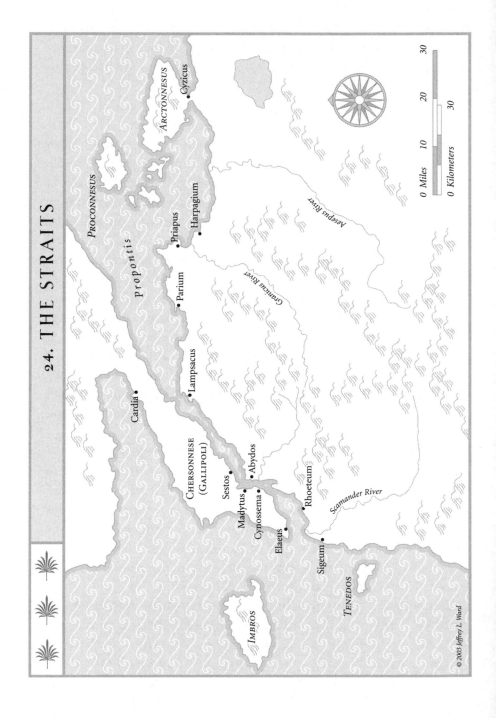

24. THE STRAITS

CHAPTER TWENTY-EIGHT

The Revolutionary Movement (411)

SINCE THE ONSET of fighting in 431 the Athenian people had demonstrated a remarkable unity through twenty years of war and cold war alike. In spite of terrible suffering caused by the loss of free use of their farms and homes in the countryside, by the need to crowd into the urban center, by the devastating plague and, finally, by the frightful losses in Sicily, they had maintained their remarkable record of avoiding coups d'état and civil war for a century after expelling tyranny from Athens. The surprising recovery of Athenian command at sea after the Sicilian disaster might have promised to undo the effects of that ill-conceived campaign, to restore the lost cities of the empire, and to raise the hope of victory in the war, but the entry of Persia into the situation darkened those prospects. In 411 the long-dormant forces hostile to democracy in Athens took advantage of the looming Persian threat and the ambitions of Alcibiades to attack the regime.

Ironically, the year 411 marked the hundredth anniversary of Athens' liberation from tyranny, which was soon followed by the establishment of the world's first democracy. In that time Athens had grown prosperous and powerful, and its people had come to regard democracy as the city's natural and normal constitution. The democratic model was still rare among the Greek cities, most of which were governed by narrow or broad oligarchies. Athenians of the upper class accepted the democracy, participating in the contests for leadership or simply standing aside, but almost all leading Athenian politicians until the Peloponnesian War were of noble birth.

THE ARISTOCRATIC TRADITION

SOME ARISTOCRATS, however, never abandoned their contempt for popular rule—a prejudice that had strong roots in Greek tradition. In the Homeric epics it was the nobles who made decisions and gave orders, while the commoners knew their place and obeyed them. In the sixth century the poet Theognis of Megara wrote bitterly as an aristocrat whose world was overthrown by political and social changes, and his ideas had a powerful influence on enemies of democracy well into the fourth century. Theognis divided mankind into two types based on birth: the good and noble, and the bad and base. Because the noble alone possesses judgment (*gnome*) and reverence (*aidos*), he alone is capable of moderation, restraint, and justice. The mass of the people lack these virtues and are, therefore, shameless and arrogant. The good qualities, moreover, cannot be taught: "It is easier to beget and rear a man than to put good sense into him. No one has ever discovered a way to make a fool wise or a bad man good. . . . If thought could be made and put into a man, the son of a good man would never become bad since he would obey good counsel. But you will never make the bad man good by teaching" (Theognis 429–438).

The views of the Theban poet Pindar, who lived past the middle of the fifth century, were also highly esteemed by the Athenian upper classes. His message mirrored that of Theognis: the nobly born were inherently superior to the mass of people intellectually and morally, and the difference could not be erased by education.

> The splendor running in the blood has much weight.
> A man can learn and yet see darkly, blow one way,
> then another, walking ever
> on uncertain feet, his mind unfinished and
> fed with scraps of a thousand virtues.
> (*Nemea* 3.40–42).

Only the natively wise can understand:

> There are many sharp shafts
> in the quiver

under the crook of my arm.
They speak to the understanding; most men need
    interpreters.
The wise man knows many things in his blood; the
    vulgar are taught.
They will say anything. They clatter vainly like
    crows against the sacred bird of Zeus.
(*Olympia* 2.86–87).

To minds shaped by such ideas, democracy was foolish, at best, and could become unfair and immoral, as well. *The Constitution of the Athenians*—a pamphlet written in the 420s by an unknown author often called "The Old Oligarch"[1]—reveals the discontent that some in Athens felt during the war. "As for the constitution of the Athenians, I do not praise them for having chosen it, because in choosing it they have given the better of it to the vulgar people (*poneroi*) rather than to the good (*chrestoi*). They use the lot for positions that are safe and pay a salary but leave the dangerous jobs of generals and commanders of the cavalry to election and the best qualified men" (*Constitution of the Athenians* 1.1.3).

What men such as "The Old Oligarch" wanted for their state was *eunomia*, the name the Spartans gave to their Spartan constitution and that Pindar had applied to the oligarchy of Corinth. Under such a constitution the best and most qualified men make the laws, and the good men punish the bad; the good men "will not allow madmen to sit in the council or speak in the assembly. But as a result of these good measures the people would, of course, fall into servitude" (1.9). The author expects that the masses will struggle to preserve democracy, "bad government" (*kakonomia*), because it is to their advantage, "But anybody who without belonging to the people prefers living in a town under democratic rule to living in one ruled by oligarchy has prepared himself for being immoral, well knowing that it is easier for a bad person to remain unnoticed in a town under democratic than in one under oligarchic rule" (2.19). It is not surprising, therefore, that men who subscribed to such beliefs looked upon the overthrow of the democracy as nothing less than a moral obligation.

[1] This is an entirely different work from Aristotle's treatise with the same name.

DEMOCRACY AND THE WAR

DURING THE PELOPONNESIAN WAR objections to the democracy had become at least as much practical as philosophical. The long drawn-out conflict, the suffering and deprivation, the failure of every strategy to achieve a definitive victory, and, most of all, the disaster in Sicily were easy to blame on the character of the regime and the men who led it. The lack of strong, respected political leaders of noble birth like Cimon and Pericles also removed one of the buffers between the democracy and its critics. In 411 the vacuum in leadership seems to have increased the power of the *hetairiai*, the clubs that played an ever more important part in Athenian politics, especially among the enemies of democracy. Their members and others in the propertied classes had been carrying unprecedented financial burdens in support of the war. The taxpaying class had, moreover, shrunk during its course, dropping from perhaps as many as twenty-five thousand adult males before the war to about nine thousand late in its progress.

By 411 many Athenians—and not only oligarchs—had begun to consider some curtailment of democratic practices, perhaps even a change of regime, in an attempt to help the war effort. The originator of this movement, however, was the exile Alcibiades, who was motivated, as ever, not by ideology but by self-interest. He shrewdly recognized that the security provided him by Tissaphernes was transitory, and that it was only a matter of time before their interests diverged. Since returning to the Sparta of Agis was out of the question, Alcibiades prepared to use his momentary influence with Tissaphernes to win a safe return to Athens.

His first step was to communicate with "the most important men among [the Athenians]"—presumably the generals, trierarchs, and other influential individuals—on Samos, asking them to mention him "to the best people" (8.47.2). They were to indicate that he would come back to Athens, bringing with him the support of Tissaphernes, if they would agree to replace the democracy with an oligarchy. The scheme worked, "for the Athenian soldiers at Samos perceived that he had influence with Tissaphernes" (8.47.2), and they began conversations with him through envoys. In an important but rarely noticed statement

Thucydides places the initiative for the oligarchic movement on Athenian leaders: "But even more than the influence and promises of Alcibiades, of their own accord, the trierarchs and the most important men among the Athenians at Samos were eager to destroy the democracy" (8.47.2).

In this case Thucydides clearly must be wrong in attributing such motives to all the Athenian leaders on Samos, for the one trierarch whose name we do know, Thrasybulus, the son of Lycus of Steiria, was never an enemy of democracy. From the beginning, when the Samian people learned of an oligarchic plot to overthrow their democracy, they came to Thrasybulus, among others, "who seemed always to be especially opposed to the conspirators" (8.73.4). Thrasybulus and his colleagues rallied to the defense of the Samian democracy and put down the oligarchic uprising. They compelled all the soldiers to swear an oath of loyalty to the democracy, and the thoroughly democratic army deposed its generals and elected reliably democratic ones in their stead, among them Thrasybulus. He spent the rest of the war as a loyal democratic leader, and after the war he was the hero who resisted and finally overthrew the oligarchy of the Thirty Tyrants and restored democracy to Athens. If Thucydides is mistaken or misinformed about motives in this instance, he may be equally wrong in other cases, so we must not simply accept his opinions without question but examine each case on its own merits.

THRASYBULUS AND THE MODERATES

SURPRISINGLY, DESPITE his democratic convictions, Thrasybulus was one of those at Samos who favored Alcibiades' return to the Athenian side. Others, therefore, might also have welcomed the renegade's reinstatement for reasons apart from hostility to the regime. From the first the leaders at Samos were split into at least two groups. One was that of Thrasybulus, of whom Thucydides says, "He always held to the same opinion, that they should recall Alcibiades" (8.81.1). That means, however, that late in 412 this lifelong democrat was willing to accept limitations on the democracy, at least temporarily, for Alcibiades could not be rehabilitated so long as the present government ruled. Alcibiades himself at first spoke openly of his support for oligarchy, but Thrasybulus and other true democrats probably forced him to temper his language, for when he met with a delegation from Samos he had modified his position, promising to bring Tissaphernes over to an Athenian alliance "if the Athenians were not under a democracy" (8.48.1). The subtle shift in language was a concession to men like Thrasybulus, who were prepared to alter the constitution, as they already had with the *probouloi*, but not to move to oligarchy.

After persuading the Athenian forces at Samos to grant Alcibiades immunity from prosecution and elect him general, Thrasybulus himself sailed across to Tissaphernes' camp to retrieve Alcibiades, for as Thucydides explains: "He brought Alcibiades back to Samos thinking that the only safety for Athens was if he could bring Tissapherness away from the Peloponnesians and over to their side" (8.81.1). Thrasybulus believed that if the Persian alliance with Sparta remained intact Athens was lost. To win the war it must win over Persia, and only Alcibiades could accomplish that.

The limitations on democracy that were acceptable to Thrasybulus can be discerned from those Alcibiades proposed to the Athenians at Samos in the summer of 411, after the oligarchs of the deepest dye had rejected the renegade as "unsuitable" to participate in an oligarchy. At that time he proposed the dissolution of the council of Four Hundred that had seized oligarchic power by violence and the restoration of the old democratic council of Five Hundred. He also called for an end to payment for public service, which would effectively exclude poor Athenians from office, and for the installation of the constitution of the Five Thousand, which restricted full, active citizenship to men of the hoplite class or higher.

For the time being, therefore, Thrasybulus must have been willing to accept such terms, but not the narrower government of the Four Hundred. The category that best suits him is the traditional designation "moderate," which in 411 indicated a man who put victory in the war as the highest priority, even if it meant compromises had to be made in the popular democracy of Athens.

THE REAL OLIGARCHS

OTHERS WHO ENGAGED in discussions with Alcibiades, however, were true opponents of democracy of any kind, and wanted to replace it permanently with some form of oligarchic rule. Two members of this conspiracy were Phrynichus and Peisander, each of whom had previously been a demagogue. A few years after the war an Athenian orator would accuse both men of helping establish the oligarchy because they feared punishment for the many offenses they had committed against the Athenian people. We cannot be certain, however, whether personal considerations did play a part in bringing these formerly popular democratic politicians over to the oligarchic conspiracy.

In any case, they were not moved to bring back Alcibiades in order to win the war. Phrynichus resisted his return throughout and "showed himself, beyond all others, the most eager for the oligarchy. . . . Once he set to work he revealed himself as the most reliable" (8.63.3). Peisander quickly turned against Alcibiades and became a leader of the most violent and narrow-minded oligarchs. He made the motion to establish the oligarchy of the Four Hundred and took a leading role in overthrowing democracies in the empire and in Athens; after the fall of the oligarchy, he went over to the Spartans.

When the "trierarchs and the most important men" at Samos sent representatives to Alcibiades, Peisander and Thrasybulus were probably members of the delegation. At their meeting Alcibiades promised to bring Tissaphernes and the Great King onto the Athenian side "if they did not retain the democracy, for in that way the King would have greater trust in them" (8.48.1). Alcibiades used his skill with words to assuage the hesitations of the moderates: "Not to retain the democracy" could be interpreted in a manner that would suit both moderates and oligarchs, in a way that "replacing the base democracy with an oligarchy" could not.

The next step was for the leaders to form "those suitable" into a functioning political entity by swearing an oath. This group probably included hoplites who had been involved in the campaign at Miletus, but the presence of Thrasybulus among them indicates that it was not merely an oligarchic conspiracy. The new group summoned the

Athenians at Samos together "and openly told the many that the King would be their friend and provide them with money if they took back Alcibiades and were not governed by a democracy" (8.48.2). If the common man did not realize that plans to establish a narrow and permanent oligarchy was the secret agenda of some members, neither did insiders such as Thrasybulus.

"The mob," as Thucydides refers to the assembly of soldiers and sailors, "even if it was somewhat annoyed at the moment by what had been done, subsided into silence because of the hopeful prospect of pay from the King" (8.48.3). This is an unfair characterization of the Athenian soldiers and sailors. Like his explanation of the popular enthusiasm for the Sicilian campaign of 415, it claims simple greed as the sole motive although there were surely far more complicated feelings and considerations. In 412 and 411 the very survival of these men as well as that of their families and their city were at stake and, beyond that, their behavior in the years to come repeatedly demonstrated their patriotism and their devotion to the Athenian democracy.

PHRYNICHUS AGAINST ALCIBIADES

WHEN THE TIME finally came to decide the matter formally, at a meeting of the leaders, everyone was ready to accept Alcibiades except Phrynichus. He dismissed the idea that Alcibiades or anyone else could bring over the Persians to the Athenian side and also challenged the notion that the abandonment of democracy would help preserve the empire. He argued against the primacy of the class struggle and internal disputes over constitutional forms and in favor of the overwhelming importance of the love of autonomy. None of the allies, he warned, "will want to be enslaved with either an oligarchy or a democracy rather than to be free under whichever of these happens to exist" (8.48.5).

Beyond even these considerations, Phrynichus insisted that Alcibiades could not be trusted. Constitutional arrangements meant nothing to him; all that concerned him was a safe return to Athens. His reappearance in the city would spark civil war and the ruin of Athens and should not be allowed. Even in the face of such arguments the

Athenian leaders were so desperate to find some way to change their city's fortunes that the meeting accepted Alcibiades' proposals. They appointed Peisander to lead an embassy to Athens, where it would attempt to negotiate the homecoming of Alcibiades and to put down the current democracy in order to win over Tissaphernes.

Phrynichus now found himself in great danger, for when news of his opposition to Alcibiades reached his enemy, he would soon come to seek revenge. In desperation Phrynicus conceived a plan to prevent the return of Alcibiades and protect himself. Scholars have long puzzled over the complicated events that followed, and while there can be no certainty about them, what follows is one possible reconstruction: Phrynichus' behavior throughout this episode is best understood as the expression of a powerful and long-standing enmity, which readily explains his willingness to speak out against the rehabilitation of Alcibiades, even without support. When he failed to persuade the meeting at Samos, he wrote a letter to the Spartan navarch Astyochus at Miletus out of fear for his own safety, in which he warned of the plot to bring back Alcibiades and of the renegade's promise to deliver Tissaphernes and Persian support to the Athenians. Unaware that Alcibiades was no longer in the Spartan camp, he assumed that Astyochus would immediately arrest him, putting an end to the plot. Although Astyochus could no longer do so, he nevertheless could not afford to ignore the warning and allow the Athenian plot to succeed.

His solution was to bring the letter to Tissaphernes at Magnesia and confront him with the plot. The satrap must have been shocked, for he surely had made no commitment to Alcibiades of any kind. Alcibiades was deeply compromised, and his standing with the satrap began to collapse at once.

Infuriated, Alcibiades wrote to Samos informing his friends of Phrynichus' letter and asking that he be put to death. Phrynichus, who had expected Astyochus to kill Alcibiades and the plot with one blow, and not to disclose the contents of his letter, wrote in a panic again to Astyochus, advising him how he could defeat the Athenians at Samos. Modern scholars find it hard to believe that he could have been so foolhardy as to send a second letter after Astyochus had betrayed the first, but the circumstances on the latter case were different. The first letter had unwittingly made an impossible request, for Alcibiades had departed and could not be arrested. The second letter, however, offered the navarch an opportunity that was not only clearly possible but promised to produce a great victory—one that might put an end to the war in a single stroke. Alcibiades was not the only Athenian politician with remarkable adaptability and grandiose personal ambitions, ready to betray his city to secure his own safety and advance his career.

Astyochus, however, feared a trap, and to put an end to the conspiracy that was intended to convince Persia to change sides he notified both Alcibiades and Tissaphernes about the second letter. Phrynichus, meanwhile, had learned that Astyochus had once again revealed the contents of his letter and so set the very trap Astyochus had feared by warning the Athenians of the forthcoming attack—an attack he himself had provoked. When Alcibiades subsequently sent a letter to warn the Athenians at Samos of Phrynichus' betrayal and the planned assault, he was disbelieved "as a man who was not trustworthy" (8.51.3). The tricky Athenian renegade had been trumped by an even more clever deceiver; instead of doing Phrynichus harm, the letter from Alcibiades confirmed the truth of his warning, and the whole affair strengthened his position, at least for for the time being, even as it increased distrust of Alcibiades in the Athenian camp. It also caused a breach between Tissaphernes and Alcibiades and destroyed any chance he had of keeping his promises to the Athenian leaders at Samos. The collapse of their negotiations with Tissaphernes put an end to the oligarchic conspirators' interest in restoring Alcibiades and led to the establishment of a new treaty between Sparta and Persia. The first attempt against democracy in Athens had failed.

CHAPTER TWENTY-NINE

The Coup (411)

PEISANDER'S MISSION TO ATHENS

LATE IN DECEMBER 412 the men on Samos planning to alter the Athenian democracy sent Peisander as leader of an embassy to Athens. They knew nothing as yet of the plots that would discredit Alcibiades, so they had gone ahead with the original plan featuring him and his promises. Because moderates like Thrasybulus, therefore, still supported the proposed changes and played an important part in the effort, the true oligarchs in the movement needed to temper their language to suit them.

The message that the ambassadors delivered to the Athenian assembly was that the very survival of the state and its victory were dependent on Persian help, that only Alcibiades could obtain it, that he, therefore, must be restored, and that the democracy had to be attenuated to make that possible. The Athenians, they assured them, could do what was needed merely by "adopting a different form of democratic government" (8.53.1). However tactful their phrasing, it did not prevent strong resistance to both parts of the proposal. Many protested any change in the democracy, and the full range of Alcibiades' enemies opposed his recall. The scene was tumultuous and rowdy, with complaints and catcalls interrupting the speakers. To this wild and unfriendly mass meeting Peisander nevertheless spoke with remarkable effectiveness. He had the advantage of being regarded as "a man of the left" because of his previous record as a radical democratic politician, and as such was more plausible than a more conservative politician, an advantage he exploited with a bold rhetorical ploy. He asked the hecklers if they had any hope for the salvation of the city while Sparta had as many ships as Athens, more allies, and money from Persia. He asked if they had any other prospects than the return of Alcibiades, bringing Persian aid with him? No one had an answer, and the scream-ing multitude grew silent. Peisander then drew the inevitable conclu-sion for the sobered Athenian democracy: they must change the constitution in order to bring back Alcibiades and Persian support with him.

Both demands were fraudulent. As we have seen, Alcibiades could not deliver Persian support for Athens, and there is no evidence that the Persians cared what constitution was in force in Athens. The oli-garchs in the movement wanted constitutional change for its own sake, and were willing to accept Alcibiades as part of the bargain. Some moderates wanted particular limits placed on the democracy, and oth-ers would have preferred to preserve it as it was; all of them, however, believed that Alcibiades was the key to winning Persian support, and because his return required a change in the constitution, they were willing to pay that price.

Peisander chose his words carefully to suit not only the views of his moderate colleagues but of the large democratic audience to which he spoke. The Athenians could not achieve their goals, he warned, "Unless we are governed more sensibly and place the offices, to a greater extent, into the hands of a few" (8.53.3). This scenario implied that the democracy would remain as it was, except for a limit on office-holding. Many could accept that as a moderate and pragmatic bow to reality; with its treasury empty Athens could not afford to pay those holding public office, so why not limit offices to those who needed no pay? A period of crisis, he argued, was no time for debates about con-stitutional forms. In any case, he reassured them, if they did not like the new constitution they could always go back to the old one.

Although the assembly did not like what Peisander had said "about the oligarchy" (8.54.1), he convinced the majority that safety lay in no other direction, so, out of fear and the belief that their action was easily reversible, they accepted his arguments. The assembly sent Peisander and ten others to negotiate with Alcibiades and Tissaphernes "in what-ever way seemed best to them" (8.54.2).

To help clear the way, Peisander eliminated the potential road-block of Phrynichus by accusing him of treason for betraying Iasus and Amorges. Technically, the charge was false, but it was understood to mean that it was he who was responsible for evading a naval battle at Miletus, now perceived to have been an error of disastrous proportions. Of this charge he was certainly guilty, and the Athenians voted to remove him and one of his colleagues, Scironides, as generals and to replace them with Diomedon and Leon. Peisander, thereby, was able to take public advantage of popular resentment to achieve his goals.

Before leaving Athens he paid visits to the *hetairiai*, most of which were oligarchic in sentiment, to "plan together to overthrow the democracy" (8.54.4). To such an audience he was free to speak bluntly and honestly, urging the establishment of a narrow oligarchy without having to trim his sails to accomodate the views of moderate allies.

THE OLIGARCHS' BREACH WITH ALCIBIADES

PEISANDER and the other envoys then sailed to the court of Tissaphernes, where they found Alcibiades, seated beside the satrap and speaking for him. But his apparently confident standing of great influence was deceiving, for by now "Alcibiades' position in respect to Tissaphernes was not very secure" (8.56.2). Until this point in his narrative Thucydides has portrayed Alcibiades as being truly respected by and influential with the satrap, so when he sent word to his friends at Samos that he could procure Persian aid he must have believed that he truly could do so. But now, Thucydides tells us, Tissaphernes had resumed his scheme of wearing out both sides, and Alcibiades' relationship with him had become insecure as a result.

The correspondence between Phrynichus and Astyochus had revealed that Alcibiades was working behind the satrap's back in his own interest and that he was secretly plotting a return to Athens without regard to Tissaphernes' wishes. This revelation must have shaken the satrap's trust in his treacherous adviser and dissuaded him from assisting Athens, if indeed he ever really had that intention. For the moment, he would return to his policy of neutrality, and he must have informed Alcibiades of that decision before the audience with Peisander and his colleagues, since the Athenian exile would serve as his spokesman.

At the meeting, therefore, Alcibiades was fully aware that he could not keep his promise and that Tissaphernes' demands would be unacceptable. All he could do, therefore, was to maintain the appearance of continued favor with the satrap and to make it seem as if the inevitable failure of negotiations with the Persians resulted from Athenian unreasonableness rather than his own incapacity. The discussions dragged out over three sessions, with Tissaphernes demanding the return of all the cities on the western coast of Asia Minor, "the adjacent islands and other things (8.56.4)." These would have included such rich and important sites as Rhodes, Samos, Chios, and Lesbos, yet the envoys agreed to surrender them. At the final session, however, Alcibiades passed on the satrap's demand that the Athenians allow "the king to build ships and to sail them along his own coasts wherever and in whatever numbers he wished" (8.56.4).

In practice, the Persians had been prevented from sending warships into the Aegean or the Hellespont since the Greeks had defeated them in 479, for the security of Athens and its empire depended on keeping Persian fleets out of these waters. Now, however, the Great King's satrap insisted on returning to the state of affairs that existed before the Persian Wars. No free Athenian assembly would accept such terms, and Peisander and his colleagues duly rejected them. The angry Athenian envoys believed that Alcibiades had deceived them, and was party to Tissaphernes' claim. The renegade, however, succeeded in one respect: the Athenians did not suspect that he was unable to deliver what he had promised but believed, rather, that for some reason of his own, he had chosen not to. Accordingly, the myth of Alcibiades' power and influence could continue to flourish.

The movement to alter Athens' democratic constitution had now come to a crisis. Alcibiades' unwillingness or inability to bring Persian help to Athens put an end to any attractions his plan originally held for moderates like Thrasybulus. Thrusybulus' next contact with the movement was as its prime enemy, although he must have taken some members of the group with him into the opposition. Those who remained had never liked Alcibiades and decided thereafter "to let Alcibiades alone, since he refused to join them, and besides, he was not a suitable man to come into an oligarchy" (8.63.4). With this act they gave up hope of gaining Persian support, but they were more determined than ever to destroy the democracy, for they had come to feel endangered because of the steps they had already taken to achieve that goal.

DIVISIONS AMONG THE PLOTTERS

BY NOW MEMBERS of the movement had made public announcements of their intention to change the constitution. It would still have been safe to drop the plan on the grounds that Alcibiades had made false representations, or that he was unable to fulfill his promises. That is precisely what the trierarch Thrasybulus and other moderates did when the negotiations with Alcibiades and Tissaphernes failed.

Of those who remained committed to the movement some were true oligarchs who wanted a revolution in government for its own sake. Others, however, were not so extreme in their views, but may have become thoroughly disillusioned with the errors of the radical democracy and fearful of the mistakes it might yet make. They were also likely to have been struck by the need for the state to practice great economy, which was incompatible with continued payment for public offices and service.

Both groups, however, found themselves in a precarious position. They could no longer claim that they aimed at a shift in Persian allegiance. The defection of Thrasybulus guaranteed that their enemies would come to learn their identities, and he would also serve them as an informed and talented leader. Those who held to their course after the possibility of Persian help had vanished would increasingly come to be seen as enemies of the democracy and potential tyrants. They resolved, nevertheless, to keep the movement alive, providing for it from their own resources money and whatever else was needed, and not to yield to Sparta.

The coalition now had to go underground and become a conspiracy, having defined three goals as the way to achieve complete success: to gain control of the naval base at Samos; to foster oligarchic revolutions throughout the empire; and to bring oligarchy to Athens. At Samos accordingly they worked to gain the support of the hoplites and farmers less attached to the radical democracy than the men who rowed the ships, and they plotted with "the important men" of the island to establish an oligarchy there.

Meanwhile Peisander, with half of the embassy that had negotiated with Tissaphernes, sailed for Athens, on their way establishing oligarchies in the empire. The other five envoys scattered throughout the Aegean to do the same but ran into trouble in the process. The general Dieitrephes, one of the conspirators, initially succeeded in putting down the democracy and instituting oligarchic rule at Thasos. Soon, however, in spite of the installation of an oligarchy in Athens, the Thasian oligarchs, reunited with other oligarchs in exile, fortified their island against a possible Athenian attack, and called in a fleet led by the Corinthian general Timolaus. The oligarchs of Thasos no longer needed an imposed "aristocracy" when they could have "freedom" in alliance with the Spartans.

The developments in Thasos supported Phrynichus' contention that replacing democracies with oligarchies would not necessarily reconcile the subject states to Athenian rule. Thucydides makes the point: "After the cities got hold of moderate government and freedom to act as they liked, they went on to absolute liberty, caring nothing for the specious *eunomia* of the Athenians" (8.64.5).

THE DEMOCRACY OVERTHROWN

IN SPITE OF this disappointment Peisander's mission still seemed promising. At Athens the extremist young aristocrats he had recruited had already assassinated a number of leading democrats, among them Androcles, the chief popular politician of the day, who was targeted not only because he was a demagogue but also to please Alcibiades. Evidently they had not yet learned of the change in the situation and of the revised goals of the leaders of the conspiracy, for they were still putting forward the program demanded by the moderates, publicly proposing the end of pay for military service and the limitation of active citizenship to no more than five thousand, restricted to those of hoplite status or higher.

At the same time, these young aristocrats were also assassinating other selected political enemies, not a course favored by the moderates. Besides Androcles, they "killed some others who were inconvenient in the same way, secretly" (8.65.2). These murders were part of a policy of terror to weaken the opposition and ease the destruction of the democracy. The popular assembly and council still met, but members of the movement now controlled the agenda and were the only ones to speak, for their opponents were terrified into silence: "If anyone should speak in opposition, he was immediately killed in some convenient way" (8.66.2). The perpetrators were tolerated, subject to neither investigations, arrests, charges, or trials. Members of the democratic faction feared to speak frankly to one another, trusting no one, for even well-known demagogues such as Peisander and Phrynichus had turned out to be oligarchic leaders.

The conspirators thus created a climate of fear in which they could gain control of the state without having to resort to a blatant use of force, protected by the guise of legality, due process, and consent. At a meeting of the assembly they suggested the appointment of a commission of thirty men (*syngrapheis*), including the ten *probouloi*, with full powers, "on a fixed day" to draft proposals "for the best management of the state" (8.67.1). This was little more than a license to propose a new constitution, and the intimidated assembly passed it without a challenge.

The commissioners made their report on the day set—not, as usual, on the Pnyx in Athens, but about a mile outside the city on a hill called Colonus Hippius. Perhaps this was done to heighten the fears of the lower classes; while the presence of an armed guard of hoplites might seem appropriate to protect a gathering held outside the defensive walls, the mere act of moving to an unfamiliar meeting place would have been an unsettling sign. The *syngrapheis* presented no suggestions for the safety or best management of the state, but offered only a single motion: "To allow any Athenian to make any proposal he liked without penalty" (8.67.2). This meant that the constitutional prohibition against introducing illegal proposals, the *graphe paranomon*, was suspended.

Within the context of the intimidating and controlled circumstances of this meeting, such a measure was not intended as a license for general free expression but only as a legal protection for those planning the revolution. Under the circumstances Peisander alone spoke, setting forth the conspirators' program. There was to be no further payment for public service not related to the war, except for the nine archons and the prytanies, who would receive a half a drachma each per day. The central element of his presentation was the establishment of a council of Four Hundred, "to rule in whatever way they thought best, with full powers" (8.67.3). This body would be chosen in a complicated and indirect manner. In so menacing a climate there was little doubt that the conspirators' choices would be elected. A list of the Five Thousand, consisting of the men of the hoplite census and above, was also to be drawn up, and the Four Hundred were empowered to summon them together whenever they saw fit.

The assembly passed these measures without dissent and dissolved; the coup had succeeded. The democracy that had reigned for almost a century would be replaced by a regime that excluded the lower classes from political life and turned the present management of the state over to a narrow oligarchy.

Although the provision made for the Five Thousand was a fraud, to the Athenians in 411 the proposals overall were apparently consistent with the program of the moderates. Payments had to be curtailed to save money for fighting the war; the radical democracy had to give way for the duration of the war to a more limited but moderate regime. The council of Four Hundred could accordingly be viewed as a temporary governing body, in power only until the Five Thousand could take over.

What remained to be dealt with was Alcibiades and his promise to bring over Tissaphernes and Persian aid. Although Peisander knew that such a prospect was no longer feasible, it is not clear whether the moderates in the movement had yet heard of the failed meeting with Tissaphernes. The moderates in Athens continued to support the coup, perhaps because they had not heard the news, but even if they had, they still had reason to stay the course. Like the moderates at Samos who had remained committed to the plan even after they learned that the element concerning Alcibiades and Persia had failed, those in Athens may have persisted "because they were already in danger" and it was therefore safer to go forward. Perhaps, too, they still genuinely wanted to save public money for the battle chest and believed that limiting active citizenship to the propertied classes was the best way to help Athens survive and win the war.

THE OLIGARCHIC LEADERS

THE LEADERS OF THE movement to overthrow the democracy were Peisander, Phrynichus, Antiphon, and Theramenes. The first two, like most of the Four Hundred, were merely self-seeking opportunists acting out of personal ambition. Antiphon, however, had a different agenda. While Phrynichus and Peisander were active and highly visible politicians, Antiphon worked behind the scenes. He seems to have been the first professional speechwriter in Athens and earned Thucydides' admiration as "the one man most able to help someone contesting both in the law courts and in the assembly." He was no friend of democracy, however, and became "an object of suspicion to the masses because of his reputation for dangerous cleverness." It was he who "had devised the whole affair and had established the way in which it had been brought to this point" (8.68.1). There is every reason to believe that Antiphon sincerely believed it best for Athens to overthrow democracy in favor of a true, narrow oligarchy, and was willing to work hard to prepare for it and to do whatever was necessary to achieve that goal. Thucydides calls him a man "inferior to no one in his own time in *arete* [courage, excellence, virtue] and the very best both in conceiving an idea and expressing it in speech" (8.68.1).

It was Theramenes, however, who turned out to play the most significant role in 411. He was also the most controversial of the four, accused by some as an oligarchic enemy of democracy, and called by his enemies *kothornos*, the tragic boot that fit either foot, but his entire career reveals him to be a patriot and a true moderate, sincerely committed to a constitution granting power to the hoplite class, whether in the form of a limited democracy or a broadly based oligarchy.

For their own particular reasons and motivated by different philosophies and goals these four men set out "to deprive of their freedom a people who not only had not been subjects but for half of the century of their freedom had been accustomed to rule over others" (8.68.4).

Peisander did not fix a date when the new regime would take control, and many Athenians must have expected their accession would be delayed until the conciliar year came to an end in about a month. But the conspirators moved swiftly and, on June 9, 411, only a few days after the meeting on Colonus, they seized power. When the Athenians went off to their military posts at the walls and the training fields, the conspirators went into action, assisted by four or five hundred armed men from Tenos, Andros, Carystus, and Aegina, who had been expressly gathered for the coup.

The Four Hundred, carrying daggers under their cloaks and supported by the 120 young aristocrats who had terrorized Athens, burst into the council house. They paid the members of the democratic council for the remainder of their terms and then ordered them out. The councilors took their money and left without protest, and no one else interfered. The Four Hundred appointed the prytanies and presiding officers by lot, as had been the practice in the old council, and performed the customary prayers and sacrifices upon taking office. They made every effort to preserve a sense of continuity, normality, and legality, but few could have been deceived. For the first time since the expulsion of the Peisistratid tyrants in 510, the state had been captured by by means of threats and force.

CHAPTER THIRTY

The Four Hundred in Power (411)

THE MEN WHO were most active in formulating the rule of the Four Hundred were not themselves moderates, but because they needed the support of the moderates they sought to cloak their agenda with promises of a more moderate future. To that end the meeting on Colonus hill appointed a board of registrars to create the list of the Five Thousand, which they never completed, as well as a committee to draft a permanent constitution for the future. These measures aimed to persuade the moderates that the rule of the Four Hundred was temporary and would give way to a new constitution of the Five Thousand when the crisis was over.

Because the extremists intended to keep the Four Hundred in control only for the time being and eventually to establish an even narrower oligarchy, however, they were forced to practice a number of deceptions. The constitutional committee, therefore, reached a "compromise," proposing two new constitutions, one for immediate use and the other for the future. The immediate constitution was a formal authorization of the extremists, conferring legal status to the council of Four Hundred with powers "to act in whatever way they thought expedient" (Aristotle, *Constitution of the Athenians* 31.2). The Athenians would be obliged to accept whatever laws they might enact in the matter of the constitution, agree not to change any, and assent not to introduce any new ones. These terms, in effect, gave license to the Four Hundred to do whatever they liked and to remain in power as long as they wished.

To maintain the allegiance of the moderates the Four Hundred also put forward a draft constitution for the future. It was fundamentally incomplete, for it said nothing about a judiciary, but it did provide for an unpaid council drawn from members of the Five Thousand over the age of thirty, divided into four sections, serving in rotation on behalf of the full council for one year. The generals and other major officials were to be chosen from the council in office at the time, so they could serve only one year in four. This arrangement was intended to thwart the rise of popular leaders, but its impracticality did not matter, nor did any of the other particular details of the document, for the oligarchs did not intend this constitution to take effect, and it never did. For the moment the moderates were satisfied with the prospect of a moderate constitution on the horizon; the specifics could be hammered out later.

Eight days after seizing power the Four Hundred formally established the new regime. The constitutional drafting committee published their two new constitutions, claiming they had been ratified by the Five Thousand. This assertion was patently false, for the list of the Five Thousand did not even exist. Yet most Athenians were too frightened, confused, or ignorant to raise any questions. Before and after this public event, the majority believed that the Five Thousand might already have been chosen. The moderates in the Four Hundred knew better, but they held their peace in the expectation that such maneuvers were a necessary part of the transition they desired. Their goal was to gain the loyalty of the Athenian force at Samos, and the apparently legal foundation of a new regime and the promise of a broad and moderate government to come were steps to achieve it.

The oligarchy arose because of a crisis in the war, but its revolutionary birth caused another crisis within the state, so it faced severe challenges from the outset. The most immediate was to make Athens secure. The Four Hundred then had to win over the Athenian forces at Samos and so unite the Athenian people under their rule. Next, decisions had to be made about how to deal with the empire, and how to proceed with the war. Should they keep fighting? If so, what should be the strategy? If not, what peace terms should they seek? In any case, what form should the Athenian government take in the long run? Significantly divided from the first, the Four Hundred set out to answer these questions.

To give the impression of moderation, legality, and continuity, they selected the council's presidents by lot, as in the democracy. To gain immediate control of the armed forces in Athens they hurried to appoint a new board of generals, a cavalry commander, and ten tribal commanders without following the procedure required by their own constitution. Of the generals whose names we know, four were extreme oligarchs, and Theramenes and one other were moderates, a representation that was probably proportionate to the balance within the Four Hundred itself. The extremists among them wanted to recall men exiled under the democratic regime, most of whom were bitter enemies of the democracy. A general rehabilitation of exiles, however, would have included Alcibiades, whom they mistrusted and feared. But excluding Alcibiades alone from such an amnesty would have alienated the moderates, who remained closely attached to him, so they held back from pursuing the matter.

From the first the ostensible purpose of the coup had been to make it possible to win the war, but as soon as the Four Hundred were in place they sought peace with Sparta. In spite of the new oligarchy's repeated assurances of their desire to go on fighting, it ought to have been evident that the destruction of democracy was incompatible with the continuation of the war. The Athenians' only hope of victory lay in the strength of the fleet, which meant depending on the cooperation of the lower classes and their democratic leaders. As long as the city's safety rested with them no assault on popular government would go uncontested for long. Even a temporary peace with Sparta, however, would leave most of the ships in their docks and their crews scattered. In those circumstances the oligarchs would be able to impose a new regime by terror and by winning over the hoplites. Then they could open negotiations to achieve a permanent peace that would leave Athens under oligarchic rule.

Even that course would not be easy, for the moderates might well insist on fighting on or, at least, demand conditions that the Spartans would not be likely to grant. While most of the extremists, no doubt, would also have preferred such provisions, they were ready to make peace "on any terms tolerable," even if that meant giving up Athens' walls, fleet, and autonomy. It was to prevent precisely such an outcome that Theramenes would soon lead a movement that drove the Four Hundred from power. He and the moderates were willing to discuss a peace that would leave Athens its independence, empire, and power, even one based on the status quo and the loss of some subject states that had rebelled, but would settle for nothing less. Despite their willingness to make far greater concessions the extremists could agree with the moderates on at least the first stage of negotiations.

The Four Hundred, therefore, sent an embassy to King Agis at Decelea offering a peace in which each side would keep those territories it now held. Agis rejected it at once: there would be no peace "unless they surrendered their maritime empire" (Aristotle, *Constitution of the Athenians* 32.3). The Spartan king regarded the Athenians' proposal as an indication of their weakness and accordingly ordered a large army from the Peloponnesus to meet him near the walls of Athens with his own force from Decelea. But the Athenians were not ready to yield, and armed forces from every class of society—cavalrymen, hoplites, light-armed soldiers, and archers—attacked when the enemy approached the walls, driving the Spartan armies away.

The determination of the Athenians made it clear that victory would not come easily. After the battle the Four Hundred continued to seek peace negotiations, and the now-sobered Agis urged the Athenians to send embassies directly to Sparta. While he did not want to seem an obstacle to peace, he was unwilling personally to discuss terms that might prove unacceptable to the Spartan government.

THE DEMOCRACY AT SAMOS

THE FOUR HUNDRED now turned to problems festering at Samos. Their original plan was to make the island an oligarchy, but the scheme quickly ran into trouble. Peisander persuaded some opportunistic Samian politicians to form a conspiracy of Three Hundred, who used terror tactics similar to the ones employed by the Four Hundred in Athens. The group murdered Hyperbolus, who had lived on the island since his ostracism in 416, as a pledge of good faith to the Athenian oligarchs, but such violence was not as effective at Samos as it had been at Athens. In response the Samian democrats looked for leadership to the most trusted Athenian friends of democracy—the generals Leon and Diomedon, the trierarch Thrasybulus, and Thrasyllus, who was only a hoplite in the ranks—men who "always seemed to be most opposed to the conspirators" (8.73.4).

The situation at Samos provides further evidence that the original conspiracy to alter the Athenian government was a nuanced affair from its inception, involving several heterogenous elements. Confronted with a national disaster, Leon and Diomedon, who were neither oligarchs nor radical democrats, must have accepted the idea of bringing back Alicibiades and altering the democratic constitution at Athens, however unhappily they viewed this plan. As generals, however, they could not have been excluded from the inner circle of the Four Hundred, which included true oligarchs like Peisander. To an outsider, therefore, they may have seemed part of the oligarchy, which would explain why the Athenian democrats on Samos later dismissed them, along with other generals and those trierarchs thought to be unreliable.

Even more striking is the democrats' confidence in the trierarch Thrasybulus, a strong supporter of Alcibiades and one of the original authors of the plan to seek Persian aid. His selection as one of only four Athenian leaders picked to save the Samian democracy reveals that those who were involved in the matter recognized that the Four Hundred were not all cut from the same cloth and that true friends of democracy walked among them.

Each of the chosen Athenians set out to warn reliable Athenian soldiers of the danger, especially to Athens' messenger ship *Paralus*, whose crew was well known for its democratic views and its hatred for oligarchy. Leon and Diomedon carefully left ships behind to guard Samos whenever they sailed off on any mission, making certain to include the *Paralus* among them. When the Samian oligarchs launched their coup, therefore, Athenian sailors, and especially the crew of the *Paralus*, were prepared to stop them. The victorious Samian democrats put thirty ringleaders of the coup to death and sent three others into exile, but declared an amnesty for the others. This showed remarkable self-restraint by the standards of the day, an effort that was soon rewarded. "Thereafter they lived under a democracy as fellow citizens" (8.73.6).

Because these events occurred shortly after the coup in Athens, the men at Samos had not yet learned that oligarchy had come to the capital. When the *Paralus* arrived in Athens to announce the great news of the democratic victory on the island, therefore, its crew was immediately placed under arrest. Chaereas, an especially zealous democrat, alone managed to escape, and he hurried back to Samos. His account of the situation at Athens was even harsher than the truth: he reported that people were being punished with the whip, that no criticism of the government was tolerated, that outrages were being committed against women and children, that the oligarchs intended to imprison and threatened to kill relatives of the men on Samos who were not friendly to their cause; according to Thucydides, "he told many other lies, as well" (8.74.3). Chaereas' speech so inflamed the Athenian soldiers that they seized "the principal authors of the oligarchy," and "those of the others who took part in it," intending to stone them to death, but "the men of moderate views" restrained them (8.75.1). The "principal authors" would have been men close to Peisander and Phrynichus, while the "others who took part" must have included moderate democrats like Leon and Diomedon, for in the passion of the moment, they were deposed from their generalships. Among the "men of moderate views" were certainly Thrasybulus and Thrasyllus, for they took the lead in the events that were now taking place. They were also instrumental in preventing violence and in bringing about what amounted to an amnesty for those who had taken part in the oligarchic movement in its early phase, since they included them in the new oath to which they swore the Athenian and Samian armed forces: "To be governed by democracy and to live in harmony, to pursue the war against the Peloponnesians vigorously, to be enemies to the Four Hundred and not to enter into negotiations with them" (8.75.2). Hereafter, both Athenians and Samians on the island would stand together against the Four Hundred in Athens as well as the Peloponnesian enemy.

The Athenian soldiers at Samos elected Thrasybulus and Thrasyllus, among others, to replace the deposed generals in an action that amounted to a declaration of sovereignty, one that claimed legitimacy for themselves as opposed to the oligarchic government at home. The new leaders encouraged their men by announcing that they, not the oligarchs in Athens, represented the majority, as well as the navy, which alone could control the empire and its income. Athens had revolted from them, not they from the city. From Samos they could both hold off the enemy and force the oligarchs to restore democracy to Athens. In any case, they were safe as long as they retained their great fleet.

Meanwhile, at their base at Miletus, not far from Samos, the Peloponnesians were having troubles of their own. Led by the furious Syracusans, many soldiers spoke out openly against their leaders. They complained of inactivity and opportunities missed while the Athenians were at war among themselves. They blamed the navarch Astyochus for shirking battle and trusting Tissaphernes. They were angry with the satrap himself for promising a Phoenician fleet that never materialized and for his inadequate and irregular payment of their wages, and they accused him of deliberately trying to wear down their strength by delay. Compelled by their assault Astyochus summoned a council, which decided to force a major battle. Having learned of the democratic attack on the Samian oligarchs, they hoped to catch the enemy in the midst of a civil war.

In mid-June, therefore, they set out for Samos with their entire fleet of 112 ships. The Athenians at Samos had only 82 vessels, but they learned of the expedition in time to send an order to Strombichides in the Hellespont to hurry back for the battle. When the Peloponnesians appeared, the Athenian fleet took shelter at Samos to await his return. The Peloponnesians camped at Mycale, on the mainland across from Samos, and prepared to sail out the next day. When they learned that Strombichides had come with ships that brought the Athenian total to 108, however, Astyochus retreated to Miletus. The Athenians pursued, hoping to provide a decisive battle, but Astyochus refused to come out of harbor. In spite of their internal difficulties, the Athenians restored the balance of power to what it had been the previous winter: the Athenian fleet, although slightly inferior in numbers, again commanded the sea.

PHARNABAZUS AND THE HELLESPONT

THE RETREAT FROM SAMOS made the Peloponnesian soldiers and sailors even more irate, and they increased the pressure on Astyochus to take effective action, even as Tissaphernes' failure to make the promised payments threatened the navarch's ability to maintain the fleet. Pharnabazus, the satrap of northern Anatolia, on the other hand, promised to support the Peloponnesian fleet if Astyochus moved it into the Hellespont. The citizens of Byzantium on the Bosporus also asked him to come and help them rebel from the Athenians. Astyochus, moreover, had not yet carried out orders from Sparta to send a force under the general Clearchus to help Pharnabazus. His policy of staying in Ionia and trying to work with Tissaphernes was clearly bankrupt, and he could delay no longer.

Late in July Clearchus set off for the Hellespont with forty ships. Fear of the Athenian fleet at Samos made him sail far to the west of the direct route, which brought him into more open sea, where he encountered one of those sudden Aegean storms so deadly to triremes. He abandoned his goal and sneaked back to Miletus when the sea was calm. Meanwhile ten ships under the bolder or luckier Megarian general Helixus made their way into the Straits and brought about the revolt of Byzantium. Soon Chalcedon, on the other side of the Bosporus, Cyzicus, and Selymbria all joined the uprising.

These developments radically changed the strategic situation, for revolts and a Spartan fleet in the Straits threatened the Athenian grain supply and consequently its ability to stay in the war. The Peloponnesians' movement into Pharnabazus' sphere of influence was also significant, since until then they had been forced to rely on the sporadic and unreliable support of Tissaphernes and were held in check by his schemes. With Pharnabazus as ally and paymaster they could hope for greater success, especially as they now stood athwart Athens' vital supply line.

ALCIBIADES RECALLED

THE ATHENIANS at Samos quickly perceived the danger in this new alliance and took steps to meet it. Thrasybulus, who had never given up on urging the return of Alcibiades as a key to winning the war, at last gained the support of a majority of the soldiers for a decree recalling him with a grant of immunity from prosecution. Thrasybulus himself sailed off to accompany Alcibiades to Samos, "thinking that the only salvation lay in bringing Tissaphernes over from the Peloponnesian side to their own" (8.81.1).

The conditions of Alcibiades' repatriation were not, however, what he had wished. He was widely distrusted and, in some quarters, hated. He had not come home to Athens but only to Samos, where his immunity protected him for the time being but not from a reckoning in the future. He would have liked to reappear in Athens at the head of a broad coalition in which he was the indispensable central figure. Instead, only one faction of moderate democrats, at the insistence of its leader Thrasybulus, brought him back to a Samos at odds with the city. His success, not to mention his future, depended on maintaining good relations with Thrasybulus, who, although a loyal friend, was a powerful man of independent mind and nobody's puppet. Alcibiades was bound to follow his lead when he arrived at the Athenian camp.

When he arrived on Samos Alcibiades spoke to the Athenian assembly there, though his words were addressed also to the oligarchic leaders in Athens as well as to the Peloponnesians. Thucydides describes his intentions as being to gain the respect of the army on Samos and restore their self-confidence, to increase the Peloponnesians' suspicion of Tissaphernes and thereby make them lose hope of victory, and to bring the fear of of his return into the hearts of those controlling the oligarchy in Athens, thereby breaking the hold of the extremist oligarchic clubs. At the heart of his speech he sustained the lies that he had great influence with Tissaphernes, and that the satrap was eager to help the Athenians. Tissaphernes would bring the Phoenician fleet, which he had promised to the Peloponnesians, to the Athenians instead—but only if they restored Alcibiades, the man he trusted, as a guarantee of their good faith. The Athenian soldiers, eager to believe that safety and victory were finally at hand, elected him general at once "and gave over to him control of all their affairs" (8.82.1).

Alcibiades' rhetoric, in fact, proved to be rather too successful, for in their enthusiasm the Athenian force wanted to sail directly to the Piraeus and attack the Four Hundred. Alcibiades, however, first needed time for a meeting with Tissaphernes, to let him know that he was no longer a man without a country, dependent on the satrap for his safety and survival, but rather the newly elected leader of the Athenian forces at Samos and a man to be reckoned with. Thucydides tells us that he "was using the Athenians to frighten Tissaphernes and Tissaphernes to frighten the Athenians" (8.82.2), but in order to do so he needed to reach the satrap before the Athenians took any action.

Meanwhile, at Miletus relations between the Peloponnesians and Tissaphernes went from bad to worse. He had used their inactivity as an excuse for holding back even more of their salaries, and by now even the officers were voicing their discontent, aiming it especially at their passive navarch Astyochus. Finding him too lenient toward Tissaphernes, they suspected him of accepting bribes from the satrap. The men from Thurii and Syracuse brought the discontent to a head by demanding their pay from Astyochus. With the arrogance typical of Spartans commanding foreign troops he answered them sharply and even raised his swagger stick to threaten Dorieus, the great athlete who commanded the Thurian force. His crews would have stoned the navarch had he not fled to an altar for sanctuary. Taking advantage of the Peloponnesians' internal strife, the Milesians seized the fort the satrap had built in their city and drove his garrison from it, earning the approval of the allies and of the Syracusans in particular. It was at this point, in the month of August, that the new navarch, Mindarus, came to relieve Astyochus.

Such turmoil must have pleased Alcibiades, who was with Tissaphernes at Miletus during part of it. Soon after he returned to Samos, an embassy from the Four Hundred in Athens arrived to try to deal with the unwelcome developments there. At first the angry soldiers shouted them down when they attempted to speak in an assembly and threatened to kill these men who had destroyed their democracy. After a while, however, they relented, and the ambassadors delivered their message. The purpose of the revolution, they explained, was to save the city, not to betray it. The new government would not be a permanent narrow oligarchy; the Four Hundred would eventually give way to the Five Thousand. Chaereas' charges were false; the soldiers' relatives in Athens were safe. These assurances did not calm the audience, however, and the proposal to attack at once the Piraeus and the oligarchs in Athens won strong support. Thucydides observes that "no one else could have restrained the mob at that moment, but Alcibiades did so" (8.86.5). Here, as so often, he ascribes too much influence to the Athenian renegade (who was probably a key source for his history), for Thrasybulus also took part in this restraint, "going along and doing the shouting, for he is said to have had the loudest voice among the Athenians" (Plutarch, *Alcibiades* 26.6).

Alcibiades answered the envoys by insisting on the adoption of the program of Thrasybulus and the moderates. "He was not opposed to the rule of the Five Thousand, but he demanded that they depose the Four Hundred and restore the council of Five Hundred" (8.86.6). He approved any economies they might have made to provide for the armed forces, and he encouraged them not to yield to the enemy, for as long as the city was safe in Athenian hands, hope for reconciliation remained. The mass of soldiers and sailors, no doubt, would have preferred a restoration of the full democracy, but their leaders still sought to establish the moderate regime they had wanted from the start, and the men acceded to their wishes.

Perhaps the chief target of Alcibiades' speech, however, was the governing body in Athens. His words were meant to strengthen the moderates' resolve to resist any excesses planned by the extremists, and perhaps to take control themselves. Even more, the goal of Alcibiades' speech was to deter the Four Hundred from making a separate peace with the enemy, handing the city over to them. The danger of such a development was real, for the army at Samos soon received conclusive evidence that the Four Hundred had tried, once again, to negotiate with the Spartans, although the envoys never reached Sparta. The crews of the ship carrying them rebelled against those they deemed "chiefly responsible for overturning the democracy" (8.86.9) and handed them over to the Argives who, in turn, delivered them to Samos.

As the summer of 411 came to an end, the men who hoped to establish a permanent oligarchy in Athens had achieved none of their goals. Their efforts at making the empire more secure by installing oligarchies only incited further rebellions. Instead of managing to place a friendly oligarchy on Samos, their attempt at a coup stirred up an angry democracy that was barely restrained from sailing to attack them. They had alienated Thrasybulus, one of the founders of the movement, and turned him into a dangerous enemy along with his friend Alcibiades, once a major element of their plan for success. Both men now demanded the dissolution of the Four Hundred, and they influenced their moderate friends within that body in Athens. Their attempt to make peace with Sparta had failed. Their only remaining hope was to convince the Spartans to save them before it was too late.

CHAPTER THIRTY-ONE

The Five Thousand (411)

ON THEIR RETURN to Athens from Samos the oligarchy's ambassadors relayed only part of Alcibiades' message to the Four Hundred. They told of his insistence that the Athenians hold out and not yield to the Spartans, and of his hopes of reconciliation and victory, but they suppressed his support of the Five Thousand, his opposition to the continued rule of the Four Hundred, and his call for a restoration of the old council of Five Hundred. Although reporting such sentiments would have deepened the rift in the movement, even the edited version heartened the moderates, who "were the majority of those taking part in the oligarchy [and] who were even before this discontented and would gladly rid themselves of the affair in any way if they could do so safely" (8.89.1).

DISSENT WITHIN THE FOUR HUNDRED

THESE DISSENTERS were led by Theramenes and Aristocrates son of Scelias. Theramenes' conduct during this period foreshadowed what would prove to be a bold and active career on behalf of a moderate regime for Athens. Aristocrates was a prominent Athenian, a general important enough to have been a signer of the Peace of Nicias and the alliance with Sparta, as well as the object of a joke in Aristophanes' *Birds* in 414. Like Theramenes and Thrasybulus he had supported the movement to limit the Athenian democracy and turned against the Four Hundred; he, too, would flourish under the restored democracy as an associate of Alcibiades.

In the discussions among the discontented Theramenes and Aristocrates announced that they feared not only Alcibiades and his army on Samos but also "those who had been sending embassies to Sparta, lest they do some harm to the city without consulting the majority." Still they were careful to avoid the language of counterrevolution lest they provoke further terror and open civil strife, which might expose the city to an easy Spartan conquest. Instead, they insisted only that the Four Hundred carry out their promise "to appoint the Five Thousand in fact and not in name and [thereby] to establish a more equal polity" (8.89.2).

Apart from any particular personal ambitions these men were motivated by fear as much as by patriotism. As the situation deteriorated, the extremists could be expected to turn against the dissidents within the Four Hundred, and they had already demonstrated their willingness to kill their opponents. If, on the other hand, Athenian democrats at Samos gained control, they were unlikely to show any mercy to the founders of the Four Hundred. With each passing day it grew more probable, therefore, that the extremists would betray the city to Sparta to save both the oligarchy and themselves. The moderates of Athens, however, were determined to preserve the independence of the city and fight the war through to victory, and events would show that their democratic fellow citizens recognized their dedication and repeatedly appointed them to military commands. All these considerations combined to pressure the moderates to take action quickly.

THE OLIGARCHIC PLOT TO BETRAY ATHENS

ALTHOUGH THE AMBASSADORS had scrupulously avoided sharing the full details of Alcibiades' message, the news from Samos nevertheless alarmed the extremist leaders to the point that they began to build a fort on the harbor at Piraeus on Eetioneia, a promontory extending south across the mouth of the harbor and dominating traffic in and out of it. Ostensibly the new construction would enable a small force to control the harbor against attacks from the land side by internal enemies, but Theramenes and the moderates immediately perceived its potential danger. Its true purpose, they protested, was "so that they could admit the enemy by land and sea whenever they wished" (8.90.3). The report of Alcibiades' return also raised the extremists' fears; they "saw that both the majority of the citizens and some of their own group whom previously they had believed trustworthy were changing their minds" (8.91.1). While they would have preferred to remain autonomous, establish oligarchy in Athens, and keep the empire intact. If they lost the empire they would seek to preserve autonomy but rather than accept a democratic restoration "they would bring in the enemy and, abandoning ships and walls, make any terms at all on behalf of their city if only they could save their own lives" (8.91.3). They accordingly hastened to finish the new fortifications at Eetioneia and sent a dozen men, including Antiphon and Phrynichus, to seek peace from the Spartans "on terms that were in any way tolerable" (8.90.2).

We can only conjecture about the specifics of the negotiations. The Athenians probably asked for a peace based on the status quo, which the Spartans refused. The embassy returned from Sparta, therefore, without a general agreement, but they did negotiate an escape for the extremists: Antiphon and his colleagues had arranged to betray their city in exchange for their own safety.

As the new walls continued to rise Theramenes complained about them with increasing openness, vigor, and courage, even though opposition to the extremists was a very risky tactic and could bring denunciation or assassination at any time. It was an assassination of a different sort, however, that finally helped launch the counterrevolution, when Phrynichus was killed in the crowded Agora, as he left the council chamber. The killer escaped, and an Argive who accompanied him refused even under torture to reveal the names of any coconspirators. At that point word came to Athens that a Peloponnesian fleet, ostensibly preparing to assist the Euboeans in a rebellion, had landed at Epidaurus before launching a raid on Aegina. That was not a stop on the route to Euboea but rather on a direct path to Piraeus. Theramenes, Aristocrates, and other moderates, both inside and outside the Four Hundred, held an emergency meeting. Theramenes had been warning for some time that the Peloponnesian fleet's true target was not Euboea but the port of Athens and now demanded action.

Aristocrates, who commanded a regiment of hoplites at Piraeus, immediately arrested Alexicles, "a general from the oligarchical faction and especially inclined to the members of the clubs" (8.92.4). This elimination of an extremist general by order of a moderate was welcomed by the hoplite army, which represented the core of the armed forces, and a group the extremists would have to control if they hoped to carry out their plan to betray the city to Sparta. When news of the uprising arrived at Athens the Four Hundred were meeting in the council chamber, and the extremists quickly turned on Theramenes, the obvious suspect. He surprised them, however, by offering to join in the rescue of Alexicles. Taken off guard, uncertain of his role in the affair, and unwilling to force an open rift at so critical a moment, they accepted Theramenes' offer and allowed him to take along another general who shared his views. The only countermeasure they could take was to send the extremist Aristarchus to accompany them as a third general.

As one army marched from Athens to face another at Piraeus, civil war seemed unavoidable. But because the force at Piraeus was commanded by moderates, and two of the three generals of the group coming from Athens were moderates as well, the result was less a decisive battle than a comic performance. When Aristarchus angrily demanded that the hoplites put their full effort into the fighting, Theramenes pretended to scold them. Most of the men, however, hesitantly asked Theramenes, "did he think that the fortification was being built to any good purpose or would it be better to destroy it?" He answered that if they thought it best to demolish it, he agreed with them. The hoplites began at once to tear down the fortification, shouting, "Whoever wants the Five Thousand to rule instead of the Four Hundred, let him get to work" (8.92.10–11).

This instigation was surely part of the moderates' plan, and while it was addressed "to the crowd" as a way of encouraging them to tear down the fortification and thwart the efforts of the extremists to betray the city to the Spartans, it was also intended as a guarantee that the new regime would be governed by the constitution they had always wanted. The soldiers who adopted and chanted the slogan probably would have preferred a direct return to full democracy, had they thought it through but, following the lead of Theramenes and his colleagues, they were satisfied with bringing down the oligarchy of the Four Hundred and preventing their treason.

The moderate leaders who were directing this activity, however, did not want it to lead to a civil war, so their goal was to make the extremists yield, not fight. The following day, after their army finished leveling the fortifications and released Alexicles, they marched toward Athens, but stopped at a parade ground where delegates from the Four Hundred had come to meet them. These representatives promised to publish the list of the Five Thousand and to allow the council of Four Hundred to be chosen from that body in any way it should decide. They urged the soldiers to be calm and not to endanger the state and everyone in it, and convinced them to hold an assembly in the theater of Dionysus on a stipulated day to discuss the restoration of harmony.

The extremists, at least, were not sincere in this offer, for they believed that "to make so many men partners in government was outright democracy" (8.92.11). Their purpose, rather, was to gain time for the Spartans to arrive to save them. A few days later news came that the Spartan fleet was sailing toward Salamis, with the intention of entering the fortifications at Piraeus, unaware that they had been destroyed. The Spartans' expedition may have been part of a plan devised with the Athenian oligarchs to land at Piraeus: if they found Eetioneia in friendly hands they could seize the harbor or block its entrance and starve the Athenians into submission. They might even have been fortunate enough to discover the Athenians torn by civil war and the harbor unguarded. If hostile forces were in control they could always sail by and head for Euboea.

Because the fortification was in ruins, however, their situation was impossible, and at the approach of the enemy fleet the Athenians ran to defend the harbor. The Spartan commander Agesandridas and his forty-two ships sailed past the city, heading south toward Sunium on the way to Euboea. Through the efforts of the moderates and the people, Athens was saved.

THE THREAT TO EUBOEA

BECAUSE EUBOEA "was everything" to the people shut up in the city of Athens, in Piraeus, and in the walled space between them, the Athenians hurried to protect the weakly defended island with a makeshift fleet under Thymochares, a moderate general. Seven miles away across the strait at Oropus, Agesandridas' fleet outnumbered the Athenians forty-two to thirty-six and had the further advantages of more experienced crews with better preparation, a rehearsed plan of battle, the element of surprise, and the collaboration of the Eretrians. Part of their strategy was to deprive the Athenians of a marketplace when they landed, so that they would have to scatter and move inland to find food. When they did so and were separated the Eretrians raised a signal, and Agesandridas attacked. The Athenians were forced to run to their ships and put to sea immediately, leaving them no time to get into formation, so they were soon driven back to shore. The Euboeans killed many who fled for their lives, though some managed to escape to safety in Chalcis and others to an Athenian fort on the island. The Athenians ultimately lost twenty-two ships and their crews, and the Peloponnesians set up a trophy of victory. With the exception of Histiaea at the northern end of Euboea, the entire island joined in the rebellion.

The panic among the Athenians in response to the defeat was greater than it had been after the Sicilian disaster. They had little money left and few ships, and were deprived of access to all of Attica outside the city walls, now including Euboea, which had been serving as a substitute for the occupied territory. The city was torn by dissension and threatened with betrayal. At any time, civil war might break out, or the Athenian fleet at Samos might attack. The populace's greatest fear was that the Peloponnesians would return and attack Piraeus, undefended by an adequate fleet. Thucydides believed that the Spartans could either have blockaded or besieged the port, provoking the fleet at Samos to come to the rescue of their relatives and their city, thereby losing the entire empire from the Hellespont to Euboea. But the Spartans, he says, were "the most convenient of all people for the Athenians to fight" (8.96.5), as they proved on this occasion and many others when they missed an opportunity.

Subsequent events, however, suggest that the Peloponnesians might not necessarily have benefited had they acted more boldly. Within Athens the threat of a Spartan assault led not to civil war but the overthrow of the Four Hundred and the unification of the state under the moderates, an outcome that a Spartan attack would only have hastened. Externally, a Spartan blockade or siege of Piraeus would surely have brought an attack by the Athenian fleet at Samos, which would easily have destroyed the much smaller force under Agesandridas and prevented defections in the empire. The result would be the reunification of the Athenian fleet under the command of moderates like Thrasybulus, and an Athens led by moderates like Theramenes and Aristocrates. A newly unified Athens could then seek out the Peloponnesian fleet with excellent prospects for victory and the recovery of lost territories. The Spartans had good reason, therefore, not to risk an attack on the Athenian port.

THE FALL OF THE FOUR HUNDRED

THE ATHENIANS, of course, did not know what to expect, so they took the necessary steps to defend themselves. After manning twenty ships to protect the harbor as best they could they met on Pnyx, the regular gathering place for the assembly under the democracy, to send a clear message that the current rule had come to an end. They formally deposed the Four Hundred, and "turned affairs over to the Five Thousand" (8.97.1), and they forbade payment for holding any public office.

This was, in effect, a ratification of the moderate program and, since the bulk of the fleet, which was manned by many members of the lower classes, was in Samos, it must have been particularly gratifying to the largely hoplite assembly that voted for it. While some of them would have favored such a constitution in itself, others would have supported it as a step toward the restoration of full democracy. The vigilance and courage of the moderate leaders had saved the city from treason and civil war and halted its movement toward oligarchy. For their actions during this crisis, Theramenes and Aristocrates, perhaps more than the glamorous renegade on Samos, deserve the accolade that they, "more than any other, were useful to the state" (8.86.4).

THE CONSTITUTION OF THE FIVE THOUSAND

IN THE NEW REGIME the rights to vote in the assembly, to serve on juries, and to hold public office were restricted to men of the hoplite census and higher. The seat of power had moved from the council of Four Hundred to the assembly, but how large in actual practice was that assembly? The figure of five thousand was actually more symbolic than real, for it included all men who could provide themselves with hoplite equipment or serve in the cavalry. In September 411, that number may have been as large as ten thousand.

There was also a council that seems to have had five hundred members, who were probably elected, not allotted, and who had greater power and discretion than the old democratic council. In other respects the constitution appears to have been the same as that of the old democracy. The court system apparently functioned in the traditional way, although the juries now excluded the lower classes. In general, apart from the class restrictions, the government of the Five Thousand seems to have functioned very much like that of its democratic predecessor.

In the end the Five Thousand lasted for less than ten months before giving way peacefully to the return of full democracy, as "the people quickly took away their control of the state" (Aristotle, *Constitution of the Athenians* 34.1). Despite its brief duration Thucydides describes the constitution of the Five Thousand as "a moderate mixture in regard to the few and the many" (8.97.2), and judges it the best government Athens had in his lifetime. Aristotle remarks that the Athenians "seem to have been governed well at that time, for a war was in progress, and the state was in the hands of those bearing arms" (*Constitution of the Athenians* 33.2).

The main weakness of the new constitution, however, was that by denying the backbone of the fleet its accustomed civic rights during a war that was predominantly naval, it was bound to encounter a significant challenge. To succeed, the newly empowered moderates would have to unite the hoplites and cavalrymen in the city with the even more important fleet at Samos; once they did so, however, it was only a matter of time until the men who rowed the ships would insist on the restoration of their full political rights. The moderates therefore faced a dilemma in that their future and their city's depended on achieving a union that would inevitably bring an end to the constitution they favored.

THE FIVE THOUSAND IN ACTION

AS A FIRST STEP in reconciling the two camps the Five Thousand voted the recall of Alcibiades and the group of exiles who accompanied him. Theramenes and the other moderates had always wanted to bring Alcibiades back to Athens and take advantage of what they judged to be his incomparable diplomatic and military talents. Just as he had almost brought ruin to the state as its enemy, he might save it when restored. Alcibiades' actions subsequent to its issuance suggest that the actual restoration decree did not provide for a complete exculpation or pardon. Since it confirmed the fleet's election of Alcibiades as general, it must have abolished his status as an outlaw as well as the threat of penalty that went with it, but it may have left him in the same position as in the autumn of 415, after his accusation but before any trial: he would have to come back to Athens to obtain full rehabilitation. Although his chief enemies were now dead or fallen from power and his friends in control, he chose not to return to Athens at once to the welcome of a grateful populace, like a man fully acquitted of all charges and free from dangers; instead, he waited almost four years until the summer of 407. As Plutarch explains, "he thought that he should not come back with empty hands and without achievements, because of the pity and the grace of the masses, but full of glory" (*Alcibiades* 27.1). More likely, he delayed his appearance out of a lasting fear of prosecution.

The new regime was by no means secure in its position. Although some extreme oligarchs fled the city at once, the situation was still so unsettled that many of them felt secure enough to remain and may even have hoped to regain power. The moderates had to proceed cautiously for, despite their leading role in unseating the Four Hundred, many of them had been members of that body. They needed not only to guard against attempts by the extremists to restore the oligarchy or betray the state but also to separate themselves in the public mind from those same extremists who had been their colleagues in the Four Hundred. One of their first official actions, however, was an odd one: the assembly voted a decree against the corpse of Phrynichus, ordering the dead man be charged with treason. When he was subsequently convicted, his bones were exhumed and removed beyond the borders of Attica, his house destroyed, his property confiscated, and the verdict and penalties inscribed on a bronze stele. Apparently, the decree was an attempt to take a reading of public sentiment by attacking a man who had many enemies and was safely dead. Even so, both Aristarchus and Alexicles spoke on Phrynicus's behalf, suggesting that both extremists still felt sufficiently safe to defend their associate.

The test case having proven successful, the moderates next moved against living extremists. Peisander apparently escaped before any sentence could be imposed, but a suit was brought against three leading oligarchs, Archeptolemus, Onomacles, and Antiphon, who were charged with treason for negotiating with the Spartans "to the detriment of the state." Onomacles seems to have fled, but Archeptolemus and Antiphon stayed to defend themselves, for Polystratus, a member of the Four Hundred, had already been released with only a fine, and many others appear to have been acquitted. These two oligarchs, however, were sentenced to death and executed with the same dishonors that were imposed on Phrynicus. Their condemnation and punishment were to be inscribed on a bronze stele to be erected near the ones bearing the decrees concerning Phrynichus, and stones were to be placed on the former sites of their houses bearing the legend "Land of Archeptolemus and Antiphon the two traitors" (Plutarch, *Moralia* 834).

The fate of Archeptolemus and Antiphon must have convinced any remaining extremists to flee, putting an end to any further threat of treason. Their condemnation probably also gained public support for the moderates and strengthened their confidence. Thymochares retained his naval command, and Theramenes felt confident enough to sail to the Hellespont, where he joined Thrasybulus and Alcibiades. The moderates could now turn their attention to the task of how to win the war.

CHAPTER THIRTY-TWO

War in the Hellespont (411–410)

THE NEW REGIME soon faced a deadly challenge from the foreign enemy when a small Peloponnesian fleet reached the key city of Byzantium on the Bosporus and brought about rebellions there and in nearby towns, threatening Athens' grain supply and the city's very survival. Pharnabazus, satrap of northern Asia Minor, urged the Spartans to send a larger fleet at once to exploit their opportunity, but Mindarus did not act quickly.

THE PHANTOM PHOENICIAN FLEET

SPARTA REMAINED bound by its treaty with Persia to cooperate with Tissaphernes in the Ionian region. Although the satrap continued his policy of sporadic and inadequate payments, he had promised to bring the Phoenician fleet into the Aegean where, if joined with the Peloponnesian fleet, the combined force might enable the Spartans to win the war at sea. It therefore seemed prudent to remain patient with Tissaphernes, however long his promise remained unfulfilled. The Phoenician fleet, 147 strong, had in fact traveled as far as Aspendus on the southern shore of Asia Minor but no further, because the satrap was still determined to wear out the Greeks on both sides.

Mindarus waited at Miletus for more than a month before receiving word that Tissaphernes was in fact deceiving the Spartans, and that the Phoenician ships were already on their way back home. This ended their expectations, released the Spartans from their treaty obligations, and freed them to join Pharnabazus in the Hellespont.

To reach there the navarch had to lead his seventy-three ships past the seventy-five Athenian triremes barring his way at Samos. Mindarus preferred to do battle in the confined waters of the Hellespont, where he would always be near land and the fleet could enjoy the support of the Persian army. Responsibility for Samos had been left with the inexperienced Thrasyllus, who, it seems, without ever having commanded a ship or regiment, had been raised from the rank of ordinary hoplite to the office of general because of the important role he had played in checking the oligarchic rebellion on Samos. After successfully containing that uprising he soon faced another challenge when rebellions broke out at the cities of Methymna and Eresus on the island of Lesbos. Athenian forces on the island were adequate to deal with Methymna, and Thrasybulus had taken a small fleet to cope with Eresus. Although Thrasyllus should have sailed to Chios at once to block Mindarus from getting through to the Hellespont, he hurried instead to Lesbos with fifty-five ships, leaving the rest to guard his base on Samos. His strategy was to attack Eresus, keeping Mindarus at Chios by placing lookouts at both ends of that island and on the mainland. He planned a long stay, using Lesbos as a base for attacking the Spartans at Chios.

Trying to accomplish too much at once, Thrasyllus failed in his major task. Mindarus stayed at Chios for only two days to load supplies for the run to the Hellespont and then shrewdly made for the narrow waters between Lesbos and the mainland, a route the Athenians did not expect him to take. He got through and by midnight arrived safely at the mouth of the Hellespont, having traveled some 110 miles in about twenty hours. He not only relocated the theater of operations but altered the course of the war, and the Athenians' failure to prevent this daring and imaginative achievement was a serious error that endangered the very existence of their city.

THE BATTLE OF CYNOSSEMA

THE ATHENIANS' PURSUIT arrived too late to keep Mindarus from joining up with the Peloponnesian fleet at Abydos, its base in the Hellespont (see Map 24). Now under the command of Thrasybulus, they spent the next five days planning and preparing for battle and then, with seventy-six ships, sailed in single file into the Hellespont close to the Gallipoli shore. Thrasybulus had little choice but to take the offensive, for the vital grain route was now at stake. Since the Spartans had no reason to come out into the open sea, the Athenians were forced to engage them within the narrow waters of the Hellespont.

With eighty-six ships the Spartans had numerical superiority, and they could also stay near their base and choose the time and place to fight. With these advantages Mindarus placed his ships in the seven-and-one-half-mile span between Abydos and Dardanus, situating the Syracusans on the right, the farthest up into the Hellespont, while he himself took command of the left wing, nearest its mouth. When the center of the Athenian column reached the point directly in front of the promontory called "Bitch's Tomb" (Cynossema), where the strait was at its narrowest, he attacked, hoping to drive the Athenians to the shore, where the superior fighting ability of his marines would be most effective. He himself took the difficult task of outflanking the enemy to cut off escape, for he intended to destroy the Athenian fleet entirely. If the Spartan center fulfilled its task, the Athenian right wing would race up to help the beleaguered Athenian center, allowing Mindarus to place himself between them and the mouth of the Hellespont, effectively trapping the Athenians. What was left of the Athenian center and the distracted left would be caught between the victorious Spartan center and Mindarus. Then it would be easy to crush the Athenian left further up the Hellespont.

Thrasyllus led the head of the Athenian column, on the left wing opposite the Syracusans, while Thrasybulus commanded the right, opposite Mindarus. The initiative lay with the enemy, so they would have to be ready to react quickly and improvise. Perhaps Thrasybulus anticipated Mindarus' strategy, for he responded brilliantly. When the Athenian center reached the narrowest part of the strait, the Peloponnesians attacked with great success. The left under Thrasyllus was engaged with the Syracusans and could not see what was happening to the center because of a promontory that cut off sight lines down the strait. Victory or defeat for the Athenians, therefore, depended on their right, under Thrasybulus. Had he rushed to the aid of the center, as expected, he would have been badly outnumbered and trapped by the combination of the enemy's center and left, and the entire Athenian fleet would have been annihilated according to Mindarus' plan.

But Thrasybulus detected the trap, and realizing that Mindarus was moving to cut off his escape, he used the greater speed of the Athenians to extend his line beyond that of the enemy. In doing so, however, he weakened the hard put center, which allowed the Peloponnesians to drive many Athenian ships aground, and to land their own troops on the shore. Here the Peloponnesians' naval inexperience and lack of discipline cost them the victory. Had they reorganized their line and joined the left wing of Mindarus in pursuit of the ships of Thrasybulus, they could have sunk or captured many of them; at the very least, they could have destroyed the forces under Thrasyllus and established firm control of the Hellespont. Instead, individual ships went off in pursuit of single Athenian triremes, until the Peloponnesian line was in disorder. At just the right moment, Thrasybulus struck, turning to face the approaching ships of Mindarus and routed them. Then he smashed into the disordered enemy center, and the Peloponnesian fleet fled without resistance toward Sestos. As they came around the bend of Cynossema the Syracusans, seeing their comrades in flight, also hastened to escape, leading the entire Peloponnesian fleet in a race for shelter at Abydos.

In histories of this period we usually see Greek naval battles through the eyes of an admiral who surveys the entire field of battle from the standpoint of the commanders, moving wings, centers, and entire fleets. In these battles at the Hellespont, however, the historian Diodorus gives us a rare glimpse from the decks of individual ships, as witnessed by individual trierarchs. Because the Peloponnesians had better marines, they were more successful in the center, where the fighting must have been at close quarters and grappling and boarding the preferred tactics. They would also have been at an advantage when the Athenians were driven to the shore, and the sea battle became a land battle. In the end, though, the Athenian steersmen, "who were far superior in experience, contributed greatly to the victory" (Diodorus 13.39.5). This factor helps to explain how Thrasybulus, at first hard put by enemy triremes, could later rout these very ships. Confusion in the Peloponnesian center led him to change his strategy. He no longer tried to avoid being blocked out but instead quickly sought battle with

Mindarus in order to take advantage of the disorder, without being caught between two organized lines of the enemy. Whenever the Peloponnesians tried to ram with their entire fleet, the skilled Athenian pilots would maneuver to meet them head-on, ram against ram. Thwarted, Mindarus arranged his ships in small groups, or in individual attacks, but again the Athenian pilots were able to outmaneuver these solo and small-group efforts, ramming and disabling the enemy (Diodorus 13.40.1–2).

Although the Athenians captured only twenty-one ships while losing fifteen of their own, Thrasybulus' crew earned the right to set up the trophy of victory atop the Cynossema promontory. The Athenians back home received word of the triumph as "unhoped-for good fortune," and its timing was excellent. Coming just after the loss of Euboea and the strife surrounding the overthrow of the Four Hundred, it lifted the spirits of the Athenians: "They were greatly encouraged, and they thought that their cause could still win out if they set to work zealously" (8.106).

This victory was of the greatest importance to the course of the remainder of the conflict. At Cynossema Thrasybulus could have lost the war in the space of a single afternoon, for had Mindarus defeated the Athenian fleet on that early October day in 411 the Athenians would probably have been soon forced to surrender. They had no funds to build a new fleet, and another loss after that of Euboea would have encouraged new defections in the empire. The victory of Cynossema prevented that and kept Athens in the war with a chance to emerge from it intact and with honor.

After Cynossema each side carried out raids against the other when opportunities arose, and each tried to increase the size of his fleet in preparation for the next significant skirmish. Well aware that the battle that followed could end the war, Mindarus ordered Syracusan commander Dorieus, who was putting down a rebellion at Rhodes, to bring his fleet north to the Hellespont.

At about the same time Alcibiades returned to Samos from the southern coast of Asia Minor, where he had gone after Tissaphernes had joined the Phoenician fleet at Aspendus. Although he no longer had influence with the satrap, he claimed credit for preventing the arrival of the Phoenicians; his real achievement, however, was in collecting money from the cities of Caria and environs, which in late September he shared with the troops on Samos, winning their favor.

While Thrasybulus fought for survival at Cynossema and both sides sought reinforcements for the next round, Alcibiades stayed at Samos, where he apparently kept watch for Dorieus' fleet, which still threatened Athenian possessions in the south. If that was Alcibiades' assignment, however, he failed to accomplish it, for when he took his fleet to reinforce the Athenians in the Hellespont, it was on the heels of Dorieus, who had slipped by him.

By now the Straits had become the focus of all attention in the region, and even Tissaphernes began to make his way there from Aspendus. With the Peloponnesian fleet no longer in the waters off his satrapy and having entered into a collaboration with Pharnabazus, he feared that his rival would gain glory and favor with Darius by defeating the Athenians, a task at which he himself had failed. But he was motivated by other concerns, as well. The Greek cities of Cnidus and Miletus had launched successful rebellions against him, and Antandrus, with Spartan help, had done the same. The Spartans were sending complaints against him to the government back home, and were no longer dependent upon him but fighting against him. There was no telling what further harm his "allies" might yet do to him.

It was the arrival of Dorieus that sparked the next contest. Before dawn on a day early in November he had tried to slip his fourteen ships into the Hellespont past the Athenian lookouts under cover of darkness, but a watchman signaled the news of his arrival to the Athenian generals at Sestos, who drove him to shore near Rhoeteum. After waiting a while he was able to make his way toward the Spartan base at Abydos, but again he was forced to the shore by an Athenian fleet, this time at Dardanus. When Mindarus learned of Dorieus' danger he raced back from Troy to his base at Abydos and sent word to Pharnabazus. With eighty-four ships he sailed to the rescue while Pharnabazus brought up an army to support Dorieus on land. The Athenians boarded their vessels and prepared for a naval battle.

THE BATTLE OF ABYDOS

WITH NINETY-SEVEN SHIPS, lined up from Dardanus all the way to Abydos, Mindarus commanded the right wing, nearest Abydos, with the Syracusans on the left. That put him opposite Thrasyllus, who commanded the Athenian left, while Thrasybulus was in charge on the right. The battle began when the commanders on each side raised a visible signal, at which trumpeters sounded the attack. The fighting was fierce and evenly matched for a long time until finally, toward evening, eighteen ships appeared on the horizon. Each side was encouraged by what it took to be the arrival of its own reinforcements, but then the fleet's commander, Alcibiades, ran up a red flag that told the Athenians the squadron was theirs.

This was not a matter of luck; the signal must have been prearranged and Alcibiades expected. What was fortunate was the timing of his arrival. While he could not have taken part in planning the tactics of the battle and showed up too late to do much fighting, his appearance was decisive.

When Mindarus realized the approaching vessels were Athenian, he led his vessels toward Abydos. The Peloponnesian forces were extended over a long distance, and many were forced to beach their ships along the shore, where they attempted to defend them on land. Pharnabazus brought up his cavalry and infantry to assist them, the satrap himself riding his horse into the sea to ward off the enemy. His intervention and the coming of darkness prevented a total disaster, but the Athenians captured thirty Peloponnesian ships and recovered the fifteen they had lost at Cynossema. Mindarus escaped to Abydos under cover of night with the remains of his fleet, and the Athenians retired to Sestos. The next morning they returned at leisure to collect their damaged ships and set up another trophy of victory, not far from the first one at Cynossema. Once again, the Athenians commanded the waters of the Hellespont.

While Mindarus repaired his vessels, sent home for reinforcements, and planned with Pharnabazus for the next campaign, the Athenians should have been requesting support of their own and trying to force a battle to annihilate what was left of the Peloponnesian fleet in the Hellespont. If Mindarus refused to fight, they ought to have set up a fleet to block enemy naval reinforcement while they recovered the cities that had rebelled from their empire in the region of the Hellespont, Propontis, and Bosporus. They were able to do none of these things, however, because the Athenian treasury was exhausted and could not even sustain the entire fleet in the Hellespont over the winter. In addition, during the battles at Cynossema and Abydos, the narrowness of the Hellespont invited hard put Peloponnesian triremes to avoid defeat by going ashore, but the Athenian forces were short of hoplites to counter such tactics. Finally, Athens also needed naval support closer to home, for Euboea was still in rebellion.

To meet that latter challenge Theramenes took a fleet of thirty ships to deal with the rebels who, aided by their new allies, the Boeotians, were building a causeway between Chalcis and Aulis, connecting the island to the mainland. Theramenes' force proved to be too small to defeat the troops defending the workers, and instead he devastated enemy land along the Euboean and Boeotian coasts, collecting considerable booty. He then proceeded to make his way around the Cyclades islands, putting down oligarchies established by the Four Hundred, gathering badly needed cash, and winning prestige for the new regime of the Five Thousand.

Having accomplished as much as he could in the Aegean, Theramenes sailed to Macedonia to help its new king, Archelaus, in his siege of Pydna. Macedonia was still the major source of timber for shipbuilding in Greece, and Archelaus appears to have supplied Athens with it and, probably, with money as well. Theramenes next went to join Thrasybulus, who had been collecting funds by plundering oligarchic Thasos and other places in Thrace. From there the combined fleets could quickly reach the Hellespont in case of emergency.

Alcibiades, meanwhile, was with the fleet at Sestos when Tissaphernes arrived in the Hellespont, and he greeted the satrap as an intimate and benefactor. The Athenians still believed that the two men were on good terms and that Alcibiades had persuaded Tissaphernes to send the Phoenician fleet home. Alcibiades kept the truth to himself and sailed with gifts to meet the Persian, but he had misjudged the situation badly, for the satrap had no wish for friendship with Athens. The Spartans had blamed Tissaphernes for their defeats, and their complaints had certainly reached the Great King, who must already have been displeased that Tissaphernes had kept his fleet at Aspendus, at great expense, without making use of it. As a result the Athenians were now in the Hellespont and the King was no closer to recovering his lost territory.

Tissaphernes had every reason to be "afraid that he would be blamed by the King" for this situation (Plutarch, *Alcibiades* 27.5). He accordingly arrested Alcibiades and sent him to Sardis for safekeeping, but within a month the clever Athenian escaped. The affair made it inescapably clear that Alcibiades no longer had any influence with Tissaphernes, and from then on his authority would depend on what he actually accomplished, rather than on what he promised to do through his Persian connection.

THE BATTLE OF CYZICUS

BY THE SPRING OF 410 Mindarus had collected eighty triremes. With only forty ships the Athenian commanders left Sestos by night and sailed to Cardia on the northern shore of Gallipoli, but Thrasybulus and Theramenes in Thrace and Alcibiades at Lesbos hurried to meet them. The fleet at Cardia now numbered eighty-six ships, and "its generals were eager for a decisive battle" (Diodorus 13.39.4). Mindarus and Pharnabazus, meanwhile, besieged Cyzicus on the southern shore of the Propontis (see Map 25) and took it by storm. The Athenian generals set out to recover the city and, moving by night to avoid detection, came to the island of Proconnesus, just northwest of the peninsula on which Cyzicus was located.

At Proconnesus Alcibiades exhorted the sailors and soldiers to "fight at sea, on land, and against fortifications, for the enemy had plenty of money from the King, but [the Athenians] would have none unless they won a total victory." (Xenophon, *Hellenica* 1.1.14; Plutarch, *Alcibiades*, 28). The fleet headed for Cyzicus in heavy rain, risking the dangers of stormy seas in return for its concealment of their approach and the actual size of their force. They sailed down the western side of the peninsula, between the mainland and the island of Haloni. At the Artaki promontory and the island of the same name not far off shore,

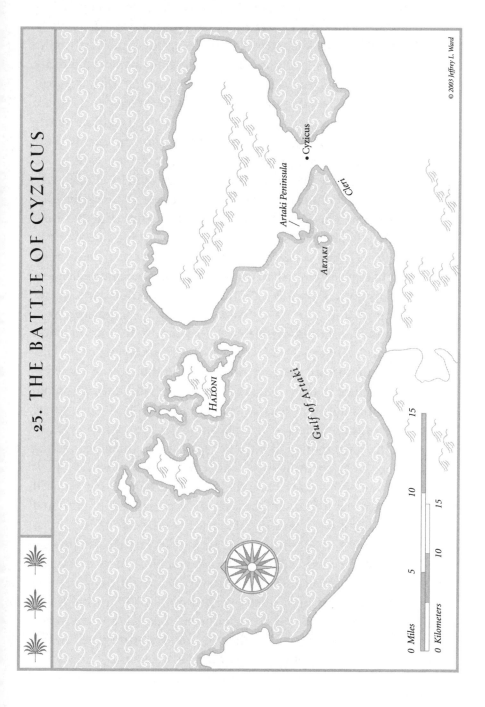

25. THE BATTLE OF CYZICUS

Cyzicus

Artaki Peninsula

Cleri

ARTAKI

HALONI

Gulf of Artaki

0 Miles   5   10   15

0 Kilometers   10   15

© 2003 Jeffrey L. Ward

they split their forces: Chaereas and his hoplites landed and marched against Cyzicus; dividing forty-six ships between them, Theramenes and Thrasybulus each hid his fleet in the little harbor to the north of the promontory; with the remaining forty ships Alcibiades moved directly toward Cyzicus. Mindarus must have thought that the Athenians had only the forty ships based in the Hellespont and were ignorant of how large his own forces had actually grown, when with all eighty triremes he sailed against them, eager to fight at what he thought were two-to-one odds. The Athenian ships fled in apparent panic to the west, in the direction of the island, but when Mindarus' ships were far enough into the harbor, Alcibiades turned to face the pursuing enemy. Meanwhile, Theramenes moved his force from behind the promontory in the direction of Cyzicus to prevent the Peloponnesians from being able to return to the city or to reach the beaches close to it. At the same time, Thrasybulus took his squadron south to cut off the escape route from the west.

Mindarus quickly perceived the trap that had been set for him and turned back in time to prevent Thrasybulus and Theramenes from completing their encirclement. He raced for safety in the one direction open to him, toward a place called Cleri, a beach southwest of the city, where Pharnabazus had encamped his army. Although the Peloponnesians pulled their triremes onto the beach, Alcibiades used grappling hooks to try to haul them back to sea. Pharnabazus now came to the rescue with his army, which outnumbered the enemy and had the advantage of the firm footing of the land, against the Athenians wading through the water. The Athenians fought well, but without help their prospects were poor. At sea Thrasybulus saw the danger and signaled Theramenes to join forces with the army of Chaereas near Cyzicus and come to the aid of the embattled Athenians while he and his marines hurried to help them from the west. Seeing Thrasybulus' approach, Mindarus sent Clearchus with a part of his own force and a contingent of Pharnabazus' mercenaries to stop him. With only the hoplites and archers from no more than about twenty-five ships, Thrasybulus was badly outnumbered and was about to be surrounded and destroyed when Theramenes arrived just in time, leading his own and Chaereas' troops. The reinforcement revived Thrasybulus' exhausted men, and a bitter battle ensued, until Pharnabazus' mercenaries and the Spartans finally fled the field.

With Thrasybulus' contingent safe, Theramenes went to the assistance of Alcibiades, who was still fighting for the ships at the shore. Mindarus now found himself caught between the troops of Alcibiades and Theramenes' corps, approaching from the opposite direction. Unfazed the Spartan commander sent half his troops to meet Theramenes, while he formed a line against Alcibiades. When he died fighting bravely among the ships, however, his men and their allies panicked and fled, and only the arrival of Pharnabazus with his cavalry halted the Athenian pursuit.

The Athenians withdrew to Proconnesus while the remaining Peloponnesians fled to the safety of Pharnabazus' camp. They later abandoned Cyzicus, which returned to the control of the Athenians, who took many prisoners, a vast collection of booty, and all the enemy's ships except those from Syracuse, whose crews had burned them before they could fall into enemy hands. The Athenians set up two trophies to commemorate their victories on land and sea.

Alcibiades remained at Cyzicus for twenty days to collect money and then set out to the north shore of the Propontis, in the direction of the Bosporus, seizing cities and funds en route. At Chrysopolis, opposite Byzantium, he built a fort as a base and as a customs house, at which the Athenians would thereafter assess a duty of one-tenth on all merchant ships passing through the Bosporus.

In Plutarch's assessment the chief result of the battle at Cyzicus was that, "Not only did the Athenians securely hold the Hellespont, they also drove the Spartans from the rest of the sea in any force" (*Alcibiades* 28.6). Perhaps as significant an effect was the blow to Spartan morale. After the battle the Athenians intercepted a letter from Hippocrates, secretary to the fallen Spartan navarch, that described the Peloponnesians' predicament with Laconic brevity: "The ships are lost. Mindarus is dead. The men are starving. We know not what to do" (Xenophon, *Hellenica* 1.1.23).

The victory at Cyzicus also removed the threat to Athens' food supply for the moment and restored its hopes of victory. Both Xenophon and Plutarch give Alcibiades exclusive credit for the triumph, but Theramenes and Thrasybulus deserve at least an equal share. Although we do not know who was responsible for the excellent naval strategy that worked so well at Cyzicus, we can be sure that Alcibiades had no hand in planning the strategies at Cynossema or Abydos, for he was absent from the first and arrived at the second only when it was almost concluded. Alcibiades fought splendidly at Cyzicus and carried out his assignment to perfection, while Theramenes's performance was also outstanding, and it was his appearance with reinforcements that ultimately assured on Athenian success.

A careful examination of the events, however, strongly suggests that once again Thrasybulus' role was decisive. Since Diodorus tells us that he was both the leader of the entire fleet and the decisive commander at Cynossema, he probably also devised the tactical plan at Abydos and had the leading strategic role at Cyzicus. For all of the brilliance of the naval portion of the fighting, the outcome was determined on land. The key moment came when Alcibiades was under attack by Mindarus and the army of Pharnabazus. If he had been left to his own devices, he would surely have been driven off and forced to abandon most of his ships, where they could be protected by Pharnabazus' infantry and cavalry. At the crucial moment, however, Thrasybulus landed with a small force that diverted a part of the enemy's troops and saved Alcibiades. No less critical was the order he gave to Theramenes that sealed the victory. At a strategist, a tactician, and a brilliant commander in the field, Thrasybulus deserves to be regarded as the hero of Cyzicus. We would do well to respect the judgment of Cornelius Nepos, a Roman biographer: "In the Peloponnesian War Thrasybulus accomplished many victories without Alcibiades; the latter accomplished nothing without the former, yet he, by some gift of his nature, gained the credit for everything" (Cornelius Nepos, *Thrasybulus*, 1.3).

Part Seven

THE FALL OF ATHENS

WHEN ADDED TO THEIR LOSSES in Sicily, the civil strife that ravaged Athens in 411 ought to have been the last straw and produced its defeat but, with remarkable resilience, the restored Athenian democracy fought on for seven more years. Even when their enemies gained the support of the Persian Empire the Athenians were able to regain the mastery of the seas and compel the Spartans to ask for peace once again. The restored democracy benefited from the victories won by the Five Thousand, dealt with the city's practical problems, and called forth again the powerful popular loyalties and energies that had brought Athens to greatness.

CHAPTER THIRTY-THREE

The Restoration (410–409)

By THE CONCLUSION of the battle of Cyzicus the Peloponnesians had lost between 135 and 155 ships within the space of a few months. Athens controlled the seas everywhere as well as access to the vital food supply from the lands of the Black Sea. Neither Persian money nor the fort at Decelea seemed to promise victory, and no other strategy seemed available. The Athenians, moreover, had taken enough prisoners to make the enemy—as it had been in 425—eager for a peace that would bring them home.

SPARTA'S PEACE OFFER

THE SPARTANS, therefore, in violation of their treaty with Persia, sued for peace. Endius, their chief negotiator and a man who was close to Alcibiades, set forth Sparta's proposal: "We wish to make peace with you, men of Athens, and that each side should keep the cities it now controls but abandon the garrisons it holds in the other's territory, ransoming prisoners, one Athenian for one Laconian" (Diodorus 13.52.1–2).

The cessation of warfare, a trade of Pylos for Decelea, and an exchange of prisoners would surely have been welcome to the Athenians, but maintaining the status quo in the empire was a different matter entirely. The Spartans still held Rhodes, Miletus, Ephesus, Chios, Thasos, and Euboea in the Aegean; a number of places on the Thracian coast; Abydos in the Hellespont; and Byzantium and Chalcedon on either side of the Bosporus. The common view is that "the most reasonable of the Athenians" favored acceptance of these terms, but the assembly rejected them, deceived by "practiced warmongers who made private profit from public troubles" (Diodorus 13.53).

The Athenians rejected peace, so goes this interpretation, because they foolishly allowed themselves to be swayed by reckless popular leaders, chief among whom was Cleophon, "the greatest demagogue at that time" (Diodorus 13.53.2). Cleophon was a favorite butt of satirical attacks by the comic poets and an object of contempt and loathing by more serious writers. The comedians dismiss him as a lyre maker (just as they denigrate Cleon as a tanner, Lysicles as a cattle dealer, Eucrates as a flax merchant, and Hyperbolus as a lamp maker), a lowly craftsman of no family background. His mother is alleged to have been a barbarian and he himself a rapacious foreigner. More serious writers describe him as a drunkard, a cutthroat, and a raving wild man in his public behavior. Although his style may well have been vehement and indecorous, this portrait is biased and inaccurate. Cleophon was an Athenian, and his father served as a general in 428/7. He himself may also have been a general and a member of the board of financial officials called *poristai*. After his death an orator could observe justly that Cleophon "had managed all the affairs of the state for many years" (Lysias 19.48). He must have owned a workshop or factory, which made him a man of means, as his father must have been.

Since the peace proposal was introduced during the constitution of the Five Thousand, Cleophon must have been a man of at least of hoplite status, though probably higher, in order to have taken part in the debate. Against the claim that he acted from motives of personal gain is the fact that we are told of no such accusation against him for peculation or corruption, at a time when such complaints against politicians were common; there is also evidence that he died a poor man.

Cleophon did take a more hopeful view of Athens' prospects in the war and argued for fighting on until it had won a total victory. No doubt he was persuasive, but many Athenians, understandably impressed by the magnificent triumph at Cyzicus and enthusiastically crediting it to Alcibiades, believed that under his leadership, "they would quickly recover their empire" (Diodorus 13.53.4). But there were more legitimate reasons for rejecting the Spartan offer than merely reveling in victory and optimism about future prospects: if the peace failed, as an earlier one had after 421, the Athenians would be in much greater danger than on the former occasion.

For the moment, the Athenian victory at Cyzicus had destroyed the Spartan fleet and left the Straits free, to the merchant ships that brought essential food to Athens from the Black Sea.

As matters now stood, however, Pharnabazus could build the Peloponnesians another fleet, and perhaps even a bigger one. From Byzantium and Chalcedon they held the choke-point of the Athenian grain route and could threaten Athens with starvation. The Athenians remained short of funds, with many sources of imperial income still in Spartan hands, so the enemy could outbid them for the services of experienced rowers from the empire. Athens would also be hard put to maintain and man a fleet that would have to be sent into the Hellespont and defeat the enemy again. There was no certainty that they could repeat such a victory, and a single major defeat would lose the war.

Swift action, on the other hand, could deprive the enemy of its bases along the route to the Black Sea and make the Straits secure. The Athenians would also have a good chance of recovering their lost territories in the Aegean, as well as capitalizing on the impression made by their victory at Cyzicus, which would encourage their friends and awe their enemies. The reclamation of lost subject cities and control of the seas would enable a restoration of Athenian finances to something like their previous level, permit the improvement of the fleet, and discourage defections by experienced rowers.

The Athenians also had reason to hope that the alliance between Sparta and Persia would not last. Tissaphernes had infuriated the Spartans and lost their trust. Further attacks on the lands of Pharnabazus, who was already stunned by the outcome at Cyzicus, might lead the Persian satrap and king to abandon their Greek involvement. The Great King, who ruled a vast empire frequently troubled with rebellions, might be compelled to abandon the war on his western boundaries if faced with a serious revolt elsewhere. Finally, the Spartans' offer of a separate peace with Athens violated their treaty with Persia and might in itself produce a breach. In light of these realities and possibilities, the Athenians' decision to reject a peace offer need not be judged foolish, but is entirely understandable.

DEMOCRACY RESTORED

WITHIN TWO MONTHS of the Athenians' refusal of the peace proposal, the Five Thousand acceded to the restoration of the full democracy that Athens had practiced before the introduction of *probouloi* in 413. The transition may have been gradual, but there had to have been a decisive moment when the exclusive powers of the Five Thousand were abolished and full political rights returned to the entire citizen body. That point may have come after the rejection of Sparta's offer of peace. However unifying was the triumph at Cyzicus, the Spartan initiative that resulted from it was terribly divisive. The moderates must have been among "the most reasonable Athenians" who favored accepting it, but the majority clearly thought otherwise. The debate over the peace—the only important event we are aware of between the battle at Cyzicus and the restoration of democracy—is likely to have been the precipitating event that led to the overthrow of the Five Thousand. Once the decision was made to continue the war, it was easy for the Athenians to conclude that those who wanted peace were no longer the men to be entrusted with leading the state to total victory. The repudiation of the Spartan offer thus amounted to the defeat of the government in a vote of confidence.

In the controversy leading to the restoration the democrats also had many advantages. They found a talented and effective leader in Cleophon, while Theramenes, the best spokesman for the moderates, was on duty at Chrysopolis; the hypnotic Alcibiades, of course, was also absent. More fundamentally, anyone then speaking in favor of democracy in Athens implicitly held the high moral ground. That form of rule was now over a century old and had the passionate attachment of a large majority, who regarded it as their traditional and natural government. Oligarchy of any kind was considered to be an innovation to which Athens had yielded only in the darkest hours of its history, when no other solution seemed possible. Accordingly, the democratic political leaders swiftly seized the chance to return to the traditional regime. By June 410 someone must have proposed the abolition of the Five Thousand and the restoration of the traditional democratic constitution; by early July the old democracy was firmly in place and passing fierce laws to defend itself against its enemies.

The policies of the newly restored democracy form a consistent, coherent, and comprehensive program for waging war under a thoroughly democratic and effective regime. The legislation introduced in 410/9 covered constitutional, legal, financial, social, and spiritual matters, and helped guide a city only recently recovered from defeat and despair to remarkable efforts and astonishing success.

The first known document of the restored democracy begins with the customary democratic formula: "Enacted by the Council and the People" (Andocides, *On the Mysteries* 96). The "People" refers to the assembly, while the "Council" is the old council of Five Hundred, chosen by allotment from all classes of citizens. After the experience of oligarchic councils, the democrats put new limits even on this very democratic one, which seems to have lost the power to impose the death penalty or fines above five hundred drachmas without the consent of the assembly or the popular courts. Another new law required members of the council to take seats assigned them by lot, which was an effort to reduce the influence of factions sitting together.

The rapid change from Four Hundred to Five Thousand and back to full democracy produced considerable confusion about the laws. Both brief regimes had appointed boards to examine, change, and introduce new legislation, which alarmed the democrats and made them eager to validate the traditional statutes. They appointed a board of registrars (*anagrapheis*) to publish an authoritative version of the laws of Solon and Draco's law on homicide.

The old rules, however, had failed to protect the democracy from subversion, so the Athenians enacted legislation providing that anyone taking part in the destruction of the democracy or holding office in a regime after its suppression be declared an enemy of Athens; such men were to be killed with impunity, and their possessions were to become public property. The people were required to swear an oath to uphold this law, which was inscribed on stone at the entrance to the council chamber and remained in force well into the fourth century.

In 409 the Athenians gave citizenship and awarded a golden crown and other benefits to the men who had killed Phrynichus two years earlier. In the years that followed there was a rash of accusations aimed at former members of the Four Hundred, men who had held office under them, and any who had served them, although membership in the Four Hundred was not a crime in itself. Penalties for conviction at a trial included exile, fines, and loss of a citizen's rights. Some of the charges were, no doubt, venal and little more than forms of extortion, arousing bitter criticism of the democrats by some in the upper classes. The Athenian democracy, however, behaved with relative restraint when compared with the the victors in civil wars in other states, who often put the losing factions to death or exiled them in great numbers merely for having been members of the ousted group. The restored democracy, on the other hand, did not outlaw the members of the Four Hundred, some of whom were elected to the highest offices in the new government, even as generals. No retroactive decrees were issued, and actions that were taken were directed against particular individuals and for specific offenses. No general executions or exiles took place, and penalties seem to have been assigned in proportion to the gravity of offenses.

With the restoration of democracy came the revival of payment for service on the council and on juries, and for other public services. The war had inflicted great suffering on the poor and brought poverty to many who had previously not been needy, so Cleophon introduced a new public subvention called the *diobelia*, because it paid each recipient two obols (a third of a drachma) daily. It was probably given to needy citizens when money was available.

In later years critics denounced the *diobelia* as a form of bribery and corruption, and as an encouragement of the base human appetite for gain that begins with small sums but inevitably increases over time. When introduced, however, such measures were necessary and could not have cost too much.

Even so, the Athenians continued to need a great deal of money to carry on the war, and while the treasury was almost empty, the revival of Athenian power and prestige after Cyzicus promised to generate income. Although subject states had already been defaulting on their payments, the Athenians in their new confidence restored the old tribute system in place of the tax on trade, expecting to collect both arrears and current assessments. The restored democracy was also willing to impose another direct war tax (*eisphora*), which made its initial appearance in 428, although it seems to have been levied on only one other occasion before the end of the war. The poor did not pay these imposts, but most Greeks, including the Athenians, found direct taxes of any kind objectionable, and even the restored democracy resorted to them only when the need was inescapable.

The resumption of the building program on the Acropolis, which had been suspended since the Sicilian expedition, also contributed to the financial burden. While the continuation of construction may have been portrayed as a form of aid to the needy, the new program was actually very small compared to the series of great works undertaken before the war, and consisted only of a new parapet for the temple of Athena Nike and the completion of the temple to Athena Polias (the Erechtheum, as it is known today). Not many workers were needed, and their term of service was brief. Inscriptions of the accounts for the project reveal that only twenty of seventy-one workers were citizens, the rest being slaves and resident aliens. That is no way for democratic politicians to organize construction projects meant to give work to the voters. We should imagine a broader purpose, an effort to revive the spirit of the great days of Pericles. The sight of great and new buildings was meant to bring confidence, hope, and courage to the men who must gain victory over formidable foes after suffering terrible misfortunes.

The parapet may have been a monument to the great victory at Cyzicus, but completion of the Erechtheum seems to have been an act of civic piety. While the Periclean era had been an age of enlightenment and the questioning of tradition, the sufferings of war, pestilence, and defeat had resulted in a turn to mystical and orgiastic foreign cults from abroad. Even with the rational and scientific Hippocratic school of medicine at its height, the Athenians imported from Epidaurus the cult of Asclepius, the god represented by a serpent, who cured by miracles.

It was in this climate that the restored democracy chose to use precious funds to finish the temple to Athena Polias, the oldest home of the patron goddess of the city, protector of the Acropolis itself. The precinct of the Erechtheum also contained the most ancient shrines of the Acropolis; sites connected with fertility cults, earth deities, and hero cults whose origins stretched into the remote Bronze Age; tombs of the ancient legendary kings; the miraculous olive tree of Athena; the trident mark and saline springs left by Poseidon; the crevice in which the child god Erechthonius was believed to guard the Acropolis in serpent form; and others.

The completion of the Erechtheum, therefore, was traditional in its aims, much like the publication of the ancient laws of Draco and Solon. Both were undertaken to win the favor of the gods and to lend self-assurance and courage to the Athenian people as they faced the tasks that lay ahead of them.

THE WAR RESUMED

IN JULY AGIS tried to take advantage of the most recent change of regime in Athens to attack the city. The united Athenians, however, had prepared a defense, and the sight of their army exercising outside the walls led him to retreat to Decelea. Before he could escape, however, the Athenians were able to pick off some enemy laggards, and their success in the skirmish bolstered the confidence of the new regime. During the same summer anti-Spartan forces gained control of Chios, and the city of Neapolis on the Thracian coast fended off an assault by the Thasians and some Peloponnesian forces, remaining loyal to Athens. The Spartans suffered an additional reverse in the winter of 410/9 when their colony at Heraclea in Trachis was defeated by its neighbors, in the course of which some seven hundred colonists and the Spartan governor perished. Of even greater damage was the entry of Carthage into a war against Syracuse in the summer of 409. Their invasion forced the Syracusans to withdraw their fleet from the Aegean and Hellespont and deprived the Spartans of their ablest, most daring, and most determined naval allies.

Despite these developments the year 410/9 brought more losses than gains to the Athenians. In the winter of 411/0, before the democratic restoration, a new civil war on Corcyra took that island out of the great war, a blow to Athens. A more serious loss was the Spartans' capture of the Athenian fort at Pylos, which removed a great annoyance to Sparta and deprived Athens of a valuable bargaining counter.

The following summer Athens also lost Nisaea to the Megarians, though the decisive theater proved to be on the sea, in the Aegean and the Straits, where the Athenians suffered setbacks as well. A Spartan fleet under the new admiral Cratesippidas returned Chios to Spartan control, but a more serious problem was the Athenians' failure to exploit the great victory at Cyzicus in the Straits. Impressive as that victory was, it nonetheless left vital cities such as Sestos, Byzantium, and Chalcedon in enemy hands. Because Pharnabazus had given the Spartans money after the battle to finance construction of another fleet as large as the one that had been destroyed, the Athenians would be forced to fight to gain supremacy in the Hellespont unless they prevented the enemy from controlling key ports. They needed to move quickly in the Aegean, as well, if they were to recover the rebellious cities and the income they could provide. From December 411 to April or May of 409, however, Thrasyllus, the general who had come home to collect reinforcements, remained in Athens, and between the spring of 410 and the winter of 409/8 the generals in the Hellespont undertook no significant campaigns.

The Athenians actually had good reasons to wait until 409 to dispatch a new force to the Hellespont. The deployment that eventually left included fifty triremes, 5,000 of their rowers equipped as peltasts and light-armed infantry; 1,000 hoplites and 100 cavalry, with 11,000 men in all. At the low rate of pay in effect after Sicily—three obols a day—the cost of such an expedition would be almost thirty talents a month, and the fleet could not set sail without several months' salary in hand. Troop and horse carriers for the hoplites and cavalry would be an additional expense, and the state would have to provide the peltasts with weapons. But funds from various sources did not become available to the depleted treasury, and the Athenians appear not to have had a sufficient number of triremes prepared, until 409.

Thrasyllus finally set out in the summer of that year, but to Ionia via Samos rather than to the Hellespont. Although the Athenians in the Straits had by now lost the advantage created by the victory at Cyzicus they did not face any immediate danger. On the other hand, Ionia offered excellent opportunities. No Spartan fleet protected it, Tissaphernes had been weakened by revolts in Miletus, Cnidus, and

Antandrus in his satrapy, and friends of Athens lurked in most Ionia cities, waiting to bring them over if the chance presented itself. Victories there would gain prestige and badly needed money and set the stage for more vital actions in the Hellespont, where Thrasyllus was ordered to go after completing his task in Ionia.

Thrasyllus arrived at Samos in June 409 and quickly landed on the Ionian mainland to recover lost subject cities, harass Tissaphernes' territory and collect booty. After achieving some small successes, including regaining Colophon, he suffered a defeat at Ephesus that forced him to give up the Ionian campaign. Instead, he sailed north along the coast and reached the Hellespont just before winter.

Thrysallus' failures on Ionia revealed his shortcomings as a general. On two occasions, he wasted time by ravaging the country and allowing the enemy to prepare for his attack. Had he moved against Ephesus at once, the Athenians might have taken the city as easily as they had recaptured Colophon. In the battle for the city he also employed faulty tactics, dividing his forces with dire results. Although the first major campaign of the new democratic regime was a failure, most of Thrasyllus' force was intact, and it still had time to achieve important results under more experienced and skillful leaders.

CHAPTER THIRTY-FOUR

The Return of Alcibiades (409–408)

ATHENS ATTEMPTS TO CLEAR THE STRAITS

WHEN THRASYLLUS' ATHENIAN reinforcements finally arrived in the Hellespont late in 409 his troops were not readily accepted by the men already posted there. Alcibiades tried to integrate the two forces, but the veterans of the battles in the Straits refused to permit Thrasyllus' men, who came fresh from defeat and disgrace, within their ranks. The two generals, nevertheless, moved all their forces to Lampsacus on the Asiatic side of the Hellespont, a base well situated for raids against Pharnabazus and for an attack on the main Spartan base at Abydos. With the addition of their land forces to their unchallenged navy, they could move down the coast and threaten the enemy from land and sea. Over the winter of 409/8 the Athenians fortified Lampsacus, and then they led an assault on Abydos.

Thrasyllus took thirty ships and landed near the city. Pharnabazus came to the rescue with infantry and cavalry, but Alcibiades was already en route over land with the Athenian cavalry and 120 hoplites, his arrival timed to strike Pharnabazus while the satrap was engaged with Thrasyllus' force. The Athenians routed the Persians, set up a trophy of victory, and raided the territory of Pharnabazus, collecting much booty. Pharnabazus' quick response had saved Abydos, which remained in Spartan hands, so the victory was a strategic failure. The triumph did, however, result in the healing of the rift in the Athenian army: "The two factions were united and returned to camp together with mutual good will and joy" (Plutarch, *Alcibiades* 29.2).

In the spring of 408, the united Athenians set out to drive the enemy from the Bosporus and gain free passage to the Black Sea, moving first against Chalcedon on the Asian side (see Map 26), whose defenses Clearchus had improved nearly two years earlier. The Spartans'

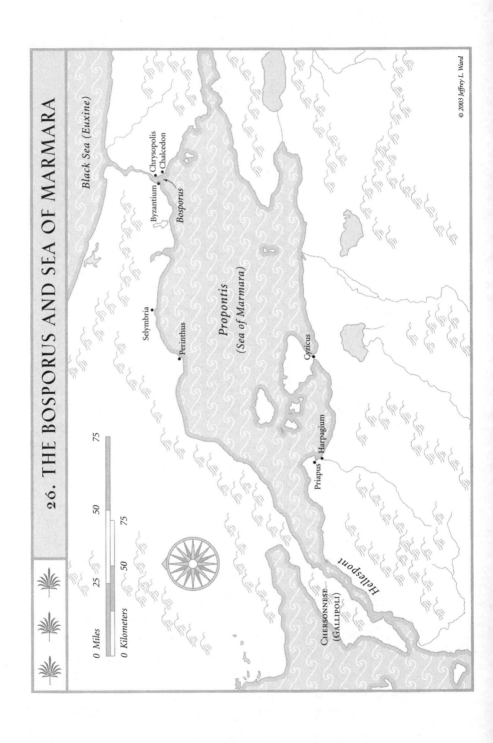

26. THE BOSPORUS AND SEA OF MARMARA

Black Sea (Euxine)

Chrysopolis
Chalcedon
Byzantium
Bosporus

Selymbria
Perinthus

Propontis
(Sea of Marmara)

Cyzicus

Harpagium
Priapus

Hellespont

CHERSONNESE
(GALLIPOLI)

0 Miles   25   50   75
0 Kilometers   50   75

© 2003 Jeffrey L. Ward

garrison there was now commanded by Hippocrates, the harmost, or governor. From his base at Chrysopolis, Theramenes began the devastation of the Chalcedonian lands and was soon joined by Alcibiades and Thrasyllus with a fleet of perhaps 190 ships.

To begin their siege of the walled city of Chalcedon the Athenians built their own wooden wall from the Bosporus to the Sea of Marmora. This enclosed the Chalcedonians within a triangle of land, with the Athenian army and the wooden palisade between them and the Persians. With the Athenian fleet in control of the sea their encirclement was complete. The Spartan army came out to fight, and Thrasyllus marched against them with his hoplites. The wall kept Pharnabazus' infantry and cavalry from joining the fight, and Alcibiades took his cavalry and a small body of hoplites into the battle after it had gone on for some time, which finally broke the Spartan resistance. Hippocrates was killed, but his army escaped to the city, closed its gates, and continued the defense. Once again the Athenians failed in the very difficult task of taking a city by means other than siege. Alcibiades departed in search of money on the Hellespontine shores, leaving the campaign in the hands of his colleagues.

Although shut in by land and sea, Chalcedon's defenders were not without hope, for Pharnabazus had a large force only a short distance away that might still get through the barrier and challenge the Athenians from the rear. That may account for the Athenian generals' negotiation of a treaty with Pharnabazus on the following terms: the Chalcedonians would pay their former level of tribute to Athens along with the arrears that had accumulated, and Pharnabazus would pay the Athenians twenty talents and take Athenian ambassadors to the Great King. The Athenians, in turn, swore not to attack the Chalcedonians or the territory of Pharnabazus until the ambassadors returned.

Unlike the usual settlements with recovered subject cities, this arrangement kept the Athenians out of Chalcedon but awarded them their tribute, arrears, and what amounted to an indemnity paid by Pharnabazus on behalf of the city. This provided the Athenians with badly needed immediate cash and promised them income in the future, saved them the cost of a siege, and freed them to move against Byzantium. The agreement, moreover, was temporary, in force only until negotiations with the Great King could be completed. It also allowed Pharnabazus to keep the city without having to withstand a siege and a battle he would rather avoid. The negotiations might make further fighting unnecessary, or other events might prevent an Athenian victory. Meanwhile he held Chalcedon, which was worth the twenty talents and a strange compromise.

Although this special arrangement left Chalcedon in enemy hands, Athenian strategy called for the ultimate recovery of all coastal cities in the straits. Alcibiades, therefore, gathered funds and Thracian troops from the Gallipoli Peninsula and attacked Selymbria, on the north shore of the Propontis. Avoiding a siege or assault, he plotted with a pro-Athenian party within the city, who opened its gates to him at night. He offered the Selymbrians reasonable terms and imposed strict discipline to see that they were observed. No harm came to the city or its citizens; the Athenians merely placed a garrison there and collected some money. It was a skillful performance that saved time, resources, and lives and still fully achieved its goal. This was the kind of warfare in which Alcibiades excelled.

To the east of Selymbria was Byzantium, the remaining key that would unlock the Bosporus and the route to the Black Sea. Alcibiades moved quickly to join Theramenes and Thrasyllus, who had gone there from the siege of Chalcedon. In spite of the Athenians' domination of the sea, their considerable land forces and adequate funds to support those forces, they discovered once again that taking a powerful walled city like Byzantium was no easy task. They repeated their strategy of building a wall to cut off the city on the landward side while their fleet prevented access by sea. Clearchus, a tough Spartan harmost, commanded the defense of the city. With him was a corps of *perioikoi* and a few *neodamodeis*, contingents from Megara and Boeotia, and a body of mercenaries; he himself was the only Spartan.

When the Athenians' assault on the city was unsuccessful Clearchus entrusted the defense of Byzantium to his subordinates and went to Pharnabazus on the Asian shore to collect pay for his troops. He also wanted to assemble a fleet to draw the Athenians away from Byzantium by attacking their allies in the Straits. Conditions in Byzantium, however, were much worse than Clearchus realized. Its people were hungry, and he was proving to be a governor in the Spartan mold, harsh and arrogant. His behavior finally angered enough influential Byzantines that they joined Alcibiades in a conspiracy. Promising the Byzantines the same leniency he had shown Selymbria, he persuaded them to let the Athenians enter the city on a fixed night. Spreading a false story of an Athenian mission to Ionia, he led the entire Athenian force away from the city as though to go there on the afternoon of the agreed-upon day.

After night fell the army stole back toward the walls of Byzantium, and the fleet sailed back into the harbor to attack the Peloponnesian vessels moored there. When the defenders abandoned their posts to help them, leaving most of the city unprotected, the Byzantine plotters let the waiting army of Alcibiades and Theramenes into the city by placing ladders at the unguarded walls. The loyal Byzantines, however, fought so bravely and effectively that Alcibiades ordered an announcement promising them safety. This guarantee convinced the citizens to turn against the Peloponnesian army, most of whom died fighting. The Athenians again honored their commitment, restoring Byzantium as an Athenian ally and neither killing nor exiling any Byzantines. The city recovered its autonomy to the extent that the Peloponnesian garrison and governor were removed, and no Athenians took their place. The Peloponnesian prisoners were not killed but disarmed and sent to Athens for judgment. All these measures represented a new policy of justness and conciliation adopted as a means of recovering the empire.

ATHENIAN NEGOTIATIONS WITH PERSIA

THE ATHENIANS' willingness to make significant concessions at Chalcedon suggests a new element in their plans for winning the war. They rejected Sparta's offer of peace partly in hopes of splitting it from Persia, and their return in force to the Straits provided an opportunity to do so. The time was ripe to test Persian intentions by talking to the Great King himself. Repeated defeats and the loss of great numbers of ships with no positive result might have persuaded him of the costliness and futility of his current policy. Besides, the Spartans' unilateral peace offer violated their treaty with Persia. If negotiations with Persia should succeed, the King would agree to stop supporting the Spartans, who would then be unable to fight at sea and would be obliged to make peace on far less favorable terms.

The trouble with this strategy was that the particular goals of each side remained in direct conflict. Both parties wanted control of the cities of Asia Minor and the revenue they provided. The temporary arrangement at Chalcedon could not serve as a model for a permanent settlement, and it is difficult to envision what an acceptable agreement might have involved. Still, the Athenians thought the effort worth pursuing. They had also heard of a Spartan mission to Susa led by Boeotius, and they may have wanted to thwart it. In any case, they had little to lose by the attempt.

After Chalcedon, Pharnabazus invited the Athenians to send ambassadors whom he would personally escort to the Great King at Susa. The satrap and the embassy made their way inland slowly, for at the onset of winter they had only reached as far as Gordium in Phrygia, where they stayed until spring. They then resumed the journey toward Susa but soon encountered the Spartan embassy led by Boeotius returning from a successful meeting with King Darius II. The Spartans announced that they had obtained everything they wished from him and proved it by presenting Cyrus, the king's son, who had come "to rule all the people on the coast and to fight alongside the Spartans" (Xenophon, *Hellenica* 1.4.1–3). That put an end to Athens' hopes for an agreement with Persia, and it would now have to formulate an alternate plan.

ALCIBIADES RETURNS

IN THE SPRING of 407 the victorious Athenian generals had already sailed out of the Hellespont on their way to Athens before they learned the bad news from Persia. The conquest of Byzantium had freed the Straits of enemy ports, except for Abydos. Although most of the Athenian soldiers and sailors had been away for years, none was as eager to head home as Alcibiades, for this was the moment he had long sought. His complicated maneuvers since his flight to Sparta in 415 made the territories of Sparta and its allies as well as the Persian Empire unsafe for him. To preserve his safety and ambitions he had to return to Athens and a public career in the military and in politics.

Even returning at the head of a victorious fleet, however, he was not completely secure. He had come to Samos as a result of a coup and had been given his first military commands by the fleet based there, not by a regular election in Athens. His return from exile had been agreed to by the Five Thousand and might not be honored by the restored democracy. Athens was still full of his enemies of various political opinions: democrats who resented his slurs on popular government and were wary of his ambition, religious conservatives, patriots who had not forgotten his treason, and other ambitious politicians who feared his rivalry. Alcibiades also needed to be on constant guard against attacks and accusations that might condemn him to death or force him into dangerous exile again. His best protection would be military success, which would bring him political popularity, but even after the victory at Abydos and the great triumph at Cyzicus, for which he received the chief credit, he still did not choose to come home. Perhaps he wanted to be certain that no other general would outshine him in his absence, and though outstanding achievements at Selymbria and Byzantium only added to his reputation, the decisive event that gave him the confidence to return was probably the ceremony sealing the agreement at Chalcedon. The generals and the satrap swore the usual oaths there, but Pharnabazus refused to consider that treaty valid without the oath of Alcibiades, which provided the Athenian the chance to emphasize the unique regard in which he was held by the Persians. He made the satrap swear the oath again on equal terms with himself, underscoring his stature at a time when the Athenians were seeking the support of Pharnabazus in their forthcoming negotiations with Darius. In the spring of 407 Alcibiades had every appearance of being not only a great general who had revived Athenian fortunes, but also once again the only man who had the power to deprive the Spartans of Persian help and win the war. Now was the moment to go back to Athens.

The Athenians left a fleet behind to guard the Straits, which enabled Thrasyllus and Theramenes to return home as well. On their voyage the Athenian forces took advantage of their command of the sea to recover more of their lost territories. Thrasybulus cleaned up the coast of Thrace, whose most important areas were the great island of Thasos and the powerful city of Abdera. Alcibiades, meanwhile, had been first to leave, heading for Samos and then south to Caria, where he collected a hundred talents before returning to Samos. From there he went to Gytheum, the main Spartan naval base in Laconia, where he saw the Spartans building ships but took no action against them. Why was he distracted by so many delays and excursions rather than making a triumphant reappearance in Athens?

The reason Alcibiades tarried at Gytheum was to see "how the city felt about him and his homecoming" (Xenophon, *Hellenica* 1.4.11), and that explanation can account equally for all his behavior since leaving the Hellespont. Specifically, he wanted to await the outcome of the elections to the generalship in the summer of 407. The results can only have been heartening to him, for the membership of the new board whose names we know included his strongest supporter, Thrasybulus, and other friends but none of his enemies.

Nevertheless Alcibiades remained cautious. Legally, he still stood condemned, as well as accursed by the most solemn religious ceremonies, and a stele bearing his condemnation and the curse against him stood on the Acropolis. Even after he dropped anchor at Piraeus he lingered on board "in fear of his enemies. Climbing onto the deck of his ship, he looked to see if his friends were there. When he saw his cousin Euryptolemus son of Peisianax and his other relatives and friends with him, he landed and went up to the city, accompanied by a party of bodyguards ready to defend him against any attack that might come" (Xenophon, *Hellenica* 1.4.18–19). No defense was needed, however, for the great numbers of people who had assembled on shore cheered and shouted their congratulations. When he landed the crowds ran alongside him clamoring for him and crowning him with wreaths in honor of his victory. There was much discussion of the cost of his absence, with many insisting that they would have won in Sicily if Alcibiades had been left in charge of that mission. He had raised Athens from a desperate condition and "not only restored its control of the sea but even brought victory over the enemy on land everywhere" (Plutarch, *Alcibiades* 32.4–5).

This warm reception, however, did not prevent him from going to the council and assembly to present a formal defense against the old charges. He declared himself innocent of the sacrilege of which he had been accused and complained of his misfortunes. Tactfully, he blamed no individuals or the people at large for them but only his own bad luck and a kind of personal evil demon that haunted him. Then he turned to address the great prospects for the future, discounting the enemy's hopes and filling the Athenians with confidence as he had in former days.

He achieved an unqualified success. No one recalled his past troubles or contested anything that he and his friends had proposed. The Athenians cleared him of all charges, restored his confiscated property, ordered the priests to revoke the curses they had called down on him, and threw the stelae bearing his sentence and other actions taken against him into the sea. The people voted him golden crowns and made him general-in-chief (*strategos autokrator*) with command on land and sea.

Even at this moment, however, at the height of his popularity, not all was well. Theodorus, high priest of the mysteries, obeyed the order to revoke the curse only grudgingly, saying: "But I invoked no evil on him if he does no wrong to the city" (Plutarch, *Alcibiades* 33.3). His reservation, no doubt, reflected the continued suspicion and ill will of some Athenians. In 407 they represented a small minority, but they served as a reminder that Alcibiades would maintain his position only so long as he was successful. Some even saw an evil portent in the fact that he had returned to Athens on the day of the ceremony called Plynteria, in which the robes on the ancient wooden statue of Athena Polias were removed and washed, and her statue was concealed from view. It was regarded as the unluckiest day of the year on which to undertake important actions. Plutarch tells us that it seemed as if the goddess had not wished to welcome Alcibiades in a friendly manner but concealed herself from him and rejected him. Xenophon says that the timing of his arrival struck some Athenians as an ill omen both for him and the state. While only a few Athenians took any real notice of the coincidence, the enemies of Alcibiades kept it in mind for future use. We can only observe the irony of the fact that, after taking such pains over his arrival, Alcibiades had forgotten about the holy day. His old rival Nicias would never have made such a mistake.

Alcibiades may have taken his first important step after his return precisely to counter this negative impression. The festival connected with the Eleusinian mysteries was perhaps the most solemn and impressive event in the Athenian religious calendar. Traditionally each year a sacred procession walked the fourteen miles to Eleusis near Attica's northwestern frontier, as initiates carried the Sacred Objects of Demeter accompanied by the image of Iacchus, in the form of a young male deity bearing a torch and attending the goddesses Demeter and Persephone. The initiates wore wreaths of myrtle, the priests were dressed in ornate robes, and bands of flute and lyre players and choruses singing hymns took part in the ceremony. In recent years, however, the presence of a Spartan fort and army at Decelea had made the processions impossible, and in 413 the initiates were forced to make the trip by sea without the splendor and pomp that were so important to it.

Alcibiades, with his keen sense of the spectacular gesture, recognized the chance to put an end to his religious problems with a single bold stroke. After consulting the relevant priests, he prepared to take part in the great procession in the traditional manner. Protected by his sentries and armed guard, he escorted the celebrants along the sacred route. They reached Eleusis without incident and returned on foot the same way. This spectacle, as an act of piety, helped disarm religious suspicions; as a demonstration of military daring and prowess it justified the extraordinary powers voted to him and raised the spirit of the Athenian army; politically it was a master stroke. No performance in the great propaganda competition between Alcibiades and Nicias could match it for timeliness or effect. Alcibiades had returned to Athens with a vengeance.

CHAPTER THIRTY-FIVE

Cyrus, Lysander, and the Fall of Alcibiades (408–406)

VICTORY IN THE HELLESPONT enabled the Athenians to turn their attention to the Ionian and the Aegean theater for what could well be the final phase of a victorious war. After the glorious march to Eleusis the assembly voted to place a force of 100 triremes, 1,500 hoplites, and 150 cavalry under the command of Alcibiades. His fellow generals were Aristocrates, Adeimantus, and Conon, all hand-picked by him. In October they led this powerful force into the Aegean to recover the areas that were still in enemy hands. These included such key Ionian cities as Miletus and Ephesus and islands as important as Chios, as well as such strategically located ones as Andros and Tenos. In the process they could restore their empire, increase essential revenues and, perhaps, crush the Spartan fleet and convince Persia to retire from the war.

PRINCE CYRUS REPLACES TISSAPHERNES

DURING THE MONTHS of Athenian inaction, however, the Spartans had been busily rebuilding their fleet, bringing the number of vessels up to seventy triremes. No less significant was the change in the enemy's leadership. King Darius had revoked the command of Tissaphernes, discredited by his breach with the Spartans and the apparent failure of his policy, and replaced him with his own younger son, Cyrus, granting Tissaphernes the lesser province of Caria. This was a remarkable decision, for Cyrus was not yet seventeen years old, and many more experienced men—including his elder brother—were available. Yet it was the untried adolescent whom the Great King sent to Sardis with the title of *karanos* (lord, or ruler) of the satrapy in western Anatolia, assigning him control of Lydia, Greater Phrygia, and Cappadocia, in addition to his command in Ionia. Darius made this surprising appointment under the influence of his wife, Parysatis, who disliked her oldest son, Arsaces.

The young prince and his mother aimed to gain for him the succession to the throne of Persia in place of Arsaces. As early as 406 Cyrus demonstrated his arrogance and ambition by putting to death two of his royal cousins, simply because they did not show him the deference owed to the Great King. Even with the aid of his mother, however, Cyrus faced a difficult road to the throne. He had powerful enemies at home and the once again formidable Athenians with which to contend. He also needed to find effective help to win his war for the succession when the time came.

His first priority was to defeat the Athenians, but this could only be done together with the Spartans and their Peloponnesian allies, who seemed unable to win at sea, no matter how many ships and how much financial support the Persians provided. Victory would require a naval commander of a quality the Spartans had never yet produced. Cyrus also had to find military support in Sparta for his personal ambitions, which promised to be a difficult task, for the Spartans and the Persians still had conflicting interests. Cyrus could not expect the Spartan kings, ephors, gerousia, and assembly to use their power to put him on the Persian throne, even if by they could find a way to win the war. He needed, therefore, to identify a faction or an individual of rare military talent who had a reason to cooperate with him and the authority to bring Sparta along with him. By a remarkable stroke of luck such a man was waiting as Cyrus made his way to Sardis in the summer of 407.

THE EMERGENCE OF LYSANDER

THE NEW SPARTAN navarch in 407 was Lysander, a *mothax*, the son of a Spartiate father and a helot mother or possibly of an impoverished Spartan who had lost his status. In either case Lysander would have been raised as the companion for his son by some Spartiate of adequate means, educated in the Spartan manner, and made eligible for full citizenship by the very unusual grant of an allotment of land.

The rise of so marginal a figure to such a high command requires explanation. Lysander's father, though poor, was of noble descent, which made the young man unusual among his fellows. Late in the war, moreover, the Spartans appointed no fewer than three *mothakes* to the position of navarch: Gylippus, the hero at Syracuse; Lysander; and his successor, Callicratidas. All through the war Spartan naval commanders had done poorly against the Athenians. As the war at sea became paramount, the Spartans were prepared to take whatever measures were necessary to gain success there, even to appoint talented men outside the charmed circle of legitimate Spartiates to the supreme naval command.

Lysander had, no doubt, demonstrated superior talents in fighting, of which we have no record, but his rise to eminence probably also owed much to powerful patronage. Young Spartiates, normally at the age of twelve, took an older man between the ages of twenty and thirty as mentor and lover. The ancient writers tend to focus on the educational, moral, and spiritual side of the relationship, but there is no question of its physical aspects, as well. Lysander was the lover (*erastes*) of the young Agesilaus, half-brother to King Agis.

These connections could also have a political significance, for the relationship between adult lover and adolescent beloved was bound to be close, and over the years it would create a strong bond between them. Lysander later played a key role in Agesilaus' ascension to the throne in Sparta and would persuade the young king to undertake a great campaign against Persia in 396.

Lysander also seems to have been on cordial terms with Agis, with whom he shared a desire to replace the Athenian Empire with a Spartan hegemony, as many Spartans did not. The two men also collaborated in shaping strategy toward the end of the war. There is good reason to support the usual view that regards Lysander and Agis as political associates, once the former had achieved eminence. It is easy to believe that Lysander benefited from this association, for he carefully cultivated personal relationships with influential Spartans in pursuit of his political ambitions. "He seems by nature to have been attentive to the men of power, beyond what was customary for a Spartiate, and to have put up pleasantly with the excesses of authority for the sake of advantage" (Plutarch, *Lysander* 2.1–3). He was notable even among the Spartans for his competitive spirit and ambition.

Lysander wanted glory, but he was also motivated by the pursuit of power. A credible tradition portrays him later in life trying to alter the Spartan constitution to allow him to become king. Such ambitions were undoubtedly already in place when he took up his naval command in 407. The strength of his personal aspirations demanded that he demonstrate his unique qualities and make himself indispensable to the Spartans, but if his own interests conflicted with those of the state, so much the worse for the latter.

In the spring of 407 Lysander set out across the Aegean for Ionia, gathering warships as he went, and by the time he reached Asia Minor he commanded a fleet of seventy triremes. He established his base not at Miletus, as earlier, but further north, at Ephesus. The shortcomings of Miletus as a base were by now clear: its position south of Samos meant that any Spartan fleet headed for the Straits could be intercepted by the Athenians. Ephesus, north of Samos, did not have that handicap and had other advantages, as well. It was, for example, much closer to the provincial Persian capital at Sardis. The city had taken on many Persian features and was congenial to Persian officials, who liked going there, so Lysander could more readily use his personal skills to influence his ally and paymaster. Lysander also found the city's aristocracy "both friendly to him and zealous in the Spartan cause" (Plutarch, *Lysander* 3.2).

Unlike his predecessors, Lysander understood the need for a port of a size, condition, population, and location able to support a large fleet and army. Because Ephesus had all these resources, he immediately set about turning it into a commercial center and an important shipyard. Doing so required some time, however, and Lysander took advantage of the Athenians' convenient delay to refine the Peloponnesians' techniques and skills in trireme warfare. He gladly allowed the time to pass without seeking battle while he readied his fleet, built his base, and trained his crews. All he needed was the money to pay for them, and Cyrus' arrival in the summer solved that problem.

The meeting between the ambitious young prince and the no less ambitious Spartan commander was one of those conjunctions in history in which the individuals involved play a decisive role in determining the course of momentous events. Lysander, the perfect man for his times, was also practical and highly skilled in the arts of winning the trust of ambitious royal youths. His mastery of concealment and subterfuge was proverbial; it was his way "to deceive boys with knuckle-bones and men with oaths" (Plutarch, *Lysander* 8.4). Lysander was the only one among the Spartans who could work so well with Cyrus and gain the support needed for victory.

THE COLLABORATION OF CYRUS AND LYSANDER

THE TWO LEADERS got on splendidly from the first. Lysander blamed previous failures and misunderstandings on Tissaphernes, a bitter enemy of Parysatis, and asked the prince to change the Persian policy and support the Spartans fully in their fight against the common enemy. Cyrus answered that he meant to do everything possible in pursuit of victory. He had five hundred talents with him and promised to spend his own money in the effort, and if that was not sufficient, he promised to break up the throne on which he sat, which was made of gold and silver. The speech contained more bravado than realism, for when Lysander asked Cyrus to double the pay of his rowers in order to encourage desertions from the Athenian fleet, the young prince had to admit that he was permitted to pay only the three obols specified in the treaty.

But Lysander put his talents as a courtier to work, and "by his submissive deference in conversation" (Plutarch, *Lysander* 4.2) won the heart of the young prince. As they parted Cyrus asked how he could please Lysander most, and the Spartan answered: "If you add one obol to the pay of each sailor" (Xenophon, *Hellenica* 1.5.7). Cyrus not only agreed but also made up the arrears in salary and gave Lysander a month's remuneration for his forces in advance. Only a royal prince, and the queen's favorite, could have raised the Spartans' pay without further authorization.

Still, Lysander was entirely dependent on the good will of the Persian prince. To strengthen his own hand he called a meeting in Ephesus of the most powerful men from the cities of Ionia and urged them to form political groups (*hetairiai*), assuring them that he would cede control of the cities to the aristocrats if he won the war. This promise brought strong support and large financial contributions. Part of his goal, of course, was to build personal allegiance to himself among these wealthy individuals which he would later use for his own purposes. As Plutarch observes, he did them personal favors, "planting in them the seeds of the revolutionary decarchies he would later bring into being" (*Lysander* 6.3–4).

The Athenians, worried by the outcome of the meeting between Cyrus and Lysander, tried to use Tissaphernes as a diplomatic intermediary. Although the former satrap was clearly the wrong man for the job, as an enemy of the royal family and a man hated and mistrusted by both sides, he urged the prince to resume the old policy of taking a position between the two Greek adversaries to wear them out. Cyrus, however, was firmly committed to a different approach, and not only rejected his advice but refused even to see the Athenian envoys. The Athenians' efforts to end the war through diplomatic agreements with Persia had failed both with Darius and with Cyrus, so the fighting would have to continue.

THE BATTLE OF NOTIUM

THE STRATEGIC SITUATION compelled the Athenians to try to force a naval battle with Lysander at Ephesus, for a victory there would enable the Athenians to dominate the Aegean and the Straits unopposed, and to bring rebellious states, and their revenues, back into the empire. By destroying still another enemy fleet they might also persuade the Spartans to make peace on acceptable terms or, if not, the Persians might at least be more willing to consider withdrawing their support. But the Athenians had to strike quickly, for every passing day might bring defections from their navy due to the higher pay offered by the Peloponnesians.

Alcibiades did not, however, sail directly for the Spartan base at Ephesus. Instead, with Euboea in enemy hands, he tried to take Andros, an island on the path taken by grain ships from the Hellespont. Although he defeated the enemy on land he could not take the island, and so left a force to continue the effort after he departed. His enemies in Athens would later use this failed attempt against him.

From Andros he sailed southeast to Cos and Rhodes in search of money and booty to pay his men. The Athenian treasury was still underfunded, and Alcibiades may not have had sufficient resources to keep his fleet at sea long enough if Lysander chose to stay in port. While it made sense for him to accumulate as much money as he could before confronting the Spartan fleet, the delay gave the enemy even more time to improve its fleet with defections and hard training.

Alcibiades next sailed to Samos and on to Notium, the port of

Colophon, which was situated on the coast to the northwest of Ephesus. Although Notium was not a major naval base, it served as a good launching point for an attack on Ephesus, as from there the Athenians could cut off Spartan ships traveling between Ephesus and Chios and prevent any attempt at an escape to the Hellespont. At Notium Alcibiades commanded eighty ships, having left twenty at Andros, while Lysander's force had grown to ninety. In spite of his advantage Lysander did not come out to fight, believing that time was on his side. His fleet had improved from its program of practice and training, while the higher wages granted by Cyrus "emptied the ships of the enemy. For most of the sailors came over to those paying more, while those who stayed were dispirited and rebellious and made trouble for their commanders every day" (Plutarch, *Lysander* 4.4).

While any Athenian commander would have appreciated the need to act quickly for the same reason that Lysander was content to bide his time, Alcibiades had reasons of his own to move swiftly. Plutarch's analysis of his rationale is sound: "It seems that if anyone was ever destroyed by his own reputation it was Alcibiades. For he was thought to be so full of daring and intelligence, from which his success was derived, that they suspected him of not trying when he failed and would not believe there was anything he could not do. If he tried, nothing could escape him" (*Alcibiades* 35.2). In spite of the special powers and large forces given him, he failed at Andros and had yet to find a way to get Lysander to risk a naval battle. Unless he achieved success soon he risked arousing the suspicions of the people and giving further encouragement to his enemies.

He stayed at Notium for a month or so but by February 406 left the bulk of his fleet there and sailed off to join Thrasybulus in the siege of Phocaea. This was probably part of a plan to force Lysander to come out and fight: if the Athenians succeeded in taking Ionian cities Lysander could not long stand by idly but must engage them. Phocaea was a good target for this strategy, as it was well situated as a base for further attacks on Cyme, Clazomenae, and even Chios. Alcibiades took only troopships with him on the mission, leaving his triremes at Ephesus to guard against the ever-growing Spartan fleet. The man he put in charge of the navy there in his absence was Antiochus, a petty officer, a helmsman or *kybernetes*, and the pilot of Alcibiades' own ship. This appointment, unique in the entire recorded history of the

444 THE FALL OF ATHENS

Athenian navy, has been assailed from antiquity to modern times. Normally a fleet of this size would have been entrusted to one or more generals, but it appears that the colleagues of Alcibiades were all away on other assignments. That being the case, the normal practice would have been to appoint a ship's captain (trierarch) who had taken part in naval warfare and had distinguished himself in previous campaigns. Among the many captains at Notium such a man must have been present. In Alcibiades' defense, however, *kybernetai* were usually men of great experience and ability in the tactics of naval warfare and had participated in many battles, typically more than any captain, and they were vital to Athenian naval excellence. In this case, moreover, Alcibiades did not expect or even desire a battle in his absence, and gave Antiochus the clear and simple order: "Do not attack Lysander's ships" (Xenophon, *Hellenica* 1.5.11). A petty officer would be far more likely to obey such a command without question and stay out of trouble than a higher-ranking and independent-minded officer. What Alcibiades needed in this situation was a man he could trust, and Antiochus, his personal helmsman and subordinate for years, must have seemed the perfect choice.

But Alcibiades had misjudged his man: Antiochus, seized by the chance for glory, devised a strategy and launched an attack. He probably based his plan on the one that won the brilliant Athenian victory at Cyzicus, perhaps the greatest naval achievement of the trireme era. But the stratagem at Cyzicus had depended on concealment and deception, making full use of geography and weather to hide the fleet's arrival, numbers, and location. None of these elements was present at Notium; there would no possibility of concealment and little point in trying similar tricks. In addition Lysander had been studying the Athenian fleet for more than a month and had received excellent intelligence about its size and its operations from the deserters who came to his camp. He was also well informed about the events at Cyzicus and the Athenian tactics there.

Antiochus modeled his opening ploy, nonetheless, on that of Alcibiades at Cyzicus. With his own ship in the lead, he sailed ten triremes directly at Ephesus, instructing the rest to be ready at Notium "until the enemy was far away from the land" (*Hellenica Oxyrhynchia* 4.1). The idea was to coax Lysander to chase his small force out into open water toward Notium. Once they were out far enough the full

Athenian fleet would try to cut them off from their harbor and force a major battle or chase them down as they fled for port.

Lysander, however, was well aware that Alcibiades was away in Ephesus and that the Athenian fleet was in the hands of a man who had never before held a command. It was an unprecedented opportunity, and presented with it Lysander decided "to do something worthy of Sparta" (Diodorus 13.71.3). He charged at the lead ship with three triremes of his own, sinking it and killing Antiochus. The nine trailing ships fled at once, chased by the entire Spartan fleet. Lysander realized that he had shocked the Athenians and ruined the timing of their plan, so hastened to take advantage of their confusion. The main Athenian force at Notium was still waiting, according to orders, until it caught sight of the Athenian vanguard racing toward it, well ahead of the pursuing enemy, before taking to sea. Instead, it saw the small force fleeing in a panic, with the entire Spartan fleet giving chase. With no time to get into good battle formation and with no directing hand to organize the force and give commands, each trierarch had to launch his ship as soon as he could, so the Athenians came to the rescue "in no order whatever" (Diodorus 13.71.4). They lost twenty-two ships in a rout, while Lysander dominated the sea and set up a trophy to mark his unexpected victory at Notium.

Alcibiades reached the scene of the battle three days later, bringing Thrasybulus' thirty triremes with him, to raise the total of Athenian ships at Notium to eighty-eight (not including the lost twenty-two). Desperate to undo the defeat, he sailed to Ephesus, hoping to draw Lysander into combat again, but the Spartan saw no reason to risk it against a fleet of equal numbers under a formidable commander. Alcibiades could do nothing but return to Samos, the loss unavenged.

Although Lysander proved his great talents in the battle and deserves the credit he gained, his victory owed much to the terrible mistakes of the Athenians. They bitterly blamed Alcibiades for their defeat, and with good reason. Whatever his purpose in going to Phocaea, it was inexcusably reckless to have left all his triremes, in clear view of a superior enemy, in the hands of a man who had never commanded. While the Athenians lost few men at Notium and still had 108 triremes in the Aegean and thus the numerical advantage, it was strategically an important defeat, reversing the momentum in the war that was flowing so strongly in the Athenian favor after Cyzicus. The Athenians would not soon recover their position in Ionia, nor would they take Andros. The morale of the Athenian soldiers and sailors at the base on Samos was also adversely affected, and desertions were bound to increase.

Alcibiades' next effort to regain the initiative did not succeed, when he led his entire force to Cyme and began ravaging the territory around the city. Taking him by surprise, the entire Cymaean army appeared and drove the Athenians back to their ships. Following so soon after the defeat at Notium, this fiasco provided additional charges for his enemies to bring against him.

THE FALL OF ALCIBIADES

WHILE ALCIBIADES WAS AWAY, events in Athens were adding to his troubles. Taking advantage of the absence of so many Athenian hoplites and cavalrymen, Agis led a large force of Peloponnesian and Boeotian hoplites, light-armed troops, and cavalry to the walls of Athens on a dark night. Although they were driven back they ravaged Attica before dispersing, which only added to the Athenians' chagrin when they learned of the defeat at Notium and the failure at Cyme. The foes of Alcibiades saw the time was now ripe for an attack. Meanwhile, a bitter enemy of Alcibiades, Thrasybulus son of Thraso had returned from the camp on Samos, full of the bitter feelings there. In the Athenian assembly he announced that Alcibiades had conducted the campaign as if it were a luxury cruise, assigning command of the fleet to a man whose only talents were drinking and telling tall sailor's tales, "so that he himself might be free to sail around collecting money and engaging in debauchery by getting drunk and visiting whores in Abydos and Ionia, even while the enemy fleet was close by" (Plutarch, *Alcibiades* 36.12). Next, ambassadors from Cyme accused him of attacking "an allied city that had done no wrong. At the same time, some Athenians blamed him for not trying to capture that city, claiming that he had been bribed by the Great King" (Diodorus 13.73.6). Others complained of his past misdeeds, his help to the Spartans, and his collaboration with the Persians, who, the charge ran, would make him tyrant at Athens after the war. Accusations old and new, true and false rained on him until someone, possibly Cleophon, proposed to remove him from office, and the motion passed.

The Athenians appointed Conon to take command of the fleet at Samos, and Alcibiades again went into exile, knowing better than to return to Athens where his many opponents were waiting with a flurry of private lawsuits and who knew what public charges. He also had to leave Samos, for the forces there had become hostile, as well, and he remained unwelcome in Spartan and Persian territory. Anticipating his possible fate, however, he had prepared a safe harbor for himself in a fortified castle he had built on the Gallipoli Peninsula during his years in service in the Hellespont, and there he went.

Many have judged this last departure of Alcibiades and his final removal from the command of the Athenian forces as a turning point in the last phase of the war, and as a disaster for Athens. While it is true his first successes as a commander on land or sea in 411 and 408 established him as a good as cavalry leader and a capable naval commander, the ablest commander in the campaigns in the Straits was not Alcibiades but Thrasybulus son of Lycus. As always, however, Alcibiades' personal ambitions proved to be a severe liability, swelling the number of his enemies and the intensity of their hatred. The eagerness with which they waited to attack him compelled him to seek extraordinary accomplishments and make promises that could not be fulfilled in order to achieve and maintain a popularity that was his only security. This drove him to take risks that another general would have avoided and that were bound to bring disaster to Athens.

He was also a serious political liability, a divisive figure who evoked powerful feelings of admiration or dislike but never steady support from a large portion of the citizenry. He could not win a reliable majority to support his own policies, nor would he subordinate himself to another for the sake of Athens. At the same time he could prevent anyone else from taking the lead, for in times of trouble, the Athenians turned to his glamour and promise for salvation. As a character in a comedy said less than a year after Notium: "They yearn for him, they hate him, but they want to have him back" (Aristophanes, *Frogs* 1425). His disgrace also brought down such able friends as Thrasybulus and Theramenes, depriving Athens of its most capable commanders when they were badly needed, which, in the end, may have been the most serious consequence of the Spartan victory at Notium.

CHAPTER THIRTY-SIX

Arginusae (406)

ALCIBIADES' DISGRACE brought his friends down with him, most notably Thrasybulus and Theramenes, who were not reelected to the generalship in the spring of 406. Factionalism was not the predominant factor, however, in the choice of a new board of generals: the voters were chiefly interested in selecting men regardless of faction, who were experienced naval commanders not close to Alcibiades.

Alcibiades himself was replaced by Conon as admiral of the Athenian fleet at Samos early in 406. The higher pay offered by Lysander and losses at Notium left him with sufficient crews to man only seventy of his one hundred ships, which prevented him from undertaking any significant campaigns. By now Lysander was in completely the opposite position. He was well funded, his fleet was growing, and the morale of his crews was high. There was but one obstacle in his path: Sparta's laws forbade the navarch to continue in command for a second year, so Lysander was compelled to hand over his fleet to his successor, Callicratidas.

THE NEW NAVARCH

THE NEW COMMANDER was also a *mothax*, but differed from his predecessor in several respects. He was very young to have attained his exalted position, probably not much over thirty, and though bold and daring he lacked the personal ambition of Lysander. Diodorus characterizes him as a man "without guile and straightforward in character," a man "not yet experienced in the ways of foreigners," but "the justest of the Spartans" (13.76.2). There is some reason to think that he shared the views of the late king Pleistoanax and his son Pausanias, who succeeded him. The father had favored peace and friendship with Athens, and the son would prove himself a formidable opponent of Lysander, leading a faction that one scholar describes as "a moderate, traditionalist group" that opposed a Spartan empire abroad. Domestically they feared the impact of the money and luxury that were the profits of empire and wanted to return to the austere principles of the Lycurgan constitution. Presumably, Lysander's close friendship with Cyrus and his organization of political clubs personally loyal to him in the Asian cities aroused suspicions in Pausanias's faction and led to the choice of Callicratidas.

Friction arose as soon as the new navarch arrived at Ephesus about April 406. Lysander handed over the fleet by proclaiming himself "as ruler of the sea and as one who has conquered in a battle at sea" (Xenophon, *Hellenica* 1.6.2). Callicratidas at once challenged those boasts, urging Lysander to sail past the Athenians at Samos and deliver his fleet at Miletus to make that claim good. This rebuke underscored the limits of Lysander's accomplishments and set both the tone of rivalry and a goal of greater victories to be achieved by the younger man.

Lysander did not rise to the bait but sailed directly home, leaving the sting behind him. His supporters among the troops at once began to undermine Callicratidas, spreading the view that he was incompetent and inexperienced. The young navarch met the taunts head-on, addressing the assembled fleet with Spartan simplicity and directness. He declared that he was prepared to give up the command "if Lysander or anyone else believes he is more expert in naval matters," but as he had been ordered to lead them he must do so as best he could. He left it to the fleet to examine his goals and to assess the criticisms raised against him and against the Spartan state for placing him in command, and then to advise him "whether I should stay or sail home and report the state of affairs here" (Xenophon, *Hellenica* 1.6.4). The speech put an end to the dissent, for no one dared suggest he disobey orders, or risked his returning to Sparta and reporting their mutinous behavior.

Lysander, however, had bequeathed a more serious legacy of trouble to his successor. When he left office he still had a portion of the money Cyrus had given him, which by right he ought to have turned over to his successor. Instead, he gave it back to Cyrus, which left Callicratidas without the funds he needed for the upkeep of the fleet but suited Lysander's goals of retaining the favor of the Persian prince and of humiliating and impeding his rival. Callicratidas was therefore obliged to go to Cyrus to ask for the money to pay his men, but the prince deliberately insulted the young navarch by forcing him to wait two days before admitting him to an interview. The meeting did not go well, as Cyrus refused his request, and the Spartan commander departed in a fury, more hostile to Lysander's policy than ever. "He said that the Greeks were in a most miserable condition because they flattered barbarians for the sake of money and if, if he got home safely, he would try his best to reconcile the Athenians and Spartans" (Xenophon, *Hellenica* 1.6.6–7). Here was the voice of the traditionalist Spartans; his words were a declaration of independence from Persian control and of his intention to reject Persian support and pursue a different policy.

Callicratidas accordingly moved the Spartan base from Ephesus back to Miletus, giving up a strategic locational advantage in order to pursue the new plan. Miletus, because it had opposed the Persians, was a better place from which to raise money for his fleet. At an assembly there he revealed his new platform and asked for funds to fight the war: "With the help of the gods let us show the barbarians that without paying homage to them we can punish our enemies" (Xenophon, *Hellenica* 1.6.11). So warmly was this appeal received by the local Greeks that even Lysander's friends did not dare withhold contributions.

With 140 ships Callicratidas had twice as many as Conon, but he knew that the Athenians were already preparing major reinforcements. Because he had rebuked Lysander for inaction after Notium and for being afraid to confront the Athenian fleet at Samos, he now needed to demonstrate his own willingness to do so. A great victory, in addition, might encourage more financial support from the Greeks of Asia Minor and the islands, so he was eager to force a battle as soon as possible. He therefore attacked and captured Athenian strongholds at Delphinium on Chios and at Teos, serving notice to Conon's fleet, which was then north of Samos. Next he seized Methymna on Lesbos and took many prisoners, but rejected advice to sell the captives as slaves for cash. Recalling Sparta's declared purpose for going to war—to bring freedom to the Greeks—he announced, "While I am in command, so far as is in my power, no Greek will be enslaved" (Xenophon, *Hellenica* 1.6.14). It was a policy and slogan aimed both to encourage cities still under the Athenian yoke to rebel, and to gain support from those already liberated. This was the only way for Sparta to win the war without Persian help, and to keep its promise to liberate the Greeks.

CONON TRAPPED AT MYTILENE

As PART OF his skillful propaganda campaign Callicratidas sent word to Conon that he meant to end his foe's "adulterous affair with the sea" (Xenophon, *Hellenica* 1.6.15), by which he branded the Athenian naval empire as illegitimate and challenged it to fight. Although Conon had used the time between clashes to get his fleet into top condition, having "prepared them for battle as no previous general had done" (Diodorus 13.77.1), he was still badly outnumbered and would not be drawn out. But the threat to Lesbos, the chief barrier to a Peloponnesian return to the Hellespont, compelled him to move his fleet to the Hekatonnesi Islands east of Methymna. When Callicratidas came after him, now with 170 ships manned by first-rate crews, Conon fled toward Mytilene, but the pursuing Peloponnesians caught them at the mouth of its harbor, taking 30 Athenian triremes. Conon barely got the remaining 40 to safety, but these were soon blocked as Callicratidas laid siege to the city by land and sea. Threatened by starvation through blockade and by betrayal on the part of the many friends of Sparta in the city, Conon was scarcely able to sneak a ship out of the harbor to go to Athens and report his plight.

Still, his escape deprived Callicratidas of a total rout, and one that might have won the war. If the Athenian fleet had been entirely destroyed, as it nearly was, the Spartans would be unopposed in taking Lesbos and Athens' undefended main base at Samos, and then moving into the equally unprotected Hellespont to block the grain route. Instead, short of money, Callicratidas was forced to conduct a siege of indeterminate length, giving the Athenians time to send out reinforcements to contest his command of the sea. Fortunately for him, however, his success convinced Cyrus that he was on the point of a complete triumph. Because a Spartan victory achieved without Persian help by a hostile commander would have been disastrous for him, he took the expedient step of changing his tactics and sent funds to pay the fleet, including a gift for the commander himself. Callicratidas, of necessity, accepted the money for his men but, in sharp contrast to Lysander's methods, remained personally cold and aloof. "There was no need," he explained, "for a private friendship between himself and Cyrus, but the agreement that had been made with all the Spartans was enough for him" (Plutarch, *Moralia* 222E). Still, a victory of the kind the navarch wanted required a quick and decisive battle, one that would take place before the Athenians recovered and before Persian money became decisive.

ATHENS REBUILDS A NAVY

CONON'S MESSENGER SHIP reached Athens about mid-June 406. The Athenians must have then had about 40 ships available, but as the result of an extraordinary effort, built their fleet up within a month to 110 triremes. The shortage of ships was only part of the problem, for the treasury was by now completely depleted. To defray the costs of construction and of salaries for the crews the Athenians were obliged to melt down the golden statues of Nike on the Acropolis and strike coins from them. Using these and other gold and silver bullion stored on the scared hill, they managed to raise a sum of more than two thousand talents in silver, which covered their expenses. Manpower presented still another problem. The best crews were already posted at Mytilene, for Conon had chosen them especially for his mission. Even experienced rowers of a lesser quality would fill only a minority of the ships preparing to leave Athens, so the Athenians were forced to use inexperienced men as rowers, including farmers, wealthy men who could afford to serve in the cavalry, and even slaves, who were offered freedom and Athenian citizenship for their service. "They embarked all those who were of military age, both slave and free" (Xenophon, *Hellenica* 1.6.24). For the first time in the war they would find them-

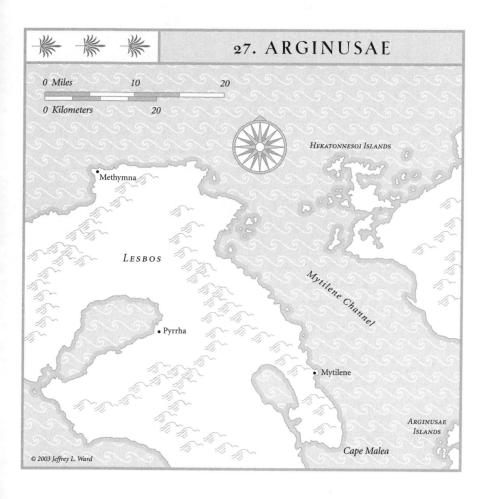

0 Miles   10   20

0 Kilometers   20

HEKATONNESOI ISLANDS

Methymna

LESBOS

Mytilene Channel

Pyrrha

Mytilene

ARGINUSAE
ISLANDS

Cape Malea

© 2003 Jeffrey L. Ward

selves in a fight at sea tactically inferior to an enemy bolstered by skilled and experienced deserters from their own forces.

Unlike any other fleet during the war, this one also had eight generals, though none of them, so far as we know, served as generalissimo. Against a bold young Spartan commander, who had already defeated Athens' best admiral, Conon, this would not seem to have been a promising arrangement. Sailing to Samos in July, the Athenians picked up 45 additional ships from their allies, bringing their number to 155 triremes. Callicratidas, preferring not to be caught between Conon's fleet in Mytilene harbor and the oncoming Athenians, left 50 ships to guard Conon while he sailed with the remaining 120 vessels to Cape Malea at the southeastern tip of Lesbos to cut the enemy off. From there he could see the Athenians at the Arginusae Islands, just off the mainland, about two miles east of the Spartan position (see Map 27). Whether or not he knew he was outnumbered, he was confident that the superior quality of his crews would bring victory.

THE BATTLE OF ARGINUSAE

CALLICRATIDAS WANTED TO repeat the surprise tactics that had succeeded against Conon by attacking at night, but was prevented from doing so by a storm. Instead at daybreak he set out into the rising sun toward Arginusae. The Spartans attacked the Athenian line abreast, 120 ships side by side, covering about twenty-four hundred yards, or a mile and a third (see Map 28). With about twenty yards between triremes they were in position to use the tactics perfected by the Athenians, which had brought them naval supremacy: the *periplous* in which greater speed permitted rowing around the end of the enemy line to hit it from the side or rear, and the *diekplous*, where a ship swiftly rowed between two enemy vessels and sharply turned to hit the side of either of them.

The Athenians, no less aware of their tactical inferiority, arranged their order accordingly, and in a manner unique in Greek naval history. They aligned their ships into three divisions, two wings and a center. Each wing consisted of sixty vessels, arrayed in two lines, one

28. THE BATTLE OF ARGINUSAE

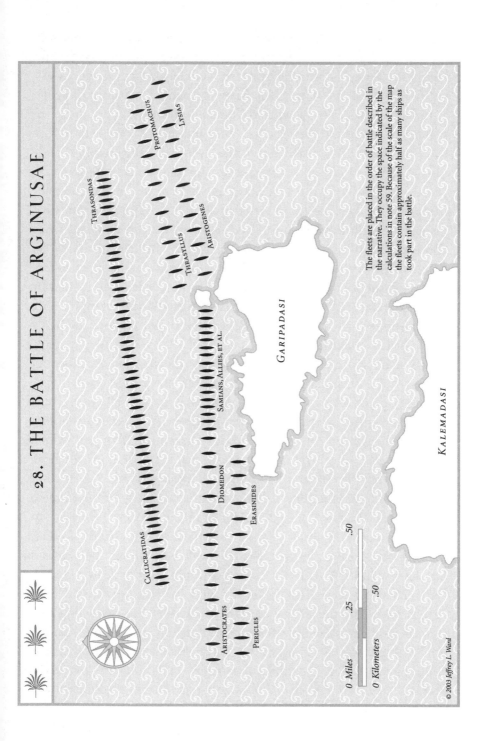

THRASONDAS

CALLICRATIDAS

PROTOMACHUS

LYSIAS

THRASYLLUS

ARISTOGENES

ARISTOCRATES

DIOMEDON

SAMIANS, ALLIES, ET AL.

PERICLES

ERASINIDES

GARIPADASI

KALEMADASI

The fleets are placed in the order of battle described in the narrative. They occupy the space indicated by the calculations in note 59. Because of the scale of the map the fleets contain approximately half as many ships as took part in the battle.

0 Miles   .25   .50

0 Kilometers   .50

© 2003 Jeffrey L. Ward

behind the other, with each ship in the rear line filling a gap between the ships in the front. The center had thirty-five ships in a single line, but these took up a position just in front of Garipadasi, the more western of the two main islands. The island prevented a Spartan *diekplous* in the center, just as the staggered double lines on the wings made the maneuver impossible there. The Athenians aligned the wings with twice the regular distance between the ships. So if the invitingly large gaps in the front line encouraged a Spartan ship to attempt the *diekplous*, the ships in the rear line could move up to stop it and allow the triremes on either side to ram it. The double gap also gave the Athenians a longer line, which protected them against the *periplous* while also enabling them to outflank the enemy. The Athenians added yet another refinement in dividing their wings into eight independent units, each under a general of its own. This apportionment would be especially beneficial on the offensive, which would take place in more open water, where the capacity of each unit to act independently would be advantageous.

As Callicratidas began his advance, "the Athenians came out against him, extending their left wing out towards the open sea" (Xenophon, *Hellenica* 1.6.29). The left, that is, which already outflanked the enemy, looped still farther to the south in a movement that threatened encirclement of the Spartan right wing. Such a ploy, which separated a squadron from the rest of the line, would normally have left a gap that the Spartans could exploit. But the double line used at Arginusae allowed the general of the front detachment on the extreme left, Pericles (the son of the great Pericles and his mistress Aspasia), to make the wide swing, leaving the rear detachment on the left, under Aristocrates, to close any gap. Whatever offensive moves Callicratidas may have planned in that part of the sea would be undone by the acute and obvious danger of encirclement, and the Spartans would have been thrown onto the defensive. Perhaps the Athenian right wing performed the same maneuver, but we are not told specifically what action it took. Even if it only moved straight ahead, however, it was already in a position to outflank the enemy on its side. The center appears to have taken no action but simply remained in place before the island.

Callicratidas commanded his right wing, and what he saw was

alarming. His personal *kybernetes*, Hermon of Megara, urged him to break off the battle, "for the Athenian triremes were more numerous by far," but the young admiral would not hear of it: "Sparta would not be the worse if he died, but to flee would be shameful" (Xenophon, *Hellenica* 1.6.32) His steadfastness was in the great tradition of Spartan courage and well suited his bold character, but in the context of this particular strategic situation it was imprudent. To fight against numerical odds while at a tactical disadvantage is unwise at any time, and the Spartans had no reason to force a battle. Time was on their side; the Athenians were out of money and could not keep the fleet at sea for long. Delay was also likely to bring further desertions from the Athenian side. A cautious commander would have left it to the Athenians to take the initiative at a site of the Spartans' choosing when the balance of forces was in the Spartans' favor.

Time, however, was not on the side of Callicratidas. He wanted a victory quickly, before he became even more dependent on Persian money and before the fighting season came to and end, robbing him for any chance at victory. What, moreover, would happen if he did take Hermon's advice and broke off the battle? He would certainly have to go to Mytilene to try to finish off Conon, and the Athenian fleet would equally certainly pursue him there. He would then have 170 ships, to the Athenians' 155 facing him, with Conon's 40 at his rear. He would thus have a fleet of 25 fewer than the Athenians, compared with his deficit of 35 at Arginusae, but that slight improvement in forces might well be offset by the need to fight an enemy at both front and rear. Whether or not he considered these factors, we need not attribute Callicratidas' decision merely to the rashness and inexperience of a spirited young man.

Faced with the threat to his flank he did what he could, and unable to extend his own line to defeat the enemy maneuver, "he divided his force, forming into two fleets, fighting a double battle, one on each wing" (Diodorus 13.98.4–5). This left him without a center and open, to attack from the single line of Athenian ships stationed in front of the island, but his situation forced him to make tactical compromises, and the primary danger of encirclement was too great to ignore. In fact, the Athenian center remained in position during the first part of the battle, which was long and hard. "First the fight was in close order, and later it was scattered" (Xenophon, *Hellenica* 1.6.33). The Athenians' attack on the flank initially concentrated the fighting into the center, leaving little opportunity for the Spartans to attempt the skilled maneuvers in which they now had the advantage. As the battle wore on, the presence of the unengaged, undamaged Athenian center became more and more threatening to the exhausted Spartans. Callicratidas was killed when his ship rammed into an enemy trireme, after which the left wing gave way and tried to escape. With the Spartan formation broken at last, the Athenian center joined in the destruction and pursuit, destroying many fleeing ships, while suffering no losses of their own. On the right the fighting continued long and fierce, until nine of the ten Laconian ships that had fought with the navarch were lost, and all the other ships had to flee. The Athenian right wing prevented any flight to the north; the only ships that got away sailed south to places like Chios, Cyme, and Phocaea. When the Spartan commander at Mytilene heard of the outcome he, too, fled, freeing Conon to join the main fleet.

According to Diodorus, Arginusae was "the greatest naval battle in history of Greeks against Greeks" (13.98.5). The Spartans lost seventy-seven ships, or sixty-four percent of their force—an astonishing number. At Cynossema, Abydos, and Notium the average loss of the defeated side was twenty-eight percent. At Cyzicus, to be sure, the entire Spartan fleet had been vanquished when the Athenians used deception, surprise, and independently commanded units to draw the enemy out to sea where he could be encircled. A comparable rout took place at Arginusae, where as the result of a brilliant plan the Spartans were once again encircled and cut off from any land nearby. Only because the Athenian left wing could not close the trap did any Spartan ships manage to get away.

The Athenians lost only 25 of their 155 ships and won a magnificent victory. Defeat in this battle would have meant defeat in the war, but with a ragtag fleet they destroyed the superior force trained and prepared by Lysander and killed the brave young admiral who succeeded him. Now, once again, Athens ruled the sea and had good reason to hope for survival and even victory in the war.

RESCUE AND RECOVERY

THEIR TRIUMPH at Arginusae saved the Athenians, but they were unable to revel in it for long, for they were soon embroiled in a bitter quarrel over its conclusion. As the battle came to an end the Athenian fleet was scattered over four square miles of increasingly stormy sea. Of the twenty-five ships lost in the contest the wrecks of twelve still floated, with perhaps a thousand men struggling for their lives, many of them clinging to the wrecks, while the bodies of scores of dead were scattered on and around the wreckage. The captains of the victorious triremes did not stop to rescue the living or to pick up the corpses for burial, but raced back to Arginusae to confer on their next step.

For the Greeks, securing a proper burial for the dead would have been almost as important a consideration as rescuing the living. In epic poetry Odysseus went to the underworld to see to the correct interment of a fallen comrade; in classical tragedy Antigone defied her king and gave her life rather than leave her dead brother unburied. What could have led the Athenians to neglect so sacred a duty?

Part of the answer lies in the unexpected nature of the battle, which took the fleet farther out to sea than usual and dispersed it over a large area. (Every other contest fought since 411 took place in a constrained area close to land.) The standard postbattle procedure would have been for the victorious fleet to land after the fighting was over and then determine how the survivors and corpses were to be collected and who would be responsible for doing so. In every case there would be sufficient time to accomplish the task. No doubt, that was the expected end of this battle, as well, for the Athenian plan to achieve a double envelopment would have brought all its ships into a containing circle not far from the Arginusae Islands. In the event, though, many enemy ships were able to escape a far distance, and when the Athenians were forced to pursue them the usual methods became impossible.

After the captains finally got their fleet back to Arginusae, a second problem arose. Conon was still twelve miles away, locked into Mytilene harbor by a Spartan blockade. When Eteonicus, the Spartan commander there, heard of the outcome of the battle he would surely flee and join the Spartan fleet at Chios. That would result in a Spartan fleet over ninety strong, which would form the basis for another armada to resume the challenge. These powerful strategic arguments compelled the Athenians to take the main fleet to Mytilene and cut off the Spartan escape, though they were surely torn between this demand and the duty toward the survivors and the retrievable bodies. Accordingly, they decided to compromise: two-thirds of the fleet, with all eight generals, hurried off to Mytilene, while forty-seven ships were left behind as a rescue squadron under the leadership of two trierarchs, Theramenes and Thrasybulus.

This decision, too, has had many critics, but it made good sense. The force going to Mytilene had to anticipate another battle if they succeeded in cutting off the ships of Eteonicus, and it was reasonable to send the generals who had planned and executed the great victory at Arginusae to finish the job. Theramenes and Thrasybulus were also not ordinary ship captains, but former generals of great talent and experience. They set to work on their mission, but encountered another difficulty when a storm developed, greatly roiling the sea and frightening the men who were to perform the collection of survivors and corpses.

Anyone who has sailed the waters of the Aegean knows how sudden and fierce storms there can be, strong enough to endanger even modern vessels. How much more menacing they must have been to men on the far less secure triremes, which were ill suited to such conditions. At Arginusae the crews under Theramenes and Thrasybulus resisted orders "because of their suffering in the battle and because of the great size of the waves" (Diodorus 13.100.2). The captains did their best, but soon conditions became so bad as to make further argument moot.

The storm also drove the main fleet back to the islands and reunited the force, at which point there were undoubtedly some unpleasant scenes. The generals must have been angry that their orders had not been obeyed and blamed the two captains assigned to the rescue mission. Theramenes and Thrasybulus must have bridled at what they judged an unfair accusation, and perhaps thought that the generals ought to have carried out the rescues and recoveries before the storm became too severe.

When the weather improved, the whole fleet set out for Mytilene, but Conon met them on the way with the news that Eteonicus and his fifty triremes had escaped. After stopping at Mytilene the Athenians pursued the Spartan force to its base at Chios, but Eteonicus was not so foolish as to risk another fight, so the Athenians could only return to their base at Samos. Their truly great victory was tarnished by the their inability to carry out the rescue and recovery operation, and by the ultimate incompleteness of their effort. These factors must have weighed heavily on the generals' minds as they considered the report they must make to the assembly in Athens. At first they wanted to present all the details of the aftermath of the battle, including the failure of the captains to carry out the rescue mission, but they were persuaded instead to omit any mention of that incident and simply to blame the storm for all that had gone wrong. They must have realized that bringing accusations against anyone was bound to start a quarrel, and that both Theramenes and Thrasybulus were popular and skilled speakers with strong political support, and would therefore be formidable opponents.

THE TRIAL OF THE GENERALS

AT ATHENS NEWS of the victory brought relief and joy, and the assembly passed a motion praising the generals responsible for it. At the same time, there was, as the naval commanders had expected, anger at the failure to deal with the survivors and the corpses. Theramenes and Thrasybulus returned to Athens from Samos at once, probably to defend themselves if necessary, but since no one in the city had learned the precise details of what took place at Arginusae, they faced no accusations, nor did any of the generals.

The Athenians' wrath, however, continued to increase, and people began to question the conduct of the generals who, so far as anyone in Athens knew, were in charge of every aspect of the campaign. When news of the public sentiment reached Samos the generals naturally assumed that the two captains were responsible for having discredited them, so they wrote to Athens again, this time revealing that the rescue mission had in fact been assigned to Theramenes and Thrasybulus.

This was a serious misjudgment, for the captains now had no

choice but to defend themselves. They did not deny the seriousness of the storm, but they blamed the generals for the rescue failure. They must also have complained that the generals wasted precious time in vain pursuit, which they could have used to retrieve the men themselves, and of the delay caused by debate at Arginusae before the orders for the rescue were given. By the time the captains received these orders the storm had rendered the mission impossible. Their defense was effective: when the generals' letters were read in the assembly the masses immediately grew angry with the captains "but after they had presented their defense the anger turned back on the generals again" (Diodorus 13.101.4). The assembly accordingly passed a motion deposing the generals and ordering them back to Athens to face trial. Two of them fled into exile at once; the procedure to which the others submitted was probably the *euthynai*, the normal review at the end of every general's term of office, starting with his financial accounts but including every aspect of his conduct in office.

The first to be tried was Erasinides, who was convicted of misappropriation of public money and misconduct in office, and he was imprisoned. Perhaps he was prosecuted first because he was an easy target, or because it had become known that he had proposed ignoring the survivors and the corpses and sending the whole fleet to Mytilene. The five remaining generals then came before the council of Five Hundred to present their accounts of the affair and returned to their original strategy of blaming the storm alone for what had happened. Perhaps when they learned that the two captains had not been held responsible for the charges against them, the generals hoped to restore the original united front. If so, they were too late, for the council voted to imprison the remaining five generals and turn them over for trial by the assembly in its judicial capacity. There, Theramenes read the generals' original letter that blamed only the storm and, along with others, he accused the generals of the loss of the survivors and the unburied bodies.

We can assume that Theramenes and Thrasybulus were angry that the generals had been first to back away from the agreed-upon explanation and had turned against them, and they must have feared that it was too late to return to the original strategy. The Athenian people, by now aware of the full story, were sure to seek culprits and punish them severely. The only remaining question was who the targets would be. By taking the offensive, Theramenes gained the upper hand, and the assembly responded by turning sharply against the generals, shouting down their defenders and not permitting them adequate time to speak in their own defense. Under such pressure they naturally turned upon their accusers, insisting that Theramenes and Thrasybulus had been given the responsibility of saving the survivors and collecting the corpses: "If it were necessary to blame any one in respect to the recovery, there was no one else to blame than those to whom the task had been assigned." Even then, however, they did not abandon their initial defense, asserting that "the violence of the storm prevented the recovery" (Xenophon, *Hellenica* 1.7.6). They brought forth pilots and sailors in support of their claims, which had a powerful effect. The assembly could easily believe that the generals had consistently held to the same account of the incident, choosing not to relate the details of the captains' assignment out of decency and because the storm made them irrelevant.

Xenophon relates that "by saying these things they were on the point of persuading the people" (*Hellenica* 1.7.6), and a moderate and sensible outcome seemed imminent when chance intervened. It grew dark before a vote could be taken, so the assembly decided to postpone its decision until the following day and ordered the council of Five Hundred to propose a procedure for conducting the trial.

By still another stroke of fortune the festival of the Apaturia fell only a few days later, which celebrated rites of birth, manhood, and marriage and brought families together from all over Attica. Ordinarily this was the occasion of great happiness and riotous pleasure, but that year the reunions only served as painful reminders of the absence of the young men who had died in the battle at Arginusae, and reawakened powerful resentments against whomever people thought responsible. When the assembly met the next day as planned, relatives of the dead, their heads shaved in mourning, demanded revenge and "begged the people to punish those who had allowed men who had gladly died in defense of their country to go unburied" (Diodorus 13.101.6).

In response Callixeinus, a member of the Five Hundred, suggested to his council a procedure most unfriendly to the generals, proposing that there be no further debate, but only a vote on their guilt or innocence. The question would be put in the most prejudicial language: whether or not the generals were guilty "for not rescuing the men who had won the victory in the naval battle" (Xenophon, *Hellenica* 1.7.9). The penalty would be death to the convicted and the confiscation of their property. Finally, the generals would be tried together, with one vote of the assembly deciding the fate of all. The council approved this proposal, unusual and prejudicial as it was, leaving the generals no opportunity to try to change the hostile mood in which this second assembly met.

The debate in the assembly was highly emotional. A man claiming to be a survivor at Arginusae recalled how drowning men in the water near him had asked him to tell the Athenians that "the generals had not rescued the men who had shown themselves the best in the service of their country" (Xenophon, *Hellenica* 1.7.11). In so heated an atmosphere Euryptolemus, cousin and close associate of Alcibiades, dared to speak on behalf of the accused. He charged Callixeinus with having made an illegal motion and in so doing called forth the *graphe paranomon*, a relatively new Athenian procedure for defending the constitution.

This measure forbade action on the proposer's motion until he himself had stood trial on the charge of making an illegal proposal and been acquitted. Some in the assembly applauded this action, but many held a different view. One of the members proposed that Euryptolemus and those who supported him be included in the charges made against the generals, a suggestion that won such great support that Callixeinus' original motion was withdrawn.

This brought the assembly back to the original motion, which would sentence all the generals to death by a single vote. However some of the prytanies—the committee of the council chosen by chance and rotation to preside over the assembly on any given day—refused to put this question to a vote on the grounds that it was illegal. Their logic rested on two strong arguments: first, that to try the accused en masse violated the traditional practice of the assembly and, more particularly, the decree of Cannonus that specifically guaranteed a separate trial for any defendant; second, that the generals had not been given the time and opportunity to speak in their own defense as prescribed by law. These arguments would have been hard to refute, but Callixeinus, sensing the hostility of the crowd against the generals, did not even attempt a rebuttal. Instead, he proposed that the same charges leveled against the generals be made to include the recalcitrant prytanies, and the people responded with a roar of agreement.

This so frightened the prytanies that they withdrew their objections and agreed to put the council's proposal to a vote. It happened by sheer chance that Socrates had been chosen by lot to serve as a council member for that year, the only public office he ever held. In addition, his tribe happened to hold the prytany for that month and, by an even greater coincidence, Socrates himself happened on that day to be serving as *prostates*, the presiding officer of the assembly. Alone among the prytranies, he held fast to his position and refused to put the question to a vote. Some years later, after the war, Plato reported his teacher's account of his behavior as Socrates defended himself before an Athenian court: "I was the only one of the Prytanies who was opposed to the illegality, and I gave my vote against you [the Athenian people]; and when the orators threatened to indict and arrest me, and you insisted and shouted out, I decided that I must run the risk on the side of law and justice rather than to be on your side against justice because of fear of prison or death" (*Apology* 32b–c). But even in the face of so principled a stand the passion of the assembly was too strong, and the hearing went forward.

Now Euryptolemus bravely rose again, suggesting different procedures that would still deal with the accused harshly but would allow them to be tried separately. He clearly believed that the strong emotions provoked by the events, the grief intensified by the Apaturia, and the emotions fanned by orators would fade after even only a little time, and that the individual trials would give the defendants a chance to make their case and to let reason rule. He made a brilliant speech that warned against illegal procedures and reminded the assembly of the great victory won by the accused generals, and he almost prevailed when a proposal to try the generals separately won a majority of votes. In the end, however, parliamentary maneuvering undid that victory. A second vote was taken, and the assembly this time voted what the council had proposed: to put all eight generals to death, including the two who had never returned.

Euryptolemus had only barely failed to save them, but he was correct in thinking that the Athenians would be unable to retain their anger. "Not long afterwards the Athenians repented and voted to bring charges against those who had deceived the people." Callixeinus was one of five so accused and arrested. They all escaped before their trial, but when Callixeinus returned to the city, "he was hated by everyone and died of starvation" (Xenophon, *Hellenica* 1.7.35).

For executing the generals the Athenians have been rightly censured through the ages, but the argument that has been made from ancient to modern times that such misdeeds are especially characteristic of democracies is far from the mark. Atrocities have been perpetrated by every kind of regime throughout history. It is precisely the general adherence to law and due process by the Athenian democracy that makes this departure from the norm so notorious. The Athenians, as we have seen, repented their error at once and did not repeat it, but it was a permanent black mark that the enemies of democracy used to attack the Athenians' government and way of life ever after.

The Athenians also suffered serious practical consequences of their decision almost immediately. Few states at war can spare eight experienced and successful military leaders. Besides the loss of the generals for 406/5, Athens also was deprived of the services of two other experienced commanders connected to the events surrounding Arginusae. Thrasybulus was not chosen as a general in the election of 405, and Theramenes, though elected, was disqualified by the board that regularly examined newly named officials. Athens now had to face the challenge posed by Sparta and Persia without the experience of most of its best commanders, and those who were selected in their stead must have been unnerved by the fate of their predecessors.

CHAPTER THIRTY-SEVEN

The Fall of Athens (405–404)

FOR ALL THEIR misfortunes after the battle, the Athenians had won a great victory at Arginusae, and the Spartans' fleet suffered badly. Although ninety triremes remained to them, no money was available to pay the crews, and the soldiers and sailors were able to escape starvation only by hiring themselves out as farm laborers on Chios. Their poverty grew so desperate that some of them planned an attack on the island's capital city, Sparta's ally. For the moment, the frightened Chians agreed to support the troops, but without Persian funding Sparta could not continue the war in the Aegean. At home, many were thoroughly discouraged by a defeat at the hands of so inexperienced an Athenian force. Spartans who shared Callicratidas' convictions, moreover, regarded collaboration with Persians against Greeks as a disgrace, and political opponents of Lysander feared his return to the command and his personal ambitions.

ANOTHER SPARTAN PEACE OFFER

FOR ALL THESE reasons the Spartans once again sought peace, this time offering to evacuate Decelea, with each side keeping every other area it held. For the Athenians this represented a better offer than the one they had rejected after Cyzicus. Although Athens had lost Pylos in 410/9 the Spartans were willing to abandon their fortress in Attica without a quid pro quo. Since 410 they had likewise been forced to cede control of Byzantium and Chalcedon, enabling the Athenians to regain freedom of the Bosporus and access to the Black Sea and the grain supplies on its shore. By now Sparta's only significant holdings were Abydos in the Hellespont, the important island of Chios off the Ionian coast, and Cyme, Phocaea, and Ephesus, significant cities on the mainland. Although the peace overture did not offer everything the Athenians would have liked, the improvement in terms since Cyzicus was considerable. It should have been attractive on other grounds, as well. If Sparta chose to continue fighting with renewed Persian assistance, it could swiftly restore numerical superiority to its fleet and continue to win over rowers from the enemy with higher pay. And, however glorious, the Athenians' victory at Arginusae was nevertheless something of a miracle, and a resumption of the war would soon exhaust their resources. Peace, on the other hand, would allow the Athenians to establish security in the empire and to collect tribute and refill the city's coffers. Sparta's withdrawal from Decelea would likewise permit Athenian farmers to return to their fields and begin producing crops again.

In spite of these temptations, Athens rejected Sparta's offer. Aristotle, among other ancient writers, blames the reckless foolishness to be expected in a democracy, and especially the "demagogue" Cleophon, who "prevented the peace; entering the assembly drunk and dressed in his military breastplate, he said he would not permit a peace agreement unless the Spartans surrendered all the cities" (*Constitution of the Athenians* 14.1). This is plainly a partisan version of events, but whatever its accuracy, the fact remains that a majority of the thousands of the Athenians present did reject the peace. The likeliest explanation for their demurral is their continuing distrust of the Spartans after their breach of faith during the Peace of Nicias: neither oaths to carry out the peace terms nor oaths ratifying a treaty of alliance were sufficient guarantee for the Peloponnesians to keep their agreements. In 406 the Athenians feared that the enemy might once again use a peace as a mere truce, providing it the time to regroup, to recover from defeat, and to negotiate again with the Persians for the funds with which to wage a renewed war to victory. They must have judged it safer to continue to press for a total victory while the Spartans were weak and discouraged and their relations with Persia strained.

THE RETURN OF LYSANDER

THE TROUBLE WITH this plan, however, was that Cyrus remained satrap, and determined to use Spartan forces for his own purposes, while Lysander bided his time to join him as his collaborator. During the winter of 406/5, in fact, Sparta's allies in the Aegean and on the Asian mainland met at Ephesus. Since Sparta's defeat at Arginusae they had been suffering badly from unopposed Athenian attacks, and together with envoys from Cyrus they petitioned the Spartans to reinstate Lysander to his command. Although two barriers stood in the way of the request—namely, Spartan politics and the Spartan constitution—both were easily swept aside, for the Athenian victory, the death of Callicratidas, and Athens' rejection of the peace offer left no choice. Because the war had to go on, Sparta's allies, both Greek and Persian, could not be denied. Any opposition to the ambitious Lysander must give way to necessity, and so must constitutional restraints. Since the law provided that a man serve as navarch only once in his life, the Spartans appointed Aracus as nominal navarch and named Lysander as his secretary (*epistoleus*) and vice-admiral. Everyone understood that this was merely a legal fiction.

The brilliant spark of Spartan naval warfare went into action at once, gathering ships from his old base at Ephesus and ordering the construction of new ones. He then quickly sought an audience with Cyrus to request the money that was so desperately needed. Although the prince remained sincerely attached to Lysander, he had to report that the Great King's money had all been spent, along with a good deal of his own. He promised, however, to continue support from his own resources, even if the King refused, and to make good on his word produced a large sum on the spot.

Cyrus needed the support of Lysander, not only for his future ambitions but also as a solution to his current troubles. His murder of his royal cousins had been met with complaints from their parents, and Darius had responded by recalling him to his court at Susa.

The young prince had little choice but to obey, and as he could trust no Persian to govern in his absence, he took a remarkable step: summoning Lysander to Sardis, he appointed the Spartan as satrap in his place over the province of the Persian Empire. He left him the entire amount of money available and assigned him the right to collect all tribute due. Trusting the Spartan's loyalty but not his prudence, he asked Lysander not to attack the Athenians until he returned. That request suited Lysander well, for his fleet would be numerically inferior for some months, and he needed time to bring his crews back up to his own high standard of training.

In Cyrus' absence, meanwhile, Lysander's personal goals required that he undo the influence of the late Callicratidas, who had awakened powerful pan-Hellenic, anti-Persian sentiments, which undermined political support for Lysander among the Greeks of the region. This was especially the case at Miletus, where a democratic government unfriendly to him held power, and his first action was to depose it. Since the city remained loyal to Sparta, he could not simply attack it, so he resorted to the trickery and deception that would always be a part of his political arsenal. Although in public he uttered approving words about the end of factionalism in Miletus, he privately encouraged his supporters to rebel against the democracy. Resorting to political murder, they killed some 340 opponents in their homes and in the marketplace and drove more than a thousand others from the city. In place of the democracy they installed their own faction at the head of an oligarchy dependent on and fiercely loyal, not to Sparta but to Lysander. His Miletus campaign was a harbinger of his methods in the future. To critics of his treacherous means, the man who boasted of cheating "boys with knuckle-bones and men with oaths" coolly justified himself by observing that "where the lion's skin will not reach, it must be patched with the fox's" (Plutarch, *Lysander* 7.4; 8.4).

To reach Miletus Lysander had been compelled to sail southward, past the Athenian fleet at Samos. As Lysander's crews were not yet in top form, the Athenians, who still outnumbered the Spartans, ought to have been on the alert for any chance to force another battle at sea, but they made no effort to intercept Lysander. Their hesitation to do so was part of the legacy of the execution and exile of the generals who had won at Arginusae, for the new generals were less experienced and lacked the confidence gained by victory. No leader had emerged from their number, and all must have been timid and suspicious, remembering the fate of their predecessors.

Their wariness was costly, for on his departure from Miletus Lysander soon turned the strategic situation to his favor. In Caria and Rhodes he stormed Athenian allied cities, killing the men and enslaving the women and children. These were acts of deliberate, exemplary terror, meant to discourage resistance by other Athenian allies. His policy was the reverse of Callicratidas'; there was to be no Panhellenism. The battle lines were drawn not between Greek and Persian but between friend and foe of Lysander. Even so, the war had to be won in the Straits, and the superior Athenian fleet at Samos that barred the way had to be circumvented. To that end he raced westward across the Aegean, taking islands, raiding Aegina and Salamis in Athens' home waters, and finally landing in Attica itself. Even the most fearful Athenian commanders could not allow such attacks to go unopposed, so their fleet set out in pursuit. Lysander evaded them by racing back across the southern Aegean to Rhodes. From there he hurried north along the coast; safely passed Samos, from which the Athenian fleet was now absent; and made his way to the Hellespont, "to prevent the merchant-ships from sailing out and against the cities that had rebelled against the Spartans" (Xenophon, *Hellenica* 2.1.18). A powerful Spartan fleet led by a brilliant and daring commander once again threatened the Athenian lifeline.

THE BATTLE OF AEGOSPOTAMI

FROM HIS BASE at Abydos (see Map 29) Lysander gathered an army, placed it under the command of the Spartan Thorax, and attacked the key city of Lampsacus by land and sea, taking it by storm. This success put the Spartans on the doorstep of the Propontis, opening the way to Byzantium and Chalcedon, control of the Bosporus, and the strangulation of Athenian trade with the Black Sea. The Athenians knew that not only would all their achievements at Cynossema, Cyzicus, and Arginusae be undone, but the survival of Athens itself would be in doubt unless Lysander could be compelled to fight and defeated decisively. Accordingly they arrived at their base at Sestos, from where they moved the fleet about twelve miles up the Hellespont to a place called Aegospotami, which lay about three miles across the strait from Lampsacus.

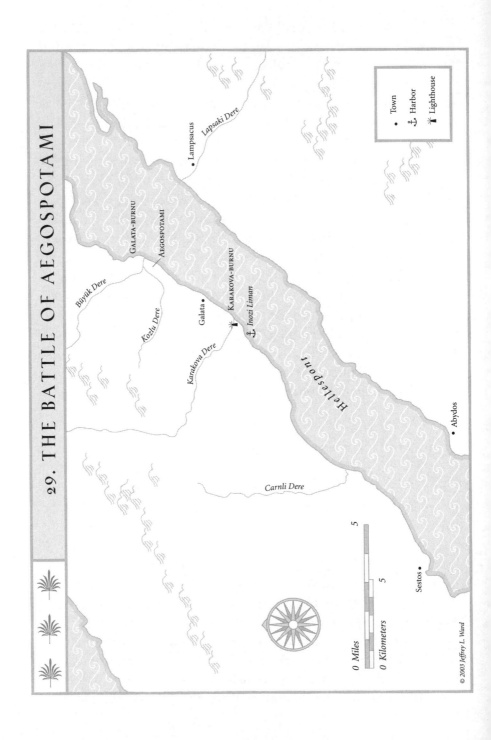

29. THE BATTLE OF AEGOSPOTAMI

Town
Harbor
Lighthouse

Lapsaki Dere

Lampsacus

GALATA-BURNU

AEGOSPOTAMI

Büyük Dere

Kozlu Dere

Galata

KARAKOVA-BURNU

Karakova Dere

Inozi Liman

Hellespont

Abydos

Carnli Dere

Sestos

0 Miles   5

0 Kilometers   5

© 2003 Jeffrey L. Ward

The decision to situate the Athenian fleet there was controversial from the first, for the area contained only a beach, without a proper harbor. The little town nearby could not begin to provide enough food and water for the approximately thirty-six thousand men on the ships, so that to obtain supplies the Athenians would have to divide and scatter their forces repeatedly to make the twenty-four-mile round trip to the main base at Sestos. Why did they not simply camp at Sestos and avoid so great a risk? The answer must lie in the strategic necessities facing them. Their first objective was to pin Lysander down and prevent him from sailing into the Propontis and toward the Bosporus; the second was to force a battle as soon as possible before their money ran out. The first would be impossible from a base twelve miles from Lysander's, while the second would be more difficult from that distance, as well as more dangerous. To challenge the Spartan fleet at Lampsacus from Sestos the Athenians would also have to row against the current and a prevailing wind, which meant they would arrive at the battle site tired and vulnerable to a rested enemy. While these reasons justify the Athenians' choice of base they do not account for their subsequent conduct of the campaign.

Six Athenian generals led the force at Aegospotami. As at Arginusae, there was no supreme commander, so the generals rotated leadership each day. Unlike the commanders at Arginusae, however, they failed to formulate a brilliantly original strategy, but relied on the obvious approach of moving their fleet to the harbor at Lampsacus each morning and challenging Lysander to come out and fight. Precise figures are not available, but the Spartans seem to have had about the same number of ships as their opponents. For four days their commander kept his fleet in the harbor. Time was speeding by, and the Athenians seemed to have no way to force Lysander into battle.

It was at this moment that none other than Alcibiades made a dramatic reappearance. He seems to have been living in exile on land he owned on the Gallipoli Peninsula, and from his castle had observed the standoff. Riding down to the Athenian camp on horseback, he offered his advice and assistance. He urged the generals to move their base to Sestos for the obvious reasons, and announced that two Thracian kings had promised him an army with which to win the war. The advice, as we have seen, was less useful than he believed, but the introduction of ground troops would have been very valuable. If the Athenians could take Lampsacus by land, Lysander would be forced to try to fight his way out of the harbor against an Athenian fleet in a stronger position, and at a time and place of their choosing. Under those conditions defeat would be certain and, with the land in hostile hands, the Spartan fleet would be destroyed as it had been at Cyzicus.

The Athenian generals, however, had good reason to doubt that the forces promised by Alcibiades would appear if summoned, for they knew all too well that similar promises in the past had not been kept. The renegade had also set unacceptable conditions for his help—namely, a share in the command of the Athenian forces. No doubt they questioned his motives, suspecting "a desire to accomplish some great deed for his country through his own efforts and through his accomplishments restore the people to their old affection for him" (Diodorus 13.105.3). Whatever their concerns, no Athenian general would have dared to yield any part of the command to an exile twice condemned by the Athenian people; still less were they inclined to accept the proposal of a man like Alcibiades, fearing that "if they were defeated they themselves would get the blame but that the credit for any success would go to Alcibiades." Instead, they told him that "they were the generals now, and not he" (Diodorus 13.105.4), and then ordered him to leave.

They now returned to the original tactics, but the delay and inaction had a deleterious effect on discipline and morale. The men became careless, going off to seek food and water as soon as their ships touched the beach, without taking proper precautions for security, and their commanders did not call them to task. The situation was difficult, and holding the crews to high standards would not have been easy in any case, but the timidity of the generals only exacerbated the problem.

On the fifth day the rotation in command fell to Philocles, who appears to have had a plan to end the stalemate and bring the enemy to battle. With thirty ships he sailed out in the direction of Sestos, leaving orders to the captains of the rest of the fleet to follow him at the appropriate time. His notion seems to have been to persuade Lysander that the Athenians had finally tired of maintaining a fruitless position at

Aegospotami and were accordingly moving to their major base down-stream. The temptation to pursue a detachment small enough to defeat easily but large enough to be a worthwhile target, he hoped, would be irresistible to the Spartans. In fact, Lysander himself had attempted something similar at Notium when he attacked Antiochus' advance squadron and then won a great victory when the rest of the Athenian fleet came to his rescue. Perhaps Philocles had taken note of that stratagem and planned to exploit it at Aegospotami. This time the detachment of an advance squadron would be a deliberate lure, and the main force would be ready to pounce on Lysander when he took the bait.

The plan was a promising one, but it would need skillful and confident command, great discipline, and excellent timing and coordination between squadrons to achieve success. On that day, however, the Athenian fleet was poorly supplied with these qualities. The enemy fleet, in contrast, was well trained, and under the command of a single leader who was justly confident of his great talent. Lysander knew that the Athenians would eventually have to decide either to withdraw or to employ some trick to draw him into battle, and he was ready for either contingency, so he patiently kept a close watch on the enemy, saw to it that his own fleet was fit, alert, and ready, and carefully prepared to strike when the chance arose. As soon as he saw Philocles' departure, he was quick off the mark and cut the Athenian squadron off before it was able to get far downstream. With superior forces he turned on Philocles, routed his unit, and then headed for the main Athenian force behind him. His movements were too fast for the Athenians, whose timing was off. Their plan had envisaged Lysander's ships chasing Philocles down the strait, with their rear invitingly exposed. Instead, the Athenians at Aegospotami were stunned to see the scattered remnants of Philocles' squadron fleeing toward them with Lysander's victorious fleet in hot pursuit. Panic and paralysis ensued, and many ships were caught on the beach without their crews.

The Athenians' confusion encouraged Lysander to put a corps of soldiers on land under Eteonicus to seize their camp, while his own victorious ships were already hauling away the beached Athenian triremes. The stunned Athenians had no organized land force to resist either offensive and ran off in all directions, with the majority heading toward Sestos to save their lives. Of the great Athenian navy all but ten ships were captured or sunk. Lysander had reversed the outcome of Cyzicus, but the defeated Athenians had no ally to restore their fortunes, and with their own treasury empty, they could not afford to build another fleet. Thus, they had lost the war.

THE RESULTS OF THE BATTLE

AFTER SWIFTLY SENDING word of his great victory to Sparta, Lysander found at Lampsacus between three and four thousand Athenian prisoners, which constituted about a tenth of the entire enemy force. In spite of his previous harshness toward defeated enemies, we cannot be certain that, were the choice his alone, he would have killed or enslaved the prisoners. His recorded atrocities do not seem to have been committed in the heat of the moment but were typically the result of cold-blooded calculation. As we have seen, he could be clement when mercy suited his purpose.

The decision, however, rested in less calculating hands, and the vengeful allies insisted on the death penalty. During the course of a war that lasted for more than a quarter-century cities such as Corinth, Megara, and Aegina had seen their land devastated, their trade cut off, their economies ruined, and their prosperity and status permanently diminished. They had suffered casualties in the fighting and been subjected to increasingly cruel treatment as the struggle continued. Atrocities on both sides had grown ever more horrible, but the Athenian massacres and enslavements of the populations of cities like Scione and Melos were especially well known, and victors commonly tend to excuse if not forget their own excesses even as they are infuriated by those they have endured. Only recently, moreover, had the Athenians, angry with the deserters from their fleet, voted to cut off the right hand of every captive. In the same mood, Philocles had ordered the crews of two captured enemy ships thrown overboard. With such actions fresh in their minds, the Spartans and their allies voted to kill all their Athenian prisoners.

Xenophon, who was probably present, reports how Athens received the news of Aegospotami:

The *Paralus* [one of two swift ships used for special missions] arrived at Athens at night and announced the disaster, and a wailing came from the Piraeus, through the Long Walls, to the city, one man passing the word to another, so that on that night no one slept. They wept not only for the men who had been killed but even more for themselves, thinking that they would suffer the kind of fate they had imposed on the Melians, colonists of the Spartans, after they had conquered them by siege, and on the Histiaeans and Scionaeans and Toroneans and Aeginetans and many others among the Hellenes. (*Hellenica* 2.2.3)

The treatment of the prisoners at Aegospotami must have only convinced them further that surrender would bring death, slavery, or exile, at the very least, so they chose to resist. The assembly voted to take all possible measures to defend the city, and the Athenians prepared for the inevitable siege.

In the Straits Lysander soon regained control of policy, and there were no further massacres. Instead he offered reasonable terms to cities allied to Athens, and they surrendered without a struggle. He even permitted Athenian garrisons and officials to leave in safety on condition that they go only to Athens. This latter gesture, though appearing benificent, was in fact a canny tactical move: Lysander knew that Athens was too strong to storm and could thus be taken only by siege, and he wanted as many hungry people in the city as possible to minimize the time it could hold out. To achieve the same purpose he placed garrisons at Byzantium and Chalcedon on either side of the Bosporus and decreed the death penalty for anyone bringing grain to Athens.

His arrangements in these two cities set the pattern for the system he meant to establish everywhere under his control. He stationed garrisons in them under commanders called harmosts, not "on the basis of aristocratic birth or of wealth, but he put control of affairs into the hands of members of his political faction and those connected to him by personal ties, and he put them in charge of rewards and punishments" (Plutarch, *Lysander* 13.4). Everywhere he found them he replaced democratic governments with oligarchies of his own loyalists, often consisting of boards of ten men called "decarchies," made up of those personally close to him. Before long the "liberator of the Greeks" was collecting tribute from the cities under his control, and the Spartan government ratified all these arrangements.

Lysander then sailed into the Aegean, taking control of cities from the Athenian Empire. Samos, alone, resisted; there the democratic ruling faction, fiercely loyal to Athens, killed its aristocratic opponents and prepared to endure the Spartan siege. Lysander left 40 ships for the purpose, taking 150 more toward Attica. On the way he restored the Melians and Aeginetans, who had been removed by the Athenians, to their native islands. Lysander had no objection to assuming the role of a liberator if it did his personal cause no harm.

THE FATE OF ATHENS

IN OCTOBER 405 Lysander finally arrived in Attica, where he met the entire Peloponnesian army at the precinct of the Academy, just outside the walls of Athens. Rather than departing with the usual two-thirds of each city's contingent, Agis had marched all his forces from Decelea, and King Pausanias had led the remainder of the army from the Peloponnese. It was the first time in more than a century that both Spartan kings were in the field simultaneously. Their intention was to intimidate the awed Athenians into immediate surrender, but even so unprecedented a show of force could not bring that about.

Some of the Athenians, at least, must have been moved by hope as well as fear of the consequences of surrender. Although their enemies were united in their hatred of the Athenian Empire, they did not necessarily share the same goals. Theban and Spartan ambitions, for example, had already come into some conflict during the war. While the complete destruction of Athens would suit the Thebans, their immediate neighbors, who might expect to move into the vacuum so created, Sparta would not benefit from an expansion of the power of its ambitious ally. In time the Spartans might see an advantage in offering better terms to the Athenians, and in any event they were not of a single mind about how to deal with their vanquished enemy. Lysander pursued an ambitious policy that aimed at replacing the Athenian Empire with a Spartan one under his control. It was unclear what Agis thought of that, but Pausanias, like his father, Pleistoanax, would soon reveal his preference for a much more conservative policy that would have the Spartans confine their activities to the Peloponnesus and seek comfortable relations with an Athens stripped of its power and empire. The king's natural influence might eventually assert itself against the temporary prestige of Lysander, and a more acceptable settlement with Athens might result. The Athenians, therefore, prepared to hold out as long as they could.

When the Spartans saw that there would be no immediate surrender they sent the army of Pausanias back home, while Lysander took the bulk of his fleet to besiege Samos, leaving enough ships to maintain the blockade of Athens. Not long before these departures they called a meeting of their allies to discuss the fate of Athens. It was probably then that Thebes and Corinth suggested its destruction, a proposal supported by both Agis and Lysander "on their own initiative and without the approval of the Spartan assembly" (Pausanias 3.8.6; the second-century A.D. author, not the Spartan king). Frightened, perhaps, by news of this decision, the Athenians sent word to Agis, who had since returned to Decelea, offering to join the Spartan alliance if they could keep their walls and Piraeus. Although under such an agreement they would have given up the claim to their lost empire, Agis responded by denying his authority to negotiate a peace and told them to take up the matter in Sparta. He obviously did not want to associate himself with such lenient terms.

When the Athenians sent ambassadors to Sparta to discuss the matter the ephors did not allow them into the city but met them at Sellasia on the Laconian frontier, where they asked them to present their proposals. On hearing the terms the Athenians had suggested to Agis, they rejected them without discussion and ordered the envoys "to go back from that very spot and, if they wanted a peace of any kind, to return with a better proposal" (Xenophon, *Hellenica* 2.2.13). At the least, they said, the Athenians must agree to breach the Long Walls for a distance of more than a mile, making them indefensible. That was a terrifying prospect, for it meant that Athens could be cut off from the sea and starved out by a siege at any time the Spartans chose to impose one.

The Spartans' very refusal even to discuss terms was a terrible hardship, for in the time needed to conduct negotiation many Athenians would starve, so close to the edge were they. A man by the name of Archestratus arose in the Athenian council and proposed the acceptance of the Spartan conditions, but even in their desperate state the Athenians would not hear of it. They imprisoned Archestratus for having made the suggestion and passed instead the motion of Cleophon to forbid in the future any similar proposal. So extreme a reaction was the product of distrust, for the Athenians believed that whatever the Spartans might say or swear to, they would kill or enslave them if they were given the slightest chance.

THERAMENES NEGOTIATES A PEACE

EVEN CLEOPHON could not postpone peace negotiations forever, however, and after an interval the pressure of hunger became intolerable. Now Theramenes—the very man who had taken part in the initiative to save Athens from defeat in 411, and who had stepped forward to overthrow the Four Hundred when they were about to betray the city to the Spartans—risked danger again in an effort to ward off disaster. His intervention was a typically moderate proposal, one that avoided the extremes of either accepting Sparta's terms or flatly refusing to negotiate. He proposed instead to seek out Lysander to learn the Spartans' true intentions—namely, did they really mean to destroy Athens and its people? At the same time, he told the assembly that he had discovered "something of great value" (Lysias 13.9) to Athens and asked the people to vote him full powers to negotiate peace. When pressed to reveal what this valuable item was, he declined to answer and urged the people to trust him. The Athenians must have realized that secrecy was critical if their negotiator was to have any chance at success, and by now they were eager for an agreement if one could be found, so they approved Theramenes' motion.

He found Lysander at Samos and stayed with him there for some three months. On his return early in March 404 he explained his long absence by saying that the Spartan had kept him there against his will and then sent him off with the same message as Agis': he had no power to discuss peace terms; for those the Athenians must go to the ephors in Sparta. That explanation is most implausible, and even the ancient writers did not believe it. They assert, instead, that Theramenes chose to stay as long as he did to allow the Athenians to grow so hungry that they would accept any peace the Spartans offered. Reason and the evidence compel a rejection of that view, however; Theramenes' absence would more likely have only prolonged resistance, for the Athenians would have been less inclined to surrender to the stated Spartan terms while their envoy was still trying to obtain a better peace. To hurry the process Theramenes need only have returned with the news that the Spartans did not in fact intend to demolish Athens but that Lysander continued to insist on the stated terms. If the Athenians believed, moreover, that he had spent so long a time with Lysander while the people suffered and then came back empty-handed they would hardly have then chosen him to lead a commission to Sparta to negotiate a peace. He must have persuaded the Athenians that he had made significant progress in the long discussions with Lysander and was now in a position to achieve a more satisfactory peace.

That, in any case, was the result, for ultimately the Spartans agreed to a settlement that left Athens intact, its people alive and free, if not fully autonomous. How did Theramenes persuade Lysander to abandon his former commitment to the destruction of Athens, and what was the "something of great value" that he claimed to have discovered? The ancient writers do not say, but reasonable speculations are possible. Theramenes hoped to salvage what he could from the situation, but he must have understood that Athens must give up its empire, its fleet, and its walls, for Sparta would accept nothing less. His goals were to save the city, its people, their freedom, and as much independence as possible. The long discussions with Lysander were needed to achieve these goals, as Lysander tried to counter the arguments of the faction that sought Athens' destruction.

The most fervent of that group were the Thebans, along with the Corinthians. It was a Theban, Erianthus, who formally proposed that "the city be leveled and the countryside left as a pasture for sheep" (Plutarch, *Lysander* 15.2). It would not have been difficult for Theramenes to persuade Lysander that razing Athens would leave its territory prey to its increasingly powerful and ambitious rival to the north. It would not be in the interests of either Sparta or Lysander to contribute to the growth of a state that had given Sparta frequent trouble during the war, had grown in size and influence in the course of it, and was currently under the control of a faction unfriendly to Sparta that was already claiming a greater share of the spoils of war. It would be far wiser, Theramenes could point out, to retain a friendly and unthreatening Athens as a buffer and a check on Theban ambitions.

In a postwar Athens Lysander would have preferred a tight oligarchy made up entirely of his close supporters—perhaps a decarchy supported by a garrison, as in the former Athenian Empire. What arguments could Theramenes have offered to persuade him, therefore, to grant the city some degree of autonomy? As it happened, Lysander's success and the extraordinary honors paid him in various cities had already made him an object of concern and jealousy to the Spartan kings and other leading figures. "He was the first Greek to whom the cities raised altars and made sacrifices as to a god" (Plutarch, *Lysander* 18.3); the restored Samian oligarchs, for example, changed the name of their chief festival from the *Heraea* to the *Lysandreia*. Both Spartan kings would soon enough reveal their hostility to Lysander's pretensions and undo the regime he would impose on the Athenians. Such antipathy must already have existed, so Theramenes could justifiably argue that the establishment of a narrow oligarchy, blatantly under Lysander's control, would give rise to a unified opposition of the kings and his other enemies to his plans. Such a regime, moreover, would antagonize most Athenians, accustomed to democracy for more than a century, and might drive them to an embarrassing resistance. It would be more stable and safer, Theramenes might argue, to install a broader, more moderate regime.

Perhaps Theramenes had another bargaining point, the "something of great value" he had mentioned to the Athenians. One critical element supporting the power of Lysander was his close relationship with the Persian prince Cyrus, on whom he counted for financial, military, and political assistance. It was Cyrus' help that had made victory possible and raised Lysander to his exalted stature, but Cyrus' own position was now in danger. Recalled to Susa, he found his father, Darius II, on his deathbed. His demise would bring to the throne Cyrus' unfriendly older brother as Artaxerxes II who, at the least, would put an end to Cyrus' command in the west and with it his power to help Lysander. That could well change the balance of power in the situation, for the new king might revert to the earlier policy of trying to prevent any single great power from emerging among the Greeks, which could lead him to support Athens against Sparta. While his backing could not reverse the outcome of the war, it could allow Athens to hold out behind its walls until even better terms could be secured, as well as encourage Lysander's Spartan opponents to undermine his position. It was very much in Lysander's interests, Theramenes could argue, to make a reasonable peace and install a friendly regime in Athens before Darius died and the news reached Greece.

Such speculations, at any rate, would explain why Theramenes could return to Athens early in March with the news that Lysander was prepared to support an acceptable peace and why the Athenians then elected him as head of the commission to negotiate such a peace at Sparta. Lysander had also sent a message to the ephors reporting on his meetings with Theramenes. His formal account was that he had given the same correct reply as Agis had made before him: the decision lay with the ephors and the Spartan citizens. Informally, he must have notified them of his own change of mind. Certainly, that view carried the day unopposed by kings or ephors, who seem to have competed in finding rhetoric to describe their noble motives. The peace terms they offered were these: the Long Walls and the walls of Piraeus were to come down; Lysander would decide how many ships Athens could keep (that number would, of course, be very small); the Athenians would give up all the cities they controlled but keep the land of Attica; they must permit all exiles to return home (most of these would be oligarchs friendly to Sparta); the Athenians would be governed by their ancestral constitution (what this meant was unclear and soon became an object of fierce contention); and the Athenians were to have the same friends and enemies as the Spartans and follow them wherever they might lead. (This in effect turned Athenian foreign policy over to Spartan control.)

These terms may seem harsh, but less so in light of the fact that the Athenians had feared that the Spartans would refuse anything short of unconditional surrender and the destruction of Athens and its people or their enslavement. When Theramenes reported the terms offered, some of his countrymen, nevertheless, rejected them. The chief opponents were the uncompromising democrats like Cleophon, who knew that capitulation would spell the end of democracy and that the return of the bitterly oligarchic exiles would mean the death of the demo-cratic leaders. So threatening was their influence that the advocates of peace believed they had to be removed; when Theramenes returned to Athens he found that Cleophon had been tried and executed. Even then, influential Athenians continued to complain to Theramenes. In response the supporters of peace, now in the majority, brought charges against the leading dissidents and had them jailed. The day after Theramenes' return the Athenians met to consider Sparta's proposal, and though to the very end some Athenians voted against it, the great majority voted to accept.

On that day in March 404, a little over twenty-seven years since it had begun, the great war between Athens and Sparta came to an end. Later in the month Lysander arrived to enforce the peace terms; the exiles who accompanied him expected this to begin a new era in Athenian history. Sparta's allies, covered with wreaths of flowers, danced and rejoiced. "With great zeal they set about tearing down the walls to the music of flute-girls, thinking that this day was the begin-ning of freedom from the Greeks" (Xenophon, *Hellenica* 2.2.3).

Archidamus' prediction that the Spartans of 431 would leave the war to their sons had come true, but he would have been astonished to learn that the conflict ended in a great naval victory for the Spartans in alliance with the very "barbarians" they had been so proud to have de-feated in 479. Pericles' predictions for the course of the war had long since been discredited. No one, in fact, had foreseen a contest so long, so bitter, so costly, and so destructive of life, property, and the ancient traditions and institutions of the Greeks. War, as Thucydides said, is a violent teacher, and no Greek war had ever been as brutal. The thin tis-sue of civilization that allows human beings to live decently and achieve their higher possibilities was repeatedly ripped asunder, plung-ing the combatant into depths of cruelty and viciousness of which only human beings at their worst are capable. The declared purpose of the victors, the liberation of the Greeks, became a mockery even before the war ended, and the peace that followed was of short duration. It was, as Thucydides called it, "the greatest movement ever to roil the Greeks, including also to some part of the barbarian peoples, even, one might say to the greatest part of mankind" (1.1.2). If it was indeed the greatest of Greek wars it was also the most terrible of Greek tragedies.

Conclusion

IN THE END, the Spartan victory brought no freedom to the former subjects of Athens, for Lysander held many Greek cities in Asia Minor, and the Persians recovered many others. The Spartans replaced the Athenian naval empire with one of their own, installing narrow oligarchies and Spartan garrisons and governors in the "liberated cities" and rcimposing tribute on them.

On Athens itself, the Spartans imposed a puppet government of oligarchs whose brutality soon earned them the name "The Thirty Tyrants." The new regime began a reign of terror consisting of widespread confiscation of property and judicial murder, first against well-known leaders of the democracy, then against rich men for the sake of gain, and finally against moderates, even those among their own number who protested these atrocities. As hostility and resistance grew, the Thirty had to call in a garrison of Spartan troops to protect them from their fellow citizens.

Having taken control of the former Athenian Empire the Spartans now dominated the Greek world, suppressing democracy and replacing it with oligarchic satellite governments everywhere. In an Athens that had become an occupied territory where even suspicion of democratic sympathies could bring death, the Athenians found a leader to challenge the situation in Thrasybulus son of Lycus. Unwilling to live under the Thirty, the bold Thrasybulus fled to Thebes, formerly hostile to Athens but now alienated from Sparta. There, escaped Athenian democrats and patriots rallied to him and formed a small army, which he established in a fort in the mountains on Athens' northern frontier. When the forces of the Thirty unsuccessfully attempted to suppress the rebels, more Athenians were encouraged to flee and join the resistance. At last Thrasybulus was strong enough to march out and capture the Piraeus and to fight a Spartan army to a stalemate. The Spartans chose to abandon Athens, and in 403 Thrasybulus and his men restored the full democracy.

Athens was free and democratic again, but the danger was not past. Angered by the outrages committed by the Thirty, many wanted to hunt down and punish the guilty men and those who had collaborated with them, a process that would have brought trials, executions, and banishments. Athens would have been torn by the very factional strife and civil war that had already destroyed democracy in so many other Greeks states. Instead Thrasybulus joined with other moderates to issue an amnesty that protected all but a few of the worst criminals. The newly restored Athenian democracy held firmly to a policy of moderation and restraint, behavior that later won extraordinary praise from Aristotle: "The reaction of [the Athenian democrats] to their previous calamities, both privately and publicly, seems to have been the finest and most statesmanlike that any people has demonstrated." Not only did they declare and enforce the amnesty, they even raised public money to remunerate the Spartans for the sum the Thirty had borrowed to fight against the democrats. "For they thought that this was the way to begin the restoration of harmony. In other cities, when democrats come to power, there is no thought of expending their own money; on the contrary, they seize and redistribute the land of their opponents" (*Constitution of the Athenians* 40.2–3). The moderation of the democrats of 403 was rewarded by a successful reconciliation of the classes and factions that enabled the Athenian democracy to flourish without civil war or coup d'état almost to the end of the fourth century.

Remarkably, the defeat that had threatened to wipe out Athens and its people, to destroy its democratic constitution, and to compromise its ability to dominate others and even to conduct an independent foreign policy, failed to accomplish any of those things for long. Within a year the Athenians had regained their full democracy. Within a decade they had recovered their fleet, walls, and independence, and Athens became a central member of a coalition of states dedicated to preventing Sparta from interfering in the affairs of the rest of Greece. Within a quarter-century they had regained many of their former allies and restored their power to the point where it is possible to speak of a "Second Athenian Empire."

To be sure, the Spartans had become the dominant force in Greece, but their victory brought no repose and much trouble. Within a few years they were compelled to abandon their empire and its tribute, but not before enough money had flowed into Sparta that its traditional discipline and institutions were undermined. Soon the Spartiates had to contend with internal conspiracies that threatened their constitution and their very existence. Abroad, they had to fight a major war against a coalition of former allies and former enemies that held them in check within the Peloponnesus, and from which they were able to emerge intact only through the intervention of Persia. For a short time they clung to a kind of hegemony over their fellow Greeks, but only so long as the Persian king wanted them to do so. Within three decades of their great victory the Spartans were defeated by the Thebans in a major land battle, and their power was destroyed forever.

The costs of the long and brutal Peloponnesian War were enormous. Loss of life was unprecedented and, in some places, devastating. The entire male populations of Melos and Scione were wiped out, while Plataea lost a great portion of its men. A decade after the end of the war the number of adult male Athenians appears to have been about half its size at the start of the conflict. The Athenians lost more people than other states, for they alone suffered from the plague that killed perhaps a third of their population, but the war's devastations of land and interference with trade brought poverty, malnutrition, and disease to other states, as well. The Athenians ruined Megara's crops and cut off its commerce for many years, leaving the Megarians so decimated and impoverished that they were forced to increase their reliance on slave labor to restore the city's prosperity. The Corinthians were able to send as many as five thousand hoplites to fight the Persians at Plataea in 479 but could provide only three thousand—surely their full force—to Nemea to defend their own territory in 394. Poverty caused by the restriction of trade during the war deprived men of the requisite wealth to serve as hoplites, but that alone can not explain the attrition. If only half the decrease was the result of a falling population that would indicate a decline in the number of adult males of some twenty percent in less than a century. The hardships of war, direct or indirect, took a comparable toll in human life throughout the Greek world, from Sicily to the Bosphorus.

Economic damage, even when it did not involve the loss of life, was severe in many places. The loss of her empire put an end to the source of Athens' great public wealth and with it the extraordinary building programs of the fifth century. Agricultural depredation took many years to repair. Not only Megara but the Aegean islands were subjected to frequent ravaging. Corinth, Megara, and Sicyon, Isthmian states for whom commerce was critical, were shut off from trade with the Aegean for almost three decades, and during most of that period their trade with the west was at least severely curtailed. In many parts of Greece, especially the Peloponnesus, poverty was so severe that many men were forced to seek their livelihood as mercenary soldiers, often in foreign armies.

Within the cities the dangers and hardships of war only exacerbated existing factional conflict. Thucydides, Xenophon, Diodorus, and Plutarch all tell of the growing prevalence of civil war, whose horrors became more commonplace as violent and vicious conflicts broke out everywhere between democrats and oligarchs. Anger, frustration, and the desire for vengeance increased as the war dragged on, and they gave rise to a progression of atrocities rarely or not at all known before that time.

Even the powerful ties of family and of the most sacred religious observances succumbed to the pressures of the long war. Its terrible effects encouraged the questioning of the traditional values on which classical Greek society rested and in the process further divided society. Some reacted by rejecting all faith in favor of a skeptical or even cynical rationality, while others tried to return to a more archaic and less rational piety.

The defeat of Athens in the war was also a blow to the prospects for democracy in other Greek cities. The influence of political systems on people outside them is closely connected with their success in war. The democratic constitution of a powerful and successful Athens was a magnet and a model for others, even in the heart of the Peloponnesus. Athens' loss in the war against Sparta was taken as proof of the inadequacy of its political system; Athenian failures were seized upon as democratic errors; ordinary human mistakes and misfortunes were judged to be the peculiar consequences of democracy. The Spartan victory over the democratic coalition at Mantinea in 418 was the turning point in the political development of Greece toward oligarchy rather than democracy, but the final defeat of Athens reinforced the trend.

In spite of its apparently decisive outcome, the war did not establish a stable balance of power to replace the uneasy one that had evolved after the end of the Persian War. It did not create a new order bringing general peace for a generation or more. Instead Sparta's victory over Athens brought only a temporary rise in Spartan influence far beyond its normal strength. The Spartans lacked the human, material, and political resources to maintain the empire they had won or to control events outside the Peloponnesus for long. Their attempts to do so only brought division and weakness to their own state and to the rest of Greece.

The settlement of 404 was finally neither a "Punic Peace" that permanently destroyed Athenian power nor a moderate, negotiated settlement whose purpose was to mollify hard feelings. Athens, moreover, had greater real and potential strength than was apparent at its moment of defeat, so that in time its power was bound to reassert itself. No sooner were the Athenians free than they began to plan for the return of the empire, power, glory, and resistance to Spartan domination of the Greek states. Athens in 404 was disarmed but unappeased, and to keep her disarmed would have required a degree of strength, commitment, cooperation, and unity of purpose not possessed by the victorious powers. Theban ambition had already grown to the point of demanding parity with the leading states and, after a while, hegemony. Sparta's vain attempts at domination of Greece brought only weakness that soon put an end to the Greeks' domination and subjected them to the control of outsiders, first to the interventions of Persia and then to conquest by Macedonia.

It is both legitimate and instructive to think of what we call the Peloponnesian War as "the great war between Athens and Sparta," as one scholar has designated it, because, like the European war of 1914–18 to which the title "the Great War" was applied by an earlier generation that knew only one, it was a tragic event, a great turning point in history, the end of an era of progress, prosperity, confidence, and hope, and the beginning of a darker time.

SOURCES FOR THE HISTORY OF
THE PELOPONNESIAN WAR

THE MAJOR SOURCE for the Peloponnesian War is the history of Thucydides, the son of Olorus, an Athenian who was born about 460 B.C. and may have lived as late as about 397. Although he was of a noble family, he became a great admirer of Pericles, the leader of the Athenian democrats. He was elected general in 424, a year in which Cleon and the more radical democrats were in favor, and assigned to command the fleet near Amphipolis in Thrace. When the city was lost to the Spartans Thucydides was held responsible, brought to trial, convicted, and sent into exile for the remaining two decades of the war.

Thucydides' work quickly won admiration, and for more than two millennia its meticulous attention to detail and objectivity have won the deepest respect. He believed that establishing the facts with the greatest possible accuracy was crucially important for his purpose: to understand and illuminate the workings of human nature, especially in the realms of politics, international relations, and war. His interpretations, however, like those of any historian, especially one deeply engaged in the events he describes, require careful scrutiny and evaluation.

Three documents, two of them contemporary to the period of the war, supplement Thucydides' account. The *Athenaion Politeia* (Constitution of the Athenians) has come down among the works of Xenophon, but scholars now agree that it cannot be his. The work appears to have been written in the 420s, and its unknown author is sometimes referred to as the "Old Oligarch," although his age at the time of writing has not been determined. Although his oligarchical sympathies are unmistakable, the pamphlet presents a hardheaded analysis arguing that the Athenian democracy, though immoral, is effective. Another *Constitution of the Athenians*, this one written in the last part of the fourth century B.C. by Aristotle or someone in his school, offers a brief history of the development of Athenian politics from the earliest times until the author's own day, about 330 B.C. Its account of the last part of the war, especially the oligarchic revolution in 411, is of particular importance. A fragment of a *Hellenica* by an unknown fourth-century author was discovered on a papyrus in Oxyrhynchus in Egypt in 1906. Most of it is an excellent and perceptive narrative of events for the year 396–95, but part of it describes the Theban spoliation of Attica in the closing days of the war. It, too, appears to have begun where Thucydides stopped, and its greatest significance is as a likely source for later historians, such as Diodorus and Plutarch.

Thucydides' narrative ends in the fall of 411, some six and one-half years before the war concluded. As the ancient writers took his work as authoritative for the period he treated, three historians who wrote of the period took up the story where he left it. Cratippus, an Athenian contemporary, carried the history of the Greek world to at least as late as 394, as did Theopompus of Chios, who was born about 378. Their works did not survive, however, and we know of them only through fragmentary quotations in later sources. Xenophon, son of Gryllus, a younger contemporary of Thucydides born about 428, also wrote a *Hellenica* that treated Greek history until 362, which has survived. Xenophon was a member of the Socratic circle and a great partisan of Sparta who served under its powerful King Agesilaus. His work lacks the analytic power of Thucydides', but it provides the major narrative account of the last years of the war.

Two very much later writers provide additional information of varying degrees of reliability and value. Diodorus of Sicily, a contemporary of Julius Caesar and Augustus, wrote a universal history in the first century B.C., some four centuries after the Peloponnesian War. The trustworthiness of his work depends on the sources he used. These included Thucydides but also others now lost to us. Of these the most important seems to have been Ephorus of Cyme, who belonged to the generation after the war and could have spoken to many who had lived through it. Ephorus, moreover, seems to have used lost passages of the Oxyrhynchus historian whose credibility is often superior to that of Xenophon. Diodorus, therefore, must be taken seriously, especially for the years after Thucydides breaks off.

That leaves Plutarch of Chaeronea, who lived in the years roughly between A.D. 50 and 120, still further removed from the events he describes. His *Lives of Illustrious Greeks and Romans*, moreover, is not the work of a historian but of a biographer who explicitly aims to draw moral lessons from the lives of great men of the past. This has led many to discount his reliability, but we do so at our peril. He had a magnificent library, including many works not available to us. He cites and refers to lost comic poets of the fifth century, histories by Thucydides' contemporaries Philistus of Syracuse and Hellanicus of Lesbos, as well as his continuators Ephorus and Theopompus. He also cites inscription from the fifth century and describes buildings, paintings and sculptures that he saw with his own eyes. The following passage from his *Life of Nicias* (1.5) gives a sense of the treasures to be found in his work: "Those deeds which Thucydides and Philistus have set forth . . . I have run over briefly, and with no unnecessary detail, in order to escape the reputation of utter carelessness and sloth; but those details which have escaped most writers, and which others have mentioned casually, or which are found on ancient votive offerings or in public decrees, these I have tried to collect, not massing together useless material of research, but handing on such as furthers the appreciation of character and temperament." In pursuing these goals he gives us precious and authentic information that we dare not ignore.

The past two centuries have also produced valuable contemporary evidence in the form of inscriptions, usually on stone. The profession of Greek epigraphy has made remarkable progress in discovering, restoring, and editing documents of major interest and importance. Perhaps the most significant achievement was the reconstruction and interpretation of the stelae on which the Athenians inscribed the annual tribute assessments imposed on their subjects from 454 B.C. until the fall of the empire. That great work was published between 1939 and 1953 by B. D. Meritt, H. T. Wade-Gery and M. F. McGregor as *The Athenian Tribute Lists*, 4 volumes, I, Cambridge, Mass., II–IV, Princeton. Apart from these, the most relevant inscriptions are collected in *A Selection of Greek Inscriptions to the End of the Fifth Century B.C.* by R. Meiggs and D. M. Lewis, revised edition, Oxford, 1992. English translations of many of the inscriptions, as well as of less accessible references in ancient writers, are provided by Charles Fornara in *Archaic Times to the End of the Peloponnesian War*, second edition, Cambridge, 1983.

Knowledge and understanding of the war were greatly enhanced by the scholarship of a number of nineteenth-century scholars, whose pioneering work is still worth reading. The greatest of these was the magnificent George Grote, the father of ancient Greek history as we know it today. His twelve-volume *History of Greece*, (London, 1846–1856) is a work of careful and profound scholarship that provides a solid foundation for many challenges to the received opinion. Grote's masterwork provoked serious thought and many responses, of which the most important are contained in multivolume histories by three German scholars. The most impressive and valuable is the vast second part of the third and last volume of Georg Busolt's *Griechische Geschichte*, Gotha, 1893–1904. It is a model of a deep and thorough knowledge of all the ancient evidence and modern scholarship up to that time and of a very successful attempt to achieve objectivity. The others are K. J. Beloch, *Griechische Geschichte*, second edition, 4 volumes in eight parts, Leipzig, 1912–1927, and Eduard Meyer, *Geschichte des Altertums*, fifth edition, 4 volumes, reprinted in 1954 and 1956 in Basel. (The first editions of the last two were begun in the nineteenth century.)

The twentieth century has also seen major contributions. Perhaps the most useful of these is *A Historical Commentary on Thucydides*, begun by A. W. Gomme and completed by A. Andrewes and K. J. Dover, (5 volumes, Oxford, 1950–1981). R. Meiggs' *The Athenian Empire* (Oxford, 1972) and G.E.M. de Ste. Croix's *The Origins of the Peloponnesian War* (Oxford, 1972) are also very valuable. The literature of special studies on the war and related subjects is vast; most of it is listed in the bibliographies at the end of each volume in my four-volume history of the war published by Cornell University Press between 1969 and 1987.

INDEX

Page numbers in *italics*
refer to maps.

Abdera, 434
Abydos, 358–59, 403–5, 407, 417, 427, 432, 467–68, 471
Abydos, battle of, 408–9, 458
Acanthus, 172–73, 179, 181, 191
Acarnania, 71, 75, 90–91, 92, 129–30, 132–36, 137, 154, 301
Achaea, 145, 218
Acharnae, 67, 68
Acharnians (Aristophanes), 154, 190, 255
Acragas, 274
Acropolis, restoration project for, 423
Acte peninsula, 177
Adeimantus, 265, 437
Aegean Sea, 3, 8, *15*, *343*
Aegina, 41*n*, 49, 71, 75, 81, 144, 158, 220, 380, 394, 471, 476, 478
Aegitium, battle of, 131
Aegospotami, battle of, 471–78, *472*
 Athenian reaction to, 476–77
Aeolidas, 167
Aeschylus, xxiii
Aetolia, 129–32
Agariste, 265
Agatharcus, 314
Agesandridas, 396–98
Agesilaus, 439
Agis, king of Sparta, 106, 125, 139–40, 299, 331, 333–34, 335, 336, 364, 424, 446, 483
 aborted uphill charge led by, 232
 advisers appointed to, 226, 229, 240–41

Alcibiades as personal enemy of, 337–38, 347
 in Argive plain campaign, 221–27
 army's lack of confidence in, 228–29, 237–38
 atrocities permitted by, 244
 in Central Greece, 333
 disgruntled troops and officers of, 234–38
 in Epidaurian campaign, 218–20
 and fate of Athens, 478–79, 480
 Four Hundred's peace offer spurned by, 384
 Lysander and, 439
 in march to Tegea, 228–30
 moves into Argive trap, 234–35
Alcamenes, 336–37
Alcibiades, 169, 222, 226, 242, 243, 244–45, 328, 335, 352, 361, 376, 394, 401, 417, 418, 420, 437, 464
 at Abydos, 408
 accused of sacrilege, 263–67
 at Aegospotami, 473–74
 Agis as personal enemy of, 337–38, 347
 Argive alliance and, 219–21
 background of, 211–12
 at Cyzicus, 429–31
 fall of, 446–47
 as fugitive, 273–74, 279, 280
 in Hellespont campaign, 406–7
 in march to Eleusis, 436
 message of, to Four Hundred, 389–91, 392, 393

Alcibiades (*continued*)
  Nicias' rivalry with, 212–13, 214,
      246–47, 250
  at Notium, 442–45
  oligarchic movement and, 364–69,
      383, 385, 390–91
  at Olympic Games of, 416, 250
  Peloponnesus expedition of, 217–18
  Pericles and, 211–12
  in plot to repatriate to Samos, 367–72
  Plutarch on, 212, 400
  regional rebellions fomented by,
      337–38, 344
  in return to Athens, 432–36
  in Sicilian expedition, 262, 269, 270,
      273, 280, 322
  in Sicilian expedition debates, 254–55
  Sparta-Argos treaty talks and, 213–14,
      215
  Spartan assembly addressed by,
      282–83
  Sparta-Persia treaty and, 339–40
  Sparta's order to kill, 347
  Thucydides on, 257–59, 347, 366, 373,
      389
  Tissaphernes' relationship with,
      347–48, 364, 366, 367, 369–70,
      372, 373–76, 378, 389–90, 406, 410
  as traitor, 280–83
Alcibiades (son of Phegus), 265
Alcidas, 105, 106, 107, 116–17
Alciphron, 224
Alcmeonides, 265
Alesion, Mount, 232, 233, 234
Alexander III (the Great), king of
      Macedonia, 168
Alexicles, 394–95, 396, 401
Ambracia, 57, 85, 90, 132
  Demosthenes' defeat of, 132–36
Amorges, 334, 339, 345, 346, 347, 350, 372
Amphilochia, 132, 135–36
Amphipolis, 171, 172, 174, 179, 181, 182,
      183, 184, 199, 203, 204, 205, 214,
      245
  Brasidas' capture of, 173–77
  and Peace of Nicias, 191–93, 197

Amphipolis, battle of, 185–87, 293
Anactorium, 57, 90, 154, 191, 193, 198, 201
Anaea, 338
Anagrapheis (registrars), 421
Anapus, battle of the, 275–78, 276
Anatolia, 437
Anaxagoras, xxiii, 12–13
Andocides, 265–66
Androcles, 376–77
Andros, 380, 437, 442, 443, 446
Antandrus, 407, 425–26
Antiochus, 443–45, 475
Antiphanes, 210
Antiphon, 379, 394, 401
Antissa, 342
Antisthenes, 351–53
Aracus, 469
Arcadia, 218, 222, 226, 331
Archelaus, king of Macedonia, 409
Archeptolemus, 401
Archesilaus, 216
Archestratus, 479–80
Archidamus, king of Sparta, 55, 63, 76,
      106, 333, 484
  death of, 125
  in exile, 40
  as peace advocate, 45, 47, 48, 51, 81,
      86
  Pericles' friendship with, 40, 44
  Plataea attack and, 88–89
  war strategy of, 59–60, 66–67, 70, 81
Argilus, 173, 191
Arginusae, battle of, 453, 454–58, 469,
      471
  Athenian alignment in, 454–56, 455
  postbattle controversy and, 459–66,
      470
  Spartan peace offer and, 467–68
Argive League, 213
  Alcibiades and, 219–21
  Corinth and, 200, 201–3, 205–7, 215,
      216
  Spartan ephors' conspiracy against,
      205–6
  Spartan peace treaty with, 208–9
Argive plain, map of, 225

Argive plain campaign, 221–27
    Argive army in, 222
    siege of Orchomenus in, 226–27
    Spartan army in, 221–22, 224
    terrain of, 222–24
    truce reached in, 224–26
    see also Mantinea, battle of
Argos, 5, 14, 76, 85, 90, 132–34, 153, 158,
        188–89, 199, 212, 216, 268, 281,
        289, 345, 391
    approaches to, 223
    Athenian treaty with, 214–15, 217
    democracy restored in, 244–45
    Epidaurus invaded by, 218–20, 221
    oligarchs rule in, 242–43
    see also Argive plain campaign;
        Mantinea, battle of
Ariphron, 211
Aristarchus, 395, 401
Aristeus, 84
Aristocles, 236–37, 238
Aristocrates, 392–95, 398, 437, 456
Ariston, 315
Aristophanes, xxiii, 68, 154, 190, 194,
        210, 255, 392
Aristotle, 4, 69, 363n, 399, 468, 486
Arrhabaeus, king of the Lyncestians,
        172
Arsaces, 438
Artaxerxes I, Great King of Persia, 84,
        86, 96, 155, 325, 332
Artaxerxes II, Great King of Persia,
        482–83
Asclepius, cult of, 423
Asia Minor, maps of, xxviii–xxix, 343
Asopius, 102
Aspasia, 456
Aspendus, 410
assembly, Athenian, 9, 69–70, 80,
        148–49, 152, 263
    Aegospotami controversy and,
        459–65
    Nicias as perceived by, 296–97
    Nicias' letter to, 293–94
    Peisander's address to, 371–72
    Pylos truce debate in, 144–45

Sicilian expedition debates in,
        254–61, 295–96
    Spartan peace offer rejected by,
        417–19, 467–68
    taxes levied by, 104–5, 328, 329,
        422–23
    see also Five Hundred, council of;
        Five Thousand, council of; Four
        Hundred, council of
assembly, Spartan, 5, 63
    Alcibiades' address to, 282–83
assembly, Syracusan, 272–73
Astacus, 71
Astyochus, 342, 346, 347, 349, 350, 359,
        369–70, 373, 387–88, 390
    advisers assigned to, 351–53
    Chios rebellion and, 342–44
Atalante, 178, 192
Athenagoras, 272
Athena Polias, temple of, 423–24
Athens, Athenian Empire, 10–11
    Alcibiades' return to, 432–36
    aristocratic tradition of, 362–63
    Corcyra civil war and, 115–17
    declining population of, 360, 452–54
    democracy of, xxiii, 8, 13, 80, 420–22,
        485–87
    deterrence policy of, 33–34, 36
    Epidamnus crisis and, 29–34
    fall of Alcibiades in, 446–47
    fate of, 478–84
    financial resources of, 57, 60–63, 75,
        86, 98, 104–5, 123, 128, 136, 189,
        190, 247, 325, 327–28, 422–23,
        442, 452, 457
    and foundation of Thurii, 20–22
    geography of, 7–8
    imperial holdings of, 8
    leadership vacuum in, 364
    Long Walls of, 9, 51, 59, 60, 68, 479,
        483
    manpower shortage of, 452–54
    Megara Decree of, 39–40, 41, 48–50,
        54, 73, 81, 162, 163
    Melos conquered by, 247–49
    moderates of, 79, 120

Athens, Athenian Empire (*continued*)
    navy of, 51–52, 57, 59–61, 247
    oligarchic conspiracy against, see
        Athens, oligarchic conspiracy
        against
    ostracism practice of, 245–46
    peace debate in, 143–47
    peace of Nicias ratified by, 192
    peace party of, 189, 190
    Pericles' death and, 99–100
    Persian relations with, 8, 13, 154–55,
        374, 431–32
    plague epidemics in, 78–79, 81, 86, 87,
        97, 113, 120, 361
    political offices of, 9–12
    Potidaea uprising and, 36–37
    regional rebellions in, 241–44, 337–38
    reserve fund of, 62, 98, 189, 341
    Spartan peace offers rejected by,
        417–19, 467–68
    Spartan rivalry with, 13–18
    taxes levied in, 104–5, 328, 329,
        422–23
    Thirty Tyrants and, 365, 485–86
    unity of, 361
    war decision of, 47–54
    war party of, 79, 85, 86, 119, 120
    see also assembly, Athenian;
        constitution, Athenian
Athens, oligarchic conspiracy against:
    Alcibiades and, 364–65, 393, 394
    Alcibiades-Persia relationship and,
        373–75
    aristocratic tradition and, 362–63
    assassinations in, 376–77
    Colonus meeting and, 377, 380, 381
    constitution and, 377–38, 381–82
    coup in, 376–80
    extremists and, 367–68, 384, 394,
        400–401
    goals of, 375–76
    leaders of, 379–80
    moderates and, 365–66, 371, 383–84,
        392
    Peisander's mission and, 371–73
    Piraeus uprising and, 393–96

    Samos counterrevolution and, 384–85
    Theramenes in, 379–80
    see also Four Hundred, council of;
        Five Thousand, council of
atrocities:
    by Agis in Argos, 244
    in Corcyra, xxiv–xxv, 115–16, 117,
        154
    execution of generals, 466
    of Lysander, 476–77
    in Mycalessus, 300
    against Peloponnesian ambassadors,
        84–85
    in Plataea, 65–66
    in siege of Scione, 203
    Thucydides on, 84–85, 117
    in Thyrea, 158–59
Attica, 7–8, 17
    Spartan invasions of, 62–68, 105–6,
        139, 299
Aulis, 409
Autocles, 157
Axiochus, 265

Belmina, 222
Birds (Aristophanes), 278, 392
Boeotia, 17, 19, 57, 64, 114, 128, 130, 146,
        147, 155–56, 189, 199, 204–5, 209,
        222, 224, 228, 299, 300, 331, 333,
        334, 353, 430
    Argive League and, 202–3, 206–7
    Athenian invasion of, 165–70, 171
    Peace of Nicias opposed by, 194, 197
    Spartan treaty with, 208, 210, 212, 213,
        214
    truce of 423 opposed by, 178
Boeotian League, 64
Bosporus, 409, 428
Brasidas, 70–71, 94, 96, 116–17, 194, 204,
        236, 332
    at Amphipolis, 185–88, 332
    assessment of, 187
    in Central Greece offensive, 125–27
    in Cleon's Thracian campaign,
        182–85
    death of, 186–88

at Megara, 164–65, 171
at Pylos, 142–43
Thracian campaign of, 171–81
Thucydides on, 172
truce of 423 reaction of, 179–80
Byzantium, 24, 413, 417, 425, 429,
    430–31, 433, 467, 471, 477
    revolt in, 388, 402

Callicratidas, 331, 439, 448–52, 467, 469,
    470, 471
    at Arginusae, 454–58
    death of, 458
Callixeinus, 463–66
Camarina, 57, 159–60, 273, 280
Camirus, 354
Cannonus, decree of, 464
Cappadocia, 438
Cardia, 410
Caria, 104, 334, 338, 434, 437, 471
Carthage, 160, 210, 257, 272, 280, 281,
    424
Carystus, 380
Catana, 270, 273, 274, 275, 278, 280,
    317–18, 320
Caunus, 352, 353, 357
Cephallenia, 71, 90, 205
Cerameicus, 186
Cerdylium, 183
Chaereas, 386, 390, 412
Chaeronea, 165, 166
Chalce, 355, 356
Chalcedon, 388, 417, 425, 432, 467, 471,
    477
    siege of, 427–30
Chalcideus, 335, 336, 337–38, 341, 347
    treaty of, 339–40, 350
Chalcidice, 38, 171, 179, 189, 192, 193, 202,
    203, 206–7, 245, 247
Chalcidic rebellion, 78, 89–90, 98
Chalcis, 397, 409
Chamberlain, Neville, 2n
Chaonians, 90
Charicles, 301
Charminus, 353
Charoeades, 118, 120

Chios, 8, 60, 76, 100, 143, 329, 359, 374,
    403, 417, 424, 425, 437, 443, 450,
    458, 459, 461, 467, 468
    rebellion in, 334, 335–36, 337–38,
    341–46, 347, 355–56
Chromon, 131
Chrysopolis, 413, 429
Cimon, 12, 14, 33, 83, 198–99, 250, 266,
    364
"Circle, The," 284, 286
Clazomenae, 338, 342, 443
Cleandridas, 283
Clearchus, 336, 352, 388, 412, 427, 430–31
Clearidas, 181, 183, 185–86, 197, 204
Cleinias, 211, 212, 257
Cleisthenes, 12, 211, 265
Cleobulus, 205–6, 207, 212, 216
Cleomedes, 248
Cleomenes, 106
Cleon, 75, 85, 118, 119, 120, 155, 156, 157,
    194, 203, 210, 248, 249, 259, 418
    assessment of, 187
    calculated terror policy of, 110–11, 179
    death of, 184, 186–87
    emergence of, 99–100
    and fate of Mytilene, 109–12
    mocking characterizations of, 68–69
    Nicias' rivalry with, 147–50
    peace debate and, 145–47
    political supremacy of, 152–53
    at Sphacteria, 150–52
    Thracian campaign of, 182–87
    Thucydides accused of treason by,
    176
    Thucydides on, 109–10, 186
Cleonae, 235, 239
Cleonymus, 181
Cleophon, 418, 420, 422, 446, 468, 479,
    483–84
Cleopompus, 78
Cnemus, 84, 90–91, 93, 96
Cnidos, 425–26
Cnidus, 353, 354
Cold War, xxv
Colonus Hippius, 377, 380, 381
Colophon, 426, 442–43

Comon, 151–52

Conon, 301, 437, 447, 448, 450, 451, 452,
    454, 458, 459, 461

constitution, Athenian, 366, 372, 374,
    375, 483
    of Five Thousand, 398–99, 418
    of Four Hundred, 381–82
    graphe paranomon and, 464
    and loss of war, 488–89
    oligarchic conspiracy and, 377–78,
        381–82
    restoration of, 420–21

constitution, Spartan, 363, 440, 469,
    488–89

Constitution of the Athenians, The
    (Aristotle), 363*n*

Constitution of the Athenians, The
    ("The Old Oligarch"), 363

Corcyra, 25–36, 26, 44, 46, 60, 70, 71, 81,
    130, 137, 139, 146, 161, 263, 268
    atrocities in, xxiv–xxv, 115–16, 117, 154
    civil wars in, 114–18, 424
    Epidamnus crisis and, 25–34

Corinth, 5, 19, 24, 57, 60, 61, 75, 77, 90,
    91, 96, 106, 119, 136, 146, 160, 193,
    204, 208, 224, 228, 331, 336, 349,
    363, 476
    Alcibiades' Peloponnesus campaign
        and, 217–18
    Argive League and, 200, 201–3, 205–7,
        215, 216
    and Athens' decision for war, 45, 48,
        50
    and battle of Sybota, 34–36, 114–15
    Corcyraean intervention and, 25–27
    Epidamnus crisis and, 25–34
    and fate of Athens, 479, 481
    Megara Decree and, 39
    Megara's boundary war with, 14–16
    Nicias' campaign in, 153–54
    Peace of Nicias opposed by, 194, 198,
        201
    in postwar era, 487–88
    and Sicilian expedition of 415, 266,
        279–81, 289–90, 291, 292, 300,
        301

Sparta's alliance with, 219–20
    and Sparta's decision for war, 42–43,
        44
    truce of 423 opposed by, 179

Corinthian Gulf, map of, 92

Coronea, battle of, 211

Cratesippidas, 425

Crete, 94, 95

Crommyon, 153

Cydonia, 94

Cyllene, 94, 116

Cyme, 342, 443, 446, 458, 468

Cynossema, battle of, 341, 346, 403–7,
    408, 409, 413–14, 458, 471

Cynuria, 188, 201, 209

Cyrus, 432, 437–38
    Callicratidas and, 449–50, 452
    Lysander's collaboration with,
        440–42, 449, 469–70, 482

Cythera, 58, 157–58, 159, 161, 177, 178, 188,
    189, 192, 198, 301

Cyzicus, 388

Cyzicus, battle of, 341, 410–13, 411, 420,
    425, 433, 444, 445, 458, 467, 471
    Spartan peace offer after, 417–19

Dardanus, 404

Darius II, Great King of Persia, 347,
    367–68, 419, 469
    Athens' failed negotiations with,
        429–32, 433, 442
    Cyrus' replacement of Tissaphernes
        and, 437–38
    emergence of, 332
    and fate of Athens, 482–83
    Persian-Spartan treaties and, 334,
        339, 340, 349, 353, 357–58

Decelea, 282, 331, 333, 351, 384, 424, 436,
    467, 468, 478, 479
    Spartan fort at, 299–300, 306, 327–28,
        417

Delian League, 8, 13, 22, 100, 247

Delium, 165, 178, 189, 198

Delium, battle of, 167–69, 170, 212

Delos, 106

Delphinium, 351, 450

democracy, xxiii
    aristocratic tradition and, 362–63
    Athenian, xxiii, 8, 13, 80
    Athens' defeat and, 488–89
    and battle of Mantinea, 241–42
    oligarchic conspiracy against, *see*
        Athens, oligarchic conspiracy
        against
    Peloponnesian War's effect on, xxiv,
        488–89
    restored to Argos, 244–45
    restored to Athens, 420–22, 485–87
Democritus, xxiii
Demosthenes, 113, 119–20, 128–52, 157,
    270, 278, 328
    Aetolia campaign of, 129–32
    Ambracians defeated by, 132–36
    death of, 321
    and invasion of Boeotia, 165–66, 170
    Megara assault and, 162–63
    in Pylos campaign, 138–47
    in Sicilian expedition, 296, 300–301,
        306, 307–10, 315, 317–21
    Spartan northwest campaign and,
        132–33
    at Sphacteria, 150–52
Demostratus, 260
Dercylidas, 358–59
Dieitrephes, 300, 376
diobelia, 422
Diocleides, 264–65
Diodorus, 240, 405, 448, 458, 488
Diodotus, 109–12
Diomedon, 342, 355, 373, 384–85, 386
Diphilus, 303
direct tax (*eisphora*), 104–5, 328, 422–23
Dorians, 119, 125, 128
Dorieus, 390, 406, 407
Draco, 421, 424

Eccritus, 300
Eetioneia, 393–94, 396
Egypt, 157
Eion, 175, 176, 183, 185, 186
eisphora (direct tax), 104–5, 328, 422–23
Eleusis, 67, 436, 437

Elis, 5, 34, 77, 94, 188, 189, 194, 197, 198,
    203–4, 214, 245
    Argive League and, 202, 222, 226,
        229–30, 241, 243
    Athenian treaty with, 215–16, 217, 281
    and battle of Mantinea, 229–30, 232
Endius, 213, 337, 338, 340, 347, 352, 417
Enyalius, 163
Epaminondas, 168
Ephesus, 155, 417, 426, 437, 443, 444, 468,
    469
    Spartan base in, 440, 442, 449, 450
    uprisings in, 329, 338
ephors (Spartan magistrates), 5–7,
    62–63, 194, 205–6, 337, 479
Epidamnus, 25–34, 26
Epidaurus, 76–77, 153–54, 217–20, 222,
    224, 241–42, 331, 394, 423
    Argive invasion of, 218–20, 221
Epilycus, treaty of, 332
Epipolae plateau, 284
    "Circle" of, 284, 286
    night attack on, 307–8
Epirus, 90
Epitadas, 142
Erasinides, 292, 462
Erechtheum, 423–24
Erechtheus (Euripides), 190
Eresus, 342, 403
Eretria, 397
Erianthus, 481
Eristratus, 253
Erythrae, 334, 338
Eteonicus, 459, 460, 461, 475
Etruria, 280, 288
Euboea, 62, 68, 71, 125–27, 299–300, 329,
    394, 406, 417, 442
    and fall of Four Hundred, 397–98
    importance of, 356–57
    rebellions in, 333, 334–35, 355–56, 408
    Spartan threat to, 396–97
Eucles, 175, 176–77
Eucrates, 109, 418
Euphemus, 280
Euphilitus, 266
Euripides, xxiii, 190, 321

Euryalus, 288, 290, 292, 307
Eurymachus, 66
Eurymedon, 113, 128, 130, 143, 328
　　Corcyraean civil war and, 117, 118,
　　　　137, 154
　　in First Sicilian Expedition, 119, 122,
　　　　159, 161–62, 283, 293
　　Pylos operation and, 137–40
　　in Sicilian expedition of 415, 296,
　　　　300–301, 306, 308, 310, 311
Euryptolemus, 434, 464, 465–66
Euthydemus, 295, 310

First Peloponnesian War, 14–18, 41n, 64,
　　　163, 188, 193
Five Hundred, council of, 9, 391, 421,
　　　462, 463
Five Thousand, council of, 366, 378,
　　　381–82, 390, 391, 409, 415, 433
　　abolition of, 420–22
　　Alcibiades repatriated by, 400
　　constitution of, 398–99, 418
　　extremists purged from, 400–401
　　Piraeus uprising and, 393–96
　　and restoration of democracy,
　　　　420–22
　　size of, 399
Four Hundred, council of, 366, 367, 378,
　　　381–91, 406, 409, 421, 480
　　Alcibiades' message to, 389–91, 392,
　　　　393
　　constitution drafted by, 381–82
　　and continuation of war, 382–83
　　counterrevolutions against, 384–87,
　　　　393–96
　　in coup, 379, 380
　　dissent within, 392–93
　　Euboea threat and, 397–98
　　fall of, 398
　　and repatriation of Alcibiades,
　　　　388–91
　　and restoration of democracy,
　　　　420–22
　　Samian counterrevolution and,
　　　　384–87

　　separate peace sought by, 384–86,
　　　　391
　　Theramenes in ouster of, 383–84

Galepsus, 177, 183, 184
Garipadasi, 456
Gela, 274, 289
Gela, Congress of, 159–61, 253, 272,
　　　293
gerousia, Spartan, 5–7
Gongylus, 289–90, 295, 309, 322
Great Harbor, battle of the, 303–5
Great King, see Artaxerxes I, Great King
　　　of Persia; Artaxerxes II, Great
　　　King of Persia; Darius II, Great
　　　King of Persia
Greece, maps of, xxviii–xxix, 72, 126
Gylippus, 283, 288, 289, 290–92, 294,
　　　295, 300, 301–2, 304, 306, 307,
　　　309, 310, 311–12, 316, 318–20, 322,
　　　331, 439
Gytheum, 434

Haerae, 338
Hagnon, 78, 83, 91, 328, 329
Halieis, 77, 153
Hekatonnesi Islands, 451
Helixus, 388
Hellespont, 334–36, 346, 352, 356, 360,
　　　374, 397, 401, 425–28, 451
　　Athenian-Persian relations in,
　　　　429–32, 467
　　battle of Abydos in, 408–9
　　battle of Aegospotami in, 471–78
　　battle of Cynossema in, 403–7
　　battle of Notium in, 442–46
　　Cyrus' replacement of Tissaphernes
　　　　and, 437–38
　　and fall of Alcibiades, 447–48
　　Miletus campaign in, 470–71
　　Phoenician fleet and, 402–3
　　post-Arginusae controversy and,
　　　　459–66
　　siege of Chalcedon in, 427–30
　　Spartan peace offer in, 467–68

Sparta's new initiative in, 358–59,
    387–88
uprisings in, 387–88
helots, 3–4, 48, 147, 152, 171, 178, 189, 205,
    220, 301
    liberated (*neodamodeis*) class of, 204,
        236, 300, 330, 430
    Sparta's fear of revolts by, 4, 14–15,
        138, 198, 200, 204, 243
Heraclea, 125, 127, 171, 216, 333, 424
Heracleum, 230, 232, 234
Heraea, 236
Hermae, sacrilege against, 262–67, 273,
    297
Hermione, 77, 331
Hermippus, 130
Hermocrates, 159–60, 161, 253, 272, 279,
    280, 302, 316, 320, 344, 348
Hermon of Megara, 457
Herodotus, xxiii
Hestiodorus, 85
Hetairiai (political clubs), 266, 364, 373,
    441
Himera, 274, 289
Hippocrates (general), xxiii, 162–66
    at Delium, 168–69
Hippocrates (governor of Chalcedon),
    427–29
Hippocrates (Spartan secretary), 413
Hipponicus, 128, 130
Hipponoidas, 236–37, 238
Homer, 79, 362
hoplite, 1, 95
Hyccara, 274
Hyperbolus, 210–11, 328, 418
    assassination of, 384
    ostracism of, 245–47
hypomeiones class, 330
Hysiae, 244

Ialysus, 354
Iasus, 345, 346, 347, 350, 372
Iberia, 281
Idomene, battle of, 151
Iliad (Homer), 79–80

Illyria, 25, 179–80
Ionia, 106–7, 108, 119, 334, 335, 338, 340,
    345–46, 352
    Thrasyllus' campaign in, 425–26
    see also Hellespont
Ischagoras, 181
Isthmian Games, 336
Istome, Mount, 137, 154
Italy, 3, *21*, 37, 57, 118–19, *121*, 137, 253, 271,
    272, 281, 302

Kapnistra, 230, 232
Kelussa, Mount, 224

Labdalum, 284, 290, 291, 295
Lacedaemonius, 33, 213
Laches, 118–20, 122
Laconia, 70, 75, 138, 166, 200, 204, 227,
    329, 330, 434
    Athenian raids on, 289, 298, 301
Lamachus, 157, 254, 255, 269, 270, 286,
    328
    death of, 287
Lampsacus, 359, 427, 471, 473–74, 476
Laurium, 299
Lebedus, 338
Leon, 213, 284, 342, 355, 359, 373, 384–85,
    386
Leontini, 118–19, 120, 122, 253, 255, 269
Lepreum, 203–4, 215, 230
Lesbos, 8, 24, 60, 76, 329, 335, 336, 356,
    374, 450, 451
    rebellions in, 333–34, 342, 345, 349,
        403
    see also Mytilene insurrection of 428
Leucas, 57, 71, 90, 129, 130
Leucimne, battle of, 29, 34, 39
Leuctra, 330
Lichas, 216, 242, 352
    third Sparta-Persia treaty and,
        353–54, 357–58
Lindus, 354
Liparian Islands, 120–22
Locris, 57, 71, 122, 128, 131, 132, 137, 228,
    268, 289, 331, 339, 353

Lycus, 365, 447
Lydia, 437–38
Lyncestians, 180
Lysander, 331, 438–45, 448, 452, 458, 467,
    471–84, 485
  at Aegospotami, 471–77
  Agis and, 439
  ambition of, 439–40, 470
  atrocities of, 476–77
  Cyrus' collaboration with, 440–42,
      449, 469–70, 482
  emergence of, 438–39
  and fate of Athens, 478–84
  as liberator, 477–78
  Miletus campaign of, 470–71
  at Notium, 442–45
Lysicles, 104, 418

Macarius, 134
Macedonia, 37, 41, 127, 409, 489
Maenalia, 236
Mantinea, 5, 188, 189, 198, 199, 203, 204,
    214, 215, 216, 217, 222, 226, 268,
    281
  in Argive League, 201
  peace conference at, 219–20
Mantinea, battle of, 228–43, 231, 258,
    281, 283, 330, 331, 489
  Agis' aborted uphill charge and, 232,
      237
  Agis' orders disobeyed in, 236–38
  Argive deployment in, 232, 235, 236
  Argive-Spartan alliance after, 242
  Argive Thousand in, 235, 238, 239–40,
      24, 242
  assessment of, 241–42
  Athenian contingent in, 232, 239, 241
  disgruntled Spartan troops in,
      234–35
  diversion of waterways in, 233–34
  Elians and, 229–30, 232
  march to Tegea in, 228–30
  political ramifications of, 240–41
  prelude to, see Argive plain campaign
  and rift in Argive army, 229–30, 232
  Spartan deployment in, 235–36

Spartan peace offer after, 242
Spartans' entrapment in, 234–35
Spartan victory in, 238–39
terrain of, 230–32
as victory for oligarchy, 241
Marathon, battle of, 88, 192–93
Marmara Sea, map of, 428
Megara, 17, 18, 19, 34, 67, 75, 96, 145–16,
    147, 155–56, 171, 178, 189, 193, 199,
    202, 204–5, 206, 217, 218, 224,
    268, 331, 430
  Athenian assault on, 162–65
  Athens' embargo decree against,
      39–40, 41, 48–50, 54, 73, 81, 162,
      163
  Corinth's boundary war with, 14–16
  effect of war on, 476, 487–88
  Peace of Nicias opposed by, 194, 197
  in Spartan Alliance, 5, 28, 57
  and Spartan decision for war, 42,
      44
  strategic value of, 16
  truce of 423 opposed by, 179
Megara Hyblaea, 269–70, 280
Megaram Decree, 39–40, 41, 48–50, 54,
    73, 81, 161, 162
Melanchridas, 335
Meletus, 266
Melian Dialogue, 248
Melos, 128, 153, 476, 477, 478, 487
  Athenian conquest of, 247–49
Menander, 295, 310, 311
Mende, 179, 180
Menedaius, 134
Messenia, 75, 129, 131, 134, 135, 138, 200,
    203–4, 205, 220, 227, 241, 289,
    301
Messina, 122, 137, 159, 268, 270, 279
Methana, 153, 157, 161, 192, 220
Methone, 70–71, 75, 77
Methydrium, 222
Methymna, 101, 342, 403, 450, 451
Metropolis, 133
Miletus, 22, 23, 349, 417, 437, 440, 449
  Athenian decision to not fight at,
      344–46, 354–55, 373

rebellions in, 329, 338, 341, 346–47, 425–26, 470
  as Spartan base, 350, 352–53, 356, 387, 390, 450
Mindarus, 390, 406, 407
  at Abydos, 408–9
  at Cynossema, 402–5
  at Cyzius, 410, 412–14
Minoa, 113, 144, 162–63, 178
Monte Climiti, 317–18, 319
mothakes class, 330–31
Mycale, 387
Mycalessus, 300
Mycenae, 224
Myrcinus, 177
Mytikas, 230, 232
Mytilene, 24, 342, 451, 458, 459–61
Mytilene insurrection of 428, 100–112
  city's surrender in, 106–7, 108
  Cleon-Diodotus debate on, 109–12
  fate of city in, 107–12
  siege in, 104–5
  Sparta and, 102–4, 106–8

Nauclides, 65
Naupactus, 85, 86, 90, 129, 131, 132, 143, 154, 220, 301, 303
  naval battles near, 91–96, 97, 98
Naxos, 270, 279
Neapolis, 424
Nemea, 224, 487
neodamodeis class (liberated helots), 204, 236, 300, 330, 430
Nepos, Cornelius, 414
Niceratus, 180
Nicias, 99, 105, 113, 119, 128, 130, 145, 195, 207–8, 210, 218, 221, 245, 281, 282, 283, 328, 435, 436
  Albiciades' rivalry with, 212–13, 214, 246–47, 250
  Cleon's rivalry with, 147–50
  Corinthian campaign of, 153–54
  in Cytheria campaign, 157–58
  death of, 321
  grandiose display of, 249–50
  illness of, 286, 297, 316

Melos conquest and, 248, 249
  peace initiative and, 189–91
  in Sicilian expedition, 264, 266–69, 270, 273–74, 275, 278–79, 284, 286–97, 303, 304, 309–11, 312, 314, 316–21, 322
  in Sicilian expedition debates, 254–57, 259–61
  Sparta-Athens alliance and, 198–99
  Thracian expedition of, 180–81
  Thucydides' eulogy of, 321
  see also Peace of Nicias
Nicostratus, 116, 118, 157
Nisaea, 96, 145, 162–65, 178, 191, 192, 193, 197, 425
Notium, battle of, 442–46, 447, 448, 458, 475
Nymphodorus, prince of Abdera, 73

Oenoe, siege of, 67
Oesyne, 177
Oeta, 125, 333
"Old Oligarch, The," 363
Olorus, 157
Olpae, 132–33
  siege of, 134–35
Olympic Games:
  of 416, 250
  of 420, 215–16
Olympieum, 304
Olynthus, 90, 191
Onomacles, 344, 401
Orchomenus, 168, 222, 228, 229, 242
  siege of, 226–27
Orneae, 5, 235, 239
Oropus, 355, 356

Paches, 104, 105, 107, 108, 111–12
Pagondas, 167, 168–69
Panactum, 191, 192, 193, 197, 206, 207–8, 210, 212, 214
Panhellenism, 20–22, 471
Paralus, 97
Paralus, 385–86, 477
Parrasia, 203
Parysatis, 438

Pasitelidas, 183
Patrae, 217–18
Pausanias, king of Sparta, 321, 449,
    478–79
Peace (Aristophanes), 190, 194, 210
Peace of Nicias, 191–94, 195, 468
    Athenian-Argive treaty and, 214–15
    Athenian ratification of, 192
    Athenian violations of, 289, 298–99
    demise of, 289, 298–99
    motivations for seeking, 188–89
    opposition to, 194, 197, 198, 201
    shortcomings of, 193–94
    Spartan-Athenian alliance and,
        198–200
    Spartan violations of, 197, 204–5, 210,
        220, 221
    Sparta's Peloponnesian offensive
        and, 203–6
    terms of, 191–92
    unravelling of, 197–98
    war-weariness and, 190
Pedaritus, 349, 351, 352, 355, 359
Pegae, 145, 162
Peisander, 385, 386, 401
    Athens mission of, 371–73
    conspiracy of Three Hundred and,
        384
    Hermae affair and, 264–65
    in oligarchic conspiracy, 367, 369,
        371–80
Peisianax, 434
Peithias, 115
Pellene, 224, 331
Peloponnesian League:
    categories of allies in, 5
    and decision for war, 46–50
    Epidamnus conflict and, 27–29, 31
    principles of, 4–5
    Samian rebellion and, 24
    states included in, 57
Peloponnesian War:
    aftermath of, 487–88
    assessments of, 75, 484, 488–90
    Athenian strategy for, 57–59
    atrocities in, *see* atrocities
    costs of, 487–88
    fractional strife in, 89–90, 114–18,
        134–35, 162, 488
    novel technology in, 169
    onset of, 1–2, 64–65
    Spartan strategy for, 57–59
    Spartan ultimatum in, 49–50
    war weariness and, 190, 198
    as world war, xxiv
Peloponnesus, maps of, 6, 58
Perdiccas, king of Macedon, 73, 98,
        171–72, 178, 182, 185, 188, 245
    end of Spartan alliance with, 179–80
Pericles (father), 43–44, 66, 87, 91, 104,
        109, 119, 144, 189, 195, 246, 248,
        249, 250, 257, 259, 269, 293, 296,
        314, 328, 329, 364, 423, 456, 484
    Alcibiades and, 211–12
    Archidamus' friendship with, 40,
        44
    assessment of, 97–98
    background and character of, 12–13
    and battle of Sybota, 36
    corruption accusation against, 83
    death of, 55, 97–98, 99
    and decision for war, 47–50
    deterrence policy of, 33–34, 52–54, 55,
        97
    Epidamnus crisis and, 32
    First Peloponnesian War and, 16–18
    and foundation of Thurii, 20–22
    funeral oration by, 73–74
    Megara Decree and, 39, 40, 54
    peace mission opposed by, 80–81
    personal prestige of, 69–70
    political attacks on, 68–70, 75, 77,
        79–80, 81–83, 85, 97
    Samian rebellion and, 22
    Thirty Years' Peace and, 193
    Thucydides on, 12, 69, 99
    war expeditions led by, 73, 76–79
    war strategy of, 50–54, 57–63, 70,
        77–78, 86, 110, 123, 146–47, 155,
        162, 169–70, 192
Pericles (son), 456
perioikoi, 3–4, 430

Persian Empire, xxiii, 78, 251, 325, 361, 415
  Athenian relations with, 8, 13, 154–55,
    374, 431–32
  Delian League and, 8, 13
  Samian rebellion and, 22
  and Sicilian campaign aftermath,
    332–33
  Spartan relations with, 84, 154–55,
    331–33, 334, 467
  Spartan treaties with, 349–50, 353–54,
    357–58, 402, 417, 419, 431–32
  in treaty of Epilycus, 332
  see also Darius II, Great King of
    Persia; Hellespont; specific
    satraps
Persian Wars, 7, 12, 13–14, 88, 198–99,
  211, 374, 489
Phaeax, 253
phalanx, 1, 51, 52, 57, 60, 167, 287
  in battle of Mantinea, 236–39
  deep wing of, 168
Phanomachus, 85
Pharax, 240
Pharnabazus, 334, 407, 419, 427, 432
  at Abydos, 408
  Athenian treaty with, 429–30, 433
  at Cyzicus, 412–13, 414
  Sparta's Hellespont campaigns and,
    335, 354, 387–88, 402, 425
Phegus, 265
Philip II, king of Macedon, 168
Philistus, 321
Philocharidas, 213
Philochorus, 311
Philocles, 474–75, 476
Phlius, 5, 221, 222, 224, 244
Phocaea, 342, 443, 445, 458, 468
Phocis, 57, 129–30, 178, 228, 331
Phormio, 85, 90, 212, 345
  Alcibiades' return opposed by, 368–70
  at Naupactus, 91–96
Phrygia, 438
Phrynichus, 376, 386, 394, 421–22
  Miletus decision and, 344–46, 355
  oligarchic conspiracy and, 367,
    372–73, 377, 379

treason charges against, 372–73,
  400–401
Pindar, 362–63
Piraeus, 9, 51, 59, 60, 68, 71, 264, 336,
  389, 390, 397–98, 479, 483, 486
  counterrevolutionary uprising in,
    393–96
  Spartan attack on, 96–98
Pissuthnes, 22, 106, 334
plague epidemics, 78–80, 327, 361, 487
  religion and, 79–80
Plataea, 1, 145, 162, 191, 203, 204, 330, 487
  atrocities in, 65–66
  fate of, 113–14
  and Peace of Nicias, 192–93
  Spartan attack on, 87–89, 109
  Theban attack on, 1, 64–66, 298
Plataea, battle of, 88
Plato, 465
Pleistonax, king of Sparta, 16, 40, 106,
  125, 188, 203, 229, 233, 238, 331, 478
Plemmyrium, 291, 295, 304, 322
  fall of, 301–3
Plutarch, 32, 36, 48, 49, 60, 80, 87, 273,
  278, 321, 435, 441, 443, 488
  on Alcibiades, 212, 400
  battle of Cyzicus assessed by, 413
  on Nicias' grandiose display, 249–50
  on Nicias in Sicily, 274, 297
Plynteria ceremony, 435
Pnyx, 398
Polles, king of the Odomantians, 183
Polyanthes, 303
Polydamidas, 180
Polystratus, 401
poristai, 418
Potidaea, 41, 43, 44, 47, 49, 62, 146, 179,
  180, 198, 203, 212, 293
  siege of, 73, 75, 77, 78, 79, 80–81, 83
  uprising in, 36–37
Prasiae, 77
Priene, 22
probouloi, 328–29, 346, 366, 377, 420
Procles, 128, 131
Proconnesus, 410, 412
Propontis, 409, 471, 473

Protagoras, xxiii
Pteleum, 192
Pulytion, 263
Pydna, siege of, 409
Pylos, 58, 138–47, 141, 148, 157, 177, 189,
        192, 220, 289, 301, 320, 417
    Athenian occupation of, 150, 152, 178,
        188, 229, 299
    continuation of war affected by, 158,
        161, 198, 205–8, 229, 298
    Demosthenes' campaign in, 138–47
    fort at, 138–39
    geography of, 140–42
    naval battle for, 142–43
    Sparta's recapture of, 424, 467
    truce debate and, 143–47
Pythen, 289, 311, 314
Pythodorus, 122, 137, 161, 293
Pythonicus, 263

Ramphias, 188, 352
Rhegium, 120, 137, 159, 268, 269, 270,
        273, 279, 283
Rheneia, 249
Rhium, 217
Rhodes, 329, 357, 374, 417, 442, 471
    rebellion in, 354–56, 406

Sadocus, 84
Salaethus, 105, 107–9
Salaminia (trireme), 266
Salaminioi, clan of, 211
Salamis, 96, 396, 471
Salamis, battle of, 339
Samian rebellion, 22–24, 31, 42, 106, 328
Saminthus, 224
Samos, 23, 91, 345, 356, 359, 374, 378, 397,
        426, 433, 445, 454, 482
    Alcibiades' repatriation to, 364,
        367–72, 388–89
    as Athenian naval base, 341, 349, 350,
        352–53, 375, 446, 447, 451, 470,
        471
    civil war in, 341–42
    democratic counterrevolution in,
        364, 365, 382, 384–87, 391, 392
    Lysander's siege of, 478–79
    see also Samian rebellion
Sarandapotamos (stream), 230, 233
Sardis, 437, 440, 469
Scandeia, 157
Scelias, 392
Scione, 179, 182–83, 191, 203, 248, 476, 487
Scironides, 344, 355, 373
Sciritae, 235–36, 239
Segesta, 253–55, 260, 268–69, 274
Selinus, 253–55, 268–69, 274, 289, 332
Sellasia, 479
Selymbria, 388, 430, 431, 433
Sestos, 359, 405, 408, 425, 471, 473,
        475–76
Sicanus, 314
Sicilian expedition of 415, 251–324, 334,
        361
    aftermath of, 327–28, 332–33
    Alcibiades' treason and, 280–83
    Athenian bases in, 268–70, 273, 279,
        280
    Athenian decision for, 254–61
    Athenian declaration of war in,
        270–72
    Athenian lack of cavalry in, 275,
        278–79
    Athenian retreat and surrender in,
        316–20
    Athenian withdrawal debate in,
        308–10
    battle of the Anapus in, 275–78
    casualties and costs of, 327
    Corinth and, 266, 279–81, 289–90,
        291, 292, 300, 301
    and demise of Peace of Nicias, 289,
        299–300
    Epipolae plateau in, 284, 286, 287–88,
        290–91, 292, 295, 306, 307–9,
        322–23
    fall of Plemmyrium in, 301–3
    fate of prisoners in, 321
    Great Harbor battle in, 303–5
    impetus for, 253–54
    inflated Athenian armada in, 260–61,
        267–68

Laconia raids and, 289, 298
lunar eclipse in, 310–12, 323
naval battles in, 302–5, 311–15
Nicias' leadership in, 288, 290–92,
    294–95, 322–23
Nicias' letter to Athens in, 293–95
Persia in aftermath of, 332–33
reinforcements in, 300–301, 306
sacrilegious incidents in, 262–67, 273
Segestan deceit in, 268–69
siege of Syracuse in, 284–97
Spartan mission to, 283, 288, 290–91
summer campaign of 415 in, 270–73
Syracusan finances and, 301–2, 309
Thucydides on, 254
unorthodox tactics in, 303–4, 305,
    313–14
Sicily, 3, 21, 37, 57, 121, 137, 138, 271
and Congress of Gela, 159–61, 253,
    272, 293
first Athenian expedition to, 118–22,
    161, 255, 272
see also Sicilian expedition of 415
Sicyon, 91, 217, 224, 242, 300, 331, 488
Siphae, 165, 166, 170
Sitalces, king of Thrace, 73, 84, 98
Socrates, xxiii, 169, 211
Arginusae controversy and, 465
Sollium, 71, 191, 193, 198, 201
Solon, 421, 424
Solygeia, 153
Sophocles, xxiii, 122, 137, 159, 283, 293
Athenian assembly's condemnation
of, 161–62
Corcyra civil war and, 154
probouloi election of, 328–29
Sparta, 6
Argive treaty with, 209, 210
Athenian rivalry with, 13–18
Boeotian treaty with, 208
Central Greece offensive of, 125–27
constitution of, 363, 440, 469
Corcyra civil war and, 115–17
declining population of, 204, 330
Epidamnus crisis and, 34
helots of, see helots

internal problems of, 204–6
Mytilene rebellion and, 102–4, 106–8
naval capability of, 59–60
naval construction program of,
    331–32
neodamodeis (liberated helots) class
of, 204, 236, 300, 330, 430
new colonies of, 125–27
Northwest campaigns of, 90–91,
    132–36
in Olympic Games of 420, 215–16
peace faction of, 177–78, 181, 204–5
Peloponnesian offensive of, 203–6
Persia's relations with, 84, 154–55,
    331–32, 334, 467
Persia's treaties with, 349–50, 353–54,
    357–58, 402, 417, 419, 431–32
political order of, 5–7
Potidaea uprising and, 37
Sicily and, 279–80, 283, 288, 290–91
social structure of, 3–4, 330–31
Theban defeat of, 487
ultimatum of, 49–50
war aims of, 57–60, 330–31
war decision of, 41–47
Spartan Alliance, Spartan League, see
    Peloponnesian League
Spartolus, 89–90, 191
Sphacteria, 58, 141, 147–48, 158, 161, 177,
    184, 186, 188, 198, 212, 241, 259,
    320
blockade of, 143–44
geography of, 140n
Spartans on, 140–41
Spartan surrender at, 150–53
Spiraeum, 337
Stagirus, 173, 183, 191
Sthenelaidas, 45
Stolus, 191
Straits, map of, 360
Stratus, battle of, 90–91, 93
Strombichides, 359, 387
Sunium, 282
fort at, 329
Susa, 469
Sybota, battle of, 34–36, 35, 37, 39, 45, 115

syngrapheis, 377
syntrierarchy, 328
Syracuse, 57, 137, 253, 269, *285*, 332, 390,
    424
    first Athenian expedition and, 118–22
    see also Sicilian expedition of 415

Tanagra, 167, 168
Taras, 20, 57, 268
Taulantians, 25
taxes, 329
    direct, 104–5, 328, 422–23
Tegea, 201, 202, 221, 222, 227, 232, 233,
    236, 241, 242
    Agis' march to, 228–30
Ten Generals of Athens, 9–12
Tenos, 380, 437
Teos, 338, 450
Teucrus, 264
Teutiaplus, 106
Thasos, 14, 376, 409, 417
Thebes, 5, 19, 28, 146, 165, 216–17, 478,
    479, 485, 489
    and battle of Delium, 168–69
    and fate of Athens, 481–82
    and Peace of Nicias, 191, 193, 197–98
    Plataea attacked by, 1, 64–66, 298
    Sparta defeated by, 487
    and Sparta's Plataea policy, 88, 113–14
Theodorus, 435
Theognis, 362
Theramenes, 398, 400, 401, 409, 420
    Arginusae rescue controversy and,
        460–63, 466
    coup and, 379–80
    at Cyzicus, 410, 412–14
    and fall of Alcibiades, 447–48
    and fall of Athens, 480–84
    in Hellespont campaign, 429–30, 431,
        433–34
    and ouster of Four Hundred, 383–84
    Piraeus uprising and, 392–94
Therimenes, 344, 346, 347
    treaty of, 349–50
Thespis, 165, 168
Thessalus, 266

Thessaly, 127, 171, 172, 178, 181, 339, 353
Thirty Tyrants, 365, 485–86
Thirty Years' Peace, 18–19, 37, 147, 193,
    298
    arbitration clause of, 18, 43, 49
    elements of instability in, 19
    Epidamnus conflict and, 30–31
    Samian crisis and, 24
Thorax, 471
Thrace, *38*, 98, 125, 127, 194, 197, 203,
    206, 247, 300, 409, 424, 434
Thracian campaign of 424–23, 171–81
    capture of Amphipolis in, 173–77
    rebellions and defections in, 177, 179
    Spartan peace faction and, 177–78
    Thucydides in, 175–77
Thraso, 446
Thrasybulus (son of Lycus), 371, 398,
    401, 409
    at Abydos, 408
    Arginusae rescue controversy and,
        460–63, 466
    at Cynossema, 404–6, 407
    at Cyzicus, 410, 412–13
    and fall of Alcibiades, 447–48
    oligarchic conspiracy and, 365–68,
        374–75
    recall of Alcibiades and, 388–91
    and restoration of democracy,
        485–86
    Samian democracy and, 384–85,
        386
Thrasybulus (son of Thraso), 446
Thrasyllus:
    at Abydos, 408
    in Argive plain campaign, 224–26
    at Cynossema, 403–4, 405
    in Hellespont campaign, 425, 427,
        429–30, 433–34, 443, 445
    Ionian campaign of, 425–26
    Samian democracy movement and,
        384–85, 386
Thrasymelidas, 139–40
Three Hundred, conspiracy of, 384
Thronium, 71
Thucles, 117

Thucydides, xxiv, 2, 4, 13, 14, 32, 43, 46, 78, 80, 83, 93, 96, 104, 107, 119, 134, 135, 140*n*, 150, 152, 173, 187, 188, 216, 228, 244, 249, 251, 262, 329, 359, 376, 385, 390, 397, 484, 488
  on Aetolian campaign, 129
  Alcibiades as characterized by, 257–59
  on Alcibiades in Persia, 347
  on Alcibiades' repatriation to Samos, 366
  on Alcibiades-Tissaphernes relationship, 373, 389
  on Antiphon, 379
  on Argive capture of Epidaurus, 218
  on atrocities, 84–85, 117
  on Brasidas, 172
  on Cleon, 109–10, 186
  on condemnation of Sophocles and Pythodurus, 161
  on Corinth's Corcyraean intervention, 25–27
  elected as general, 157
  on Epidaurian campaign, 76–77
  and fall of Amphipolis, 175–77, 178, 293
  historical works of, xxv–xxvi
  on Melos attack, 128
  on "the mob," 368
  Naupactus naval battle described by 92
  on Nicias, 189
  Nicias eulogized by, 321
  on oligarchic movement, 364–65
  on origin of war, 45, 57
  on Pericles, 12, 69, 99
  on Pylos peace talks, 144
  on Sicilian expedition of 415, 254, 255, 270, 278, 280, 284, 296, 312, 321–22
  on Spartan fighting style, 240
  on Sparta's attack on Plataea, 88
  on Sparta's reaction to fall of Cythera, 158
  on Thracian campaign, 175–77, 183–84
Thurii, 20–22, 24, 390
Thymochares, 396–97, 401
Thyrea, 71–72, 158–59
  atrocities in, 158–59
Thyssus, 203
Timolaus, 376
Tisias, 248
Tissaphernes, 346, 352, 419, 425–26, 441, 442
  Alcibiades' relationship with, 347–48, 364, 366, 367, 369–70, 372, 373–75, 378, 389–90, 406, 410
  Cyrus' replacement of, 437–38
  Hellespont campaigns and, 334, 335, 356–57, 387, 388, 402, 407, 409–10
  at Miletus, 344–45
  Persia-Sparta treaties and, 339–40, 350, 353–54, 357–58
  and promise of Phoenician fleet, 348–49, 351, 387
Torone, 179, 180, 181, 182–83, 184, 191
Trachis, 125, 216, 333, 424
Tretus Pass, 224
Troezen, 77, 145, 153, 178, 331
truce of 423, 178–80
  conditions of, 178–79

Ukraine, 9

Vienna, Congress of, 18

Westphalia, Peace of, 18
World War I, xxv

Xanthippus, 97
Xenares, 205–6, 207, 212, 216
Xenophanes, 255
Xenophon, 85, 89, 413, 435, 463, 476, 488
Xerxes, 68
xymbouloi (advisers), 226, 240, 351–53

Zacynthus, 84, 85, 90, 140
Zanovistas (stream), 230, 233